# PATTERN-DIRECTED
# INFERENCE SYSTEMS

# PATTERN-DIRECTED INFERENCE SYSTEMS

*Edited by*

## D. A. WATERMAN
## FREDERICK HAYES-ROTH

*The Rand Corporation
Santa Monica, California*

ACADEMIC PRESS    New York   San Francisco   London     1978
*A Subsidiary of Harcourt Brace Jovanovich, Publishers*

ACADEMIC PRESS, INC.
111 Fifth Avenue, New York, New York 10003

*United Kingdom Edition published by*
ACADEMIC PRESS, INC. (LONDON) LTD.
24/28 Oval Road, London NW1 7DX

**Library of Congress Cataloging in Publication Data**

Workshop on Pattern-Directed Inference Systems,
     Honolulu, Hawaii, 1977.
     Pattern-directed inference systems.

     Selected papers from the Workshop.
     Bibliography: p.
     Includes indexes.
     1.   Artificial intelligence—Congresses.
2.   Cognition—Congresses.   I.   Waterman, Donald
Arthur.   II.   Hayes-Roth, Frederick.
III.   Title.
Q334.W67   1977          001.53'5          78-6981
ISBN 0-12-737550-3

# CONTENTS

*v*

## CONCLUSION

# LIST OF CONTRIBUTORS

Numbers in parentheses refer to the pages on which authors' contributions begin.

BUCHANAN, BRUCE G. (297), Computer Science Department, Stanford University, Stanford, California 94305

DAVIS, RANDALL (99), Computer Science Department, Stanford University, Stanford, California 94305

DUDA, RICHARD O. (203), Artificial Intelligence Center, Stanford Research Institute, Menlo Park, California 94025

FAUGHT, WILLIAM S. (383), The Rand Corporation, Santa Monica, California 90406

FEIGENBAUM, EDWARD A. (483), Computer Science Department, Stanford University, Stanford, California 94305

FORGY, C. (177), Department of Computer Science, Carnegie-Mellon University, Pittsburgh, Pennsylvania 15213

HARRIS, GREGORY (25), Department of Computer Science, Carnegie-Mellon University, Pittsburgh, Pennsylvania 15213

HART, PETER E. (203), Artificial Intelligence Center, Stanford Research Institute, Menlo Park, California 94025

HAYES-ROTH, BARBARA (333), The Rand Corporation, Santa Monica, California 90406

HAYES-ROTH, FREDERICK (3, 431, 471, 557, 577), The Rand Corporation, Santa Monica, California 90406

HOLLAND, JOHN H. (313), Department of Computer Science, University of Michigan, Ann Arbor, Michigan 48104

JOSHI, ARAVIND K. (241), Department of Computer and Information Science, University of Pennsylvania, Philadelphia, Pennsylvania 19104

KLAHR, PHILIP (223), System Development Corporation, 2500 Colorado Avenue, Santa Monica, California 90406

LENAT, DOUGLAS B. (25, 577), Department of Computer Science, Carnegie-Mellon University, Pittsburgh, Pennsylvania 15213

McDERMOTT, J. (155, 177), Department of Computer Science, Carnegie-Mellon University, Pittsburgh, Pennsylvania 15213

McDONALD, DAVID (431), Department of Computer Science, Carnegie-Mellon University, Pittsburgh, Pennsylvania 15213

MITCHELL, TOM M. (297), Stanford University, Stanford, California 94305

MOORE, J. (155), Department of Computer Science, Carnegie-Mellon University, Pittsburgh, Pennsylvania 15213

MOSTOW, DAVID JACK (471), Department of Computer Science, Carnegie-Mellon University, Pittsburgh, Pennsylvania 15213

NEWELL, ALLEN (135, 155), Department of Computer Science, Carnegie-Mellon University, Pittsburgh, Pennsylvania 15213

NII, H. PENNY (483), Computer Science Department, Stanford University, Stanford, California 94305

NILSSON, NILS J. (203), Artificial Intelligence Center, Stanford Research Institute, Menlo Park, California 94025

REITMAN, JUDITH S. (313), Department of Psychology, University of Michigan, Ann Arbor, Michigan 48104

REITMAN, WALTER (503), Mental Health Research Institute, University of Michigan, Ann Arbor, Michigan 48104

RIEGER, CHUCK (69), Computer Science Center, University of Maryland, College Park, Maryland 20742

RIESBECK, CHRISTOPHER K. (399), Department of Computer Science, Yale University, New Haven, Connecticut 06510

ROSENSCHEIN, STANLEY J. (525), The Rand Corporation, Santa Monica, California 90406

RYCHENER, MICHAEL D. (135), Department of Computer Science, Carnegie-Mellon University, Pittsburgh, Pennsylvania 15213

SCHANK, ROGER C. (415), Department of Computer Science, Yale University, New Haven, Connecticut 06510

SCHMIDT, C. F. (361), Department of Psychology, Rutgers University, New Brunswick, New Jersey 08903

SIMMONS, ROBERT F. (455), Department of Computer Sciences, University of Texas at Austin, Austin, Texas 78712

SRIDHARAN, N. S. (361), Department of Computer Science, Rutgers University, New Brunswick, New Jersey 08903

SUTHERLAND, GEORGIA L. (203), Artificial Intelligence Center, Stanford Research Institute, Menlo Park, California 94025

THORNDYKE, PERRY W. (347), The Rand Corporation, Santa Monica, California 90406

VERE, STEVEN A. (281), Department of Information Engineering, University of Illinois at Chicago Circle, Chicago, Illinois 60680

WATERMAN, D. A. (3, 261, 577), The Rand Corporation, Santa Monica, California 90406

WILCOX, BRUCE (503), University of Michigan, Ann Arbor, Michigan 48104

WILENSKY, ROBERT (415), Department of Computer Science, Yale University, New Haven, Connecticut 06510

ZISMAN, MICHAEL D. (53), Sloan School of Management, Massachusetts Institute of Technology, Cambridge, Massachusetts 02139

ZUCKER, STEVEN W. (539), Department of Electrical Engineering, McGill University, Montreal P.Q. H3C 3G1, Canada

# PREFACE

Studies of concept formation, language understanding, problem solving, inferential reasoning, and memory organization have been conducted by researchers in both artificial intelligence and cognitive psychology, with noticeable benefits resulting from the cross fertilization of research. One recent focus for this exchange of ideas has been systems that look for interesting or important situations (defined by patterns in input and memory data) to guide their overall activity. We have called this type of system a *pattern-directed inference system,* or PDIS. The success of pattern-directed inference systems has been based, in part, on the simple, uniform structure of the schemes employed to represent situation-driven behavior rules. This structure has facilitated the formal analysis of complex systems and has provided insight into the difficult problem of understanding and representing the learning process. The rapid developments in studies of these inference systems over the past few years have been the motivating force behind the compilation of this book.

The collected state-of-the-art articles in this book describe the design and implementation of pattern-directed inference systems for a variety of applications. In addition, a number of papers address the theoretical significance of PDISs for artificial intelligence and cognitive psychology. It is our hope that this book will act both as a mechanism for communicating the similarities and differences in various approaches that have been taken to pattern-directed inference as well as a stimulus to further research in this area.

The book is organized into eight sections. The introduction provides a brief overview of pattern-directed inference systems, including a historical perspective, a review of basic concepts, and a survey of current work in this area. The second section focuses on architecture and design. It contains most of the papers relating to conventional or "pure" production system design and efficiency. More novel system architectures are also covered in this section, including some that embed rule-based systems in graphs and nets. The third section addresses deductive inference and presents some interesting methods for accessing and controlling rule-based systems. The fourth section, on learning, comprises four chapters describing methods for obtaining adaptive behavior via rule-based systems. Cognitive modeling is discussed in the fifth section, relating the

PDIS formalism with work in constructing models of human information processing. The sixth section, on natural language understanding, illustrates how a modular rule-based formalism can assist in both the conceptualization and implementation of conversational systems. The seventh section, on multilevel systems and complexity, describes recent work with complex multilevel systems and discusses general issues related to earlier papers in this volume. The last section discusses the earlier chapters in the book and provides a unifying set of principles for the PDIS formalism.

Contributions to this volume have been selected from the papers presented at the Workshop on Pattern-Directed Inference Systems, held May 23–27, 1977, in Honolulu. Other papers presented at the workshop have been published in the workshop proceedings, a special edition of the *SIGART Newsletter,* **63,** June 1977. The workshop was supported in part by the Mathematical Social Sciences Board of the National Science Foundation. We are grateful to Ed Feigenbaum for his assistance in developing the workshop and to Doris McClure, who played critical roles in organizing workshop communications and preparing this manuscript. We also appreciate the roles that B. J. Gritton and Bob Anderson have played in creating the supportive research environment at Rand that was necessary for undertaking this project.

# Introduction

# AN OVERVIEW OF PATTERN-DIRECTED INFERENCE SYSTEMS

D. A. Waterman and Frederick Hayes-Roth
*The Rand Corporation*

*Pattern-directed inference systems are programs that look for interesting or important situations occuring as patterns in their input or memory data. These patterns select pieces of program code to be executed. In this chapter a brief overview of pattern-directed inference systems is presented, including an historical perspective, a review of basic concepts, and a survey of current work in this area. Examples of the best known type of pattern-directed inference system, the production system, are presented and discussed in detail.*

## 1.0 BASIC CONCEPTS

During the past few years researchers have become interested in topics at the intersection of artificial intelligence, cognitive psychology, and pattern recognition. One focus for this interest has been a very simple but powerful idea: a program organization based on data or event-driven operations. Here the program responds directly to a wide range of data or events (possibly unanticipated) rather than operating on expected data in known formats using a prespecified and inflexible control structure, as found in conventional programs. Such an organization can be characterized as *pattern-directed*: patterns occurring in the data select pieces of code in the system to be activated. Systems organized this way have been used primarily for deductive inference, and, to a lesser extent, for inductive inference or learning. We shall call a system that exploits patterns in the input data to select and trigger activities a *pattern-directed inference system* (PDIS). A PDIS has three basic components: (1) a collection of substructures

*3*

called *pattern-directed modules* (PDMs), which can be activated or "fired" by patterns in the data, (2) one or more data structures that may be examined and modified by the PDMs, and (3) an executive (also called an interpreter) that controls the selection and activation of the PDMs [F. Hayes-Roth77h]. Examples of PDISs are production systems, grammatical inference systems, or any deductive or inductive inference system that uses patterns or rules to guide the decision-making process.

An important type of PDIS is the *rule-based system* (RBS), in which the PDMs consist of antecedent-consequent pairs called *rules*. The distinguishing characteristic of a rule-based system is the separation of *data examination* from *data modification*. The examination of data generally takes place in the antecedent or left-hand side of a rule, while data modification is normally handled by the consequent or right-hand side. No further assumptions are made concerning the representation of either antecedents or consequents, the structure of the data they manipulate, or the type of control structure determining how rules make contact with data.

Data examination consists of comparing the patterns associated with the antecedents to the elements in the data structures. The patterns may be defined in many ways: as simple strings, complex graphs or semantic net structures, or even arbitrary segments of code capable of inspecting data elements. Data modification can be as simple as asserting that some proposition is true, or as complex as firing arbitrary actions to modify data, rules, or the environment (via output operations). Information in the data structures can be in the form of lists, trees, nets, rules or any other useful representations. Even the control structure can range from a simple implicit one as used in many production systems to a complex explicit one based on special heuristics or *metarules*.

*Production systems* are a well-known type of rule-based system in which the control structure can be mapped into a relatively simple *recognize-act* paradigm. A production system typically consists of a data base, a set of production rules of the form *antecedent → consequent*, and an interpreter that embodies a mechanism to examine the data and determine which rules to fire.

Production systems most often have antecedents comprising *conditions* that characterize the data base and consequents comprising *actions* that manipulate the data base. The execution of this type of production system can be defined as a series of recognize-act cycles, as diagrammed in Fig. 1. Each cycle involves deciding which rule to fire and then executing the actions associated with that rule. Since the effect of executing the actions may change the data base, different rules may fire on successive cycles.

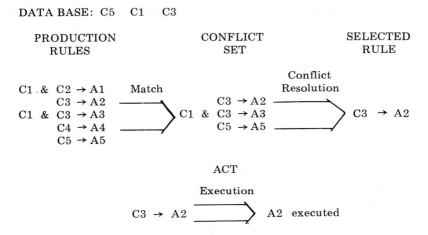

RECOGNIZE

DATA BASE: C5   C1   C3

| PRODUCTION RULES | | CONFLICT SET | SELECTED RULE |

Figure 1. Production system recognize-act cycle

The *recognize* portion of the cycle consists of comparing rule conditions to the data base to search for matches. The *conflict set* comprises all rules that are satisfied by the current data. In Fig. 1, a rule matches the data base if all the C's in its antecedent are found in the data base. Then *conflict resolution*, the process of deciding which satisfied rule to fire, is applied to the conflict set. Once a rule is selected the cycle concludes with the *act* step during which the actions in the consequent of the rule are executed.

The history of the production system is summarized succinctly in Newell and Simon [Newell72b]:

> The production system was one of those happy events, though in minor key, that historians of science often talk about: a rather well-prepared formalism, sitting in wait for a scientific mission. Production systems have a long and diverse history. Their use in symbolic logic starts with Post (see, [Post43], from whom the name is taken. They also show up as Markov algorithms [Markov54]. Their use in linguistics, where they are also called rewrite rules, dates from Chomsky [Chomsky57]. As with so many other notions in computer science, they really entered into wide currency when they became operationalized in programming languages, first in string manipulation systems (COMIT, see [Yngve58]; and SNOBOL [Farber64]) and in compiler translation languages [Floyd61].

One of the first uses of production systems in psychological modeling was the work of Newell and Simon [Newell65] in chess analysis and [Newell67, 68] in the analysis of cryptarithmetic problems. In both cases the intent was to use production systems to model human problem solving in specific task areas. The basis for the research was a method of protocol analysis [1] in which subjects were instructed to "think aloud" as they solved a problem. The resulting *protocol* or verbalization of their problem solving effort was used to infer productions that could account for the behavior noted in the protocol. Newell and Simon [Newell72b] consider the production system to be a good candidate for modeling human cognitive processes for a number of reasons, the most important being:

(1)   They have the computational generality of universal Turing machines, providing the models with a wide range of potential information processing capabilities.

(2)   Since production rules tend to represent independent components of behavior, the creation and addition of rules can be incremental; i.e., new rules can be added one at a time.

(3)   Under certain assumptions, the production system data base models the functional characteristics of human short-term memory, and the production rules provide a possible model of human long-term memory.

Production systems usually represent antecedents as logical combinations of predicates whose truth values can be determined by examining the data. Consequents are usually represented either as procedures to alter the data, rules, or environment, or as assertions about the truth value of statements. The production system illustrated in Fig. 1 is *antecedent-driven*; i.e., during the matching process it makes initial contact with the data through the conditions in its antecedents. Rule-based systems that make initial contact with the data via the consequents have also been termed "production systems." These *consequent-driven* RBSs have rules analogous to logical implication statements. Thus, $A \& B \& C \rightarrow D$ in such a system would be interpreted as "if A, B, and C are true then D is true." Consequent-driven behavior involves searching for preconditions to justify or confirm the consequents.

## 2.0 STRUCTURE OF PATTERN-DIRECTED INFERENCE SYSTEMS

Contemporary PDISs have evolved from a humble beginning, the

---

[1] For details on protocol analysis see [Waterman71, 76c].

Post production systems [Post43, Minsky67]. The symbol manipulation systems of Post were composed of grammarlike rules called "productions" used for specifying string replacement operations. A rule in a Post production system would typically have the form [A$x$B → A$y$B], stating that an occurrence of the string $x$ in the context of A and B would be replaced by the string $y$. Imposing an implicit control structure on a collection of ordered string replacement rules leads to the concept of the Markov normal algorithm [Markov54, Galler70]. In a Markov algorithm the rules are tested against a data base that is a simple string of symbols, and the first rule found to be applicable is applied, resulting in an alteration of the string. After that rule is applied, testing resumes, beginning with the highest priority rule. This *test-apply* cycle is repeated until no rules are applicable. Figure 2 illustrates a Markov algorithm that transforms any string composed of a's and b's into the string AB [Waterman76b].

| Alphabet: | a, b, A, B |
|---|---|
| Variables: | $x$ |
| Productions: | (1) . aa → a |
| | (2) . bb → b |
| | (3) . a$x$ → $x$a |
| | (4) . a → A |
| | (5) . b → B |

Fig. 2. A simple Markov normal algorithm for mapping strings of a's and b's into the string AB.

The productions are arranged in order with highest priority first. After any production is applied, testing begins again with rule 1. If the data base is the string abaaba, rules 1, 3, 1, 2, 3, 1, 4, and 5 are applied in that order to produce the string AB. Note that the highest priority productions must be applied first to insure that the algorithm will terminate and give the correct result.

Production systems can be thought of as a generalization of Markov normal algorithms. The early production systems for modeling human cognition [Newell72a, b, 73, 75, Hunt74, D. Klahr73] have a simple form: a small data base or working memory contains a collection of active memory elements (symbols or lists), and a long-term memory contains condition-action rules selected for execution by comparing rule antecedent with the elements in memory. The rule consequents are actions that add, delete, or modify memory elements. Figure 3 illustrates a production system of this type that performs subtraction (P - Q) by iterated counting operations.

Data Base: (START) (P 5) (Q 3)

Variables: $x1$ $x2$

Rules:

1.                            (START) → delete ((START))
                                              deposit ((COUNT 0))

2. (COUNT $x1$) & (P $x2$) & (Q $x2$) → say ($x1$)
                                          stop()

3.       (COUNT $x1$) & (Q $x2$) → replace ($x1$, s ($x1$), (COUNT $x1$))
                                          replace ($x2$, s($x2$), (Q $x2$))

Actions:

| | |
|---|---|
| delete(b): | removes b from the data base. |
| deposit(b): | puts b into the data base. |
| replace(b, c, d): | replace b with c in data element d. |
| print(b): | prints b at terminal. |
| stop( ): | stops production system execution. |
| s (b): | returns the successor of b (i.e., b+1). |

Fig. 3. A production system for performing the integer subtraction, P minus Q (see Fig. 4).

The highest priority rule (topmost) matching the data base fires on each cycle. Thus rule 1 fires first, deleting the memory element (START) and adding the element (COUNT 0). Next rule 3 fires repeatedly, incrementing the numbers associated with COUNT and Q until the numbers associated with P and Q are equal, causing rule 2 to fire. The $x$'s are variables that are instantiated during the match process and evaluated during the execution of the actions. Note that the two occurrences of the same variable ($x2$) in rule 2 means that the condition is satisfied only when the numbers associated with P and Q are identical.

Of course, production systems are not restricted to the use of simple matching techniques on a list-structured data base. The matching process can evaluate arbitrary predicates on the data base. Similarly, the action components can specify a variety of executable procedures. To illustrate the contrast, the production system of Fig. 3 has been written in RITA [R.H. Anderson76a, b, 77a, b], a high-level production system language. The RITA equivalent of Fig. 3 is shown in Fig. 4. Note that the two systems are isomorphic and have their rules executed in exactly the same order. In RITA the data base is a collection of object-attribute-value triples, rather than an arbitrary list structure, and reserved words (shown in boldface) abound. Also, the LHSs explictly state how they should be evaluated relative to the data base, while in the example of Fig. 3 this match or evaluation is implicit.

| Data Base: | **OBJECT** start; | **OBJECT** p | **OBJECT** q |
|---|---|---|---|
| | | value **IS** 5; | value **IS** 3; |

| Rules: | Rule 1: | **IF**: | **THERE IS** a start |
|---|---|---|---|
| | | **THEN**: | **DELETE** the **OBJECT** start |
| | | | & **CREATE** a count **WHOSE** value **IS** 0; |
| | Rule 2: | **IF**: | **THERE IS** a count |
| | | | & the **VALUE OF** p **IS** the value **OF** q |
| | | **THEN**: | **SEND** the value **OF** count **TO** the **USER** |
| | | | & **RETURN SUCCESS**; |
| | Rule 3: | **IF**: | **THERE IS** a count |
| | | | & **THERE IS** a q |
| | | **THEN**: | **SET** the value **OF** count **TO** 1 + value **OF** count |
| | | | & **SET** the value **OF** q **TO** 1 + value **OF** q; |

Fig. 4. A RITA production system for performing the integer subtraction, P minus Q (see Fig. 3).

Figures 2, 3, and 4 illustrate the operation of antecedent-driven production systems, where matching is based on the antecedent properties. In consequent-driven systems, however, matching is based on rule consequents. A consequent-driven system is usually given a premise to "prove" through deductive inference. The consequents of the rules are examined to find those which could confirm the given premise. From this set of rules one is chosen and examined to see if all the premises in its antecedent are true relative to the data base. If they are, the rule is fired and the given premise is proved. If they are not, the process continues recursively in an attempt to deduce the validity of each premise in the antecedent of the rule. This process of working backward through the rules from consequents to antecedents in search of a causal chain that will prove the given premise is called *backward chaining* or *consequent reasoning*.

An abstract example of this type of system is shown in Fig. 5. The letters represent data base elements and are considered true if in the data base. In this simple system, the action of firing a rule inserts the right-hand side letter into the data base.

DATA BASE:    B  C

RULES:    (1) .   B & D & E   →   F
          (2) .         D & G   →   A
          (3) .         C & F   →   A
          (4) .             C   →   D
          (5) .             D   →   E
          (6) .             A   →   H

Fig. 5. A simple consequent-driven production system.

Assume the given premise is that "H is true." Since H is not in the data base it must be deduced by backward chaining through the rules. The system first chooses rule 6 and attempts to show that A is true, since A implies H. Unfortunately A is not in the data base and must itself be deduced. This can be attempted through either rule 2 or 3. Assume the system first tries rule 2. It must now show that both D and G are true. D is easy; it can be inferred from rule 4. G is another matter; nothing can be inferred about G since no rules contain G on the right-hand side. The system now backs up and tries to infer A through rule 3. This time it succeeds since C is true and F can be inferred by showing that B, D, and E are true. A causal chain has now been produced that proves the given premise "H is true," as shown in Fig. 6.

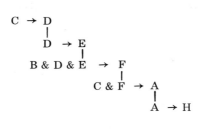

Fig. 6. Causal chain for inferring H from B and C, using the data base and rules of Fig. 5.

Pattern-directed inference systems, in general, are characterized by a separation of data, rules, and a control schema. The control schema can be characterized as having four basic parts: selection, matching, scheduling, and execution, as shown in Fig. 7.

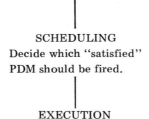

Fig. 7. The control schema of pattern-directed inference systems.

Selection consists of deciding what subset of procedural task knowledge (PDMs) and declarative state knowledge (data or working memory elements) should be considered for use during the next cycle of operation of the system. In production systems selection may be trivial, e.g., on each cycle all rules and all data elements can be considered, or may be quite complex, e.g., special filters [J. McDermott77a] can be designed to eliminate from consideration many rules that could not possibly match the current data. In sophisicated rule-based systems selection may involve the use of hierarchies, state transitions, metarules, or complex control schemes like Petri nets to narrow the set of rules considered.

The process of selection can take many forms. It may involve tagging rules as new data elements are added and deleted, e.g., in Fig. 8 if C3 were added to the data base, rules 2 and 3 would be tagged and would remain tagged until C3 were deleted. Selection in this case involves choosing the set of tagged rules [J. Mcdermott77a].

| (1) | C1 & C2 | → | A1 |
|-----|---------|---|-----|
| (2) | C2 & C3 | → | A2 |
| (3) | C3 & C4 | → | A3 |
| (4) | C4 & C5 | → | A4 |
| (5) | C5 & C6 | → | A5 |
| (6) | C6 & C7 | → | A6 |

Fig. 8. A single level production system.

Alternatively, rules may be partitioned into sets or hierarchies, and selection may consist of applying metarules to choose one particular rule set. For example, suppose set A contains rules 1 and 2 from Fig. 8, set B contains rules 3 and 4, and set C contains rules 5 and 6. The metarules might state that if condition X exists set A should be selected, otherwise if Y exists B should be selected, otherwise set C should be used. Selection is determined by evaluating these metarules. The same effect could be achieved by arranging the rules into a hierarchy as shown in Fig. 9. In this and subsequent figures, the minus symbol before a data element (e.g., -X) in a condition denotes that the data element must be absent from the data base for the condition to be satisfied.

Here the actions P1 and P2 mean that the named production systems are to be executed (selected), and each production system is assumed to be ordered with highest priority rules first. The rule sets

P1:    (0)    −X &Y → P2
       (1)    C1 & C2 → A1
       (2)    C2 & C3 → A2

P2:    (0)  −X & −Y → P3
       (1)    C3 & C4 → A3
       (2)    C4 & C5 → A4

P3:    (0)      X → P1
       (1)    C5 & C6 → A5
       (2)    C6 & C7 → A6

Fig. 9. Hierarchical production systems.

could also be associated with nodes in a graph or net as shown in Fig. 10.

A selection mechanism similar to this but more complex, making use of Petri nets instead of finite state transition networks, is used by Zisman [Zisman 77a].

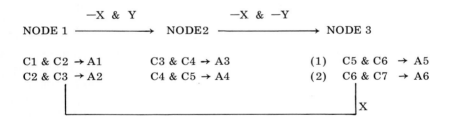

Fig. 10. Transition network production system.

Matching consists of searching the selected rules and comparing them against the selected data, looking for rules whose conditions are satisfied. The matching operation can be time-consuming, as it may involve instantiating many variables; this is one reason for using selection—it can significantly improve the overall efficiency of the system.

Once the satisfied rules are identified, the scheduling process (also called conflict resolution) decides which rule to fire. The scheduling mechanism may be implicit in the system or may be explicit as a set of metarules or procedures describing how to choose the rule to fire. Metarules permit the application of dynamic conflict resolution heuristics in a straightforward and understandable way.

Execution consists of firing the chosen rule, i.e., accessing and executing the procedures associated with the pattern elements that matched the current data. The result of execution is a modification of data elements or structure, or I/O operations.

## 3.0 EARLY WORK WITH PATTERN-DIRECTED INFERENCE SYSTEMS

Following the seminal work of Newell and Simon in the 1960s (see earlier references), production systems have attained a prominent position in artificial intelligence and cognitive psychology research. One of the first uses of production systems in a purely artificial intelligence application was work on the representation and learning of heuristics in a game-playing environment [Waterman68, 70]. Heuristics for generating favorable moves were represented as production rules and were learned over the course of playing a few games. This approach, which separates the problem of knowledge acquisition (theory formation) from the program that applies the theory, is reflected in the separation between Meta-DENDRAL [B.G. Buchanan72, 76a, b, 77], a program designed to formulate rules of mass spectrometry, and Heuristic DENDRAL [B.G. Buchanan69, Smith74], a performance program that applies such rules to the analysis of molecular structure. sis of molecular structure.

In the early 1970s, the use of production systems as models of cognition was one focus of research at Carnegie-Mellon University. This work included models of small group interactions [Friend73], cognitive development [D. Klahr73, 76, Young73,], human memory [Newell72a, 73], symbolic imagery [Moran74], and cognitive processes in writing computer programs [Brooks75]. More AI-oriented work included learning grammarlike productions for concept identification [Hedrick74, 76, F. Hayes-Roth76a, c], development of adaptive production systems [Waterman75, 76a], applications of production systems for speech understanding [F. Hayes-Roth75, 76j, 77g], and the use of production systems as AI programming languages [Rychener76]. At the same time, at Stanford University, Meta-DENDRAL was being pursued and MYCIN [Shortliffe73, 75b, 76], a rule-based system for advising physicians regarding antimicrobial therapy, was developed.

More recently, the use of pattern-directed inference systems as a framework for knowledge organization in AI work has spread to new areas, such as program synthesis and natural language understanding. In the next section recent work in new areas will be reviewed.

## 4.0 CURRENT USE OF PATTERN-DIRECTED INFERENCE SYSTEMS

Much research is being undertaken currently within the PDIS framework. In fact, there has been a veritable explosion of interest in this formalism during the past few years as evidenced by the huge number of recent papers generated on this subject. This work can be divided into six main areas: program synthesis, system architecture, knowledge acquisition, knowledge engineering, natural language understanding, and cognitive modeling. Each of these is discussed in turn.

### 4.1 Program Synthesis

In the area of program synthesis the problem of creating programs from examples of their traces is being investigated in the domain of man-machine interface software [Waterman77d]. Here the user creates "agents" (programmed procedures) to perform useful tasks by supplying an *exemplary programming* (EP) system with examples of the desired behavior. The EP system "looks over the shoulder" of the user and transforms the sample interaction between the user and the computer into a general procedure capable of performing that class of tasks in the future. The agents being created are represented as sets of rules to facilitate their incremental growth.

Program synthesis systems are being developed that produce conventional rather than rule-based programs, but organize their knowledge about how to construct programs as sets of rules. One example is PMB (program model builder), a module of the PSI program synthesis system designed to create programs from natural language descriptions and traces [Barstow76, Green76]. PMB's knowledge about synthesizing programs is represented as a set of rules whose antecedents test the state of the current program fragment being generated and whose consequents modify that fragment or create new subgoals [McCune77]. Another example is a production rule mechanism for generating LISP code from examples of input-output pairs [Biermann77]. The information for coding recursive loops and branches in LISP is represented in production rule schemata. These general formats can be instantiated by user-provided information to yield a set of production rules pertinent to the problem at hand. When these rules are executed they generate the desired LISP code. PECOS, a knowledge-based system for automatic program synthesis [Barstow77a, b], also represents its programming expertise via condition-action rules about programming. The target program is initially specified as an abstract algorithm, and through successive application of programming rules the specification is gradually refined into the specific code. In a program synthesis system called SYNSYS [Manna77] high-level specifications are accepted in mathematical notation, and transformation rules are used to map this description into the desired primitive program. Production rules also have been used to drive a program transformation system, where the goal is to transform high-level, inefficient program descriptions into efficient but lower-level code [Kibler77].

## 4.2 System Architecture

In the area of system architecture, a variety of languages for knowledge representation have been implemented that contain special implicit pattern-matching capabilities. These include PLAN-NER [Hewitt71], QA4 [Rulifson72], KRL [D.G. Bobrow77, a], OWL [Szolovits77], and TELOS [Travis77]. AMORD [de Kleer77] is a language for expressing pattern-evoked procedures that monitor a pattern-indexed data base. Rules are used to perform antecedent reasoning on assertions in the data base. Several production system languages have also been developed, including PSNLST, a general programming language for AI applications [Rychener76]; RITA, an English-like rule-based language for building small, intelligent programs called "user agents" that couple the user to the computer and perform routine interactions for him [R.H. Anderson76b, 77a, Waterman77b]; OPS, a production system language for building large, instructable systems [Forgy77a, Rychener77]; EPS [Brooks77], an experimental production system language similar to PSG; and APRIL, a production system language for modeling problem solving in a CAI environment [M.J. Smith77]. Aspects of production system efficiency have also been investigated [F. Hayes-Roth75, J. McDermott77a, b, Forgy77, Zucker77b, Rosenchein77a, Rhyne77].

In some cases, new system architectures have been designed to fit particular tasks. For example, AM, a rule-based system for the discovery of new mathematical concepts [Lenat76, 77a, b, c, d], uses over 200 heuristic rules that communicate via an agenda mechanism to discover set- theoretic concepts such as *singleton sets* and *natural numbers*. A system for modeling language comprehension has been developed that uses rules in the form of "trigger" patterns and associated procedures [Rieger77a, b, c]. The trigger patterns are located in associative "trigger trees" that monitor the flow of information through a data channel and can "fire" to insert or modify data in the channel. A system for modeling office processes has been designed that uses a Petri net to control the selection of production rules [Zisman76, 77a].

This permits modeling concurrent, asynchronous processes in a fairly efficient manner. All three of these systems are based on interesting architectures that are potentially extensible to a range of tasks beyond the original goals of the designers.

There are many examples of pattern-directed inference system architectures making clever use of deductive and inductive inferencing techniques. For example, Klahr [P. Klahr77] uses a planning process to select promising rules for deductively inferring desired conclusions. Planning involves finding chains of rules that connect the assumptions with the goals. This is accomplished by searching forward from the assumptions and backward from the goals simultaneously, looking for rules that link forward and backward chains (see also [Kellog77]). NASL [D. McDermott77a, b] controls rule selection by a set of metarules that help it deduce which task-oriented rules are likely to lead to a solution during the backward chaining search. Joshi [Joshi77] approaches the problem of inference based on partial information by permitting only a small amount of data in the active portion of the data base at one time, and then firing the collection of rules that best "accounts for" or matches this active data. Thus rules that only partially match the data (have some unmatched predicates in the antecedent) can be accessed. Representing rules in a semantic net structure [Duda77, Shapiro77] has facilitated the use of subset and inclusion relations and provides a way to include the same relation in several different premises and conclusions.

## 4.3 Knowledge Acquisition

In the area of knowledge acquisition, considerable recent progress has been made. TEIRESIAS [Davis76a, 77b, c, e], facilitates the transfer of knowledge from a human expert to the knowledge base of a task-oriented system by applying general data structure schemata to construct new, specific inference rules. Waterman [Waterman77a] has developed techniques by which man-machine interface programs can acquire the rules they need to perform personalized tasks for individual users, such as tutoring or creating reactive messages. A number of rule-based systems are able to infer new rules. Meta-DENDRAL contains the expertise of an organic chemist and is able to infer rules of fragmentation of molecules in a mass spectrometer [B.G. Buchanan77, Mitchell77]. Hayes-Roth and McDermott [F. Hayes-Roth76c, 77f] induce condition-action rules from examples by partial-matching the examples and generalizing their identified commonalities. Vere's approach is similar but separates rule antecedents into two parts, a static context and a modifiable premise, and generalizes each part differently when producing one general rule from many specific ones [Vere77a, b, c]. Other approaches include applying generalization heuristics to variable-valued logic decision rules [Larson77], generalizing examples of simple numerical patterns to produce rules relating the patterns to desired responses [D. Brown75, 77], and using feedback to evolve rules that enable a learning system to adapt best in an artificial environment [Holland77]. Additional uses of partial matching techniques [F. Hayes-Roth77b, f] have been made in rule-based systems for inferring new concepts, pattern templates, syntactic categories, and problem-solving rules.

### 4.4 Knowledge Engineering

Knowledge engineering has been defined as "bringing the principles and tools of AI research to bear on difficult applications problems requiring experts' knowledge for their solution" [Feigenbaum77]. Programs constructed in this knowledge engineering framework embody domain-specific knowledge from an expert and apply it to produce useful inferences for the user. Much current work of this sort exploits a pattern-directed or rule-based organization.

A good example of an "expert" knowledge system is DENDRAL [Feigenbaum71], a performance program developed for the analysis of molecular structure. It makes use of mass spectrometry rules formulated by Meta-DENDRAL [B.G. Buchanan77, Mitchell77] and by experts. MOLGEN, a knowledge-based system for experiment planning in molecular genetics, uses data schemata to represent procedural knowledge. Instances of schemata act as rules expressing transformational and problem solving knowledge [Martin77]. The MYCIN system [Shortliffe76, Davis77d] contains rules for inferring the diagnosis of blood infections and recommending appropriate treatment. Expert knowlege is acquired via a related system called TEIRESIAS [Davis77b], which permits the user to interact with the knowlege system, adding new rules or modifying old ones. Other pattern-directed knowledge systems in medicine include IRIS, a medical consultation system that uses semantic nets and decision tables to make proper diagnoses [Trigoboff76, 77], and KAMM [Walser77], a program that accepts rules about management of chorioretinal diseases in ophthalmology and integrates them into the MEDICO system [Walser76], a knowledge-based consultant organized as a production system.

The use of multiple levels of abstraction in pattern interpretation has been the key to success in many recent projects, including the SU/X program, which takes continuous acoustic signal data and tries to identify their sources, and SU/P (also known as CRYSALIS), which infers 3-D models of protein molecules from an electron density map of crystallized protein [Nii77]. These programs use a global data base (blackboard) for integration of relevant knowledge and a multilevel representation of the partial solution hypotheses. Multiple knowledge sources, organized as sets of rules, are used to generate inferences about both the solution and the overall strategy for applying the knowledge sources to various aspects of the problem. The form of multilevel knowledge representation in both programs was patterned after the Hearsay-II speech understanding system, which embodied a variety of independent, cooperating, pattern-directed knowledge sources [F. Hayes-Roth77e, g, Lesser77a]. One particular knowledge source, a production system for syntax and semantics, was abandoned because of its inability to control the combinatorial explosion arising from partial matching of conditions by incomplete and errorful data [F. Hayes-Roth77b, Mostow77]. Other recent work adopting similar multilevel architectures for pattern-directed inference includes a system that acquires knowledge about action-oriented competitive games (e.g., baseball) in the form of schemata that act as rules for interpreting and predicting future events [Soloway77], a system that constructs intentional interpretations of an observed sequence of human actions [Sridharan77], and a system for playing Go that recognizes and updates pattern interrelations and uses this knowledge to drive high-level planning and problem-solving functions [W.R. Reitman77].

Many other expert knowledge-based systems are now under development that use a rule-based formalism for knowledge representation. EL, an electrical network analysis program has been implemented in ARS, a problem-solving language employing rules as demons that monitor an associative data base [Sussman75b, 77, Stallman76]. Deductions are made by backward chaining, as in MYCIN, and the sequence of rules used in a deductive chain can be examined by the user. PONTIUS-0 [Goldstein77] is a production system for achieving skill in attitude instrument flying, where the goal is to maintain steady climbs, turns, descents, or level flying. This system uses "annotated" production rules; i.e., each rule is associated with a formal commentary describing caveats, rationales, plans, and control information. Other tasks performed by expert knowledge-based systems include automatic theory formation in mathematics [Lenat76, 77a], consultation about mineral exploration [Duda77], business consultation [Mark77], air traffic control [Wesson77], information management in criminal court proceedings [J.R. Buchanan77], and modeling foreign policy decision making [Sylvan77, R. A. Miller76].

## 4.5 Natural Language Understanding

Research in natural language understanding is now moving toward rule-based formalisms for representing knowledge about goals, motivation, and causality. A recent version of PAM

[Schank77b], a system for story understanding, incorporates knowledge about the goals of the story characters as a production system that can build a structure in memory describing the points (dramatic events) of the story in terms of a problem and its solution. The production rules are used primarily to fill the gaps in the meaning representation that the understander is trying to build. ELI, the English language interpreter used by the SAM and PAM story understanding systems, is organized as a production system that maps input text into a conceptual dependency structure. Riesbeck [Riesbeck77] describes the system and discusses mechanisms used to reduce the problems caused by the use of large numbers of production rules. Schank [Schank77a] uses condition-action rules to map sentences given to children into conceptual dependency representations of the meaning that the sentences have to the children. This is part of a system for modeling the linguistic development in a child from one to two years of age. A production system is also used to map sentences into a semantic network in a system designed to infer the meaning of phrases from the constituent words [McDonald77]. Simmons [Simmons77] uses rules to transform English discourse describing a story into semantic case predicates, then applies causal rules to these predicates to produce a net of causal relations among elements of the story, and finally is able to apply generative rules to such internal representations to produce natural language texts. Faught [Faught77b] discusses a rule-based model of conversational action that describes and predicts speech acts in natural language dialog. The model makes use of overlapping and parallel rules to predict and generate overlapping linguistic events, and uses the emotional context of the dialog to help resolve the ambiguous interpretations that arise.

### 4.6 Cognitive Modeling

In the area of cognitive modeling based on pattern-directed inference, current work is heavily influenced by the earlier work of Newell with PSG [Newell72a, 73]. Young [Young77] has developed production system models of children's behavior in seriation and subtraction tasks. The models use PSG-like production rules and attack the problem of representing a mixture of problem-solving strategies within a single integrated production system such that each strategy maintains its uniqueness as a separate collection of rules. Klahr and Wallace [D. Klahr76] use PSG-like production systems to model cognitive development, in particular, tasks associated with Piaget's concrete operational stage. Models are produced that account for task behavior within a particular substage, and these are analyzed to determine how they could be modified to account for behavior at the next substage.

Another current approach to modeling human memory is embodied in the ACT system [J.R. Anderson76, 77a, b]. Memory is a propositional network of interconnected nodes, a small portion of which may be active at any one time. Operating on this memory is a set of production rules whose conditions test for the existence of certain features in the active portion of memory and whose actions can change the memory structure. Linear growth in computation time with the size of the data base or the number of production rules is avoided by only considering data in the active part of memory when rules are applied and by associating with each node a list of rules that reference the node. When the node is activated the associated rules are selected for consideration. Thus the number of rules being tested against memory at any time depends on the number of currently active nodes rather than the size of the production system. Faught [Faught77a] extended his use of production rules in a conversational action paradigm to include a model of affect (emotion) activation and response. The affect levels are used in the left-hand sides of production rules to provide a context for interpreting situations that the model is in (e.g., threatening situations), and in the right-hand sides of rules to effect responses to situations. Hayes-Roth [B. Hayes-Roth77d] evaluates human pattern processing and its relation to artificial knowledge systems in the light of recent psychological studies. Thorndyke [Thorndyke77b] describes a view of human text comprehension, memory, and recall that assumes information processing is guided by hierarchical patterns of abstract conceptual relations.

## 5.0 CONCLUSIONS

Pattern-directed inference systems have three fundamental characteristics. First, they are data- or event-driven, and thus respond directly to observed patterns in the environment. Second, there is modularity of control knowledge; control of the way the pattern components make contact with the data can be described independently of the structure and function of the task knowledge. Finally, there is modularity of task knowledge. Both the knowledge that constitutes the data and knowledge that constitutes the heuristics for manipulating the data are organized into separate, although not necessarily independent, units (e.g., data elements, rules) that can be accessed, applied, or themselves manipulated with some degree of autonomy. This simplifies the problem of isolating useful units of knowledge and facilitates the development of learning systems.

Two factors underlying the desirability of employing PDISs are environmental complexity and the diversity of the responses it necessitates. When intelligent behavior consists of numerous specialized responses to widely varying and largely unpredictable situations, the antecedent-consequent structure of PDMs isolates and represents the appropriate logic of such data- directed behavior in a natural way. In some cases, the complexity and scope of individual PDMs, the *granularity* of the PDIS, may be an option in the design and implementation of the system. It is important that the grain size match the problem domain characteristics. If the PDIS is too fine-grained for the particular task it may be laborious to program and difficult to understand. If the grain size is too coarse the PDIS may not perform as well as possible because of its nondiscriminating nature. Often the adoption of fine-grained, separable PDMs, so characteristic of production systems, leads to individual rules that can be induced from examples, separately evaluated and verified, and even explained or understood at a local level. Of course, it is sometimes preferable to employ PDMs that are individually so complex that these putative benefits are not realizable. In exchange, the more coarsely segmented system is often easier to comprehend *in toto* since individual PDMs can be interpreted as more macroscopic behavior generators. Ultimately, the choice of grain-size should reflect an attempt to minimize the disparity between the task characteristics and the chosen problem representation.

Although pattern-directed inference systems have been in use and under development for a number of years, only recently has the range of task domains expanded to encompass many areas of artificial intelligence. The current interest in these systems and the success to date are good indications that this formalism provides a promising framework for the development of intelligent inference systems.

# Architecture and Design

# DESIGNING A RULE SYSTEM THAT SEARCHES FOR SCIENTIFIC DISCOVERIES[1]

Douglas B. Lenat and Gregory Harris
*Carnegie-Mellon University*

*Some scientific inference tasks (including mass spectrum identification [Dendral], medical diagnosis [Mycin], and math theory development [AM]) have been successfully modeled as rule-directed search processes. These rule systems are designed quite differently from "pure production systems." By concentrating upon the design of one program (AM), we shall show how 13 kinds of design deviations arise from (1) the level of sophistication of the task that the system is designed to perform, (2) the inherent nature of the task, and (s) the designer's view of the task. The limitations of AM suggest even more radical departures from traditional rule system architecture. All these modifications are then collected into a new, complicated set of constraints on the form of the data structures, the rules, the interpreter, and the distribution of knowledge between rules and data structures. These new policies sacrifice uniformity in the interests of clarity, efficiency, and power derivable from a thorough characterization of the task. Rule systems whose architectures conform to the new design principles will be more awkward for many tasks than would "pure" systems. Nevertheless, the new architecture should be significantly more powerful and natural for building rule systems that do scientific discovery tasks.*

## 1.0 THE BASIC ARGUMENT

Although rule-based computation was originally used for formal and systems purposes [Post,Markov,Floyd], researchers in artificial intelligence (AI) found that the same methodology was also useful for

[1] This work was supported in part by the Defense Advanced Research Projects Agency (F44620-73-C-0074) and monitored by the Air Force Office of Scientific Research.

modeling a wide variety of sophisticated tasks. Many of these early AI rule-based programs (called "production systems") served as information processing models of humans performing cognitive tasks in several domains (digit recall [Newell73], algebra word problem solving [D. G. Bobrow68], poker playing [Waterman68], etc. [Moran73, Newell72b]).

There were many design constraints present in the classical formal rule-based systems. Many of these details were preserved in the AI production rule based programs (e.g., forcing all state information into a single string of tokens), but there were many changes. The whole notion of "what a rule system really is" changed from an effective problem statement to a tendency to solve problems in a particular way. One typical corollary of this change of view was that instead of *no* external inputs whatsoever, there was now a *presumption* of some "environment" that supplied new entries into the token sequence. In Section 2 (see Table 1) is an articulation of these *neo*classical (i.e., AI circa 1973; see [Davis76b]) principles for designing "pure" production systems.

Due to the early successes, psychological applicability, and esthetic simplicity afforded by production systems, AI researchers began to write rule systems (RSs) to perform informal inductive inference tasks (mass spectrum identification [B. G. Buchanan75], medical diagnosis [Shortliffe74] and consultation dialogue [Davis76a], speech understanding [McCracken77], nonresolution theorem proving [Bledsoe75], math research [Lenat76], and many more).

Yet it seems that most of the large, successful RSs have violated many of the "pure production system" guidelines. The purpose of this chapter is to show that such "exceptions" were inevitable, because any system satisfying the neoclassical design constraints, though universal in principle, is too impoverished to represent complex tasks for what they are.

The essence of the neoclassical architecture is to opt for simplicity in all things, since there is very little one can say about RSs in general. As more becomes known about the task of the RS, it turns out that some of that new knowledge takes the form of specific constraints on the design of the RS itself (as distinct from what specific knowledge we choose to represent within that design). Sometimes a new constraint directly contradicts the early, domain-independent one; sometimes it is merely a softening or augmentation of the old constraint.

After examining the "pure" architecture, we shall examine in detail the design of one particular rule system that discovers and studies mathematical concepts. Deviations from the pure architecture will be both frequent and extreme. Subsequent sections will analyze these differences. It will be shown that each one is plausible, usually for reasons that depend strongly on the "scientific discovery" domain of the RS. Some of the limitations of this RS will be treated, and their elimination will be seen to require abandoning still more of the original design constraints.

When these modifications are collected, in Section 5, we shall have quite a different set of principles for building RSs. Not only will naivete have been lost: so will generality (the breadth of kinds of knowledge representable, the totality of tractable tasks). Rule systems conforming to the new design will be awkward for many tasks (just as a sledge hammer is awkward for cracking eggs). However, they should be significantly more powerful and natural for scientific inference tasks.

## 2.0 EARLY DESIGN CONSTRAINTS

By a *rule system* (RS) we shall mean any collection of condition-action *rules*, together with associated *data structures* (DS; also called *memories*), which the rules may inspect and alter. There must also be a policy for *interpretation*: detecting and firing relevant rules.

These definitions are deliberately left vague. Many details must be specified for any actual rule system (e.g., What may appear in the condition part of a rule?). This specification process is what we mean by *designing* a RS.

Table 1 contains an articulation of the design of the early general-purpose AI production rule systems. Notice the common theme: the adequacy of simplicity in all dimensions.

Table 1. Neoclassical Rule System Architecture

1.  *Principle of Simple Memories.* One or two uniform data structures define sufficient memories for a rule system to read from and write into. The format for entries in these structures is both uncomplicated and unchanging.
2.  *Principle of Simple DS Accesses.* The primitive read and write operations are as simple and low-level as possible; typically they are simply a membership-test type of read, and an insert-new-element type of write. More complicated, algorithmic operations on the memories are not available to the rules.
3.  *Principle of Isolated DS Elements.* Elements of the uniform DS cannot point to (parts of) other elements. This follows from the preceding principle: if we are not allowed to *chase* pointers, there might as well not be any.
4.  *Principle of Continuous Attention.* In addition to the one or two simple data structures, there may be an external envi-

ronment that continuously inserts stimuli into the DS. The interleaving of stimuli and internally generated symbols is managed quite trivially: (a) The stimuli are simply inserted into the DS as new elements; (b) Each rule is so small and quick that no "interruption" mechanism is necessary. The interpreter may ignore any suddenly added stimulus until the current rule finishes executing. The RS may be viewed as "continuously" attending to the environment.

5.   *Principle of Opaque Rules.* Rules need not have a format inspectable by other rules, but rather can be coded in whatever way is convenient for the programmer and the rule interpreter; i.e., the set of rules is not treated as one of the RSs data structures. For example, the condition parts of rules may be barred from fully analyzing the set of productions [Rychener76], and the action parts of rules may not be allowed to delete existing rules [Waterman75].

6.   *Principle of Simple Rules.* Rules consist of a left- and a right-hand side, which are quite elementary: The left-hand side (lhs, situation characterization, IF-part, condition) is typically a pattern-match composed with a primitive DS read access, and the right-hand side (rhs, consequence, THEN-part, action) is also simply a primitive DS write access. There is no need for sophisticated bundles of DS accesses on either side of a rule. Thus several extra rules should be preferred to a single rule with several actions.

7.   *Principle of Encoding by Coupled Rules.* A collection of interrelated rules is used to accomplish each subtask; i.e., wherever a subroutine would be used in a procedural programming language. For example, programming an iteration may require many rules "coupled" by writing and reading special (i.e., otherwise meaningless) loop control notes in the data structure.

8.   *Principle of Knowledge as Rules.* All knowledge of substance should be, can be, and is represented as rules. This includes all nontrivial domain-dependent information. The role of the DS is just to hold simple descriptive information, intermediate control state messages, recent stimuli from the environment, etc.

9.   *Principle of Simple Interpretation.* The topmost control flow in the RS is via a simple rule interpreter. After a rule fires, it is essential that any rule in the system may potentially be the next one to fire (i.e., it is forbidden to locate a set of relevant rules and fire them off in sequence). When the rhs of a rule is executed, it can (and frequently will) drastically

alter the situation that determined which rules were relevant.

10.   *Principle of Closure.* The representations allowed by (1-9) are sufficient and appropriate for organizing all the kinds of knowledge needed for tasks for which a given RS is designed.

This design was plausible *a priori*, and worked quite well for its initial applications (the simulation of simple human cognitive processes [Moran73, Newell73, Waterman75]). But is this design proper for *any* RS, regardless of its intended task? In particular, what about scientific inference tasks? Over the years, several rule-based inference systems for scientific tasks have been constructed. With each new success have come some deviations from the above principles [Davis76b]. Were these mere aberrations, or is there some valid reason for such changes in design?

We claim the latter. The task domain — scientific discovery — dictates a new and quite different architecture for RSs. To study this phenomenon, we shall describe in Section 3 one particular RS that defines new mathematical concepts, studies them, and conjectures relationships between them. Subsequent sections will explore the deviations of its design from the neoclassical constraints in Table 1.

## 3.0 AM: A RULE SYSTEM FOR MATH THEORY FORMATION

A recent thesis [Lenat76] describes a program called AM that gradually expands a base of mathematical knowledge. The representation of math facts is somewhat related to Actors [Hewitt76] and Beings [Lenat75] in the partitioning of such domain knowledge into effective, structured modules. Departing from the traditional control structures usually associated with Actors, Beings, and Frames [Minsky75], AM concentrates on one "interesting" miniresearch question after another. These "jobs" are proposed and rated by a collection of approximately 250 situation-action rules. Discovery in mathematics is modeled in AM as a rule-guided exploration process. This view is explained in Section 3.1. (See also [Polya54].) The representation of knowledge is sketched next, followed by a much more detailed description of the rule-based control structure of AM. Finally, in Section 3.5, the experimental results of the project are summarized.

### 3.1 Discovery in Mathematics as Heuristic Rule-Guided Search

The task that AM performs is the discovery of new mathematics concepts and relationships between them. The simple paradigm it follows for this task is to maintain a graph of partially developed concepts , and to obey a large collection of "heuristics" (rules that frequently lead to discoveries), which guide it to define and study the most plausible thing next.

For example, at one point AM had some notions of sets, set-operations, numbers, and simple arithmetic. One heuristic rule it knew said *"If f is an interesting relation, Then look at its inverse".* This rule fired after AM had studied "multiplication" for a while. The rhs of the rule then directed AM to define and study the relation "divisors-of" (e.g., divisors-of(12) = {1,2,3,4,6,12}). Another heuristic rule that later fired said *"If f is a relation from A into B, then it's worth examining those members of A which map into extremal* members of B". In this case, f was matched to "divisors-of," A was "numbers," B was "sets of numbers," and an extremal member of B might be, e.g., a very *small* set of numbers. Thus this heuristic rule caused AM to define the set of numbers with no divisors, the set of numbers with only 1 divisor, with only 2 divisors, etc. One of these sets (the last one mentioned) turned out subsequently to be quite important; these numbers are of course the primes. The above heuristic also directed AM to study numbers with very *many* divisors; such highly composite numbers were also found to be interesting.

This same paradigm enabled AM to discover concepts that were much more primitive (e.g., cardinality) and much more sophisticated (e.g., the fundamental theorem of arithmetic) than prime numbers. We shall now describe the AM program in more detail.

### 3.2 Representation of Mathematical Knowledge

What exactly does it mean for AM to "have the notion of" a concept? It means that AM possesses a framelike data structure for that concept. For instance, Fig. 1 shows how one concept looked after AM had defined and explored it.

### 3.3 Top-Level Control: An Agenda of Promising Questions

AM was initially given a collection of 115 core concepts, with only a few facets (i.e., slots) filled in for each. AM repeatedly chooses some facet of some concept, and tries to fill in some entries for that particular slot. To decide which such job to work on next, AM maintains an *agenda* of jobs, a global queue ordered by priority [D. G. Bobrow77]. A typical job is *"Fill-in examples of Primes".* The agenda may contain hundreds of entries such as this one. AM repeatedly selects the top job from the agenda and tries to carry it out. This is the whole control structure! Of course, we must still explain how AM creates plausible new jobs to place on the agenda, how AM decides which job will be the best one to execute next, and how it carries out a job.

NAME: Prime Numbers
DEFINITIONS:
      ORIGIN: Number-of-divisors-of(x) = 2
      PREDICATE-CALCULUS: Prime(x) iff
        (For-all z) (z|x implies z=1 XOR z=x)
      ITERATIVE: (for x>1): For i from 2 to x-1, not (i|x)

EXAMPLES: 2, 3, 5, 7, 11, 13, 17
      BOUNDARY: 2, 3
      BOUNDARY-FAILURES: 0, 1
      FAILURES: 12
GENERALIZATIONS: Numbers, Numbers with an even
   number of divisors,
             Numbers with a prime number of divisors
SPECIALIZATIONS: Odd Primes, Prime Pairs, Prime
   Uniquely-addables
CONJECS: Unique factorization, Goldbach's conjecture,
   Extrema of Divisors-of
ANALOGIES: Maximally-divisible numbers are converse
   extremes of Divisors-of
INTEREST: Conjec's tying Primes to Times, to Divisors-of, to
   closely related operations
WORTH: 800

Fig. 1. A typical concept.

If the job were *"Fill in new Algorithms for Set-union"*, then *satisfying* it would mean actually synthesizing some new procedures, some new LISP code capable of forming the union of any two sets. A heuristic rule is *relevant* to a job if and only if executing that rule brings AM closer to satisfying that job. Potential relevance is determined *a priori* by where the rule is stored. A rule tacked onto the domain/range facet of the Compose concept would be presumed potentially relevant to the job *"Fill in the Domain of Insert-o-Delete"*. The lhs of each potentially relevant rule is evaluated to determine whether the rule is truly relevant.

Once a job is chosen from the agenda, AM gathers together all the potentially relevant heuristic rules, the ones that might accomplish that job. They are executed, and then AM picks a new job. While a rule is executing, three kinds of actions or effects can occur:

(1) Facets of some concepts can get filled in (e.g., examples of primes may actually be found and tacked onto the "Examples" facet of the "Primes" concept). A typical heuristic rule which might have this effect is

*If examples of X are desired, where X is a kind of Y (for some more general concept Y), then check the examples of Y; some of them may be examples of X as well.*

For the job of filling in examples of Primes, this rule would have AM notice that Primes is a kind of Number, and therefore look over all the known examples of Number. Some of those would be primes, and would be transferred to the examples facet of Primes.

(2) New concepts may be created (e.g., the concept "primes that are uniquely representable as the sum of two other primes" may be somehow be deemed worth studying). A typical heuristic rule that might result in this new concept is

*If some (but not most) examples of X are also examples of Y (for some concept Y), then create a new concept defined as the intersection of those 2 concepts (X and Y).*

Suppose AM has already isolated the concept of being representable as the sum of two primes in only one way (AM actually calls such numbers "uniquely-prime-addable numbers"). When AM notices that some primes are in this set, the above rule will create a brand new concept, defined as the set of numbers that are both prime and uniquely prime addable.

(3) New jobs may be added to the agenda (e.g., the current activity may suggest that the following job is worth considering: "Generalize the concept of prime numbers"). A typical heuristic rule that might have this effect is

*If very few examples of X are found, then add the following job to the agenda: "Generalize the concept X."*

The concept of an agenda is certainly not new: schedulers have been around for a long time. But one important feature of AM's agenda scheme *is* a new idea: attaching—and using—a list of quasi-symbolic reasons to each job that explain why the job is worth considering, why it is plausible. It is the responsibility of the heuristic rules to include reasons for any jobs they propose. For example, let us reconsider the heuristic rule mentioned in (3) above. It really looks more like the following:

*If very few examples of X are found, then add the following job to the agenda: "Generalize the concept X," for the following reason: "X's are quite rare; a slightly less restrictive concept might be more interesting."*

If the same job is proposed by several rules, then several different reasons for it may be present. In addition, one ephemeral reason also exists: "focus of attention" [F. Hayes-Roth76g]. Any jobs that are related to the one last executed get "focus of attention" as a bonus reason. AM uses all these reasons to decide how to rank the jobs on the agenda. Each reason is given a rating (by the heuristic that proposed it), and the ratings are combined into an overall priority rating for each job on the agenda. The jobs are ordered by these ratings, and so it is trivial to select the job with the highest rating. Note that if a job already on the agenda is reproposed for a new reason, then its priority will increase. If the job is reproposed for an already-present reason, however, the overall rating of the job will *not* increase. This turned out to be an important enough phenomenon that it was presented in [Lenat76] as a necessary design constraint.

AM uses each job's list of reasons in other ways. Once a job has been selected, the quality of the reasons is used to decide how much time and space the job will be permitted to absorb, before AM quits and moves on to a new job. Another use is to explain to the human observer precisely why the chosen top job is a plausible thing for AM to concentrate upon.

## 3.4 Low-Level Control: A Lattice of Heuristic Rules

The hundreds of concepts AM possesses are interrelated in many ways. One main organization is that provided by their generalization and specialization facets. The concepts may be viewed as nodes on a large lattice whose edges are labelled Genl/Spec. The importance of this organization stems from various *heritability* properties. For example, Spec is transitive, and so the specializations of numbers include not only primes but all *its* specializations as well.

Let us describe a second, very important heritability property. Each of the 250 heuristic rules is attached to the most general (i.e., abstract) concept for which it is deemed appropriate. The relevance of heuristic rules is assumed to be inherited by all its specializations. For example, a heuristic method that is capable of inverting any function will be attached to the concept "Function"; but it is certainly also capable of inverting any permutation. If there are no known methods specific to the latter job, then AM will follow the Genl links upward from Permutation to Bijection to Function..., seeking methods for inversion. Of course the more general concepts' methods tend to be weaker than those of the specific concepts.

In other words, the Genl/Spec graph of concepts induces a graph structure upon the set of heuristic rules. This permits potentially relevant rules to be located efficiently. Here is one more example of how this heritability works in practice: Immediately after the job "fill in examples of Set-equality" is chosen, AM asks each generalization of Set-equality for help. Thus it asks for ways to fill in examples of any Predicate, any Activity, any Concept, and finally for ways to fill in examples of Anything. One such heuristic rule known to the Activity concept says: *"If examples of the domain of the activity f are already known, Then actually execute f on some random members of its domain."* Thus when AM applies this heuristic rule to fill in examples of Set-equality, its domain facet is inspected, and AM notes that Set-equality takes a pair of sets as its arguments. Then AM accesses the examples facet of the concept Set, where it finds a large list of sets. The lhs is thus satisfied, and so the rule is fired. Obeying the heuristic rule, AM repeatedly picks a pair of the known sets at random, and sees if they satisfy Set-equality (by actually running the LISP function stored in the algorithms facet of Set-equality). While this will typically return False, it will occasionally locate—by random chance—a pair of equal sets.

Other heuristics, tacked onto other generalizations of Set-equality, provide additional methods for executing the job "fill in examples of Set-equality." A heuristic stored on the concept Any-concept says to symbolically instantiate the definition. After spending much time manipulating the recursive definition of Set-equality, a few trivial examples (like $\{\} = \{\}$) are produced. Notice that (as expected) the more general the concept is, the weaker (more time-consuming, less chance for success) its heuristics tend to be. For this reason, AM consults each concept's rules in order of increasing generalization.

### 3.5 Behavior of This Rule System

As Sections 3.1 to 3.4 indicate, the dynamic behavior of AM was as follows: a job is chosen from the agenda, potentially relevant rules are located by their position in the Genl/Spec lattice, their lhs's are evaluated to find those which actually trigger, they are then executed (in order of decreasing specificity) until they are all executed (or until some *local*, self-imposed limit on time or space is exceeded), and the cycle repeats. AM has a modest facility that prints out a description of these activities as they occur. The following is a tiny excerpt of this self-trace monologue:

\** Job 65: \** Fill in Examples of the concept "Divisors-of."

3 Reasons: (1) No known examples of Divisors-of so far.
    (2) TIMES, which is related to Divisors-of, is now very interesting

(3) Focus of attention: AM recently defined Divisors-of.

26 examples found, in 9.2 seconds, e.g., Divisors-of(6) = {1 2 3 6}.

** Job 66: ** Consider numbers having small sets of Divisors-of.

2 Reasons: (1) Worthwhile to look for extreme cases.
(2) Focus of attention: AM recently worked on Divisors-of.

Filling in examples of numbers with 0 divisors.
0 examples found, in 4.0 seconds.
Conjecture: no numbers have precisely 0 divisors.

Filling in examples of numbers with 1 divisors.
1 examples found, in 4.0 seconds. e.g., Divisors-of(1) = {1}.
Conjecture: 1 is the only number with precisely 1 divisor.

Filling in examples of numbers with 2 divisors.
24 examples found, in 4.0 seconds. e.g., Divisors-of(13) = {1 13}.
No obvious conjecture. May merit more study.
Creating a new concept: "Numbers-with-2-divisors."

Filling in examples of numbers with 3 divisors.
11 examples found, in 4.0 seconds. e.g., Divisors-of(49) = {1 7 49}.
All numbers with 3 divisors are also Squares. Definitely merits more study.
Creating a new concept: "Numbers-with-3-divisors."

** Job 67: ** Consider the square-roots of Numbers-with-3-divisors.

2 Reasons: (1) Numbers-with-3-divisors are unexpectedly also Perfect Squares
(2) Focus of attention: AM recently worked on Nos-with-3-divisors.

All square-roots of Numbers-with-3-divisors seem to be Numbers-with-2-divisors
e.g., Divisors-of(Square-root(169)) = Divisors-of(13) = {1 13}.

Even the converse of this seems empirically to be true, i.e., the square of each No-with-2-divisors seems to be a No-with-3-divisors.
The chance of coincidence is below acceptable limits.

Boosting the interestingness rating of each of the concepts involved.

** Job 68: ** Consider the squares of Numbers-with-3-divisors.

3 Reasons: (1) Squares of Numbers-with-2-divisors were interesting.

                (2) Square-roots of Numbers-with-3-divisors were interesting.

                (3) Focus of attention: AM recently worked on Nos-with-3-divisors.

Now that we have seen how AM works and we have been exposed to a bit of "local" results, we shall take a moment to discuss the totality of the mathematics that AM carried out. AM began its investigations with scanty knowledge of one hundred elementary concepts of finite set theory. Most of the obvious set-theoretic concepts and relationships were quickly found (e.g., de Morgan's laws; singletons), but no sophisticated set theory was ever done (e.g., diagonalization). Rather, AM discovered natural numbers and went off exploring elementary number theory. Arithmetic operations were soon found (as analogs to set-theoretic operations), and AM made surprising progress in divisibility theory. Prime pairs, Diophantine equations, the unique factorization of numbers into primes, and Goldbach's conjecture were some of the nice discoveries by AM. Many concepts that we know to be crucial were never uncovered, however: remainder,[2] gcd, greater-than, infinity, proof, etc.

All the discoveries mentioned were made in a run lasting one cpu hour (Interlisp + 100k, SUMEX PDP-10 KI). Two hundred jobs in toto were selected from the agenda and executed. On the average, a job was granted 30 cpu seconds, but actually used only 18 seconds. For a typical job, about 35 rules were located as potentially relevant, and about a dozen actually fired. AM began with 115 concepts and ended up with three times that many. Of the synthesized concepts, half were technically termed "losers" (both by the author and by AM), and half the remaining ones were of only marginal interest.

Although AM fared well according to several different measures of performance (see Section 7.1 in [Lenat76]), of greatest significance are its *limitations*. This subsection will merely report them, and the next section will analyze whether they were caused by radical departures from the neoclassical production system architecture, or from departing not far enough from that early design.

As AM ran longer and longer, the concepts it defined were further and further from the primitives it began with. Thus "prime pairs"

---

[2] This concept, and many of the other "omissions," *could* have been discovered by the existing heuristic rules in AM. The paths that would have resulted in their definition were simply never rated high enough to explore.

were defined using "primes" and "addition," the former of which was defined from "divisors-of," which in turn came from "multiplication," which arose from "addition," which was defined as a restriction of "union," which (finally!) was a primitive concept (with heuristics) that we had supplied to AM initially. When AM subsequently needed help with prime pairs, it was forced to rely on rules of thumb supplied originally about *unioning*. Although the heritability property of heuristics did ensure that those rules were still valid, the trouble was that they were too general, too weak to deal effectively with the specialized notions of primes and arithmetic. For instance, one general rule indicated that A union B would be interesting if it possessed properties absent both from A and from B. This translated into the prime-pair case as "*If $p+q=r$, and $p,q,r$ are primes, Then $r$ is interesting if it has properties not possessed by $p$ or by $q$.*" The search for categories of such interesting primes $r$ was of course barren. It showed a fundamental lack of understanding about numbers, addition, odd/even-ness, and primes.

As the derived concepts moved further away from finite set theory, the efficacy of the initial heuristics decreased. AM began to "thrash," appearing to lose most of its heuristic guidance. It worked on concepts like "prime triples," which is not a rational thing to investigate. The key deficiency was the lack of adequate *meta*rules [Davis76a]: heuristics that cause the creation and modification of new heuristics.

Aside from the preceding major limitation, most of the other problems pertain to missing knowledge. Many concepts one might consider basic to discovery in math are absent from AM; analogies were underutilized; physical intuition was absent; the interface to the user was far from ideal; etc.

## 4.0 REEXAMINING THE DESIGN

Let us now consider the major components of RS design and how AM treated them: the DS, the rules, the distribution of knowledge between DS and rules, and the rule interpretation policy. For each component, AM's architecture failed to adhere strictly to the pure RS guidelines. Were these departures worth the loss of simplicity? Were the deviations due to the task domain (scientific discovery), to the task view (heuristically guided growth of structured theories), or to other sources? These are the kinds of questions we shall address in each of the following subsections.

## 4.1 Data Structures

We recognize that a single uniform DS (e.g., an infinite STM [Newell73]) is universal in the Turing sense of being *formally* adequate: One can encode any representation in a linear, homogeneous DS. The completeness of such a DS design notwithstanding, we believe that encouraging several distinct, special-purpose DSs will enhance the performance of a discovery system. That is, we are willing to sacrifice esthetic purity of DSs for clarity, efficiency, and power. In this section we will explore this tradeoff.

The data structures used in AM are unlike the uniform memories suggested by the first design constraint (see Table 1). One DS—the agenda—holds an ordered list of plausible questions for the system to concentrate on, a list of jobs to work on. Another DS is the graph of concepts AM knows about. Each concept itself consists in much structured information (see Fig. 1). The reasons AM has for each job have information associated with them. Still other information is present as values of certain functions and global variables: the cpu clock, the total number of concepts, the last thing typed out to the user, the last few concepts worked on, etc. All these types of information are accessed by the lhs's of heuristic rules, and affected by rhs's (some "deliberately" in the text of the rule, some "incidentally" through a chain of if-added methods).

Why is there this multitude of diverse DSs? Each type of knowledge (jobs, math knowledge, system status) needs to be treated quite differently. Since the primitive operations will vary with the type of information, so should the DS. For *jobs*, the primitive kinds of accesses will be picking the highest-rated job, deleting the lowest-rated one, reordering some jobs, merging new ones. A natural choice to make these operations efficient is to keep the system's goals in a queue ordered by their rating or partially ordered by those ratings that are commensurable. For *resource information*, the usual request is for some *statistic* of some class of primary data. To maintain a table of such summary facts (like how much the CPU clock has run so far, or how many concepts there are) is to introduce an unnecessary DS and incur exorbitant costs to maintain many *short-lived* entries that will, most probably, never be used. It is far more reasonable to run a summarizing procedure to develop just that ephemeral, up-to-date information that is needed. For *math concepts*, we have a much less volatile situation. We view them as an ever-growing body of highly interrelated facts. Knowledge in this form is stable and rarely deleted. When new knowledge is added, a great many "routine" inferences must be drawn. In a uniform, linear memory, each would have to be drawn explicitly; in a structured one (as the Genl/Spec graph structure provides) they may be accomplished through the tacit (analogical) characteristics of the representation, simply by deciding *where* to place the information.

Each kind of knowledge dictates a set of appropriate kinds of primitive operations to be performed on it, which in turn suggest natural data structures in which to realize it. The generality of this perspective on rule-based systems is made more plausible by examining other RSs that deal with many types of knowledge (e.g., [B. G. Buchanan75]). If this is so, if the design proceeds from "knowledge to be represented" to "a data structure to hold it," then fixing *a priori* the capabilities of the DS access primitives available to rules is suspect.

Therefore, we advocate the opposite: the RS designer is encouraged to name every combination of "machine" operations that together comprise a single conceptual access of data by rules. In AM, it is quite reasonable to expect that a request like "find all generalizations of a given concept" would be such a primitive (i.e., could be referred to by name). Even though it might cause the "machine" (in this case, LISP) to run around the Genl/Spec graph, a single rule can treat this as merely an "access" operation. The use of complex tests and actions is not new; we simply claim that it is *always* preferable to package knowledge (for which a reasonably fast algorithm is available) as a single action (though it may have side-effects in the space of concepts) or a single test (so long as its sole side-effect — modulo caches — is to signal). Primitive tests and actions should be maximally algorithmic, not minimally computational. The neoclassical view of designing a production rule system was that of defining a machine. Our present view is that RSs do not *compute* so much as they *guide attention*. In adopting this view (thereby separating the controller from the effector), we recognize that we are giving up an attractive feature of pure rule systems: a homogeneous basis for definition. For example, the rule system designer must now spell out in detail the definitions of the DS accessing functions; but the designer of a neoclassical RS is simply able to take as *givens* the matching and inserting operations (as specified in neoclassical principle 6, Table 1), and he builds each more complicated one out of these primitives.[3] In giving up the old view of the RS as an abstract computing machine, the RS designer must use another homogeneous substrate (e.g., LISP) in terms of which to define his DSs and especially the procedures that process them. In exchange, he obtains a clear distinction between two kinds of knowledge contained in the neoclassical rule: plausible proposals for what to do next, and how to accomplish what might be proposed.

---

[3] Either by stringing out a sequence of primitives on one side of a rule, or by handcrafting a tightly coupled bundle of rules (so firing such a rule would simulate traversing one link of the kind that abound in AM's DSs).

We have seen that admitting complicated and varied DSs leads to stylized sets of DS accesses. The DSs and their sets of read/write primitives must in turn be explicitly defined (coded) by the designer. This seems like a high price to pay. Is there any bright side to this? Yes, one rather interesting possibility is opened up. Not only the RS designer, but the RS *itself* may define DSs and DS access functions. In AM, this might take the form of dynamically defining new kinds of facets (slots). For example, after "injective function" is defined, and after some of its properties have been discovered, it would be appropriate to introduce a new facet called "inverse" for each (concept representing an) injective function. In AM, the actual definitions of the facets of every concept are complex enough (shared structure), interrelated enough (shared meaning), and interesting enough (consistent heuristic worth) that a special concept was included for each one (e.g., a concept called "examples") that contained a definition, description,. . . of the facet. Thus the same techniques for manipulating and discovering math concepts may be applied to DS design concepts. Not only do math theories emerge, so can new DS access functions (new slots; e.g., "small boundary examples," "factorization," or "inverse").

It should be noted that in opting for nonuniform DSs, we have not in general sacrificed efficiency. One has only to compare the time to access a node in a tree, versus in a linear list, to appreciate that efficiency may, in fact, be *increased* by nonuniformity.

Just how tangled up a DS should we tolerate? Should memory elements be permitted to refer to ("know about") each other? We believe the answer depends upon the *type* of data structure involved. For the homogeneous DS called for in the neoclassical design, much simplicity is preserved by forbidding this kind of interrelationship. But consider a DS like AM's graph of concepts. It is growing, analogically interrelated, and it contains descriptions of its elements. This richness (and sheer quantity) of information can be coded only inefficiently in a uniform, non-self-referential manner. For another example, consider AM's agenda of jobs. One reason for a job may simply be the existence of some other job. In such a case, it seems natural for part of one entry on the agenda (a reason part of one job) to point to another entry in the same DS (point to another specific job on the agenda). Thus, interelement pointers *are* allowed, even though they blur a "pure" distinction between a DS and its entries.[4] Interelement references play a necessary role in organizing large bodies of highly interrelated information into structured modules.

There is yet another motivation for special-purpose DSs when the task of the RS includes sensing an external environment. Using a

---

[4] In Section 4.3 we shall mention work that blurs this distinction even further.

uniform memory, external stimuli are dumped into the working memory and rub shoulders with all the other data. They must then be distinguished from the others. ("Must" because to freely intermingle what one sees or is told with what one thinks or remembers is to give way to endless confusion.) How much cleaner, less distracting, and safer it is for stimuli to arive in their own special place — a place that might well be a special-purpose store such as an intensity *array* (not even a list structure at all), or a low-level speech-segment *queue*. A linear memory (e.g., an infinite STM) is of course adequate; one could tag each incoming environmental stimulus with a special flag. But the design philosophy we are proposing is aimed at maximizing clarity and efficiency, not uniformity or universality.

We know that this view of DSs means making a specialized design effort for each class of knowledge incorporated into the RS. But that is desirable, since it buys us three things: (1) system performance is increased, (2) some forms of automatic learning are facilitated, (3) knowledge is easier to encode.

## 4.2 Rules

In the "pure" view of RSs, the rule store is not a full-fledged DS of the RS. For example, in Waterman's [Waterman75] poker player, rules may not be deleted. Rychener [Rychener76] states that the only way his RS may inspect rules is by examining the effect of those rules which have recently fired. Although AM had no explicit taboo against inspecting rules, such analyses were in practice never possible, since the rules were *ad hoc* blocks of LISP code. This eventually turned out to be the main limitation of the design of AM. The ultimate impediment to further discovery was the lack of rules that could reason about, modify, delete, and synthesize other rules. AM direly needed to synthesize specialized forms of the given general heuristic rules (as new concepts arose; see the end of Section 3.5.)

We want our heuristic rules to be added, kept track of, reasoned about, modified, deleted, generalized, specialized, . . . whenever there is a good reason to do so. Note that those situations may be very different from the ones in which such a rule might fire. For example, upon discovering a new, interesting concept, AM should try to create some specially tailored heuristic rules for it. They would not actually *fire* until much later, when their lhs's were triggered. After having constructed such rules, AM might subject them to criticism and improvement as it explores the new concept.

In sum, we have found that the discovery of heuristic rules for using new math concepts is a necessary part of the growth of math knowledge. Hence, following the argument in Section 4.1, the rules themselves should be DSs, and each rule might be described by a concept with effective (executable) and noneffective (purely descriptive) facets. This lesson was made all the more painful because it was not new [B. G. Buchanan75]. Apparently the need for reasoning about rules is common to many tasks.

The current recoding of AM does in fact have each rule represented as a concept. What kinds of noneffective "facets" do they have? Recall that one of the features of the original AM (as described in Section 3.3) was that with each rule were associated some symbolic *reasons* that it could provide whenever it proposed a new job for the agenda. Thus one kind of facet that every rule can possess is "reasons." What others are there? Some of them *describe* the rule (e.g., its average cost); some facets provide a road map to the space of rules (e.g., which rule schemata are mere specializations of the given one); some facets record its derivation (e.g., the rule was proposed as an analog to rule X because . . .), its redundancy (some other rules need not be tried if this one is), etc.

There are some far-reaching consequences of the need to reason about rules just as if they were any other concepts known to AM. When one piece of knowledge relates to several rules, then one general concept, a rule *schema*, should exist to hold that common knowledge. Since each rule is a concept, there will be a natural urge to exploit the same Genl/Spec organization that proved so useful before. Heritability still holds; e.g., any reason that explains rule R is also somehow a partial explanation of each specialization of R.

Rule schemata have cause to exist simply because they generalize — and hold much information that would otherwise have to be duplicated in — several specific rules. They may tend to be "big" and less directly productive when executed, yet they are of value in capturing the essence of the discovery techniques.[5] We put "big" in quotes because sheer length (total number of lhs tests allowed, total number of rhs actions) is not directly what we are talking about here. A general rule schema will capture many regularities, will express an idea common to several more specific rules. It will contain dual forms of the same rule, sophisticated types of variable-binding (for the duration of the rule application), and searching may even be required to find the actions of such a general rule. We may even wish to consider every rule in the RS as a rule schema of some level of generality, and much processing may go on to find the particular instance(s) of it that should be applied in any particular situation.

Let us consider a rule schema called the "rule of enthusiasm." It

---

[5] In AM, even the specific rules may be "big" in the sense that their very precise knowledge may involve much testing to trigger and, once triggered, may conclude some elaborate results.

subsumes several rules in the original AM system (pp. 247-8 of [Lenat76]), e.g., those that said

*If concept G is now very interesting, and G was created as a generalization of some earlier concept C,*

*Give extra consideration to generalizing G, and to generalizing C in other ways.*

and

*If concept S proved to be a dead-end, and S was created as a specialization of some earlier concept C,*

*Give less consideration to specializing S, and to specializing C in other ways in the future.*

The proposed rule schema is

*If concept X has very high/low interest and X can be derived from some concept C by means m,*

*Give more/less consideration to finding (and elaborating) concepts derived from C, X (and their "neighbors") by means analogous to m.*

There are four variables to be matched and coordinated in the lhs of this rule: a concept X, the direction (high or low) of its extreme interest rating, a derivation procedure m, and an associated source concept C. The action itself is to search for jobs of a certain type and give them a corresponding (high or low) rating change. Three types of matching are present: (1) ranging over a set of alternatives that are known at the time the rule is written (e.g., the "high/low" alternative); (2) ranging over a set of alternatives that can be accessed easily at any moment the rule is run, like the set of concepts and connections between them now in existence (e.g., the variables X and C range over this kind of set); (3) ranging over a set of alternatives that must be heuristically searched for as part of the rule execution (e.g., "analogous" and "neighbors" only make sense after a nontrivial amount of searching has been performed).

Since the "rule of enthusiasm" is very general, it will only be tried if no more specific rules (such as the two that were listed just above it) are relevant at the time. Ideally, the search to specify the action should create a new, specialized form of the rule of enthusiasm to catch this situation and handle it quickly, should it arise again. Note that versions of this schema that mention generalization or specialization are also schemata (without any specification search); they are simply less general schemata than the rule of enthusiasm itself. Whenever a new subject for discovery gets defined, the abstract, hard- to-execute rule schemata can be specialized (compiled, refined, etc.) into efficient heuristics for that subject.

Another use of a rule schema might be to *name* a collection of neoclassical rules that are coupled by together fulfilling a single function. Consider a collection of rules that is tightly coupled, say to perform an iteration. Much knowledge about the iteration loop as a whole may exist. Where is such descriptive information to be stored and sought? Either it must be duplicated for each of the coupled rules, or there must be a rulelike concept that "knows about" the iteration as one coherent unit. We conclude that even if some intertwined rules *are* kept separate, an extra rule (a schema) should exist that (at least implicitly) has a rhs that combines them (by containing knowledge common to all of them). Thus rule schemata do more than just unify general properties of rules: there must also be schemata of the kind that relate function to mechanism.

Another problem crops up if we consider what happens if one of the coupled rules is modified. Often, some corresponding change should be made in all its companions. For example, if a term is generalized (replacement of "prime" by "number" everywhere) then the same substitution had probably better be done in each rule with which this one is supposed to couple. What we are saying is that, for RSs that modify their own rules, it can be dangerous to split up a single conceptual process into a bunch of rules that interact in more or less fixed ways when run, without continuing to reason about them as an integrity, *like any other algorithm* composed of parts. Here again, we find pressure to treat RSs as algorithms, not vice versa.

Finally, let us make a few irresistable observations. The whole notion of coupling via meaningless tokens is esthetically repugnant and quite contrary to "pure" production system spirit. By "meaningless" we mean entries in DS that provide a narrow hand-crafted channel of communication between two specific rules that therefore "know about each other."[6] At the least, when a coupled rule deposits some "intermediate-state" message in a DS, one would like that message to be meaningful to many rules in the system, to have some significance itself. We can see that entries in a DS have an expected meaning to the read access functions that examine the DS.[7] If this purity is maintained, then any apparent "coupling" would be merely superficial: each rule could stand alone as a whole domain-dependent heuristic. Thus no harm should come from changing a single rule, and more

---

[6] By contrast, a "meaningful" DS entry will embody a piece of information that is specific to the RS's task, not to the actual rules themselves.

[7] Perhaps this "meaning" could even be expressed formally as an invariant that the write access functions for the DS must never violate.

rules could be added that act on the "intermediate message" of the coupling. Such meaningful, dynamic couplings should be encouraged. Only the meaningless, tight couplings are being criticized here.

## 4.3 Distribution of Knowledge between Rules and DS

A common "pure" idea is that all knowledge of substance ought to be represented as rules. Independent of such rules, the DS forms no meaningful whole initially, nor has it any final interpretation. The "answer" that the RS computes is not stored in the DS; rather, the answer consists in the process of rule firings.[8] The DS is "just" an intermediate vehicle of control information.

Contrary to this, we say that rules ought to have a *symbiotic* relationship to DSs. The DSs hold meaningful domain-dependent information, and rules process knowledge represented in them. For RSs designed to perform scientific research, the DSs contain the theory, and the rules contain methods of theory formation. But much domain-dependent knowledge is conditional. For example, "If n and m are relatively prime and divide x, then so must nm." Shouldn't such If/ Then information be encoded as rules? We answer an emphatic *No*. Just as there is a distribution of "all knowledge of substance" between rules and DSs, so too must the conditional information be partitioned between them. We shall illustrate two particular issues: (1) Much information can be stored implicitly in DSs; (2) Some conditional knowledge is inappropriate to store as rules.

When designing a DS, it is possible to provide mechanisms for holding a vast amount of information *implicitly*. In AM, e.g., the organization of concepts into a Genl/Spec hierarchy (plus the assumed heritability properties; see Section 3.4) permits a rule to ask for "all concepts more general than primes" as if that were a piece of data explicitly stored in a DS. In fact, only direct generalizations are stored ("the immediate generalization of primes is numbers"), and a "rippling" mechanism automatically runs up the Genl links to assemble a complete answer. Thus the number of specific answers the DS can provide is far greater than the number of individual items in the DS. True, these DS mechanisms will use up extra time in processing to obtain the answer; this is efficient since any particular request is very unlikely to be made. Just as each rule knows about a general situation, of which it will only see a few instances, that same quality (of wide potential applicability) is just as valuable for knowledge in DSs. These are situations where, like Dijkstra's multiplier [Dijkstra72], the mech-

---

[8] The sequence of actions in time. In addition, perhaps, the "answer" may involve a few of their side-effects, e.g., (Respond 'YES').

anism must provide any of the consequences of its knowledge quickly on demand, but in its lifetime will only be asked a few of them.

Now that we have seen how tacit information *can* be encoded into DSs, let us see some cases where it *should* be, i.e., where it is not appropriate to encode it as rules of the system. Many things get called implication, and only some of them correspond to rule application. For instance, there is logical entailment (e.g., if A and B then A), physical causation (e.g., if it rains, then the ground will get wet), probable associations (e.g., if it is wet underfoot, then it has probably been raining.) These all describe the way the world is, not the way the perceiver of the world behaves. Contrast them with knowledge of the form "If it is raining, then open the umbrella." We claim that this last kind of situation-action relationship should be encoded as rules for the RS, but that the other types of implication should be stored declaratively within the DS. Let us try to justify this distinction.

The situation-action rules indicate imperatively how to behave in the world; the other types of implication merely indicate expected relationships and tendencies within the world. The rules of a RS are meant to indicate potential procedural actions that are obeyed by the system, while the DSs indicate the way the world (the RSs environment) behaves in terms of some model of it. The essential thing to consider is what relations are to be *caused in time;* these are the things we should cast as rules. The lhs of a rule measures some aspect of knowledge presently in DSs, while the rhs of the rule defines the attention of the system (regarded as a processor feeding off of the DS) in the immediate future.

This is the heart of why rule-sets are algorithms. They are algorithms for guiding the application of other (DS processing) algorithms. It also explains why other kinds of implications are unsuitable to be rules. Consider causal implication ("raining $\rightarrow$ wet"). While the lhs could be a rule's lhs (it measures an aspect of any situation), the rhs should *not* be a rule's rhs (it does not indicate an appropriate action for the system to take).[9]

Most purist production systems have (often implicitly!) a rule of the form "If the left side of an implication is true in the database, Then assert the right side." This is only one kind of rule, of course, capable of dealing with implications. For example, MYCIN and LT [Newell57]

---

[9] In a RS that aspires to any generality at all, an antecedent theorem of the form "if *you know that* it is raining, then *assert that* it is wet" is not the appropriate form to store this knowledge; it is too compiled a form, standing alone. If "told" (or given) a rule like this, a learning system should "parse" it as a familiar kind of deduction, file the residue of new information away as a conjectured tendency of wetness to follow rain, and start checking for exceptions. A sophisticated (and lucky) discovery RS might thereby develop the concept of "shelter."

(implicitly) follow a very different rule: "If the rhs of an implication will satisfy my goal, Then the lhs of the implication is now the new goal." Other rules are possible; many rules for reasoning may feed off the same "table" of world knowledge. The point is that the implications themselves are declarative knowledge, not rules. In summary, then, it may be very important to distinguish rules (attention guides) from mere implications (access guides), and to store the latter within the DSs. This policy was not motivated by the scientific inference task for our RS. We believe it to be a worthwhile guideline in the design of *any* RS.

## 4.4 Interpreter

After a rule fires, the neoclassical interpretation policy (9 in Table 1) demands that *any* rule in the system can potentially be the next one selected to fire. This is true regardless of the speed-up techniques used in any particular implementation (say, by preprocessing the lhs's into a discrimination net [Rychener76]). But consider RSs for scientific discovery tasks. Their task—both at the top level and frequently at lower levels — is quite open-ended. If 20 rules trigger as relevant to such an open-ended activity (e.g., gathering empirical data, inducing conjectures) then there is much motivation for continuing to execute just these 20 rules for a while. They form an ad hoc plausible search algorithm for the agenda item selected.

A RS for discovery might reasonably be given a complex interpreter (rule-firing policy). AM, for example, experimented with a two-pass interpreter: first, a best-first, agenda-driven resource allocator and attention focuser selects the job it finds most interesting; second, it locates the set of relevant rules (typically about 30 to 40 rules) for the job, and begins executing them one after another (in best-first order of specificity) until the resources allocated in the first step run out [Norman75b]. The overall rating of the job that these rules are to satisfy determines the amount of cpu time and list cells that may be used up before the rules are interrupted and job is abandoned.

For example, say the job were "Find examples of primes." It is allotted 35 cpu seconds and 300 list cells, due to its overall priority rating just before it was plucked from the agenda. Say, 24 rules are relevant. The first one quickly finds that 2 and 3 are primes. Should the job halt right then? No, not if the real reason for this job is to gather as much data as possible, data from which conjectures will be suggested and tested. In that case, many of the other 23 rules should be fired as well. They will produce not only *additional* examples, but perhaps other *types* of examples.

The jobs on AM's agenda are really just miniresearch questions that are plausible to spend time investigating. Although phrased as specific requests, each one is really a research proposal, a topic to concentrate upon. We found it necessary to deviate from the simplest uniform interpreter for clarity (e.g., a human can follow the first-pass (job selection) taken alone and can follow the second-pass (job execution) by itself), for efficiency (knowing that all 24 rules are relevant, there is no need to find them 35 times), and for power (applying qualitatively different kinds of rules yields various types of examples). We claim this quality of open-endedness will recur in any RS whose task is free concept exploration. This includes all scientific discovery but not all scientific inference.

## 5.0 SPECULATIONS FOR A NEW DISCOVERY SYSTEM

The spirit of this chapter has been to give up straightforward simplicity in RSs for clarity, efficiency, and power. Several examples have been cited, but we speculate that there are further tradeoffs of this kind that are applicable to RSs whose purpose is to make new discoveries. Often there are several possible ways the designer may view the task of (and subtasks of) the intended RS. We wish to add the notion of "proof" to AM, say. Should we represent proof as a resolution search, as a process of criticism and improvement [Lakatos76] spiralling toward a solution, as a natural deduction cascade? Although any one of these task views might perform respectably, we advocate the incorporation of all of them, despite the concomitant costs of added processing time, space, and interfacing. In fact, we wish never to exclude the possibility of the system acquiring another task-view.

We look for the development of further discovery tools in the form of domain-independent metaheuristics that synthesize heuristic rules, and in the form of abstract heuristic schemata that specialize into efficient rules for each newly discovered domain. These discovery tools are all part of "getting familiar" with shallowly understood concepts, such as synthesized ones tend to be initially. It may even be that symbolic analogy techniques exist, cutting across the traditional boundaries of knowledge domains. We contemplate a system (called EURISKO) that keeps track of (and has methods with which it attempts to improve) the design of its own DSs, its own control structure, and perhaps even its own design constraints. Although working in (a collection of) specific domains, this would be a general *symbol system discoverer*, capable of picking up and exploring formulations, testing them and improving them.

### 5.1 A New Set of Design Constraints

Table 2 gives 13 principles for designing a RS whose task is that of scientific theory formation. They are the result of reconsidering the original principles (Table 1) in the light shed by work on AM. Most of the "pure" principles we mentioned in Table 1 are changed, and a few new ones have emerged.

### Table 2. Scientific Discovery RS Architecture

1. *Principle of Several Appropriate Memories.* For each type of knowledge that must be dealt with in its own way, a separate DS should be maintained. The precise nature of each DS should be chosen so as to facilitate the access (read/write) operations that will be most commonly requested of it.

2. *Principle of Maximal DS Accesses.* The set of primitive DS access operations (i.e., the read tests that a rule's lhs may perform, and the write actions that a rhs may call for) are chosen to include the largest packages (clusters, chunks,. . .) of activity that are commonly needed and that can be performed efficiently on the DS.

3. *Principle of Facetted DS Elements.* For ever-growing data structures, there is much to be gained and little lost by permitting parts of one DS item to point to other DS items. In particular, schematic techniques of representing content by structure are now possible.

4. *Principle of Rules as Data.* The view that the RS designer takes of the system's task may require that some rules be capable of reasoning about the rules in the RS (adding new ones, deleting old ones, keeping track of rules' performance, modifying existing rules,. . .). Some of the methods the RS uses to deal with scientific knowledge may be applicable to dealing with rules as well. In such cases, the system's rules may thus be naturally represented as new entries in the existing DS, which holds the scientific theory.

5. *Principle of Regularities among Rules.* Each rule is actually a rule *schema.* Sophisticated processing may be needed both to determine which instance(s) are relevant and to find the precise sequence of actions to be executed. Such schemata are often quite elaborate.

6. *Principle of Avoiding Meaninglessly Coupled Rules.* Passing special-purpose loop control notes back and forth is contrary to both the spirit of pure RSs and to efficiency. If rules are to behave as coupled, the least we demand is that the notes they write and read for each other be meaningful entries in DS (any other rule may interpret the same note, and other rules might have written one identical to it).

7. *Principle of Controlled Environment.* For many tasks, it is detrimental to permit external stimuli (from an environ-

ment) to enter any DS at random. At the least, the RS should be able to distinguish these alien inputs from internally generated DS entries.

8. *Principle of Tacit Knowledge.* In designing the DS, much knowledge may be stored *implicitly,* e.g., by where facts are placed in a hierarchical network. The DS should be designed so as to maximize this kind of concentrated, analogical information storage. Hence, hard-working access functions are needed to encode and decode the full meaning of DSs.

9. *Principle of Named Algorithms.* When basic, "how to" knowledge is available, it should be packaged as an operation and used as a part of the lhs or rhs of various rules. Embodying this chunk of knowledge only as several coupled rules is not recommended, for we will want to manipulate and utilize this knowledge as a whole.

10. *Principle of Rules as Attention Guides.* Knowledge should be encoded as rules when it is intended to serve as a guide of the system's attention, to direct its behavior. Other kinds of information, even if stated in conditional form, should be relegated to DSs (either explicitly as entries, or implicitly as special access functions).

11. *Principle of Inertial Interpreter.* In tasks like scientific research, where relevant rules will be performing inherently open-ended activities (e.g., data-gathering), such rules should be allowed to continue for a while even after they have nominally carried out the activity (e.g., gathered one piece of data). In such cases, the occasional wasted time and space is more than compensated for by the frequent acquisition of valuable knowledge that was concentrated in the later rules. For scientific discovery, no single rule (however "appropriate") should be taken as sufficient: a single rule must necessarily view the task in just one particular way. All views of the task have something to contribute; hence variety depends on a policy of always applying several rules.

12. *Principle of Openness.* A discovery rule system can be enriched by incorporating into its design several independent views of the knowledge it handles. Never assume everything is known about a class of knowledge. All appropriate formulations of a knowledge class have something to contribute; hence variety depends on openness to new formulations.

13. *Principle of Support of Discovery by Design.* By representing its own design explicitly (say, as concepts), the RS could study and improve those concepts, thereby improving itself. This

includes the DS design,[10] the access function algorithms, how to couple them, the function of various rules, the interpretation policy of the RS, etc. This suggests that the study of designs of computational mechanisms may be a worthy area for a discovery system to pursue, whether its own design is available to it or not.

Rule systems whose designs adhere to these guidelines will be large, elaborate, and nonclassical. We have mentioned throughout the paper several new complications that the principles introduce. Trying to produce such a RS for a task for which a pure, neoclassical production rule system was appropriate will probably result in disaster. Nevertheless, empirical evidence suggests that RSs having this architecture are quite natural — and relatively tractable to construct — for open-ended tasks like scientific discovery.

# ACKNOWLEDGMENTS

This research builds upon Lenat's Ph.D. thesis at Stanford University, and he wishes to deeply thank his advisers and committee members: Bruce Buchanan, Edward Feigenbaum, Cordell Green, Donald Knuth, and Allen Newell. In addition, he gladly acknowledges the ideas he received in discussions with Dan Bobrow, Avra Cohn, and Randy Davis. Similarly, ideas received by Harris in two long and fruitful associations, with John Seely Brown and with Roger Schank, have contributed to this work. Many of our ideas have evolved through discussions at CMU this past year, notably with Don Cohen, John McDermott, Allen Newell, Kamesh Ramakrishna, Paul Rosenbloom, James Saxe, and especially Herbert Simon.

---

[10] For example, the facet specifications. If the input/output requirements change with time, so should the rule system's data structures.

# USE OF PRODUCTION SYSTEMS FOR MODELING ASYNCHRONOUS, CONCURRENT PROCESSES

Michael D. Zisman

*University of Pennsylvania*

*Because of the event-driven nature of asynchronous, concurrent processes, production systems (PSs) are an attractive modeling tool. The system of interest can be modeled with a large number of independent states, with independent actions, and the knowledge base can be conveniently encoded declaratively. However, asynchronous, concurrent processes normally have strict requirements for interprocess communication and coordination; this requires a substantial degree of interrule communiation in the PS. The result of this is that a complex control structure is embedded in the short-term memory (STM); this is generally considered unattractive for a number of reasons. This chapter proposes a separate, explicit control structure for modeling asynchronous, concurrent processes with PSs. Specifically, the use of a Petri net is addressed. A system of asynchronous, concurrent processes can be modeled using PSs to model the individual processes or events and using a Petri net to model the relationships between the processes. Furthermore, a hierarchy of such networks is proposed; an allowable production rule action is the instantiation of another network. This is supported with a structured, hierarchial STM.*

## 1.0 INTRODUCTION

Davis and King [Davis76b] suggest that production systems (PS) are most useful in problem domains that are generally modeled by a large number of independent states, with independent actions, and where the knowledge base is best encoded declaratively as opposed to procedurally. Furthermore, they suggest that a fundamental characteristic of PSs is their restriction on the interaction between rules. To produce a degree of interaction between rules requires the introduction of indirect communication through the short-term memory (STM). This results in using the STM both for data and for complex control mechanisms.

This chapter investigates the possibility of introducing a separate explicit control structure for PSs where there is a need for substantial interaction between rules. Specifically, we are interested in developing a formalism for modeling a system that is composed of a collection of asynchronous concurrent events . The particular problem domain of interest to us is that of office procedures. We are interested in developing a formalism with which we can model procedures that exist in many office environments; we choose to view instances of these procedures as asynchronous concurrent processes. Modeling office procedures in this way is attractive because an office can be viewed as an environment in which a large number of independent tasks are in progress and these tasks tend to be primarily event driven (i.e., recognize/act logic).

PSs initially seem attractive for modeling in this domain since the domain has many of the positive characteristics outlined in [Davis76b]. There are generally a large number of independent (asynchronous and concurrent) states and the knowledge base can be conveniently encoded declaratively (because of its event-driven nature). However, most systems of asynchronous, concurrent processes have strict requirements for interprocess communication and coordination. To handle this communication with standard PSs would require a large number of state variables for interrule communication, resulting in a complex control structure being embedded in the STM. We are faced with a situation then where certain characteristics of the problem domain make a PS representation very attractive and where other characteristics seriously discourage the use of PSs.

We suggest that by augmenting the PS representation to explicitly deal with complex interrule interaction we can mitigate some of the difficulties of PSs and still capitalize on the advantages of the PS representation. Here we will suggest that Petri nets be used to provide this explicit control structure. We will use PSs to model each individual process (event) and the Petri net to model the interaction and temporal relationships between these events. The Petri net will be used to dynamically extract from all of the available rules about the system, those rules which are relevant given the present system state (the present state being defined as the union of all enabled transitions). In this way, the Petri net adds structure to the PS formalism.

Before developing this model further, an example of a "typical" office procedure will be useful. Consider the procedure whereby a journal editor might process papers submitted for publication. When the paper is submitted to the journal secretary, an acknowledgment letter is sent to the author and a request is made of the editor for the names of referees for the paper. If the editor does not respond within a certain time period a reminder message is sent to him. When he does respond with the names of referees, a message is sent to each referee asking if he might review the paper. Each returns a postcard indicating whether or not he can review the paper; if he cannot, the editor must choose another referee. If he can review the paper, he is given a reasonable amount of time in which to do so; if he does not submit the review in this amount of time, a reminder letter is sent to him. When all of the referees have submitted their reports, a decision is requested of the editor. When the editor makes a decision, the author is informed.

## 2.0 PROCESS REPRESENTATION

Let us assume for the moment that the PSs are a useful formalism for modeling each individual process in a system of asynchronous, concurrent processes. In this section, we will look at various formalisms for modeling the relationships between these processes. We will call this the process representation, as opposed to the knowledge representation. Here, we will review formalisms for representing systems that are composed of a sequence of asynchronous and possibly concurrent events (e.g., an office procedure composed of several steps handled by different people). We will consider finite-state machines, partial orderings (PERT networks), and finally Petri nets.

## 2.1 State Machines

A state machine is a finite state automaton that can be represented either by a state diagram (a directed graph) or by a state transition table.

In graphical form, a state machine consists of a number of states, which are nodes in the graph, and a number of directed arcs connecting states. Some state is labeled as the initial state.

At any time, the system is in one and only one state. Based on input to the system, or more generally some observation about the environment, the system takes an action and changes states. By definition, this is a sequential process. Although it is physically possible to represent concurrent processes with a state machine, the number of states will grow exponentially with the number of tasks to be performed concurrently.

The difficulties with state machines in our problem domain are easily illustrated by considering three variations of the same modeling problem. First, assume that there are a number of tasks to be performed in a fixed order and only one task can be performed at a time.

A state machine will easily represent this system and the number of states will grow linearly with the number of tasks. Next, consider the case where the tasks still must be performed one at a time but where we remove the specific ordering constraint. This would be the case if the tasks were independent but all required some unique resource. In any state, we would like to know which tasks have been completed, and which task, if any, is now in progress. In this case, the number of states will grow exponentially with the number of tasks. Lastly, consider the case where the tasks can be performed in any order and where any degree of concurrency is allowed. Again, if we wish to know, for each state, which tasks have been completed and which are in progress, the number of states will grow exponentially with the number of tasks.

As can be seen, the representation of concurrency is possible in a state machine, but it becomes unwieldy for a large number of tasks.

## 2.2 Partial Orderings

A partial order for a set of events is represented by a directed graph where the arcs represent events to be completed and the nodes represent the termination and commencement of events. The events on a path of the graph represent events that must occur in a fixed order (i.e., the order of their occurrence in the path). Events not on the same path have no ordering relation. All arcs in the graph must be traversed.

Consider again the examples we used to analyze state machines. Representing n tasks that must be performed in a fixed order is simply a partial-order graph with one path. One arc is required for each task, and so we will need n arcs and $n+1$ nodes. The graph will grow linearly with the number of tasks.

If we wish to represent the case where the tasks can be performed in any order with any degree of concurrency, partial-order graphs are still satisfactory. This is simply a graph with 2 nodes and n arcs. The graph will grow linearly with the number of tasks.

Partial-order graphs cannot be used to represent the case where the tasks can be performed in any order, but only one at a time. For each possible ordering, we would need a separate graph, or n! graphs. The difficulty here is that partial-order graphs can represent only two extremes: fixed order and complete concurrency. Either two events have a precedence relation or they have no relation. There is no way to represent the case where two events can proceed in any order but one must wait for the completion of the other. This capability is obviously fundamental to resource allocation.

As we can see, the problem with partial order graphs is that they are a fixed representation for what is inherently a dynamic system.

We must determine a priori all of the precedence relations in the system. For example, in PERT networks, we first determine how long each event will take to complete; this allows the PERT system to determine all of the precedence relationships. Partial-order graphs have no power for describing *coordination* between events that do not have a strict precedence relation.

This ability to represent coordination among concurrent processes is crucial to our representation of office processes. Resource allocation is an obvious example. Another example is the need to make a choice among alternative actions and to resolve conflicts among competing events. We have shown that state machines can represent choice and conflict but are very unwieldy for representing concurrency. Partial-order graphs, on the other hand, can represent concurrency but cannot represent choice, conflict, and coordination among processes. We now turn our attention to a representation that will address these problems.

## 2.3 Petri Nets

In 1962, C.A. Petri devised a general graphical representation for systems [Petri66]. His work was extended in the late 1960s by Anatol Holt [Holt70, 71]. Holt called his representation "Petri nets" since they were based on the work of Petri.

We will assume here that the reader has some acquaintance with Petri nets and only a brief description will be given here. An excellent tutorial can be found in Holt [Holt71].

Like state machines and partial-order graphs, Petri nets are represented as directed graphs. They have been used in the study of parallel computation, multiprocessing, and computer systems modeling as well as the modeling of other physical processes and human activity processes. The following definition of Petri nets is from Miller [R.E. Miller73].

A Petri net is a graphical representation with directed edges between two different types of nodes. A node represented as a circle is called a *place* and a node represented as a bar is called a *transition*. The places in a Petri net have the capability of holding *tokens*. For a given transition, those places that have edges directed into the transition are called *input places* and those places having edges directed out of this transition are called *output places* for the transition. If all the input places for a transition contain a token, then the transition is said to be *active*. An active transition may *fire*. The firing removes a token from each input place and puts a token on each output place. Thus a token in a place can be used in the firing of only one transition. A simple example of a Petri net is shown in Fig. 1. Here tokens are shown as black dots. The

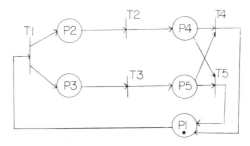

Fig. 1.

starting condition has a token only in place P1. The activity of the net (or process) is then described by the successive firings of transitions. In this example, T1 can fire followed by T2 and T3. Only after both T2 and T3 have fired are T4 and T5 active. Either T4 or T5 can fire but not both. When either T4 or T5 fires it brings the net back to its starting condition and the process is ready to repeat.

We note here that state machines and partial-order graphs are both restricted forms of Petri nets. A state machine is a Petri net where each transition can have exactly one input place and exactly one output place. Since each arc then has just one transition, we remove the bar from the diagram. A partial-order graph is a Petri net where each place has exactly one input arc and exactly one output arc (in Petri net terms, this is called a marked graph). Since each arc then has exactly one place, we remove the circle from the graph and simply place a dot on each arc where a token resides.

We now turn our attention to the same problem we used to study state machines and partial-order graphs. First we wish to represent the case where n tasks are to be performed in a fixed order, one at a time. Figure 2a shows the Petri net for this case. Two states are required for each task (since we want to represent the system at rest as well as busy), and so the number of states will grow linearly with the number of tasks.

Next we consider the case where the tasks are to be performed in any order, but only one at a time. Figure 2b represents this case. Each letter indicates a distinct task. Letters before the "/" indicate tasks already completed and letters after the "/" indicate tasks in progress. Place P1 is the resource allocator and the token in P1 represents the unique resource. Once it is "assigned" to one task, it is unavailable until that task completes. All other tasks will be held up until the active task completes. This scheme will work for any number of resources and competing tasks. We simply initialize the net with one token for each resource. The number of states required for this representation is three for each task and one for the resource allocator, and so growth is linear with the number of tasks.

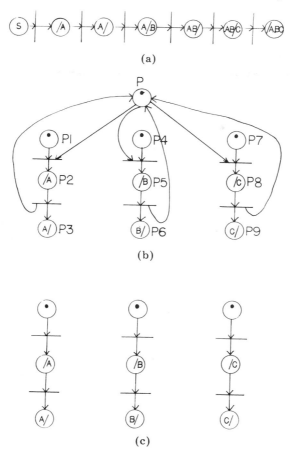

(a)

(b)

(c)

Fig. 2.

The last case we consider is where the tasks can be performed in any order and any degree of concurrency is allowed. Figure 2c shows the Petri net for this representation. In this case three states are required for each task (not started, in progress, and complete), hence the number of states still grows linearly with the number of tasks.

It is instructive to compare this representation to the state machine example. With the state machine, the machine could be in only one state at a time. This forced us to code all relevant information about the process into each state. With Petri nets, we effectively partition the state into a number of components. Each place represents a possible assertion about the total system state. If there is a token in a place, that component of the state is asserted. A token in P2 of Fig. 2b is an assertion that task A is in progress. Thus we can represent all 27 combinations of a three-task problem with only 9 places. With a state machine, we need a state for each possible combination and hence 27 states. To represent 20 tasks requires 60 places in a Petri net and 3.5 billion states with a state machine for the same level of information content. When we place the state machine restriction on Petri nets, we allow each transition to have only one input and only one output place. This means that the total information about when a transition can fire must be stored in only one place and all of the information associated with a transition firing must flow to only one place. In the more general Petri net, we allow information from several places to influence the occurrence of events, thus partitioning the total system state into logical components.

Comparing Petri nets to partial orderings, the key addition is a coordination mechanism. Although implicit in coordination, it is worth noting that Petri nets also provide for communication among processes. This coordination is achieved by allowing a place to be input to more than one transition. Although a very simple construct, it proves very powerful in describing required coordination. Note that this construct is specifically not allowed in the partial-order graph restriction of Petri nets.

## 2.4 Choice of Process Representation

As can be seen, state machines and partial order graphs are restricted forms of Petri nets. Partial order graphs do not have the capability to model coordination among concurrent processes and choice among alternative actions, which we require for our representation of asynchronous, concurrent processes. While state machines can represent choice and conflict easily, they are very unwieldy for representing concurrency because the number of states grows exponentially. Petri nets can represent asynchronous, concurrent processes, process coordination, and choice and conflict among events. They can also be used to model resource allocation. Since Petri nets subsume the other formalisms we have discussed, it is clear that we should use Petri nets for our problem.

To gain an appreciation for the descriptive power of Petri nets as they apply to office processes, we show a simple example. In the journal editing case, there are several instances when a message is sent from the system to the environment for which a reply is expected within a certain period. When the response arrives, the activity continues. However, if the response does not arrive within the specified period, some other action must be taken (such as generating another document). Figure 3 shows the Petri net representation for this. When we are in state P1 we are waiting for a reply within a certain period. Note that both T1 and T2 are enabled, hence we have a conflict. This Petri net is nondeterministic since we cannot state with certainty

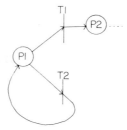

Fig. 3.

whether T1 or T2 will fire. If the reply arrives within the specified period, T1 fires. If it does not arrive, however, T2 fires. The actions specified at T2 are taken and a token is placed back in P1, once again enabling T1 and T2. This will let us wait another time period before taking remedial (T2) action. We have not stated how we shall resolve the conflict between firing T1 and T2. Clearly, conflict resolution requires that we have some knowledge about the conflict. We shall directly address this issue in the next section when we take up knowledge representation.

## 3.0 KNOWLEDGE REPRESENTATION

One of the major research efforts in the field of artificial intelligence concerns the representation of knowledge. For a program to exhibit intelligence, it must possess knowledge. The difficulty lies in determining the proper structure for representing the knowledge applicable to the problem domain. Obviously, this difficulty increases as the scope of the problem domain broadens.

In representing asynchronous, concurrent processes, we clearly would like to encode knowledge about each process into our representation. This allows the system interpreting the representation to exhibit at least limited intelligence about the problem domain.

A number of formalisms for knowledge representation could be considered for this problem. Plannerlike formalisms could be employed (e.g., in our example, we could have a goal of judging a paper, which could be decomposed into a number of subgoals) or we could use a form of frame system formalism. However, given the event-driven nature of these problems, production systems seem ideally suited.

### 3.1 Production Systems

A PS consists of a set of rules, or "productions," which are of the form (condition)→(action), a database or "context," which maintains state data, and a rule interpreter. The condition portion of each rule (left-hand side or LHS) is tested. If the condition is true, the consequent action (right-hand side or RHS) is executed. In a "pure" PS [Davis76b], the rules are in a sequential list, and rules are evaluated one at a time according to their order in the list. When a rule is found that is true in the current context, the RHS is executed and rule testing begins again at the top of the list of rules. When no rules have true LHSs or a "halt" RHS is executed, the system terminates processing.

In some uses of PSs, the methods for choosing which rules to evaluate and in what order, varies. However, the reader should note that the method chosen for determining "rule priority" is crucial to the efficiency and correctness of the production system.

The use of production systems varies from simple string rewriting rules to the modeling of human cognitive processes [Newell72b], a system for assisting in medical diagnosis [Shortliffe74], and the development of an intelligent terminal agent [R.H.Anderson76b]. The rules can be as simple as testing and replacing substrings in an input string or as general as predicate conditions that perform subtle pattern matching on the database and invoke arbitrary procedures that modify the database and produce side effects.

A simple example of production systems provides some interesting insights. This example deals with rewriting rules. These are used to examine an input string that is normally a sentence from some grammar and to reduce it according to the production rules.

Figure 4a is a set of production rules for reversing a string from an alphabet that does not contain the symbols $ and * (these are used as "marker" symbols). This is what we have called a "pure" production system so rules are chosen for testing according to their order in the rule list. For each rule, the input string is examined from left to right with a moving window looking for a match with the LHS of the rule being tested. If a match is found, the input string is modified by replacing the matched substring in the input string with the RHS of the production rule. Rule testing then resumes with P1. If any rule does not have a match in the input string, then the next rule in the list is tested. If no rules match, then the system halts. Figure 4b shows how the input string ABC is modified during this process.

Upon first examining the production system in Fig. 4a, it may appear that the relatively simple task of reversing a string should not require six rules for its proper specification. The reason six rules are required here is because of the lack of control structure; we must be very careful that the actions of rules do not interfere with each other. In fact, this is precisely why two marker variables are required instead of just one. Furthermore, the ordering of rules in this example is crucial. If the relative ordering of certain rules is changed, the

P1: $$ → *
P2: *$ → *
P3: *x → x*
P4: * → null.
P5: $xy → y$x
P6: null →$

(a)

ABC => $ABC P6
    => B$AC P5
    => BC$A P5
    => $BC$A P6
    => C$B$A P5
    => $C$B$A P6
    => $$C$B$A P6
    => *C$B$A P1
    => C*$B$A P3
    => C*B$A P2
    => CB*$A P3
    => CB*A P2
    => CBA* P3
    => CBA P4

(b)

P1: $$ → null (P4)
P2: $xy →$x (P2)
P3: null → $ (P1)
P4: $ → null (P4)

(c)

Fig. 4. Production rules for string reversal. (a) Pure production system, (b) appli-
cation of rules to string ABC, (c) modified production rules for string reversal.

system will not operate as desired. For example, the reader should
consider the effect of switching P1 and P6, or of switching P2 and P4.

It is, of course, possible to add control structure to the production
system model and thereby increase its efficiency and/or decrease the
number of rules required. One possibility is to add some information
to each rule, which we will call a branch label. This will be the label
of some rule in the rule set. When a rule LHS is tested and found to
be false, the next rule in the list is tested. However, if the rule LHS
is found to be true, the RHS is executed and the next rule selected for
testing is the one specified in the branch label.

It seems intuitive that once a certain rule is tested and found to
be true, this should give us some clue as to which other rules are now
likely to be true. Pure production systems do not use this information,
but blindly resume their search at the top of the rule list at each cycle.
As we implied above, one way to make use of this information is to
append to each rule a rule number that should be tried next if this rule

is true. This branch instruction gives the system advice on how to proceed.

Fig. 4c shows the production system for reversing a string with this added control structure. This added structure allows us to reduce the number of rules by one-third and the number of marker variables by one-half in this particular example. We argue that this makes the entire production system easier to understand. As far as efficiency is

Figure 4c shows the production system for reversing a string with this added control structure. This added structure allows us to reduce the number of rules by one-third and the number of marker variables by one-half in this particular example. We argue that this makes the entire production system easier to understand. As far as efficiency is concerned, reversing the three-character string required 57 rule tests in the production system without branching and only 18 rule tests in the production system with branch labels.

Adding control structure to the production system by the "branch if successful" label allows us to neatly represent the system as a state machine. (The original production system can also be represented by a state machine, but this is of little use.) Each rule is a state and each state has two outgoing arcs, marked true and false. When the system enters a state, it tests the rule in that state. If the LHS is true, the RHS is executed and the system follows the arc marked true to its next state. If the LHS is not true, the RHS is not executed and the system follows the arc marked false to its next state. The process terminates when the "eureka" state is reached. Figure 5 shows the state machine corresponding to the production system in Fig. 4c.

Since a production system of this sort can be represented by a state machine, and a state machine is a restricted form of Petri net, it is certainly possible to represent a production system in a Petri net.

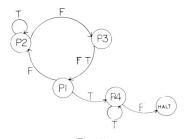

Fig. 5.

## 4.0 A REPRESENTATION FOR ASYNCHRONOUS, CONCURRENT PROCESSES

In the last two sections, we have discussed formalisms for process representation and formalisms for knowledge representation. Now we wish to derive a formalism suitable for the representation of asynchronous, concurrent processes. It is our contention that there is a real advantage, at least initially, in viewing process representation and knowledge representation separately. In those problems which exhibit some sort of flow characteristic, the current state of the system can often be used to determine which "chunks" of knowledge are likely to be useful in determining what to do next. Stated in a slightly different way, knowledge about the process flow can be a very useful aid in partitioning the total knowledge set into useful subsets (not necessarily disjoint).

We suggest that each process in a system of asynchronous, concurrent processes be modeled as a set of productions. We can then develop a Petri net structure for this system of processes. Each transition in the net represents a process; since these processes are described by productions, the transition is really a "home" for the rules describing the process. When a transition is enabled (all input places have at least one token), its firing will be determined by the rules "residing" at the transition. All rules at all enabled transitions (the fact that there can be more than one enabled transition is key) will constitute what we will call the *active rule set*. Obviously, membership in this active rule set is transitory. The PS interpreter will continually cycle through rules in the active rule set; when a rule LHS becomes true, the rule actions will be executed and the transition from which this rule came will be fired. This will enable some transitions and disable others, thus modifying the active rule set. The Petri net will be used to dynamically extract from all of the available rules about the system those rules which are relevant given the current state of the system (the current state being defined as the union of all enabled transitions).

In this way, the Petri net adds structure to the PS formalism. The firing of a rule provides direct information (through the Petri net) to the rule interpreter about which other rules are now applicable. This provides, in essence, for direct rule interaction.

We will call this combined formalism an *augmented Petri net*. It is possible, and oftentimes advisable, to describe a system of asynchronous, concurrent processes as a hierarchy of augmented Petri nets. For example, we may want to describe the journal editing system as two augmented Petri nets, one from the viewpoint of the editor and one from the viewpoint of the referee. One of the allowed production rule actions is the (concurrent) instantiation of another augmented Petri net. Attached to each Petri net is its own STM. Lower level networks inherit the STM's of all parent nodes; the result is a structured, hierarchical STM.

We note the similarity between augmented Petri nets and augmented transition networks (ATN) [Woods70]. Just as the ATN is a generalization of state machines, the augmented Petri net is a generalization of Petri nets. The registers in an ATN are analogous to our STMs and the conditions and actions on ATN arcs are equivalent to the production rules that reside at transitions. The main difference, of course, is that in the augmented Petri net, a number of transitions can be enabled simultaneously.

## 5.0 AN EXAMPLE

We will now describe the journal editing process in the augmented Petri net representation. First we list the states in which the system can exist:

(1) waiting for a paper to arrive;
(2) waiting for the editor to designate referees;
(3) waiting for the referee to respond;
(4) waiting for the referee to submit his report;
(5) waiting for all reports to arrive;
(6) waiting for the editor to make a decision.

Next we describe what can happen in each of these states:

(1) When a paper arrives, generate an acknowledgment letter to the author and request that the editor designate referees.

(2) If the editor does not respond within two weeks, generate a reminder letter to him and continue to do so every two weeks. When he does respond, generate letters to each of the referees requesting their services.

(3) If the referee does not respond within two weeks, generate a reminder letter to him. If he does respond and states that he cannot review the paper, inform the editor and request that another referee be designated. If the referee agrees to review the paper allow one month for him to submit his report.

(4) If the referee does not respond within one month, generate a reminder letter. When the report is received, inform the editor of its arrival.

(5) When all of the reports are in, request that the editor make a decision.

(6) If the editor does not make a decision within two weeks after all reports are in, generate a reminder letter. When he does make a decision, inform the author and executive editor.

At each step in the process, we wish to generate the proper documentation and to "file" it appropriately. Figure 6 is an augmented Petri net description of this system. Note that the system is described by two nets, one for the editor and one for the referee. The rule in T02 of the editor net instantiates the referee process for each referee selected by the editor. The two nets communicate through the hierarchical STM.

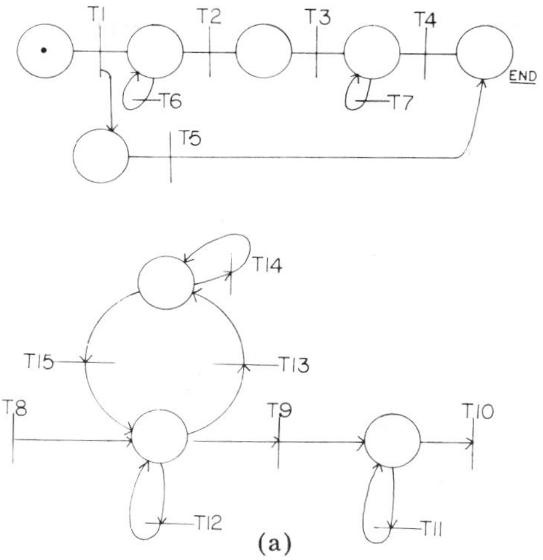

(a)

T01: If a paper is received => send acknowledgement letter to author and request names of referees (any number) from editor.

T02: If the editor supplies the names of referees => instantiate the referee process for each referee.

T03: If all of the referee activities terminate (i.e., fire T10) => request that the editor make a decision.

T04: If the editor supplies a decision on the paper => generate final documentation to author and editor-in-chief.

T05: If the author withdraws the paper => instantiate termination procedure.

T06: If the editor does not respond within two weeks of T06 enabling => send reminder letter to editor.

T07: If the editor does not make a decision within two weeks from T07 enabling => send reminder letter to editor.

T08: If (null condition, fires upon instantiation) => send letter to referee requesting services.

T09: If the referee returns postcard and can review the paper, then allow one month for report.

T10: If report is received => send thank-you letter to referee.

T11: If referee does not send report within one month from enabling of T11 => send reminder to referee.

T12: If referee does not return postcard within two weeks from enabling of T12 => send reminder letter to referee.

T13: If referee returns postcard and cannot review paper => request that editor supply another referee.

T14: If editor does not respond with two weeks from enabling of T14 => send reminder letter to editor.

T15: If editor does supply referee name => send letter to referee requesting services.

(b)

Fig. 6. (a) Top: editor; bottom: referee. (b) Production rules.

## 6.0 CONCLUSION

In this chapter, we have developed a representation that we feel is useful for describing asynchronous, concurrent processes. This was done by separately studying the formalisms available for process representation and those available for knowledge representation. For reasons discussed throughout, we have chosen to integrate PSs, a formalism for knowledge representation, with Petri nets, a formalism for process representation. We call this an augmented Petri net. By adding the Petri net as an explicit control structure for PSs, we have provided a formalism wherein a system of asynchronous, concurrent processes can be modeled with a collection of interrelated PSs sharing a common, structured STM. This extends the use of PSs to new problem domains.

A computer system for processing the augmented Petri nets in an office automation environment has been implemented on the Wharton School DEC-10 [Zisman76, 77]; and is currently being used to manage the workflow for an associate editor of CACM. This is a particular use of the system; it accepts as input a general augmented Petri net and then interfaces with a number of office systems (e.g., mail system, document generators, filing systems, etc.) to carry out the work specified in the net.

# ACKNOWLEDGMENTS

The author wishes to acknowledge the assistance and encouragement of Dr. Howard L. Morgan during the course of this work.

# SPONTANEOUS COMPUTATION AND ITS ROLES IN AI MODELING[1]

### Chuck Rieger
### *University of Maryland*

*There are, broadly speaking, two significantly different styles of programming for digital computers: demand-based computing, where code runs on demand for specific reasons, and spontaneous computing, where reactive computations themselves determine when to run and contribute information. This chapter is about spontaneous computation, its engineering (as it has been implemented in the CSA system), and its theoretical roles in cognitive modeling. It is an attempt to suggest theoretical demarcations between these two styles of computing, and to suggest how they ought to interact cooperatively.*

## 1.0  INTRODUCTION

Broadly, the form of any computation on a digital computer can be classified in one of two categories: *demand-based*, or *spontaneous*. A "demand-based" computation is one that is invoked only on request from another computation (or the outside world) in order to fulfill a specific need. The solicitation of a demand-based computation's services may occur either by a direct, hard-wired call, or by a pattern-based request for help. In the former case, the linkage between the requesting and requested computations is via a precompiled calling sequence that is a very local phenomenon; in the latter case, the demand-based computation is identified as relevant, then run, on the

[1] The research described in this report was funded in part by the Office of Naval Research under grant N00014-76C-0477, and in part by the National Aeronautics and Space Administration under grant NSG-7253. Copies of the CSA SC code (Wisconsin LISP for Univac 1110) are availble on request.

basis of a pattern match between its advertised expertise and the current demand, or goal. "Spontaneous" computation on the other hand is unsolicited; conceptually, it is a generalization of the notion of an interrupt in digital hardware. Although the mechanism by which spontaneous code is triggered might be very similar to the pattern matching process that initiates pattern-invoked demand-based computation, the two styles of computing play very different theoretical roles in models of human intelligence. Spontaneous computation, and its theoretical roles in cognitive models are the topics of this chapter.

Specifically, our purposes are twofold: (1) to present (briefly) a technique for implementing and controlling spontaneous computation and (2) to suggest and explore some aspects of AI modeling for which spontaneous computation (hereafter abbreviated SC), as opposed to demand-based computation, seems most appropriate.

## 2.0 BACKGROUND

### 2.1 General Background

MICROPLANNER [Sussman71], based on Hewitt's PLANNER [Hewitt71], is generally recognized as the first major AI programming language that heavily incorporated the notion of pattern-directed invocation as a substitute paradigm for the conventional "subroutine call" structure of prior languages. In MICROPLANNER, there are conceptually three systemwide communication paths: (1) a "hot line" where pattern-based requests to a population of demand-based computations (called THCONSE "theorems") are posted, (2) a data entry path into a central database of LISP $n$-tuples, and (3) an exit path from that database. Attached to the entry and exit paths of the database are populations of computations that can gain control immediately after the assertion or erasure of a fact (which matches at least one of their invocation patterns). These populations are called THANTE and THERASING "theorems," respectively.

The THCONSE theorem population and associated hot line of MICROPLANNER comprise an instance of pattern-directed, demand-based invocation, and do not capture the notion of spontaneity. However, the THANTE and THERASING theorems, insofar as they react as the result of an assertion or erasure of a fact, and do so without solicitation, are illustrative of spontaneous computation.

Since MICROPLANNER, there has been somewhat of a cultural revolution in AI control structures. Most engineering advances fall into one of two categories: either an elaboration or enrichment of pattern-directed, demand-based computation, or an extension of the notions of spontaneous computation originally suggested by MICRO-PLANNER. CONNIVER [D.McDermott74], QA4 [Rieger77d], QLISP/INTERLISP [Reboh73, Teitleman74], and POPLER [Davies73] are representative of the former type of contribution to AI control structures. Contributions to the engineering of true spontaneous computation have recently come primarily from production systems, where knowledge is phrased in terms of co-equal or hierarchical collections of rewrite rules (see [Davis76b, Newell72b, Tesler73] for examples).[2]

## 2.2 Engineering or Theory?

Although bigger and better control structures are probably a necessary condition for the development of advanced AI models, they are certainly not sufficient. In a sense, most systems to date are guilty of selling a product they do not fully back: you get a tool, but no theory manual telling you when and how to use it. The resulting phenomenon, as nearly everyone now recognizes, is that engineering is several steps ahead of theory; we simply haven't identified the theoretical ingredients of intelligence well enough to know whether or when to apply existing engineering.[3]

In presenting yet another model of SC engineering in the first half of the chapter, I will probably be as guilty as everyone else in attempting to sell a product I'm not fully certain how to use. However, I attempt to atone in the second half by suggesting some do's and don't's of applying the engineering to theory, focusing primarily on problem solving, interference, and language comprehension.

## 2.3 Specific Background

Up to this point in my own research, I have been interested in processes that are most properly classified as doers. The research, called The Commonsense Algorithm (CSA) Project, has so far been concerned mainly with the development of a representation for com-

---

[2] The recent KRL notion of "procedural attachment" [D.G. Bobrow77] is also suggestive of a highly distributed type of spontaneous computation.

[3] There have been exceptions. Charniak [Charniak72], for example, proposed a theory of story comprehension that demanded application of some then-state-of-the-art SC engineering. His thesis was that story comprehension is primarily a matter of sowing predictions earlier in the story, hoping they fire as the result of later developments, thus relating cause-effect events, etc. I personally agree that some such mechanism is central to comprehension, but would argue that Charniak overused SC in his model. Marcus [Marcus74] provides another example of a possibly sound theoretical application of some rather exotic SC-based control structures in natural language parsing. He employs SC as a vehicle for encoding English grammar in hierarchical populations of demons, which monitor the state of sentence, phrase, and clause level buffers.

monsense cause and effect knowledge, and the development of an organization that permits the storage and access of large numbers of so-called CSA patterns in useful ways.

The CSA theory has been an attempt to unify some ideas about language comprehension and problem solving; it is described in [Rieger75a, 76a, b]. Because this unification has been my goal, the doers in the existing CSA model are, abstractly speaking, twofold:

(1)  The *plan synthesizer*, which given an agent and a goal (expressed via the set of state and statechange predicates known to the system), will construct a plan (i.e., build a novel CSA pattern up from its knowledge store of smaller patterns) that could be employed by the agent to accomplish the goal; and

(2)  The *language interpreter*, which given a situation and an action will search "backwards" through the knowledge base of CSA patterns and arrive at a most reasonable interpretation (i.e., reason) for the action in the situation. Interpretations are thus sensitive to the context defined by the situation; because of this, I feel this represents the kernel of a reasonably powerful story comprehender.

The central theme in these segments of the CSA research has been that *intelligent selection* is the basic issue with regard to demand-based computation. The general statement CSA is making is that demand-based "doers" must have good reasons for solving a given problem (or answering a given question) in the way they decide to do it. My belief (which is, of course, not unique!) is that intelligent selection at every step where selection is possible is a necessary (and almost sufficient) cornerstone of human intelligence.

However, it was recognized early in the CSA research that doers are only half of the model—that SC is an equally important aspect of some CSA ideas. It is only recently that our group has gotten into the business of SC, and our interest was initially motivated by a facet of CSA having to do with *mechanism description and simulation*. By "mechanism," is meant any man-made device that reflects useful cause-effect behavior.

Using the CSA representation we have represented a variety of mechanisms from a digital flip-flop [Rieger77d] to a home gas-forced air furnace [Rieger77a]. Since, among others, one of our goals was to be able to use the CSA pattern describing an arbitrary device as the basis of a *mechanism simulator* (which in turn is scheduled to become the heart of a CAI "Mechanisms Laboratory"), we were confronted with the design of a simulator. Inspired by Sussman's work with electronic circuit analysis using a simple SC basis [Sussman75b], we adopted the following strategy for our simulator: convert the CSA pattern, which describes a mechanism to a population of SC-based procedures, each of which models one local aspect of the flow of causality within the mechanism, then light the fuse by presenting the population with a starting pattern, and watch it go!

The mechanisms simulator is now running [Rieger 76c, 77a], and represents the first fully developed application of the CSA SC component (to be described), which itself has been under development for the past several months.

However, since the initial ideas about the simulator, I have grown more interested in SC for its own sake, and as the basis of certain classes of inference in story comprehension (described later). Also, I have grown more and more interested in the nature of *interactions between demand-based computation and spontaneous computation*, specifically those between "watchers" and the doers in the existing CSA model.

The main questions are

(1) What is the division of labor between these two computational paradigms?

(2) How do demand-based computations and spontaneous computation constructively coexist and cooperate?

Hence, the remainder of the chapter will be about a CSA-independent theory of spontaneous computation, but motivated from within the specific CSA framework. The first part is design and engineering; the second part is theory.


## 3.0 SPONTANEOUS COMPUTATION

### 3.1 Simple CSA SC Activation Patterns

Conceptually, there are two components of a spontaneous computation: the part that causes it to fire, called its activation, or trigger pattern, and the part that affects the interrupted model at the time of firing, called its body. In production systems, the activation pattern is the left-hand side of a rule, while the body is thought of as the rule's right-hand side. In the case of production systems, both components usually adhere to a tight structural syntax, but in general, the body can be an arbitrary computation. Although our current implementation ambivalently accepts an arbitrary computation as the body, as we shall see later, there are probably good reasons to restrict both its form and capabilities.

The basic data structure for the CSA system's SC trigger facility is a rather obvious LISP construct, the nested $n$-tuple $<nn>$. Figure

1 shows the syntax for this most elementary trigger pattern component. The semantics of the variables in a trigger n-tuple are similar to those employed in other systems, in that variables with identical names must be consistently bindable to the same symbol in the constant pattern to which the trigger n-tuple is being matched.

<nn> := <constant> | <variable> | (<nn> ... <nn>)
<constant> := <LISP atom>
<variable> := -<LISP atom> (read as a hyphen sign)

Fig. 1. Simple CSA trigger pattern syntax.

Examples of CSA trigger *n*-tuples are

(LOCATION BLOCK-1 TABLE)
(SUPPORTS BLOCK-1 -X)
(INHEAD -X (KISS -Y -Z))
(INHEAD -X (LOVES -Y -X))

## 3.2 Complex Trigger Patterns

Trigger patterns at about this level of complexity (with some embellishments allowing for slightly more sophisticated variable handling during pattern matching) form the basis of SC in systems such as MICROPLANNER and CONNIVER. Although such a level of sophistication is probably adequate in principle for carrying out general theories of SC, it is quite restrictive to use in practice. Among other things, such primitive trigger patterns will generally provide only very superficial evidence that an SC is ready to fire, with the remaining bulk of relevance testing left to the body. There are at least three engineering disadvantages to this approach: (1) overly coarse (simple) trigger patterns will cause many false alarms, resulting in the premature running of SC bodies simply to complete the relevance testing, (2) trigger patterns involving N multiple components tied by an OR relation must be modeled awkwardly by N SCs whose bodies will be essentially the same, and (3) it is structurally unclear which components of the body are simply more relevance tests (conceptually prefatory to the true firing of the SC) and which components comprise the substantive body.

Another, more insidious disadvantage of low-complexity triggers has to do with the degree to which they focus a researcher's thoughts and modeling goals. It is obviously advantageous that the limitations inherent in the form of trigger patterns hamper the theorist as little as possible when he attempts to express his possibly complex theories, say, of inference, story character interaction schemata, and so forth. Hence, there is also a *theoretical* need for SC facilities with more expressive trigger patterns.

Such deficiencies of low-complexity trigger patterns suggest a rather obvious, but important extension to this elementary syntax, namely, to allow for the composition of numerous trigger *n*-tuples using logical connectives. Since the major step is taken by permitting compositions based on AND and OR, the CSA trigger facility incorporates only these extensions, leaving other more elaborate relations for specific future needs.

The resulting complex trigger pattern syntax, and that which is presently used in the CSA system, is shown in Fig. 2. The underlying semantics are as follows. Each trigger pattern is composed of primitive elements, using the relations AND, OR, and ANY (zero or more), nested to any reasonable depth. The primitive elements are one of:

(1) a trigger *n*-tuple, $<nn>$, representing an *associative* component of the complex pattern, i.e., one that can instigate a firing of the SC;

(2) a trigger *n*-tuple, $<nn>$, representing a *nonassociative* component, i.e., one that cannot instigate firing but must nevertheless be deducible at trigger time in order for firing to occur;

(3) an arbitrary LISP computation, called a *computable*, that must evaluate non-NIL at trigger time in order for firing to occur but cannot instigate triggering.

The associative components of a trigger pattern will be woven into the systemwide activation control of SC, whereas the nonassociative and computable components will simply be retained in a form accessible for deductive purposes at trigger time.

```
<tp> := <assoc> | <non-assoc> | <computable> | <complex>
<asoc> := (+ <effort> <nn>)
<non-assoc> := (-<effort> <nn>)
<computable> := <LISP-S-expression>
<complex> := (AND <tp> ... <tp>)
| (OR <tp> ... <tp>)
| (ANY <tp> ... <tp>)
```

Fig. 2. Complex trigger pattern syntax.

Examples of complex trigger patterns are

(AND (+ 1 (LOCATION BLOCK-1 TABLE))
    (OR (+1 (CLEARTOP BLOCK-1))

```
(AND (+1 (SUPPORTS BLOCK-1 -Y))
     (-1 (CLASS -Y PYRAMID)))))

(AND (+ 1 (LOVES -X -Y))
     (+ 1 (INHEAD -X (KISS -Z -Y)))
     (- 1 (SEX -X MALE))
     (- 1 (SEX -Y FEMALE))
     (- 1 (SEX -Z MALE))
     (NOT-EQUAL -X -Z))
```

The first would be triggered whenever BLOCK-1 comes to be located on the table, whenever its top is clear, or whenever it supports an object. Full firing will occur only when BLOCK-1 is on the table either with a clear top or supporting a pyramid. The plus signs denote associative components, the minus signs denote nonassociative components. The integer following the plus or minus governs the amount of energy the deductive component may expend when attempting to deduce the truth or falsehood of components other than the one responsible for initial triggering; energy expenditure is measured as the number of database fetches, in this example all single fetches. The second pattern would fire in situations in which jealousy is liable to be a key feature, since it demands that X's lover be kissed by a third party, and that X know about it.[4]

This concludes the description of CSA trigger pattern structure, which has of necessity been brief. Rieger [Rieger76d] includes a more substantive discussion of the philosophy and decisions that lead to this final product. Since the systemwide organization of trigger patterns from this mold will be important, I shall turn now to a brief description of the data structures that synthesize many trigger patterns into useful higher-level reactive populations.

### 3.3  Trigger Trees

The organization of CSA SC trigger patterns is based upon a structure I call a *trigger tree* (sometimes abbreviated TT). A trigger tree is a central struture into which all the associative components of all SC trigger patterns in a given population of SCs can be knit. It will then become possible to speak in terms of "populations of SCs," meaning a tree of triggers, and in terms of "planting" the associative components of an SC's complex trigger in some trigger tree.

Mechanically, the problem of planting a complex trigger pattern consists of two operations:

---

[4] Patterns of this and greater complexity are emerging in our story comprehender, and will be documented in future reports.

(1) fragmenting the pattern, extracting all its associative components for subsequent implantation in a specified tree;

(2) implanting each of these components in the tree, back-linking each planted component, A, to the entire SC (the body), and additionally specifying other components of the pattern L(A) (implied by the pattern's logical composition) that, in conjunction with the planted component, would comprise sufficient evidence for firing the SC.

These operations are carried out by the CSA SC-planting function, $PLANT:

($PLANT <complex trigger> <body> <trigger tree>)

To illustrate, pursuing the example of jealousy begun above, we might encode a rule of inference as an SC that would be defined and implanted in a trigger tree of human emotion inferences:

```
($PLANT '(AND (+ 1 (LOVES -X -Y))
              (+ 1 (INHEAD -X (KISS -Z -Y)))
              (- 1 (SEX -X MALE))
              (- 1 (SEX -Y FEMALE))
              (- 1 (SEX -Z MALE))
              (NOT-EQUAL -X -Z))
         '(LAMBDA (X Y Z) (INFER (LIST 'JEALOUS X Z)))
         'HUMAN-EMOTION-INFERENCE-TREE)
```

This would cause the two associative components to be entered into the existing human emotion tree (or such a tree to be begun). Assuming these are the first patterns to be stored in this tree, the trees initial structure would then be as shown in Fig. 3.

Briefly, the structure of a trigger tree is as follows. Each node corresponds to a nested *n*-tuple position. Each node has three general classes of offspring: constants, variables, and complexes (another nested *n*-tuple). As a pattern being implanted or matched is traversed left-to-right, depth-first, some path is followed through the tree, beginning at the root. A successful match ends at a terminal node of the tree; and the terminal nodes contain back-linking information to the original SC.[5]

Trigger trees are accessed either in $PLANT mode, $KILL mode (which removes a pattern from the tree), or $ACTIVATE mode, the associative lookup mode wherein a stimulus pattern is filtered down

[5] Again, there is a more complete discussion of the rationale behind the choice of this data structure in [Rieger77d]. [Rieger77d] also provides more details and documentation of trigger trees (for example, variable management, binding and mapping), which might interest some readers.

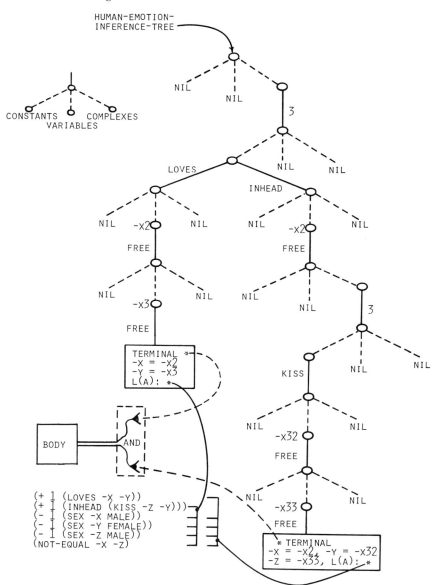

Fig. 3. Trigger tree.

the tree in search of all trigger patterns that match it. $ACTIVATE mode is effected by calling either the function $ACTIVATE or the trigger tree itself (which is made to appear semantically as a function of one argument):

($ACTIVATE <stimulus> <trigger tree>)

or

(<trigger tree> <stimulus>)

as in

($ACTIVATE '(KISS BILL MARY)
                    'HUMAN-EMOTION-INFERENCE-TREE)

or

(HUMAN-EMOTION-INFERENCE-TREE '(KISS BILL MARY))

In either case, the call results in a conceptually breadth-first descent through the tree, terminating in a set of candidate SCs that have nibbled at the bait. A "polling" function, $ALLBINDS, is then applied to each SC so located to determine whether or not it is fully triggered. This polling will, in general, cause considerable interaction with the database and deductive component of the system, suggesting some theoretically interesting SC/demand-based computation interactions (which will be discussed later). If there are multiple ways to bind the complex pattern of some SC, $ALLBINDS will return all the possibilities. The end product of a tree's application to a stimulus pattern emerges in the form of a list of SCs to be invoked spontaneously, together with all binding information applicable to each. The next section will describe how spontaneous invocation is controlled system-wide.

This approach to SC trigger pattern organization makes it natural to group SCs into populations, in the sense that each trigger tree could, e.g., be thought of as a functional group of watchers tuned to some specific part of the environment, some specific phase of an operation, or some specific context. There may then either be one large, system-wide population, as there is in PLANNER and CONNIVER, or there may be numerous small trees. In the latter arrangement, trees would perhaps pay exclusive attention to one arena of activity, or perhaps each tree would gather its perceptions from several arenas.

This natural tendency to split the SC population into functional subgroups suggests, conceptually at least, the idea of elevating the notion of a SC trigger tree to the status of a programming language data type, manipulable as a single entity at some still higher level. Regarding SCs in this way suggests a notion of *trigger tree attachment* to a process. Attaching a trigger tree TT to a process P would amount to allowing the population of SCs represented by TT to fishbowl P's activity, reacting to it in ways that are either transparent to P, or in ways that alter or destroy P.

## 3.4  Channels

If this is our vision of SC populations, to what are we to attach trigger trees? In PLANNER and CONNIVER, there is one large population attached to the store function, one large population attached to the erase function, and one large population more or less hard-wired into the central control for the system, i.e., the hot line. From these ideas, I have developed a control structure called a *channel*.

A channel is defined to be the medium whereby one LISP function calls (posts requests to) another LISP function. Doing this will essentially allow us to "make public" what is ordinarily the private calling protocol between functions, the locus of all the real work in LISP. This metaphor of a channel gives rise to a CSA programming construct, the CHANNEL (!), to which trigger trees may now be attached.

We can visualize a channel as follows:

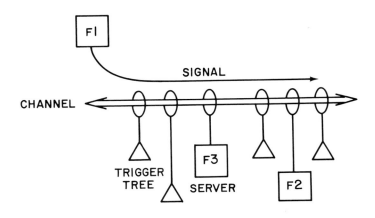

Fig. 4. Channel.

Now, wherever function F1 used to call function F2 via the standard LISP protocol, we shall require F1 to post all requests to F2 on this intermediate construct, the channel. Possibly unbeknownst to either F1 or F2, there is now the possibility of one or more trigger trees, as well as other functions (such as F3 in Fig. 4), being attached to this channel, either as "transparent," benign watchers, or as "modifying," possibly inimical watchers.

Since all the work in a LISP environment transpires via function calls, if we give watchers the ability to see calling sequences, we shall have in some sense a "most general" SC attachment paradigm. Although I tend to regard the new channel construct as a state of mind (i.e., a convention not enforced by LISP), one could imagine enforcing this style of communication by restructuring LISP's control. Doing so would bring us into a realm of thinking akin to Hewitt's "actors" and "messages" paradigms [Hewitt 77]. (In fact, in retrospect, the whole concept of channels and trigger tree attachment fits in very nicely with Hewitt's view of computation.

Specifically, a channel is a construction with the following features:

(1)  It is one-dimensional.

(2)  Other constructs can be attached to it at *tap points*; there is no limit to the number of tap points.

(3)  The left-right ordering of tap points is significant.

(4)  Each tap point is either a *watcher* or a *server*, and has mode either *transparent* or *modifying*; a modifying watcher or sever may alter either the passing signal, or any other aspect of the system.

(5)  Signals (either requests to a server or a response from a server) may be injected on a channel at arbitrary starting points, and propagate either left or right.

(6)  Both channels and tap points are context-sensitive, so that reconfiguring the medium by which one function calls another is relatively simple.

The user-level channel-related functions in the current CSA system are

($CONNECT <object> <channel> <mode> <type> <in-relation-to>
          <other-point>)
($DISCONNECT <object> <channel>)
($INJECT <signal> <server> <channel> <in-relation-to>
          <other-point> <prop-direction>)

Since a channel is both spatial and directional, we shall imagine a signal to propagate from some starting point in some direction with finite speed. As it passes by a tree of watchers, any relevant watchers in the tree will be triggered and run, and (1) allow the signal to continue as is, (2) modify the signal but allow it to proceed, or (3) block the signal altogether. If and when the signal reaches the requested server, the server will be run unconditionally on the (possibly modified) signal. Its response will then be momentarily held while the signal is allowed to propagate to the end of the channel, or until is it blocked. At that time, the server's response will be injected on the channel, starting at the server's tap point. The response is defined simply as the LISP value the server returns, and it will propagate from the server back to the point on the channel at which the original request was injected. On its way back, the response might pass over a set of "response watchers," which similarly can have the potential for altering or blocking the response as it passes on its way back to the requester.

As an illustration, consider how a rather simple channel configuration that models the THANTE capability in MICROPLANNER can be set up. (This will amount to activating any relevant watchers *after* some pattern has successfully entered the system's database.) The CSA calls required to set up this channel are

($CONNECT '$STORE 'DB-IN-CH 'TRANSPARENT 'SERVER
        'AT 'RIGHT-END)
($CONNECT 'TRIGGERTREE1 'DB-IN-CH 'TRANSPARENT
        'WATCHER 'AFTER '$STORE)

The possibilities for complex channel hierarchies are limitless. Figure 5, for example, illustrates how signals flowing on a primary, top-level channel might be parceled off to subchannels by trigger trees whose SCs classify the main-channel signals.

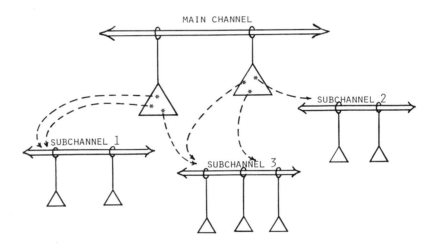

Fig. 5. Channel hierarchies.

Although the engineering of channels on sequential machines obviously does not come without cost, there are what I regard as compelling conceptual arguments in their favor. The first is that channels and trigger trees help to modularize a theory by providing data structures that suggest how to group knowledge into natural populations.[6] Sec-

---

[6] This includes masking and manifesting entire populations in context-sensitive fashions, since the implementation provides for the individual masking of SCs within trigger trees, of entire trigger trees (by detaching them from their channels), and of entire channels themselves.

ond, channels can serve as a literal translation of the ubiquitous "block diagram" of AI models by regarding each interbox connection as a channel. Although there are certainly numerous possible communication paradigms for coordinating the subprocesses of large models, I would argue that the metaphorical channel is one of the more powerful ones.

This concludes the first half of the chapter on SC engineering issues. Readers interested in more detail are referred to [Rieger77d].

## 4.0  THEORETICAL ROLES OF SC IN AI MODELS

At this point, we are ready to move into some more theoretical considerations about how SC can be put to use in cognitive models. I shall begin with the interesting question: What is the relationship between the SC component and the deductive component of the system as manifest during the polling process? In particular, what effect ought partially triggered SCs to have on a model?

### 4.1  Partially Triggered SCs and SC Splitting

Each SC trigger pattern may be regarded as a spiny urchin (sophomoric metaphors notwithstanding!); when any of its spines are touched associatively by some passing object, the rest of the spines are set in motion, by a polling process. (Is this the way a real urchin works?) While the triggering is purely associative, the polling process that ensues is very deductive or goal-directed in the sense that in its subsequent behavior, the system becomes (at least momentarily) motivated to seek out other conditions requisite to the SCs full firing. In a very important way, therefore, SCs will comprise a basic source of goal direction.

One interesting question is: What ought to happen when some trigger fires associatively on some stimulus, causing polling to occur, but then not all the required components of the trigger pattern can be derived deductively? Two obvious things could happen: (1) the SC could simply be put back to sleep, retaining no memory of its partial activation, or (2) all the partial results of the initial association and subsequent polling could somehow be remembered. I shall call these two general strategies the *pulse* model and the *pressure* model of SC activation respectively. The term "pressure" is intended to suggest a cumulative buildup of evidence in favor of running the SC. The term "pulse" is intended to suggest the transient nature of SC trigger patterns that have no memory of past partial successes; unless all required components of a pulse SC's trigger pattern are found to be true simultaneously, a pulse SC never fires.

There will be applications where we can get by with a pulse model. However, the pressure model is far more interesting theoretically, both because it conserves what it has discovered as partial evidence (via what may have been a very costly deductive process), and because it can be made to give rise to "lingering motivations" within the system, i.e., to focus what happens in the future on the basis of what has happened in the past. Therefore, how might we implement a pressure model?

The metaphor for managing pressure is one of digital AND and OR gates with symbolic inputs and outputs (i.e., each connecting "wire" represents an antecedent or consequence relation, and signals are binding lists rather than zeroes and ones). A symbolic AND gate that encodes a simple inference is illustrated in Fig. 6. While this metaphor may some day be taken literally by digital engineers,[7] we cannot use it in precisely this form on today's machines. We are therefore concerned with techniques for capturing this notion within the current SC framework.

A solution to pressure management in the present framework is as follows. Suppose SC X's trigger pattern is initially stimulated by stimulus A; suppose the polling process, interacting with the deductive mechanism, ascertains that certain ones of the other required components of the pattern are satisfied, but that one or more remain unsatisfied (that is, not all of L(A) is satisfied).

If the parts satisfied by the polling process are $X_1, \ldots X_j$, and the unsatisfied parts are $Y_1, \ldots, Y_k$, we can conserve much of the effort expended to that point by splitting off the as-yet unsatisfied portion of the pattern, $Y_1, \ldots, Y_k$, and instantiating as much of it as possible with the various bindings derived from those parts $A, X_1, \ldots, X_j$, which have been satisfied.

In general, this may give rise to numerous partially instantiated patterns, corresponding to each possible binding set (way to perform a partial instantiation of $Y_1, \ldots, Y_k$) derived from $A, X_1, \ldots, X_j$. I shall call this process *SC splitting.*

SC splitting will amount to a narrowing of the scope of applicability of the original SC, S, to some subset of the original class of situations to which S is applicable. In this sense, SC splitting provides not only an implicit memory for what has happened (i.e., it creates simpler AND gates whose *existence* represents some combination of backed up binding lists), but also a theoretically important strategy for narrowing the system's future focus according to what it has become aware of in the past.

---

[7] It is interesting indeed to ponder what a digital machine with symbolic gates with memories might look like. Are there analogies to flip-flops, counters, shift-registers, etc.?

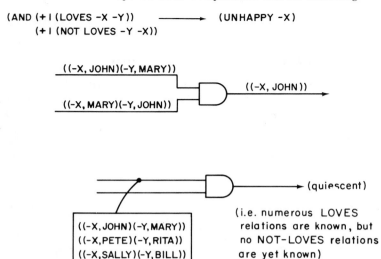

Fig. 6. A symbolic AND gate, and its memories of lovers' backups.

As an example of SC splitting, suppose some trigger tree modeling the activities of space life contains an SC planted by

($PLANT '(AND (+ 1 (LOCATION -SPACECRAFT OUTER-SPACE))
                (+ 1 (CONTAINS -SPACECRAFT -HUMAN))
                (+ 1 (CAUSE S -HUMAN (OPEN -HATCH)))
                (- 1 (CLASS -HATCH OUTER-HATCH))
                (- 1 (PART -OF -HATCH -SPACECRAFT)))
         '(LAMBDA (SPACECRAFT HUMAN HATCH)
                (INFER (LIST 'DEAD HUMAN)))
         'SPACE-LIFE-TREE)

and suppose that the autopilot of a freshly launched vehicle ENTER-PRISE has just injected the symbolic observation (derived from its external sensors)

(LOCATION ENTERPRISE OUTER-SPACE)

onto the main spacecraft-wide CSA channel. Suppose further that there is exactly one external hatch on the vehicle, and that the vehicle is transporting exactly one astronaut, JOE. Then, possibly among numerous others, this SC will be triggered, causing it to gather most of the information it requires to fire. Unfortunately (for JOE, fortunately) a critical trigger component (OPEN HATCH-1) is missing. It would be computationally quite inefficient to waste the potential energy represented in this nearly triggered SC's current state by allowing the

SC to doze off again, losing all recollection of its near-triumphant moment. Theoretically, it would also be wasteful not to preserve some record of the near miss, since this SC has now ascertained some important features of local context, namely, that the spacecraft is in outer space, that its astronaut is Joe, and so forth. Such context can be extraordinarily useful later in focusing the concerns and motivations of the system. This is perhaps not obvious when we consider only one SC. However, since there may be quite a number of SC's that partially trigger on the stimulus (LOCATION ENTERPRISE OUTERSPACE), if all of them retain a memory of past partial contexts, then collectively they will capture the general concept of what it means to be in outer space.

Suppose, therefore, that we catch the SCs that fire on (LOCATION ENTERPRISE OUTERSPACE) before they doze off, yank out the unmet components of the trigger pattern, then replant these components as a simpler trigger pattern in some tree, pointing the new SC at a partially instantiated and correspondingly simpler body. Then, if we rely primarily on these new, more context-focused SCs, the model will start behaving in ways that reflect an implicit conditioning to known sectors of the general context.

In this particular example, the resulting split SC would be created via

> ($PLANT '(+ (OPEN HATCH-1))
> '(LAMBDA () (INFER '(DEAD JOE)))
> <some trigger tree>)

The precise choice of which trigger tree should receive such a split pattern is a topic of considerable interest, but since I have no convincing ideas, one that will not be discussed here. A syntax for SC splitting (to be included in the call to $PLANT) is, however, under development for use in our story comprehension project. This syntax includes a specification of the subsets of the trigger pattern that, if fulfilled, would constitute interesting split points, as well as a "destruct-when" set of conditions, which govern the split SC's continued existence.

## 4.2  SC Splitting, Context, and Frames

If we now visualize what begins to happen systemwide in a model that splits SCs, we can see the possibility for many SCs becoming partially aroused and fulfilled by some stimulus, such as (LOCATION ENTERPRISE OUTER SPACE). That subpopulation of SCs that nibbles at such a stimulus constitutes (in a very real sense, I feel) the model's composite (SC-based) understanding of the concept of being in outer space; after all, the "meaning" of such a concept can be no more than the sum of all larger patterns in which it participates.

The act of splitting and instantiating all SCs that nibble at some stimulus involving being in outer space therefore amounts to conditioning the system with an implicit awareness that this concept is relevant to the current context. The manner in which the system behaves subsequently will then reflect this conditioning through the population of specialist SCs spawned by the splitting process.

If we regard the population of SCs that would nibble at some given stimulus as the frame [Minsky75] for that stimulus, then the event of splitting and instantiating that population for some instance of the stimulus will correspond to instantiating its frame with specific terminals (to use Minsky's terms). In other words, all instantiated and split SCs that would nibble at (LOCATION ENTERPRISE OUTER-SPACE) will collectively represent a copy of the "spaceship in outer space" frame, instantiated with respect to JOE and the ENTERPRISE.

This similarity between partially activated SCs and frames is esthetically pleasing, since it seems to tie some ideas together. All the ideas have to do with a model being able to "tune" itself automatically to a situation in order to access the most relevant world knowledge in the most efficient manner at the most opportune moment. I have previously been interested in this idea of tuning within a totally different, demand-based computaion framework as described in [Rieger7-6a]. In that framework, tuning means planting so-called bypasses in the selection networks of the other theoretical half of the CSA system, the more goal-directed components.

## 4.3  SCs as Character Followers in Story Comprehenders

In *The Magic Grinder* story that we have been using to focus our story comprehension research, there is a very natural application of this notion of SC splitting that has to do with modeling the story characters.

As each character is introduced, or as each new characteristic of a character is discovered,we dangle the new features over the population of SC generalists, then catch, split, and instantiate all the nibblers to capture or refine the "frame" for the character whose features have been nibbled at. Then we plant the resulting split SCs in a tree associated with the character. I imagine there to be a tree for each story character, and we call the tree for each character a *character follower*.

Character follower trees will represent fragments of the generalist knowledge that have been tuned to the idiosyncrasies of each character. Because of this, they can do a more efficient job in the role of spontaneous inference (including predictions) where the character is concerned; character follower trees hence represent a significant form of search reduction in the processes that will predict what any given character is likely to do, or how he is likely to react to any given situation.

Character traits in the CSA story comprehender are defined by collections of SCs. GREED, for example, is compositely defined by a collection of pointers to SC patterns that illustrate the concept in its various manifestations. We have found these patterns to be very large, primarily because we are attempting to be as precise and thorough as possible in their specification. But to illustrate the concept with a simplified example, one manifestation of GREED might be expressed as

```
($PLANT '(AND (+ 1 (PERSONALITY -X GREEDY))
              (- 1 (POSSESSES -Y -Z))
              (NOT-EQUAL -X -Y)
              (- 1 (INHEAD -X (POSSESSES -Y -Z)))
              (+ 1 (WANTS -X (POSSESSES -X -Z)))
              (- 1 (PHYSICALLY-SUPERIOR -X -Y)))
         '(LAMBDA (X Y Z)
                  (PREDICT (LIST 'STEAL-FROM -X -Y -Z)))
         'HUMAN-EMOTION-PREDICTION-TREE)
```

i.e., if X is a person who is greedy and physically superior to Y, who has object Z (an object that X wants), and if X knows that Y has this object, then X might attempt to steal the object from Y. (This in fact is one manifestation of greed that is pivotal to the comprehension of the "Magic Grinder," the children's story we are using.) In the comprehender's present organization, there is one trigger tree to represent each basic character trait; it is into this tree that all patterns illustrative of that particular trait are planted. All character trait trees are then connected to a single channel, HUMAN-CHARACTER-TRAITS, which is one branch of the channel structure of the comprehender, and which receives stimuli from both the language interface that is doing the reading and the inference mechanisms (attached to higher channels). It should be noted that the information in patterns such as the one above can be accessed from numerous points of view: we might be told explicitly that Lord Gurr is greedy, in which case *all* the triggers in the GREED tree would respond, or we might infer Lord Gurr's greed from evidence built up from the (partial) firings of individual greed manifestation SCs.

## 4.4  Spontaneous Computation and Inference

Inference is perhaps the most prevalent single notion in artificial intelligence. Unfortunately, however, the term "inference" has almost as many connotations as there are subdisciplines in AI. For the purposes of this discussion, I shall concentrate not on the logical categories of inferences, but on the times at which various categories are manifest during comprehension. Thus, for example, although deduction is normally regarded as a type of inference, I shall regard deduction and inference as distinct enterprises by distinguishing the times at which they are invoked in AI models. Specifically, I shall regard deduction as a demand-based computation that occurs in response to specific needs (e.g., to answer a database query), whereas I shall use the terms "inference" to suggest the unsolicited introduction of new information via something more spontaneous. Using this terminology, we can examine some categories of inference which ought, and ought not, to be implemented as spontaneous computation.

### 4.4.1 Algorithmic Inference

In the CSA model of the more goal-directed (described in [Rieger75a, 76a, b]), I have been concerned with a special class of inference dealing with actions and knowledge about cause and effect. I call knowledge about cause and effect *algorithmic knowledge*, and therefore term inferences that arise from this knowledge "algorithmic inferences." Since, as proposed in [Rieger75a, 76a, b], algorithmic knowledge is highly structured, and accessible only in orderly, "refereed" manners, it is necessary to make a clear distinction in theory between algorithmic inference and other classes of inference for which, it is proposed, SC should serve as a basis.

In [Rieger75a, 76a, b], I have argued that cause-effect knowledge (say, as used by a problem solver) is highly structured, and accessible only in orderly, "refereed" manners. In brief, the process of *algorithmic inference* goes as follows: state S or action A is perceived to be (respectively) desired or performed by some actor; the system's goal is to produce a context-sensitive explanation of this desire or action.

In the CSA setting, there is a large number of relatively small cause-effect schemata, called "abstract algorithms," which describe specific ways for causing states and statechanges to occur. The abstract algorithms are organized into "causal selection networks," one network for each state and statechange concept known to the system. For example, there is a statechange LOCATION network that serves as the organizing structure for thousands of (in principle, not in the running model!) strategies for changing the location of various types of objects from a starting point to a terminal point. Clearly, the strategy will be dependent on both the objects and places involved in the statechange of location, who will be effecting the strategy, and a general awareness of the context in which the strategy will be effected. It is the purpose of a causal selection network to ask an orderly progression of questions to illuminate as much of the relevant information as required about the situation so that an intelligent selection of *one* strategy from among the large number of contenders that may exist at the terminals of the selection network can be made.

But if the system has an algorithmic base of thousands of cause-effect schemata, each tuned to a small part of the world, we can also confer upon it the reverse ability to determine of any given state or action X where X *could conceivably* participate in cause-effect strategies. Knowing where X could participate, it is then possible to trace upward (backward) through layers of CSA patterns and causal selection networks from the set of starting points (strategies) in which X might be participating. By applying the questions in the network as this upward climbing occurs, it seems to be possible to rule out most possible "interpretation paths" quickly, because of failures of the situation in which X participates to agree with the tests in the network. (This is described in more detail in [Rieger77d], and the concept is generically related to the concept of "backward chaining" employed by the MYCIN project; see, e.g. [Davis76a].)

The final interpretation, i.e., the algorithmic inference, from X is the path (or collection of paths) that survives long enough to connect up with a prediction[8] that has been made concerning the actor associated with desire or action X.

I propose that this type of inference, inasmuch as it interacts with a highly structured knowledge about cause and effect, ought *not* to be modeled by spontaneous computation. Without the tremendous search-restricting and mediating influence of the causal selection networks, the system would explode combinatorially with possible interpretations of actions and desires in context. Fundamentally, SCs are local entities that are independent of one another. They are inherently resistant to organization into the kinds of larger structures that seem to be appropriate for cause and effect knowledge, and I believe that it is incorrect to attempt to cast them in this mold by building "spontaneous computation selection networks." SCs are simply not intended to be selected among, and are hence intrinsically ill-suited for algorithmic inference.

### 4.4.2  Nonalgorithmic Inference

Algorithmic inference is easy to describe; unfortunately, its complement is not. However, one hallmark of nonalgorithmic inference is an absence of intentionality; that is, nonalgorithmic inferences are

---

[8] The CSA system's predictions at any given moment have been derived from other CSA patterns, primarily ones involving the so-called *inducement* and *motivation* links. These are described in [Rieger76b].

inferences that do not involve purposeful choice of actions, reasoning about the possible outcomes of actions, or the third-party understanding of others' actions. I find it difficult to offer a concise definition of nonalgorithmic inference, but nevertheless feel that it is to this (large) residue of nonvolitional inference types that SC-based inference ought to be limited; to actionless situations, "settings" that convey information via state descriptions that have not been purposefully caused by actors. As illustrated earlier this will embrace things like descriptions of characters in stories, scenes laying out spatial or emotional relationships, and patterns delimiting how a story character might be expected to behave in general situations. In other words, SC-based inference ought to deal only with nonpurposeful aggregates of states, which are the way they are for no particular reason, but which nevertheless will represent an often-rich basis for inference.

## 4.5  Spontaneous Computation in Problem Solving

### 4.5.1  SCs as Models of CSA Tendencies

In the CSA model, there are five theoretical types of events: actions, states, statechanges, wants, and tendencies [Rieger75a]. A tendency is defined to be an actionlike event, in the sense that it causes new states and statechanges, but an event in which there is no animate actor. A tendency is therefore a nonintentional force that must occur whenever its set of enabling conditions occurs.

For example, my commonsense notion of gravity tells me that whenever an object X is in an unsupported state and close to a very large mass, it will begin changing its location from where it is toward the large mass. In CSA syntax, we write this as shown in Fig. 7.

CSA distinguishes the notions of *enablement* and *gating*. An enablement is a condition (state) that must be in effect in order for an

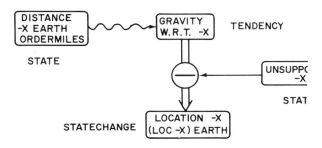

Fig. 7. Commonsense earth gravity.

action to proceed, regardless of what the action is intended to accomplish. For example, if one wishes to pick up an object, he might grasp after having ensured that his hand is hovering around the object he intends to pick up. In this situation, regardless of whether or not the *gating* state (AROUND (HAND P) OBJECT) has been satisfied, in order for the action GRASP even to begin, the *enabling* condition

(MOBILE (FINGERS (HAND P))

must be true, and must remain true for the duration of the GRASP movement. Enablements therefore are associated with the context-free requirements of actions in isolation, while gates describe the context in which the action must be performed in order to achieve some desired result.

This separation of enablements from gates in the CSA theory meshes naturally with the notions of spontaneous computatons we have been developing here. Roughly speaking, every tendency is a purely associative or state-based inference, which we are obligated to make whenever we can. Thus for example, we may model the tendency COMMONSENSE-GRAVITY by an SC whose trigger pattern might appear as

(AND (+ 1 (DISTANCE -X EARTH ORDERMILES))[9]
(+ 1 (UNSUPPORTED -X)))

Somehow, the two conditions on this pattern do not have equal status; the support status of an object is, conceptually at least, far more apt to vary than the object's distance from EARTH, and besides, the distance from earth governs gravity's *existence* (with respect to that object), whereas support relations govern its *effects*. Since the CSA theory categorizes these two conditions differently, why not reflect this in the SC implementation of gravity?

We can do so by retaining only the second condition about unsupportedness as the SC's trigger pattern, and placing the SC itself in a tree that models an entire population of SCs that share the DISTANCE condition as an existence enablement. Then by turning the entire tree on and off on the basis of knowledge bout our distance to the earth, we shall be able to model large-scale shifts in context (e.g., leaving the earth's influence) quite naturally.

I therefore imagine populations of tendencies modeled by trees of

---

[9] ORDERMILES is a fuzzy concept that specifies a range of acceptable values. Fuzzy concepts are noticed and properly matched by the CSA pattern matcher.

SCs. A tendency's inclusion in a population is a function of the tendency's enablements, while the tendency's trigger pattern within the tree is derived from its gate conditions. In this setting, there might be some SCs whose sole job would be to turn on and off entire trees of tendencies on the basis of large scale context changes which arise, say, as the result of executing a plan, or as the result of entering some hypothetical context during the course of synthesizing a plan to solve some problem.

### 4.5.2  SCs as Subgoal Annihilation Interrupts

There are several other interesting ways such populatins of tendencies can interact with a problem solver. Another form of interaction has to do with ordering problems in the synthesis of complex plans. Often, it will happen that subgoals are not compatible, or at least are incompatible with respect to some particular ways of solving them. Thus, as recognized for some time now [Waldinger75, Sacerdoti75b, Sussman75a], there is the danger of a purely recursive plan synthesizer first solving a subgoal but, in the synthesis of the next subgoal, causing conditions that would destroy the effects presumed to have been achieved by the first subgoal's solution. Since subgoals are states of the world that usually must be in effect *simultaneously* at plan execution time, if solving one destroys another, the plan simply will not work. Sussman has called this problem "prerequisite clobbers brother goal," and it was precisely this problem that motivated much of his dissertation research [Sussman75a]. I shall refer to this problem as "subgoal annihilation."

Subgoal annihilation may happen for one of two reasons: either the CSA pattern the synthesizer has adopted as a strategy is conceptually faulty (e.g., it may have been incorrectly learned, or may have been learned and works for one case, but not for another) or the pattern is not conceptually faulty, but the *ways* the synthesizer has gone about solving the subgoals are inimical to each other.

We have recently applied spontaneous computation in the CSA system in what seems to be a general technique for (a) detecting and (b) correcting subgoal annihilation problems that stem from inopportune orderings [Rieger77b]. (This technique has been implemented and incorporated in the existing CSA plan synthesizer that is described in [Rieger76a].) Briefly,the operation of the detection phase is as follows. As a solution strategy emerges from the selection process of the plan synthesizer, it will introduce a subgoal reduction pattern that is usually of the form

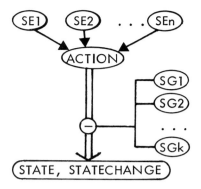

i.e., providing enabling states $SE_1,\ldots, SE_n$ are in effect to permit the performance of ACTION, then ACTION will produce STATE (or STATECHANGE), provided gating states $SG_1,\ldots,SG_k$ are simultaneously true. Having selected such a strategy, the synthesizer's tasks are (1) to solve (recursively) any gating or enabling states that cannot be presumed true at plan execution time, (2) to add ACTION to the action stream (which constitutes the synthesizer's solution), and finally (3) to assert the newly caused STATE or STATECHANGE.

The protection paradigm is this: as each subgoal (gate, enablement) is solved, it is "protected" by planting an SC that will trigger whenever conditions that are inimical to the protected state materialize. Currently, these so-called guardian clusters are rather primitive, reacting only to the direct erasure of the protected state or to the assertion of another semantically opposite state; however, they can be made as comprehensive as necessary to provide reliable detection of annihilation problems. ([Rieger77b] discusses some of the tradeoffs here.)

Ordinarily, the synthesis of all gate and enablement subgoals will proceed smoothly, ending in a condition in which all are protected, and simultaneously true. At that point, the synthesizer (1) adds the action to the action stream, (2) unprotects each protected subgoal (by masking its SCs), and (3) protects the state or statechange assumed to have been caused by the action. The synthesis thus proceeds in a purely recursive fashion, with the protection and unprotection of subgoals following the recursion. However, when a guardian cluster fires, the recursive structure of the synthesis is interrupted. At that time, the violated state is "unravelled," i.e., deasserted and unprotected, graciously backing off so that the interrupting subgoal synthesis may proceed. Simultaneously, the action that originally achieved the violated state is recalled from the action stream, and the gates and enablements relating to this action are revived by reactivating their guardian clusters. The net effect is that actions get rearranged, and parts of the plan that once were thought to be independent come to coexist in time (i.e., they must all get along with one another). Secondary and higher-order violations incurred by primary unravellings are handled naturally by this technique.

I feel this detection-unravelling strategy is both universal, in that it does not rely on any details of the CSA representation, and noncombinatorial, in that it forces remedial actions only for the portions of the plan that absolutely require rearrangement. Furthermore, this interaction between the SC system and the plan synthesizer is a nearly ideal illustration of the possible types of fruitful theoretical complicity between demand-based and spontaneous computation.

## 4.6  SCs as Hierarchical Situation Characterizers

It is natural to think of SCs in terms of numerous populations, each population tuned to specific facets of the environment, to specific contexts, or to specific levels of resolution. In other words, SCs can be structured and put to use hierarchically. They can be regarded either as data-driven or as goal-driven, because of the way they interact with the deductive components of the system during the polling process.

Hierarchically structured populations of SCs can be put to use in interesting ways to convert context-free information at the data level into progressively higher, more semantic, and context-dependent assessments of a situation. Consider a chess game. Context-free information in a chess game presumably has forms such as: "PAWN1 is attacking KNIGHT2," "ROOK2 is not in immediate danger," "QUEEN has the following three moves," and so forth. The context free information is that which can be gathered on a very local and mechanical, piece by piece basis, with no regard for its contextual implications.

Now imagine a population of SCs whose job it is simply to watch this level of characterization. The trigger pattern of a typical SC in this population will be a mixture of context-free parts and more semantic and contextual parts, perhaps things like "Does the bishop play a role in constraining the opponent's rook?" Now, when the SC triggers on the basis of very *syntactic* information, it will (via the polling process) pose the as yet unanswered semantic and contextual questions in its trigger pattern to the deductive component of the system.

The deductive component, being fishbowled by yet other SCs, will pose a new generation of questions designed to answer this question, possibly giving rise to new SC invocations. Thus, regardless of the answer's outcome, the very fact that the original SC *posed* the question can give rise to an upward spiraling of more semantic awareness about what is happening on the board. At another higher level, I would imagine yet more abstract SCs designed to react to lines of constraint, lines of force, mounds of power, or whatever. Presumably, these top level characterizers would correspond closely with the concepts a chess expert employs.

This deceptively simple notion — mixing the syntactic with the semantic and contextual in SC trigger patterns — seems to be the key to many problems of context. It provides the system with a starting point at which to begin making semantic conjectures; these conjectures, whether or not they prove to be true, can be important catalysts for higher-level SCs via questions sought during the deductive processes. In this sense, SCs provide a significant source of "upward awarenesses," which at some point hopefully make contact with the strategy, algorithmic, or goal-directed levels of the system.

## 5.0 SUMMARY

In this chapter, I have presented some of the engineering techniques and theoretical applications of spontaneous computation as it might be of use in models of human cognition. I have contrasted the SC style of computation with the more traditional style of demand-based computation and, hopefully, have suggested some model regions where the two styles of computation can cooperatively interact.

The main conclusion is that any model must contain a mixture of demand-based and spontaneous components. Typical of the types of tasks for which demand-based computation is best suited are strategy selection during directed problem solving, and algorithmic inference, where the same orderly problem solving knowledge is used in reverse to infer intentions, causes, enablements, and so forth. Typical of tasks best suited for spontaneous computation are nonalgorithmic inference (character followers, more static situational inferences, etc.), subgoal protection and optimization during plan synthesis, and simulation. In each of these, SC is used to realize a generalized interrupt reflex that can either be tightly controlled by demand-based computation, or more free-wheeling, as it would be, in say, a large data-driven inference system.

A future report will describe in more detail the applications of spontaneous computation in the CSA story comprehender.

# ACKNOWLEDGMENTS

I wish to thank the members of the CSA group (Phil London, Milt Grinberg, Mache Creeger, John Boose, George Fekete) who have helped me focus many of the ideas described in this chapter.

# KNOWLEDGE ACQUISITION IN RULE-BASED SYSTEMS—KNOWLEDGE ABOUT REPRESENTATIONS AS A BASIS FOR SYSTEM CONSTRUCTION AND MAINTENANCE[1]

Randall Davis
*Stanford University*

*Recent research efforts aimed at task-oriented systems have emphasized the importance of large stores of domain-specific knowledge as a basis for high performance. But assembling the required knowledge base is a difficult task that often extends over several years, and involves numerous modifications to the knowledge base. Given the difficulty of making even small changes to a program, this presents a challenging problem in system construction.*

*We have studied this issue in the context of TIERESIAS, a program designed to function as an assistant in the task of building large knowledge bases. TIERESIAS facilitates the interactive transfer of expertise from a human expert to the knowledge base of the system, in a dialog conducted in a restricted subset of natural language.*

*One such knowledge transfer task involves teaching the system about a new conceptual primitive from which new inference rules can be built. We show that by providing a program with a store of knowledge about its own representations, this acquisition of new concepts can be carried out in a high-level dialog that transfers information efficiently. The necessary knowledge about representations includes both structural and organizational information, and is specified in a data structure schema, a device used to describe representations.*

[1] This work was supported in part by the Bureau of Health Sciences Research and Evaluation of HEW under Grant HS-01544 and by the Advanced Research Projects Agency under ARPA Order 2494. It was carried out on the SUMEX Computer System, supported by the NIH under Grant RR-00785.

## 1.0 INTRODUCTION

The difficulty of making even relatively simple changes to any sizable program is a well-known phenomenon. It is often referred to as the "one-plus-$\epsilon$" bug problem, since the changes made to fix a single known bug may introduce more than one new bug. The problem arises with respect to both code and data structures, and has inspired techniques based on a number of different approaches [Dahl72, Schneiderman74, Suzuki76].

This chapter examines the problems of making changes to a large collection of data structures, and considers in particular the difficulties encountered in adding new instances of existing data types. It explores the character of the errors commonly made and determines the kinds of information required to avoid them. Finally, it describes an approach to organizing and representing that information, and shows how this approach can be used to make the process of data structure management both easier and less prone to error.

## 2.0 PERSPECTIVE

We begin by noting that the terms *data structure, extended data type,* and *representation* will be used interchangably. Equating the first two implies extending the idea of data types to cover every data structure in a system. The utility of this view appears to be widely accepted, and in the case at hand will influence our approach to determining what information about data structures is relevant and how that information should be organized.

The equivalence of the last two suggests the perspective in this chapter on the design and implementation of knowledge representations. These two tasks—design and implementation—are typically decoupled, and indeed the desirability of transparency of implementation has been stressed from many quarters [Bachman75, Balzer67, Liskov74]. But what might we learn by considering them simultaneously? That is, what can we learn about representation design by considering issues that arise at the level of implementation and technical details? Conversely, what can we learn about the organization or design of data types by viewing them as knowledge representations? We examine these questions and others in the remainder of the chapter.

## 3.0 THE PROBLEM

Consider now the standard approach to adding a new instance of an extended data type to a large system. The programmer attempting the task will have to gather a wide range of information, including the structure of the data type and its interrelations with other data types in the system. Such information is typically recorded informally (if at all), is often scattered through a range of sources, and might be found in comments in system code, in documents and manuals maintained separately, and in the mind of the system architect. Just finding all of this information can be a major task, especially for someone unfamiliar with the system.

In this situation, two sorts of errors are common: the new instance may be given the wrong structure, or it may be improperly integrated into the rest of the system. Since an extended data type may be built from a complex collection of components and pointers, it is not uncommon that a new instance receives an incorrect internal organization, that extraneous structures are included, or that necessary elements are inadvertently omitted. Since data structures in a program are not typically independent, the addition of a new instance often requires significant effort to maintain the existing interdependencies. Errors can result from doing this incorrectly (by violating the interrelationships of existing structures) or (as is more common) by omitting a necessary bookkeeping step.

The fundamental source of difficulty here is size. There are often a large number of different data types, each of which may have its own structural organization, its own set of interrelations with other data types, and its own set of requirements for integration into the system. There is also typically a large number of instances of each data type. Since modifications to a data type design have to be carried out on all of its instances, the efficient retrieval and processing of this set is another problem involving the handling of large numbers of structures.

## 4.0 THE SOLUTION

In the simplest terms, the solution we suggest is to give the system a store of knowledge about its representations, and to use this as a basis for construction and management of them.

In more detail, we view every data structure, every knowledge representation in the system as an extended data type. Explicit descriptions of each data type are written, descriptions that include all the information about structure and interrelations that was noted earlier as often widely scattered. Next, we devise a language in which all of this can be put in machine-comprehensible terms, and write the descriptions in those terms, making this store of information available to the system. Finally, we design an interpreter for the language, so that the system can use its new knowledge to keep track of the details of data structure construction and maintenance.

This is of course easily said and somewhat harder to do. The difficult questions include, *What knowledge about its representations does a system require in order to allow it to do a range of nontrivial management tasks? How should that knowledge be organized? How should it be represented? How can it be used?*

This chapter is concerned primarily with issues of what knowledge is required and how it can be used.[2] We demonstrate in particular that the relevant knowledge includes information about the structure and interrelations of representations, and show that it can be used as the basis for interactive transfer of domain-specific expertise.

The main task here, then, is the description and use of knowledge about representations. To accomplish this, we use a *data structure schema*, a device that provides a framework and language in which representations can be specified. The framework, like most, carries its own perspective on its domain. One point it emphasizes strongly is the detailed specification of many kinds of information about representations. It attempts to make this specification task easier by providing an organization for the information and a relatively high-level vocabulary for expressing it.[3]

The schemata were developed as a generalization of the concept of record structures, and strongly resemble them in both organization and use. Many of the operations with the schemata can be seen in terms of variations on the task of creating a new instance of a record-like structure. We shall see that these operations proceed in a mixed-initiative mode: the need to modify a data structure is made evident by an action on the part of the user; the system then takes over, retrieving the appropriate schema and using it to guide the rest of the interaction.

The aim of the work described here is to develop a language for describing representations and techniques for managing them. Some of the representations that the language can describe are those illustrated further on; later sections of this chapter examine the limits of its expressive power. Within the range of representations permitted by the framework, the techniques used are domain independent, and

---

[2] The interesting and difficult questions of knowledge organization and representation are covered in more detail elsewhere [Davis76a]. Here we describe the representation and organization scheme chosen, but omit detailed justifications.

[3] Work in other areas has addressed some of these same issues. The *CODASYL Data Base Task Group Report* (ACM, 1971), for instance, describes a major effort to provide a language for specifying descriptions for COBOL data structures. More generally, the notion of a "data description language" is a common one in work on data base management (see, e.g., [Lucking75]).

have a degree of representation independence as well. Nothing here is specific to a particular domain, or to the attribute-object-value representation, which we will see employed. To illustrate the design of the language and use of the techniques developed, we consider next a specific example.

## 5.0 BACKGROUND: THE PERFORMANCE PROGRAM AND INTERACTIVE TRANSFER OF EXPERTISE

Assembling the required knowledge base for a task-oriented, domain-specific program (e.g., DENDRAL [Feigenbaum71], MACSYMA [Mathlab74]) is an ongoing task that may involve numerous man-years of manual effort. A key element in the construction process is the transfer of expertise from a human expert to the program. Since such programs typically make use of a complex collection of knowledge representations, this transfer of expertise process involves numerous examples of data structure construction and maintenance, and hence offers an excellent case study.

In addition, since the domain expert often knows nothing about programming, the interaction between the expert and the performance program typically requires the mediation of a human programmer. If the construction and maintenance of data structures could be assumed by the system, the need for outside assistance might be reduced or eliminated, simplifying the task of creating high performance systems. Part of our goal then is to establish a discourse at a high enough level that the expert is insulated from the details of representation implementation.

We seek to create a program that might supply much the same sort of assistance as the programmer — that is, an assistant that will help build the knowledge base for intelligent programs. The system we have implemented is called TIERESIAS [Davis76a, 77a, b, c], a large INTERLISP program designed to offer assistance in the interactive transfer of knowledge from a human expert to the knowledge base of a high performance program.

A companion paper [Davis77b] focuses on using TIERESIAS as an aid to the acquisition of new inference rules for the performance program. Here we examine the process of acquiring the conceptual primitives from which rules are built. Since these primitives form a large set of structures with a range of formats and a rich set of interrelationships, they provide a useful case study involving issues of both representation management and interactive transfer of expertise.

### 5.1 Perspective on Knowledge Acquisition

Our model for the interaction between the domain expert and

performance program is that of a teacher and student. That is, the expert should be able to challenge the program with a problem, observe its performance, discover the rationale for its results, and then comment on their correctness. The discovery of a faulty piece of reasoning would then provide impetus for the transfer of information from the expert to the program, in order to improve performance.

Note that this model of the interaction assumes we can make a clear distinction between the *problem-solving paradigm* used by the performance program, and its *degree of expertise*. That is, we assume that the program's basic approach to the problem is correct, and that the deficiency lies in its store of knowledge about the domain. At the level of code and data structures, this means assuming that the program's control structure and knowledge representations can be considered separately from its knowledge base. The former are assumed debugged and acceptable, the latter is the focus for continued growth. This has implications for the expert, since it means that he will take as given the set of available control structures and representations (i.e., the question of *how* knowledge is encoded and used is assumed settled), and concentrate on improving the content of the knowledge base (i.e., improving *what* it is the program knows).

### 5.2 The "Student"

Figure 1 suggests the architecture of the sort of performance programs we shall be considering. (The program described here is modelled after the MYCIN system [Shortliffe76, Davis77d], which provided the context within which TIERESIAS was actually developed; we have abstracted out here just the essential elements of MYCIN's design.) The *knowledge base* is the program's store of task specific knowledge that makes possible high performance. The *inference engine* is an interpreter that uses the knowledge base to solve the problem at hand.

The main point here is the explicit division between these two parts of the program. This design is in keeping with the assumption noted above that the expert's task would be to augment the knowledge base of a program whose control structure (inference engine) was assumed both appropriate and debugged. If all of the control structure information has been kept in the inference engine, then we can engage the domain expert in a discussion of the knowledge base and be assured that the discussion will have to deal only with issues of domain specific expertise (rather than with questions of programming and control structures).

In this discussion we assume the knowledge base contains information about selecting an investment in the stock market; the performance program thus functions as an investment consultant. (The domain has been shifted from medicine to keep the discussion phrased

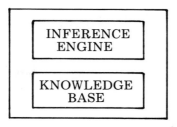

Fig. 1. Architecture of the performance program.

in terms familiar to a wide range of readers, and to emphasize that neither the problems attacked nor the solutions suggested are restricted to a particular domain of application. The dialog shown is a real example of TIERESIAS in action with a few word substitutions, e.g, *primary bacteremia* became *Georgia Pacific, infection* became *investment*.)

Knowledge is in the form of a collection of associative triples (attribute, object, value), which characterize the domain, and inference rules built from them (Fig. 2). The rule is stored internally in INTERLISP, and the English version shown is generated from that with simple template-based mechanisms. Each rule is a single "chunk" of domain specific information indicating an action (in this case a conclusion) that is justified if the conditions specified in the premise are fulfilled.

The premise is a Boolean combination of one or more clauses, each of which is constructed from a predicate function with the associative triple as its argument (Fig. 2b). These items—the attributes, objects, and values—are some of the conceptual primitives we will be concerned about acquiring from the expert, to increase the performance program's vocabulary of concepts for expressing knowledge.

RULE027

If   [1]   the time-scale of the investment is long-term, and
       [2]   the desired return on the investment is greater than 10%, and
       [3]   the area of the investment is not known,
then there is evidence (.4) that the name of the stock to invest in is AT&T.

(a)

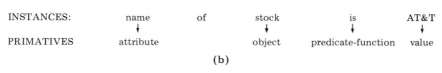

Fig. 2. (a) Example of an inference rule.
(b) Attribute-object-value triples and the predicate function.

We distinguish between acquiring a new instance of an existing primitive (e.g., a new ATTRIBUTE, OBJECT, VALUE, or PREDICATE-FUNCTION), and acquiring a new kind of primitive (e.g., a new primitive in addition to these four). While TIERESIAS is capable of both, the example in this chapter concerns only the former. Detailed examples of the latter are found in [Davis76a].

## 5.3 Knowledge Acquisition in Context

An example of the program in action is shown in Section 6. The program interviews the user, requesting various pieces of information that are relevant to selecting the most appropriate investment, then prints its recommendations. In the remainder of this chapter the "user" will be an expert running the program in order to challenge it, offering it a difficult case, and observing and correcting its performance.

Note that this means knowledge acquisition occurs in the context of a shortcoming in the knowledge base (the error uncovered by the expert). This has proven to be quite useful. It provides the expert with a large amount of contextual information that makes it easier for him to determine what it is the performance program needs to know, and how to express it. The same contextual information is useful to TIERESIAS as well, which uses it to help guide the acquisition process.

## 5.4 A Word About Natural Language

Since this work has not focused on natural language understanding, a range of simple technques has been used to provide the level of performance required. All questions and responses from TIERESIAS are either preformed or based on a simple template completion mechanism (as evidenced by the appearence of phrases like "a area"). Responses from the user are of three general types: single-token answers to multiple choice questions, strings belonging to a synthetic language with a formal grammar, and heavily stylized natural language sentences using a restricted vocabulary (examples of all of these are seen below). The first is handled in the obvious way, the second relies on a simple parser that matches user input against a BNF specification of valid responses, and the last relies on straightforward keyword analysis. This has served thus far to keep the interaction acceptably "natural," without unreasonable processing overhead.

This approach appears to be viable where unrestricted dialog is not the goal, and in domains where there is available a semiformal technical language with a low degree of ambiguity. Since in our experience technical interchange in such domains is often ungrammatical (relying instead on technical terms to convey meaning), a heavily grammar-based approach might not have fared well in any case.

## 6.0 EXAMPLE: ACQUISITION OF A NEW VALUE

In the dialog shown below, the expert is challenging the investment advisory program with a particular case, observing the program's performance, and then making the necessary correction to the knowledge base. (The process of tracking down the error has been edited out here to shorten the trace; a detailed example is found in [Davis77b].) The error in this case is a rule missing from the knowledge base concerning the selection of a particular stock that the system doesn't know anything about yet. Thus the attempt to teach the system the new rule also triggers the acquisition of a new instance of the concept VALUE.

In the trace below, computer output is in mixed upper- and lowercase in this font, user responses follow a double asterisk and are in **BOLD CAPITALS**, and commentary appears as {*indented italics inside braces*}.

Investment Advisory Program
Special options?
** **RD**
Hello, Randy.

{*The expert identifies himself to the program, and then describes a particular case as a test of performance.*}

1) Investor's name?
***ALBERT JONES**

2) Age?
***40**

3) Present income?
***28,000**

4) Number of dependents?
***1**

5) Occupation?
***PHYSICIAN**

6) Amount of previous investment experience? (slight = less than one year; moderate = 2 to 4 years; extensive = more than 4 years)

## **MODERATE

.

.

.

*{This interviewing process continues until the system has gathered all necessary information; the remainder of it is omitted. We continue with the program printing out its conclusions.}*

The following investments appear to be the most appropriate at
  this time:

Crown-Zellerbach
General-Electric

*{At this point* TIERESIAS *steps in, and since the interaction is with an expert (rather than an ordinary user), requests an evaluation of the performance program's results. From here on the dialog takes place between* TIERESIAS *and the expert, with the performance program in the background being manipulated by* TIERESIAS.*}*

Are all these correct?
++** **N**

*{The expert indicates that the results are incorrect. . .}*

Are there any missing?

++** **Y**
Which one(s)?
++** **GEORGIA-PACIFIC TEXASGULF**
Are there any that shouldn't have appeared?
++** **Y**
Which one(s)?
++** **GENERAL ELECTRIC**

*{. . .and then specifies the problems.}*

Do you want to
1] track down the problem yourself, or
2] allow me to guide the debugging, or
3] ignore it for now and fix it another time?
Type 1, 2 or 3
++** **2**

.

.

.

*{The expert allows* TIERESIAS *to help him track down the error by having it "unwind" the sequence of rules that led to the incorrect*

*result. The problem in this case proved to be a rule missing from the knowledge base. We continue at the point where the expert is typing in the new rule.}*

The new rule will be called RULE384

If 1 - **THE DESIRED RATE OF RETURN ON THE INVESTMENT IS GREATER THAN 10%**
  2 - **THE AMOUNT OF INVESTMENT EXPERIENCE OF THE CLIENT IS MODERATE**
  3 - **THE AREA OF THE INVESTMENT IS NATURAL RESOURCE DEVELOPMENT**

**Then**

  1 - **THERE IS EVIDENCE (.5) THAT THE NAME OF THE STOCK TO INVEST IN IS GEORGIA PACIFIC**

Sorry, but I don't understand

+ +** THERE IS EVIDENCE (.5) THAT THE NAME OF THE
+ +** STOCK TO INVEST IN IS GEORGIA PACIFIC

because these words are unknown: GEORGIA PACIFIC

*{TIERESIAS finds it cannot generate any interpretations of the text, so it reprints the original line, and specifies where the trouble is. This makes it possible for the expert to figure out what it is that is new to the system.}*

Would you care to try rephrasing that?
+ +** **Y**

(Please use *'s to mark what you think might be a new attribute or a new value of an existing attribute)

  1 - **THERE IS EVIDENCE (.5) THAT THE NAME OF THE STOCK TO INVEST IN IS * GEORGIA PACIFIC ***

*{While the language in this example is very simple, there are more complex cases where it would be quite hard to decide from the context what sort of new item the expert had in mind. To avoid the necessity for more sophisticated natural language handling, he is asked to mark off the new word or phrase with asterisks.}*

It looks as though

GEORGIA PACIFIC

refers to a new value of an attribute, correct?

$++^{**}$ **Y**
. . .is it a name of a stock?
$++^{**}$ **Y**

{. . .*and with the new item clearly marked, the system can then do some very simple pattern matching to decide what's going on.*}

Now please tell me a few things about it. . .

{TIERESIAS *retrieves the schema for a stock, and "reads" it to find out what it needs to know about any stock.*}

Please give the full, formal name for "GEORGIA PACIFIC"
$++^{**}$ **GEORGIA PACIFIC**
= GEORGIA-PACIFIC

{*Many companies have long names and numerous abbreviations, so* TIERESIAS *starts by requesting the formal name. (Hyphens are inserted to make a single identifier out of it.)*}

Now please give all synonyms or abbreviations for GEORGIA-PACIFIC which you would like the system to accept.
[type an empty line when done]
$++^{**}$ **GP**
$++^{**}$

{*The system requests abbreviations (e.g., the ticker symbol) so that they can be used in the future. The first of them is then used through the rest of the dialogue.*}

Please give a short description of GP.
$++^{**}$ **?**
[e.g., for UTAH-INTERNATIONAL, the description is"MULTI-NATIONAL MINING COMPANY, INVOLVED PRIMARILY IN COAL AND RELATED RESOURCES."]
[type an empty line when done]
$++^{**}$ **MAJOR PRODUCER OF WOOD AND WOOD**
$++^{**}$ **PRODUCTS, OPERATING MAINLY IN THE**
$++^{**}$ **PACIFIC NORTHWEST**
$++^{**}$

{*Two useful capabilities are displayed here. First, the expert is asked to describe every structure he creates, providing a form of on-line documentation for all data structures. Since the documentation is acquired incrementally along with the rest of the knowledge base, the task is much easier than attempting to document an entire system at once. Second,* TIERESIAS *can generate sample answers for any of its questions. In some previous session, the expert had evidently taught*}

*the system about UTAH INTERNATIONAL. Since each schema has
an indication of all of the instances which were created from it, the
system picks one of those instances, and displays the answer to this
question for that instance.}*

On what markets is GP traded?
The answer should be in the form of 1 or more of the following:

<market name> <year first traded>

[Type 1 set to a line, then an empty line when done.]
+ +** **NYSE 1945**
+ +** **PCE 1968**
+ +**

*{Each of the questions from the system is prompted by the attempt to
fill in some component of the data structure being built, according to
the representation conventions indicated by the schema. One of those
conventions indicates that the market name and risk class (below) are
stored as part of the stock (on its property list). The schema also indicates the format for each piece of substructure, and this is displayed
as instructions to the user.}*

What is the current risk classification of GP?
The answer should be in the form of a

<risk classification>

+ +** **AMEX**

Sorry, but the following are invalid:

AMEX is not a recognized <risk classification>

Please answer again [use the same answer if you really meant
    it.]

+ +** **BLUE-CHIP**
+ +**

*{The formatting information also allows a check on the validity of
each answer, to ensure that all information added to the knowledge
base is properly structured. This time the expert made a mistake. It can
happen, however, that the answer is correct but the performance program simply hasn't heard of it yet. Early in its "education," the knowledge base may, for instance, not have information about all the risk
classes yet, and this might become evident in the course of teaching it
about a new stock. Examples of this are found in [Davis76a], which
demonstrates that TIERESIAS sets up new subtopics as required.}*

[Adding GP to STOCKNAMELIST]

{*As in any fairly large and complex program, it isn't enough simply to create the new structure. In addition, a number of other (existing) structures must be "informed" about its existence, and updated accordingly. TIERESIAS now begins working on a number of such updating tasks. The first is very simple, and involves adding the new stock name to an internal list. (The message is printed simply to indicate that the proper step has been taken.)*}

[Adding GP to HILOTABLE]

Please indicate the high and low price for the current year for GP.
The answer should be in the form of

<high price> <low price>

**41 25**

{*The second task involves updating a table of high and low prices, and requires some information from the expert.*}

Should this new item be added to -
- those stocks for which voting rights are cumulative
**N**

{*. . . as does the next task.*}

Should this new item be added to-
     1 - the list of common stocks, or
     2 - the list of preferred stocks, or
     3 - the list of cumulative preferred stocks, or
     4 - the list of participating preferred stocks
Select one of the above
++** **3**

[Adding GP to CUMULATIVEPFD]

{*The fourth task involves adding the new stock to one of four mutually exclusive lists.*}

Please indicate the dividend rate for this preferred stock.
The answer should be in the form of

<dollar amount>

++** **4.25**

{*Another structure keeps track of dividend rates on all preferred stocks.*}

Please indicate the years and amounts of any omitted dividends.
The answer should be in the form of 0 or more of the following-
<year> <dollar amount>

[Type 1 set to a line, then an empty line when done.]
++** 1954 3.75
++** 1955 3.75
++** 1961 4.25
++**

{*And the last structure requiring updating keeps track of part of the stock's performance record. Note that all of this information is required for every new stock added to the system.*}

Ok, done with GP now... Back to the rule.
This may take a few moments.

{*Having finished acquiring the new stock, the system returns to parsing the new rule, and with some help from the expert gets the correct result (the parsing process is omitted here, see [Davis77b] for a detailed example).*}

This is my understanding of your rule:

If 1 - the desired rate of return for the investment is greater than 10%
   2 - the amount of investment experience of the client is moderate
   3 - the area of the investment is natural-resource-development

Then
1 - there is evidence (.5) that the name of the stock to choose
    is georgia-pacific

## 7.0 KNOWLEDGE ABOUT REPRESENTATIONS: ORGANIZATION

Acquisition of new conceptual primitives depends on an extensive store of knowledge about the underlying representations. There are several levels of organization of this knowledge (Fig. 3 below). At the highest level, a schema hierarchy links the schemata together, indicating what categories of data structures exist in the system and the relationships between them. At the next level of organization, there are the individual schemata, the basic unit around which knowledge about representations is organized. Each schema indicates the structure and interrelationships of a single type of data structure. At the lowest level are the slotnames (and associated structures) from which the schemata are built; these offer knowledge about specific conventions at the programming language level. Each of these three levels supplies a different sort of information; together they compose an extensive body of knowledge about the structure, organization, and implementation of the representations.

schema hierarchy    — indicates categories of representations and their organization
individual schema    — describes structure of a single representation
slotnames    — the schema building blocks, describe implementation conventions

Fig. 3. The levels of detail of knowledge about representations.

We begin by examining the organization of the hierarchy.

## 7.1 The Schema Hierarchy

The schemata are organized into a generalization hierarchy that has several useful properties. Part of the hierarchy for the current system is shown in Fig. 4.

KSTRUCT-SCHEMA (knowledge structure) is the root of the network; its schema is empty. Below it are the schemata for value and attribute; each of these is further subdivided into more specific schemata. The right branch of the network illustrates the fact that a schema can have more than one parent.

The major contribution of the hierarchy is as an organizing mechanism, indicating the global organization of representations in the system, and offering as well a convenient overview of them. The right branch in Fig. 4, for instance, indicates that in the current performance program there are two different breakdowns of the set of attributes, one indexed according to the objects with which they are associated, the other according to the type and number of values they can have (see [Davis76a] for details).

Acquisition of a new *instance* of one of these primitives is (as we shall see) in part a process of descent through this hierarchy. The hierarchy thus provides a useful structuring of the dialog. Acquisition of new *types* of conceptual primitives is viewed as a process of adding new branches to this network. It is therefore important that network growth be reasonably smooth and convenient. As examples in [Davis76a] demonstrate, this growth does in fact arise as a natural part of the knowledge acqusition task, and is automatically reflected in future dialogs.

Extensive use is made in the network of the concept of inheritance of properties. The left branch in Fig. 4, for instance, indicates that investment area and stock name are more specific categories of the data type VALUE. All of the characteristics that investment area and

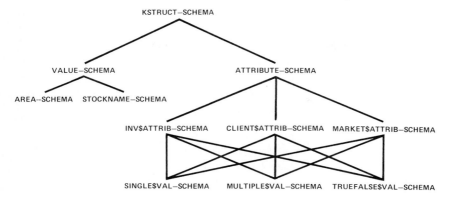

Fig. 4. Part of the schema hierarchy.

stock name have in common as VALUEs are stored in the VALUE-SCHEMA. Thus, for instance, the structure description part of the VALUE-SCHEMA describes the structural components that are common to all VALUEs. The network then branches at this point because an investment area is a different type of data structure than a stock name, and differs in details of organization and structure. As Section 7.2 illustrates, this inheritance of properties is used for all the different types of information stored in the schema.[4]

## 7.2 Schema Organization

The schemata are the second of the three forms of knowledge about representations. Each contains several different types of information:

(1) the structure of its instances
(2) interrelationships with other data structures
(3) a pointer to all current instances
(4) inter-schema organizational information
(5) bookkeeping information

Figure 5 shows the schema for a VALUE, Fig. 6 shows the schema for a stock name. In both, information corresponding to each of the categories listed above is grouped together (the numbers at right in the figures are for reference only).

---

[4] This hierarchical distribution of information also offers a way of describing data types at different levels of abstraction, since the hierarchy stores at each level only those details relevant to that particular level. In this sense it is similar to the sort of hierarchy often represented with the *class* construct in SIMULA.

VALUE-SCHEMA

| | | | | |
|---|---|---|---|---|
| PNTNAME | ATOM | ASKIT | | [1 |
| VAL | PNTNAME | INSLOT | | [2 |
| PLIST | [( INSTOF | VALUE-SCHEMA | GIVENIT | [3 |
| | DESCR | STRING | ASKIT | [4 |
| | AUTHOR | ATOM | FINDIT | [5 |
| | DATE | INTEGER | CREATEIT) | [6 |
| | | CREATEIT] | | [7 |
| | | | | [8 |
| STRAN | "the value of an attribute" | | | [9 |
| FATHER | (KSTRUCT-SCHEMA) | | | [10 |
| OFFSPRING | (STOCKNAME-SCHEMA   AREA SCHEMA) | | | [11 |
| DESCR | "the VALUE-SCHEMA describes the format for a value of an attribute" | | | [12 |
| AUTHOR | DAVIS | | | [13 |
| DATE | 1115 | | | [14 |
| INSTOF | (SCHEMA-SCHEMA) | | | |

Fig. 5. Schema for a value.

STOCKNAME-SCHEMA

| | | | | |
|---|---|---|---|---|
| PLIST | [( INSTOF | STOCKNAME-SCHEMA | GIVENIT | [15 |
| | SYNONYM | (KLEENE (1 0) < ATOM >) | ASKIT | [16 |
| | TRADEON | (KLEENE (1 1 2) < (MARKET-INST FIRSTYEAR-INST) >) | ASKIT | [17 |
| | RISKCLASS | CLASS-INST | ASKIT | [18 |
| | CREATEIT] | | | [19 |
| | | | | [20 |
| RELATIONS | ( (AND* STOCKNAMELIST HILOTABLE) | | | [21 |
| | (OR* CUMVOTINGRIGHTS) | | | [22 |
| | (XOR* COMMON PFD CUMPFD PARTICPFD) | | | [23 |
| | ((OR* PFD CUMPFD PARITCPFD) PFDRATETABLE) | | | [24 |
| | ((AND* CUMPFD) OMITTEDDIVS) ) | | | [25 |
| INSTANCES | (AMERICAN-MOTORS AT&T . . . XEROX ZOECON) | | | [26 |
| STRAN | "the name of a stock" | | | [27 |
| FATHER | (VALUE-SCHEMA) | | | [28 |
| OFFSPRING | NIL | | | [29 |
| DESCR | "the STOCKNAME-SCHEMA describes the format for a stock name" | | | [30 |
| AUTHOR | DAVIS | | | [31 |
| DATE | 1115 | | | [32 |
| INSTOF | (SCHEMA-SCHEMA) | | | |

Fig. 6. Schema for a stock name.

Note that since the VALUE-SCHEMA is the parent of the STOCK-NAME-SCHEMA in the hierarchy, information in the former need not be reproduced in the latter. Hence the complete specification for a stock name is given by considering information in both.

### 7.2.1 Instance Structure [Lines 1-7, 15-19]

The part of the schema that describes the structure of its instances is the element that corresponds most closely to an ordinary record descriptor. The current implementation takes a very simple view of

LISP data structures. It assumes that they are composed of a print name, a value, and a property list, with the usual conventions for each: the print name is a single identifier by which the object is named, the value is an atom or list structure, and the property list is composed of property-value pairs. The first three items in the schema of Fig. 5 deal with each of these in turn.

Each item is expressed as a triple of the form

<slotname> <blank> <advice>

(We use the term "slot" from the work on frames [Minsky75] since the concept is similar, but the schemata grew out of and are fundamentally an extension of the idea of a record structure.)

For the print name of any value of an attribute then, the *slotname* is PNTNAME, the *blank* is ATOM, and the *advice* is ASKIT.

The *slotname* labels the "kind" of thing that fills the *blank*, and serves as a pointer to other information that aids in the knowledge transfer process. Slotnames are the conceptual primitives around which much of the "lower-level" knowledge in the system is organized. All of the semantics of a print name, for instance, are contained in the PNTNAME slot and the structures associated with it (see Section 7.3).

The *blank* specifies the exact format of the information required. A translated form of it is printed out when requesting information from the expert; it is then used to parse his response and to ensure syntactic validity.

The *blank* has a simple syntax, but can express a range of structures. The term KLEENE, for instance, is taken from the Kleene star, and implies a repetition of the form within the angle brackets. The parenthesized numbers that follow it indicate the typical, minimum, and maximum number of occurrences of the form. The appearance of a term of the form <datatype>-INST indicates some instance of the <datatype>-SCHEMA. Thus

(KLEENE (1 1 2) <(MARKET-INST FIRSTYEAR-INST)>)

from the stock name schema above indicates that the market on which a stock is traded is given by one or two lists of the form (<market> <year first traded>). A more detailed specification of the syntax is given in [Davis76a].

The *advice* suggests how to find the information. Various sorts of information are relevant in the course of acquiring a new concept from the expert. Some of it is domain specific (e.g., the risk classification of a stock), and clearly must be supplied by the expert. Other parts of it are purely representation specific. These should be supplied by the system itself, not only because they deal with information that the system already has (and therefore should not have to ask), but because the expert is assumed to know nothing about programming. Even a trivial question concerning internal data structure management would thus appear incomprehensible to him. The *advice* provides a way of expressing instructions to the system on where to find the information it needs. There are five such instructions that can be given (Fig. 7).

ASKIT          — ask the expert
CREATEIT       — manufacture the answer
FINDIT         — the answer is available internally, retrieve it
GIVENIT        — use the contents of the blank as is (like QUOTE in LISP)
INSLOT         — use the contents of the slot indicated

Fig. 7. Five types of advice.

The first triple in Fig. 5 (line 1) indicates then that the print name is an atom and that it should be requested from the expert. The second (line 2) indicates that the stock name should evaluate to its print name, and the third (lines 3-7) indicates the form of the property list. Note that the *blank* for the last of these consists in turn of a set of *slotname - blank - advice* triples describing the property list.

### 7.2.2 Interrelationships [Lines 20-24]

A second main function of the schema is to provide a record of the interrelationships of data structures. The RELATIONS slot contains this information, expressed in a simple language for expressing data structure interrelationships (see [Davis76a] for details of the language).

As lines 20-24 of Fig. 6 show, the data structure STOCKNAME is richly interconnected with a number of other structures in the system. Line 20 names two other structures that each contain an entry for every stock name; line 21 indicates a structure that may or may not contain an entry; while line 22 indicates that the four structures it names are a mutually exclusive and exhaustive set of classifications for each stock name. Lines 23 and 24 specify conditional interrelationships: line 23 says that PFDRATETABLE has an entry for each stock contained in any of the three structures listed; while line 24 indicates that the structure OMITTEDDIVS contains an entry for every stock in the structure CUMPFD.

The key point here is to provide the system architect with a way of making explicit all of the data structure interrelationships upon which his design depends. The approach we use differs slightly from the one more typically taken, which relies on a demon-like mechanism that uses the full power of the underlying programming language. We have avoided the use of an arbitrary body of code and emphasized instead the use of a task-specific high level language.

This formalization of knowledge about data structure interrelationships has several useful applications. First, since the domain expert can not, in general, be expected to know about such representation conventions, expressing them in machine-accessible form makes it possible for TIERESIAS to take over the task of maintaining them. Second, having TIERESIAS attend to them ensures a level of knowledge base integrity without making unreasonable demands on the expert. Finally, it keeps knowledge in the system accessible, since the RELATIONS make explicit the sort of knowledge that is often left implicit, or embedded in code and hence inaccessible. There are several advantages to this accessibility of knowledge. For example, by adding to TIERESIAS a simple analyzer that could "read" the RELATIONS, a programmer could ask questions like *What else in the system will be affected if I add a new instance of this data structure?*, or *What are all the other structures that are related to this one?* This would be a useful form of on-line documentation.

### 7.2.3 Current Instances [Line 25]

Each schema keeps track of all of its current instances, primarily for use in knowledge base maintenance. If it becomes necessary to make changes to a particular representation, for instance, we want to be sure that all instances of it are modified appropriately. Keeping around a list of all such instances is an obvious but very useful solution.

### 7.2.4 Organizational Information [Lines 8-10, 26-28]

FATHER indicates the (more general) ancestors of this schema in the hierarchy, and OFFSPRING indicates its more specific offspring. STRAN is an English phrase indicating what sort of thing the schema describes and is used in communicating with the expert.

### 7.2.5 Bookkeeping Information [Lines 11-14, 29-32]

Every data structure in the system is automatically tagged with its AUTHOR and DATE of creation; in addition the author is asked to furnish a DESCRiption of it. All of these provide a useful form of documentation in keeping track of a large and growing knowledge base. INSTOF is the inverse of INSTANCES, and indicates which schema was used to create this data structure. (Note that in the current example it is the stock name schema itself that is being described by all of this bookkeeping information, and as shown, it is an instance of the SCHEMA-SCHEMA, described in Section 9.)

### 7.3 Slotnames and Slotexperts

The most detailed knowledge about representations is found in the slotnames and the structures associated with them. They deal with aspects of the representation that are at the level of programming language constructs and conventions. The information associated with a slotname is shown in Fig. 8.

<slotname>
| | |
|---|---|
| PROMPT | an English phrase used to request the information to fill the slot |
| TRANSLATION | an English phrase used when displaying the information found in the slot |
| EXPERT | the name of the slotexpert |

Fig. 8. Information associated with a slotname.

The PROMPT and TRANSLATION are part of the simple mechanism that makes the creation of a new data structure an interactive operation. The former is used to request information, the latter is used when it is necessary to display information that has previously been deposited in a slot. (These have been adapted from work in [Shortliffe76].)

Associated with each slotname is a procedure called a *slotexpert* (or simply *expert*). It serves primarily as a repository for useful pieces of knowledge concerning the implementation of the representations. For example, names of data structures have to be unique to avoid confusion or inadvertent mangling. Yet in knowledge acquisition, new data structures are constantly being created, and many of their names are chosen by the user. Part of the task carried out by the *expert* associated with the PNTNAME slot is to assure this uniqueness.

The experts are organized around the different sorts of advice that can be used in a slot. Their general format is shown in Fig. 9. Since not all pieces of advice are meaningful for all experts, not every expert has an entry for every piece of advice.

[SELECTQ can be thought of as a *case* statement for symbolic computation. The code in Fig. 9 is equivalent to if ADVICE = ASKIT then ... else if ADVICE = CREATEIT then ... etc.]

The individual chunks of code that make up the parts of the *experts* are the smallest units of knowledge organization in our framework. They embody knowledge about things like where to find or how to create the items needed to fill the *blank* for a particular slot. For

```
( <slotexpert> [LAMBDA  (BLANK ADVICE)
                (SELECTQ ADVICE
                    (ASKIT     · · ·)
                    (CREATEIT · · ·)
                    (FINDIT     · · ·)
                    (INSLOT     · · ·)
                    (GIVENIT   · · ·)        etc. ])
```

Fig. 9. The structure of a slotexpert.

instance, we noted that the *expert* associated with the PNTNAME slot insures the uniqueness of names that are supplied by the user. This routine would be found in the ASKIT section of the *expert*. Code in the CREATEIT section uses a number of heuristics that help to generate print names that are between 4 and 10 characters long and are reasonably mnemonic. This is used when the system itself creates a name for a new internal data structure.

Recall that we set out to describe representations in order to make possible the interactive acquisition of new conceptual primitives. The slotname and associated expert organize the knowledge needed and provide the English to make the operation interactive. The blank provides an indication of the format of the answers to questions, and a check on their syntax. The advice allows the embedding of an additional sort of knowledge, which makes the process function efficiently and "intelligently."

## 8.0 KNOWLEDGE ABOUT REPRESENTATIONS: USE

We next consider how to use this information about representations to allow the expert to teach the system new instances of conceptual primitives. [Other uses (e.g., as a basis for information retrieval and storage) are described in [Davis76a].]

### 8.1 Schema Function: Acquisition of New Instances

Assume that a schema in the network has been selected as a starting point for the acquisition process (Section 8.2 explains how this decision is made). Since information is distributed through the schema network, the first step is to get to the root, keeping track of the path while ascending. TIERESIAS "climbs" up the FATHER links, marking each schema along the way. (If it encounters a schema that has multiple parents, it jumps directly to the network root. This is a suboptimal solution; a better approach would have a more sophisticated treatment of the network. It might, for instance, be able to recognize the situation in which all the parents had a common "grandparent," and thus jump only two levels (over the ambiguous section), rather than straight to the root.)

The system eventually arrives at the root, with all or some part of the path marked back down to a terminal schema. (Parts may be unmarked either because it jumped over nonunique parents, or because the starting point chosen was not a terminal of the network. The latter case would arise if, for instance, TIERESIAS knew only that expert wanted to create a new kind of value, but was not able to discover which type.)

The next step is to descend back down the network along the marked path, using each schema along the way as a further set of instructions for acquiring the new instance. If the process encounters a part of the path that is not marked, the expert's help is requested. (This is done by displaying the English phrase (the STRAN) associated with each of the OFFSPRING of the current schema, and asking the expert to choose the one that best describes the item being constructed.)

At each node in the network the acquisition process is directed by a simple "schema interpreter" whose control structure consists of three basic operations: (1) use the structure description part of the schema to guide the addition of new components to the instance, (2) attend to any updating according to the information specified in the RELATIONS, and (3) add the new item to the schema's list of instances. (For the sake of efficiency, only schemata at the leaves of the network keep track of instances. Each new item carries a record of its path through the network (in its INSTOF property), and this allows disambiguation when a schema has more than one parent in the network.)

### 8.1.1 Adding to the Structure of the New Concept

The process of adding new components to the new instance is viewed conceptually in terms of filling in slots. Computationally, the process involves invoking the associated *expert* with the *blank* and *advice* as its arguments. The segment of code in the *expert* associated with the *advice* then determines how to go about filling in the *blank*.

### 8.1.2 Attending to Updates

The next step — dealing with necessary updates to other structures — relies on the information specified in the RELATIONS slot. The basic idea is to consider this information as a list of potential updating tasks to be performed whenever a new instance of the schema is acquired.

Maintaining existing interdependencies of data structures in the face of additions to the system requires three kinds of information:

(1) What other structures might need to be updated in response to the new addition?

(2) If those other structures are not all independent, what interrelationships exist between them?

(3) What effect should the new addition have on each?

The "language" of the RELATIONS is a syntax of data structure interrelationships that provides a way of expressing the answers to questions 1 and 2. For instance, line 22 of Fig. 6;

(XOR* COMMON PFD CUMPFD PARTICPFD)

indicates (1) which structures are potentially affected, and (2) the constraint of mutual exclusion.

The information for question 3 is supplied by updating functions (described below), which are included in some of the schemata.

As an example, consider the acquisition of a new stock name shown earlier. The first step is to determine which structures should actually be updated. If the "switch" is OR* or XOR*, the expert's help is requested (otherwise the system itself can make the decision). Since the switch here is XOR*, the system displays the DESCRiptions for the four choices, and asks the expert to select one.

The rest of the process can best be viewed by adopting the perspective of much of the work on "actors" [Hewitt75] and the SMALLTALK language [Goldberg72], in which data structures are considered active elements that exchange messages. In these terms, the next step is to "send" the new stock name to the target selected (CUMPFD), along with the command to the target to "add this to yourself." The target "knows" that knowledge about its structure is stored with the schema of which it is an instance, and so it finds a way to pass the buck: it examines itself to find out which schema it is an instance of, determining that it is an instance of the schema for alphabetically ordered linear lists (the AOLL-SCHEMA). It sends a request to this schema, asking the schema to take care of the "add this" message.

Recall that the schema is a device for organizing a wide range of information about representations. Part of that information indicates how to augment existing data structures. The AOLL-SCHEMA (like some others) has an "updating function" capable of adding new elements to its instances without violating their established order. Thus, in response to the request from CUMPFD, the AOLL-SCHEMA invokes its updating function on the new stock name and the list CUMPFD, adding the new element to the list in the proper place.

To review,

(a) STOCKNAME-SCHEMA asks the expert if the new stock is common, preferred, cumulative preferred, or participating preferred.

(b) The expert indicates cumulative preferred.

(c) STOCKNAME-SCHEMA sends the new stock name to CUMPFD, with the message "add this to yourself."

(d) CUMPFD examines itself, finds it is an instance of AOLL-SCHEMA, and sends a message to AOLL-SCHEMA saying "add this new stock to me."

(e) The updating function associated with AOLL-SCHEMA adds the new stock to CUMPFD.

The advantages to this distribution of knowledge are discussed in more detail in [Davis76a]. Briefly, the important issues are the organization and indexing of knowledge that concerns more than one data structure, and the degree of flexibility that results from various approaches to the problem. For a range of systems designs, the approach we have taken offers a high degree of flexibility.

The techniques described are also applicable to a wide range of data structures. OMITTEDDIVS, for instance, is (conceptually) a table listing dividends omitted by a given preferred stock, and is indexed by stock name (row) and year (column). Each new preferred stock is "sent" to OMITTEDDIVS as part of the response to the updating command in line 24 of Fig. 6. In this case, OMITTEDDIVS sends a request to the schema of which it is an instance (the TABLE-SCHEMA); this schema then invokes its updating function, which results in the interaction seen earlier in the trace (Please indicate the years and amounts of any omitted dividends). The answer is used to create a new row in the table.

## 8.2 Where to Start in the Network

The description of the use of schemata to guide acquisition assumed that the question of where to start in the schema hierarchy had already been settled. While the mechanisms used to make this decision are not complex, they illustrate an interesting issue.

One mechanism provides a default starting place for the case in which the user indicates, outside the context of any consultation, that he wants to teach the system about some new instance. Since there is no context to rely on, the default is to start at the root of the schema network and ask the expert to choose the path at every branch point. This presents a reasonable dialog, since it requests from the expert a progressively more detailed specification of the concept he has in mind. Each individual inquiry will appear sensible, since without contextual information there is no way the system could have deduced the answer.

When a new concept is mentioned during acquisition of a rule, however, there is an extensive amount of context available. The same sort of default approach would look "dumb" in this case, since there are numerous clues indicating which kind of data type is being mentioned. In the example in Section 6, for instance, it was not difficult to discover that the concept was the name of a new stock.

As indicated, this is accomplished by some simple pattern matching. Each schema in the network has one or more patterns associated with it. For example, the pattern

the <attribute> of <object> is —

is associated with the VALUE-SCHEMA. Each of these patterns is tested against the line of text that prompted acquisition of the new item, and the outcome supplies a starting place in the network. (If all matches fail, the system starts as before with the root of the network.)

The patterns thus make it possible to use contextual information from the rule acquisition dialog to select a starting place in the schema network. Note that this link between the natural language dialog and the data type hierarchy represents part of the semantics of each data type. Since the schemata were designed initially to represent only the syntax of the data types, at present they contain only a very limited amount of somewhat ad hoc semantic information, like that in the patterns. Such information is clearly needed, however, and would represent a useful and natural extension to the current implementation. It would mean that, along with the syntax of each data type, some of its semantics would be described, perhaps in the form of a more systematic set of patterns than those currently in use, or other more sophisticated devices. The system would then always start at the root of the network, and could use the semantic information stored with each schema to take advantage of context from the dialog, guiding its own descent through the network.

## 9.0 "KNOWLEDGE ABOUT KNOWLEDGE ABOUT REPRESENTATIONS"

TIERESIAS was designed to make possible interactive transfer of expertise. As we have seen, one kind of expertise it can transfer is domain specific information, the kind supplied by an expert to improve the operation of a performance program. But recall that high performance on this knowledge transfer task required a store of knowledge about representations. If TIERESIAS is designed to make possible interactive transfer of expertise independent of domain, why not apply it to the task of acquiring and maintaining the requisite base of knowledge about representations? That is, why not push this back a level, and consider the knowledge about representations as a candidate for interactive transfer of expertise.

This has been done, and involves using TIERESIAS in two phases (Fig. 10). As we have seen, the domain expert uses TIERESIAS to teach the performance program about the domain of application. High performance on this task is made possible by the base of knowledge about representations provided by the schemata. But the system architect can also use TIERESIAS to teach about a particular set of representations. High performance on this task is made possible by the *schema-schema*, a base of "knowledge about knowledge about representations," which is used to guide the process of describing a new representation.

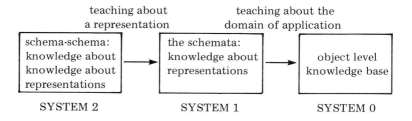

Fig. 10. The multilevel process of knowledge acquisition.

It is in effect a set of instructions describing how to specify a representation (Fig. 11). Since the instructions are in the same format as those in an ordinary schema, the process of following them is identical. As a result, we need only a single "schema interpretation" process. Teaching about a representation (acquiring a new schema) is thus computationally identical to teaching about the domain (acquiring a new instance of a schema); indeed both teaching tasks shown in Fig. 10 are done with a single body of code.

## 10.0 LEVELS OF KNOWLEDGE

The mechanisms reviewed above provide an extensive amount of machinery for encoding knowledge about representations. But it is not enough simply to provide the machinery — if the result is to be something more than "yet another knowledge representation formalism," there must be some sense of organization and methodology that suggests how all this ought to be used.

```
SCHEMA-SCHEMA

PNTNAME          ATOM         CREATEIT
STRUCT           PNTNAME      INSLOT
PLIST
        [ (PNTNAME      (BLANK-INST ADVICE-INST)     ASKIT
          STRUCT       (PNTNAME INSLOT)             GIVENIT
          PLIST
                [ (INSTOF        (  (PNTNAME INSLOT) GIVENIT )                      CREATEIT
                  DESCR         (STRING   ASKIT)                                   GIVENIT
                  AUTHOR        (ATOM     ASKIT)                                   GIVENIT
                  DATE          (INTEGER CREATEIT)                                 GIVENIT
                  KLEENE        (SLOTNAME-INST   (BLANK-INST ADVICE-INST))         ASKIT)
                  CREATEIT
          FATHERMOD    SCHEMA-INST              FINDIT
          INSTANCES    LIST                     ASKIT
          STRAN        STRING                   FINDIT
          INSTOF       SCHEMA-SCHEMA            GIVENIT
          DESCR        STRING                   CREATEIT
          AUTHOR       ATOM                     ASKIT
          DATE         INTEGER                  CREATEIT
          OFFSPRING    (KLEENE (0) < SCHEMA-INST >)  ASKIT
          RELATIONS    (KLEENE (0) < (UPDATECOM-INST >) KLEENE (1)
                                 <(SWITCHCOM-INST KLEENE (1)    <KSTRUCT-INST>)>)>)
                          ASKIT

          CREATEIT]
FATHERMOD    (SCHEMA-SCHEMA)
INSTANCES    ((ALLSCHEMA))
STRAN        "knowledge structure"
INSTOF       (SCHEMA-SCHEMA)
DESCR        "the schema-schema describes the format for all other schemata"
AUTHOR       DAVIS
DATE         876
OFFSPRING    NIL
RELATIONS    ((ADDTO (AND* ALLSCHEMA)))
```

Fig. 11. The schema-schema.

This organization is provided by a common theme that serves to unify all of the proposed mechanisms: the notion of *levels of knowledge*. There are several different (and independent) stratifications of knowledge implicit in the formalism developed above. Two of the most important involve (a) describing knowledge in the system at different levels of detail, and (b) classifying it according to its level of generality. In both cases, the important contribution is a framework for organizing the relevant knowledge about representations. The idea of different levels of detail indicates that representations (e.g., VALUE or ATTRIBUTE) can be described at the level of global organization (as in the schema hierarchy), at the level of logical structure (as in the schemata), and at the level of implementation (as in information associated with the slotnames). These levels provide an organizational scheme that makes it easier to specify and keep track of the large store of information about representations required by the acquisition task. The different levels of generality for classifying knowledge include domain specific, representation specific, and representation independent. As explained below, the idea of maintaining clear distinctions between these different kinds of knowledge is an important contributor to much of TIERESIAS's current range of application.

## 10.1 Level of Detail

As noted in Section 7, the schema hierarchy, individual schemata, and slotnames each encode their own form of knowledge about representations. The hierarchy indicates the global organization of representations in the system, and provides a foundation for both the acquisition of new instances of existing primitives (a process of descent through the hierarchy and instantiation of the schemata encountered), and the acquisition of new kinds of primitives (a process of adding new branches to the hierarchy, see [Davis76a]).[5] The schemata describe the logical structure and logical interrelationships of individual representations, and as prototypes provide a focus for the organization of knowledge about a representation. The slotnames have associated with them information concerning the implementation of a specific representation, information at the level of programming language constructs and conventions (e.g., variable name uniqueness).

## 10.2 Level of Generality

Much of the range of applicability of TIERESIAS results from the isolation and stratification of the three kinds of knowledge shown in Fig. 12. The base of *domain specific* knowledge at level 0 consists of the collection of all instances of each representation.

The base of *representation specific* knowledge at level 1 consists of the schemata, which are in effect the declarations of the extended data types. These have a degree of domain independence, since they describe what an attribute is, what a value is, etc., without requiring *a priori* knowledge of the domain in which those descriptions will be instantiated.

The base of *representation independent* knowledge at level 2—the schema-schema—describes what a declaration looks like. At this level resides knowledge about representations in general, and about the process of specifying them via declarations.

While level 2 is formed by hand, it is the only body of knowledge in the system for which this is true, and it forms a small core of

---

[5] Note that the entire schema hierarchy is viewed here as dealing with information at a single level of detail (viz., global organization of representations). Viewed by itself, it is, of course, yet another (independent) structuring of knowledge in the system into various levels.

(0)  the knowledge base of the performance program contains:
     *object level* knowledge that is
     *domain specific*, and is formed by
     instantiating the appropriate schema to form a *new instance of an existing conceptual primitive*

(1)  the knowledge about representations (the schemata) contains:
     *meta level* knowledge that is
     *representation specific*, and is formed by
     instantiating the schema-schema, to form a *new type of conceptual primitive*

(2)  the schema-schema contains:
     *second order meta level* knowledge that is
     *representation independent*, and is formed by
     hand

Fig. 12. Levels of generality of knowledge about representations.

knowledge from which everything else can be built. For example, the schema hierarchy shown in Fig. 4 (and all associated structures) was constructed in this fashion, bootstrapping it from the schema-schema and a few associated structures. The single process of schema interpretation was used to guide the construction of the base of representation-specific knowledge (the hierarchy and schemata), and then used to instantiate it to build a small object level knowledge base.

One reason this is a practical approach is the great leverage in the notion of a schema as a prototype. The knowledge base of a real investment advisory program, for instance, might require knowledge of several hundred stocks, but a single stock-name schema serves to characterize every one of them. There might be on the order of a hundred or so different representations in such a system, requiring a hundred schemata, yet a single schema-schema serves to characterize all of them.

It was in fact precisely such utilitarian considerations that motivated the initial creation of the schema-schema. Recall that the schemata were developed because there were many details involved in creating a new object and adding it to the system. But there turned out to be a large number of details involved in creating all the necessary schemata, too. The schema-schema was thus the result of the straightforward application of the basic idea back on itself, for precisely the same reason.

## 10.3 Impact

The direct advantages of these stratifications arise from the capabilities they support. The compartmentalization of knowledge suggested by the levels of generality, for instance, provides an increased range of applicability of the system. The single schema-instantiation process can be used with the core of representation-specific knowledge in a range of different domains, or can be used with the representation-independent knowledge over a range of representations (see Section 11). Describing representations at different levels of detail, on the other hand, offers a framework for organizing and keeping track of the required information. It also provides a useful degree of flexibility in the system, because the multiple levels of description insulate changes at one level from the other levels. Thus modifications to information associated with the slotnames can change the implementation of a representation without impacting its logical structure (exactly in the manner of record structures [Balzer67]), and changes can be made to logical structure (the schemata), without impacting the global organization of representations (the hierarchy).[6]

In a more general sense, both stratifications provide guidance in using the representational machinery proposed above. In both cases we have a set of general guidelines that suggest the appropriate mechanism to use for each of the forms of knowledge necessary for the acquisition task. Those guidelines (Figs. 3 and 12) deal with dimensions of knowledge organization that are broadly applicable, and hence not limited to a single domain of application or a single representational formalism. They thus help to "make sense" of the representation scheme outlined here.

## 11.0 RANGE OF APPLICABILITY

The approach we have used and the techniques developed make a number of important assumptions about the kind of data structures being built and managed. These assumptions are outlined below, to give a feeling for the likely range of applicability of our formalism.

(1) Data structures have a well specified syntax. That is, they have a certain static quality, and maintain the same structure and organization over a lifetime that includes a number of access, storage, and creation operations. One obvious set of candidates are those structures that do not change while the program is executing. On the other hand, applying this to temporary structures that are quickly modified would be less successful.

(2) Data structures can be specified in terms of distinct subunits, each of which has a straightforward syntax and is for the most part independent of the others.

---

[6] Changes at one level may quite possibly require additional changes at that same level in order to maintain consistency of data structure specifications, or to assure continued operation of the program. But by organizing the information in the levels described, the effects of changes will not propogate to the other levels of description.

(3) Data structures may be interdependent. Thus, part of the task of specifying a new representation is to describe any interrelationships it may have with other structures.

(4) There is more than one instance of each data type. The utility of the schemata as a tool for dealing with program complexity is dependent on a useful instance-to-schema ratio. If every data structure in a program were distinct (a 1:1 ratio), the schemata would offer little advantage in knowledge base maintenance.

(5) The different data types in a program can be organized into a generalization hierarchy. We rely on this to provide another tool for dealing with complexity. Little would be gained in constructing a hierarchy for a system that used a large number of unrelated data types, but it can provide a useful organizational overview when there are a number of related categories. It can then also offer a useful framework for adding new data types to a system, as illustrated in [Davis76a].

In general, then, the techniques we have outlined are applicable to a large collection of data structures subject to change during program development but relatively stable during program execution. For small collections of well-established structures, or those which do not fall within the description given above, the overhead of using this technique would outweigh the benefits gained.

## 12.0 CAPABILITIES OF THE CURRENT IMPLEMENTATION

In the introduction we noted that a global goal for TIERESIAS was to provide, as far as possible, the same sort of assistance as a human intermediary. Let us now specify this more precisely and consider how close we have come.

First, TIERESIAS ought to be able to assure knowledge base integrity. That is, the expert should not be able to introduce inconsistent data structures in augmenting or modifying the knowledge base via the schemata. In fact, TIERESIAS offers a level of integrity that is useful, but imperfect. The system can assure a form of completeness, by making sure that the expert is reminded to supply every necessary component of a structure, and that all other appropriate structures will be informed about the newly added item. It can also assure syntactic integrity. There is complete type checking, and no interaction with the expert will result in incorrect data types in the knowledge base. Finally, it can assure an elementary level of semantic integrity. The semantics of any individual data structure will be properly maintained, so that, for instance, a new attribute will be given all the descriptors appropriate to it, in the correct form. It can also assure some semantic consistency in two or more related structures, but this is as yet incomplete, since inconsistencies can arise that require knowledge about the domain not easily expressed in the current formalism.

This inability to deal with more complex interrelationships of representations is currently the system's primary shortcoming. Related attempts to formalize such information have come from many directions (e.g., [Spitzen75, Stonebreaker75, Suzuki76]) and encountered similar difficulties. Specifying complex integrity constraints is fundamentally a problem of knowledge represention, and confronts many of the same difficult issues.

Second, TIERESIAS should present the expert with a dialog that is coherent, i.e., one that involves only questions the expert will find comprehensible and that TIERESIAS could not have answered with the information currently available. This means asking the expert questions restricted to domain specific knowledge. Other mechanisms were employed for dealing with questions concerning data structure implementation and manipulation (e.g., the structure and interrelationship descriptions in the schemata), and for making use of information already available (e.g., the *advice* and *slotexpert* mechanisms). As a result, the goal of a coherent dialog has for the most part been achieved.

## 13.0 MULTIPLE PERSPECTIVES ON KNOWLEDGE

At the beginning of this chapter we suggested that it would be instructive to consider the terms *knowledge representation, extended data type,* and *data structure* as equivalent, and see what might be learned by viewing each of them in the perspective normally reserved for one of the others. A number of the key ideas involved in the design and use of the schemata were inspired by this mixing of perspectives.

The fundamental idea of *a base of knowledge about representations,* for instance, was suggested by the view of representations as extended data types and motivated by the desire to organize and represent knowledge about those data types. It strongly influenced the design of the schemata by indicating what sort of information they ought to contain (e.g., structure and interrelationships). This view also suggested the organization of that information and led to *organizing it around representational primitives* (e.g., attribute, object, value), which were in turn *represented as prototypes* (the schemata), and *instantiated to drive the interactive transfer of expertise process.*

Viewing extended data types from the perspective of knowledge representations led to incorporating in those data types the *advice* mechanism. This provided an additional source of knowledge about those structures, and allowed a "high level" dialog that was coherent to the domain expert.

Finally, blurring the distinction between data type and knowledge representation offers an interesting consideration for knowledge base design. A less obvious factor that added to the coherence of the acquisition dialog earlier was the somewhat fortuitous correspondence between data structures and domain specific objects (e.g., stocks). This means the acquisition dialog can be made to appear to the expert to be phrased in terms of objects in the domain, while to the system it is a straightforward manipulation of data structures. Such a correspondence helps to bridge the gap in perspectives and the purposeful attempt to ensure its presence in a system can be a useful consideration in initial design of a knowledge base.

## 14.0 SUMMARY

The schemata and associated structures offer a language and framework in which representations can be described. That framework strongly emphasizes making explicit many different kinds of knowledge about representations, and offers an organization for it. The schema hierarchy, individual schemata, and slotnames each support their own variety of that knowledge. The result can be a useful global overview of the organization and design of all the representations in a system.

For both the system engineer and the application domain expert, the capabilities for interactive transfer of expertise supported by the schemata offer a very organized and thorough assistant who can

(1) Attend to many routine details. Some of these are details of data structure organization and format, and with these out of the way, the task of specifying large amounts of knowledge becomes a good deal easier. The emphasis can be placed on specifying its content rather than attending to details of format. Others are details of data structure management, and having the system attend to them means the expert need know nothing about programming.

(2) Show how knowledge should be specified. In terms of the three systems pictured earlier, the assistant's intelligence always lies at the level above that of the knowledge being specified. While it cannot choose a representation for a stock, it can indicate how the representation should be specified. Similarly it cannot suggest what the risk classification of a new stock might be, but it can indicate that every stock must have one, can describe exactly how it should be specified, and can assure at least the syntactic validity of the answer. It is this ability to structure the task and lead the user through it that is most useful.

(3) Make sure that the user is reminded of all the required representation construction and management tasks. Since knowledge base construction is viewed as a process of knowledge transfer, the assistant's thoroughness offers some assurance that the transfer operations will not inadvertently be left incomplete.

In summary, the assistant cannot supply answers, but it does know what all the proper questions are and what constitutes a valid answer for each. The application domain expert can rely on the assistant to show him how to transfer his knowledge to the program, while the system designer can use the assistant as an aid in knowledge base management, using it to help him keep track of the large number of representations that may accumulate during the construction of any sizable program.

# ACKNOWLEDGMENTS

The work described here was performed as part of a doctoral thesis supervised by Bruce Buchanan, whose assistance and encouragement were important contributions. Elaine Kant, Nancy Martin, and Bill Clancey made a number of helpful comments on earlier drafts of this paper.

# AN INSTRUCTABLE PRODUCTION SYSTEM: BASIC DESIGN ISSUES[1]

Michael D. Rychener and Allen Newell
*Carnegie-Mellon University*

*The full advantages of the incremental properties of production systems have yet to be exploited on a large scale. A promising vehicle for this is the task of instructing a system to solve problems in a complex domain. For this, it is important to express the instruction in a language similar to natural language and without detailed knowledge of the inner structure of the system. Instruction and close interaction with the system as it behaves are preferred over a longer feedback loop with more independent learning by the system. The domain is initially an abstract job shop. The beginning system has capabilities for solving problems , processing language , building productions, and interacting with the task environment. All parts of the system are subject to instruction. The main problem-solving strategy, which permeates all four system components, is based on means-ends analysis and goal-subgoal search. This is coupled with an explicit representation of control knowledge. The system's behavior so far is restricted to simple environmental manipulations, a number of which must be taught before more complex tasks can be done.*

## 1.0 INSTRUCTION TASKS AND LARGE PRODUCTION SYSTEMS

### 1.1 Introduction and Overview

This chapter reports the beginnings of a system-building project.

[1] This paper draws ideas from an ongoing project involving C. Forgy, J. McDermott, Kamesh Ramakrishna, and P. Langley, in addition to the authors. Forgy and McDermott have been responsible for the implementation of the OPS production system architecture and other system facilities described here. We acknowledge the joint role these people have played in developing the ideas in this paper, but they are not responsible for our detailed expression or interpretation of them. This research was supported in part by the Defense Advanced Research Projects Agency under Contract no. F44620-73-C-0074 and monitored by the Air Force Office of Scientific Research.

*135*

The aim is to build a large, generally intelligent system by gradual instruction , starting from a small initial system. At present, the large system is still in the future. This description is limited to describing a promising initial system, along with the rationale for believing it has significant potential for further work. Likewise, the task domain of the eventual system is not yet determined, although there is an initial domain.

Production systems are the system architecture most consonant with the project's aims. Their basic condition-action form, along with the global and open nature of their action, indicates their usefulness for a task involving incremental growth, recognition-based problem solving, responsiveness to unexpected conditions, and other attributes discussed below. The initial task domain is based on the problem of scheduling a job shop. This has unusual features that allow tests of basic instruction issues, particularly a wide range of tasks with simply produced variants. Thus the potential exists for instructing the system on one variant and then introducing perturbations to which it must dynamically adjust, evoking the need for further instruction. There are several constraints on what instruction is and on what the instructors can know about the internal content of the system.

The remainder of this section discusses in more detail the basic task and system issues, and introduces a suitable production system architecture. Section 2 discusses the rationale for our approach to building the initial system, called the Kernel. The Kernel embodies a set of assumptions about problem solving, language use, the particular task, and augmentation. Section 3 presents an instruction protocol that the system has performed. Section 4 summarizes our current status.

## 1.2 Building a Large Production System

Production systems (abbreviated "PSs") have a brief but illustrious history within artificial intelligence (AI) and cognitive psychology. For general background, the reader is referred to [Davis76b, Newell-72a, 72b]. There are four architectural components of the kind of PS used here: production memory, working memory, recognize-act cycle, and conflict resolution principles . Action arises from the system as a result of conditions (left-hand sides) of productions being recognized true of the current working memory state. The recognition leads to the performance of associated actions (right-hand sides). This is the basic recognize-act step, except that in general the conflict resolution principles must be applied to distinguish between productions whose conditions are simultaneously true, making a selection before actions are actually performed. The performance of actions results in a new working memory state, and the recognize-act step is repeated.

We have chosen PSs for our instructable system for a number of reasons. All productions are sensitive to a single working memory, with no control organization imposed on them, and with all necessary control achieved by goals and other data conventions within working memory. In practice, productions tend to be small (only a few conditions and actions) and relatively independent of each other. Thus they are attractive where structure is to be added gradually and incrementally. Their feasibility, power, transparency, flexibility, and conciseness have been shown empirically by implementing well-understood AI systems [Rychener76]. The importance of having actions conditioned on the recognition of aspects of a global state is central. Actions are not evoked directly by other actions, but are performed whenever the appropriate conditions emerge. Thus intelligence is distributed rather than concentrated in a complex control executive or other orchestrating mechanism. Since intelligence requires the ability to respond to important aspects of complex states, the high degree of conditionality of action in PSs appears to have merit.

In building the system, the PS architecture is used according to specific conventions. All long-term knowledge is kept as productions, and working memory is used exclusively for short-term, dynamic state. This is in contrast to a possible view of working memory as a long-term data base, with "facts" stored in it, to be manipulated by "procedures" coded as productions. Though working memory may become large, our convention is to store as productions such data-base-like things as facts about objects in the world or relational structures (semantic networks).

A large intelligent system of the sort envisioned places new demands on PSs and on system-building capabilities in general. Building such systems is interesting in its own right, raising issues of representation, accommodation, and a whole range of activities associated with intelligence [Moore74]; see also [D. G. Bobrow75b]. To study many of these issues fruitfully, as many have noted, an uncommonly large-scale knowledge base is necessary. From a pure PS research standpoint, building a large system (on the order of several thousand productions), especially including a rich diversity of knowledge, allows us to test hypotheses about PS efficiency, openness, modularity, automatic augmentation, representational flexibility, and feasibility. The system is to develop, eventually, past the current state of the art in AI.

## 1.3 The Abstract Job Shop Task

Several criteria are essential to our choice of an initial task for an instructable system. The task domain should be rich in problems of sufficient challenge to require instruction; it should be amenable to the instructional mode (see Section 1.4); and it should not be amenable to a general solution mechanism, which, once constructed, would make further instruction unnecessary. Among the general task areas that might be appropriate are a tutor in some domain, an intelligence-test taker, an automatic programming system, and the higher, cognitive levels of an image understanding system. We have chosen for the time being a toy task, the abstract job shop (AJS). The job shop has as its objective to produce objects with specified desired properties from raw materials according to some schedule. The shop contains stacks of materials and partial products, machines that must be started with explicit commands, and means for transporting objects from one place to another within the shop. The details of the particular implementation of this idea are given in Section 1.5. This toy task has a number of close analogs that are potential applications of any useful techniques developed: real-world production scheduling, the general problem of functional design, scheduling in computer operating systems, and coding computer programs (to name just a few). It also contains within it the possibility of exploring the full range of AI tasks known as the "toy blocks world."

If all goes well, the AJS task has attributes that are the extra bonus for immediate purposes. AJS has an unusual number of variants, including the basic task of producing desired objects, the allocation of scarce resources, advanced kinds of planning, and production under time constraints. After the system has been instructed in a number of basic variants, perturbations to the tasks and to the environment (the job shop) can pose major difficulties for the system. Among these perturbations are changes in the profit-objective function for various mixes of outputs, spoilage of materials, error in machines, accidents in moving objects, additional time constraints, and last-minute changes in orders. The difficulties of the basic task should preclude any advance planning on the part of the instructor to have the system respond gracefully to such basic task changes. Thus, the system's behavior will be interesting, whether it can adjust easily or not. The effectiveness of the entire approach, including the use of PSs, will be measured by the adequacy of the system's behavior over a set of such perturbations.

## 1.4 The Instruction Mode

Posing the task as one of growing a large system through instruction introduces additional issues. Some of these might seem irrelevant to the main aims, but others are directed toward important questions with respect to the study of the representation and use of knowledge. The following attempts to justify this third major concern, instruction, which is in addition to the concerns with building a generally intelligent system and using PSs as a basis.

The instruction mode used here forces the automatic encoding of knowledge as productions. This allows the verification of essential properties of PSs, particularly those dealing with the independence or modularity of the knowledge in the PS. If the PS were augmented by simply composing and adding Ps, there would still be a possibility for the system to be very intricately contrived, with implicit global coordination of production action sequences. A language of instruction is used that states each new item of knowledge in a human-readable, plausibly independent form, with no reference to internal structure.

Instruction takes place under the following constraints:

(1) The instructor (Ins) can see what the system (IPS, Instructable PS) is doing in the environment, and can communicate with IPS, but cannot examine the internal structure of the system directly.

(2) Interaction between Ins and IPS is in an external language, analogous to natural language, rather than in internal representations, either of working memory or production memory forms.

(3) The initiative for interaction is mixed. IPS's behavior can be interrupted by Ins at any time, for corrective instruction or interrogation. Likewise, IPS may communicate to Ins and interrupt him.

(4) Instruction may be about any topic within the total environment: the structure of the environment, how to perform a task, the language of communication, the detection and correction of errors, how to learn about the environment, etc. Also, the instruction may be at whatever level Ins wishes or can achieve: specific behavior sequences, general methods, abstract principles, models, theories, etc.

(5) Knowledge gained through instruction accumulates over the life of the system.

Having the system be instructable adds to its capabilities as a total man-computer interactive system, so that in ultimate real applications the performance of the combination system can be expected to be higher than either participant alone. As a practical measure, making the system instructable also reduces the possibility of internal coding conventions that would prohibit multiple instructors from understanding the existing system. That is, all communication is forced to be in a language of instruction, which may be more easily shared than program conventions. If instructability can be achieved, it should be worth the extra initial effort.

The instruction mode can be contrasted with a learning mode in which the system is set tasks and then required to learn on its own from the environment. Here Ins gives incomplete or approximate instructions and watches very closely for opportunities to interrupt IPS and refine them. It is "incomplete or approximate instructions" because too much preplanning by Ins is bound to be futile, given Ins's imperfect knowledge of IPS's internal structure, and given a task sufficiently complex to make anticipation difficult and ineffective. With Ins watching IPS so closely, the need for learning by the system on its own is minimized, but such independent learning is not excluded. It can eventually arise in the way IPS interacts with and gathers knowledge from the task environment, in the way IPS uses the external language, and in other knowledge-acquisition mechanisms. Presumably the best strategies of instruction and performance require that IPS be able to learn for itself about a changing environment. The sequence of novel but related tasks is intended in part to arouse this. Nor does the futility of preplanning rule out giving IPS general methods, anticipating certain types of difficulties. Such general methods, however, are bound to have incompleteness similar to that of specific ones.

### 1.5 The Production System Architecture and Task Environment

Before detailing the PS architecture used for IPS, a few distinguishing features of our overall PS approach are pointed out. The way that action develops from the PS differs from some others in being a forward recognition-driven cycle, rather than a backward-chaining, goal-driven cycle, as in the MYCIN system [Davis77d]. The system is controlled by signals and symbol structures in the global working memory, called goals, which are included explicitly in production conditions when appropriate. This is in contrast to MYCIN and to DENDRAL [B. G. Buchanan73]. The PS architecture is used as the total system, rather than having it be one of a number of procedural components. Other systems have employed additional, non-PS procedures for such activities as modifying and analyzing the PS. Working memory is arbitrary list structures in an extensive data-base-like structure, with a vast majority of items explicitly stored rather than represented as computable predicates. Production conditions make use of general pattern-matching capabilities, as is common in other recent AI languages [D. G. Bobrow74]. Though the general architecture derives from concern for human cognition [Newell72a, 72b], little consideration is given to psychological constraints.

The particular architecture and language used for IPS is called OPS (Official, at least locally, PS) [Forgy76] and is an iteration on earlier designs [Newell75, Rychener76]. Production memory in OPS is an unstructured, unordered set of productions. Working memory is likewise an unordered set of list structures, without duplications. It is bounded in size, by deleting elements whose last assertion occurred more than some arbitrary number of system actions in the past (currently 300). The recognize-act cycle is (1) form a conflict set of productions whose conditions are currently satisfied; (2) apply the conflict resolution principles to select a unique element from the conflict set; and (3) execute the actions of the selected production.

For conflict resolution (the most distinctive component of OPS) the following rules apply, in order. These rules are experimental in nature, and are expected to change as understanding of instructability increases [J. McDermott77b].

(1) Refraction: a production is not fired twice on the same data (instantiation of a pattern) unless some part of that data has been reinserted into working memory since the previous firing. This prevents most infinite loops and other useless repetitions.

(2) Lexicographic recency: the production using the most recently inserted elements of working memory is preferred. "Most recent" is determined lexicographically, i.e., if there is a tie on the most recent element used, the next most recent elements are compared, and so on; use of any element is considered more recent than using none, e.g., (A X) is ordered before (A). Recency order discriminates at the level of individual actions within productions, rather than taking all the actions performed by a production to be of equal recency. This rule serves to focus the attention of the system very strongly on more recent events, allowing current goals to go to completion before losing control.

(3) Special case: a production is preferred that has more conditions, including negative conditions that do not match to specific memory elements. Most of the meaning of having one production be a special case of another is captured by rule 2, since a special case that uses more data than a general one is lexicographically more recent. Preferring special cases to general ones follows the expectation that a specific method is more appropriate to a situation than a more general one. Also, this is consonant with a strategy of augmentation by providing more discriminative rules.

(4) Production recency: the more recently created production is preferred. This allows identically conditioned rules (with perhaps contradictory actions) to be distinguished and assumes that a more recent instruction is more correct.

(5) Arbitrary: a selection is made among multiple matches to the same production using the same data.

As a matter of practice, conflict resolution rarely requires more than the first two rules.

OPS has several other distinguishing features. The pattern matching allows a limited form of segment variables , namely, a variable may match an indefinite-sized tail of a list. The Pattern-And (Pand) feature allows an expression to be matched to several patterns, and then bound to a variable. OPS allows complex negative conditions to be specified, for instance, including the negation of an entire production condition within the condition of another production. Productions in OPS are compiled into an efficient network form, rather than interpreted [Forgy77]. OPS has an operator for adding productions to production memory that have been formed (in terms of an appropriate data structure) in working memory; such additions are done directly into the compiled network during the runtime cycle without excessive cost.

A subsystem of OPS provides the task environment (TE) for instruction. The TE is represented as an array of discrete locations, within which objects can be placed, plus a set of "perceptual" and "motor" operators. Each location and object is represented as a list of pairs in attribute-value form, with certain attributes given special interpretations. For example, the external display of a location in the TE (L15), would be

L15
```
W 6
W 98
W 72
```

with the internal representation,

```
L15: ( NAME         L15
       TYPE         STACK
       MEMBER       TE-ARRAY
       POSITION     (2 3)
       COMPOSITION  (W6 W98 W72) )
```

The object W98 might be defined as

```
W98: ( NAME       W98
       TYPE       WOOD
       MEMBER     L15
       POSITION   (2)
       SHAPE      TRIANGULAR
       LENGTH     5
       WIDTH      7
       COLOR      RED )
```

Objects are potentially hierarchical, with values of attributes composed of other objects. Relations between positions of the TE and objects can be determined by the following TE operators.

(1) View: the attribute-value pairs for an object or location appear in working memory.

(2) Scan: the TE is searched for an object satisfying a pattern, and if it is found, it is viewed.

(3) Trans: an object is transferred from one location to another within the TE.

(4) Start: a machine in the TE is started, consuming a set of inputs (specified as values of INPUT attribute) and producing a set of outputs (specified as values of OUTPUT). The machine operates once, not continuously.

(5) Compare: two attribute-value pairs are compared, with results depending on the values compared. For instance, if the values are pairs of numbers, as for POSITION, the result is a spatial relation, amounting to, say, "northwest."

## 2.0 THE INITIAL INSTRUCTABLE SYSTEM

The instructable system is initialized with a relatively small set of hand-coded productions called the Kernel. The Kernel design includes a minimal set of components that can support all of the present instruction goals and provide an interface to the TE. The components at present achieve minimal capabilities for (1) solving problems, (2) processing language, (3) building productions, and (4) interacting with the TE.

A number of design issues influenced the Kernel. These derive from a wish to maintain easy instructability within the rules laid out above for the instructional mode.

(1) Everything in the system is potentially instructable and improvable. This includes especially the components of the Kernel and the results of instruction that the Kernel produces. The Kernel itself may eventually be superseded by productions gained through instruction, and commitments to techniques and representations in the Kernel may eventually be altered.

(2) The system should be instructable without detailed knowledge of internal structures. Thus the Kernel design must include some capability for mapping from external to internal forms, and vice versa.

(3) Knowledge should not be globally coordinated or preplanned, but should develop in locally plausible, concrete increments. This particularly affects the form of problem-solving methods and language-processing techniques.

(4) The construction of the Kernel should not embody a commitment to focusing on a particular kind of problem, e.g., language, but should be amenable to instruction in a number of problem areas.

## 2.1 The Problem-Solving Component of the Kernel

The Kernel has two general forms of problem-solving unit, corresponding to two uses of the basic condition-action form of productions. The first recognizes a goal and proposes means to achieve it:

goal & conditions => possible means.

The means to achieving a goal can be one or more subgoals, direct actions on the TE, or requests to Ins.

The second form of production serves as a test or recognizer:

goal & conditions => goal success or failure or consequences.

The growth philosophy for the IPS revolves around means-ends analysis [Newell72b]. Knowledge added to the system forms a conceptual network of connections between goals, means to achieving them, and tests on the results of applications of means. Goals constitute the most meaningful portion of the dynamic state of the system (working memory), while means and tests are permanent productions added gradually through instruction and learning. It is important that this network of means and ends is defined at the level of individual productions rather than, say, at some higher level of organization with productions used to code an interpretive mechanism for the network. For the means-ends structure must be applicable to creating, shaping, and correcting all aspects of the behavior of the system, down to the finest detail.

Augmentation of networks of means-ends structures leads to a flexible but highly inefficient computational structure. Strategies for converting or compiling these structures are a necessary component of the growth philosophy outlined here, which however will not be discussed further.

Two basic conventions built into the system help to make the basic production form adequate for general problem solving: the lexicographic event order conflict resolution rule and a taxonomy of PS control, represented in a particular way. Recall that the conflict resolution principle orders production firings based on the relative recency of data used. This gives a depth-first emphasis, focusing on recently proposed goals before older ones and allowing successes to propagate in orderly fashion. It does not preclude, however, having emerging conditions unexpectedly satisfy an older goal and lead to action quite distinct from what was the immediately preceding focus.

While the conflict resolution principle is built into the PS architecture, the Kernel's knowledge of control is by way of modifier tags that appear in most working memory elements. The current system of representation is based on an analysis of past PSs [Rychener76]. The basic representation form is

(Primary Secondary Modifier Body)

A primary is a verb or main data structure name, while a secondary is an object of a verb, an attribute of a structure, or the name of a substructure. Some examples of primary-secondary pairs are examine object, interrogate value, object color, and phrase boundary. The modifier is a list with positions occupied by values from predefined classes: goal values, data values, process values, truth values, and degrees of completion. By combining values from various classes, a large number of meanings can be assumed by a modifier, which in turn affects the interpretation by productions of the representational unit containing it.

Space does not permit giving the entire modifier system, but the main entities that are used in the Kernel are as follows (examples of actual representations appear in Section 3). The most important goal value indicates "Want," and marks units that are currently desired goals. Other goal values indicate "Old," "Don't-want," and "Neutral." Evocation, intermediate control, and results of processes employ goal values in combination with process and data values: "Activate," "Iterate," "Hold," "Result", and "Continue." Truth values are "True," "False," and "Unknown."

Modifier values are made coherent by certain established knowledge about control. For instance, a process is usually initiated by a "Want Activate" signal, which then becomes "Want Continue," if it has several steps to be performed. The steps are indicated by using degrees of completion, which are simply ordinals. When the process is started, the "Want Activate" becomes "Old Activate," but the content of the initiation signal itself is still available, should it become necessary later to examine it. Similarly, control for a process can go into a dormant "Hold" status until some preset condition arises, whereupon it reverts to its former status. When a process finishes, it may produce an item with modifier "Neutral Result."

The use of these explicit modifiers in the basic representational units makes the behavior of the system open for detailed self-examination, when combined with the basic openness of working memory. Such a simple scheme for managing control knowledge is based on the ease of control in PSs generally, and its feasibility has been tested extensively on typical AI tasks [Rychener76], though its suitability for the present instruction task has yet to be verified in large-scale practice. As shown below, control knowledge can be easily expressed in the external language by using key phrases corresponding to modifier variants. The available knowledge and basis of control can similarly be expanded.

The Kernel itself is a problem solver (in the domains of language, building productions, etc.), and is written using the conventions just sketched. But it is also the producer of programs embodying the same conventions. Thus, initial instruction is constrained to be close to such forms. Later on, as IPS becomes more sophisticated, internal problem-solving method forms should be producible from instruction requiring more difficult mappings. Incidentally, the Kernel itself is simple enough that a straightforward instruction sequence should be able to reproduce it.

## 2.2 External Language Capabilities of the Kernel

The Kernel is built to understand a limited external language. The language capability has three aims: to make interactions with IPS readable by the instructors and by other AI researchers; to make the interactions occur in something other than a PS language; and to encode a number of representational conventions, so that instructors can refer to the same internal entity in a variety of ways, i.e., a mapping or assimilation facility, relating external to internal structures. To keep the Kernel simple, an initial language with rather rigid format has been chosen.

Language expressions are processed primarily in a bottom-up fashion, with only a few keywords having specific meanings to start with. That is, a keyword is recognized and classified, and a number of the actions associated with it (its semantics) are performed. A default action is taken for words with no known classification. Occasionally, a keyword sets up anticipations for actions later in the input, giving the processing a partial top-down orientation. The default action for unclassified words is easily superseded, using the special-case conflict resolution principle. Along with the careful design of the Kernel to allow all of its goals and subgoals to be discussed in the external language, this use of special cases forms the basis for extensibility. A similar bottom-up approach, though not coded strictly incrementally, has been used successfully in a toy blocks domain [Rychener76].

The main form in the language is an image of a production or of a closely related set of productions. The form starts with "To," with an expression of a condition following, then a sequence of actions. "To" is taken as an abbreviation of "If you want to." For example,

*To* examine an object in *some* location , *do* view *that* location .

In this example, the keywords have been italicized. The other words are given in an ordering that corresponds to the basic primary-secondary form discussed above. Thus "examine object" is the essence of a representational unit forming the goal in a condition-side of a production to be built. Most of the keywords not shown deal with the formation of conjunctions and sequences of units, so that productions can test more complex conditions and perform more complex actions: "and," "then," and "if." "Some," "that," and a few other keywords allow the specification of match variables, as opposed to constants. Detailed examples of the use of the language in a simple instruction protocol are shown in the following section.

Another main keyword in the language is "Next." "Next" is followed by text very much like the "To" clause above. This allows a process for achieving some goal to be expressed as a set of closely related productions, related by being continuations or steps in the common process. That is, the "To" clause of an instruction signals the main or first step in the solution of some goal (the phrase immediately following the "To"). When "Next" clauses follow the "To" clause, they give succeeding steps in the process, which presumably test the outcome of the first step and take further actions accordingly. Some form of the main goal appears in all of the productions constructed within such a set of clauses. This loose content-based association of productions is called a module, though nothing structural in the architecture distinguishes it. The productions in such a module share internal assumptions, since they arise from a contiguous instruction sequence. The module is known to other modules usually only through its main goal unit, which is its evoking condition. To connect this with the discussion on means-ends analysis above, the language allows the local (intramodule) sharing of assumptions about means to achieve a goal.

## 2.3 Building Productions and the Interface to the TE

The Kernel's third and fourth components are minimal: the system's abilities to build productions and to manipulate the TE effectively are expected to develop as system behavior develops and as considerations arise from the task that vary from our present preconceptions.

Basically only simple, direct ways exist for telling IPS what to store in production memory and what to do in the TE. Both capabilities rely on the closeness of external language expressions to internal forms. The main sentence form is an image of a production, so the operation needed to build an actual production is a simple iteration over a list of units extracted from an input string. The current strategy for adding to production memory treats the memory as an unordered set. To specify a TE operator, the instructor uses the keyword "do" and follows it with a phrase in the proper form for the operator. The expandability of both components rests on the basic openness of their Kernel representation, rather than on specific structural design. The simple goals by which they are presently achieved are expressed using a small set of primaries and secondaries, along with a few modifier tags to indicate partial results and iterations.

## 2.4 Discussion of the Kernel Design

To recap the basic strategy in building the Kernel, focus is placed on a primitive language capability embodying definite problem-solving and goal search methods. This is not because language issues are most important, but because language seems to provide the shortest path to easier instruction, to flexibility, and to the encoding of basic problem-solving method assumptions. That is, an instructable language system leaves a large amount of openness for further instruction without precluding desirable options. Our experience over the short history of our attempts, covering a dozen or so initial abortive Kernels, indicates that the best strategy is to rely more on spontaneous ad hoc methods arising from interactions than on initial knowledge about aspects of problem solving. This ensures that important aspects of the system relating to the problem-solving task are themselves instructable, rather than "cast in concrete."

## 3.0 SAMPLE SYSTEM BEHAVIOR

The Kernel starts with essentially no behavioral capability with respect to the TE. Thus, it must be instructed in some basic TE tasks to build up a network of goals for doing more significant tasks. A sequence of progressively more complex tasks has been established to build complex abilities from the simple ones in the Kernel.

The first task attempted is to instruct IPS to look at the top of a stack of objects in a TE location. This will involve viewing the location (in the TE sense of View defined above), checking to see that there is in fact a stack of objects there, and then finding the top of that stack and viewing it. Instructing it to achieve these goals gives it some material to work with on tasks that follow this first one, which include looking at objects other than the top one in a stack, determining the type of an object (which requires that it be looked at first), and comparing the types of two objects. More complex tasks include rearranging objects and determining the requirements and effects of machines in the TE.

The instruction sequence to be given now consists first of giving IPS a top-level subgoal sequence to achieve the goal. Then a concrete task is given, involving that goal, so that its behavior gives rise to subgoals that it cannot solve, at which points further instruction is given.

IPS starts by asking for input, and it is given the following:

*To examine an object the top in some location , want do view that location then want test the status of the value of that location composition , Next ...*

In the text, "..." indicates that more is to come below; it does not appear in actual input. Note that the language is very primitive in expression, a consequence of our desire to include only the minimum necessary for communication of basic ideas, thus excluding familiar linguistic elaborations.

The system uses the word "next" to act as a temporary boundary for the input, and forms the following production before continuing to scan further.

R1    (examine object (want activate) top in =location) $ =c1
→    (view.TE =location (want activate))
     (test status (want activate) value =location composition)
     (examine object (want continue 1) top in =location)
     (examine object (old activate) top in =location)
          (delete =c1) ;

The OPS notation for productions gives the name R1, followed by the condition side, followed by →, followed by the action side and terminated by semicolon. The equals sign is used to mark variables , as in "=location," which makes "location" a variable. $ stands for Pattern-and, which allows two match expressions to use the same working memory expression. In R1, "$" is used to bind the single condition element and the variable c1 to a single working memory element. A production is executed as a result of matching its condition, which results in binding its variables to elements or subelements of working memory. Firing the production then results in asserting or deleting working memory elements according to the action-side forms ("assert" is implicit, "delete" explicit), in such a way that the leftmost action becomes the most recent working memory element, for purposes of conflict resolution.

The phrase between "To" and the first comma has been formed into the condition side of R1. The mapping of text to representational unit is direct, with the Kernel supplying the "want activate" modifier and the "$ =c1," which is used to delete the "want activate" form after it is converted to "old activate" at the end of the action side. "Direct mapping" means that words are added to a unit in the same order as given in the text. The remainder of the text is converted to a sequence of two representational units, the first two in the action side. This conversion is also quite direct. These serve as subgoals, the first of which, view.TE, will be achieved by Kernel mechanisms, and the second, by further instruction. The third action element is a signal that will stay in working memory until the first and second action elements have been recognized and their consequences followed up, at which time it will become most recent, and productions using it will become candidates for firing.

The first segment of the instruction has established a topic for the entire sequence up to the next period, namely, the goal of "examine object." The next segment of the instruction for this goal is

*. . ., Next if the result of test the status is non-empty is the value of that location composition, want find the top of the value of that location composition , Else . . .*

This results in forming a second production, including as a condition the "want continue" unit from R1 and a unit corresponding to the text between "if" and the comma:

(test status (neutral result) non-empty value = location composition)

The production tests the result of the second subgoal of R1 (to test the status of the composition attribute of the viewed location) and proceeds with a further subgoal (to find the top of the composition list) if appropriate. To do the continuation, it includes a "want continue 2" unit with the form of the main topic.

The next phrase tells IPS what to do if another condition arises as a result of that second R1 subgoal.

*. . ., Else if the result of test the status is empty is the value of that location composition , the result of examine the object is failure , Next . . .*

This fragment gives one of the possible results of the topic goal, which indicates a failure (at present, in a noninformative way).

The next segment forms a production to recognize the result of the "find top" subgoal, view that result, and leave the name of the result in working memory (a "neutral result" form similar to the one above):

*. . ., Next if the result of find the top is some object , want do view that object and the result of examine the object is that object .*

The system has now taken that instruction sequence and formed four productions. It then awaits further input, which is the following:

*Try examine the object top in L23*

This tells IPS to actually try to achieve an "examine object" goal for a particular TE location. It would not get very far before stopping, in need of further instruction to allow it to achieve the "test status" goal (the second goal in the action side of R1). Ins determines what the system is in need of (if he cannot remember) by asking it, "What want ?", IPS answers by finding its most recent "want"-modified unit. Instruction for the "test status" goal can be given so that the system can achieve it directly. That is, a single production suffices to perform the test and return a result, without further subgoals. After that, it needs instruction on the "find top" goal, which can also be achieved directly.


## 4.0 CONCLUSIONS

The aim of this initial examination of the problem of an instructable PS has been to motivate the starting assumptions, to discuss some broad issues for PSs and for instructable systems, and to give some detail on where the project stands as a result of several design iterations.

A PS architecture has been developed that builds on substantial experience with past architectures. Its conflict resolution scheme appears to be compatible with incremental additive growth, and it essentially abandons the use of static orderings of the productions. A small kernel system of about 150 productions currently exists, embodying an incremental approach to solving problems, processing language, representing knowledge as productions, and interacting with a toy environment. The system's problem-solving capabilities exploit a form of knowledge that is natural for PSs, means-ends analysis. With that, a taxonomy of some simple control mechanisms in PSs provides the system with the capability to do complex tasks.

The initial ingredients assembled seem ideally suited to attaining the incremental growth of a complex understanding system. Experimentation with a sequence of progessively more difficult tasks will reveal whether this is the case. However, it may not happen quickly. Experience so far, expressed in a good dozen kernels, has shown how difficult it is to get the details right, even while the general features of the scheme hold up rather well. Partly the difficulty is that our design intuitions imply a substantial "kernel" of capabilities in place, whereas it is necessary to grow (instruct) that "kernel" through a much leaner initial system, which is certainly highly atypical and counterintuitive in many ways. Any attempt to lay down this larger "kernel" by an act of design (in the usual system-building fashion) seems sure to create a beast that is uninstructable except along limited dimensions. Thus a regimen of iteration and back-tracking at primitive levels seems necessary.

One issue that has arisen about the particular ingredients can serve to summarize and illuminate the current state of understanding of the approach. If the observable behavior of the PS is to be organized completely as a means-ends network, then what role do the properties of the PS architecture play? Would not any other architecture or basic programming system do as well?

To see the force of this, consider what makes means-ends analysis attractive for the instructable-system task. It permits simple addition to the existing system, since increments are made by attaching new (alternative) methods to existing goals, from which other goals and methods may freely branch. Its network of goals and methods can be driven down to any fineness of processing detail, permitting the scheme to be used for any processing. If care is taken initially, then all aspects of the system will be formed as a means-ends structure; hence, all aspects will be open to modification by further means-ends construction. To utilize such a scheme requires of the underlying programming system (which constitutes the operators and associated data structures through which the means-ends net works) only that it be complete, have a fine enough grain of action, and perhaps be rather simply composable.

These properties constitute a significant fraction of the claimed advantages of PSs. What do PSs provide that is not already latent in an approach that focuses purely on construction of means-ends networks?

Means-ends analysis dictates (hence provides) a structure of goals, methods, goal-tests, operators, and operands (data structures). But it only provides functional roles, not the programming system. Subject to the conditions of fineness of detail and completeness, we do not see that PSs have a striking advantage over other homogeneous architectures for realizing these processes in general.

In a performance system the instances of these structures are provided by the system creator. In a learning system they must be provided by the system itself, and the properties of the architecture become relevant to how easy or hard that will be. An instructable system, though it can shade into a programmed system (especially initially), is fundamentally a learning system.

Without being exhaustive, some of the important functions to be performed in learning a means-ends structure are the detection of error and/or the opportunity for learning, the construction of hypothesized means-ends structures, their installation so as to supersede selected pre-existing structure, their validation and debugging, and a secure environment within which learning experimentation can occur. Means-ends itself does help on some of these functions, notably installation and (possibly) supersession, but does not provide help with most of them.

PSs appear to be a useful architecture for a number of these aspects, though no claim can be made that it is especially perspicuous across the board. Detection, validation, and debugging seem to require wide-band access to the existing knowledge in the system at all times, i.e., in a monitoring-like mode. This is distinctly a feature of PSs. Although not quite so obvious, wide-band access seems important also to the construction of new hypothesized goals and methods. Successful modifications depend not just on some fixed procedure for correcting failed goals, but on detecting and attending to highly various features of the environment and to equally various aspects of past experience. The problem of memory search to make contact with relevant but disparately represented experience is not solved in PSs just by the recognition scheme, but the architecture seems a useful one for approaching the problem.

The extreme simplicity of the ultimate forms of both goal tests and method steps in PSs is probably also important. They can consist simply of throwing together some hopefully relevant distinctions on the environment as conditions along with some likewise hopefully relevant actions, then adding the collection to the program memory without further ado. This is a fundamentally task-oriented operation, unencumbered by syntactic ceremonies or other detailed knowledge. That the elementary form of functionally relevant additions can be so simple rests upon two other aspects that PSs seem to provide in some measure. The first is security, which is provided by all behavior in a PS being effectively monitored (by the whole production memory). It can be brought under interpretive control at any time to dampen the prospects of "sudden death." The second aspect is the related ability to program by debugging, i.e., by adding fragments and modifying the system later on the basis of self-observed behavior.

Our present assessment is that the ingredients will cooperate together in a mutually supporting way. However, it has taken a long time to evolve reasonable conflict resolution rules, to take an important recent example [J. McDermott77b]. It may also take a while, for example, to evolve systems that map to distant experience appropriately [Moore74] but that can be serviced by the limited recognition abilities inherent in efficient recognize-act cycles.

# THE EFFICIENCY OF CERTAIN PRODUCTION SYSTEM IMPLEMENTATIONS[1]

J. McDermott, A. Newell and J. Moore[2]
*Carnegie-Mellon University*

*The obvious method of determining which productions are satisfied on a given cycle involves matching productions, one at a time, against the contents of working memory. The cost of this processing is essentially linear in the product of the number of productions in production memory and the number of assertions in working memory. By augmenting a production system architecture with a mechanism that enables knowledge of similarities among productions to be precomputed and then exploited during a run, it is possible to eliminate the dependency on the size of production memory. If in addition, the architecture is augmented with a mechanism that enables knowledge of the degree to which each production is currently satisfied to be maintained across cycles, then the dependency on the size of working memory can be eliminated as well. After a particular production system architecture, PSG, is described, two sets of mechanisms that increase its efficiency are presented. To determine their effectiveness, two augmented versions of PSG are compared experimentally with each other and with the original version.*

## 1.0 INTRODUCTION

As considerable recent work in artificial intelligence shows, production systems provide an interesting alternative for how to organize an intelligent system [Davis76b, Newell73]. This chapter is concerned

---

[1] This work was supported in part by the Defense Advanced Research Projects Agency (F44620-73-C-0074) and is monitored by the Air Force Office of Scientific Research.

[2] J. Moore is now at Information Sciences Institute, University of Southern California.

with the efficiency of implementation of production systems. If implemented straightforwardly according to their definition (as is done in most initial and demonstration versions), they are quite expensive, especially for large systems. Thus, alternative implementations are needed. Here we explore several schemes and give some experimental results.

A production system consists of a *production memory* and a *working memory*. Working memory, WM, is a collection of *memory elements*. Production memory, PM, is a collection of *productions*; each of which is a conditional statement composed of zero or more *condition elements* and zero or more *action elements* (written P: $(C_1 \ C_2 \ \ldots \ \to$ $A_1 \ A_2 \ \ldots)$). Whenever each condition element in a production is matched by a memory element in WM, the production is satisfied and may be fired. When a production is fired, each action element in the production is executed. This ordinarily causes WM to be modified in some way; for example a new element might be added to WM or an element in WM might be deleted. The basic unit of behavior is the *recognize-act cycle*. The cycle has two parts: (1) discovering the *conflict set*, the subset of satisfied productions, and selecting one or more of the productions in the conflict set as the productions to be fired; and then (2) firing the productions selected, that is, executing their action elements. Processing continues, cycle follows cycle, until either no production is satisfied or an action element explicitly stops the processing.

The cost of executing a production system is simply the per-cycle cost of finding the conflict set and executing the action elements in the production selected to be fired. If one uses the obvious method of determining which productions are members of the conflict set—testing them one at a time against the elements in WM—then the time needed to discover the conflict set can be much greater than the time needed for the second part of the cycle. Indeed, if a production system has either a large number of productions or a large number of memory elements, the cost of the first part can be prohibitive.

We will present some results of an attempt to reduce the cost of discovering the conflict set. Throughout, we will use a particular production system architecture, PSG [Newell73, 75], but the considerations will be applicable generally. In Section 2 we describe how production systems processed by PSG discover the conflict set and the heuristics we have used to make this processing more efficient. In Section 3 we present formulas for the costs of these various schemes. In Section 4 we compare experimentally the time requirements of PSG when the heuristics are used with the time requirements of PSG alone.

## 2.0 IMPLEMENTATION ALGORITHMS

A production system processed by PSG has memory elements (Ms) that are list structures and condition elements (Cs) that are list structures with variables. To determine if a production is satisfied, the following three criteria are used: (1) every C must match a distinct M; (2) a C and an M match only if they have the same name, or the C is a matching variable, or they match as expressions; (3) a C and an M match as expressions only if the subelements of the C and the subelements of the M are in the same order, the first subelement of the C matches the first subelement of the M, and each subsequent subelement of the C matches a subelement of the M. Thus, consider the following WM containing three elements

WM: ((E (F) G) D ((I H)))

and the five productions (where X and Y are variables)

P1: ((E (F) X) ((I X)) → . . .)
P2: (((F) G) → . . .)
P3: ((E (F) X) ((I Y)) → . . .)
P4: (D (E G) → . . .)
P5: (((I H G)) → . . .)

P3 and P4 are satisfied, while the others are not.

PSG computes the conflict set in the following way: At the beginning of each cycle, the first condition element in the first production is matched against each memory element until a match is found. Then the second condition element is matched against each memory element. This continues until an attempted match fails, or until all of the condition elements have been found to be supported, in which case the production is inserted into the conflict set. This procedure is repeated for each of the productions. We can schematize this as follows:

```
for every P
    SUCCESS ← true
    while SUCCESS
        for every C
            FOUND ← false
            while not FOUND
                for every M
                    if match(C, M)
                    then
                        FOUND ← true
                        if final C then add P to CONFLICT SET
                else if final M then SUCCESS ← false
```

Two alternative methods are provided for resolving conflict in the case of more than one production being satisfied. If *production order* is used, productions are tested in order until the first satisfied one is found; then that production is fired. For production order, no explicit conflict set is formed. If *memory order* is used, all productions are tested; the first of those productions supported by the memory element that is more recent than any other memory element supporting a production is fired.

PSG does not avail itself of any of the knowledge that could be obtained before execution by determining which productions contain identical (or similar) condition elements. Nor does it make use of the information actually computed during previous cycles. Knowledge of which productions are satisfied, which condition elements are supported, and what memory elements are in WM is lost at the end of each cycle and must be continually rediscovered. This leads to much redundancy in processing. There are three knowledge sources, KSs, that can be used to eliminate this inefficiency:

(1) The *Condition-membership* KS provides knowledge about the occurrence of condition elements in productions.

(2) The *Memory-support* KS provides knowledge about the memory elements that support condition elements.

(3) The *Condition-relationship* KS provides knowledge about the relationship among condition elements *within* each production.

A *filter* is any body of code that uses these sources of knowledge to reduce the number of productions tested by a production system architecture. A filter admits to further testing that subset of productions not known to be unsatisfied on the basis of whatever information is available in its KSs. The set of productions passed through the filter for further evaluation is called the $P^+$ set. To be useful in a filter, a KS must contain enough information so that a significant number of productions can be excluded from consideration. The filter must also be able to store this information in such a way that accessing and updating is significantly less costly than processing the excluded productions.

Knowledge of which conditions occur in the productions permits rejection of productions whose conditions elements are not supported by elements in WM. Filters based on the Condition-membership KS admit to further testing productions whose conditions elements all appear to be supported by memory elements. This does not guarantee that such productions will be satisfied: the condition elements may not match the memory elements in detail (if the filter is using only partial knowledge); or all conditions might match individually, but not when considered together (e.g., due to instantiation of variables). Given

P10:  (D E → . . .)
P11:  (E F → . . .)
P12:  (F D → . . .)

P13:  (D D → . . .)
WM: (D F)

and given a KS containing the information that P10, P12, and P13 contain D, P10 and P11 contain E, and P11 and P12 contain F, a filter could match the condition elements D, E, and F against the elements in WM and generate P': {P12 P13}. Only three condition elements would be matched against the elements in WM by PSG, rather than the seven that would have to be matched if the information in the Condition-membership KS were not available.

The Memory-support KS contains the knowledge of which condition elements are supported by a memory element at the beginning of a cycle. This knowledge complements that in the Condition-membership KS. If a filter makes use of both of these KSs, then (continuing the above example) since the Memory- support KS would contain the information that the condition elements D and F are supported, no matching would be necessary at the beginning of the cycle to generate P': {P12 P13}. The knowledge in the Memory-support KS must be updated at the end of each cycle. This involves matching the elements added to and deleted from WM with each condition element, and the cost of doing this is primarily the cost of doing the matching. To determine how the updating cost compares with the cost of matching each condition element with the elements in WM at the beginning of each cycle, one must know the ratio of the number of memory elements added or deleted per cycle to the number of elements in WM. If the ratio is 1 to 1, then the two costs are approximately the same.

The third KS, the Condition-relationship KS, is probably of value only if the other two KSs are also being used. Like the Memory-support KS, it contains knowledge that must be updated during each cycle. This knowledge can be used to determine whether a production, each of whose condition elements is supported when considered individually, is actually satisfied. It can also be used to determine whether a production is satisfied even though some of its condition elements appear to be unsupported when considered in isolation. Consider

P13:  (D D → . . .)
P14:  (X (E X) → . . .)
P15:  (X (E X) ABS → . . .)
WM: (D (E F))

where X is a variable and the symbol ABS negates the condition element preceding it.[3] The knowledge from both the Condition-mem-

---

[3] A production containing a negated condition element is satisfied only if that condition element is *not* supported by any element in WM.

bership and Memory-support KSs would not indicate that either P13 or P14 is unsatisfied, though both are. Moreover, unless negated condition elements are ignored, it would indicate falsely that P15 is not satisfied. The Condition-relationship KS would contain the information that P13 can be satisfied only if D occurs twice in WM, that P14 can be satisfied only if the variable X can be bound to the same symbol each time it is instantiated, and that P15 can be satisfied if the variable X is bound to an element that does not occur as a subelement in an element whose first subelement is E.

Our interest in this chapter is with filters that make only a limited use of the first two of these KSs. If one builds a filter that makes full use of all three, that filter can generate conflict sets (i.e., $P^+$ sets containing only satisfied productions). Two such filters have been designed, one by Hayes-Roth and Mostow [F. Hayes-Roth75], the other by Forgy [Forgy77]. The two filters were developed independently, but are organized in much the same way. Both are networks of tests, each of which incorporates some small piece of knowledge of one of the three sorts described above. Productions are associated with different subsets of these tests. Tests at the lowest level of the network are applied to data elements entering (or leaving) WM. Those elements that satisfy one or more of these initial tests are passed up the network to other tests. When all of the tests associated with a particular production have been satisfied by some subset of data elements, that production is known to be satisfied.

Part of the efficiency of each of these filters is due to the fact that their tests can be arranged in such a way that those which are both highly discriminating and inexpensive are applied first. The strategy embodied in the filters described below is to make use of only very inexpensive tests like those applied at the lowest level of the networks. Since these tests cannot guarantee that the productions in the $P^+$ set are satisfied, this subset of productions will then have to be retested. However, it seems highly likely that for many production systems, the retesting cost will be less than the cost of maintaining the network of sufficient tests.

### 2.1 A Condition-Membership Filter

One of the two filters we have constructed makes use of the Condition-membership KS exclusively; we call this filter CmF. The KS is a discrimination net that indicates which productions contain similar condition elements. Here similar means having the same first named symbol or *primary feature* (PF). Each node in the network is a single primary feature and thus represents all condition elements having that feature as their first named symbol. The full CmF has nodes corresponding to each feature in the production system being processed. A partial CmF has nodes corresponding to only some of the features.

At the beginning of a run, a list of pairs is generated; each pair contains a primary feature and the set of productions that do *not* contain a condition element with that feature. This list is ordered by increasing size of the sets of productions. Then the primary feature with the smallest set of associated productions (i.e., the feature whose absence excludes the largest number of productions) is selected as the top node of the discrimination net. This node has two successors. Its same-set-successor is the feature on the list that excludes the second largest number of productions; the same-set-successor of this node is the feature on the list that excludes the third largest number of productions, and so on. The subset-successor of the top node (and of each of the other nodes in the tree) is found by reordering the list on the basis of how many additional productions are excluded by each remaining feature; the feature that excludes the largest number of additional productions is the subset-successor; its same-set- successor is the feature on the reordered list that excludes the second largest number of productions, and so on, as above. Nodes continue to be generated until the list of features is empty or until the net is of a stipulated size.[4]

At the beginning of each cycle, a set containing the primary feature of each memory element in WM is generated. Then the discrimination net is traversed by testing whether the current node is a member of this feature set. If it is not, then only the productions associated with the terminal node descendants of that node can possibly be satisfied, so the subset-successor is tested. If, on the other hand, the current node is a member of the feature set, no information has been gained; to discover which productions (if any) can be excluded, the same-set-successor is tested. When a terminal node is encountered, the list of possibly satisfied productions associated with that node becomes the P[+] set. Schematically,

```
for every M add PF of M to WM FEATURE SET
for I ← 1 thru N where N is depth of NET
    if NODE I is in WM FEATURE SET
        then descend to the SAME-SET-SUCCESSOR
        else descend to the SUBSET-SUCCESSOR
P+ SET ← productions associated with NODE N
```

## 2.2 A Condition-Membership Memory-Support Filter

We have implemented three versions of a second filter that uses

---

[4] The reordering procedure is useful only for partial nets; it guarantees that the net produced is the most effective net of its size.

both the Condition-membership and the Memory-support KSs. The three versions, CmMsF1, CmMsF2, and CmMsF3, differ from one another only in the set of features they use to represent condition elements.

CmMsF1, like CmF, uses only the primary feature to represent a condition element. At the beginning of a run a set of associations are established. Each primary feature is associated with the list of those condition elements it represents; then each condition element is associated with the list of productions containing it. In addition, the number of condition elements contained in each production is associated with that production; this number is the initial measure of the support needed in order for that production to be satisfied.

During each cycle, whenever a memory element enters or leaves WM, its primary feature is generated; the condition elements associated with this feature are found and also each of the productions containing one of these condition elements. If the memory element is entering WM, then for each of these productions, the measure of its needed support is decremented by one and, if the resulting number is less than or equal to zero, the production is tagged as possibly satisfied. If the memory element is leaving WM, then for each of the productions the measure of its needed support is incremented by one, and if that number is positive, the production is tagged as unsatisfied. Before each cycle, those productions tagged satisfied are put into the $P^+$ set. Schematically,

$X \leftarrow$ PF of M entering WM
for every C with X as PF
    for every P with C
        decrement NEEDED SUPPORT MEASURE by 1
        if NEEDED SUPPORT MEASURE < 1 then tag P possibly
        satisfied

$X \leftarrow$ PF of M leaving WM
for every C with X as PF
    for every P with C
        increment NEEDED SUPPORT MEASURE by 1
        if NEEDED SUPPORT MEASURE > 0 then tag P unsatisfied

for every P
    if P is tagged possibly satisfied then put P in $P^+$ SET

CmMsF2 is identical to CmMsF1, except in its representation of condition elements. CmMsF2 uses both a primary feature and a list of *secondary features* indicating the position, but not the depth, of each named symbol. For example, the condition element (D ((E) F)) is represented as (1D 2E 3F), where 1, 2, and 3 simply indicate the order of the named subelements. CmMsF2 is more discriminating than CmMsF1. At the beginning of a run, CmMsF2, instead of directly associating each primary feature with a set of condition elements, associates each primary feature with a set of secondary feature lists (SFLs); each feature list is then associated with the set of condition elements it represents. During each cycle, after the primary feature of the memory element entering or leaving WM has been generated, the list of secondary features of that memory element is generated; the secondary feature lists associated with the primary feature are then matched with the list of secondary features of the memory element. A condition element feature list matches a memory element feature list if all of its elements are contained in the memory element feature list and are in the same order. A feature representing a variable matches any element. The productions containing the condition elements represented by the secondary feature lists matching successfully are updated as in CmMsF1.

CmMsF3 uses both a primary feature and a list of secondary features indicating the depth as well as the position of each named symbol to represent condition elements. For example the condition element (D ((E) F)) is represented as (1D1 2E3 3F2), where the numbers following the named subelements indicate the depth of that subelement. CmMsF3 is more discriminating than CmMsF2; it differs only in the procedure used to match condition element feature lists with memory element feature lists.

## 3.0 ESTIMATED-COST FORMULAS

In this section we give formulas that predict the costs of PSG and the two filters. The formulas arise from an analysis of the structure of the algorithms (as embedded in the actual code) coupled with various simplifying statistical assumptions about the nature of the task environment. We are primarily interested in assessing the major factors affecting the cost of a cycle, T.CYCLE. This could be accomplished by using the formulas to argue for the *form* of the relationship and then verifying this with experimental data, determining the constants so as to produce a good fit to the data. Alternatively, the formulas can be made sufficiently precise to produce absolute predictions of the time taken under various experimental conditions. We have chosen this later course, since an interesting side question is how good such cost formulas can be.

It should be evident from our description of PSG's basic algorithm that two important factors determining its cost are the size of PM and the size of WM. This shows up in the simplest approximation to the actual per cycle cost of PSG, which is

$$(1) \ \text{T.CYCLE} = \text{CONDITION COST} + \text{ACTION COST}$$
$$= (P * M * \text{T.MCH}) + ((A/P) * \text{T.ACT})$$

where P is the number of productions in PM, M the number of elements in WM, T.MCH the time to match a condition element with a memory element, A the number of action elements, A/P the average number of actions per production, and T.ACT the time to execute one action element. This formula actually yields a value that is close to a lower bound for the cost when memory order is used for conflict resolution. If the number of condition elements in each production is close to 1, or if the number of first condition elements supported by elements in WM is close to 0, this formula is a fair approximation.

For production systems whose conflict resolution strategy is production order, a better approximation is

$$(2) \ \text{T.CYCLE} =$$
$$(((P + 1)/(\text{CS} + 1)) * M * \text{T.MCH}) + ((A/P) * \text{T.ACT})$$

where CS is the average number of productions in the conflict set. The system quits as soon as it finds the first acceptable production, and so it searches only $(P+1)/(\text{CS}+1)$ productions instead of P.

These two formulas make clear that with either conflict resolution regime the basic algorithm is linear jointly in P and M. The cost addition of the action side will be negligible for large systems (either large P or M), as long as the number of actions per production remains modest (which is true of all systems envisioned to date, since the action sequence is required to be unconditional and hence is limited).

When a filter is added to PSG, the simplest approximation to the per-cycle cost would seem to be

$$(3) \ \text{T.CYCLE} = \text{T.FILTER} + (P' * M * \text{T.MCH}) + ((A/P) * \text{T.ACT})$$

where $P'$ is the number of productions in the $P^+$ set that are tested. For production order, $P' = (P^+ + 1)/(\text{CS} + 1)$, and for memory order, $P' = P^+$. The main effects of the filter according to formula (3) are to cut down the effective number of productions (from P to essentially $P^+$), leaving everything else unchanged, and to add a cost due to the filter, which is unknown until specific designs are considered.

The principal inadequacy of this formula is that it does not take into account the possibility of a filter decreasing the number of memory elements with which a condition element is matched. We need to decompose the middle term in formula (3) to allow this to be estimated. A useful form for this decomposition is

(4) T.CYCLE =
(4.1) T.FILTER +

(4.2) THE COST OF SUCCESSFUL MATCHES ON Ps THAT
    FAIL +
(4.3) THE COST OF UNSUCCESSFUL MATCHES ON Ps
    THAT FAIL +
(4.4) THE COST OF SUCCESSFUL MATCHES ON Ps THAT
    SUCCEED +
(4.5) THE COST OF UNSUCCESSFUL MATCHES ON Ps
    THAT SUCCEED +
(4.6) (A/P) * T.ACT

The formulas based on (4) for PSG and for PSG augmented by the two filters are rather involved and are given in the appendix. Their main features can be summarized as follows. The filter cost for CmF is roughly linear in the product of M and PF. However, PF grows slowly and so the principal factor is M. The filter cost for CmMsF is dependent only on the number of elements added to or deleted from WM per cycle. (In the case of CmMsF1, since PF grows slowly, there is an additional dependency on the number of condition elements associated with each primary feature.) In PSG, the condition cost (the sum of the costs given in lines 2-5) is primarily the cost of the unsuccessful matches on productions in the $P^+$ set that fail; the number of these matches is dependent on both P and M. For PSG augmented by either filter, the entire condition cost becomes insignificant for large P compared to filter cost. The condition cost of CmF is linear with M, while for CmMsF the condition cost has almost no dependence on M. The three formulas all predict the same action cost.

To the extent that our formulas are accurate, we can make the following general statements about the efficiency of production system architectures: (1) An architecture without a filter has a total cost that is roughly linear in the product of P and M. Each unsatisfied production tested involves at least M matches. An additional N * M/2 matches will be needed for each unsatisfied production whose first N condition elements are supported by memory elements; however, for large P and small M, this number will be insignificant. To test a satisfied production, C/P * M/2 matches are needed; this number likewise will be insignificant for large P unless M (or CS) is correspondingly large. (2) A production system architecture augmented by a filter using a Condition-membership KS has a cost that is roughly linear in the product of $P^+$ and M. Because production systems typically have many productions, but only a small WM, the Condition-membership KS can be viewed as the most crucial of the knowledge sources since it eliminates the cost dependency on P. (3) An architecture augmented by a filter using both a Memory-support KS and a Condition-membership KS has a cost that is linear only in $P^+$. By providing information that makes the searching of WM unnecessary, the Memory-support KS eliminates the cost dependency on M.


## 4.0 EXPERIMENTAL RESULTS

This section is divided into three parts. Each part considers one of the three production systems we used for gathering cost data, and includes a brief description of the production system involved, a table displaying the predicted and measured costs for the runs, with and without filtering, and a discussion of the discrepancies between the predicted and measured costs.[5]


## 4.1 PSCC1: Testing Variations in Processing

The first set of cost data attempts to test the reliability of our estimated-cost formulas. We wanted to determine whether the discrepancies between the measured and predicted costs of a production system would vary if the size of PM and the size of WM were held constant, but the stimuli presented to the production system were varied. We reasoned that if the discrepancies between measured and predicted costs did not remain relatively constant, then the cost of a production system would be too highly task dependent for our formulas to be considered meaningful. The production system we selected for this test, PSCC1, was designed to simulate the performance of human subjects on a task described by Chase and Clark [Chase72]. They used this task to study the mental processes people use in deciding whether or not a sentence is an accurate description of a picture. The task involves presenting a subject with (1) one of the eight sentences that can be formed by using *star* or *plus* as subject, *is* or *isn't* as verb, *above* or *below* as preposition, and then *plus* or *star* (whichever was not used as subject) as the object of the preposition, and (2) a picture of a * and a +, one above the other. The subject indicates whether the sentence is true of the picture. For instance, if *star is above plus* and */+ are presented, the subject says *yes* (see Table 1).

We presented 3 of the 16 possible sentence-picture combinations to PSCC1. Each set of inputs was run on PSG, PSG.CmMsF1, PSG.CmMsF2, and PSG.CmMsF3. PSG.CmF was not used; given the number of productions in PSCC1, space limitations made the use of the full CmF impossible, and the diversity of features in PSCC1 was such that no partial CmF was more than minimally discriminatory. Al-

---

[5] A technical report, of the same title, containing additional data and a more complete discussion of the adequacy of the formulas is available from the authors.

Table 1

Per Cycle Times (in msec) for PSCC1

| | Stimulus Set 1 Predicted Measured | | Stimulus Set 2 Predicted Measured | | Stimulus Set 3 Predicted Measured | |
|---|---|---|---|---|---|---|
| **PSG** | | | | | | |
| Filter cost | 0 | 0 | 0 | 0 | 0 | 0 |
| Condition cost | 5988 | 9423 | 6230 | 9328 | 6261 | 9389 |
| Action cost | 145 | 170 | 145 | 183 | 145 | 179 |
| Total cost | 6134 | 9593 | 6376 | 9512 | 6406 | 9569 |
| **PSG.CmMsF1** | | | | | | |
| Filter cost | 121 | 139 | 121 | 160 | 121 | 151 |
| Condition cost | 252 | 948 | 252 | 1093 | 252 | 1118 |
| Action cost | 145 | 173 | 145 | 198 | 145 | 199 |
| Total cost | 520 | 1262 | 519 | 1452 | 519 | 1469 |
| **PSG.CmMsF2** | | | | | | |
| Filter cost | 254 | 296 | 254 | 307 | 254 | 338 |
| Condition cost | 221 | 928 | 221 | 930 | 221 | 967 |
| Action cost | 145 | 186 | 145 | 194 | 145 | 197 |
| Total cost | 621 | 1411 | 621 | 1432 | 621 | 1502 |
| **PSG.CmMsF3** | | | | | | |
| Filter cost | 418 | 463 | 418 | 491 | 418 | 498 |
| Condition cost | 219 | 929 | 219 | 922 | 219 | 952 |
| Action cost | 145 | 192 | 145 | 197 | 145 | 197 |
| Total cost | 783 | 1585 | 783 | 1610 | 783 | 1648 |

though there are, as Table 1 shows, significant discrepancies between the measured costs for this task and the costs predicted by the formulas given in the appendix, the discrepancies remain constant across all of the runs and are due to some of the distribution assumptions that we made, not to an incorrect characterization of the interdependencies among the production system parameters. The measured costs for each of the PSSC1 runs on PSG are greater than our predicted costs by about a factor of 1.5. This discrepancy can be accounted for almost entirely by our inability to estimate accurately the number of productions that need to be considered before the first satisfied production is found. The formula that we use to estimate this number presupposes that the satisfied productions are evenly distributed among the productions in PM and thus that roughly P/CS productions will be tried in each cycle. In PSCC1, however, one production, the 34th, is fired far more frequently than any of the others, and consequently, on the average, 19 productions are tried before the first satisfied one is found. The discrepancies between the predicted and measured costs in PSG.CmMsF1, PSG.CmMsF2, and PSG.CmMsF3 are primarily due to our inability to estimate accurately the size of the $P^+$ set. Our estimate is low for all of these runs because our PSG.CmMsF formula assumes that negated condition elements can be ignored. Ignoring negated condition elements results, on the average, in two additional productions being admitted to further testing on each cycle.

## 4.2 PS20Q: Testing Variations in the Number of Productions

The second set of cost data attempts to determine the relationship between the number of productions in PM and the cost of processing a production system. To measure the effect of varying PM size, we used a production system containing productions almost all of the same form. The production system, PS20Q, plays the game of 20 questions. Except for three control productions, each production in the system is a member of a three-production set that encodes information about a category. One production in the set associates a category with a subcategory. Another associates the category with another category within the same supercategory. The third provides a mechanism by which the production system can acquire knowledge of additional subcategories. For example, the following information about the category *citrus fruit* might be represented: (1) A lime is a citrus fruit. (2) A banana is another kind of fruit. (3) If there is another citrus fruit besides the lime, it should be associated with the lime. Because information about each category is encoded in a homogeneous fashion, the values of the production system parameters vary directly with the number of productions.

The first run of PS20Q was with 50 productions; before each of the two subsequent runs, an additional 50 productions were added to PM. In all three cases, the production system (unbeknownst to itself) was looking for the same answer. For each set of productions, runs on PSG, PSG.CmF, PSG.CmMsF1, and PSG.CmMsF2 were made. PSG.CmMsF3 was not used since PSG.CmMsF2 was fully discriminating; that is, the $P^+$ set was the conflict set. The PSG.CmF runs were with a partial filter; only four features were used. PS20Q uses memory order for conflict resolution; thus in this case, PSG finds all satisfied productions before selecting one to fire.

As is evident from Table 2, the predicted costs for the PS20Q runs are much closer to the measured costs than was the case in the previous task. This is due partly to the similarity in form of most of the productions and partly to the use of memory order rather than production order as the conflict resolution strategy. Figure 1, which plots total cost as a function of the size of PM, shows very clearly the value of the two filters. The only two significant discrepancies between the predicted and measured costs for PS20Q occur in the PSG.CmMsF1 and PSG.CmMsF2 runs. In both, the measured filter costs and condition costs increase with the size of PM, whereas the predicted costs remain relatively constant. This suggests that there is a dependency in both cases on the number of productions in PM — a dependency that our formula does not capture. For the condition cost, there is such a dependency. The filters have been implemented so that rather than updating the $P^+$ set at the beginning of a cycle, they simply update a

Table 2

Per Cycle Times (in msec) for PS20Q

| | 50 Productions Predicted | Measured | 100 Productions Predicted | Measured | 150 Productions Predicted | Measured |
|---|---|---|---|---|---|---|
| **PSG** | | | | | | |
| Filter cost | 0 | 0 | 0 | 0 | 0 | 0 |
| Condition cost | 8407 | 9422 | 16816 | 18880 | 25009 | 27269 |
| Action cost | 594 | 450 | 566 | 454 | 558 | 443 |
| Total cost | 9002 | 9872 | 17383 | 19334 | 25567 | 27713 |
| **PSG.CmF** | | | | | | |
| Filter cost | 126 | 122 | 126 | 130 | 126 | 141 |
| Condition cost | 2331 | 2266 | 4428 | 4615 | 6477 | 6681 |
| Action cost | 594 | 422 | 566 | 448 | 558 | 440 |
| Total cost | 3051 | 2811 | 5121 | 5194 | 7162 | 7122 |
| **PSG.CmMsF1** | | | | | | |
| Filter cost | 382 | 252 | 475 | 506 | 470 | 758 |
| Condition cost | 144 | 250 | 147 | 324 | 147 | 377 |
| Action cost | 594 | 464 | 566 | 476 | 558 | 478 |
| Total cost | 1129 | 966 | 1188 | 1307 | 1176 | 1615 |
| **PSG.CmMsF2** | | | | | | |
| Filter cost | 908 | 775 | 1094 | 1298 | 1087 | 1894 |
| Condition cost | 140 | 251 | 143 | 325 | 143 | 412 |
| Action cost | 594 | 478 | 566 | 472 | 558 | 479 |
| Total cost | 1643 | 1504 | 1804 | 2096 | 1789 | 2786 |

flag on each production that indicates whether or not it is satisfied. PSG then generates the $P^+$ set by checking the flag. The cost of this check is approximately 1.5 msec per production. For the filter cost though, the dependency is only apparent. The actual dependency is on the number of condition elements associated with each primary feature. However, in PS20Q the number of condition elements associated with four of the primary features is directly proportional to the number of productions in PM.

## 4.3 PSSTRN: Testing Variations in the Size of WM

The third set of cost data attempts to determine the relationship between the size of WM and the cost of processing a production system. To determine the effect of WM size, we used PSSTRN, a production system that can do three related tasks: (1) It can do the Sternberg binary classification task [Newell73]. In this task, the subject is given a small set of symbols, called the positive set, and then another symbol, called the probe; the task is to determine whether the probe is in the positive set. (2) It can determine whether the same probe has been given before. (3) It can look for a pattern in its yes or no answers to the Sternberg task. The effect of WM size was determined by selecting three different-sized WMs so that the same sequence of productions fired, but different numbers of condition elements (the number being

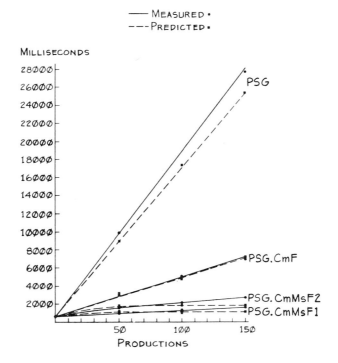

Fig. 1. Per cycle cost of PS20Q on PSG, PSG.CmF, PSG.CmMsF1, and PSG.CmMsF2

proportional to the number of memory elements) were supported during each run.

For the first run of PSSTRN, four elements were in WM, for the second, an additional three, and then three more for the third run. For each WM, runs on PSG, PSG.CmF, PSG.CmMsF1, and PSG.CmMsF2 were made. As with PS20Q, PSG.CmMsF2 was fully discriminating and so PSG.CmMsF3 was not used. The predicted costs for the PSG.CmF runs are for the complete 17 level (17 PF) net; however, space limitations made it impossible to use the full filter and so the runs were made with a net of ten levels instead. This partial filter was as discriminating as the full filter would have been; so except for a slight difference in filter cost, our measured costs are the same as they would have been had we been able to use the full filter. Memory order was used as the conflict resolution strategy.

As Table 3 shows, the discrepancies between the predicted and measured costs for PSSTRN are not completely consistent across the runs. This is primarily because there is a wide variance in the number of condition elements that each of the memory elements support or appear to support. The effect of this lack of uniformity of support can be seen in Fig. 2, where total cost is plotted as a function of WM size.

Table 3

Per Cycle Times (in msec) for PSSTRN

|  | 4 Memory Elements Predicted Measured | | 7 Memory Elements Predicted Measured | | 10 Memory Elements Predicted Measured | |
|---|---|---|---|---|---|---|
| **PSG** | | | | | | |
| Filter cost | 0 | 0 | 0 | 0 | 0 | 0 |
| Condition cost | 4130 | 5595 | 8057 | 8498 | 11254 | 11760 |
| Action cost | 162 | 222 | 162 | 225 | 162 | 226 |
| Total cost | 4292 | 5817 | 8219 | 8723 | 11416 | 11986 |
| **PSG.CmF** | | | | | | |
| Filter cost | 176 | 117 | 308 | 197 | 440 | 286 |
| Condition cost | 1098 | 1562 | 4582 | 3560 | 6422 | 5865 |
| Action cost | 162 | 220 | 162 | 220 | 162 | 218 |
| Total cost | 1436 | 1899 | 5052 | 3978 | 7024 | 6369 |
| **PSG.CmMsF1** | | | | | | |
| Filter cost | 156 | 106 | 156 | 107 | 156 | 108 |
| Condition cost | 209 | 386 | 224 | 418 | 237 | 495 |
| Action cost | 162 | 225 | 162 | 227 | 162 | 227 |
| Total cost | 528 | 718 | 543 | 753 | 556 | 831 |
| **PSG.CmMsF2** | | | | | | |
| Filter cost | 369 | 206 | 369 | 207 | 369 | 208 |
| Condition cost | 198 | 356 | 211 | 417 | 222 | 494 |
| Action cost | 162 | 226 | 162 | 228 | 162 | 228 |
| Total cost q | 729 | 789 | 742 | 852 | 754 | 931 |

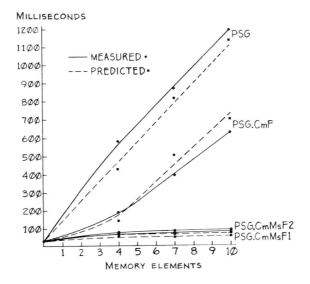

Fig. 2. Per cycle cost of PSSTRN on PSG, PSG.CmF, PSG.CmMsF1, and PSG.CmMsF2

## 5.0 CONCLUSIONS

As stated, our purpose in generating the estimated-cost formulas was primarily to provide a means for studying the effect of a variety of production system parameters on the cost of processing a production system. In spite of various inadequacies in the statistical assumptions, the cost formulas do capture the most important dependencies. Though many things are involved, the factor that stands out as the single most important determinant for a production system architecture not augmented by a filter is the number of attempted matches of a condition element in an unsatisfied production with a memory element that does not support it. It is this factor that our two filters deal with most successfully.

The two graphs (Figs. 1 and 2) show clearly that the cost of running a production system on PSG is almost directly proportional to the product of the number of productions in PM and the number of elements in WM. The filter (CmF) that makes use of just the Condition-membership KS eliminates the dependency on the number of productions by making the number of unsatisfied productions tested dependent on CS rather than on P. The filter (CmMsF) that utilizes both the Condition-membership KS and the Memory-support KS eliminates the memory size dependency as well by eliminating the need to search WM.

CmF and CmMsF both show that large increases in efficiency can be gained by using simple filtering mechanisms. Although a CmF, because it cannot eliminate the WM dependency, is perhaps not of much use in practical applications, CmMsFs appear to have the necessary power: neither the cost of maintaining the KSs nor the cost of finding the satisfied productions is dependent on PM or WM size. Moreover, CmMsFs are highly effective even when the information in the Condition-membership and Memory-support KSs is very incomplete, as is the case with CmMsF1.

## APPENDIX

Three formulas are given below. Formula (5) estimates the cost of PSG; formula (6) the cost of PSG augmented by CmF, and formula (7) the cost of PSG augmented by CmMsF. The formulas all have the same form: The first line indicates the cost of the filter, the second line the cost of $MCH^+P^-$ (the number of successful matches on productions that fail), the third line the cost of $MCH^-P^-$ (the number of unsuccessful matches on productions that fail), the fourth line the cost of $MCH^+P^+$ (the number of successful matches on productions that succeed), and the fifth line the cost of MCH$^-$P$^+$ (the number of unsuccessful matches on productions that succeed). The sixth line indicates the cost of executing the action elements in the productions selected to be fired. The formulas accurately reflect the structure of the algorithms down to the level of matching routines. Thus each time constraint corresponds to a particular isolated body of code. Each routine was timed independently by running loops involving only that body of code. All times are in milliseconds.[6]

The estimated-cost formula for PSG is

(5) T.PSG $=$

(5.1) $0\ +$

(5.2) $P'^- * (1/(CD - 1)) * T.MCH^+\ +$

(5.3) $P'^- * (((1/(CD - 1)) * ((M - 1)/2)) + M) * T.MCH^-\ +$

(5.4) $P'^+ * (((C - C.ABS) + NTC)/P) * T.MCH^+\ +$

(5.5) $P'^+ * (((((C - C.ABS) + NTC)/P) * ((M - 1)/2)) + ((C.ABS/P) * M)) T.MCH^-\ +$

(5.6) $(A/P) * T.ACT$

> P$'^-$ is the number of unsatisfied productions tested:
> > For production order, $P'^- = (P - CS)/(CS + 1)$
> > For memory order, $P'^- = P - CS$
> CD is the number of distinct, nonnegated condition elements
> T.MCH$^+$ is the time it takes to match a supported C with its supporting M:
> > $T.MCH^+ = (LPF * 28) + (((F - FV)/C) * 6) + ((FV/C) * 18) + 15$
> LPF is the average depth of the primary feature
> F is the number of features (named symbols)
> FV is the number of features that are variables
> T.MCH$^-$ is the time it takes to attempt to match a C with an M that does not support it:
> > $T1.MCH^- = (LPF * 28) + 15$
> P$'^+$ is the number of satisfied productions tested:
> > For production order, $P'^+ = 1$
> > For memory order, $P'^+ = CS$
> C is the number of condition elements
> C.ABS is the number of negated condition elements
> NTC is the number of action elements that perform a match
> T.ACT is the time it takes to execute one action element:
> > $T.ACT = 72$

---

[6] The version of PSG used is coded in the list-processing implementation language L*(H) (see [Newell77]) and run on a PDP-10, model KA. The system was run in a basically interpretive mode with no attempt to optimize the code locally.

In line (5.2), $MCH^+P^-$ is approximated by taking the product of the number of unsatisfied productions tested and the average number of supported Cs in each production before the first unsupported one is found. In (5.3) $MCH^-P^-$ is approximated by taking the sum of two products: the first gives the number of Ms tested before a successful match is found; the second product is simply the number of unsatisfied productions tested multiplied by the number of elements in WM. In (5.4) $MCH^+P^+$ is approximated by multiplying the number of satisfied productions tested by the number of nonnegated Cs (including NTCs) per production. In (5.5) $MCH^-P^+$ is approximated by taking this same product and multiplying it by the number of Ms tested before a successful match is found; then the number of negated Cs per production times the number of Ms in WM is added to that product. In (5.6) the action cost is estimated by multiplying the average number of action elements in each production by the cost of executing an action element.

The estimated-cost formula for PSG.CmF is

(6) T.PSG.CmF =

(6.1) M * (T.SET + (PF * T.NET)) +

(6.2) $P'^- $ * (1/((P$^+$8+) * (C/P)) − 1)) * T.MCH$^+$ +

(6.3) $P'^-$ * (((1/((P$^+$ * (C/P)) − 1)) * ((M − 1)/2)) + M) * T.MCH$^-$ +

(6.4) $P'^+$ * (((C − C.ABS) + NTC)/P) * T.MCH$^+$ +

(6.5) $P'^+$ * (((((C − C.ABS) + NTC)/P) * ((M − 1)/2)) + ((C.ABS/P) * M)) * T.MCH$^-$ +

(6.6) (A/P) * T.ACT

T.SET is the time it takes to generate the PF of one M:
 T.SET = 10

PF is the number of primary features

T.NET is the time it takes to test whether the PF of a
 C is the same as the PF of one M:
 T.NET = 2

$P'^-$ is the number of unsatisfied productions tested:
 For production order, $P'^-$ = (P$^+$ - CS)/(CS + 1)
 For memory order, $P'^-$ = P$^+$ - CS

P$^+$ is the number of productions admitted to further
 testing:
 P$^+$ = CS * (((C - C.ABS)/PF) exp (P/(C - C.ABS)))

$P'^+$ is the number of satisfied productions tested:
 For production order, $P'^+$ = 1
 For memory order, $P'^+$ = CS

In line (6.1), T.FILTER is approximated by multiplying the time it takes to generate the PF of one M plus the time it takes to search the net given one M by the number of elements in WM. The rest of (6) is identical to (5) except that in (6.2) and (6.3) $P^+$ is substituted for P in $P'^-$ and the probability that a C (in a production in the $P^+$ set) matches an M is $1/(P^+ * (C/P))$ instead of $1/CD$.

PSG.CmF is useful as a partial filter only when some subset of features, PRTF, essentially partitions the production system into a number of sets equal to the number of features in that subset. When this situation obtains, the cost formula is the same as (6), except that $P^+$ is $(1/PRTF) * P$ and the filter cost is $M * (T.SET + (PRTF * T.NET))$.

The estimated-cost formula for PSG.CmMsF is

(7) $T.PSG.CmMsF =$

(7.1) $((A/P) * (C/F') * LPF * (T.PFT + (K * T.FLT)) +$

(7.2) $P'^- * (1/((P^+ * (C/P)) - 1)) * T.MCH^+ +$

(7.3) $P'^- * (((C - C.ABS)/C) + ((C.ABS/C) * (M/2))) * T.MCH^- +$

(7.4) $1 * (((C - C.ABS) + NTC)/P) * T.MCH^+ +$

(7.5) $1 * ((C.ABS/P) * M) * T.MCH^- +$

(7.6) $(A/P) * T.ACT$

    $F'$ is the number of distinct PFs or SFLs:

        For PSG.CmMsF1, $F' = PF$

        For PSG.CmMsF2 and PSG.CmMsF3, $F' = SFL$

    K is the factor by which T.FLT is multiplied depending
        on which version of CmMsF is being used

        For PSG.CmMsF1, $K = 0$

        For PSG.CmMsF2, $K = 1$

        For PSG.CmMsF3, $K = 2$

    T.PFT is the time it takes PSG.CmMsF1 to keep track
        of the degree to which each production is supported:

        $T.PFT = 30$

    T.FLT is the time it takes PSG.CmMsF2 to keep track
        of the degree to which each production is supported:

        $T.FLT = 78$

    $P'^-$ is the number of unsatisfied productions tested:

        $P'^- = (P^+ - CS)/(CS + 1)$

    $P^+$ is the number of productions admitted to further
        testing:

        $P^+ = CS * (((C - C.ABS)/F') \exp (P/(C - C.ABS)))$

    $T.MCH^-$ is the time it takes to attempt to match a C
        with an M that does not support it:

        $T.MCH^- = (LPF * 28) + 21$

In (7.1) T.FILTER is approximated by multiplying the number of modifications to WM by the number of Cs associated with each distinct PF or SFL and that by the average depth of the PF and then multiplying this product by the time it takes to keep track of the degree to which each production is supported. Lines (7.2) and (7.3) are the same as (6.2) and (6.3) except $P'^-$ is always $(P^+ - CS)/(CS + 1)$; each C is matched with approximately one M rather than with half of the elements of WM for supported Cs and all of the elements of WM for unsupported Cs; and the time it takes to attempt to match a C with a nonsupporting M is slightly greater since no C is matched with an M that does not have at least the same PF. Lines (7.4) and (7.5) are the same as (6.4)

# PRODUCTION SYSTEM CONFLICT RESOLUTION STRATEGIES[1]

J. McDermott and C. Forgy

*Carnegie-Mellon University*

*Production systems designed to function and grow in environments that make large numbers of different, sometimes competing, and sometimes unexpected demands require support from their interpreters that is qualitatively different from the support required by systems that can be carefully hand crafted to function in constrained environments. In this chapter we explore the role of conflict resolution in providing such support. Using criteria developed here, we evaluate both individual conflict resolution rules and strategies that make use of several rules.*

## 1.0 INTRODUCTION

The typical artificial intelligence system of the 1960s labored within a highly constrained environment. The recent development of a number of powerful programming tools has made it feasible to build systems that can function intelligently in more interesting environments. The production system control structure [Davis76b, Newell73, Rychener76] is one such tool. In this chapter we argue that the production system control structure—provided it makes use of a carefully devised conflict resolution strategy—is particularly suitable for systems that must respond in reasonable fashion to frequent, sometimes competing, and sometimes unexpected demands from their environments.

[1] This work was supported in part by the Defense Advanced Research Projects Agency (F44620-73-C-0074) and monitored by the Air Force Office of Scientific Research.

*177*

A production system consists of a collection of productions held in *production memory* and a collection of data elements held in *working memory*. A *production* P is a conditional statement composed of zero or more condition elements C, and zero or more action elements A; a production has the form

$$P_j \ (C_1 \ C_2 \ldots C_n \to A_1 \ A_2 \ldots A_m).$$

Most action elements modify working memory by deleting, adding, or modifying a data element. Condition elements are templates; when each can be matched by an element in working memory, the production containing them is said to be instantiated. An *instantiation* is an ordered pair of a production and the elements from working memory that satisfy the conditions of the production. The production system interpreter operates within a control framework called the *recognize-act* cycle. In recognition, it finds the instantiations to be executed, and in action it executes them, performing whatever actions occur in their action sides. The recognize-act cycle is repeated until either no production can be instantiated or an action element explicitly stops the processing. Recognition can be further divided into *match* and *conflict resolution*. In match, the interpreter finds the *conflict set*, the set of all instantiations of productions that are satisfied on the current cycle. In conflict resolution, it selects from the conflict set one or more instantiations to be executed.

We will explore the role of conflict resolution in production systems designed to function intelligently in dynamic environments. In Section 2 we propose a set of criteria for determining the adequacy of conflict resolution rules. In Section 3, several specific rules are described. Then in Section 4, these rules are evaluated in terms of the proposed criteria. It will become evident in this section that for systems designed for dynamic environments, no single rule is adequate, and thus that several rules have to be used in conjunction with one another. Finally, in Section 5, we describe a number of different combinations of rules that do meet the criteria of adequacy.

## 2.0 CONFLICT RESOLUTION

If a system is to be capable of functioning intelligently in an environment that makes varied and sometimes unexpected demands, it must meet two requirements. First, it must be responsive to its environment. When the environment makes a demand, the system must be able to attend to that demand, decide what action is necessary, and then take that action. Second, it must be able to learn. When encountering a new aspect of the environment or when shown that a previously learned behavior is inadequate, the system must be ready to acquire a new behavior. Systems that are both responsive to their environment and able to augment and refine their knowledge of that environment would, given sufficient time and instruction, be able to behave appropriately in any situation.

A production system, if it is to meet both of these requirements, must be given substantial support by its interpreter. Because a production system becomes aware of changes in its environment only during the recognize phase of the recognize-act cycle, responsiveness suffers if too much time is spent in the act phase. Thus to meet the responsiveness requirement, the number of productions fired on each cycle must be limited. Perhaps the most obvious way to limit the number fired is to make them applicable to mutually exclusive situations. But to do this requires that the productions be given knowledge of each other's domains of applicability, and this severely restricts the system's ability to learn. For in order for a production system to add productions to its production memory without having to modify many of the productions already there, the productions must have a high degree of autonomy. Using conflict resolution to limit the number of productions fired enables the necessary degree of autonomy to be maintained. Since conflict resolution can select on the basis of global considerations unknown to the individual productions, each production is required to say only that if no other production more applicable to the current situation is ready, it is. As other productions are added, as more knowledge becomes available, as the overall goals of the system change, the role of individual productions remains the same; each has to say only that it understands and is ready to respond to some tiny piece of the current situation.

If a production system is to function by performing only a small number of actions per cycle, as we just argued it must in order to be responsive to its environment, it must meet a requirement in addition to the two mentioned above. Since some of the system's behaviors will involve long sequences of actions, it must be able to coordinate the firing of several productions, each of which will perform only a few actions. The most obvious way to effect this coordination is to require that each production explicitly evoke its successor. But if this path is taken, production autonomy is lost. Again, conflict resolution can provide a solution. With conflict resolution to make the final choice of the productions to be fired, a production need specify only what is to be done, rather than who is to do it. A small distinction, but enough. New productions may be added to a system employing this mechanism for control with no knowledge required of the existing system beyond the knowledge of the names of a few goals.

A production system that is responsive to the demands of its environment will be said to display *sensitivity*. One that is able to maintain continuity in its behavior will be said to display *stability*. We have argued that the function of conflict resolution is to provide a mechanism that can preserve sensitivity and stability without sacrificing production autonomy. The following two subsections consider in detail what characteristics an interpreter must have in order for production systems having both stability and sensitivity to be implemented easily. Later sections will show how particular conflict resolution rules contribute to sensitivity and stability.

### 2.1 Sensitivity

Attempts to build production systems capable of operating in dynamic environments have shown that such systems are significantly easier to construct when the interpreter provides support of certain kinds. Below we list five characteristic kinds of support that have proven useful. Of course, we make no claim of completeness.

(1) The interpreter should aid the system in its attempts to remain sensitive to multiple aspects of its environment while it focuses attention on a particular task.

(2) The interpreter should aid the system in its attempts to be sensitive simultaneously to multiple aspects of its own processing.

(3) The interpreter should aid the system in its attempts to deal intelligently with the existence in working memory of conflicting data.

(4) The interpreter should recognize when multiple instantiations are attending to aspects of the same situation and take some reasonable action.

(5) All actions taken by the interpreter should be observably deterministic to the system.

In the following paragraphs we describe these five characteristics more fully.

Although the needs of sensitivity and stability are not conflicting, an implementation strongly biased toward one could be weak in its treatment of the other. The first characteristic above implies only that the interpreter should ignore neither. (Since this characteristic concerns the interaction between sensitivity and stability, it could have been proposed instead in the following subsection.)

The second characteristic, like the first, concerns the interaction between the need for sensitivity in a system and the need for direction in the system's processing. For the second characteristic, however, the sensitivity is sensitivity to the results of its own actions. As the system engages in activity directed toward a particular goal, there is the possibility that, at any time, an important but unexpected event may transpire as a side effect of its processing. For example, the system might generate evidence (such as a repeated state) that it is looping, or it might, while working on one piece of a problem, transform the problem in some significant way. In such cases, it is certainly desirable for the system to recognize what has happened and take action accordingly.

A production system, with its single global data base (working memory) and no local memory, is particularly vulnerable to the frame problem. For example, a group of productions might communicate using structures similar in form to structures used earlier by another group, or the environment might force information on the system that conflicts with information already in working memory. An interpreter that possesses the third characteristic can aid production systems in their attempts to deal with the problem of distinguishing relevant information from information that is no longer relevant.

In contrast to the first three characteristics, which are concerned with ways in which the interpreter can aid a production system in its quest for sensitivity, the fourth characteristic is concerned with a sensitivity that the interpreter itself must possess. Since a production system needs knowledge of varying degrees of specificity to function in a complex environment, a given demand will often find more than one production ready to respond. Preventing this situation is quite beyond the power of a production system; whenever a more specific production is satisfied, the more general ones will necessarily be satisfied as well. Thus, it must be the responsibility of the interpreter to recognize the situation and either decide itself what is to be done or evoke a production that is able to make the decision.

The fifth characteristic, that the actions of the interpreter be observably deterministic[2], is important if systems using the interpreter are to learn from experience. Experience would, after all, be of small value in a world without causality.

## 2.2 Stability

As pointed out in the previous subsection, attending too closely to the needs of either stability or sensitivity can result in a loss of the other. In particular, if sensitivity is not to be lost, the designer of a production system must walk a narrow path when building stability into his system, carefully dividing the responsibility for stability between the interpreter and the system itself. The designer cannot put all of the responsibility on the interpreter, in essence adding a program counter to the production system, without losing the potential

---

[2] Presumably all actions taken by a computer are deterministic, but that determinism is of little value to the system if it depends on state variables the system cannot examine.

for sensitivity. Neither can he put all of the responsibility on the production system, essentially using the production system to program an interpreter for another language, for this extreme also results in a system that has lost the potential for sensitivity.

The method employed here to arrive at a reasonable division of responsibility was to determine the forms the needed coordination of firings could take, and then to determine the minimum support that must be provided by the interpreter in order to allow these forms to be implemented without the use of executive productions. The forms the coordination can take were determined by an examination of existing production systems. It could be argued that the number of existing production systems is too small to give validity to results obtained in this fashion. However, this worry seems unfounded. The forms of coordination that we found correspond closely to the major control constructs used in conventional languages, and the few deviations are easily explained. These forms will be presented below in terms of the analogous conventional control constructs.

In general, there is only one way to coordinate production firings and that is by modifying the contents of working memory. A data element placed in working memory to enable the firing of some production or group of productions will be called a *signal*. Signals can have a significance beyond their control function, but only the control function is of interest here. A data element used to effect control will be called a signal regardless of any other uses.

The basic control construct in conventional languages is the GOTO (and sequential execution, which is, after all, just a variant of the GOTO). The use of signals to evoke productions and groups of productions is closely analogous to the use of GOTOs — provided there is assurance that the enabled productions will be the next to fire.

The FOREACH construct provides iteration over a set of data. Since the condition part of a production describes elements of a set, an analogous control construct in production systems is one that allows each of the instantiations of a single production to be executed once, effectively causing the production to loop over the set of data it selects from working memory.

As the FOREACH provides for iteration over a set of data, the FORK-JOIN provides for iteration over a set of processes. At the FORK a number of parallel processes (parallel in the weak sense that there is no specified ordering among them) are initiated; at the JOIN the multiple control paths are merged back into one. In production systems, the FORK enables a number of productions without giving a preferred order of firing. The JOIN is a production that fires upon completion of the processing initiated by the enabled productions.

One control construct often used in production systems has no close analog among the conventional control constructs. (It has, perhaps, a distant analog in the ASSIGN-GOTO.) This construct, called EXTERNAL SEQUENCING, allows one production to enable multiple productions and to specify the order in which their instantiations are to be executed.

To implement SUBROUTINEs requires the capabilities of transfering control to the SUBROUTINE, passing data to the SUBROUTINE, and returning control to the calling process. Transfer of control to the SUBROUTINE entails only the execution of a GOTO, discussed above. Return of control to the calling process in conventional languages entails execution of a GOTO to an address passed to the SUBROUTINE. Something similar can be accomplished in production systems by passing to the SUBROUTINE a signal encoded so that it will not take effect immediately and then relying on the SUBROUTINE to decode the signal as its last operation. It is perhaps simpler, though, to use EXTERNAL SEQUENCING to cause the production at the return point to be fired on termination of the SUBROUTINE. In this case the SUBROUTINE need do nothing to effect the return. Data can be passed to a SUBROUTINE reliably only if it can be guaranteed both that the SUBROUTINE will get all of the data passed to it and that it will be able somehow to distinguish these data from all other elements in working memory.

Since a single control construct used in isolation provides little power, an ability to create hierarchies of control constructs is necessary. If the system is using one construct and some production initiates another type of control, the first must be suspended until the second completes. If, for example, a production in a FORK-JOIN initiates a FOREACH, the FOREACH must be allowed to finish before the FORK-JOIN resumes. If strictly hierarchical control is assumed, nothing more than a stack of control signals is needed.

Two control constructs commonly used in conventional languages, the IF and the WHILE-DO, are seldom explicitly constructed in production systems. The IF is already provided, of course, in the form of productions. The WHILE-DO is provided in the recognize-act control paradigm, which on every cycle determines if there is anything to do (i.e., if there is at least one instantiation ready to be executed) and if so, does it (i.e., executes one or more of the instantiations).

## 3.0 POSSIBLE CONFLICT RESOLUTION RULES

In this section we describe 13 rules. The rules have been divided into five classes on the basis of the criteria by which they judge the adequacy of an instantiation. Each subsection below describes the rules in one class. Within each class the rules are distinguished on the basis of their selectivity and on the basis of the sources of knowledge they use in making their choices. The rules vary greatly in their selectivity; some eliminate only a small fraction of the instantiations in the conflict set, others eliminate almost all instantiations. All of the rules presented here use one or more of three knowledge sources, production memory, working memory, and a state memory maintained by the interpreter. Production memory holds the productions and information such as the order in which the productions were entered into the system. Working memory holds the data elements and information such as the relative age of those elements. The interpreter's state memory holds information such as the name of the last production fired and the subset of data elements that it matched. The rules that we present do not cover the space of possible rules.[3] Our aim was simply to select a few representative rules having interesting properties. We have included most of the conflict resolution rules used by existing production systems.

Figure 1 will be referred to as we present the rules. For some of the rules it will be necessary to know the order in which the productions were entered into the system and for others the relative age of the data elements. Assume that the elements are ordered in working memory from most recent, (P S), to least recent, (W T). Assume further that the first two elements were asserted on the previous interpreter cycle, the next two on the cycle before that, (Q S) and (P V) three cycles in the past, and (W V) and (W T) 101 cycles in the past. Assume the productions were entered into the system in the order shown, P1 first and P4 last. Note that the symbol = in a production signifies that the symbol immediately following it is to be treated as a variable. If the same variable occurs more than once on the condition side of a production, all occurrences must be bound to the same value in order for the match to succeed. The symbol ¬ preceding a condition element signifies that the match is to fail if there is an element in working memory that matches the condition element.

## 3.1 Production Order Rules, POs

Production order rules use a preestablished priority ordering on productions as their criterion of selection. Their source of knowledge then is always production memory. We shall consider only two such rules. Under the first, which we shall call PO1, the relation of dominance totally orders the productions. The first rule entered into the system dominates all the others, the second rule dominates all but the

---

[3] In particular, we do not consider rules that can be appropriately used only by systems that place very weak restrictions on the amount of processing that can be done during the action phase of a cycle. For a discussion of such rules, see Hayes-Roth and Lesser [F. Hayes-Roth77e].

WM  ( (P S) (Q T) (P T) (R V) (Q S) (P V) ... (W V) (W T) )
P1  ( (Q =X) (P =X) → ... )
            I1₁ [ P1 ((Q T) (P T)) ]
            I1₂ [ P1 ((Q S) (P S)) ]
    P2  ( (P S) (P =X) (W =X) → ... )
            I2₁ [ P2 ((P S) (P T) (W T)) ]
            I2₂ [ P2 ((P S) (P V) (W V)) ]
        P3  ( (=X S) (=X =Y) (W =Y) (R =Y) (Q S) → ... )
            I3  [ P3 ((P S) (P V) (W V) (R V) (Q S)) ]
    P4  ( (Q S)¬(U S) (P =X)¬(U V)¬(U T) → ... )
            I4₁ [ P4 ((Q S) (P S)) ]
            I4₂ [ P4 ((Q S) (P T)) ]
            I4₃ [ P4 ((Q S) (P V)) ]
PO1 {I1₁ I1₂}
PO2 {I1₁ I1₂ I3}
SC1 {I2₁ I2₂ I3 I4₁ I4₂ I4₃}
SC2 {I1₁ I2₁ I3 I4₂}
SC3 {I1₁ I2₁ I3 I4₁ I4₂ I4₃}
R1  {I1₂ I2₁ I2₂ I3 I4₁}
R2  {I1₁ I1₂ I2₁ I2₂ I3 I4₁}
R3  {I1₁}
R4  {I1₁ I1₂ I4₁ I4₂ I4₃}
R5  {I2₁}

Fig. 1. Conflict resolution using special case and recency rules.

first, etc. The second rule, PO2, is a generalization of rule PO1. The relation of dominance under PO2 is given by a directed graph where the vertices in the graph represent productions and the edges represent dominance relations between the productions. The graph for PO2 is disconnected. Each component of the graph contains productions all of which are applicable to the same task, and hence there is no relation of dominance between productions related to different tasks.

PO1 is a strongly selective rule. Given a completely ordered set of productions and the set of instantiations of those productions, it prefers instantiations of the production that is highest in the priority ordering. Thus in Fig. 1 the instantiations of production P1, I1₁ and I1₂, are chosen by rule PO1. This rule is, of course, of limited usefulness to systems designed to function in multitask domains in which the productions germane to different tasks cannot be meaningfully ordered. In such domains, a less constrained rule, such as PO2, is more appropriate.

PO2 is much less selective than PO1. Using the preestablished dominance relation on productions to establish a dominance relation on instantiations, PO2 prefers every instantiation not dominated by another. Since the graph for PO2 is disconnected, each component of the graph that contains an enabled production will contribute at least one instantiation to the set of preferred instantiations. Moreover, since the productions within each component need not be completely ordered, each component may contribute several instantiations. Assume in Fig. 1 that production P1 dominates P2, that P3 dominates P4, and that there are no other dominance relations. Then rule PO2 will select $I1_1$, $I1_2$, and I3.

Unlike the other rules we will describe, production order rules require the production system to specify for each production built where in the priority ordering that new production is to lie. One scheme for adding productions to a system using a production order rule was proposed by Waterman [Waterman75]. His system, which uses PO1, inserts a newly built production just before the first production that has either a condition element or an action element in common with the new production. The rationale for this scheme is that a production being added should mask (or at least partially mask) other productions with a similar function, but should do so in a way that interferes as little as possible with the already established ordering. The system uses as a heuristic the assumption that if two productions have a condition or action element in common, they have a similar function.

### 3.2 Special Case Rules, SCs

Special case rules use the presence of a special case relationship between instantiations as their criterion of selection. Because many pairs of instantiations will fail to have a special case relationship, SC rules are only weakly selective. They may use production memory, working memory, or both as their sources of knowledge. We will present three special case rules, SC1 to SC3. Each defines the special case relationship in a different way, but they all take the same action when they determine that a special case relationship exists. If instantiation $I_s$ is determined to be a special case of instantiation $I_g$, $I_s$ is preferred. In addition, if there exists an instantiation $I_n$ that is neither a general nor a special case of any other instantiation, $I_n$ is preferred. Thus, these rules only prevent the execution of instantiations that are general cases of other instantiations.

SC1, which has production memory as its knowledge source, is sensitive to a special case relationship between the productions of instantiations. It defines the special case relationship in the following way: A production $P_s$ is a special case of another production $P_g$ if (1) $P_s$ has at least as many condition elements as $P_g$, (2) for each condition element in $P_g$ containing constant elements, there is a corresponding condition element in $P_s$ containing those elements as a subset, and (3) $P_s$ and $P_g$ are not identical.[4] According to these rules, P4 in Fig. 1 is a special case of P1. Whenever P4 has an instantiation, any instantiations of P1 are excluded by SC1. P2 and P3 are neither special nor general cases of the other productions. Thus, SC1 prefers instantiations $I2_1$, $I2_2$, I3, $I4_1$, $I4_2$, and $I4_3$.

SC2, which has working memory as its knowledge source, is sensitive to a special case relationship between the data of instantiations. It considers instantiation $I_s$ to be a special case of instantiation $I_g$ if $I_s$ contains as a proper subset all of the data elements contained in $I_g$. According to this rule, I3 in Fig. 1 is a special case of $I1_2$, $I2_2$, $I4_1$, and $I4_3$. Thus, SC2 prefers I3 and the remaining instantiations: $I1_1$, $I2_1$, and $I4_2$.

SC3, which uses both production memory and working memory as knowledge sources, defines the special case relationship in much the same way that SC2 does. It simply augments SC2's definition in such a way that negated condition elements are taken into account. For SC3, $I_s$ is a special case of $I_g$ if (1) $I_s$ contains all of the data elements contained in $I_g$ as a proper subset, and (2) $P_s$ (i.e., the production from $I_s$) has more condition elements than $P_g$. SC3 is thus a weaker rule than SC2; it will prefer every instantiation preferred by SC2 plus some that SC2 does not prefer. In Fig. 1, it prefers $I1_1$, $I2_1$, I3, and $I4_2$ for the same reason that SC2 prefers them. It also prefers $I4_1$ and $I4_3$, which SC2 does not. Because P4 has the same number of condition elements as P3, SC3 does not consider P3's instantiations to be a special case of P4's instantiations.

### 3.3 Recency Rules, Rs

Recency rules use the amount of time that elements have been in working memory as their selection criterion. Two different measures of time are in common use. Some rules consider the age of a data element to be the number of interpreter cycles that have elapsed since its assertion. Others consider the age to be the number of other actions that have been performed since the action that asserted the element. It is possible for two elements to be equally recent under the first measure (two elements are equally recent if they were asserted on the same cycle). No two elements can be equally recent under the second measure. In most cases, and for a number of different reasons, the

---

[4] SC1 could have been presented as a production order rule. We chose to present it as a special case rule because (1) it is worthwhile to compare its use of a special case relationship with other rules making use of that relationship, and (2) most systems that make use of production order use criteria for ordering productions that are more complex (or at least less easy to make explicit) than the special case criterion given above.

rules favor more recent elements. All recency rules use working memory as their knowledge source. We will consider five recency rules, R1 to R5.

The first rule, R1, measures time in number of actions that have been performed since the assertion of an element. This rule orders instantiations on the basis of the most recent data element contained in each. If the most recent data element of one instantiation $I_r$ is more recent than the most recent data element of $I_e$, $I_r$ is preferred. Since every pair of instantiations can be compared under this rule, it is highly selective. For example, in Fig. 1 there are some instantiations that contain (P S) in their data part. Because it is the most recent element in working memory, instantiations containing it are preferred to all the other instantiations. The preferred instantiations are $I1_2$, $I2_1$, $I2_2$, I3, and $I4_1$.

R2 is similar to R1 in that it also orders instantiations on the basis of the most recent data element that each contains. R2, however, uses the other measure of time: the number of interpreter cycles that have elapsed since the element was asserted. With its more liberal definition of recency, R2 is somewhat less selective than R1. In Fig. 1, there are two elements, (P S) and (Q T), that were asserted on the interpreter cycle just completed. The instantiations that contain one or the other of these are preferred to the other instantiations. Thus, R2 prefers $I1_1$, $I1_2$, $I2_1$, $I2_2$, I3, and $I4_1$.

R3 orders instantiations on the basis of the least recent element that each contains; it prefers the instantiation whose least recent element is most recent. R3 measures time like R1 in number of actions since assertion. Because of an anti-special-case property, it is somewhat more selective than R1. In applying this rule, the least recent element of each instantiation must be examined. One of these least recent elements will be the most recent. The instantiations that have that element as their least recent element are preferred to all others. In Fig. 1, instantiation $I1_1$ has (P T) as its least recent element. The least recent elements of all of the other instantiations are less recent than this one. Thus, R3 prefers instantiation $I1_1$.

R4, like R3, orders instantiations on the basis of the least recent elements contained in each, but it is far less selective than R3. R4 uses the number of elapsed interpreter cycles as its measure of time. Instantiations whose least recent elements have been in working memory for 100 cycles or less are preferred to instantiations whose least recent elements have been in for 101 cycles or more. In Fig. 1, there are three instantiations whose least recent elements are more than 100 cycles old and five whose least recent elements are less than 101 cycles old. R4 prefers those five: $I1_1$, $I1_2$, $I4_1$, $I4_2$, and $I4_3$.

The final recency rule, R5, makes more complete use of the available recency information than the other rules do. It uses the number of actions since assertion as its measure of recency. Unlike the other recency rules, R5 considers the recency of all data elements of an instantiation. To order two instantiations, it first compares their most recent elements; if those elements are equally recent, it compares their next most recent elements, and so on. When it finds a pair of elements that are not equally recent, it prefers the instantiation containing the more recent element. If it exhausts the data of one instantiation without finding a pair of differing recency, it prefers the instantiation not exhausted. Only if the instantiations are exhausted simultaneously, and hence, contain exactly the same data, are they considered equivalent under R5. In choosing from the instantiations in Fig. 1, R5 would first compare the most recent elements of the instantiations. All but the five instantiations that contain (P S) as their most recent element would be eliminated after this step. Next it would compare the second most recent elements of these five. One, $I2_1$, has (P T) as its second most recent element. This element is more recent than any of the second most recent elements of the other four instantiations, so $I2_1$ is preferred. Although this example does not show it, R5 has the properties of a special case rule as well as the properties of a recency rule. If an instantiation $I_s$ would be preferred to $I_g$ by SC2, it would also be preferred by R5 either because $I_s$ would contain an element more recent than the corresponding element of $I_g$, or (if the data of $I_g$ were the most recent data of $I_s$) because the data of $I_g$ would be exhausted first. This rule is the most strongly selective of the recency rules.

## 3.4 Distinctiveness Rules, Ds

Distinctiveness rules select on the basis of the similarity or dissimilarity of the instantiations in the conflict set to previously executed instantiations. Knowledge of what instantiations have been executed is provided by the interpreter's state memory. We will describe two rules, D1 and D2, both of which are weakly selective.

D1 considers two instantiations to be distinct if the productions of those instantiations are different. D1 only looks one firing back in the past in deciding which instantiations to prefer. It prefers instantiations that are distinct from the instantiation just fired. In short, D1 tries to prevent any production from firing on consecutive cycles.

D2 uses a stronger criterion. It considers two instantiations to be distinct if either the productions or the data of the two are different. In addition, its uses the entire past history of the system in deciding which instantiations to prefer. It prefers instantiations that are distinct from the instantiations that have already fired. More simply, D2 discourages instantiations from firing twice. For D2 "same data" does not mean "EQUAL (the Lisp predicate) data." Asserting a new element results in instantiations that are distinct from all previous instantiations, even if the element is EQUAL to an existing element.[5]

## 3.5 Arbitrary Decision Rules, ADs

The final rule that we will consider, AD1, stipulates what is to be done in the absence of any information that would indicate that $I_j$ should be preferred to $I_k$. This rule simply selects one instantiation at random.

## 4.0 EVALUATION OF THE RULES

In this section we evaluate the rules described in Section 3 using the criteria developed in Section 2. We indicate first which rules support which of the sensitivity and stability characteristics. Then we show the degree to which each of the rules considered in isolation provides an adequate basis for conflict resolution.

## 4.1 Rules Supporting Characteristics 1 and 2

The first two characteristics are concerned with the problem of building systems that display both sensitivity and stability. The first characteristic is concerned with a system's sensitivity to its environment, the second with a system's sensitivity to the results of its own actions. The problem can be solved by building systems that are sensitive, not to the state of working memory, but to changes in the state of working memory. Sensitivity of this type is quite sufficient to yield a system able to interrupt its processing and respond to important events. It is, at the same time, the basis of coherence in processing; if the system is strongly sensitive to change, the changes made by the firing of one production will strongly influence the choice of which production to fire on the next cycle. Four of the rules that we have studied promote a sensitivity to change of state.

Three of these rules, R1, R2, and R5, are recency rules. Since they achieve their effect by dynamically ordering instantiations on the basis of the most recent element contained in each, these rules are

---

[5] Unless the interpreter is capable of computing the entire conflict set, rule D2 will be very expensive to implement. The interpreters that make use of D2 all have the property that they find each instantiation on the cycle on which it becomes legal [Forgy77]. On such interpreters it is possible to implement D2 without actually storing the entire history of the system. The conflict set is partitioned into two parts, Used and Unused. When an instantiation is first found, it is marked as Unused. After execution it is marked as Used. Thus, the only history that needs to be kept is an indication for each current instantiation of whether it has been executed.

strongly sensitive to change. If there are instantiations that make use of elements added on the previous cycle, whether by the system itself or by the environment, these instantiations will be preferred by all three rules. The slightly different interpretation of recency used by R2 makes its response to change somewhat more uniform than is the case with the other two. Since R2 considers all elements added during a single cycle to be equally recent, the response of a system using R2 to an element added to working memory by the environment will be the same regardless of whether the element is added before, during, or after the action part of the interpreter's cycle.

D2 also promotes a sensitivity to change, but in a manner different from, though complementary to, that of the recency rules. If D2 is used in combination with R1, R2, or R5, the resulting strategy will display an eminently useful form of sensitivity to change. The recency rule will encourage the system to go forward either with its current task or with some other more urgent task; when progress can no longer be made, the combined strategy will cause the system to go back to the last choice point still open (the recency rule will discourage the system from backing any further than necessary) and take an alternate path.

The other rules are essentially indifferent to these first two characteristics. If any of the other rules are used in conjunction with rules that support characteristics 1 or 2, they do not (or at least do not necessarily) weaken the support. Neither, however, do they do anything to promote these two characteristics.

## 4.2 Rules Supporting Characteristic 3

The third characteristic is concerned with the problem of dealing with conflicting data elements. Implicit in characteristic 3 is the notion that the interpreter must make some decision about the relative usefulness of the conflicting data. A reasonable heuristic for a system trying to function in a changing environment is to assume that the older information is, the more likely it is to describe a no longer existing state. Hence, a conflict resolution rule that makes the system ignore old data when there are more recent data available supports characteristic 3. Rules R1 to R4 have this property; rule R5 does not since it would prefer an instantiation containing a very recent and a very ancient element to an instantiation containing only moderately recent elements. A second heuristic is to assume that if information has already been used, then it should make way for other information. By this heuristic, the use of D2, which prefers instantiations that have not been executed to those that have been executed, is justified.

R3 provides more support for characteristic 3 than any of the other recency rules. R1 and R2 provide only the weakest of support. If one of the conflicting elements is most recent, R1 and R2 will make the necessary distinction, otherwise they will not. R4 provides much more support, but the support is of an arbitrary nature. R4, which effectively disables all instantiations containing an element that has been in working memory for more than 100 cycles, in essence stipulates that all data more than 100 cycles old be considered suspect. R3, with its relative definition of recency, does not tie the probability that an element accurately represents a current state of the environment to the element's absolute age.

## 4.3 Rules Supporting Characteristic 4

The fourth characteristic, like the third, implies the need for a decision by the interpreter. The decision to be made in this case is whether two instantiations are attending to the same situation. Either working memory or production memory can provide knowledge on which to base this decision. If the interpreter uses working memory, it may base the decision on any of a number of possible criteria, from requiring that the data of one instantiation be a subset of the data of another, to requiring only that the data of the instantiations have at least one element in common. Since much of the data in working memory may have global significance, it is hard to justify any but the first of these criteria. If the interpreter uses production memory as its only knowledge source, it is restricted in the decision criteria it may use. Productions typically do not change after they enter production memory; new productions may be added to the system, and old productions deleted, but old productions are seldom modified. Thus, once a special case relationship is determined to exist between two productions, the relationship is likely to remain forever unchanged. Four of the rules described above are useful in determining which instantiations attend to the same situation and in prescribing a response.

Rules SC1 to SC3 and R5 are consonant with the demands of characteristic 4. If a system is to respond intelligently in situations where there is little information about how to satisfy the current demand of the environment as well as in situations where there is a good deal of information, the system must have a range of methods, from weak to strong. A system that chose a weak method in preference to a strong method when both were apparently applicable would not be behaving in a reasonable way. All of these rules would, in choosing the instantiation making the strongest informational demand, choose the strong method.

Among the four rules, there are three different definitions of special case. SC1 defines the relation using information from production memory only. SC2 and R5 use working memory only. SC3 uses both memories. Of the three rules that use working memory as a knowledge source, SC2 is the only one that employs exactly the criterion suggested above, finding one instantiation to be a special case of another if the data of the first are a superset of the data of the second. R5 is somewhat stronger since it will order all instantiations having that relation, plus others that do not. SC3 is weaker since it requires more than the above relation before it will consider one instantiation to be a special case of another.

Since SC3 requires more evidence than either SC2 or R5 before it will grant that two instantiations have a special case relationship, it might seem to provide more support for characteristic 4. What this observation misses is that the more evidence a rule demands, the more likely it is that the rule will fail to recognize two instantiations that are attending to aspects of the same situation. Thus the danger that two instantiations might be falsely viewed as bearing on the same situation must be weighed against the danger that two instantiations that do bear on the same situation might not be recognized as such.

## 4.4 Rules Supporting Characteristic 5

All of the rules except AD1, because their effects are observably deterministic, support characteristic 5. Thus, any conflict resolution strategy not employing AD1, or a similar rule, will support characteristic 5. Unfortunately, the use of AD1 is often necessary to prevent the loss of sensitivity that results from executing multiple instantiations. None of the other rules presented here is sufficient by itself to produce a preferred set containing only a single instantiation. Certain combinations of rules are sufficient to produce such a set, but most are not. If the conflict resolution strategy used by a system has the property that it will not generate a unique choice, the system will sometimes execute multiple instantiations and, as pointed out in the general discussion of sensitivity, lose some sensitivity because of the lengthened cycle. To avoid this problem, the interpreter can be made to arbitrarily select a unique instantiation when necessary. In making this arbitrary choice, the interpreter is implicitly using AD1 or a similar rule.

## 4.5 Rules Supporting Stability

Rules R1, R2, and R5 support GOTOs; rule D1 is somewhat in conflict with the needs of GOTOs. A GOTO cannot be implemented in production systems unless it is possible for a production to specify that some subset of the set of instantiations is to be preferred. Rules R1 and R5 make this possible. If the final action performed by a production asserts a signal that enables a group of productions, then the instantiations of these productions will have precedence over all other instantiations. Rule R2, if applied in isolation, also guarantees that instantiations containing a signal asserted on one cycle will be executed on the next cycle. However, instantiations not containing that signal may be executed as well. Thus if R2 is used in combination with other rules, instantiations not containing the signal may be selected in preference to those containing the signal. Rule D1 would work against a production performing a GOTO to itself.

Two forms of the FOREACH are in common use. Each requires different support. A FOREACH can be implemented either by executing all instantiations on one cycle or by executing each on a separate cycle. Executing all instantiations on one cycle requires only that rule AD1 not be used. Executing the instantiations on separate cycles is made easier by the use of rule D2 and is made more difficult by the use of D1. When D2 is used there is no need to explicitly disable each instantiation after it is executed. Use of rule D1 makes it impossible to have a one production loop.

As with the FOREACH, there are two ways to implement a FORK-JOIN, executing all instantiations on one cycle, or executing each on a separate cycle. Executing all on one cycle again requires only that AD1 not be used. If the instantiations are to be executed on separate cycles, there must be a way to guarantee that the JOIN production is the last to be executed. Use of PO1 or PO2 with the JOIN production having lower priority than the other productions is one possibility. If the JOIN production is made the general case of every other production in the FORK-JOIN, use of SC1, SC2, SC3, or R5 is appropriate. D2 is again helpful in eliminating the need to disable instantiations after they are executed, though it is less essential here than in the case of FOREACH.

The simple implementation of EXTERNAL SEQUENCING requires a conflict resolution strategy that orders instantiations on the basis of the most recent element each contains and that measures time in actions rather than in cycles so that the production performing the EXTERNAL SEQUENCING can order its signals as required. Only rules R1 and R5 meet these conditions.

As discussed above, the only mechanism needed to implement SUBROUTINEs, given GOTOs, is a parameter-passing mechanism. The parameter-passing mechanism must ensure that the subroutine will process exactly the data passed to it, and nothing more nor less. No rule described here can guarantee that the subroutine will process all of its data before terminating. Rule R3 can, however, guarantee that the subroutine will not process more data than it should. The data to be passed must be asserted after the signal that enables the production that terminates the subroutine. The other productions of the subroutine will then be unable to fire on data that were asserted before the signal. Any instantiation that includes such data will be dominated by the instantiation of the subroutine terminating production.

If a strictly hierarchical control discipline is used, no more machinery is needed to implement nested control structures than is needed to implement single control structures. In such a control discipline, the order of instantiations in the control stack is exactly the order of their enabling. Hence, a conflict resolution rule sensitive to that order, such as R1, R2, or R5, is suitable for implementing the stack.

An overview of the relationships between each of the 13 rules and the characteristics of an adequate interpreter is given in Fig. 2. A plus indicates that a rule supports a characteristic, though in some cases additional rules are required in order to fully support that characteristic. A minus indicates that if the rule is used, even in combination with other rules, then the characteristic cannot be realized. The absence of a plus or minus indicates that the rule neither actively supports nor actively works against the characteristic, and that the rule can generally be combined with rules that do provide support without weakening the support.

## 5.0 COMBINATIONS OF CONFLICT RESOLUTION RULES

Since, as Fig. 2 shows, no single rule supports all of the characteristics, any conflict resolution strategy using only one rule will be deficient. In this section we will show how rules can be combined so that all of the characteristics can be supported at least to some extent.

The most frequently used technique for combining rules is to place a priority ordering on the rules and then select the instantiations to be executed by means of a lexicographic sort. In other words, the first rule is applied to the instantiations in the conflict set to yield a subset of preferred instantiations; then the second rule is applied to this subset, and so on. Use of this technique gives the first rule the greatest significance and the last rule the least significance. In those cases in which one wants two or more rules to be equally significant, an alternative technique can be used. Each of the rules is applied to the same set of instantiations; the intersection of the resulting subsets is the set of preferred instantiations. A single conflict resolution strategy may use both of these techniques. More precisely, the lexicographic technique can be modified so that at each step either a single rule or a set of rules is applied to the current set of preferred instantiations. We will use the connective $\times$ to indicate that two rules are to be applied to the same set of instantiations and the intersection of the resulting subsets used, and the connective $\rightarrow$ to indicate that the second of two rules (or sets of rules) is to be applied to the set of instantiations preferred by the first; ($\times$ always has precedence over $\rightarrow$).

It is possible that when a rule is applied to a set of instantiations, no instantiation will be preferred. This would occur, for example, if D2

| | 1 | 2 | 3 | 4 | 5 | GOTO | FRCH | F-J | E-S | SUBR | HIER |
|---|---|---|---|---|---|---|---|---|---|---|---|
| P01 | | | | | + | | | + | | | |
| P02 | | | | | + | | | + | | | |
| SC1 | | | | + | + | | | + | | | |
| SC2 | | | | + | + | | | + | | | |
| SC3 | | | | + | + | | | + | | | |
| R1 | + | + | + | + | + | | | + | | | + |
| R2 | + | + | + | + | + | | | − | | | + |
| R3 | | | | + | + | | | | | + | |
| R4 | | | | + | + | | | | | | |
| R5 | + | + | | + | + | + | | + | + | | + |
| D1 | | | | | + | − | | − | | | |
| D2 | + | + | + | | + | | | + | + | | |
| AD1 | | | | | − | − | | − | | | |

Fig. 2. Rule contributions.

were applied to a set of instantiations all of which had been previously fired. Thus, for each rule (or set of rules) that proscribes certain instantiations, it is necessary to specify what is to be done if the set of preferred instantiations is empty. The alternatives, of course, are either to execute no instantiation or to continue with the lexicographic sort on the non-preferred set. If the instantiations in the non-preferred set are there because they are believed to be inappropriate (as opposed to less appropriate), then none of them should be executed. In our discussion below of specific conflict resolution strategies, we will indicate by enclosing a rule (or set of rules) in brackets that it excludes from further consideration all instantiations not in its preferred set.

The remainder of this section is devoted to brief descriptions of four conflict resolution strategies that are among the more adequate combinations of rules from Section 3. Since the rules are chosen from the same small set, these four strategies are all rather similar. Figure 3, which contains the same production system as Fig. 1, will be used to illustrate the workings of these strategies. Again it should be assumed that (P S) and (Q T) were asserted on the previous cycle, (P T) and (R V) two cycles ago, (Q S) and (P V) three cycles ago, and (W V) and (W T) 101 cycles ago. In addition, assume that $I2_1$ has already been executed.

The first of these strategies is [D2] → R1 → SC2 → R3. If this strategy were applied to the production system in Fig. 3, first $I2_1$ would be excluded by rule D2, then {$I1_2$ $I2_2$ I3 $I4_1$}, all of which contain (P S), would be given preference by rule R1, and then since I3 is a special case of $I1_2$, $I2_2$, and $I4_1$ under rule SC2, SC2 would select I3; rule R3 would not be applied. If we ignore negative interactions among these

WM ( (P S) (Q T) (P T) (R V) (Q S) (P V) ... (W V) (W T) )
P1 ( (Q =X) (P =X) → ... )
        I1₁       [ P1 ((Q T) (P T)) ]
        I1₂       [ P1 ((Q S) (P S)) ]
P2 ( (P S) (P =X) (W =X) → ... )
        I2₁       [ P2 ((P S) (P T) (W T)) ]
        I2₂       [ P2 ((P S) (P V) (W V)) ]
P3 ( (=X S) (=X =Y) (W =Y) (R =Y) (Q S) → ... )
        I3 [ P3 ((P S) (P V) (W V) (R V) (Q S)) ]
P4 ( (Q S)¬(U S) (P =X)¬(U V)¬(U T) → ... )
        I4₁       [ P4 ((Q S) (P S)) ]
        I4₂       [ P4 ((Q S) (P T)) ]
        I4₁       [ P4 ((Q S) (P V)) ]
[D2] → R1 → SC2 → R3 {I3}
[D2 × R4] → R1 → SC2 {I1₂ I4₁}
[D2 × R4] → R5 {I1₂ I4₁}
[D2 × R4] → R5 → PO1 → AD1 {I1₂}

Fig. 3. Conflict resolution using combinations of rules.

rules, then this strategy, which has at least one rule supporting each of the characteristics, has no apparent weaknesses. And in fact, combining the rules in this order causes few negative interactions. One of the few is between R1 and R3. Preceded by R1, rule R3 no longer gives effective support to the SUBROUTINE construct. To reverse the order and put R1 after R3 is unacceptable, however. If R1 were preceded by R3 it would no longer support any of the characteristics. Another effect that should be noted is that since SC2 precedes R3, an instantiation $I_s$, which is a special case of another instantiation $I_g$, will be preferred to $I_g$ even if it contains an element that is less recent than the least recent element contained in $I_g$. This effect could be eliminated by putting SC2 after R3. We elected not to do so because the justification for the R3 → SC2 combination, which would severely restrict the scope of the special case rule, seems rather weak. Finally, there is a positive interaction between R1 and SC2. Preceding SC2 by R1 causes the strategy, in effect, to use data recency (R1) to choose what to do next and then to use special case relationships (SC2) to choose how to do it.

    The second strategy is like the first except that R3 is replaced by R4. One apparent advantage of R3 over R4 is that R3 helps in the implementation of subroutines while R4 does not. But, as pointed out above, R3 loses this advantage if it follows R1. Since R4 is used to exclude instantiations from consideration, it is applied first (together with D2). Thus, this second strategy is [D2 × R4] → R1 → SC2. If this strategy were applied to the production system in Fig. 3, $\{I2_1\ I2_2\ I3\}$ would be excluded by D2 and R4, then $\{I1_2\ I4_1\}$ would be selected by R1; since neither $I1_2$ nor $I4_1$ is a special case of the other under SC2, SC2 would not give preference to either instantiation. Because R4 comes first in the strategy and its nonpreferred instantiations are never allowed to fire, it excludes from consideration any instantiation that contains a data element more than 100 cycles old. An obvious way to implement this rule is to delete data elements automatically when they reach the age of 101 cycles. This implementation has a positive side effect: Since a production containing a negated condition element will be enabled only if no element in working memory matches that condition element, an indefinitely long working memory makes using negated condition elements somewhat difficult. When working memory has a limited size, negation has an essentially local effect that complements characteristic 3.

The third strategy is $[D2 \times R4] \to R5$. This strategy takes advantage of the fact that R5 has both data recency and special case characteristics to allow this one rule to replace the two rules R1 and SC2 used in the first two strategies. The support provided by this strategy is virtually identical to that provided by the second strategy. Since R5 is a stronger ordering rule than R1, the number of instantiations executed on each cycle is likely to be less under this third strategy than under the second.

The first three strategies all allow multiple firings. Since multiple firings can result in a large number of actions being performed during a single cycle and thus in a possible loss of sensitivity, a strategy that always produces a unique preferred instantiation may be desirable. Such a strategy results if the third strategy above is extended with PO1 and AD1 to give $[D2 \times R4] \to R5 \to PO1 \to AD1$. An interaction between PO1 and R5 causes them almost always to prefer a unique instantiation. The equivalence class of instantiations preferred by R5 will have exactly the same data; each will be an instantiation of a different production unless one or more of the productions can instantiate the same set of data elements in more than one way. Consequently, PO1, since it uses a complete ordering on productions as its ordering criterion, will ordinarily select one instantiation. In the rare case in which PO1 selects more than one instantiation, AD1 will produce a unique instantiation.

## 6.0 CONCLUDING REMARKS

There are three principal sources for the knowledge on which conflict resolution rules base their selection: production memory, working memory, and the state memory maintained by the interpreter. We have argued that if all three sources are carefully exploited it is possible to create a conflict resolution strategy that is adequate to support systems that must function intelligently in dynamic environments. We do not claim that the support is in any sense optimal; surely no conflict resolution strategy that places all of the responsibility on the interpreter can be right for all situations.

One line of research that appears particularly promising at the moment is bringing the production system itself into the selection process.[6] If the selection provided by the production system can be made to mesh smoothly with the selection provided by the fixed conflict resolution rules of the interpreter, a more nearly optimal form of conflict resolution should emerge. The fixed (and therefore rather inflexible) rules of the interpreter will provide fast selection in the simple cases. The flexible and extensible selection provided by the production system itself will provide somewhat slower, but more intelligent, selection in the difficult cases.

# ACKNOWLEDGMENTS

The development of many of the ideas discussed above owes much to the members of a production system project at Carnegie-Mellon University. The members of this project, in addition to the authors, are P. Langley, A. Newell, K. Ramakrishna, and M. Rychener.

[6] One approach to the use of productions (meta rules) in conflict resolution is described by Davis [Davis76a].

# Deductive Inference

# SEMANTIC NETWORK REPRESENTATIONS IN RULE-BASED INFERENCE SYSTEMS[1]

Richard O. Duda, Peter E. Hart, Nils J. Nilsson,
Georgia L. Sutherland
*Stanford Research Institute*

*Rule-based inference systems allow judgmental knowledge about a specific problem domain to be represented as a collection of discrete rules. Each rule states that if certain premises are known, then certain conclusions can be inferred. An important design issue concerns the representational form for the premises and conclusions of the rules. We describe a rule-based system that uses a partitioned semantic network representation for the premises and conclusions.*

*Several advantages can be cited for the semantic network representation. The most important of these concern the ability to represent subset and element taxonomic information, the ability to include the same relation in several different premises and conclusions, and the potential for smooth interface with natural language subsystems. This representation is being used in a system currently under development at SRI to aid a geologist in the evaluation of the mineral potential of exploration sites. The principles behind this system and its current implementation are described here.*

## 1.0 INTRODUCTION

The use of production rules for knowledge representation has led to systems that have achieved impressive levels of performance in their particular domains [B.G. Buchanan69, Shortliffe76]. The advantages of this approach stem from the fact that the representation is

---

[1] This work was supported in part by the internal research and development program of Stanford Research Institute, and in part by the Office of Resource Analysis of the U.S. Geological Survey under Contract No. 14-08-0001-15985.

*203*

modular and declarative. This provides conceptual clarity, encourages incremental development, and makes the knowledge base directly accessible, so that, for example, the program can explain its own reasoning processes.

Davis and King have observed that the production system formalism is more appropriate for some domains than others, being particularly natural when the knowledge can be expressed as a more or less independent set of "recognize-act" pairs [Davis76b]. In particular, it might be natural to represent judgmental knowledge by a set of production rules, but unnatural to use the same mechanism to represent other relevant knowledge, such as taxonomic (subset/element) relations among objects in the domain.

This chapter describes a way to use semantic network representations in rule-based inference systems. This combination allows a designer to retain the desirable modularity of a rule-based approach, while permitting an explicit, structured description of the semantics of the problem domain. Since semantic nets are among the leading internal representations used in computational linguistics, their use should also simplify the development of a natural language interface between the system and its users.

The examples used throughout are drawn from a geological consultant system currently being developed at SRI. This system is intended to help geologists in evaluating the mineral potential of exploration sites. Our approach to designing the system has been influenced by various developments in artificial intelligence. Shortliffe's MYCIN program for diagnosing and treating bacterial infections has been the dominant influence, primarily through its use of production rules to represent judgmental knowledge, and its inclusion of formal mechanisms for handling uncertainty [Shortliffe73, 74, 76]. We share with Pople's INTERNIST (nee DIALOG) program an exploitation of taxonomic structures, a concern for the use of volunteered information (event- driven, bottom-up, forward-chaining, or antecedent reasoning), and a need for more flexible control strategies [Pople75]. There are also parallels between our work and that of Trigoboff, who has developed different but related methods for propagating measures of uncertainty through a semantic network [Trigoboff76]. Finally, we have been influenced by the generality and power of Hendrix's partitioned semantic networks [Hendrix75, 76b], and have employed such networks in our system.

The following sections present the basic principles behind our system. Section 2 briefly reviews the rudiments of partitioned semantic networks and shows how individual rules are represented. Section 3 describes our use of Bayesian procedures to propagate information through a network of rules. Section 4 describes our current implementation, and gives an example of the operation of the existing system.

Finally, Section 5 discusses a number of unresolved design issues, whose presence should forewarn the reader that the ideas presented are not yet fully mature.

## 2.0 PARTITIONED SEMANTIC NETWORKS

### 2.1 Background

We are using a semantic network formalism (proposed by Hendrix) that uses "partitions" as a way of grouping parts of the net into meaningful units [Hendrix75, 76b]. Partitioned semantic networks possess all of the expressive power of predicate calculus; quantification, implication, negation, disjunction, and conjunction are easily represented. As compared with most computer implementations of predicate calculus representations, however, semantic networks have the additional advantages of two-way indexing, direct set-subset-element representations, classification of variables according to type, and a capacity for representing modal statements. In this section we give a brief overview of partitioned semantic nets and how we use them.

### 2.2 Elements of Semantic Networks

A semantic network consists of nodes linked together by directed arcs. Two main types of nodes are distinguished: object nodes and relation nodes. These two types play roughly the same role as do terms and predicates, respectively, in the predicate calculus. For example, the statement "Entity-1 is composed of rhyolite," could be represented by the net structure shown in Fig. 1. Here the "composed-of" relation node has two arguments, entity and value. In this net, these arguments are filled by the object nodes ENTITY-1 and RHYOLITE, respectively. Arcs in the network are used to connect relation nodes to other nodes; they are labeled with the name of the argument they represent.

Some relations, such as set membership, are so common that as a shorthand they are represented by special arcs rather than by a configuration of relation nodes and arguments. The net structure shown in Fig. 2, with its "s" and "e" arcs, includes a representation of the statement "Galena is an element of the lead sulfides that is a subset of the sulfide minerals that is a subset of the minerals." Net structures of this sort are obviously useful in representing taxonomic hierarchies.

Each particular instance of a relation is an element of the set of all relations of that type. Thus, the net shown in Fig. 1 depicts just one

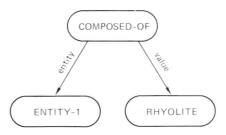

Fig. 1. Representation of the statement "Entity-1 is composed of rhyolite"

instance of all "composed-of" relations. If this particular instance were labeled C1, the resulting structure would be as shown in Fig. 3. The set of all "composed-of" relations forms a relation family. Our present system employs several types of relation families to express concepts such as composition, form, physical location, distance, and special properties. Each relation family is represented in the network by a structure called a "delineation" in which the types of the arguments are explicitly shown. For example, the delineation for the "composed-of" relation is shown in part in Fig. 4.

This structure shows our first use of partitions. The structure within the partition (box) delineates the "composed-of" relation. In particular, it shows that the "composed-of" relation has two arguments. One argument is an "entity" E drawn from the set PHYSICAL OBJECTS (of which ENTITY-1 is an example); the other argument is a "value" V drawn from the set MATERIALS. The partition serves to isolate the delineation, which is really like a definition, from other actual instances of relations in the network. Structures within a partition are treated specially and do not have the same "existential" character as unpartitioned nodes. In particular, we use nodes within partitions as variables that can be bound to constants outside the partition.

A complete network characterization of a large body of knowledge would interconnect many structures of the type mentioned. The simultaneous occurrence of several relation nodes in a partition represents their logical conjunction. Partitions are also used to isolate the components of disjunctions, implications, and negations. For details on these and related topics, such as quantification, see [Hendrix75, 76b].

## 2.3 Rules

Much judgmental knowledge about mineral exploration can be represented in the form of "rules" such as

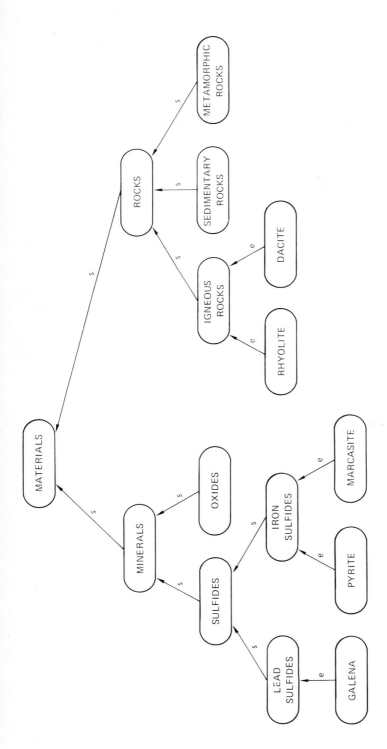

Fig. 2. A taxonomy of materials

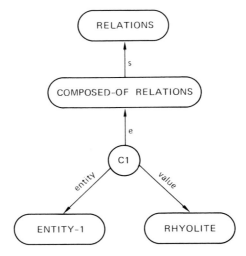

Fig. 3. C1 as an instance of a 'composed-of' relation

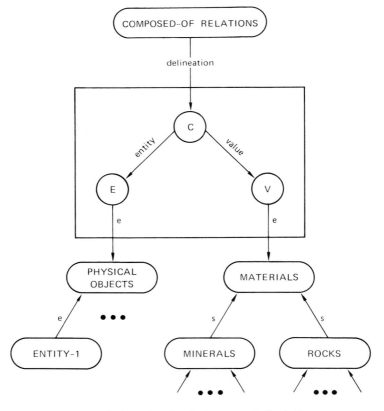

Fig. 4. Delineation for the 'composed-of' relation

"Limonite casts suggest the probable presence of pyrite"

or

"Barite overlying sulfides suggests the possible presence of a massive sulfide deposit."

These rules are in the form of simple implicational statements such as E1 & E2 & ... & EN => H, where the Ei are individual pieces of evidence and H is a hypothesis suggested by the evidence. Seldom can any of the implications be made with absolute certainty; usually the English versions of the rules contain phrases such as "strongly suggest" or "is mildly important for."

The representation of rules of this sort must specify the individual pieces of evidence, the hypothesis, the implication, and its strength. To represent the implication, separate partitions are created for the antecedent and the consequent. Each rule is represented by a structure having the form shown in Fig. 5. The individual partitions for antecedent and consequent contain the appropriate network structures. A property list attached to the rule node includes a measure of the strength of the implication. (This actually requires the specification of two numbers, as will be discussed in the next section.)

Using this formalism, the rule "Barite overlying sulfides suggests the possible presence of a massive sulfide deposit" is represented as shown in Fig. 6. A literal English statement of the antecedent might

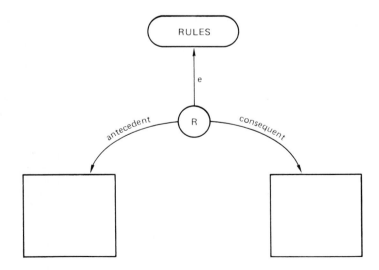

Fig. 5. General form of the representation of a rule

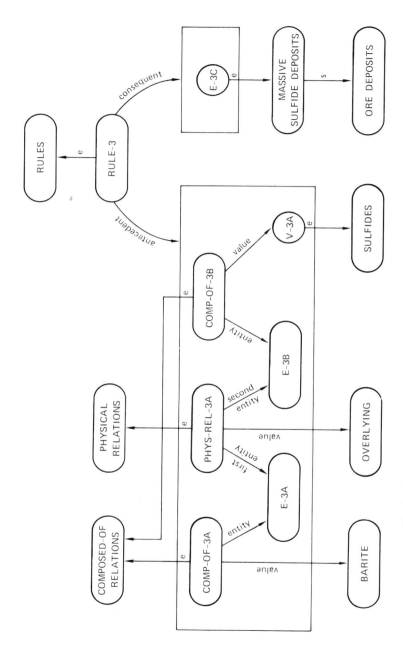

Fig. 6. Representation of the rule "barite overlying sulfides suggestes the possible presence of a massive sulfide deposit"

be something like "There is some entity, called E-3A internally, that participates in an overlying relation (PHYS-REL-3A) with some other entity, E-3B. Furthermore, E-3A is composed of barite, and E-3B is composed of some material, V-3A, that is a member of the sulfides." Note that the nodes for BARITE and SULFIDES lie outside of the partitions; these concepts "have existence" in their own right, independent of the example rule.

## 3.0 INFORMATION PROPAGATION IN INFERENCE NETWORKS

### 3.1 Inference Networks

The production rules used to represent judgmental knowledge typically are not independent, but are linked together in various ways to form what we call an inference network. Explicit links arise when the hypothesis (consequent) of one rule is the evidence (antecedent) for another. Several examples of this appear in Fig. 7, which is a simplified representation of 7 of the 34 rules currently used to draw conclusions about a possible Kuroko-type massive sulfide deposit. For example, the observation of bleached rocks would suggest the possibility of a reduction process (Rule 27), which in turn suggests the existence of clay minerals (Rule 28), which are often associated with a Kuroko-type massive sulfide deposit (Rule 24).

It is not necessary that all parts of a consequent and a related antecedent match. For example, rhyolite appears as part of the antecedent for Rule 14: "Galena, sphalerite, or chalcopyrite filled cracks in rhyolite or dacite is very suggestive of a massive sulfide deposit." Rules can also be linked implicitly through so-called e-s (element-subset) chains. For example, suppose that an entity composed of galena is observed. Since galena is an element of the set of lead sulfides, which in turn is a subset of the sulfide minerals, this observation is relevant to Rule 3: "Barite overlying sulfides is mildly suggestive of a massive sulfide deposit." Thus, information can propagate through the network in two ways, either directly through chained rules or indirectly through e-s chains.

### 3.2 Variables

In the general case, the links shown between rules in Fig. 7 should be viewed as potential rather than actual links. The object and relation nodes within any partition are variables and can be bound in various ways. Thus, for example, the particular entity composed of galena

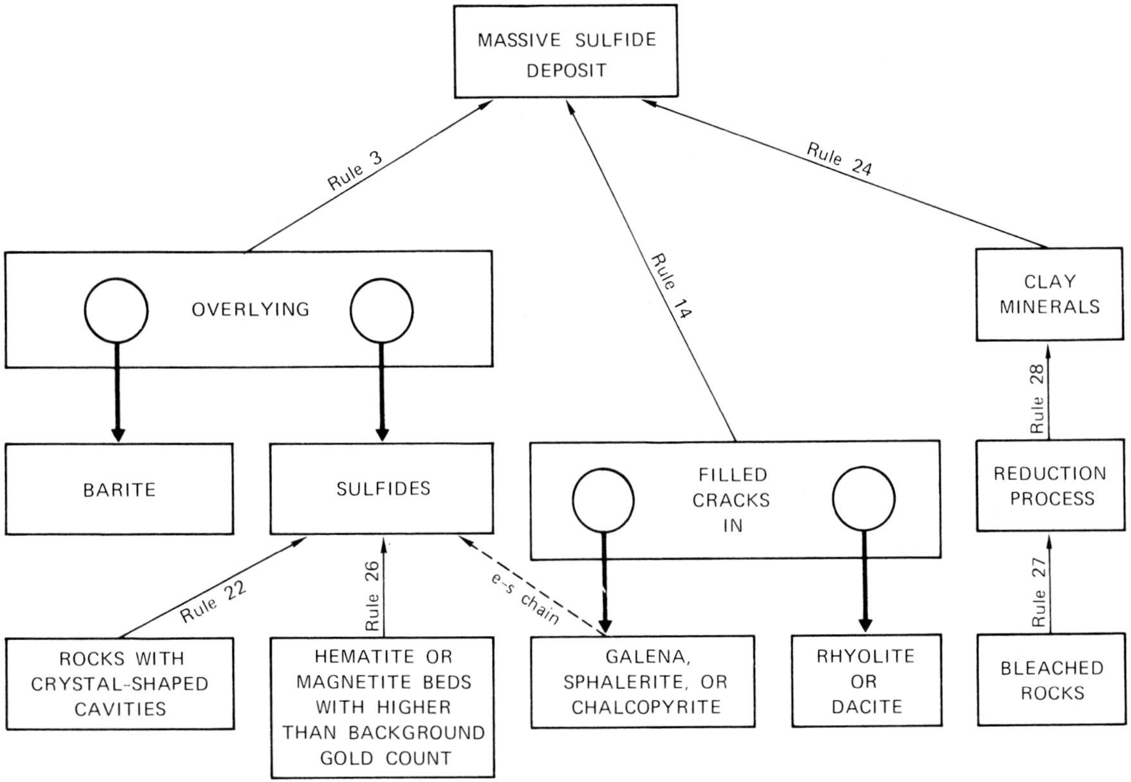

Fig. 7. Simplified representation of part of the massive sulfide deposit inference net

used in Rule 14 might be different from the physical entity composed of galena used to reach sulfides in Rule 3; one might satisfy one set of relations, the other another.

As a result, the rules cannot be linked statically, but must be connected by pattern matching at run time. While this situation is simplified by the fact that the potential matches are relatively few in number and can be precomputed, it still gives rise to a number of complications. As a temporary expedient, our current implementation tacitly assumes that any variable can be bound in only one way, so that, for example, only one entity composed of galena would be allowed. However, the representation used is general, permitting the unrestricted use of variables that ultimately will be needed.

## 3.3 Uncertainty

To account for uncertainty in both the evidence and the rules, we associate a subjective probability with every relation and a pair of strength values with every rule. Thus, rather than saying definitely that "Entity-1 is composed of rhyolite," we would say that "Entity-1 is composed of rhyolite with probability P1," and would associate P1 with the composed-of relation, rather than with the entity or the value. The interpretation is subjective, meaning that we interpret P1 as a measure of degree of belief rather than as the long-run relative frequency of occurrence [Fine73].

In general, the antecedent of a rule is a logical function of the relations involved. Rule 3 illustrates the typical case of logical conjunction; for the antecedent to be true, we must have an entity E-3A composed of barite, an entity E-3B composed of one of the sulfide minerals, and an overlying relation between E-3A and E-3B (see Fig. 6). To compute the probability of the antecedent we make recursive use of Zadeh's fuzzy-set formulas [Zadeh65]:

$$Pr(A \ \& \ B) = \min \ \{Pr(A), Pr(B)\}$$
$$Pr(A \ v \ B) = \max \ \{Pr(A), Pr(B)\}$$
$$Pr(\sim A) = 1 - Pr(A).$$

Given the probability associated with an antecedent, we use a form of Bayes' rule, modified to accommodate possible inconsistencies between subjectively determined probabilities, to determine the probability of the consequent. Unlike the mechanism used in MYCIN, this procedure does not require separate treatment of belief and disbelief, nor does it require the attainment of a given level of certainty before a rule can be used. Any time the probability of the antecedent changes, the rule can be "applied" again to update the probability of the consequent. This feature is particularly valuable if the user modifies previously given information, thereby forcing a reevaluation of the situation.

A derivation and justification for our procedure is given in [Duda76]; for completeness, we summarize the final results briefly. Let E denote the antecedent and H the consequent of a rule. Let O(E) be the prior odds on E, and let O(H) be the prior odds on H, where odds O are uniquely related to probabilities P by

$$O = \frac{P}{1 - P} .$$

Let E' denote all of the evidence we have for believing E to be true (or false). Through the rule, this evidence affects the posterior odds on H, O(H E'). Of all of the possible situations regarding our knowledge of the truth of E, three are particularly interesting: E known true, E known false, and E believed true with the prior probability P(E). The last case is trivial, in that it leaves the odds on H unchanged at O(H). For the other two cases, Bayes' rule yields

$$O(H|E) = \lambda \, O(H)$$

and

$$O(H|{\sim}E) = \bar{\lambda} \, O(H) .$$

Here $\lambda$ is the likelihood ratio for E true, and $\bar{\lambda}$ is the likelihood ratio for E false. We sometimes say that $\lambda$ measures the degree of sufficiency, since a very large value for $\lambda$ means that E is sufficient for H. Similarly, $\bar{\lambda}$ measures the degree of necessity, since a very small value for $\bar{\lambda}$ means that E is necessary for H. The values of $\lambda$ and $\bar{\lambda}$ taken together define the strength of the rule.

For the general case, let P(E|E') denote our present degree of belief in E based on E'. We compute P(H|E') as the piecewise-linear function of P(E|E') shown in Fig. 8, which amounts to interpolating linearly between the three special cases just described. This in turn defines the desired posterior odds O(H|E'), and an effective likelihood ratio $\lambda'$ defined by

$$\lambda' = \frac{O(H|E')}{O(H)} .$$

An effective likelihood ratio is associated with every rule. Unlike $\lambda$ and $\bar{\lambda}$, it varies in value as information is gained, starting initially at unity (indifference) and approaching either $\lambda$ if E is determined to be true, or $\bar{\lambda}$ if E is determined to be false. If several rules all bear on the same hypothesis, the effective likelihood ratio provides the mechanism for combining their effects. Assuming that the separate rules

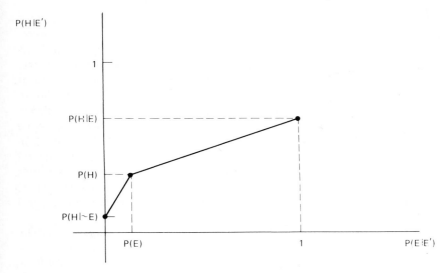

Fig. 8. The function used to determine the posterior probability of the consequent for a single rule

bear on H independently, we compute the posterior odds $O(H|E')$ by multiplying the prior odds $O(H)$ by the product of all of the incoming effective likelihood ratios. Repeated application of this computationally simple procedure allows the effects of the alteration of any probability to propagate through the network.

## 4.0 CURRENT IMPLEMENTATION

The current implementation of our system is called PROSPECTOR. It is coded in INTERLISP, and makes direct use of Hendrix and Slocum's semantic net package. In addition to providing the data structures described in Section 2, PROSPECTOR contains an executive program and facilities (or hooks for facilities) for the following tasks:

(1) accepting volunteered information
(2) propagating consequences
(3) determining needed information
(4) asking questions
(5) answering questions
(6) augmenting the knowledge base.

While some of these facilities are fairly sophisticated, the current implementation is still rather new, and little attention has been devoted to the important topic of handling English input and output. This means that the interactions involved in Topics 1, 4, and 5 are currently rather clumsy. In particular, to volunteer information to the current system, one must know the internal net representations and evaluate the appropriate LISP functions. A more convenient but still rudimentary question-answering facility based on Hendrix's LIFER package [Hendrix77] allows the user to use constrained English to ask certain kinds of questions about either the taxonomy or the rules. Answering questions posed by the system is straightforward, although even here no attempt has been made to have PROSPECTOR pose the questions in graceful English. Thus, the human engineering features so important for inexperienced users are currently minimal.

The main parts of PROSPECTOR are domain independent. Domain- specific information is kept in separate taxonomy and rule files. Special facilities are available for reading and writing taxonomy files, acquiring taxonomic information interactively, and constructing semantic net structure corresponding to a taxonomy. A formal description language has been designed for representing the rules in the rule files. Facilities are also available for reading and writing the rule files, and automatically constructing the corresponding semantic-net representations. The present rule base contains 34 rules for Kuroko- type massive sulfide deposits and 16 rules for Mississippi-Valley-type lead/zinc deposits. These rules have been entered manually, although we have experimented with and recognize the ultimate usefulness of automatic rule acquisition [Davis76a].

Whenever new information is entered, the procedures described in Section 3 are used to propagate the consequences. In particular, this will usually affect the probabilities associated with certain "top- level" nodes that correspond to important hypotheses. After the user has finished volunteering information and propagation has terminated, the system must determine what additional information will be most effective in establishing the top-level hypotheses with greater certainty. This is the so-called control problem, and it raises many unsolved problems.

Our current strategy resembles the depth-first strategy used by MYCIN, with two important exceptions: we allow for volunteered information at any time, and we use a simple evaluation function for dynamic rule ordering. The hypothesis selected initially is the top-level hypothesis having the highest current probability. Every untried rule having that hypothesis as a consequent is scored according to the function

$$|\log \frac{\lambda}{\lambda'}|P(E|E') + |\log \frac{\lambda'}{\lambda}|[1-P(E|E')].$$

and the highest scoring rule is selected. If its antecedent is askable (and has not been asked about before), the user is asked about it. If the user can provide even a partial answer, those results are propagated and the rules are rescored. However, if the antecedent is not askable, or if the user has no information to offer, that antecedent becomes the new hypothesis, and the same procedure is applied recursively.

The particular scoring function used computes the expected change in $|\log O(H|E')|$ under the assumption that E will be found to be true with probability $P(E|E')$ or false with probability $1 - P(E|E')$. When E is unlikely a priori, this criterion initially favors rules with small values of $\overline{\lambda}$ (necessary conditions), and as E becomes more likely it favors rules with large values of $\lambda$ (sufficient conditions). However, low scores are assigned if the truth or falsity of E becomes well established, so that there is little to gain in trying to make knowledge about the antecedent more certain.

The following example, edited for the sake of brevity, illustrates the operation of the present system. The interaction was designed to display the various aspects of the program, including favorable and unfavorable evidence, linked rules, subquestions, etc., and does not correspond to an actual exploration problem.

———————————————— START ————————————————

PROSPECTOR, an experimental computer-based consulting system, is designed for use both in searching for ore deposits and in evaluating the mineral potential of large geographic areas. Being in the early research stages, PROSPECTOR knows only one exploration model, specifically, Park's model for Kuroko-type massive sulfide deposits.

In using PROSPECTOR, you will be asked questions, or you may volunteer information about a particular mineral prospect. The program will use your information and the rules it contains to draw conclusions about possible ore deposits on the prospect.

Indicate your answers as follows:

  2 — VIRTUALLY CERTAINLY PRESENT
  1 — PROBABLY PRESENT
  0 — NO OPINION ONE WAY OR THE OTHER
−1— PROBABLY ABSENT
−2— VIRTUALLY CERTAINLY ABSENT

————————————Program execution is now starting————————————

Do you want to volunteer any evidence? YES

  A. Space name of evidence: SPACE-25L
      New likelihood of (Widespread Igneous Rocks) : 2
  B. Space name of evidence: NIL

Proceeding to establish the likelihood of (Massive Sulfide Deposit):

1. Do you have anything to say about (Volcanic province and major fault zone) ? 1
2. Do you have anything to say about (Mineralization) ? 0
3. Do you have anything to say about (Near shore depositional sequences of andesites, rhyolites, or dacites) ? 0
4. Do you have anything to say about (Pillow structures) ? 2
5. Do you have anything to say about (Breccia) ? NO
6. Do you have anything to say about (Rhyolite or dacite plug) ? YES
6a. Have you anything to say about an entity with the composition of (OR RHYOLITE DACITE) ? 1

This entity will hereafter be referred to as ENTITY-1

6b. Have you anything to say about whether ENTITY-1 has the form of PLUG ? 2
7. Do you have anything to say about (Galena, sphalerite, or chalcopyrite filled cracks in rhyolite or dacite) ? YES
7a. Have you anything to say about an entity with the composition of (OR GALENA SPHALERITE CHALCOPYRITE) ? 2

This entity will hereafter be referred to as ENTITY-2

7b. Have you anything to say about whether ENTITY-1 has the property of CONTAINING-CRACKS ? 2
7c. Have you anything to say about whether ENTITY-2 is CONTAINED-IN ENTITY-1 ? 1

.
.
.

10. Do you have anything to say about (Olivine or alkaline andesite) ? 2
11. Do you have anything to say about (Calc-alkaline andesite) ? NO

.
.
.

14. Do you have anything to say about (Clay Minerals) ? 0
15. Do you have anything to say about (Reduction process) ? 0
16. Do you have anything to say about (Bleaching of rocks) ? YES
16a. Have you anything to say about an entity with the composition of ROCKS ? 2

This entity will hereafter be referred to as ENTITY-4

16b. Have you anything to say about whether ENTITY-4 has the property of BLEACHED ? 1

.
.
.

22. Do you have anything to say about (Prospect within a few miles of known MSD) ? NO

In summary, the following have been observed:

The most likely deposit type is (Massive Sulfide Deposit) Its current probability is 0.01465

The most encouraging observations were: (Galena, sphalerite, or chalcopyrite filled cracks in rhyolite or dacite) and (Rhyolite or dacite plug)

The only discouraging observation was: (Olivine or alkaline andesite)

The most useful additional information would be: (Mineralization) and (Breccia)

———————————————— DONE ————————————————

This example represents a typical interaction between the current program and a user. After the initial description and instructions have been given, the system permits the user to input relevant knowledge he may wish the program to use. Since language understanding is absent, internal names must be used. In this run, the user asserts the existence of widespread igneous rocks by knowing that SPACE-25L represents this concept; the system responds with an appropriate translation, and then accepts the probability assignment.

After the volunteered evidence phase, the system's control strategy selects the most likely top-level hypothesis, scores all incoming rules, and selects the highest scoring rule in order to obtain evidence about the hypothesis. Questions 1, 2, 3, 5, 6, 7, 10, 11, 14, and 22 all represent rules that give evidence for the top-level hypothesis. Questions 4, 15, and 16 represent rules at a deeper level in the net. Questions 6a, 6b, 7a, 7b, 7c, 16a, and 16b are subquestions that establish the likelihoods of the different relations that make up an antecedent.

The user has a variety of possible responses to any question. A YES answer causes the system to pursue the question further, whereas a NO answer terminates interest in that evidence. The answer 0 indicates "no opinion" or "don't know," and causes the system to pursue the question if it has deeper rules that can be used to infer the desired evidence. A nonzero numerical answer is used directly to assign probabilities and to propagate inferences through the net.

The propagations are not shown in the example, but each nonzero numerical response triggered a propagation, many of which had an effect on the likelihood of the top hypothesis. The sequence of changes to the probability value of the top hypothesis was $0.001 \to 0.003985 \to 0.004312 \to 0.03241 \to 0.711 \to 0.002968 \to 0.01465$. In particular, the response to Question 7 was highly favorable, while the response to Question 10 was highly unfavorable for a Kuroko-type massive sulfide deposit. The final summary represents a simple evaluation of the session, and is based entirely on the final $\lambda'$ values for the rules.

## 5.0 DISCUSSION

As the example of the preceding section showed, we have made some progress in developing a system that both represents and uses judgmental knowledge about a specific problem domain. Most of the remaining technical problems are shared with other production-system approaches to consultant systems, and the most important of these problems deserve at least brief mention.

A major problem concerns the acceptance of volunteered information, which could ultimately include diagrams and maps as well as text. Our present procedure, which requires the user to know the internal naming conventions, is obviously a temporary expedient, while the use of unrestricted natural language is not technically feasible. Our decision to use semantic net representations was at least partly motivated by the hope for fairly flexible English input/output, but the development of such an interface is a major unfinished task.

A second major research area concerns control strategies. Any attempt to determine strategies that are optimal in a decision-theoretic sense is probably computationally infeasible, particularly when the networks are large and when unrestricted use of variables is allowed. Pople's ideas on focusing are very attractive here [Pople75], and further work along these lines is needed.

Another important part of any consultant program is the explanation system. As MYCIN has demonstrated, quite informative explanations of conclusions can be produced merely by doing a "back-trace" of the applied rules. However, the rules themselves are often the consequence of more fundamental considerations (such as the effects of certain underlying ore genesis processes in our geology example), and are not always satisfactory as explanations. Kulikowski's work on causal networks is evidently relevant in this regard [Kulikowski72], and the intermixed use of procedural and declarative models is a natural and intriguing extension of this kind of work.

The use of production rules to encode the judgmental knowledge and the use of partitioned semantic networks to represent the structured knowledge about a domain provide a general and potentially powerful framework for building a consultant system. This combination has clear advantages and has provided us with what we consider to be a strong base for further development.

## ACKNOWLEDGMENTS

We would like to thank Dr. Charles F. Park, Jr., and Dr. Alan N. Campbell, who were the source of the specific rules in our current system, and who played a major role in helping us translate geological concepts into computer representations. In addition, we want to acknowledge Dr. Gary Hendrix and Mr. Rene Reboh for their help in the system implementation.

# PLANNING TECHNIQUES FOR RULE SELECTION IN DEDUCTIVE QUESTION-ANSWERING

Philip Klahr
*System Development Corporation*

*Deductive planning techniques are described for rule selection in question-answering systems. Rules typically represent inferential knowledge applicable to a given domain of discourse. Given a question-answering system containing a large number of such rules, a crucial problem arises in selecting those rules that are relevant and needed to answer particular input queries. A planning process has been implemented to find chains of rules that deductively infer the desired conclusions. The processes of forward chaining from assumptions and backward chaining from goals are combined to form middle-term chains, which provide the basis of the planning mechanism. The applicability and generality of these techniques for use in other rule-based systems is also discussed.*

## 1.0 INTRODUCTION

An increasingly important problem in rule-based inference systems is one of selecting rules that are relevant to answer a user's input query or to solve a particular problem. This rule-selection problem becomes crucial in systems containing a large number of such rules. Given a query that needs deductive support, i.e., a query that cannot be answered by direct retrieval from the file of specific facts, the system must find its way among the potentially large set of general statements (rule-based knowledge) and discover a subset that is relevant and sufficient to answer the given query. Without significant guidance and direction, the system may get hopelessly lost in generating irrelevant inferences. New planning techniques have been de-

*223*

signed and implemented for selecting relevant rules. Although the techniques have been developed, and will be discussed, within the framework of a question-answering system [Kellogg76, P. Klahr75], they should be applicable to other systems that use rules as the basis for inferring and deducing new or implicit knowledge.

Early work in question-answering used special-purpose deductive mechanisms. The most common was the set-inclusion logic of SIR [Raphael64], CONVERSE [Kellogg71], and SYNTHEX [Schwarz70]. With the development of the "resolution principle" in mechanized theorem-proving [Robinson65], several researchers have incorporated resolution techniques into question-answering systems for purposes of more general-purpose (domain-independent) deduction. Most notable among these was the system developed by Green [Green69]. But problems with explosive search space, even for small numbers of axioms and theorems, and with canonical forms that are difficult for users to comprehend, have led many researchers to find alternative representations and deductive techniques. Even with the various resolution strategies that have been developed (Chang and Lee [Chang73] discuss most of these), very few current systems use resolution as a basis for question answering (the Maryland system [Minker73] being a notable exception).

As an alternative to resolution, the use of more "natural" deduction techniques have become common in question-answering, problem-solving, and even theorem-proving systems. Such techniques usually involve the use of goal-oriented backward chaining or subgoal generation as a basis for deduction. Given an input query or goal, rules whose consequents match the goal are invoked, and the antecedents of the rules are set up as subgoals. The process repeats recursively. Such backward-chaining techniques are found in several rule-based systems, e.g., in production systems such as MYCIN [Davis77d] and RITA [R.H. Anderson76b]; in PLANNER-like language systems [Hewitt71, D. G. Bobrow74] where rules are in the form of procedures; and in several theorem-proving systems [Bledsoe72, Nevins74, Reiter73]. Rule selection in these systems ranges from an emphasis on user interaction in choosing rules [Bledsoe74], to having an ordered recommendation list of rules to apply [Hewitt71], to picking up all applicable rules [Davis77d].

The process of backward-chaining proceeds in one direction, backward from a goal. In many cases, backward-chaining will lead to dead ends, i.e., subgoals that cannot be deduced, found in the data base, or supplied by the user. As backward-chaining proceeds, rules are applied if their consequents match the desired goal. Substitutions for variables in the rules occur during the matching process and are passed on to variables in rules selected for further backward-chaining.

This process thus verifies the consistency of the variable substitutions in the course of selecting and applying rules. But the effort expended in this verification is wasted for those cases where chaining leads to dead ends. The planning mechanism discussed below separates the selection process from the verification process. Verification (consistency of substitutions) is delayed until a set of rules has been selected as being relevant to the particular problem, thus avoiding the verification of many fruitless deductive paths.

The approach to rule selection taken here is one of generating derivation plans, or proof skeletons, representing possible deductions needed to answer queries. The planning process combines backward-chaining from goals with forward-chaining from assumptions to form deductive chains through the rules. The generation of these resultant "middle-term" chains is the basic mechanism used for rule selection. In generating middle-term chains, the system is aware of the deductive interactions among the rules but it is not concerned with the verification of variable substitutions within chains or proof plans. Such verification occurs after proof planning. This chapter focuses on defining middle-term chaining and showing how it is used in proof planning.

## 2.0 ORGANIZATION AND REPRESENTATION OF KNOWLEDGE

Within our knowledge base, we will distinguish between facts and rules. Facts are represented in a relational format, i.e., a relation (predicate) followed by its arguments. Examples of facts are GREEK(-Socrates), ATTEND(Smith,ACM76), CONDUCTS-RESEARCH-AT(Jones,MIT). Rules are general statements that the system uses to deduce new or implicit knowledge.They are in the form of implications. The left-hand side of a rule represents the set of assumptions or conditions of the rule, while the right-hand side represents the set of goals or actions of the rule. Conjunctions, disjunctions, and negations can occur on either side of the implication. An example rule is &(ATTEND(x,z), ATTEND(y,z)) ⊃ SCIENTIFIC-CONTACT(x,y), which states that if two scientists (x and y) attend the same conference (z) then scientific contact can occur between them. All variables occurring in rules in this chapter will be considered universally quantified (with optional domain class restrictions, e.g., scientists, conference). For the use of rules containing existentially quantified variables, see Klahr [P. Klahr75].

The primary motivation for distinguishing rules and facts is that the deductive processor operates on the rules, while a data management system accesses and retrieves facts. This organization is in sharp contrast to most resolution-based systems, which combine rules (axioms and theorems) and facts into a single file. The distinction between rules and facts being made here is similar to the separation of rules and data base found in typical production systems [Davis76b]. However, the control structure and the interface between rules and data base is more constrained in our system. We are concerned with domains containing large numbers of rules and facts. Our primary focus is on developing techniques for locating relevant rules within our deductive processor. The problem of searching over a large file of facts is also a significant problem, but it is not one we are addressing here. The data management system we have written is satisfactory for use in our initial experimentation, but we are seeking to interface the deductive system with a more sophisticated data management system for retrieval over much larger files of specific facts. We want this interface to be efficient and infrequent and to be used only when facts are needed in a proof. The last example presented here involves such an interface.

## 3.0 DEDUCTIVE INTERACTIONS

Before describing middle-term chains and proof planning, we will first show some simple examples of the use of rules in deduction. Figure 1a shows that if we know or assume some proposition A and if we have a rule that states that A implies B, then we can infer B. Figure 1b shows that we can deduce that Joe is a human, given that he is a man and that all men are human. This deduction requires the substitution of "Joe" for the variable x. This substitution is found by a pattern matcher that operates on the argument strings of the relation being considered. We will refer to a successful pattern match as a "unification" (after Robinson [Robinson65]). Unifications represent deductive interactions and are shown as vertical lines in Fig. 1 and in subsequent figures.

In Fig. 1c, two rules are needed to deduce that Joe is a mammal. The two rules deductively interact through a unification between the two occurrences of the predicate HUMAN. Note the consistency of the variable substitutions in the three unifications: The variable x must equal Joe; the variable y must equal x; and y must equal Joe. We will later see how these variable substitutions are combined and used in proof-plan verification. Note also the structural pattern in Fig. 1c, a unification followed by an implication, followed by a unification, etc., forming a deductive implication chain between MAN(Joe) and MAMMAL(Joe) through the two given rules.

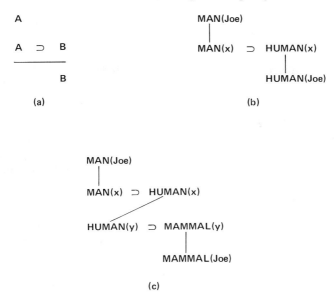

Fig. 1. Simple examples of rule-based deduction.

## 4.0 MIDDLE-TERM CHAINS

Consider the example in Fig. 2. For purposes of simplicity, only predicate names are shown in the query and in the rules. The argument strings of the predicates have been suppressed. The input query is broken down into the assumption A and the goal D. Suppose the three given rules are known to the system. The subscript attached to each predicate serves to identify the rule number in which the predicate occurs. Suppose that unifications exist between the two occurrences of B and between the two occurrences of C. Suppose, further, that unifications exist between the assumption A and the occurrence of A in rule 1, i.e., $A_1$, and between the goal D and $D_3$. Then we have the middle-term chain shown in Fig. 2. $A_1$, which unifies with the assumption, implies $B_1$, which in turn unifies with $B_2$, which implies $C_2$, etc. The relations B and C are *middle-term predicates*, i.e., relations needed to deductively link the assumption to the goal. The predicate occurrences $B_1$, $B_2$, $C_2$, and $C_3$ are middle-term predicate occurrences. $A_1$ and $D_3$, the chain endpoints, are occurrences of the assumption and the goal, respectively.

The proof plan involving this middle-term chain is also shown in Fig. 2. The plan becomes a completed proof if the variable substitutions involved in the unifications are consistent, i.e., no variable takes

Query:     $A \supset D$

Assumption:    A

Goal:    D

Rules:

(1)    $A_1 \supset B_1$

(2)    $B_2 \supset C_2$

(3)    $C_3 \supset D_3$

Middle-Term Chain:

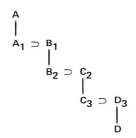

Proof Plan:

Fig. 2. Middle-term chaining.

on two different constants as its value. Plan verification will be shown in later examples.

## 5.0 PREDICATE CONNECTION GRAPH

In generating middle-term chains, the system uses a net structure called the *predicate connection graph*. This graph is an abstraction of the rules known to the system. It contains information about the deductive interactions among the rules and the implications within the rules. As rules are entered into the system, unifications between them and the other rules are precomputed and stored. The existence of unifications is stored in a unifications array while the substitution lists associated with the unifications are stored in a variable-substitutions array. The chain-generation and proof-planning processes use the information about the existence of unifications but need not be concerned with the substitution lists required by the unifications. Once a global plan has been developed, the plan verifier will combine the substitution lists of the unifications in the plan and check for substitution consistency.

The predicate connection graph bears some resemblance to the graphs used in the proof procedures of several theorem-proving systems [Kowalski75, Shostak76, Sickel76]. The similarity lies mainly in representation, i.e., using a graph to represent deductive interactions. The primary difference is in the way the graph is used. Here the graph is used as a planning tool to generate possible deductive paths through the rules. The emphasis is on using the graph to locate potentially relevant rules from a large set. The graph does not, by itself, generate proofs, as it does in these other systems.

For the simple example in Fig. 2, we note that if assumption A and goal D were removed from the proof plan shown, the resulting structure would essentially be identical to the predicate connection graph that would exist for the three given rules. The chain-generation process finds deductive paths through this graph. For larger rule sets, a proof plan would typically be a small subset of the deductive interactions contained in the predicate connection graph.

It is important to summarize the use of the pattern matcher and the use of the substitution lists that result. First, the pattern matcher is invoked when a new rule is entered into the system. Unifications of the new rule with existing rules are determined and stored. Second, for a given input query, the pattern matcher determines possible chain initialization points, i.e., it finds predicate occurrences within the rules that unify with query assumptions and goals. And third, after proof planning, the substitution lists of the unifications in the plan are combined and verified. During proof planning the existence of unifications, as determined by the pattern matcher, is used, but the pattern matcher itself is not invoked.

Thus most of the work done by the pattern matcher occurs in a preprocessor for entering rules into the system and in proof-plan verification, which fills out the details of the proof. This is in contrast to most resolution-based systems, production systems, and PLANNER-like systems, which continually verify substitutions in the course of finding a proof or answering a given query. Although the idea of suppressing details is not new (e.g., Newell *et al.* [Newell60]), very few systems use different stages of processing to operate on varying levels of detail. A notable exception is the work of Sacerdoti [Sacerdoti74, 75b], whose problem-solving systems show considerable promise in the use of global planning and the suppression of details for later processing.

## 6.0 FORWARD- AND BACKWARD-CHAINING

The middle-term chaining process can be visualized as one that generates expanding wave fronts forward from assumptions and backward from goals. The query assumptions are unified with occurrences of the same predicates in the rules. The successfully unified occurrences represent possible chain starting points. Similarly, those occurrences unifying with query goals represent possible chain endpoints. From then on the system uses the predicate connection graph exclusively to find implication links and unifications in each direction. In the forward direction, implication links from the unified assumption occurrences are extracted from the predicate connection graph. Then occurrences unifying with the implied occurrences are extracted, etc. The same process occurs backward from the goal occurrences. When an intersection occurs between the two wave fronts, the system has found a middle-term chain. (See Nilsson [Nilsson71] for a general discussion of graph-searching techniques and Pohl [Pohl71] for strategies in bidirectional graph searching and intersecting.)

Let us look at an example of how the chain in Fig. 2 was found for the given query from a larger set of rules. Suppose that in addition to the three rules shown in Fig. 2, the following rules also existed in the system: (4) $A_4 \supset E_4$, (5) $E_5 \supset F_5$, (6) $G_6 \supset H_6$, and (7) $H_7 \supset D_7$. Suppose also that unifications exist between $E_4$ and $E_5$, between $H_6$ and $H_7$, between $A_4$ and the query assumption A, and between $D_7$ and the query goal D. The predicate connection graph for the seven rules is shown in Fig. 3. Possible chain starting points are $A_1$ and $A_4$. Possible chain endpoints are $D_3$ and $D_7$. Forward-chaining from $A_1$ and $A_4$ yields $B_1$ and $E_4$. Unifications from $B_1$ and $E_4$ are $B_2$ and $E_5$. Implications from $B_2$ and $E_5$ are $C_2$ and $F_5$. Backward-chaining from $D_3$ and $D_7$ yields $C_3$ and $H_7$. Unifications from $C_3$ and $H_7$ are $C_2$ and $H_6$. There is now an intersection point between the two wave fronts at $C_2$. The resulting chain is $A_1$-$B_1$-$B_2$-$C_2$-$C_3$-$D_3$. In actual operation, forward- and backward-chaining proceed alternately one step at a time until a chain is found (or until effort limits have been exceeded). The chain found is the only one that exists for this example set of seven rules. Forward-chaining to $F_5$ is a dead end as is backward-chaining to $H_6$ (and further back to $G_6$).

Note that the chaining processes found in most other systems will verify as they proceed, i.e., substitutions for variables in the argument strings will be found and combined as the system proceeds from $A_1$ to $B_1$ to $B_2$, etc. Similarly they would also verify as they proceed from $A_4$

**Rules:**

(1) $A_1 \supset B_1$         (4) $A_4 \supset E_4$

(2) $B_2 \supset C_2$         (5) $E_5 \supset F_5$

(3) $C_3 \supset D_3$        (6) $G_6 \supset H_6$

                            (7) $H_7 \supset D_7$

**Predicate Connection Graph:**

**Middle-Term Chaining:**

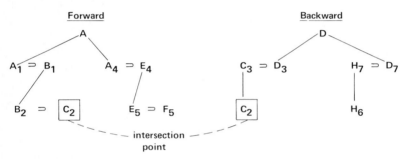

Fig. 3. Middle-term chaining through a larger rule set.

to $E_4$ to $E_5$ to $F_5$. Our system verifies only after a proof plan (in this case the single middle-term chain) has been found. The verification of dead ends in this example is avoided.

The process of chain generation is quite fast, owing largely to the representation and storage of information within the predicate connection graph. Each predicate occurrence in the rules is assigned a unique integer, e.g., $A_1$ is assigned 1, $B_1$ is 2, $B_2$ is 3, etc. The set of unifications out of a particular occurrence is given simply by a list of integers, those representing the unifying occurrences. The unifications are stored in an array indexed on the occurrence integers. Thus, to find the unifications existing out of the predicate occurrence whose assigned integer is 2, i.e., $B_1$, the system simply accesses the second element in the unifications array. A similar process occurs in the storage and retrieval of implication links occurring within rules.

These implications are stored in another special-purpose array. Thus, once chain initialization points are found, the system executes its forward- and backward-chaining by indexing into the two arrays.

The segmentation of information into different arrays has greatly facilitated the organization and processing efficiency of the system. The plan verification processor, for example, uses only the variable-substitutions array to retrieve the substitution lists of the unifications involved in a proof plan. Such segmentation will be of great importance when main memory cannot accommodate a very large set of rules. The various arrays can be swapped in and out of main memory along with the associated processor. In the current version of the deductive system, seven arrays are used. Implementation details are given in Klahr [P. Klahr75].

Even with such efficient storage and retrieval of deductive and implication information, the expanding wave fronts can become quite large, especially if there are a large number of deductive interactions among the rules. Three primary methods are used in reducing and ordering the implications and unifications picked up at any point in middle-term chaining. These include the use of semantic information, user-supplied advice, and plausibility measures.

The pattern matcher finds unifications between predicate occurrences by finding substitution lists that make the argument strings of the occurrences identical. While matching two argument strings, the pattern matcher also checks the domain classes of the variables and constants being matched. When rules or queries are entered into the system, the user can specify domain classes for any variables or constants involved. For example, he could specify the variable x as being a scientist, the variable y as being a politician, and the constant "Einstein" as being a scientist. Then the pattern matcher would allow the substitution of Einstein for x, but would not allow the substitution of Einstein for y nor the substitution of x for y, since they belong to different domains. Domain-class specifications can also include conjunctions, e.g., scientist and teacher; disjunctions, e.g., scientist or politician; and negations, e.g., not scientist. The use of such semantic domain types can greatly reduce the number of deductive interactions that exist among the rules as well as reduce the number of chain-initialization points for a given query.

We are currently expanding the use of domain types to include domain subsets and supersets. This would allow successful matches to occur between elements belonging to domains in which one domain is a subset of the other, e.g., between a variable that is a scientist and one that is a human.

The system also allows the user to supply advice to the system. Advice can be entered for a particular query or it can be stored in a more permanent advice file, which the system accesses for each goal.

The user can specify that particular predicates and rules be used in deductive chaining. The advice is transformed into predicate and rule alert lists (as well as negative alert lists for negative advice), which serve to order implications and unifications within middle-term chaining. In the case of advised predicates, the system attempts to find chains through occurrences of those predicates. For advised rules, the system tries to chain through them whenever possible. Unifications are ordered at each point in the chaining process so that unifications to advised rules are given priority. Ordering rules in this way is similar to the use of meta rules to order rule-selection in [Davis77d], although here it occurs in proof planning.

The use of advice gives a user much flexibility. If he can aid the system by specifying particular rules or predicates as being important, the system can take advantage of this. In addition, he can try to find alternative proofs using different advice to see if certain rules are appropriate or to get alternative derivations. In question-answering systems it is often useful to find alternative proofs to give more credence to the conclusion, particularly if rules have varying degrees of plausibility. The system does not necessarily stop with the first completed proof. At the user's request, it will continue to find alternative derivations with or without advice.

The final method used in ordering and selecting elements in middle-term chaining is through the use of plausibility measures. These measures are similar to the certainty factors used in MYCIN [Davis77d]. The plausibility of a rule represents the degree of certainty that the antecedents of the rule imply the consequents. Plausibilities can be reset by the user at any time. Unifications are ordered during chaining so that those associated with highly plausible rules are picked up first, although advised rules are given highest priority regardless of plausibility.

## 7.0 GENERATING AND VERIFYING PROOF PLANS

For each middle-term chain generated, the system extracts the rules containing the chain occurrences and determines if any subproblems result from the rules. In Fig. 4, the middle-term chain shown is the same as the one generated in Fig. 2. (Once again, argument strings have been suppressed.) However, the rules are more complex. In the first rule, both $E_1$ and $A_1$ are needed as conditions for inferring $B_1$. Thus $E_1$ is set up as a subproblem. In the second rule, $F_2$ is not a subproblem since $B_2$ infers $C_2$ independently of $F_2$. Similarly, $G_3$ is not a subproblem in the third rule. $H_3$, however, is a subproblem. To infer $D_3$ by this proof, we must show the negation of $H_3$ to be true.

$$A$$
$$\uparrow$$
$$\&(E_1, \; A_1) \supset B_1$$
$$\big|$$
$$B_2 \supset \&(C_2, \; F_2)$$
$$\big|$$
$$v(G_3, \; C_3) \supset v(D_3, \; H_3)$$
$$\big|$$
$$D$$

Fig. 4. Chaining through more complex rules.

Each subproblem is set up for either deductive support through the rules, for data-base support from the file of specific facts, or for computation. The latter occurs for predicates that are defined by user-supplied procedures. When such a predicate occurs as a subproblem, its corresponding procedure is executed to determine its truth value (e.g., predicates such as GREATER-THAN). The user can also specify that certain predicates be given data-base support. These would typically be predicates that are completely defined by the set of facts to which they apply, or predicates about which the user can supply the missing information. In the later case the system would output conditional answers, i.e., answers that can be concluded if the user can supply the remaining information. All other predicates occurring as subproblems are set up for deductive support to be obtained by recursive calls on the deductive system.

Let us look at more concrete examples. Consider the example shown in Fig. 5. The system needs to find a value for y, the place where Socrates lives, given the two assumptions. Suppose the system found the middle-term chain given by the occurrences involved in the unifications $u_1, u_2$, and $u_3$. The two rules shown state that if someone is the husband of another then they are married; and married people live in the same place. The resulting subproblem LIVES-IN($x_4, x_5$) is resolved directly from an assumption as shown by unification $u_4$. The resulting structure represents a plan and is not yet a proof, since we have not analyzed the variable substitutions in the plan. This is done by the plan verifier when there are no remaining deductive subproblems (although data-base and compute subproblems may still exist).

The plan verifier extracts the substitutions of the unifications in the plan and creates *variable-flow classes*. Each class specifies a list of elements, i.e., variables and constants, that must be equal for the proof to be logically valid. In the example, $x_1$ must equal Socrates from unification $u_1$. From $u_2$, it must also equal $x_3$, which in turn must equal Socrates from $u_3$. The variable-flow class (Socrates, $x_1$, $x_3$) is thus

Query:  &(HUSBAND(Socrates,Xanthippe), LIVES-IN(Xanthippe,Athens))

⊃ LIVES-IN(Socrates,y)

Assumptions:  HUSBAND(Socrates,Xanthippe), LIVES-IN(Xanthippe,Athens)

Goal:  LIVES-IN(Socrates,y)

Proof Plan:

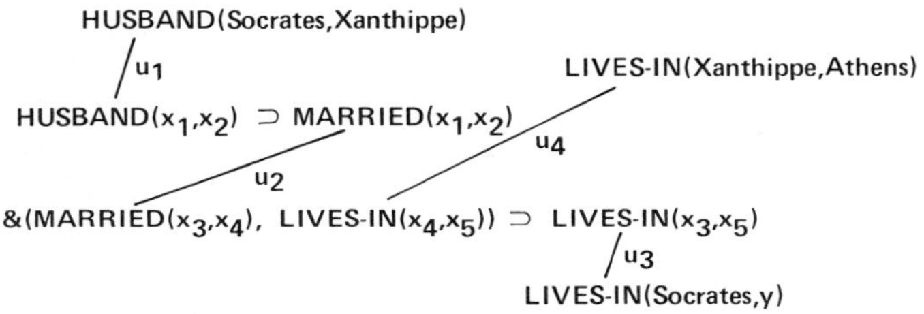

HUSBAND(Socrates,Xanthippe)

$u_1$

LIVES-IN(Xanthippe,Athens)

HUSBAND$(x_1,x_2)$ ⊃ MARRIED$(x_1,x_2)$

$u_4$

$u_2$

&(MARRIED$(x_3,x_4)$, LIVES-IN$(x_4,x_5)$) ⊃ LIVES-IN$(x_3,x_5)$

$u_3$

LIVES-IN(Socrates,y)

Variable-Flow Classes:    (Socrates, $x_1$, $x_3$)    (Xanthippe, $x_2$, $x_4$)

(Athens, $x_5$, y)

Data-Base Requests:  None

Answer:    y = Athens

Fig. 5. Deduction showing proof plan and variable-flow (verification) classes.

formed. Following another variable flow, we see that $x_2$ equals Xanthippe from $u_1$, and equals $x_4$ from $u_2$. The variable $x_4$ in turn equals Xanthippe from $u_4$. The resulting variable-flow class is (Xanthippe, $x_2$, $x_4$). Finally, if we follow the flow of y, we see that from $u_3$, y equals $x_5$, which in turn equals Athens from $u_4$, forming the class (Athens, $x_5$, y). Note that in each class there is at most one distinct constant. If any variable-flow class contains two different constants, the proof plan fails to verify. In this example, there are no substitution inconsistencies, and the plan successfully verifies.

Since the proof plan contains no remaining subproblems needing evaluation or data-base search, the plan is a complete proof. The system then outputs an answer. If variables were specified in the input query, values for these variables would be displayed. If no variables exist, the system would respond affirmatively if it found a successful derivation. In the example, the variable y occurs in the query. The system locates the variable-flow class in which y occurs. Since the constant "Athens" is in the same class, it becomes the value of y and the answer to the query.

Consider the example in Fig. 6. The query asks whether MIT knows about Newlisp, which was originated by Smith. The three rules used are concerned with knowledge transfer among scientists and laboratories: If the originator of a result has scientific (professional) contact with another scientist, the latter will know the result. Scientific contact between scientists can exist if they attend the same conference. If a scientist knows a certain result and conducts research at a particular laboratory, then the laboratory also knows the result.

The middle-term chain generated involves the unifications $u_1$, $u_2$, and $u_3$. Two subproblems are formed. The occurrence of CONDUCTS-RESEARCH-AT is to be given data-base support. This was specified previously by the user either because the data-base has considerable knowledge about the relation or because it can be easily determined or found by the user (e.g., knowledge about where researchers work).

The other subproblem involves SCIENTIFIC-CONTACT, which is to be given deductive support. The system was unable to find a middle-

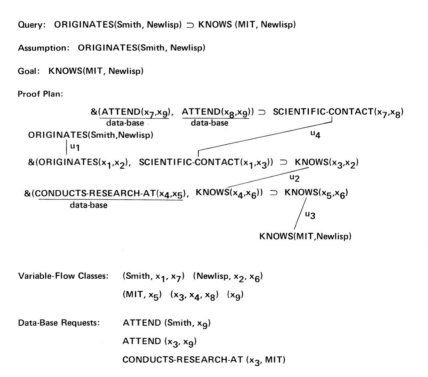

Fig. 6. Deduction requiring data-base facts.

term chain for this subgoal, and so it chained back to the rule shown via unification $u_4$. (Backward-chaining will occur whenever middle-term chains cannot be found between assumptions and goals or when no assumptions exist. In such cases, the middle-term chain generator defaults to using only backward-chaining. Techniques are being developed whereby the system can generate appropriate assumptions for goals when no assumptions exist so that middle-term chaining can be attempted. One such technique involves finding facts whose predicates apply to constants that occur in the goal, and using these predicates as assumptions [P. Klahr75].) Two more subproblems result, both requiring data-base support. The resulting proof plan has three subgoals to be resolved by data-base search.

The plan verifier forms the variable-flow classes. No conflicts occur, and the data-base subproblems are set up with respect to the classes. The subproblem ATTEND($x_7$,$x_9$) becomes ATTEND(Smith,$x_9$), since the constant "Smith" is in the same class as $x_7$. ATTEND($x_8$,$x_9$) becomes ATTEND($x_3$,$x_9$). In this case, the variable-flow class containing $x_8$ does not contain a constant. The variable is then replaced by the first member in its class. This is done so that all variables within the same class will be specified as being identical for data-base searching. Thus $x_3$ is also substituted for $x_4$ in CONDUCTS-RESEARCH-AT($x_4$,$x_5$), which becomes CONDUCTS-RESEARCH-AT($x_3$,MIT), MIT being substituted for $x_5$. Thus, the deductive system can conclude that MIT knows about Newlisp if there is a scientist who works at MIT and who also attended a conference that Smith attended.

The data-base search requests are then sent to a data management system (currently a relational data management system written in LISP by the author [P. Klahr75]), which attempts to find values for the open variables that would satisfy the subproblems. For example, if it found that Smith attended ACM76, which Jones also attended, and that Jones works at MIT, then the system would repond "yes" to the original query. If insufficient information about the subgoal relations existed in the data base, the system would output a conditional answer. In a sense, the deductive system can be used without any data base. All data-base search requests would be simply given to the user as remaining subproblems for him to resolve.

We can also use the example in Fig. 6 to show how variable and constant domain-class specifications can be used to reduce search space. For example, a user could specify that $x_1$, $x_3$, and $x_4$ are scientists. These variables occur in predicates concerned with scientists originating results, knowing results, working at laboratories, etc. Similarly, $x_5$ could be specified as being a laboratory, indicating that KNOWS($x_5$,$x_6$) refers to laboratories knowing results. In the query, MIT could be typed as a laboratory. The pattern matcher will check domain-class compatibility when finding deductive interactions. Thus

MIT would match $x_5$, since they are of the same domain type, but would not match $x_3$. KNOWS(MIT,Newlisp) will thus unify with KNOWS($x_5,x_6$) but will not unify with KNOWS($x_3,x_2$), thereby reducing the number of potential unifications.

## 8.0 SUMMARY AND RESULTS

The main focus of the research described here has been on developing techniques to find relevant rules in deductive question answering. However, we feel that these techniques can be used in most rule-based systems, including those using production rules and those using rules in the form of predicate calculus implications. The processes of forward- and backward-chaining have been used in previous rule-based systems, but here they are combined to find middle-term chains that form the basis of a planning process designed primarily for rule selection. Middle-term chains are found through the use of a predicate connection graph that contains information about the existence of deductive interactions between rules and the existence of implications within rules. Middle-term chains are expanded into proof plans that are verified when there are no remaining subgoals that require deductive support. Remaining data-base subgoals are sent to a data management system for retrieval from the file of specific facts. Answer extraction is straightforward, given the variable-flow classes produced during plan verification and updated after data-base search (returned data-base values for variables are added to the variable-flow classes).

The primary features of the deductive system may be summarized as follows:

(1) Separation of rules and facts; deductive system operates on the rules while a data management system retrieves needed facts.

(2) Precomputation of deductive unifications between new rules and existing rules when rules are added to the system; efficient storage and retrieval of deductive information within a predicate connection graph.

(3) Process of middle-term chaining to find deductive paths through the rules. When there are no assumptions or when there are no goals, middle-term chaining defaults to backward- or forward-chaining, repetively.

(4) Separate processing phases for rule selection (planning using middle-term chains) and verification.

(5) Use of semantic domain classes to reduce search space.

(6) Use of user guidance about which rules or predicates may be appropriate.

The deductive planning system is implemented in LISP and is operational on an IBM 370/158. Our initial experimentation involves the use of about 30 rules containing approximately 40 deductive interactions. Results so far have been promising. Queries requiring the use of six or seven rules average about one second of processing time, which includes a call on the data management system to resolve about four data-base subgoals. A more comprehensive set of rules is being developed for more extensive testing. One of the problems in generating a large number of rules is that of knowledge acquisition and finding experts in particular knowledge domains to aid in the generation of appropriate and meaningful rules.

We are also concerned with computational comparisons with other deductive systems. But such comparisons are difficult to generate and obtain. Our system involves the generation and then validation of proof plans. This approach is in sharp contrast to most other deductive systems. There is a difference in emphasis. Our system attempts to find relevant rules before those rules are actually used (verified). Thus it would be difficult to compare our system with, for example, resolution techniques that have comparison measures such as number of clauses generated, proof level, etc., for an example set of queries. For a small number of rules, other deductive approaches may be more efficient, since rule selection may be less important. But as the number of rules increases, the problem of rule selection becomes more significant, and we feel certain that some form of planning must be done. We are encouraged by our progress and results, and feel that the planning techniques that we have developed hold considerable promise for rule-based deduction.

## ACKNOWLEDGMENTS

Much credit is due to my colleagues Charles Kellogg and Larry Travis, for their many suggestions and insights in the design and development of the deductive system. The research reported here has been supported in part by the Advanced Research Projects Agency of the Department of Defense and monitored by the Office of Naval Research under Contract N0014-76-C-0885.

# SOME EXTENSIONS OF A SYSTEM FOR INFERENCE ON PARTIAL INFORMATION[1]

Aravind K. Joshi
*University of Pennsylvania*

*Some extensions of a system for inference on partial information, which uses production rules, are described. Basically, the system consists of RULES, an active set of rules (a subset of potentially large set of rules), partially ordered by specificity, and FACTS, a small active set of facts (a subset of potentially large set of data base facts). The critical feature of the inference method is that only a partial match of the antecedent of a rule is needed. Some selected extensions of the system are presented. These concern some approaches to the problems of selecting from an ambiguous response and, more important- ly, transforming or dynamic clustering of FACTS and RULES. This latter problem is important because partial match is defined over the sets RULES and FACTS, and unless these sets are reasonably small, partial match can be an unmanageable operation. Several issues concerning the use of this infer- ence system in certain applications are also briefly discussed.*

## 1.0 INTRODUCTION

We will describe some extensions of a system for inference on partial information that uses production rules.[2] Basically, the system

[1] This work was partially supported by NSF Grant MCS 76-19466. I wish to thank Bill Dolson, Jerry Kaplan, and Ron Lee for many very profitable discussions with them. Bill Dolson has implemented the system (M.S. Thesis, University of Pennsylvania, March 1978).

[2] Some theoretical and design considerations are treated in [Rosenschein75a] and further details about the matching procedure used in the implemented system are described in [Rosenschein77b]. Stan Rosenschein has implemented the system in MTS-LISP. Some applications of an earlier implementation were described in [Joshi75]. The system has been used for exploring issues in inference, particularly those relating to decomposition of predicates into primitives, as well as other defined predicates other

consists of RULES, a small active set of rules (a subset of potentially large set of rules, LRULES), partially ordered by specificity, and FACTS, a small active set of facts (a subset of potentially large set of data base facts, LFACTS). The critical feature of the inference method is that only a partial match of the antecedent of a rule is needed. The other important features are easy implementation of "default" and "overide" and control of bottom-up and top-down inference by the form of the rules alone.

Except for some well-structured domains and aside from most logical systems, inference is never in the context of total information. In conversational situations, and in general, in the context of dynamic and interactive situations, at each stage of interaction, interpretations have to be made, accounting for all of the input. Hence, a flexible system for inference is essential. The problems of partial match and best match are central to such flexible inference systems. The inference system described in Section 2 structures the pattern space in a specific way, enabling us to set up internal (structural) criteria for best match. We shall illustrate the working of the system by several examples.

Several extensions of the inference system are under investigation.[3] We will present some selected extensions that have been implemented to varying degrees so far. In Section 3, we shall discuss some of the approaches to the problem of selecting from an ambiguous response (conflict resolution), which arises when two or more rules are selected by the matching criterion. In Section 4, we deal with the problem of synthesizing a multiple response, which arises when one rule is not adequate to cover FACTS, and two or more rules are required. In this case, often one is justified in not just instantiating the consequents of the selected rules, but rather instantiating a composite consequent. This issue is related to the capability of describing intermediate concepts. Flexible inference systems are appropriate for this purpose. Finally, in Section 5, we deal with the important question of transforming FACTS and RULES. We are interested here in investigating techniques for dynamically clustering facts and rules depending on the current FACTS and RULES. We shall be especially interested here in implicit transformations of FACTS and RULES, and not in explicit transformations achieved by the control or by the use of special symbols, as pointed out in [Davis76b], although such explicit

---

than those implicit in the primitive expressions to which they will be ultimately reduced [Joshi76]. Another application is in scene analysis, which is being carried out by Bajcsy and Sloan [Sloan77].

[3] Extensions of the system that involve extending the partial order to data types other than those described in Section 2, e.g., sets and sequences mutually embedded to any level as with QLISP data types, have been discussed also in [Rosenschein77b].

transformations will be always needed. The problem of transformations of FACTS and RULES is also important because partial match is defined on the sets FACTS and RULES, and unless these sets are reasonably small, partial match can be an unmanageable operation. In the concluding section (Section 6), we shall discuss briefly several issues concerning the use of this inference system in certain applications.

Although we have described a specific system and its extensions, it is useful to place such work in a larger framework of "the role of partial and best matches in knowledge systems" [F. Hayes-Roth77b]. Hayes-Roth has given an excellent discussion of the necessity of partial match and best match (i.e., inference on partial information). He has also examined several applications of partial match and best match schemes. His discussion of the principal characteristics of the partial matching problem appears to be particularly relevant to some of the basic ideas in our papers, especially those in Section 5.

## 2.0 DESCRIPTION OF THE INFERENCE SYSTEM

First we need some definitions.

LRULES: User defined, potentially large set of productions (rewrites).

RULES: A small subset of LRULES, which is *active* at any given time. The rewrite rules in RULES are partially ordered by specificity in a manner similar to LISP 70 [Tesler73]. RULES is the *current focus* of LRULES.

LFACTS: A potentially large data base of facts.

FACTS: A small subset of LFACTS, which is *active* at any given time. FACTS is the *current focus* of LFACTS.

Let CONS and VARS be sets of constants and variables (including predicate variables), respectively. The set of forms (FORMS) is defined as follows:

(1)  $A \in CONS \to A \in FORMS$; ( ) $\in FORMS$
(2)  $?X \in VARS \to ?X \in FORMS$
(3)  $A \in CONS \& F1, F2, \ldots Fn \in FORMS \to (A\ F1\ F2\ \ldots\ Fn) \in$ FORMS[4]
(4)  Nothing else.

---

[4] It is understood that A is a predicate constant with rank n, the number of arguments of A. Predicate variables appear only as arguments of a predicate constant and not as the leftmost element of a form. This definition of FORMS is restrictive, but it is adequate for our purpose.

*Examples 2.1*

(1)  (P A B) ;P,A,B are constants, P is a predicate constant.
(2)  (HIT JOHN BILL)
(3)  (P ?X ?Y)
(4)  (HIT ?X ?Y)
(5)  (WANT ?X (DO ?X ?P)) ;WANT has DO as an argument, ?P is a predicate variable.
(6)  (WANT JOHN (DO JOHN (BUY BOOK)))
(7)  (HIT JOHN/?X BILL/?Y) ;?X has been bound to JOHN and ?Y to BILL

LFACTS and FACTS are sets of forms. The productions or rewrite rules are defined as follows. Each rule is of the form

<antecedent> → <consequent>

where <antecedent> and <consequent> are lists (representing sets) of forms.[5] Rules in RULES are partially ordered by specificity. The antecedent may contain an item of the form (MUST <x>), or its abbreviated equivalent \$<x>. In this case, <x> is taken as necessary for the match to succeed. Otherwise, <x>'s absence on occasion may be overlooked by the inferencer, when the whole rule is a good approximation for FACTS, according to the inference rule described later.

For our present purpose we can briefly describe the partial ordering on RULES as follows. Rule Ri is equal to or less than rule Rj if and only if the antecedent of Ri (represented as a set of forms) is a subset of the antecedent of Rj (represented as a set of forms). Thus R1: (P Q R) → E1 is less than R2: (P Q R S) → E2, (R1 is the minimal of the two), but it is not comparable to R3: (P Q U V) → E3, since the antecedent of R1 is not a subset of the antecedent of R3 and vice versa. Further if Ri' is like Ri, except that some unbound variable in Ri is bound in Ri', then Ri' is less than Ri (Ri' is more specific than Ri); (P ?X B/?Y is less than (P ?X ?Y). (Some theoretical considerations of the ordering are described in [Rosenschein75a, 77b].)

The consequent of the rule may contain items of the form (EXEC <x>). In this case, <x> is evaluated for effect in LISP when the rule is invoked. EXEC is primarily used for calling INPUT and producing OUTPUT.

The symbol % in the consequent is an abbreviation for <antecedent>. Thus

(A B C) → (%D)

---

[5] These rules are similar to the relational productions of Vere [Vere77a].

is equivalent to

(A B C) → (A B C D)

*Examples 2.2*

(1)    ((P ?X ?Y)         ((P ?X ?Y)
       (Q ?Y ?Z))    →   (Q ?Y ?Z)
                               (R ?Z))

(2)    ((P ?X ?Y)         (%
       (Q ?Y ?Z)    →   (T ?Y ?Z))
       (S ?Z))

(3)    ((MUST(P ?X ?Y))   ((P ?X ?Y)
       (Q ?Y ?Z))    →   (Q ?Y ?Z)
                               (R ?Z))

(4)    ((BELIEVE ?X (ABLE ?Y (DO ?Y ?Z)))) →
       (%)

(5)    ((WANT ?X (DO ?Y ?P))
       (BELIEVE ?X (ABLE ?Y (DO ?Y ?P)))) →
       ( %
       (POSSIBLE (FUTURE
                  (REQUEST ?X ?Y (DO ?Y ?P))))))

(6)    ((ASK-WHETHER ?X ME ?P)
       (BELIEVE ?X ?P)) →
       ((RHETORICAL-QUESTION (ASK WHETHER ?X ME
            ?P))
       (BELIEVE ?X ?P)
       (EXEC (PRINT ' (YOU ALREADY KNOW THAT ?P))))

(7)    ((WANT ?X (DO ?Y ?P))
       (BELIEVE ?X (ABLE ?Y (DO ?Y ?P)))
       (ASK-WHETHER ?X ?Y (INTEND ?Y (DO ?Y ?P)))) →
       ( %
          (REQUEST ?X ?Y (DO ?Y ?P)))

The operation CLEAR can be used to clear either RULES or FACTS. The operations

(ADDRULE <antecedent> <consequent>)
(INPUT <expression>)

are used to add a rule or fact. The operation

(REWRITE)

transforms FACTS with respect to RULES in the following manner:

A subset $S \subseteq$ FACTS is *maximal* if S identifies one or more rules in RULES and for all $S' \subseteq$ FACTS and $S' \supset S$, $S'$ does not identify any rule in RULES. If FACTS is the only maximal subset then we choose the minimal rule that covers FACTS. Otherwise, for each maximal subset we find the minimal rule that covers the subset, i.e., no single rule was able to cover FACTS; we needed more than one rule to cover FACTS, one for each maximal subset. We will call this multiple response (see Examples 2.3). The result of the application of a rule (or rules) is (the union of) the instantiated consequent(s) of the rule(s) corresponding to the maximal subset(s). The set of these instantiated consequents become the new FACTS.[6] The critical feature of this inference system is that it is not necessary to match the left hand side of the rewrite rule in its entirety. With suitable variable bindings, the antecedent covers as much of the FACTS as possible, while (1) covering any item explicitly marked as necessary and (2) containing no more unneeded items than any other such cover that is comparable to it (in terms of the partial ordering on RULES).

The inference system can be represented by Fig. 1. In the usual production system [Davis76b], the productions are sequenced and the control determines how they will be used in matching. In our system, the control structure has been merged with the antecedent matcher to yield a matching criterion that depends on the *entire* rule set RULES, and not on one production only, i.e., *it depends on the entire set of antecedents and their interrelationships.* Such a criterion provides a sound basis for use of partial information in inference.

Note that after a rule is selected and applied, the set of instantiated consequents becomes the new FACTS. Thus some old facts may continue to be in the new FACTS, depending on the rule selected, but there will also be some new facts i.e., the inferred facts. (In Section 3, we will consider some other possibilities of transforming FACTS as well as RULES.)

*Examples 2.3.* In the first four examples, let us assume for simplicity that the forms have constants only.

*Example 2.3.1.* Let RULES be

R1:   $(P\ Q\ R\ S\ M) \rightarrow (P\ Q\ R\ S\ M\ U)$

R2:   $(P\ Q\ R\ S\ T\ G) \rightarrow (P\ Q\ R\ S\ T\ G\ V)$

---

[6] Ambiguous response is possible in both the single or the multiple-response case. Two different instantiations of the same rule can also cause ambiguous response. At present, one response is chosen at random. See Section 3 for some other approaches.

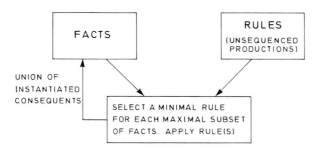

Fig. 1. Inference on partial information.

R3:    (P Q R) → (P Q R W)

If FACTS = (P Q) then antecedents of R1, R2, and R3 all cover FACTS. (P Q) is the only maximal set. R3 is minimal because it has the fewest unmatched items as compared to the other covers that are comparable to it, in terms of the partial order on RULES; this is so because (P Q R) is a subset of both (P Q R S M) and (P Q R S T G). Hence, we choose R3 and instantiate the consequent, so now FACTS = (P Q R W). Note that R was not matched, but since R3 has been selected, R has been instantiated also i.e., it has been inferred. W has been inferred also. (In this example there are no MUST forms).

*Example 2.3.2.* Let RULES be the same as before. If FACTS = (P Q M G) then there are two maximal sets, (P Q M) and (P Q G). R1 covers (P Q M) and R2 covers (P Q G). Hence, the result is the union of the instantiated consequents of R1 and R2, i.e.,

(P Q R S T G V M U)

Again, R, S, T have been instantiated, although not matched in the antecedent of R1 or R2.

(P Q R S T G V M U)

is the new FACTS.

Note that there is no nondeterminism here. One rule was unable to cover FACTS; hence, we needed more than one rule (in this case two).

*Example 2.3.3.* Suppose in R3 we make R a MUST predicate i.e., we have (instead of R3) R3′: (P Q (MUST R)) → (P Q R W).

Let FACTS = (P Q) as in Example 2.3.1. Now R3 will not be selected because R has not been matched. R1, and R2, are both minimal because they are noncomparable. At present, one will be chosen at random. Hence, the result will be either (P Q R S M U) or (P Q R S T G V).

*Example 2.3.4.* Let RULES be

R1:   (P Q L) → (P Q L U)
R2:   (P Q M) → (P Q M W)

If FACTS = (P Q), both R1 and R2 are minimal. At present, one of them will be picked at random. See Section 3 for some other approaches.

*Example 2.3.5.* In order to give a more detailed example using variable bindings, we will take RULES to be the set of rules 4 thru 7 in *Example 2.1:*

If FACTS =   ((WANT SAM (DO HARRY (WRITE HARRY
             PAPERS))
             (ASK-WHETHER SAM HARRY
             (INTEND HARRY (DO HARRY (WRITE
             HARRY PAPERS)))

then after REWRITE,

FACTS =   ((WANT SAM (DO HARRY (WRITE HARRY
          PAPERS)))
          (ASK-WHETHER SAM HARRY
             (INTEND HARRY (DO HARRY (WRITE
          HARRY PAPERS))))
             (BELIEVE SAM (ABLE HARRY (DO HARRY
          (WRITE HARRY PAPERS))))
             (REQUEST SAM HARRY (DO HARRY
          (WRITE HARRY PAPERS))))

Note that rule 7 was selected. The (BELIEVE . . .) antecedent was also instantiated and added to FACTS, thus completing a set of preconditions that was matched on partial information.

## 3.0 SELECTING FROM AN AMBIGUOUS RESPONSE

As we have seen in Section 2, sometimes we get an ambiguous response, i.e., we find that more than one rule in RULES is minimal. (Note that an ambiguous reponse must not be confused with multiple response, where we need more than one rule to cover FACTS because no single rule is able to cover the entire FACTS. Multiple response is simply a generalization of the case when only one minimal rule is adequate to cover FACTS.)

We must **now** select one rule from the set of responses. One simple approach is to select a rule from the ambiguous set at random. Other approaches have been described in [Davis76b]. Here, we will describe only two approaches, which are some of the extensions carried out so far.

## 3.1 Minimum Number of Unmatched Predicates

As described earlier, if two rules, which are comparable in terms of the partial order on RULES, cover FACTS, then the matching criterion will select the rule that has the minimum number of un-matched predicates. Hence, the set of rules in the ambiguous set must be noncomparable (see Example 2.3.3). We will now adopt the follow-ing criterion: select the rule from the ambiguous set that has the minimum number of unmatched predicates (i.e., we are extending the requirement of minimum number of unmatched predicates to the non-comparable rules also). Thus, in Example 2.3.3, we will select R1 over R2. This criterion assigns equal importance to all unmatched predi-cates.

## 3.2 Weighting of Rules

For each predicate in each rule in LRULES we will assign two types of weights (following an idea in [Pople75]). The first type of weight for a predicate (called the evoking weight, $e_\omega$) reflects the certainty with which the consequent can be inferred, if the predicate is matched (in the given rule). The second type of weight for a predi-cate (called the frequency weight $f_\omega$) reflects the certainty of finding this predicate, if we were to hypothesize the consequent.

*Example 3.2.1.*

$$( P \quad Q \quad R ) \to T$$
$$e_\omega \quad 0.9 \ 0.2 \ 0.5$$
$$f_\omega \quad 0.3 \ 0.6 \ 0.4 \quad \text{(The values of the weights are between 0 and 1.)}$$

Thus if P is matched, we are fairly confident of inferring T because its $e_\omega$ weight is high; however, if T is hypothesized, we may not necessari-ly find P because its $f_\omega$ weight is rather low.[7]

We now proceed as follows. For each rule in the ambiguous set, we calculate its weight in the following manner. We take all the predi-cates that are matched in the antecedent and have their $e_\omega$ weights make a positive contribution to the weight of the rule. For the un-matched predicates in the antecedent, we take their $f_\omega$ weights and have them make a negative contribution to the weight of the rule. The

---

[7] If a predicate is a MUST predicate as in Example 2.3.3, its $f_\omega$ weight is 1.

exact function for combining these weights is not important here, as long as it has the properties described above.

Thus, for example, if

Rk (P Q R) → (T)

is a rule in the ambiguous set, and if P and Q were matched (because P,Q $\in$ FACTS), but R was not, (because R $\notin$ FACTS), then the weight of Rk, W(Rk), is

W(Rk) = $\Phi$ (e$_\omega$(P),e$_\omega$(Q),f$_\omega$(R))

where $\Phi$ is appropriately defined.

We then select the rule with the largest weight (of course, we may still get two rules having the same weight!). This weighting facility is implemented so that it can be turned on if it is meaningful to assign weights of the kind discussed above; otherwise, it is turned off. The weights play no part in the matching criterion itself; the matching criterion is structural in the sense described in Section 2. Note that the e$_\omega$ and f$_\omega$ weights are assigned to the components of each rule *a priori*, but the weight of the rule is computed dynamically.


## 4.0 MODULATION OF PREDICATES

We now consider the case of a multiple response, which arises when one rule is not adequate to cover FACTS and two or more rules are needed. In this case, all these rule will be selected and the union of their consequents will be instantiated. In most cases, such multiple responses come from a set of rules that are interrelated and have a kind of *coherence*. Such sets are used in characterizing certain event types [Joshi76]. Each rule characterizes a specific event, while the entire set characterizes some event type.[8] Two rules in such a set are usually related not only in the sense of being members of the same set, but also by virtue of the fact that they share certain components. When responses belonging to such sets are instantiated, we proceed as follows.

*Example 4.1.* This is no doubt an impoverished example; however, it is adequate to illustrate the idea. Let E be WALKING and F RUNNING, two events in the space of locomotive (human) events. Let the predicates be defined as follows: P, change of location; Q, one foot on the ground at all times; R, speed less than some constant, say s; Q', both feet off the ground from time to time; R', speed greater than s.

---

[8] KRL [D.G. Bobrow77] allows for representations of different views of an event but does not seem to allow relations (transformations) among them.

R1: ((P?X) (Q ?X) (R ?X)) → ((WALKING ?X)) = E
R2: ((P ?X) (Q' ?X) (R' ?X)) → ((RUNNING ?X)) = F

Let FACTS = ((P JOHN) (Q JOHN) (R' JOHN)). Then the response is

((WALKING JOHN)(RUNNING JOHN)). We can now modulate E by F or F by E.

These two cases can be represented as

(F (E)) i.e., (RUNNING(WALKING JOHN))     (1)
(E(F)) i.e., (WALKING(RUNNING JOHN))     (2)

(1) can be paraphrased as *John is almost running* (or as *John is runningly walking*, if we had an adverb such as *runningly*) and (2) can be paraphrased as *John is almost walking* (or as *John is walkingly running*, if we had an adverb such as *walkingly*).

We thus can construct a composite consequent. We choose R1 (or R2) (the choice determined by contextual criteria) and then the response is (1) or (2). Thus *the form of the selected response will carry information about the alternate responses*. Language has the facility for carrying composite interpretations where one interpretation is favored but it is *modulated* by the other interpretations.[9] There is a variety of modulations and they appear to serve a number of functions. We have investigated this phenomenon and some of its generalizations within our system for inference on partial information, and these have been partially implemented.

## 5.0 TRANSFORMING FACTS AND RULES: DYNAMIC CLUSTERING

For given FACTS and RULES, the basic operation (SELECT-APPLY) consists of selecting a rule (according to the criterion described earlier) and applying it; the set of instantiated consequents becomes the new FACTS. Some old facts will continue to be in the new FACTS, but there will be also some new facts, i.e., the inferred facts. In this section, we consider some other possibilities of transforming FACTS and RULES.

When a rule is selected and applied the <EXEC> part of the rule can, of course, be used to bring out arbitrary sets of facts and rules from LFACTS and LRULES into FACTS and RULES, respectively. LFACTS and LRULES can be structured in certain ways (some gross classification being the simplest way) and this global structuring can be used by the <EXEC> part of the rule to determine the new FACTS

---

[9] This phenomenon appears to be related to hedging.

and RULES. We will call such transformations explicit. Some capability of explicit transformations will always be needed (and is indeed incorporated in varying degrees in the specific applications of the inference system); however, such transformations are not quite in the spirit of the approach taken in this section (and also not in the spirit of pure production systems). We are interested here in implicit transformations, which allow us to cluster *dynamically* rules and facts, depending on the current FACTS and RULES.

We shall briefly describe a transformation called *local context closure* (LCC) whose purpose is to minimally augment the given FACTS and RULES (using LFACTS and LRULES) such that all facts and rules that are "immediately relevant" are pulled together.[10] LCC is carried out prior to SELECT-APPLY. After a rule is selected and applied, explicit transformations may be carried out, if specified by the rule selected. We then apply LCC before the next SELECT-APPLY, etc.

## 5.1  Local Context Closure (LCC)

LCC can be viewed as a two-step operation. Given FACTS and RULES we shall augment RULES by adding to RULES, all rules in LRULES whose antecedents have one or more predicates that appear in FACTS. Let RULES' be the augmentation of RULES. We now augment FACTS to FACTS' by adding to FACTS, all facts in LFACTS that pertain to predicates appearing in the antecedents of rules in RULES'. We shall first give a somewhat more precise definition from which we can show that it is indeed a closure; further iterations would not contribute more "relevant" facts or rules. We shall then give a simple example to illustrate the idea.

A substitution $\theta$ is defined in the conventional sense; i.e.,

$$= \{A_i/?X_i \mid A_i \in \text{CONS} \cup \text{VARS}, ?X_i \in \text{VARS}\}.$$

Let LRULES/FACTS be a quotient operation with respect to a substitution $\theta$, defined as follows.

$$\text{LRULES/FACTS} = \{\alpha \mid ((\alpha \in \text{LRULES}) \land (\text{FACTS} \cap \alpha \, \theta \neq \phi))\}$$

Let LFACTS/RULES be a quotient operation with respect to a substitution $\theta$, such that FACTS $\subseteq$ RULES $\theta$ is defined as follows.

$$\text{LFACTS/RULES} = \{f \mid (\exists \alpha \in \text{RULES})((f \in \text{LFACTS}) \land (f \in \alpha \, \theta))\}$$

---

[10] This section has been revised considerably since the original version of the chapter was submitted. I have profited from some of the ideas of Bill Dolson, in particular, those concerning LCC. These and other related ideas are under investigation now; these results will be reported at a later date.

Hence,

$$\text{RULES}' = \text{RULES} \cup \text{LRULES/FACTS} \qquad (1)$$

and

$$\text{FACTS}' = \text{FACTS} \cup \text{LFACTS/RULES}' \qquad (2)$$

If we apply (1) again with FACTS', we obtain

$$
\begin{aligned}
\text{RULES}'' &= \text{RULES}' \cup \text{LRULES/FACTS}' \\
&= \text{RULES} \cup \text{LRULES/FACTS} \cup \\
&\quad \text{LRULES}/(\text{FACTS} \cup (\text{FACTS}'\text{-FACTS})) \\
&= \text{RULES} \cup \text{LRULES/FACTS} \cup \\
&\quad \text{LRULES}/(\text{FACTS}'\text{-FACTS})
\end{aligned}
$$

Now, SELECT-APPLY will never pick a rule from LRULES/(FACTS'-FACTS). This is so because a rule in LRULES/(FACTS'-FACTS) pertains to predicates that are in FACTS' but not in FACTS; thus for any $r_i \in$ LRULES/(FACTS'-FACTS), there is an $r_j \in$ LRULES/FACTS, such that $r_j$ will always cover more of FACTS than $r_i$, and hence $r_i$ will never be selected. Therefore,

$$\text{RULES}'' = \text{RULES} \cup \text{LRULES/FACTS} = \text{RULES}'$$

and obviously FACTS'' = FACTS'. The two-step operation (LCC) is thus a sort of closure that allows us to augment the local context minimally. We call it "local" because it is with respect to the current FACTS and RULES.

Fig. 2 diagramatically illustrates LCC.

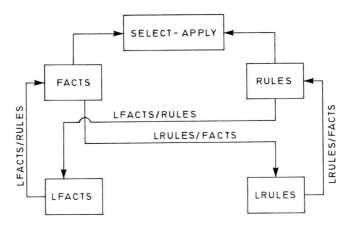

Fig. 2. Local context closure.

*Example 5.1.*

Let LRULES be

R1:     ((P ?X ?Y)        ((P ?X ?Y)
        (Q ?Y ?Z))   →   (Q ?Y ?Z)
                         (R ?X))

R2:     ((P ?X ?Y))       ((P X? ?Y)
        (Q ?Y ?Z)    →   (Q ?Y ?Z)
        (S ?Z))          (M ?X ?Y ?W))

R3:     ((M ?X ?Y ?W)     ((M ?X ?Y ?W)
        (N ?U)       →   (N ?U)
        (Q ?Y ?Z))       (Q ?Y ?Z)
                         (L ?W)

Let LFACTS be

((P A B)
 (S C)
 (N D)
 (M A B E))

Let FACTS be ((P A B)) and RULES be ( ). Then RULES' is

R1:     ((P ?X ?Y)        ((P ?X ?Y)
        (Q ?Y ?Z))   →   (Q ?Y ?Z)
                         (R ?X))

R2:     ((P ?X ?Y)        ((P ?X ?Y)
        (Q ?Y ?Z)    →   (Q ?Y ?Z)
        (S ?Z))          (M ?X ?Y ?W))

FACTS' is

((P A B)
 (S C))

The result of LCC is thus FACTS' and RULES'. It is clear that rule R2 will be selected and applied. Thus FACTS now becomes

((P A B)
 (Q B C)
 (M A B ?W))

LFACTS and LRULES will also be updated. Thus the new facts (Q B

C) and (M A B ?W) will be added to LFACTS, and LRULES will now
be not just {R1, R2, R3} but rather {R1, R2, R3, R1′, R2′, R3′},[11] where

R1′:   ((P A/?X B/?Y)          ((P A/?X B/?Y)
       (Q B/?Y C/?Z))    →     (Q B/?Y C/?Z)
                               (R A/?X))

R2′:   ((P A/?X B/?Y)          ((P A/?X B/?Y)
       (Q B/?Y C/?Z)     →     (Q B/?Y C/?Z)
       (S C/?Z))               (M A/?X B/?Y ?W))

R3′:   ((M A/?X B/?Y ?W)       ((M A/?X B/?Y ?W)
       (N ?U)            →     (N ?U)
       (Q B/?Y C ?Z)           (Q B/?Y C/?Z)
                               (L ?W))

This example illustrates LCC as well as how LFACTS and
LRULES have been transformed. There are several problems concerning the updating of LRULES and LFACTS with respect to the treatment of partially bound forms, consistency, etc., which we will not
discuss here. How to treat the facts in FACTS that were not used (in
our example, there were none) is another problem. At present, these
are removed from FACTS, but, of course, not from LFACTS.


## 6.0 CONCLUSIONS

We have described some extensions of a system for inference on
partial information. The extensions deal with conflict resolution, and
more importantly, with implicit transformations of current FACTS
and RULES prior to the SELECT-APPLY operation. Several related
issues were briefly discussed also.

Aside from most logical systems, inference is always in the context
of partial information. The necessity of partial match and best match
(i.e., inference on partial information) has been briefly discussed in
Section 1. Our work on inference on partial information has been
primarily motivated by the appropriateness of such schemes in the
context of dynamic, interactive, or conversational situations. At each
stage of interaction, interpretations have to be arrived at, while ac-

---

[11] Here, for ease of exposition, we have simply augmented the rule set by the
transformed rules. The implementation (by Bill Dolson) does not quite proceed in this
manner. Also, this feature appears to be related to [Rieger77d].

counting for all of the input. A flexible system for inference is therefore required.

We shall briefly describe some of the applications we have made so far and some that are under development at present.

(1) Applications to lexically motivated inferences, especially in the organization of lexicon of speech act verbs were carried out by Rosenschein [Rosenschein75a].

(2) In the conversational context, one is forced to "summarize" (for event interpretation and consequent lexicalization), while accounting for all of the input. This act of summarizing invariably forces the system (one of the participants) to imply more than what is in the input, i.e., to make inferences, or to put it more appropriately (in the conversational context), the system expects the hearer to make these extra inferences. The necessity of using lexical items for interpretation of events *r*equires summarizing by appropriate lexical items and hence inference on partial information. The ability to summarize as soon as possible, with the possibility of recognizing the need for unpacking the summaries and being able to do it, is useful in modeling certain conversational and question-answer situations. Such investigations were carried out in [Joshi76].

(3) This inference system has been also used in scene analysis systems [Bajcsy78, Sloan77]. Partially ordered world models have found usefulness in scene analysis.[12]. Hence, the present system turns out to be appropriate for this domain. In particular, in the interactive mode, simple *a priori* tagging of rules is not adequate. The facts and rules have to be dynamically clustered depending on the context (current state of the system) and the demand (determined by the visual interaction or the user interaction), [Bajcsy78]. Some of the transformations of FACTS and RULES provide such mechanisms.

(4) Since the system has been used both in the context of lexical inference and in scene analysis, we believe that it will serve as a natural interface for a question-answer system for a visual data base. Such work is currently in progress.[13]

(5) Inference on partial information is also relevant to question-answer systems for data bases. In particular, we are developing a system that will attempt to answer questions in an approximate manner in the following sense: For a question Q, if the system's answer A is somehow judged by the system as uninteresting or uninformative, the system will try to answer a question Q' (related to Q in a systematic manner) by an answer A'; A' is then an approximate response to Q.

---

[12] Earlier work in this context was carried out by Tidhar [Tidhar74].

[13] In collaboration with Ruzena Bajcsy, Charles Berg, and Dave Rosenthal.

Some features of the inference system described in this chapter (in particular, the notion of summarizing) are relevant to this work.[14]

Some suggestions for further research are as follows:

(1) **Integrated systems for inference on partial information with the formal deductive systems.** Such an integration will enable the incorporation of goal-directed behavior into a data directed system, which is a more natural domain for the type of inference system described here.

(2) Alternate schemes (analogous to LCC) for implicit transformations for dynamic clustering of facts and rules are worth exploring, especially from the point of view of defining schemes with interesting formal properties.

(3) Systematic ways of integrating explicit and implicit transformations should be investigated; these schemes will be useful in relating local and global structures of LFACTS and LRULES (see [F. Hayes-Roth77b]).

---

[14] In collaboration with Jerry Kaplan and Ron Lee.

# Learning

# EXEMPLARY PROGRAMMING IN RITA

D. A. Waterman
*The Rand Corporation*

*This chapter describes the development of a RITA agent for exemplary programming (EP). The EP agent learns new procedures for data manipulation and represents them as programs called "user agents." Both the EP agent and the programs it creates are written as sets of IF-THEN rules (production systems) in RITA: the rule-directed interactive transaction agent system. The programs produced by the EP agent act as personalized software designed to perform a variety of tasks for the user. Program creation is a cooperative effort between the user and the EP agent: the user illustrates what he wants done by performing a series of operations on the computer, and the agent watches and asks the user pertinent questions during the demonstration. The information thus gained is synthesized by the EP agent into a program or user agent for performing the given task.*

## 1.0 INTRODUCTION

Recent work on personal computer architecture [R.H. Anderson76b] has pointed out the usefulness of software tailored to the requirements of individual users. The idea is to provide users with a set of small, personalized programs, called *agents*, that can act either as interfaces to external operating systems or as assistants to perform useful but often mundane tasks for the user. Since the needs and demands of users are not static, these agents need to be easy to create and modify. Moreover, each user must be treated as a distinct individual and must be given a set of agents designed to facilitate his particular interactions. The problem is how to provide each user with software handcrafted especially for him. The approach proposed here is to provide a method by which users can create agents without having to worry about all the details of program creation and debug-

*261*

ging. This approach to the problem is called *exemplary programming* (EP), which means synthesizing programs from examples of traces of the activity one would like the program to perform. Here the examples are complete protocols of user-machine interactions, including all the input typed by the user and all elicited system responses. The protocols are generated by the user, with the help of another user familiar with the task to be accomplished. The user performs the operations he wants the agent to mimic, and by watching the user perform the task, a special EP agent creates a program (another agent) to perform the same task or generalized variants of it.

In this chapter a first attempt at developing an exemplary programming agent is described. The agent and the programs it creates are written in RITA, a production system programming language. These RITA programs are called *user* agents (or interactive transaction agents) and are particularly useful in man-machine interface applications. Typical uses of these agents include network accessing [Waterman77b], message handling [R.H. Anderson77a], reactive message creation, and tutoring functions [Waterman77a].

Section 2 describes the RITA architecture and its relation to other production system architectures. Section 3 discusses the design of user agents in the context of the exemplary programming task. Section 4 describes EP-1, an exemplary programming agent written in RITA, and concluding remarks are presented in Section 5.

## 2.0 RITA ARCHITECTURE

RITA is a specialized software system combining production system (PS) control structure with man-machine interface technology [R.H. Anderson76a, b]. The RITA architecture is interesting and useful for three reasons: first, the use of a PS control structure provides the degree of simplicity and modularity needed to organize and modify programs easily. Second, the system is human-engineered in the sense that the programs or user agents are composed of rules that have a restricted but English-like syntax making them easy to write and understand. As a result, the agents can be completely self-documenting. Finally, language primitives in RITA permit the user to interact with other computer systems, even to the extent of initiating and monitoring several jobs in parallel on external systems.

RITA is the embodiment of a particular PS architecture that makes it possible to create specific applications-oriented programs called agents. A PS is a collection of rules of the form *conditions* → *actions* [Newell72b, Davis76b, Waterman76b, Rosenschein77a], where the conditions are statements about the contents of one or more data bases and the actions may include procedures for altering the contents of the data bases. PS architectures have been developed to facilitate adaptive behavior [Waterman70, 75, 76a, B.G. Buchanan77, Vere77b], model human cognition and memory [Newell72b, 73, D. Klahr76], and study rule-based control structures in artificial intelligence tasks [Lenat77d, Rychener76, 77,]. These systems are predominantly left-hand side (LHS) or antecedent-driven, i.e., when all conditions in the antecedent of a rule are true with respect to the data base the rule "fires," causing the actions associated with the right-hand side or consequent to be executed.

Another type of PS architecture currently in use is based on a right-hand side (RHS) or consequent-driven[1] control structure [R. H. Anderson76a, Davis76a, Duda77, P. Klahr77, Shortliffe76]. When the system is given a condition to be inferred, it examines the RHSs of rules to find one that could make the desired condition true. If such a rule is found its LHS is examined to see if all conditions are true. If so, the rule is fired; if not, the process continues recursively in an attempt to make each condition in the LHS of the rule true.

The RITA architecture encompasses both LHS and RHS control schemes. It is possible to create user agents that are entirely LHS-driven, entirely RHS-driven, or some combination of both. The production rules accessed from the LHS are called RULES, those accessed from the RHS are called GOALS, and both operate on a data base composed of objects defined by attribute-value pairs. The control structure of RITA is based on the standard production system recognize-act cycle [Waterman77e]. The rules are *ordered*, i.e., the highest priority (topmost) rule with satisfied conditions is selected and executed during each cycle.

An example of a simple user agent composed of one RULE and one GOAL is shown in Fig. 1. When this agent is executed RULE 1 fires, because all three parts of its premise are true. Firing the rule results in the execution of its actions, in this case a DEDUCE and a SEND. When the DEDUCE is executed it initiates a deduction for "the type of the operating-system." This means that all goals are searched to find one whose actions modify "the type of the operating-system." Since GOAL 1 is applicable, it is used to deduce this information, and its premises are tested against the data base. Since the premises of GOAL 1 are true, the goal is fired and the attribute-value pair type = TENEX is added to the object "operating system<1>" in the data base. Finally the second action of RULE 1, the SEND, is executed and the sentence, "This is a TENEX system," is printed at the user's terminal.

The RITA system is patterned closely after MYCIN [Shortliffe76] and offers the user many of the same facilities as MYCIN. For exam-

---

[1] Also referred to as goal-driven or backward chaining.

## DATA BASE

OBJECT operating-system <1>:
        host-computer      IS  "PDP-10",
        prompt-character  IS  "@",
        net-address       IS  "sumex-aim";

OBJECT operating-system <2>:
        type             IS  "UNIX",
        host-computer      IS  "PDP-11",
        prompt-character  IS  "%",
        net-address       IS  "rand-unix";

## RULE SET

RULE 1:
    IF: THERE IS an operating-system
        WHOSE host-computer IS KNOWN
        AND WHOSE prompt-character IS KNOWN
        AND WHOSE type IS NOT KNOWN

    THEN: DEDUCE the type OF the operating-system
        AND SEND concat( "This is a ",
            the type OF the operating-system,
            " system") TO user;

GOAL 1:
    IF: the host-computer of the operating-system IS "PDP-10"
        AND the prompt-character of the operating-system IS "@"

    THEN: SET the type OF the operating-system TO "TENEX";

Fig. 1. An example of a user agent using both LHS-driven and RHS-driven production rules. (RITA reserved words are shown in uppercase.)

ple, if the system reaches a dead end during a deduction attempt and cannot find appropriate goals to fire to obtain the information it needs, it will query the user for the information before either backing up and trying another path through the goals or giving up entirely. RITA is able to "explain" to the user why it needs the information being sought, by showing the user the goals it is currently trying to satisfy.

## 3.0 USER AGENTS

A user agent is a relatively small program that can reside in a user's terminal (or in a portion of a remote timesharing system) to act as an interface between the user and computer facilities he wants to employ [Waterman77a]. The agent typically displays many of the characteristics of a human assistant. For example, it may have the ability to carry on a dialog with either the user or external computer systems. It may have specific knowledge about particular users, e.g., user A wants his mail retrieved from system X every Friday at 10 am, or user B tends to accidently invert pairs of letters when he types, often typing "lgoin" for "login." It may also have the ability to interact with other agents that are currently operational in the terminal or even create other agents and initiate their operation.

User agents can be classified along two dimensions, one describing the way the agent relates to the user and another describing the knowledge acquisition capability of the agent. The agent can relate to the user in a very direct way, and hence be considered an *active* agent, or in a somewhat indirect way as a *passive* agent. Neither of these classifications is absolute, since actual agents can exhibit both active and passive properties to varying degrees. Figure 2 illustrates the major difference between active and passive agents.

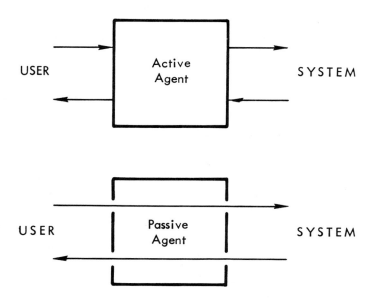

Fig. 2. Active and passive user agents.

An active agent stands between the user and the external system, hiding the characteristics of that system. The agent may carry on a dialog with the user in one language while communicating with the external system in another, never permitting the user to talk directly to the external system. This type of agent can take the user's input, translate it into something the external system will understand, and immediately send it to the system. Or it may gather a large amount of knowledge from the user, process it, and then use it later to perform some task for the user. Alternatively, without actually interacting with the user, the agent may autonomously perform some periodic and routine task, leaving the result where the user can find it when he so desires.

In contrast, a passive agent passes the user's input directly to the external system and the reply of the system directly back to the user. By maintaining such a low profile, the agent gives the impression that the user is talking directly to the other system. A passive agent allows the user to take the initiative and guide the course of the interaction; e.g., the user may ask the agent questions, give the agent commands, and generally maintain control of the situation. The active agent, on the other hand, may try to accomplish a particular task in some pre-specified way. It maintains control, querying the user when task-specific information is needed and supplying results to the user when the task is completed.

The second dimension along which the user agent can be classified is its capacity for knowledge acquisition. The agent can either be *static* (incapable of permanently acquiring new knowledge) or *dynamic* (able to acquire new knowledge and use it in new situations). This chapter is particularly concerned with dynamic agents, especially those which can be called *creative*.

A creative agent is one that creates, builds, or modifies another agent. It acquires information and then represents this information in a form suitable for incorporation into some other agent. Figure 3 illustrates the operation of a creative agent. The creative agent contains rules specifying how to map the information it receives from the user and external systems into knowledge that can be used by the new agent. This knowledge is either in the form of RITA objects (data) or RITA rules (program) and is saved as part of the new agent. In Section 4 the operation of a creative user agent called EP-1 is described in detail.

## 4.0 EXEMPLARY PROGRAMMING

Exemplary programming (EP) is a type of program synthesis by example that relies on program specification from examples or traces

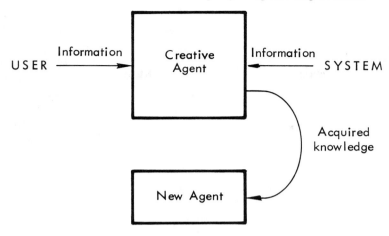

Fig. 3. A creative user agent.

of the activity to be performed (see also [Biermann74, 76, Siklossy75, Green76]. It is a special case of the more general problem of *learning by example* [F. Hayes-Roth78]. Variants of this problem have been studied by researchers in both artificial intelligence and cognitive psychology, particularly in the areas of concept formation [Hunt62, B. Hayes-Roth77b, Winston75], serial pattern acquisition [Simon63, Waterman76a], and rule induction from examples [F. Hayes-Roth76a, c, Vere77b, Waterman75].

In exemplary programming the user specifies the desired function to the EP agent by actually doing it rather than by presenting a general description for synthesis. The primary problem arising in this approach is providing the EP system with techniques for making generalizations about what the user has done. This can be accomplished either by building into the system domain-specific knowledge regarding invariant versus generalizable aspects of the process examples, or by permitting the system to interact with the user to extract this information.

An important aspect of this approach to exemplary programming is that program creation is really a cooperative venture between the user and the machine, i.e., they work together to do the job. In its most basic form exemplary programming involves the user and the machine working together to provide the machine with the knowledge it needs to perform some task for the user. The user and the EP agent create a program, primarily by having the user illustrate what he wants done, and answer questions asked by the agent. Once a superficial program has been created, it can be generalized by applying domain-specific knowledge or by having the user act as part of the inference-generalization-debugging loop in an interactive way. For example, a program for transferring file "mail.box" via the ARPAnet from computer site A to site B could be generalized to a program capable of transferring any file from any site to site B. This would necessitate having the EP agent incorporate into the program general information about hosts, sites, file names, account names, passwords, etc.

Thus exemplary programming is a form of learning by example, where the user is the teacher and the machine is the pupil. In this chapter the EP approach to program creation will be illustrated by describing a first attempt at implementing an EP agent.

## 4.1 An Exemplary Programming Agent

Program creation within a production system framework can proceed quite naturally in discrete steps or increments. The EP agent to be described uses just such an approach. A program is created incrementally, but debugging (in the form of extending and refining the program) is saved for a later step.[2] The rationale behind this approach is to create a complete program quickly that performs the task correctly most of the time, only applying sophisticated debugging techniques as needed later to fine-tune the program so it will produce the correct output through its entire range of inputs. Because program-creating agents can be designed to avoid syntax errors, such debugging is chiefly concerned with conceptual errors made by the EP agent.

The EP agent, called EP-1, watches the user interact with an external computer system and then creates a new agent called a task agent, to perform the task it saw the user perform. The information used to create the task agent is derived two ways: (a) passively, as EP-1 observes the actions of the user and the associated responses of the external system, and (b) actively, as EP-1 queries the user about what he is doing during the interaction. Thus EP-1 has both passive and active characteristics, although it is primarily a passive agent. A diagram of the information flow between the user, the EP agent, and the external system is shown in Fig. 4.

Initially, the user sends task commands to the external system and receives system responses using EP-1 as an intermediary that passes messages back and forth and asks questions about what is happening. The knowledge acquired from this interaction is used to create the task agent incrementally, as the user performs the task. When the user is finished, the task agent is complete and the user can then have

---

[2] The alternate approach is to have the program modified in accordance with feedback identifying errors in the current code [Waterman75, 76a]. Such a system would in effect be writing and debugging the program simultaneously.

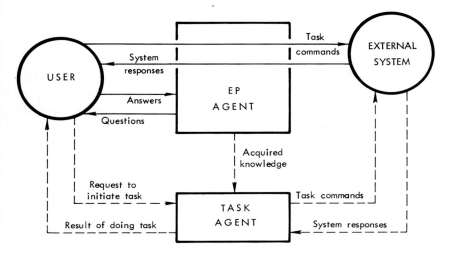

Fig. 4. Information flow in EP agent.

the same task performed by the task agent, as shown by the dashed lines in Fig. 4.

The task agent can be more complex than is indicated in Fig. 4. It may be interactive and require the user to supply information of a variable nature as it is running. Also, the agent will not always be able to handle all possible external system responses. To deal with these cases the agent must be put through a training phase for refining and generalizing its rules.

The tasks best suited to this type of analysis and program creation are those whose search space is relatively linear (sequential), i.e., all solution paths through the space have many states in common. Tasks of this type include network accessing tasks, where the common states might be "logging on," "initiating a series of requests," and "logging off," and library subroutine tasks, where the common states might be "calling the library routine," "supplying it with data," and "retrieving the results."

## 4.2 Modes of Operation

The EP agent is designed for two modes of operation: the acquisition mode and the training mode.[3] In the acquisition mode the agent watches the user perform some interactive task, asks the user appropriate questions about the task, and then writes a set of RITA rules

---

[3] The training mode is not currently implemented.

to perform that task. The acquisition mode is essentially a program writing mode in which the EP agent, with the help of the user, is able to write a program from scratch.

In contrast, the training mode is a debugging mode, in which the EP agent can debug the program it creates during acquisition. Here the situation is reversed: the user watches the EP agent run a rule set to perform some interactive task, and when the rule set produces an incorrect response, the user specifies the correct response and the reason it is correct. EP-1 then uses this information to modify the rule set accordingly. This can be accomplished by either adding new rules or modifying existing ones, as was done in TEIRESIAS [Davis76a].

### 4.3 Acquisition Mode

Ideally, we would like EP-1 to monitor and analyze the behavior of the user and then create new RITA agents to duplicate that behavior without having to interrogate the user. The questioning of the user by EP-1 is necessary because the current version is quite general: no domain-specific knowledge is built into the agent. The questioning of the user may be reduced or eliminated by adding such knowledge, but additional care must be taken to ensure that created rules include only essential premises, and that variables used in the rules have mnemonic names.

The current implementation of EP-1 is a working RITA program operating in the acquisition mode. It watches the user perform a task and then creates a new RITA agent capable of performing the same task. The operation of EP-1 during acquisition consists of an initialization step and a basic cycle (see Fig. 5.)

To illustrate this sequence, assume the user tells EP-1 that the following three types of information are relevant.

(1) the name of the current-system (the name of the operating system or program the user is currently accessing),

(2) the state of the agent (a term describing what the agent is currently trying to accomplish, e.g., "logging in" or "giving password"),

(3) the response of the system (the response the user receives from the external system, e.g., "host:" from the file transfer program, ftp.)

In addition, the user specifies that this particular "response of the system" is output information from the external system. After EP-1 tells the user to start the protocol, assume the user types a carriage return, gets back a "% ", and declares to EP-1 that the name of the current-system is "unix" and the state of the agent is "use ftp." In this

INITIALIZATION

\*     The user supplies a name for each type of
data object relevant to this task.

BASIC CYCLE

\*     The user sends a message to the external
system and receives its reply.

\*     The user is asked for the current values of
the data objects declared relevant during
initialization.

\*     A RITA rule is created. Its premises reflect
the values of the data objects before the
user sent his last message to the external
system. Its actions reflect the content of
his last message and its effect on the data
objects.

\*     The user continues, repeating the cycle
until he wishes to quit. At this time he
types "\*finished\*".

Fig. 5. Operation of EP-1 during acquisition.

situation the dialog shown in Fig. 6 would lead to the creation of a new
rule.

At this point EP-1 creates a rule using the information just elicited
from the user and the information elicited in the previous cycle. In this
case the rule created would be similar to the one shown below. Note
that the information acquired in the first cycle in Fig. 6 is used to
create the premises in Rule N, while the information from the second
cycle is used to create the actions. Thus a new rule is created at the
juncture of each cycle.

RULE N:

IF: the name OF the current-system IS "unix"
    & the state OF the agent IS "use ftp"
    & the response OF the system CONTAINS { "% " }

THEN: SET the name OF the current-system TO "file
        transfer program"
    & SET the state OF the agent TO "give the host
     name"
    & SET the response OF the system TO " "
    & SET the reply OF the agent TO "ftp";

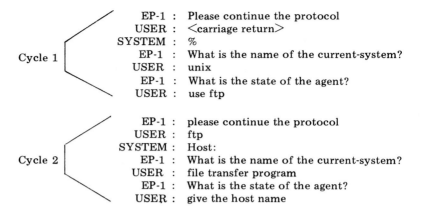

|  |  |  |
|---|---|---|
| EP-1 | : | Please continue the protocol |
| USER | : | <carriage return> |
| SYSTEM | : | % |
| EP-1 | : | What is the name of the current-system? |
| USER | : | unix |
| EP-1 | : | What is the state of the agent? |
| USER | : | use ftp |

Cycle 1

|  |  |  |
|---|---|---|
| EP-1 | : | please continue the protocol |
| USER | : | ftp |
| SYSTEM | : | Host: |
| EP-1 | : | What is the name of the current-system? |
| USER | : | file transfer program |
| EP-1 | : | What is the state of the agent? |
| USER | : | give the host name |

Cycle 2

Fig. 6. Two cycles of dialog needed for rule creation in EP-1.

A predefined rule at the beginning of the rule set being created sends the reply of the agent, in this case "ftp", to the external system. Thus when rule N is fired it will send "ftp" to unix and set the values of the relevant objects appropriately.[4]

As the user interacts with the external system, the EP agent monitors the interaction, asks questions, creates RITA rules, and stores them in a file. When the user terminates his task, the EP agent is also finished with the job of creating the new rule set or agent. This rule set is now available for immediate use; the user need not examine or modify it before using it to again perform the desired task.

To illustrate more fully the operation of EP-1 during acquisition, the initial, middle, and final portions of an actual protocol of a user-EP interaction are shown below. The task is to transfer a file over the ARPAnet from a remote host to the local host. User input is shown in italics, EP agent response in normal type, and system response in boldface.

What task are you going to perform?
*the file transfer*
What things are relevant?
*the name of the current-system*
What else?
*the state of the agent*
What else?

---

[4] The third action of rule N sets the value of "response of the system" to the empty string, indicated by the double quotation marks. This is needed so that each time the system response is read the value of "response of the system" will reflect only the current response (see rule 16 in Fig. 7).

*nothing*
What I/O is relevant?
*the response of the system*

This initial set of queries provides EP-1 with the names of the pieces of information deemed relevant by the user. The agent uses these names in the rules it creates and obtains their values at different points in the demonstration by repeatedly querying the user.

Please start the protocol to be learned

*ftp*
**Host:**

What is the name of the current-system?
*file transfer program*
What is the state of the agent ?
*give the host name*

Here the user calls ftp, the file transfer program, and answers EP-1's queries about the current values of the relevant information.

Please continue the protocol to be learned

*cmu-10a:What system shall I retrieve the file from?. . .*
**Connections established.**

**300 CMU10A 8.3/DEC 6.02VM FTP Server 4(31)**
**>**

At this point the user names "cmu-10a" as the host from which the file should be transferred, but also indicates that this is a "variable" piece of information, one that may change each time the file transfer agent being created is used. The user indicates this by supplying the prompt, ":What system . . .," along with the host name. EP-1 builds this prompt into the rule it is currently creating, so that the file transfer agent will ask for the name of the system from which the file should be retrieved, and will only retrieve from cmu-10a if it doesn't receive a reply within $n$ seconds (where $n$ is a parameter to EP-1).

For brevity, a portion of the protocol is omitted at this point. It contains a trace of the user logging in, supplying his user name, password, and the command "retr" to initiate the retrieval. The last system output in this portion of the trace is a request from the ftp program to provide the name of the "remotefile" (the file to be retrieved).

Please continue the protocol to be learned

*mail.box[a330dw28]:What file do you want retrieved?...*
**localfile:**

What is the name of the current-system ?
<*carriage-return*>
What is the state of the agent ?
<*carriage-return*>

Here the user indicates that he wants to retrieve mail.box-[a330dw28], and wants this file name considered a variable with the associated prompt "What file do . . . ." The ftp program asks him for the localfile name (the destination of the retrieved file), but before he responds he answers EP-1's queries about the current values of the relevant information. The carriage return is the user's way of indicating that this information is unnecessary for the rule that will control this interaction.

Again, for brevity, the last portion of the protocol is omitted. In this trace the user names the destination of the retrieved file, exits the ftp program, and types "*finished*" to terminate EP-1.

A total of sixteen RITA rules were written by EP-1 during the above interaction. The rules corresponding to the portions of the protocol listed above are shown in Fig. 7.

The task agent partially specified in Fig. 7 automatically retrieves files from remote sites on the ARPAnet, copying them into a RAND-UNIX file. The first three rules in Fig. 7 are always generated to handle the mechanics of sending messages specified by the other rules to either the user or the external system. The last two rules are generated to look for the response from the external system and limit the time expended so the agent won't loop if the external system fails to respond. The other rules carry out the dynamics of the file transfer, and constitute the core of the file transfer agent.

Figure 8 contains a sample protocol produced by running the file transfer agent created by EP-1. For clarity, the entire trace is shown, both commands sent by the task agent and responses received from the external system. In normal use this trace is suppressed, and the user only sees queries for the following information:

(1)   remote-site name
(2)   account-name at that site
(3)   password at that site
(4)   name of file to be retrieved
(5)   new name for retrieved file.

If at any point the user fails to respond to the question within a reasonable length of time (currently 15 seconds) the agent uses the default answer for that question and continues. As the agent obtains

RULE 1:
    IF: the prompt OF the agent IS KNOWN
  THEN: SEND the prompt OF the agent TO user
      & RECEIVE the NEXT
        {**ANYTHING 'line-contents'** FOLLOWED BY <carriage return>}
        FOR 15 SECONDS FROM the user
      & SET the new-reply OF the agent TO 'line-contents'
      & SET the prompt OF the agent TO NOT KNOWN;

RULE 2:
    IF: the new-reply OF the agent IS KNOWN
      & the new-reply OF the agent IS NOT " "
  THEN: SET the reply OF the agent TO the new-reply OF the agent
      & SET the new-reply OF the agent TO " ";

RULE 3:
    IF: the reply OF the agent IS KNOWN
  THEN: SEND the reply OF the agent TO system
      & SEND " " TO user
      & SEND concat( "sent: ", the reply OF the agent ) TO user
      & SET the reply OF the agent TO NOT KNOWN;

RULE 4:
    IF: the name OF the current-system IS NOT KNOWN
      & the state OF the agent IS NOT KNOWN
      & the response OF the system CONTAINS { " "}
  THEN: SET the name OF the current-system TO "file transfer
        program"
      & SET the state OF the agent TO "give the host name"
      & SET the response OF the system TO " "
      & SET the reply OF the agent TO "ftp";

RULE 5:
    IF: the name OF the current-system IS "file transfer program"
      & the state OF the agent IS "give the host name"
      & the response OF the system CONTAINS {"Host:   "}
  THEN: SET the state OF the agent TO "login"
      & SET the response OF the system TO " "
      & SET the reply OF the agent TO "cmu-10a"
      & SET the prompt OF the agent TO
      "What system shall I retrieve the file from?...";

[Rules 6 through 10 are omitted]

RULE 11:
    IF: the response OF the system CONTAINS {"remotefile:   "}
  THEN: SET the response OF the system TO " "
      & SET the reply OF the agent TO "mail.box[a330dw28]"
      & SET the prompt OF the agent TO
      "What file do you want retrieved?...";

[Rules 12 through 14 are omitted]

RULE 15:
    IF:  the input OF the system IS " "
       & the count OF the system IS less THAN 20
  THEN:  RECEIVE FOR 5 SECONDS FROM system AS the input OF
       the system
       & SET the count OF the system TO 1 + the count OF the
       system;

RULE 16:
    IF:  the count OF the system IS less THAN 20
  THEN:  SET the response OF the system TO
       concat( the response OF the system, the input OF the
       system)
       & SET the input OF the system TO " "
       & SET the count OF the system TO 0
       & SEND concat( "got: ", the response OF the system ) TO
       user;

Fig. 7. Rules created during a user-EP-1 interaction.[5]

the information it needs, it calls the local file transfer program, answers its questions, and initiates the retrieval. When the retrieval is complete the agent informs the user and halts. During one particular execution of the file transfer agent there were some cases in which the messages sent by the agent were garbled during transmission, leading to unexpected error messages from the external system. In these cases the agent correctly backed-up to the appropriate spot in the sequence of operations and repeated the messages until they were correctly transmitted and received.[6] For details of the operation of this agent see the expanded version of this chapter [Waterman77b].

### 4.4 Extensions of the Current Implementation

There are a number of ways this initial version of an EP agent could be expanded to make the acquisition phase more effective. First, a more sophisticated method could be developed for determining what part of the external response (the I/O information) should be used in the creation of each rule. For example, when the response consists of many lines and is not always the same for a given input to the external system then something more sophisticated than using the entire re-

---

[5] The RECEIVE statement in rule 1 reads the next line typed in by the user and calls it 'line-contents', stripping off the terminating carriage return. In the actual RITA program the control character "Êj" is used rather than <carriage-return>. The second action of rule 3 sends a carriage return to the user.

[6] The addition of a rule limiting the number of times the same response could be received repeatedly from the external system would prevent infinite looping in this situation.

sent: ftp
got:  Host:
What system shall I retrieve the file from?. . .*sri-ai*

sent: sri-ai
got:  Connections established.

> > 300 SRI-AI FTP Server 1.44.0.0 – at THU 20-MAY-77 10:21-PDT

sent: user
got:  username:
What is your user name on this system?. . .*rand*

sent: rand
got:  330 User name accepted. Password, please.
>

sent: pass,
got:  Password:
What is your password on this system?. . .*abcdef*

sent: abcdef
got:
230 Login completed.
>

sent: retr
got:  remotefile:
What file do you want retrieved?. . .*test.bas*

sent: test.bas
got:  ?Command argument too long
> >

sent: retr
got:  ?Command argument too long
> >

sent: retr
got:  ?Command argument too long
> >

sent: retr
got:  remotefile:
What file do you want retrieved?. . .*test.bas*

sent: test.bas
got:  localfile:
What do you want to call the retrieved file?. . .

```
sent: newdata
got:   255 SOCK 3276932611
250 ASCII retrieve of <RAND>TEST.BAS;1 started.

sent: bye
got:   231 BYE command received.
%
the file transfer has been completed
```

Fig. 8. Protocol produced by the file transfer agent. (User input is in italics, file transfer agent response in normal type.)

sponse is needed. In the current implementation of EP-1 the problem is handled by simply using the first few characters of the last line of the external system response. This could be improved by using the first few characters of both the first and last lines. However, to effect any significant improvement one would need to build into EP-1 specific knowledge about the tasks it could be asked to learn, plus rules telling it how to decide what components of the system response are likely to be invariant. A time-consuming alternative would be to have EP-1 discover invariant components through empirical verification.

Also, EP-1 could be modified to supply for itself the values of the relevant objects at each step, rather than interrogating the user. This would reduce the work load on the user but would introduce several difficulties: (a) the mnemonics created by the agent would not be as intelligible as those created by the user, unless the agent had clever heuristics for inferring good mnemonics from the trace of the user-system interaction; and (b) global knowledge about the task being performed would have to be built into the agent so it could infer the values of the relevant objects, e.g., it would have to know that if the user types a <carriage return> and gets back a "% " the name of the system the user is interacting with is unix.

## 5.0 CONCLUSIONS

The work in exemplary programming using RITA agents has a number of implications for knowledge-based systems. First, the production system framework can be used for implementing dynamic programs, programs that create new data and code. In particular, the RITA architecture facilitates creation of new RITA agents through combined user-agent interactions. The modularity of production systems is viewed as the critical factor underlying the successful approach taken to program creation. That is, the success obtained with RITA agents creating other RITA agents is attributable to the fact that the programs being created, the new agents, are all based on the RITA production system architecture.

Second, it has been demonstrated that user agents can be applied to the problem of program creation and produce programs having practical applications. The agent produced by EP-1 is a viable, general program for file transfer. EP-1 has also been used to create agents to access the New York Times Information Bank and retrieve abstracts of news articles pertinent to the user's current interests.

Finally, the potential that exemplary programming has for man-machine interface applications has been demonstrated. It is a first step in helping the naive user create programs without learning a programming language or other artificial language for expressing the task to be performed. This technique is effective for programs involving repetition of similar sequences of processing, especially when the solution paths through the problem space often converge, resulting in many common states. The crux of the learning problem in exemplary programming is how to generalize the program after seeing only a few paths to the solution, i.e., one or two examples of how the task can be accomplished. This important problem appears to be solvable and deserves to have considerable time and effort spent on its solution.

## ACKNOWLEDGMENTS

The comments and criticisms of Rick Hayes-Roth, Bob Anderson, and other members of the Information Sciences Department staff at The Rand Corporation are gratefully acknowledged. This research was supported by the Defense Advanced Research Projects Agency under Contract No. DAHC15-73-C-0181.

# INDUCTIVE LEARNING OF RELATIONAL PRODUCTIONS

Steven A. Vere
*University of Illinois at Chicago Circle*

*Relational productions provide a mathematically tractable formal model for operators in discrete systems. Two paradigms for the inductive learning of such operators are considered: before-and-after situation pairs and situation sequences. An operational theory for the generalization of productions for these paradigms is then developed, based on previous work in concept induction. This theory has been computer implemented. In examples three "blocks world" operators are learned from six before-and-after pairs and also from a sequence of fifteen blocks world situations. A transformational grammar learning example of Hayes-Roth is repeated with an improvement in speed of two orders of magnitude.*

## 1.0 INTRODUCTION

The concept of an operator is a fundamental one in artificial intelligence. Usually operators are postulated. However, the *acquisition* of operators from experience is an important, underdeveloped topic. This chapter is concerned with the learning of operators from experience. Relational productions [Vere77a, 76] will be used as the model for operators. The relational production is a well-defined, mathematically tractable formal model for describing change in discrete systems. It is an amalgamation of two familiar ideas: string productions [Post43] and STRIPS operators [Fikes72].

Two closely related paradigms for the learning of operators will be considered. In the first, a number of "before-and-after" situation pairs are presented and the problem is to learn a minimal set of operators capable of causing the observed changes between the first situation and the second. In the second paradigm, a situation sequence is presented, i.e., a sequence of symbolic "snapshots" of a discrete system undergoing change. Each adjacent pair of situations can be regarded as a before-and-after pair, and again the problem is to learn a minimal set of operators capable of causing the changes observed in the sequence.

Building on previous work in generalization of concepts [Vere75], a formal method is presented for generalization of productions. A SNOBOL4 program called Thoth-p has been developed to implement this theory. Several example problems run on Thoth-p are presented. In one, three "blocks world" operators are learned from six before-and-after situation pairs. In another, these operators are learned from a sequence of 15 blocks world situations involving five blocks. In a third, a transformational grammar learning problem was successfully solved with a computation time two orders of magnitude faster than that reported for a program by Hayes-Roth [F. Hayes-Roth77f].

Significantly, the operator learning theory of this chapter also provides a formal solution for the class of analogy problems studied by Evans [Evans68], without requiring ad hoc constructs such as the "rval" evaluation function. This interesting topic is discussed elsewhere [Vere77c].

Previous work closely related to the topic of this paper is by Hayes-Roth [F. Hayes-Roth77f], Soloway [Soloway76], Waterman [Waterman75], Egan [Egan74], and Hedrick [Hedrick76]. The Hayes-Roth program demonstrated the ability to learn a single operator from before-and-after description pairs. As mentioned above, it seems comparatively slow, and no formal model for operators is employed. The goal of Soloway's work is nearly the same as ours: learning the "rules" for actions from a sequence of situation snapshots, in particular, the rules of baseball. The tone of his work is frankly empirical, rather than analytical, and at last report a working program was still under development. The productions studied by Waterman are quite different from relational productions, despite the name similarity. They more resemble the if-then statements of a programming language than a formal system, and are ordered like Markov algorithm rules. Mathematical tractability of these productions has not been demonstrated and is doubtful. While "programs" composed of these productions are often compact, they seem difficult for humans to comprehend. Nevertheless, very interesting learning behavior has been demonstrated. Egan and Greeno are concerned with integrating models for the acquisition of patterns or rules for human behavior. Their orientation is to the psychology of human learning. Hedrick describes a program capable of learning his own variety of production systems. A semantic net provides information that may be used in learning the productions.

The organization of this chapter is as follows. In Section 2, the concept of a relational production is informally introduced. In Section 3, the two operator learning paradigms are described in detail. In Section 4, the theory of relational production generalization is developed. In Section 5, examples run on the Thoth-p implementation are presented.

## 2.0 INTRODUCTION TO RELATIONAL PRODUCTIONS

Relational productions have been previously introduced [Vere77a, 76]. A relational production is a relation revision mechanism, analogous to string productions. String productions specify possible *revisions* of a string of symbols; relational productions specify possible *revisions* of a conjunction of literals. For the moment, a literal will be taken to be an ordered list of terms, and a term will be a constant or a variable.

For our purposes, a relational production , has the form $\alpha \rightarrow \beta$, where $\alpha$ and $\beta$ are conjunctions of literals. The substrate that a set of productions may revise is called a *situation*, which is also a conjunction of literals.

To illustrate the structure and application of relational productions, consider a "blocks world" consisting of a number of cubic blocks of uniform size. Figure 1 shows schematically a "blocks world" situation containing three blocks. We will use three types of literals to describe this world:

(1)  (on .X .Y) means block X rests directly on top of block Y;

(2)  (ontable .X) means block X rests directly on the table;

(3)  (clear .X) means the top of block X is clear, i.e., no block rests on X.

The convention is that variables are identified by a period prefix. Otherwise, strings of letters and digits are constants.

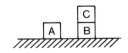

Fig. 1. A simple blocks world situation.

Using these literal types, a description of the situation of Fig. 1 is:

(clear a)
(ontable a)

(on c b)
(ontable b)
(clear c)

The following relational production specifies the unstacking of a block:

(clear .X)          (clear .X)
(on .X .Y)      →   (ontable .X)
                    (clear .Y)

In words, this specifies that if a block X is clear and rests on block Y, then the situation may change into one in which X rests on the table and Y is clear. We emphasize that a production is *not* a predicate calculus implication, since the literals on the left of the production are *deleted* from the situation. This will be described precisely below.

Of course, a production may not be applicable in a given situation. For example, an unstacking operation can occur only if one block rests on another. Let $\sigma$ represent a situation and $\theta$ a conventional substitution of the kind used in deductive theorem proving, and having the form $\{t_1/v_1, \ldots, t_r/v_r\}$, where each $t_i$ is a term and each $v_i$ is a variable. Then production $\alpha \to \beta$ is *applicable* to situation $\sigma$ iff $\alpha\theta \subseteq \sigma$. In this relation, the conjunctions $\alpha$ and $\sigma$ are regarded as sets of literals. Thus the unstacking production above is applicable to the situation of Fig. 1 since

$$\begin{bmatrix} \text{(clear .X)} \\ \text{(on .X .Y)} \end{bmatrix} \quad \{c/.X, b/.Y\} = \begin{bmatrix} \text{(clear c)} \\ \text{(on c b)} \end{bmatrix} \subseteq \begin{bmatrix} \text{(clear a)} \\ \text{(ontable a)} \\ \text{(on c b)} \\ \text{(ontable b)} \\ \text{(clear c)} \end{bmatrix}$$

To specify the new situation after a production has revised a situation, we will use additional set operators:

$$\sigma' = \sigma \cap \overline{\alpha\theta} \cup \beta\theta$$

Here ∪ and ∩ denote set union and intersection, respectively, and the overbar denotes set complement. $\theta$ is any substitution that satisfies the applicability relation. In the absence of parentheses, intersection takes precedence over union in expressions.

Continuing the example above, if the unstacking production is applied to the situation of Fig. 1, the new situation is determined as follows:

$$
\sigma' = \begin{bmatrix} \text{(clear a)} \\ \text{(ontable a)} \\ \text{(on c b)} \\ \text{(ontable b)} \\ \text{(clear c)} \end{bmatrix} \cap \overline{\begin{bmatrix} \text{(clear .X)} \\ \text{(on .X .Y)} \end{bmatrix}} \quad \{c/.X, b/.Y\}
$$

$$
\cup \begin{bmatrix} \text{(clear .X)} \\ \text{(ontable .X)} \\ \text{(clear .Y)} \end{bmatrix} \quad \{c/.X, b/.Y\}
$$

$$
= \begin{bmatrix} \text{(clear a)} \\ \text{(ontable a)} \\ \text{(ontable b)} \\ \text{(clear c)} \\ \text{(ontable c)} \\ \text{(clear b)} \end{bmatrix}
$$

Thus the production serves to unstack a block. Similar productions can be formulated to transfer a block from one stack to another and to stack blocks. By continuing to apply productions, a situation can be revised repeatedly. The notation $\sigma \overset{p}{=}> \sigma'$ will denote that production p transforms situation $\sigma$ into situation $\sigma'$.

Beyond artificial intelligence applications, relational productions are also capable of modeling the semantics of computer programs, including list processing and structured data [Vere76].

*The Context Form for Relational Productions*

The antecedent $\alpha$ and consequent $\beta$ of a production may contain common literals. Let $\gamma = \alpha \cap \beta$. This set of common literals $\gamma$ will be called the *context* of the production. Consideration of the applicability relation $\alpha\theta \subseteq \sigma$ and next situation relation $\sigma' = \sigma \cap \overline{\alpha\theta} \cup \beta\theta$ shows that adding or deleting literals in the context affects applicability of a production, but not the transformation caused by that production. The context form of a production $\alpha \to \beta$ is

$$[\alpha \cap \beta] \, \alpha \cap \overline{\beta} \to \overline{\alpha} \cap \beta$$

For example, the context form of the blocks world unstacking production

$$
\begin{array}{cc} \text{(clear .X)} & \text{(clear .X)} \\ \text{(on .X .Y)} \to & \text{(ontable .X)} \\ & \text{(clear .Y)} \end{array}
$$

is

$$
[\text{(clear .X)}] \, \text{(on .X .Y)} \to \begin{array}{c} \text{(ontable .X)} \\ \text{(clear .Y)} \end{array}
$$

In productions, the context will always be enclosed in square brackets. The context form has two motivations. First, it is a notational convenience that saves writing certain literals twice. More importantly, it will be seen in Section 4 that literals in the context must be generalized in a different manner from literals in the sets $\alpha \cap \bar{\beta}$ and $\bar{\alpha} \cap \beta$.

## 3.0  TWO PARADIGMS FOR LEARNING RELATIONAL PRODUCTIONS

This section presents two paradigms for the learning of relational productions: the "before-and-after" paradigm, and the "situation sequence" paradigm.

In the before-and-after paradigm, pairs of situations are presented that describe a situation both before and after an action has occurred. Hayes-Roth [F. Hayes-Roth77f] used the term "before-and-after" to refer to situation pairs involving only a single action. Here we will allow a single set of pairs to exemplify an arbitrary number of actions.

An example of the first paradigm, Fig. 2 presents six blocks world before-and-after pairs. Note that some of the pairs involve a stacking action, others an unstacking, and others the transfer of a block from one stack to another. Each situation would be described by a conjunction of literals, as seen in Section 2.

Each before-and-after pair $(\sigma_b, \sigma_a)$ may be viewed as a single production $\sigma_b \to \sigma_a$. That this production exactly transforms $\sigma_b$ into $\sigma_a$ is easily seen from the relation $\sigma' = \sigma \cap \bar{a} \, \theta \ \cup \beta \theta$ of Section 2. Consequently, a set of before-and-after pairs may also be regarded as a set of productions, each consisting entirely of ground literals. These productions may then be generalized as described in Section 4.

The before-and-after paradigm is somewhat unrealistic in that it assumes a teacher is available to present examples of the effect of a set of actions. A closely related but more interesting paradigm is the situation sequence paradigm. Here a sequence of situation snapshots are presented, describing a discrete system undergoing change. The task of the learning mechanism would then be to formulate a minimal set of productions, one of which is capable of causing the transformation between any adjacent pair of situations in the sequence.

Suppose the situation sequence is $\sigma_1, \sigma_2, \ldots, \sigma_n$. Then from this sequence can be extracted the set of ground productions

$$\sigma_1 \ \to \ \sigma_2$$
$$\sigma_2 \ \to \ \sigma_3$$
$$\cdot$$
$$\cdot$$
$$\cdot$$
$$\sigma_{n-1} \to \sigma_n$$

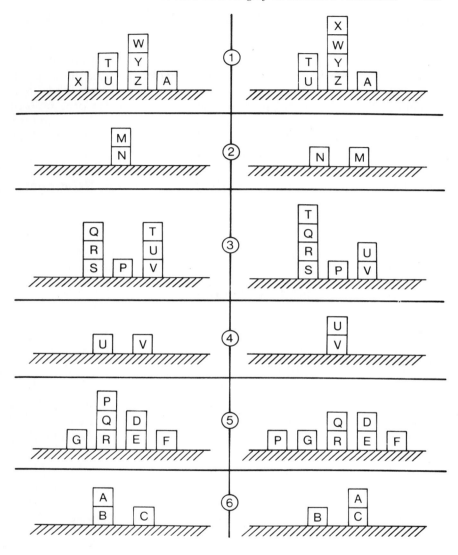

Fig. 2.

In context form these are

$$[\sigma_i \cap \sigma_{i+1}] \, \sigma_i \cap \bar{\sigma}_{i+1} \rightarrow \bar{\sigma}_i \cap \sigma_{i+1}, \, (1 \leqslant i \leqslant n-1).$$

This set of productions can then be generalized just as for the before-and-after pair paradigm.

## 4.0  GENERALIZATION OF RELATIONAL PRODUCTIONS

Given a set of productions, we would like to be able to find a minimal set of generalized productions capable of producing any transformation that could be caused by a production in the original set. This section develops an analytic, operational theory for accomplishing this task. First, "generalization" is defined for productions; then properties of generalizations are reviewed; finally, a method for generalizing productions is developed based on an earlier method for generalizing simple conjunctions of literals.

### 4.1  Definition and Theorem for Generalization of Relational Productions

The following definition is useful for our purposes:

Production $p_1$ is a *generalization* of production $p_2$, denoted $p_1 \leqslant p_2$, iff for all situations $\sigma$ and $\sigma'$,

$$(\sigma \overset{p_2}{=\!\!>} \sigma') \text{ implies } (\sigma \overset{p_1}{=\!\!>} \sigma').$$

In other words, if $p_1$ is a generalization of $p_2$, then $p_1$ can cause any transformation caused by $p_2$, and possibly others as well.

*Relational Production Generalization Theorem*

If $p_1 = ([\gamma_1] \, a_1 \to \beta_1)$ and $p_2 = ([\gamma_2] \, a_2 \to \beta_2)$ are two relational productions, and $\forall \theta \; a_1\theta \cap \beta_1\theta = \emptyset$ and $a_2\theta \cap \beta_2\theta = \emptyset$, then $p_1 \leqslant p_2$ iff there exists a substitution $\theta_a$ such that $\gamma_1\theta_a \subseteq \gamma_2$, $a_1\theta_a = a_2$, and $\beta_1\theta_a = \beta_2$.

*Proof:* Given that $\gamma_1\theta_a \subseteq \gamma_2$, $a_1\theta_a = a_2$, and $\beta_1\theta_a = \beta_2$, it is straightforward to show that $p_1 \leqslant p_2$. To prove the implication in the other direction, note that $p_1 \leqslant p_2$ implies the following relations:

$\forall \sigma \; \forall \theta_2$ such that $(a_2 \cup \gamma_2)\theta_2 \subseteq \sigma \; \exists \theta_1$ such that

$$(a_1 \cup \gamma_1) \, \theta_1 \subseteq \sigma, \tag{1}$$

and

$$\sigma \cap \overline{a_1\theta_1} \cup \beta_1\theta_1 = \sigma \cap \overline{a_2\theta_2} \cup \beta_2\theta_2 \tag{2}$$

Applying Karnaugh map analysis to (1) and (2), together with the theorem conditions $\forall \theta \; a_1\theta \cap \beta_1\theta = \emptyset$ and $a_2\theta \cap \beta_2\theta = \emptyset$ shows that

$$\forall \theta_2 \; \exists \theta_1 \; a_1\theta_1 = a_2\theta_2 \text{ and } \beta_1\theta_1 = \beta_2\theta_2. \tag{3}$$

From (1) and (3) it follows that

$$\forall \theta_2 \, \exists \theta_1 \; \gamma_1 \theta_1 \subseteq \gamma_2 \theta_2. \tag{4}$$

From (3) and (4) it can be inferred that $\exists \theta_a \, \gamma_1 \theta_a \subseteq \gamma_2$, $a_1 \theta_a = a_2$, and $\beta_1 \theta_a = \beta_2$ by the following argument. Suppose $\forall \theta_2 \, \exists \theta_1 \; a_1 \theta_1 = a_2 \theta_2$ but no $\theta_a$ exists such that $a_1 \theta_a = a_2$. Let $\theta_2$ be the null substitution. Then $a_1 \theta_1 = a_2 \theta_2 = a_2$, which is a contradiction, and so it must be true that $\exists \theta_a \, a_1 \theta_a = a_2$.

## 4.2  Properties of Generalizations

In this section we briefly review some of the properties of generalizations.

### Strict Generalizations

If production $p_1$ is an alphabetic variant of production $p_2$, it follows immediately from the generalization definition for productions that $p_1 \leqslant p_2$. If $p_1 \leqslant p_2$ and $p_1$ is *not* an alphabetic variant of $p_2$, then $p_1$ is a *strict* generalization of $p_2$, denoted $p_1 < p_2$.

### Common Generalizations

If $p_1 \leqslant p_2$ and $p_1 \leqslant p_3$ it is natural to say that $p_1$ is a *common generalization* of $p_2$ and $p_3$. It is also useful to talk of the common generalization of more than two productions.

### Maximal Common Generalizations

Loosely speaking, a maximal common generalization is one containing all the common features of the productions of which it is a generalization. More precisely, a production $p_1$ is a *maximal common generalization* of productions $p_2$ and $p_3$ iff:

(1)  $p_1 \leqslant p_2$ and $p_1 \leqslant p_3$ (i.e., it is a common generalization);
(2)  no $p_1'$ exists such that $p_1 < p_1'$, $p_1' \leqslant p_2$, and $p_1' \leqslant p_3$ (i.e., it is maximal).

As an example, consider the four productions

$p_1 = \{[(\text{window open})] \quad (\text{at mky a1}) \rightarrow (\text{at mky a2})\}$
$p_2 = \{[(\text{window open})] \quad (\text{at mky a7}) \rightarrow (\text{at mky a8})\}$
$p_3 = \{[(\text{window open})] \quad (\text{at mky .X}) \rightarrow (\text{at mky .Y})\}$
$p_4 = \{[] \; (\text{at mky .U}) \rightarrow \quad (\text{at mky .V})\}$

$p_4 \leqslant p_1$ and $p_4 \leqslant p_2$. However, $p_4$ is not a maximal common generalization of $p_1$ and $p_2$, because $p_3$ is also a common generalization and $p_4 < p_3$. In fact, $p_3$ is a maximal common generalization (mcg).

*A Maximal Common Generalization Is Not Necessarily Unique.*

Consider the following abstract example:

$p_1 = \{[(a\ c\ e)(b\ e\ c)]\ (g\ a) \rightarrow (g\ g)\}$
$p_2 = \{[(a\ d\ f)(b\ g\ d)(b\ f\ h)]\ (g\ c) \rightarrow (g\ g)\}$

There are two distinct maximal common generalizations of these two productions:

$p_3 = \{[(a\ .X\ .Y)(b\ .Z\ .X)]\ (g\ .U) \rightarrow (g\ g)\}$
$p_4 = \{[(a\ .X\ .Y)(b\ .Y\ .Z)]\ (g\ .U) \rightarrow (g\ g)\}$

Multiple distinct mcgs occur frequently in real problems, but are usually too complex for a short example.

### 4.3  Computing Maximal Common Generalizations of Two Productions

In previous work [Vere75] we have presented a procedure for computing the maximal common generalizations of two conjunctions of literals. This procedure is the basis for the computation of maximal common generalizations of two productions. For purposes of generalization, a production may be regarded as an ordered list of three conjunctions of literals: the context $\gamma$, the antecedent $a$, and the consequent $\beta$. Given two productions $p_1$ and $p_2$, their mcgs are obtained by computing the mcgs of each of their three components. However, generalization of the antecedent and consequent are special cases. To see why, consider three productions $p_1 = \{[\gamma_1]\ a_1 \rightarrow \beta_1\}$, $p_2 = \{[\gamma_2]\ a_2 \rightarrow \beta_2\}$, and $p_3 = \{[\gamma_3]\ a_3 \rightarrow \beta_3\}$. It follows immediately from the theorem and definitions of Sections 4.1 and 4.2 that if $p_3$ is an mcg of $p_1$ and $p_2$, then $\gamma_3\theta_a \subseteq \gamma_1$, $\gamma_3\theta_b \subseteq \gamma_2$, $a_3\theta_a = a_1$, $a_3\theta_b = a_2$, $\beta_3\theta_a = \beta_1$, and $\beta_3\theta_b = \beta_2$ for some substitutions $\theta_a$ and $\theta_b$. Thus the contexts $\gamma_1$ and $\gamma_2$ need not have the same number of literals, but $a_1$ and $a_2$ and $\beta_1$ and $\beta_2$, respectively *must* have the same number. Consequently $a_3$ must not only be an mcg of $a_1$ and $a_2$, but it must also have exactly the same number of literals. The same is true for $\beta_3$.

For example, consider the two productions

$p_1 = \{[\ ]\ (at\ mky\ a1) \quad \rightarrow \quad (at\ mky\ a2)\}$
$p_2 = \{[\ ]\ (at\ mky\ b1) \quad \rightarrow \quad (at\ mky\ b2)$
$\qquad\quad (at\ box\ b1) \qquad\qquad (at\ box\ b2)\}$

The mcg of the antecedents is (at mky .X), and the mcg of the consequents is (at mky .Y). However, for both antecedent and consequent these generalizations have fewer literals than the antecedent and consequent of $p_2$. Hence no mcg of $p_1$ and $p_2$ exists.

In summary, to find the mcg of two productions $p_1$ and $p_2$, compute the mcgs of their respective components. However, if $\alpha_3$ or $\beta_3$ has fewer literals than the corresponding components of $p_1$ or $p_2$, no mcg exists.

## 4.4 Computing a Minimal Set of Maximal Common Generalizations of an Arbitrary Number of Productions

A procedure for computing the maximal common generalizations of two productions was discussed in Section 4.3. This procedure is the basis for the computation of a minimal set of mcgs for N productions, where $N > 2$. If $p_1$ and $p_2$ are two arbitrary productions, let $mcg(p_1,p_2)$ denote the set of mcgs of $p_1$ and $p_2$. If X is an arbitrary set of productions, let M(X) be defined as $\{p:(\forall p_1 \in X) (\forall p_2 \in X) \, p \in mcg(p_1,p_2)\}$. In other words, M(X) is the set of all mcgs of all pairs of productions in set X. Let $P_0$ denote the original set of productions to be generalized. Define $P_1 = M(P_0)$ and $P_r = M(P_{r-1})$ for $1 \leqslant r \leqslant m$. Terminate the process when $P_m = $ null. This will always occur in a finite number of iterations m.

As was pointed out in Section 4.3, it is possible that the mcg of two arbitrary productions is empty. If X is an arbitrary set of productions, let S(X) be defined as $\{x: x \in X$ and $(\forall x' \in X) \, x \neq x' => mcg(x,x') = $ null$\}$. In words, S(X) is the set of all productions in X from which no generalization can be formed with any other production in X. Define $S_1 = S(P_0)$ and $S_r = S(P_{r-1})$ for $1 \leqslant r \leqslant m$. Thus a production in $S_i$ is one that has "dropped out" of the generalization process on the ith iteration. Now consider their union:

$$G = \underset{i=1}{\overset{m}{\cup}} S_i.$$

Using the transitive property of generalizations, it is easy to prove that, for any subset of the original set $P_0$ of productions with mcg $\delta$, a $\delta' \in G$ exists such that $\delta' \leqslant \delta$. Given a list of those productions in $P_0$ generalized by each $g \in G$, a minimal set $G_m \subseteq G$ can be easily computed such that $(\forall p \in P_0)(\exists q \in G_m) \, q \leqslant p$; i.e., every production in the original set is "covered" by a generalization in the minimal set of generalized productions. The next section documents results of an implementation of this procedure.

## 5.0 EXAMPLES RUN ON THE THOTH-P IMPLEMENTATION

This section documents four example problems run on the Thoth-p computer implementation of the production generalization theory of Section 4. Thoth-p is written entirely in SNOBOL4 and consists of about 1400 executable statements. It runs in 256K bytes of memory on the IBM 370 model 158.

## 5.1 A "Blocks World" Before-and-After Pairs Problem

The input for this problem is the six "blocks world" pairs shown schematically earlier in Fig. 2. There are two examples of each action, but the program is merely given the six pairs, without being told which pairs exemplify the same action. Thoth-p generated the three productions shown below in 8.5 seconds, along with the information that the first production covers pairs 1 and 4, the second production pairs 2 and 5, and the third production pairs 3 and 6.

$$
\begin{bmatrix} \text{(clear .N10)} \\ \text{(ontable .N9)} \end{bmatrix} \quad \begin{matrix} \text{(ontable .N10)} \\ \text{(clear .N11)} \end{matrix} \quad \rightarrow \quad \text{(on .N10 .N11)}
$$

$$
\begin{bmatrix} \text{(clear .N7)} \\ \text{(ontable .N8)} \end{bmatrix} \quad \text{(on .N7 .N6)} \quad \rightarrow \quad \begin{matrix} \text{(ontable .N7)} \\ \text{(clear .N6)} \end{matrix}
$$

$$
\begin{bmatrix} \text{(clear .N3)} \\ \text{(ontable .N2)} \\ \text{(ontable .N1)} \end{bmatrix} \quad \begin{matrix} \text{(on .N3 .N5)} \\ \text{(clear .N4)} \end{matrix} \quad \rightarrow \quad \begin{matrix} \text{(clear .N5)} \\ \text{(on .N3 .N4)} \end{matrix}
$$

Note that the first production is a stacking operator, the second an unstacking, and the third a transfer between stacks.

## 5.2 A "Blocks World" Sequence Problem

Figure 3 shows a sequence of 15 "blocks world" situations. Between each pair of situations a block stacking, unstacking or transfer operation has occurred. This sequence was input to the program Thoth-p, which extracted 14 ground productions, representing each of the 14 transformations between pairs of adjacent situations, as described in Section 3. For example, comparing the first two situations the program generated the production

$$
\begin{bmatrix} \text{(clear a)} \\ \text{(ontable b)} \\ \text{(ontable c)} \\ \text{(clear c)} \\ \text{(ontable d)} \\ \text{(ontable e)} \\ \text{(clear e)} \end{bmatrix} \quad \begin{matrix} \text{(on a b)} \\ \text{(clear d)} \end{matrix} \quad \rightarrow \quad \begin{matrix} \text{(on a d)} \\ \text{(clear b)} \end{matrix}
$$

These 14 productions were then generalized as described in section 4, and the following three productions were computed with a total execution time of 175 seconds:

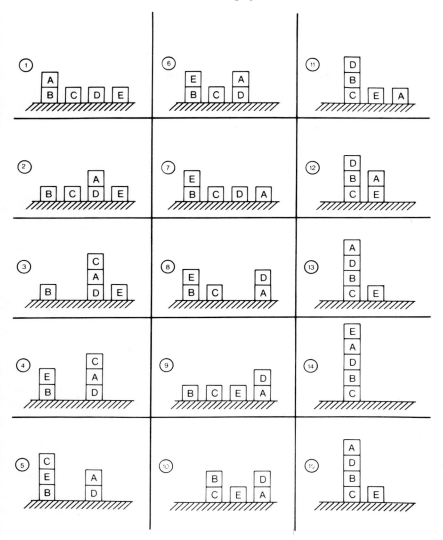

Fig. 3.

$$
\begin{bmatrix} \text{(ontable .N13)} \\ \text{(ontable .N12)} \\ \text{(clear .N10)} \end{bmatrix} \quad \begin{array}{l} \text{(clear .N11)} \\ \text{(on .N10 .N9)} \end{array} \rightarrow \begin{array}{l} \text{(on .N10 .N11)} \\ \text{(clear .N9)} \end{array}
$$

$$
\begin{bmatrix} \text{(ontable .N6)} \\ \text{(clear .N7)} \\ \text{(on .N5 .N6)} \end{bmatrix} \quad \begin{array}{l} \text{(clear .N8)} \\ \text{(ontable .N7)} \end{array} \rightarrow \begin{array}{l} \text{(on .N7 .N8)} \end{array}
$$

$$
\begin{bmatrix} \text{(clear .N4)} \\ \text{(ontable .N2)} \\ \text{(on .N1 .N2)} \end{bmatrix} \quad \begin{array}{l} \\ \text{(on .N4 .N3)} \end{array} \rightarrow \begin{array}{l} \text{(ontable .N4)} \\ \text{(clear .N3)} \end{array}
$$

The second and third productions illustrate idiosyncrasies of this sequence. In every case, when a stacking or unstacking action occurred, it happened to be true that one block was already on another. This idiosyncrasy is reflected in the context relations (ontable .N6) (on .N5 .N6) and (ontable .N2) (on .N1 .N2), respectively, of these two productions. The generalization mechanism is such that any common feature appears in the generalization, whether that feature is coincidental or "significant."

### 5.3  Grammatical Transformations

In this problem we repeat a grammatical transformation learning example by Hayes-Roth [F. Hayes-Roth77f]. Given the deep-structure representations of the following three pairs of sentences, the problem is to induce the rule of grammar which transforms the first sentence into the second. This is the before-and-after pairs paradigm.

(1)  The little man sang a lovely song. A lovely song was sung by the little man.
(2)  A girl hugged the motorcycles. The motorcycles were hugged by a girl.
(3)  People are stopping friendly policemen. Friendly policemen are being stopped by people.

To represent the deep-structures of these sentences we use a capability of the program not discussed here because of space limitations. The terms of a literal may themselves be conjunctions of literals, and so on. For example, the "hierarchical literal" representation of the deep-structure of the first sentence of pair 1 is

(S (NP (DET THE)(ADJ LITTLE)(NOUN (NST
    MAN)(NUMBER SINGULAR)))
(VP (AUX (AUXST HAVE)(TENSE PRESENT)(NUMBER
    SINGULAR))(VERB

(NUMBER SINGULAR)(VST SING)(TENSE PASTPART)(NP
    (DET A)(ADJ
LOVELY)(NOUN (NST SONG)(NUMBER SINGULAR)))))

Thoth-p generated the following generalization of the three pairs in 31
seconds:

(S (NP (DET .N4)(ADJ .N3)(NOUN (NST .N2)(NUMBER
    .N1)))(VP
(AUX .N11)(VERB (NUMBER .N1)(VST .N7)(TENSE .N8))(NP
    (DET .N10)
(ADJ .N9)(NOUN (NST .N6)(NUMBER .N5))))) →

(S (NP (DET .N10)(ADJ .N9)(NOUN (NST .N6)(NUMBER
    .N5)))(VP
(AUX .N11)(PB (NUMBER .N1)(PBST BE)(TENSE .N8))(VERB
    (NUMBER
(ADJ .N3)(NOUN (NST .N2)(NUMBER .N1))))))

Of the 31 seconds, 16 seconds is consumed in converting the three
pairs into the internal representation used by the program, and the
remaining 15 seconds in actual computation of the generalized production and conversion back into the string form required for output. The
Sprouter program of Hayes-Roth consumed 33 minutes in computing
the equivalent generalization, with input conversion time not reported.

## 6.0  CONCLUSION

We have developed and implemented a theory for learning operators from situation sequences and before-and-after pairs. This work
is completely independent of the problem domain, and requires only
that situations be describable by a conjunction of predicate calculus
literals. In an extension of this work [Vere77c], we permit a common
body of "background information" to supply relevant facts about objects mentioned in the "foreground" situations.

# MODEL-DIRECTED LEARNING OF PRODUCTION RULES[1]

Bruce G. Buchanan and Tom M. Mitchell
*Stanford University*

*The Meta-DENDRAL program is described in general terms that are intended to clarify the similarities and differences to other learning programs. Its approach of model-directed heuristic search through a complex space of possible rules appears well suited to many induction tasks. The use of a strong model of the domain to direct the rule search has been demonstrated for rule formation in two areas of chemistry. The high performance of programs that use the generated rules attests to the success of this learning strategy.*

## 1.0 INTRODUCTION

Knowledge-based artificial intelligence programs derive their power from the richness and depth of their knowledge bases. It follows that careful construction of the knowledge bases is an obvious prerequisite for high performance in such systems, yet we have few alternatives to hand-crafting these for each new program. We are better off than we were several years ago, however, for it is no longer necessary to hand-craft a whole program. A rather general program, e.g., a production rule interpreter, can constitute the problem-solving machinery for common problems in a variety of domains. The task-specific knowledge is then encoded in tables of inference rules, definitions, and procedures that test predicates in the domain and execute task-specific actions.

[1] This work was supported by the Advanced Research Projects Agency under contract DAHC 15-73-C-0435, and by the National Institutes of Health under grant RR 00612-07.

Waterman's early work [Waterman70] showed the advantages of using a production rule encoding of knowledge. It also provided a model for learning productions by a program. Davis has made a significant contribution to our understanding of interactive knowledge acquisition [Davis76a] in which a human expert's knowledge is elicited and checked by a sophisticated acquisition program.

The Heuristic DENDRAL programs [Feigenbaum71] are structured to read much of their task-specific knowledge from tables of production rules and to execute the rules under rather elaborate control structures. These programs interpret analytic data from organic chemical samples in order to help chemists determine the molecular structures of the samples. For a number of reasons, we made little progress with the interactive approach to building a knowledge base for DENDRAL. Instead we constructed another set of programs, collectively called Meta-DENDRAL, that aid in building the knowledge base. Meta-DENDRAL is described below in general terms that are intended to clarify the similarities and differences to other learning programs (see [R.G. Smith77]).

## 2.0 THE TASK DOMAIN

### 2.1 Rule Formation

The rule formation task that Meta-DENDRAL performs is similar to the tasks of grammatical inference, sequence extrapolation, and concept formation [Hedrick74, Hunt75, Winston75]. Programs that perform these tasks can all be characterized as "induction" programs. Broadly speaking, the induction task is to find general rules that can generate, classify, or explain a training set of specific instances, and correctly predict new instances. The training set can be thought of as a set of I/O pairs from a "black box" machine; the induction program is supposed to discover the generating principles used in the machine. Often there is a single generating principle to be found; Meta-DENDRAL expects to find several.

### 2.2 Mass Spectrometry

As described previously [B.G. Buchanan76a], the black box whose behavior we are attempting to characterize is an instrument for chemical analysis known as a mass spectrometer. The mass spectrometer bombards a small sample of an unknown chemical with high energy electrons, breaking individual molecules into many fragments and causing atoms to migrate between fragments. Results of these processes are observed in a recording of the masses of the fragments that are collected. The data are usually presented in a bar graph of the relative abundance of each fragment (Y-axis) plotted against fragment mass (X-axis). From these data and a strong model of mass spectrometry, a skilled chemist can reconstruct much of the molecular structure of the unknown compound.

Throughout this chapter we will use the following terms to describe the actions of molecules in the mass spectrometer:

(1) Fragmentation: the breaking of an individual graph (molecule) into fragments by breaking a subset of the edges (bonds) within the graph.

(2) Atom migration: the detachment of nodes (atoms) from one fragment and their reattachment to a second fragment. This process alters the masses of both fragments.

(3) Mass spectral process, or process: a fragmentation followed by zero or more atom migrations.

One I/O pair for the instrument is considered to be (INPUT), a chemical sample with uniform molecular structure (abbreviated to "a structure"), and (OUTPUT), one X-Y point from the bar graph of fragment masses and relative abundances of fragments (often referred to as one peak in the mass spectrum). An example of an I/O pair is the following:

INPUT    CH3-CH2-CH2-NH-CH2-CH3
OUTPUT Fragment mass (X) : 58
        Relative abundance (Y) : 0.38

Since the spectrum of each structure contains 50 to 100 different data points, each structure appears in many I/O pairs. Thus, the program must look for several generating principles, or processes, that operate on a structure to produce many data points. In addition, the data are not guaranteed correct because these are empirical data from an electronic instrument that produces some background noise. As a result, the program does not attempt to explain every I/O pair. It does, however, choose which data points to explain on the basis of criteria given by the chemist as part of the imposed model of mass-spectrometry.

## 2.3 Syntax of Rules

Rules of mass spectrometry actually used by chemists are often expressed as production rules. These rules (when executed by a program) constitute a simulation of the fragmentation and atom migration processes that occur inside the instrument. The left-hand side is a description of the graph structure of some relevant piece of the molecule. The right-hand side is a list of processes that occur: specifically, bond cleavages and atom migrations. For example, one simple rule is

(R1)   N - C - C - C  →  N - C * C - C

where the asterisk indicates breaking the bond at that position and recording the mass of the fragment to the left of the asterisk. No migration of atoms between fragments is predicted by this rule.

Although the vocabulary for describing individual atoms in subgraphs is small and the grammar of subgraphs is simple, the size of the subgraph search space is immense. For example, for subgraphs containing 6 atoms, each with any of roughly 20 attribute-value specifications, there are roughly $20^6$ possible subgraphs. In addition to the connectivity of the subgraph, each atom in the subgraph may have up to four (dependent) attributes specified: (a) atom type (e.g., carbon), (b) number of connected neighbors (other than hydrogen), (c) number of hydrogen neighbors, and (d) number of doubly bonded neighbors.

The language of processes (right-hand sides of rules) is also simple: one or more bonds from the left-hand side may break and zero or more atoms may migrate between fragments.

### 2.4 Semantic Interpretation of Rules

The interpretation of rule (R1) in the above example is that *if* a molecule contains a nitrogen atom and three carbon atoms bonded as N-C-C-C *then* it will fragment in the mass spectrometer between the middle two carbon atoms, and the piece containing the nitrogen will be recorded. In a large molecule, this rule may apply more than once. For example, the spectrum of CH3-CH2-CH2-NH-CH2-CH2-CH2-CH3 will contain data points at masses 72 and 86 corresponding to the two fragments derived from the application of this rule:

CH3-CH2-CH2-NH-CH2

and

CH2-NH-CH2-CH2-CH2-CH3

For a number of reasons the data points are not uniquely associated with a single fragmentation and atom migration process (rule). For example, a single process may occur more than once in a molecule (as in the above example), and more than one process may produce identical fragments (and thus produce peaks at the same mass points in the bar graph).

### 2.5 Space of Instances

In order to learn rules of this form, the Meta-DENDRAL program is presented with many examples of actual I/O pairs from the mass spectrometer. Each I/O pair is described as a molecular graph structure, together with a data point from the mass spectrum for that structure. The rules to be learned constitute a description of the relevant transformations in the black box. Typically we start with a training set of 6-10 related molecules and their associated bar graphs, each containing 50-150 data points. These are drawn from an infinitely large space of possible instances, of which only a few for each structural class of molecules are available from libraries of spectra.

# 3.0 THE WORLD MODEL

## 3.1 Reasons for Introducing Strong Biases

Purely statistical learning programs find associations that are indicated by the data without introducing judgments about the meaningfulness of those associations. This is an advantage at times when an investigator's bias inhibits seeing associations or when an investigator is merely looking for all associations. It is a disadvantage, however, when the number of associations is so large that the meaningful ones are lost in the chaff. Statistical pattern recognition programs have been applied to mass spectrometry with some success [Jurs74].

In contrast to statistical approaches, Meta-DENDRAL utilizes a semantic model of the domain. This model has been included for two important reasons. First, it provides guidance for the rule formation program in a space of rules that is much too large to search exhaustively, especially when the input data have ambiguous interpretations. Second, it provides a check on the meaningfulness of the associations produced by the program, in a domain where the trivial or meaningless associations far outnumber the important ones.

## 3.2 The Half-Order Theory

The base-level or zero-order theory of mass spectrometry states that every subset of bonds within a molecule may break, and that the resulting fragments plus or minus migrating atoms will all be recorded. This zero-order model of mass spectrometry is not specific enough to effectively constrain the rule search. Therefore, some general guidelines have been imposed on it in the so-called half-order theory.

The half-order theory asserts that bonds will break and atoms will migrate to produce data points, according to the following constraints.

Constraints on fragmentations:

> Double bonds and triple bonds do not break.
> No aromatic bonds break.
> Only fragments larger than two carbon atoms show up in the data.
> Two bonds to the same carbon atom cannot break together.
> No more than three bonds break in any one fragmentation.
> No more than two complete fragmentations occur in one process.
> At most two rings fragment in a multiple step process.

Constraints on atom migration:

> At most two hydrogen atoms can migrate after a fragmentation.
> At most one H2O unit is lost after any fragmentation.
> At most one CO unit is lost after any fragmentation.

One of the most helpful features of this model is its flexibility. Any of the parameters can be easily changed by a chemist with other preconceptions. Any of these assumptions can be removed and, as discussed in the following section, additional statements can be added. **This power to guide rule formation will result in the program discovering only rules within a well-known framework. In addition, it also results in rules that are meaningful for the domain.**

### 3.3 Augmenting the Half-Order Theory

A chemist will often know more about the mass spectrometry of a class of molecules than is embodied in the half-order theory. In these cases it is important to augment the program's model by specifying class-specific knowledge to the program. This also provides a way of forming rules in the context of additional intuitions and biases about mass spectrometry. A chemist can thus see the "most interesting" rules (as defined by the augmentations) before the other rules. For example, one might be interested first in rules that mention at least one nitrogen atom before the numerous (and generally less interesting) rules that mention only carbon and hydrogen substructures.

### 4.0 THE LEARNING STRATEGY

We began with the assumption that numerical parameter estimation methods were not sufficient for the kinds of rules we wanted the program to discover in this domain due to the large number of variables required to describe subgraphs. We also wanted a chance to explore the power of heuristic search in a learning program, in the belief that efficient selection of alternative explanations is a large part of scientific discovery. As mentioned above, we also wanted to make rule discovery a model-directed procedure.

As described in more detail below, the learning program is based on a generator of production rules of a predetermined syntax operating under the constraints of a semantic world model. In common with other induction programs, it also contains an instance selection component and a critic for evaluating potential rules.

## 4.1 Instance Selection

Unlike the sophisticated instance selection procedure described by Simon and Lea [Simon73], Meta-DENDRAL merely looks at the *next* I/O pair, which is the next data point for the current molecule or, when there are no more for this molecule, the first data point for the next molecule. For each iteration through the learning cycle, training data consist of several spectra presented at a time, which are interpreted and summarized before any rule formation takes place. In Hunt's terms [Hunt75] the data are presented in parallel, rather than sequentially, for each iterative step.

Some interesting variations can be introduced to improve the instance selection procedure. For example, we have suggested elsewhere [B.G. Buchanan76a] allowing the program to request new data that will answer specific questions raised upon examination of the current best rule set. However, the cost of obtaining new data can be prohibitive in cases where chemical samples are difficult to obtain. Thus, the program cannot assume that it will receive each training instance that it requests.

## 4.2 The Critic

Any learning system must employ a critic to compare current performance with some desired standard. In Meta-DENDRAL there are two critics: one associated with rule generation and the other with rule modification. Both critics rely heavily upon examining evidential support for rules in the training data. Each rule is evaluated in terms of its positive evidence (correct explanations of data points) and its negative evidence (incorrect predictions associated with the rule). Both critics treat evidence that is uniquely explained by a rule (unique positive evidence) differently from evidence that is shared by several rules. In particular, a data point that can be explained by only one rule is stronger evidence for the rule than a data point that has several alternative explanations.

The rule generation critic analyzes candidate rules in terms of their positive evidence only; for reasons of efficiency it does not consider negative evidence. If the positive evidence of a candidate rule exhibits characteristics typical of good rules, then the critic adds this candidate rule to the list of output rules. Otherwise it decides whether the candidate rule should be further refined and reconsidered or should be abandoned.

The rule modification critic analyzes both positive and negative evidence of individual rules in order to fine-tune each rule. Since rule modification involves several distinct tasks (explained below) the critic makes several types of decisions. The criteria used for making all of these decisions can be summarized as follows.

(1) The set of rules as a whole should be made as compact and correct as possible without decreasing the positive evidence of the rule set.

(2) Rules should be modified to increase their positive evidence without increasing negative evidence.

(3) Rules should be modified to decrease their negative evidence without decreasing their unique positive evidence.

### 4.2.1 Credit Assignment

After evaluating performance, the critic must assign credit (or blame) to specific rules or components of rules. This credit assignment problem is an instance of a large class of such problems that have been recognized for some time [Minsky63] as important to learning programs. When blame for poor performance can be assigned to a component of a rule, modifications to that component are attempted.

For the rule generation critic, credit assignment is quite simple. During the rule search it must credit individual features in the left-hand side of a rule for the evidence covered by the rule. Therefore, as each new feature is added to a rule its effect on the rule's supporting positive evidence is examined. If the effect is unfavorable (see Section 4.3.2) the new feature receives the blame and is removed immediately from the rule.

There are three credit assignment problems during rule modification corresponding to the three decision criteria listed above.

(A) In order to make the rule set more concise, the critic must assign credit among redundant rules for explaining a specific data point. Credit is assigned to the rule with the strongest evidence over the entire training data set. Strength of evidence is a measure of a rule's positive and negative evidence weighted by the average intensity (Y-component) of the data points that the rule explains. In the event that two redundant rules have equally strong evidence, credit is given to the rule with the simpler left-hand side.

(B) In order to increase the positive evidence of a rule, some attribute value in the left-hand side of the rule must be made less specific. The critic must search for an overly specific feature to blame for excluding additional positive evidence for the rule. Currently the critic must search by trial and error for such a feature.

(C) In order to remove negative evidence from a rule, the critic must assign blame to some overly general feature. The set of attribute values common to positive evidence instances provides a menu of possible rule attribute values. Attribute values from this list are added to the rule to remove the negative evidence.

## 4.3 The Learning Cycle

The learning cycle is a series of "plan-generate-test" steps as found in many AI systems [Feigenbaum71]. After prescanning a set of several hundred I/O pairs, the program searches the space of rules for plausible explanations and then modifies the rules on the basis of detailed testing. When rules generated from one training set are added to the model, and a second (or next) block of data examined, the rule set is further extended and modified to explain the new data. That is, the program can now iteratively modify rules formed from the initial training set (and add to them), but it is currently unable to "undo" rules. Details of each of these processes are provided below.

### 4.3.1 Data Interpretation

The planning step in the procedure includes reinterpretation of all the given I/O pairs in terms of the vocabulary of the specified model (the augmented half-order theory). That is, the output half of each I/O pair is reinterpreted to be a list of fragmentation and atom migration processes (potential right-hand sides of rules) that are feasible explanations of the data point within the specified model. This must be done since we want the final rules to propose the underlying mass spectral processes that produce data points, not just the data points themselves. Notice that the association of processes with data points may be ambiguous. For instance, in the molecule CH3-CH2-CH2-NH-CH2-CH3 a spectral peak at mass 29 may be attributed to a process that breaks either the second bond from the left or one that breaks the second bond from the right. This planning step is called INTSUM, for interpretation and summary of the initial data. For each molecule in a given set, INTSUM produces the plausible mass spectral processes that might occur, i.e., breaks and combinations of breaks, with and without migration of atoms. INTSUM then examines the data points associated with each molecule, looking for evidence (spectral peaks) for each process. Finally the planning step produces a summary showing the total evidence associated with each possible process. This summary is used during rule generation to avoid considering uninstantiated candidate rules.

### 4.3.2 Rule Generation

After the data have been interpreted in INTSUM, control passes to a heuristic search program known as RULEGEN, for rule generation. RULEGEN creates general rules by selecting "important" features of the molecular structure around the site of the fragmentations proposed by INTSUM. These important features are combined to form a subgraph description of the local environment surrounding the broken bonds. Each subgraph considered becomes the left-hand side of a candidate rule whose right-hand side is INTSUM's proposed process. Essentially RULEGEN searches within the constraints of the half-order theory through a space of these subgraph descriptions looking for successively more specific subgraphs that are supported by successively "better" sets of evidence.

Conceptually, the program begins with the most general candidate rule, X*X (where X is any unspecified atom and where the asterisk is used to indicate the broken bond, with the detected fragment written to the left of the asterisk). Since the most useful rules lie somewhere between the overly general candidate X*X and the overly specific complete molecular structure (with specified bonds breaking), the program generates refined descriptions by successively specifying additional features. This is a coarse search; for efficiency reasons RULE-GEN sometimes adds features to several nodes at a time, without considering the intermediate subgraphs.

The program systematically adds features (attribute-value pairs) to subgraphs, starting with the subgraph X*X, and always making each successor more specifi: than its parent. (Recall that each node can be described with any or all of the following attributes: atom type, number of nonhydrogen neighbors, number of hydrogen neighbors, and number of doubly bonded neighbors). Working outward, the program assigns one attribute at a time to all atoms that are the same number of atoms away from the breaking bond. Each of the four attributes is considered in turn, and each attribute *value* for which there is supporting evidence generates a new successor. Although different values for the same attribute may be assigned to each atom at a given distance from the breaking bond, the coarseness of the search prevents examination of subgraphs in which this attribute is totally unimportant on *some* of these atoms.

A portion of the rule search tree leading to R1 is shown in Fig. 1. Starting with the parent subgraph S0, the "number of neighbors" attribute is specified for each atom adjacent to the break in subgraph S1. "Atom type" is then specified for atoms adjacent to the break in S2, and for atoms one bond removed from the break in S3. At each step in the search there are also many other possible successors corresponding to assignments of other values to these same attributes, or assignment of values to other attributes.

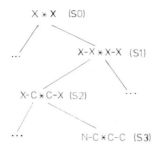

Portion of the RULEGEN Search

Fig. 1. Portion of the RULEGEN search.

Each descendant is checked to see if the supporting evidence is "better" (see below) than the evidence for the parent. Those which satisfy the test become new parents for a next level of descendants with one more feature specified. The program adds specifications to candidate rules until it finds a rule that is (a) specific enough to make correct predictions and (b) general enough to account for more than a few special cases.[2] Subgraph S3 in Fig. 1 meets these conditions, and is output by the program as rule (R1):

(R1)  N - C - C - C  →  N - C * C - C

In (R1) the only important features are the atom types and the connections of four atoms; the other features and atoms have been

---

[2] The program judges a rule to be an improvement over its parent if three conditions hold: (a) the new rule predicts fewer fragments per molecule than the parent (i.e., the new rule is more specific); (b) it predicts fragmentations for at least half of all the molecules (i.e., it is not too specific); and (c) either the new rule predicts fragmentations for as many molecules as its parent or the parent rule was "too general" in the following sense: the parent predicts more than two fragments in some single molecule or, on the average, it predicts more than 1.5 fragments per molecule.

generalized away. The point of generalizing is to abstract away unimportant attributes of atoms and unimportant atoms.

### 4.3.3 Rule Modification

The last phase of the program (called RULEMOD) evaluates the plausible rules generated by RULEGEN and modifies them by making them more general or more specific. In order to extend the range of applicability of the rules, RULEMOD uses a less constrained model than RULEGEN. Rules generated by RULEGEN under an augmented half-order theory, e.g., in which only fragments containing a nitrogen atom were considered, cannot immediately be applied by a performance program using a more general model. Therefore RULEMOD refines the rule so that it can stand on its own under a more general model. In contrast to RULEGEN, RULEMOD considers negative evidence (incorrect predictions) of rules in order to increase the accuracy of the rule's applications within the training set. RULEGEN performs a coarse search of the rule space for reasons of efficiency, whereas RULEMOD performs a localized, fine search to refine the rules.

RULEMOD will typically output a set of **5 to 10** rules covering substantially the same training data points as the input RULEGEN set of approximately **25 to 100** rules, but with fewer incorrect predictions. This program is written as a set of five tasks (corresponding to the five subsections below), which we feel are closely analogous to this aspect of human problem solving.

*Selecting a Subset of Important Rules.* As a first step, the selection procedure is applied to the whole set of rule candidates produced by RULEGEN. The local evaluation in RULEGEN has ignored negative evidence and has not discovered that different RULEGEN pathways may yield rules that are different but explain many of the same data points. Thus there is often a high degree of overlap in those rules and they may make many incorrect predictions.

To select rules, scores are calculated (see Critic section), the rule with the best score selected, and the evidence peaks supporting that rule removed from the supporting evidence for other rules. Then the whole process is repeated until either (a) all scores are below a selected threshold or (b) all evidence has been explained. The scoring function[3] applies the standard of performance of the RULEMOD critic discussed above.

*Merging Rules.* Although most of the redundant rules have been deleted in the first step of RULEMOD, there may still remain sets of

---

[3] The scoring function is Score $= I * (P + U - 2N)$, where $I =$ the average Y-component (fragment abundance) of positive evidence data points; $P =$ the number of positive evidence instances for the rule; $U =$ the number of unique positive evidence instances for the rule; $N =$ the number of negative evidence instances for a rule.

rules that explain many of the same data points. For any such set of rules, the program attempts to find a slightly more general rule that (a) includes all the evidence covered by the overlapping rules and (b) does not bring in extra negative evidence. If it can find such a rule, the overlapping rules are replaced by the single compact rule.

*Deleting Negative Evidence by Making Rules More Specific.* RULEMOD tries to add attribute-value specifications to atoms in each rule in order to delete some negative evidence while keeping all of the positive evidence. This involves local search of the possible additions to the subgraph descriptions that were not considered by RULEGEN. Because of the coarseness of RULEGEN's search, some ways of refining rules are not tried, except by RULEMOD. For example, rule (R1') below would be a specification of (R1) that RULEGEN would miss because it specifies different attributes (not just different values) for atoms that are the same distance from the broken bond (asterisk):

(R1')   N - CH2 - C - C   →   N - CH2 * C - C.

In this case, the number of hydrogen neighbors is specified for the first left-hand atom from the broken bond, but not for the first right-hand one.

*Making Rules More General.* RULEGEN often forms rules that are more specific than they need to be. At this point we have a choice whether to leave the rules as they are or to seek a more general form that covers the same (and perhaps new) data points without introducing new negative evidence. Rule (R1') for example, could be made more general by removing the atom type specification on one of the first atoms next to the asterisk, and by removing completely the rightmost atom in the subgraph; resulting in rule (R1'').

(R1'')   N - CH2 - X   →   N - CH2 * X

Again, because of the coarseness of its search, RULEGEN could not have considered this form of the rule. We assume here that RULEGEN produces good approximations to rules and that RULEMOD can refine them.

*Selecting the Final Rule Set.* The selection procedure applied at the beginning of RULEMOD is applied again at the very end of RULEMOD in order to remove redundancies that might have been introduced during generalization and specialization.

*Evaluating the Rules.* Rules may be evaluated by measuring how well they explain, or "cover," the given spectra. We call this the "explanatory power" of the rules. We also want to be able to estimate how well they can be used to discriminate the most plausible structures from the rest in a list of candidate explanations of an unknown spectrum (from a known class). We call this the "discriminatory power" of the rules (see [B.G. Buchanan76b] for details).

### 4.3.4 Integrating Subsequent Data

A requirement for any practical learning program is the ability to integrate newly acquired data into an evolving knowledge base. New data may dictate that additional rules be added to the knowledge base or that existing rules be modified or eliminated. New rules may be *added* to the rule base by running RULEGEN on the new data, then running RULEMOD on the combined set of new and previously generated rules.

When an existing rule is *modified*, the issue is raised of how to maintain the integrity of the modified rule on its past training instances. To see this consider an example. A new training instance is acquired and, after credit assignment questions are resolved, it is decided that rule R incorrectly "triggered" on some situation S. The left-hand side of rule R must be modified so that it will no longer match S. In general there will be many possible changes to R that will disallow the match to S, but some will be better choices than others. The correct changes to R are those which do not alter past correct applications of R. Of course there is no way of knowing which of the possible changes to R will turn out to be correct upon examining still more data, and once a single change is selected the possibility exists that backtracking will be necessary at some future point. This whole issue may be viewed as a problem of credit assignment among the features that make up the left-hand side of R.

Different learning programs have taken different approaches to this problem of ensuring that rule modifications are consistent with past training instances. Some [Samuel63] have assumed that the correct performance of each rule on past data need not be preserved. Other programs [Waterman75] reexamine past training instances to evaluate later changes to rules, and to allow backtracking in cases where incorrect changes to rules were made. Many programs [Winston75] use domain specific heuristics to select the most likely change to R in order to minimize the need for backtracking.

We are currently developing a method [Mitchell77] for representing all versions of the left hand side of a rule that are consistent with the observed data for all iterations thus far. This representation is referred to as the "version space" of the rule. By examining the version space of R, we can answer the question "Which of the recommended changes to R will preserve its performance on past instances?" The answer is simply "Any changes that yield a version of the rule contained in the version space." By using version spaces we avoid the problem of selecting a single unretractable modification to R, and therefore eliminate the need for backtracking when the training data are consistent. Instead all the elements of the version space that do not match some negative instance S are retained, and those which do match S are eliminated. Similarly, when new data are encountered in which a situation S′ is found to correctly trigger R, only those elements of the version space that match S′ are retained.

## 5.0 RESULTS

One measure of the proficiency of Meta-DENDRAL is the ability of the corresponding performance program to predict correct spectra of new molecules using the learned rules. One of the DENDRAL performance programs ranks a list of plausible hypotheses (candidate molecules) according to the similarity of their predictions (predicted spectra) to observed data. The rank of the correct hypothesis (i.e., the molecule actually associated with the observed spectrum) provides a quantitative measure of the "discriminatory power" of the rule set.

The Meta-DENDRAL program has successfully rediscovered known, published rules of mass spectrometry for two classes of molecules. More importantly, it has discovered new rules for three closely related families of structures for which rules had not previously been reported. Meta-DENDRAL's rules for these classes have been published in the chemistry literature [B.G. Buchanan76b]. Evaluations of all five sets of rules are discussed in that publication. This work demonstrates the utility of Meta-DENDRAL for rule formation in mass spectrometry for individual classes of structures.

Recently we have adapted the Meta-DENDRAL program to a second spectroscopic technique, 13C-nuclear magnetic resonance (13C-NMR) spectroscopy [Mitchell78]. This new version provides the opportunity to direct the induction machinery of Meta-DENDRAL under a model of 13C-NMR spectroscopy. It generates rules that associate the resonance frequency of a carbon atom in a magnetic field with the local structural environment of the atom. 13C-NMR rules have been generated and used in a candidate molecule ranking program similar to the one described above. 13C-NMR rules formulated by the program for two classes of structures have been successfully used to identify the spectra of additional molecules (of the same classes, but outside the set of training data used in generating the rules).

The rule-based molecule ranking program performs at the level of a well-educated chemist in both the mass spectral and 13C-NMR domains. We view this performance as indicative of the quality of the rule base discovered by Meta-DENDRAL.

## 6.0 SUMMARY

We believe that automated knowledge base construction is feasible for constructing high-performance computer programs. The functional components of Meta-DENDRAL are common to other induction programs. The Meta-DENDRAL approach of model-directed heuristic search through a complex space of possible rules appears well suited to many induction tasks. The use of a strong model of the domain to direct the rule search has been demonstrated for rule formation in two areas of chemistry. The high performance of programs that use the generated rules attests to the success of this learning strategy.

# COGNITIVE SYSTEMS BASED ON ADAPTIVE ALGORITHMS[1]

John H. Holland and Judith S. Reitman
*The University of Michigan*

*The type of cognitive system (CS) studied here has four basic parts: (1) a set of interacting elementary productions, called lassifiers, (2) a performance algorithm that directs the action of the system in the environment, (3) a simple learning algorithm that keeps a record of each classifier's success in bringing about rewards, and (4) a more complex learning algorithm, called the genetic algorithm, that modifies the set of classifiers so that variants of good classifiers persist and new, potentially better ones are created in a provably efficient manner.*

*Two "proof-of-principle" experiments are reported. One experiment shows CS's performance in a maze when it has only the ability to adjust the predictions about ensuing rewards of classifiers (similar to adjusting the "weight" of each classifier) vs. when the power of the genetic algorithm is added. Criterion was achieved an order of magnitude more rapidly when the genetic algorithm was operative. A second experiment examines transfer of learning. Placed in a more difficult maze, CS with experience in the simpler maze reaches criterion an order of magnitude more rapidly than CS without prior experience.*

## 1.0 OVERVIEW

In broadest terms, the cognitive systems described here infer environmental patterns from experience and associate "appropriate" response sequences with them. To determine appropriate response sequences the systems keep track of selected performance measures

[1] Research reported in this paper was supported in part by the National Science Foundation under grant DCR 71-01997 and by the Horace H. Rackham School of Graduate Studies under grant 387156.

*313*

such as the rate of accumulation of certain resources or the rate of reduction of predetermined needs. These performance measures enter directly into determining what patterns and associations are inferred and preserved. Because behaviors (patterns and associations) required for good performance in a given environment may be difficult to determine a priori, the systems of interest to us must be capable of learning most behaviors falling within the limits set by the system's basic capacities (inputs, outputs, memory capacity, and procedures given a priori). In particular, the systems must be capable of organizing these behaviors into "cognitive maps" appropriate to the environment and usable for prediction and lookahead.

It follows that the core of such a cognitive system (CS) is the learning algorithm—its way of inferring patterns, associations, and predictions. This emphasis on learning is reinforced by the observations that intelligent systems inevitably require a steady succession of changes as experience is gained. CS makes these changes itself, rather than requiring the designer to supply them. The problems encountered are familiar: learning of new productions, generalization, focus of attention and conflict resolution between competing productions, access and use of knowledge already acquired and the use of information not directly associated with the performance measures. (Discussion of these problems occur, for example, in Hayes-Roth and Burge [F. Hayes-Roth76e], McDermott and Forgy [J. McDermott77b], Samuel [Samuel63], Soloway and Riseman [Soloway77], and Waterman [Waterman70]. The systems we study approach these problems by generating and combining elementary productions (simple condition-action rules) to generate behavior. Learning is accomplished through a powerful and flexible algorithm belonging to the class of provably efficient genetic algorithms [Holland75].

The designer of an intelligent system should give possible changes careful consideration from the outset, even if he intends to make all the changes himself. Without such consideration it is unlikely that the changes dictated by experience will be easily implemented. Since it is impossible to determine, at the outset, which changes experience will require, the designer should consider the full range $A$ of systems that could result from various combinations of changes. If the designer concentrates only on his initial design, a single variant in $A$, he gains little insight into $A$ as a whole. Not knowing much about $A$, he wanders through it blindly as experience accumulates, making "local improvements" but searching $A$ very inefficiently. In the literature of artificial intelligence, Samuel's [Samuel63] approach to game-playing is a particularly good example of such prior consideration of $A$. He characterizes the range of strategies $A$ by specifying allowable changes, then searches $A$ by making progressive changes in the strategy initially tried.

It is vital that the changes allowed for, i.e., the range $A$, be rich enough to give a reasonable chance of correcting faults in the initial design. In other words, the system should not only learn, but some guarantee should be given that it can adapt to a wide range of situations. Given any program of behavior falling within CS's basic limits (storage capacity, etc.), $A$ should contain a variant that can carry it out. One way of assuring sufficient richness is to find a set of allowable changes that makes $A$ computationally complete within CS's basic limits. ($A$ is computationally complete if each procedure executable by a general-purpose computer can be effected by some system in $A$. For CS this means that any complex of behaviors that can be defined precisely can be attained by some sequence of changes. The learning algorithm now becomes a procedure for searching $A$, making changes in accord with the patterns it finds in the environment.

Because learning has a central role, all parts of CS have been designed with a view to their suitability as part of the domain of the learning algorithm. The basic elements of the domain are elementary productions called classifiers. Each classifier is defined by specifying a set of conditions to which it is sensitive—collectively called a *taxon*—and a signal it broadcasts when these conditions are fulfilled. A classifier can be sensitive to signals broadcast by other classifiers as well as to signals from the environment. That is, the taxon specifies conditions on both kinds of signals.

In more detail: CS encodes all signals by using an array of *detectors*, $\delta_i$, $i = 1, \ldots, \beta$, each detector being sensitive to some attribute of the environment or some attribute of the (set of) signals from other classifiers. Using $I_1$ to denote the set of environmental conditions, and $I_2$ to denote all possible sets of broadcast signals, the i-th detector can be thought of as a function

$$\delta_i : I_j \rightarrow \{0,1\} \quad i = 1, \ldots, \beta \quad j = 1 \text{ or } 2$$

where $\delta_i$ takes the value 1 ("on") whenever detector $i$ detects the appropriate attribute in a signal; and otherwise takes value 0 ("off"). Each combination of environmental and internal signals $s$ yields an $\beta$-digit binary number $(\delta_1[s], \ldots, \delta_\beta[s])$ via the detectors. More formally, the set

$$\{\delta_1(s), \delta_2(s), \ldots, \delta_\beta(s) : s \in I_1 \times I_2\}$$

constitutes a set of representations of all combinations of signals $I_1$-$\times I_2$.

The taxon of a classifier specifies a subset of the $\beta$-tuples, any one being sufficient to cause the classifier to broadcast its signal. In the simpler versions a taxon specifies, for each detector, whether or not the classifier attends to that detector and, if it does, what value (0 or 1) it requires. In this case, the taxon is defined by an $\beta$-tuple

$$(\lambda_1, \lambda_2, \ldots, \lambda_\beta)\ \lambda_i\ \epsilon\ \Lambda\ =\ \{\#,0,1\}\ i\ =\ 1, \ldots, \beta$$

where $\lambda_i = \#$ indicates that the classifier does not attend to detector i (it "doesn't care"), and $\lambda_i = 0$ (or 1) indicates that detector i must be off (or on) for the overall detector configuration to satisfy the taxon. The task of the learning algorithm is to manipulate these taxa so that the appropriate signals are emitted to control CS under the various environmental conditions it faces.

Two broad principles guide the learning algorithm in the manipulation of taxa:

The first principle concerns the level of generality of a taxon. A taxon that is too general (too many #s) will give rise to inconsistent performance by signaling in inappropriate situations. A taxon that is too specific (too few #s) wastes memory capacity by specifying a situation that recurs infrequently or not at all. The learning algorithm must put a steady selective pressure upon the population of classifiers, replacing taxa that are too general or too specific by more appropriate taxa.

The second principle concerns prediction as a means of using the (usually extensive) information acquired on the way to a goal (attainment of resources, reduction of needs, etc.). Generally, when a goal is attained after a long sequence of responses, many of the responses along the way are inconsistent in the sense that they delay attainment of the goal. (As an example, consider a board game such as Go; cf. W. Reitman [W.R. Reitman77].) The learning algorithm must rid the system of such inconsistencies. Stated the other way around, the algorithm should select classifiers that produce consistent goal-directed sequences of responses. This selection depends much more on information acquired on the way than on information received at the time the goal is attained. Inconsistencies along the way can be discovered if each classifier predicts the anticipated long-term effect of its activation. Then, if a subsequently activated classifier makes a different prediction, an inconsistency is revealed. The procedure here was foreshadowed by Samuel's [Samuel63] use of a position evaluator as a predictor. When Samuel's evaluator gives a different value at a subsequent position, thereby revealing an inconsistency in expectations, weights are revised to bring the earlier prediction more in line with the subsequent evaluation. Here, inconsistencies are reconciled by having the learning algorithm punish (select against) activated classifiers making predictions that are subsequently contravened. Chains of consistent goal-oriented responses are rewarded (selected for) with the eventual result that the first element of the chain predicts the ultimate outcome.

Using these principles as guides, a genetic algorithm was modified to serve as a learning algorithm. Briefly, the genetic algorithm selects classifiers based on their predicted performance, and operates on their taxa to build classifiers that potentially respond to important regularities in the environment. It does this by making intensive use of particular combinations of 0s, 1s, and #s consistently associated with above-average performance (see below). A primary reason for this choice is the provable efficiency of *genetic algorithms* (see Chapter 7 of Holland [Holland75]). This efficiency is most easily understood by considering special classes of taxa called *schemata*. (More formally, schemata are hyperplanes in $A$). Schemata name or identify particular combinations of attributes and don't cares (0s, 1s, and #s) that aid in producing goal-oriented classifiers. The object of the learning algorithm then is to discover good schemata and use them in building taxa.

Formally, schemata are defined in terms of a $\beta$-tuple representation of $A$'s elements by using an additional symbol, $\Box$. $\Box$ is a schema-level "don't care." For example the schema $(1, \Box, \#, \Box, \Box, \ldots, \Box)$ names the *set* of all $\beta$-tuples in $A$ that have a 1 at the first position, a # at the third position, and any values whatsoever from $\Lambda = \{\#,0,1\}$ at the other $\beta$-2 positions. In full generality, the set $\Xi$ of schemata is the set of all $\beta$-tuples formed by substituting $\Box$s at various positions in $\beta$-tuples from $A$. (Formally, $\Xi = \{\Lambda \cup \{\Box\}\}^{\beta}$). A schema $\xi = (\nu_1, \ldots, \nu_\beta)$ from $\Xi$ names a subset of $A$ as follows: $A = (\lambda_1, \ldots, \lambda_\beta) \in A$ belongs to $\xi = (\nu_1, \ldots, \nu_\beta)$ if and only if, for each position j, $\lambda_j = \nu_j$ if $\nu_j \in \Lambda = \{\#,0,1\}$; otherwise, when $\nu_j = \Box$, $\lambda_j$ can be any element of $\Lambda$.

The following are important, provable properties of genetic algorithms regarding schemata:

(1) If $A$ is regarded as a sample space then *each* taxon is a legitimate sample point for each of the $2^\beta$ schemata (sets) of which it is an instance. The genetic algorithm uses this information to alter its estimates of the value of a large proportion of the schemata involved. In fact, each time the genetic algorithm is applied to the set of M taxa being used by the cognitive system, the estimated values of about $M^2 \times 2^{\beta/2}$ implicitly associated schemata are adjusted. This occurs even though only M taxa are modified—a phenomenon called *intrinsic parallelism*. It cannot be emphasized too strongly that this tremendous "speed-up" plays a critical role in the performance of this system. In effect $M^2 \times 2^{\beta/2}$ different combinations of 0s, 1s, and #s are tried, evaluated, and used to generate taxa each time the genetic algorithm is applied.

A more formal statement gives a more precise idea of what is actually occurring. Let $B = \{A_1, \ldots, A_M\}$ be the set of taxa maintained by the cognitive system at some time t, and let $\{\mu_1, \ldots, \mu_M\}$ be the associated performance predictions. That is, $\mu_j$ is a *prediction* of the value of the goal that will be attained if the classifier with taxon $A_j$ is activated. Consider a schema $\xi$ having instances in B. (A taxon $A_j$ is an instance of a schema $\xi$ if it belongs to the subset of $A$ named by $\xi$, i.e., if it has the particular attributes named by $\xi$). Let $\mu_\xi$ be the average of the predicted performances of the instances of $\xi$. (Formally, $\mu_\xi = [\Sigma_{j|A_j\epsilon\xi}\mu_j]/[\text{number of } A_j\epsilon\xi]$). It can be proved that each time the genetic algorithm is applied to B, about $M^2 \times 2^{\beta/2}$ schemata will have the number of their instances in B changed by amount proportional to $\mu_\xi$. The exact statement is

$$M_\xi(t+1) = (\mu_\xi/\mu) \times (1\text{-}\epsilon) \times M_\xi(t)$$

where $M_\xi(t)$ is the number of instances of $\xi$ in B at time t, $\mu$ is the average predicted performance of all the taxa in B, and $\epsilon << 1$ for the $M^2 \times 2^{\beta/2}$ schemata of interest. (See Lemma 7.2 of Holland [Holland75].)

(2) Under the selective pressure on schemata described in (1), the number of instances in B of a given schema comes to reflect its usefulness in generating new taxa. That is, the cumulative effect of the genetic algorithm is the *ranking* (and use) of a great many schemata. The *rank* of a schema $\xi$ is simply the number $M_\xi$ of taxa in B at time t that are instances of $\xi$. This rank reflects the system's experience with $\xi$ prior to time t; in general, the higher the rank, the more useful the schema in generating new taxa, the higher the estimated value of that particular combination of 1s, 0s, and #s. Recall that each *taxon* is an instance of $2^\beta$ distinct schemata; here, several taxa serve to determine the rank of a given schema. It follows that a given taxon can participate in the ranking (count) of many schemata. Thus the rank of a great many schemata can be stored with the help of a few dozen selected taxa. The net result is the compact storage of a great deal of information gleaned from experience. The genetic algorithm automatically accesses and uses this information to generate new taxa. The higher the rank of a schema, the more frequently the corresponding combination of 0s, 1s, and #s is used.

(3) Because the set of schemata is such a rich cover of the space of possibilities $A$, almost any interactions (or correlations) between attributes (detectors) will be "discovered" by some schema. Combinations of attributes that correspond to useful regularities in the environment will give rise to corresponding high-ranking schemata in B. Because of the way in which the genetic algorithm processes schemata, high dimensionality and complex interactions pose no difficulties; the genetic algorithm actually exploits them to make an efficient search of $A$. (In another context, genetic algorithms have been used to find the global optimum of high-dimensional, nonlinear functions. See

DeJong [DeJong75]. Hayes-Roth's [Burge76] SLIM makes a similar use of schemata, but without the intrinsic parallelism.)

These properties, taken together, augur well for genetic algorithms as learning algorithms. By using the predicted performances $\{\mu_j\}$ the algorithm directly incorporates the two principles discussed earlier. A taxon that is too general cannot yield consistent performances or predictions. Hence it will be associated with a low predicted performance $\mu$. Similarly a taxon that is associated with an invalid prediction will have its $\mu$ lowered (see the next section for details). In both cases, the genetic algorithm selects against such taxa (relative to taxa at more appropriate levels of generality and prediction). At the same time, the algorithm displaces too-specific taxa (because they "age" more rapidly—see the next section) to make room for newly generated taxa. Only taxa that are above average in their predictions and levels of generality will be favored. More importantly, the schemata they instance will be favored in the generation of new taxa. The resulting speed-up, a consequence of the algorithm's intrinsic parallelism, provides rapid and flexible learning.

## 2.0 DESCRIPTION OF COGNITIVE SYSTEM LEVEL 1 (CS-1)

CS-1 consists of a general memory store containing classifiers and three important processes that act on information in memory. The first process directs CS-1's performance by coding the situation and finding in memory actions that are appropriate to both the specifics of the situation and CS-1's goals. The second process is a form of simple learning; after a series of actions, it stores in memory information about the consequences of these actions. The third process is a more complex learning process that changes the contents of memory to allow good productions (classifiers) to endure, bad ones to be deleted, and new, potentially good productions to be created for subsequent trial. The novelty of the model is not so much in the performance or simple learning processes, but rather in the process that changes memory.

*Structure.* Figure 1 illustrates the structural parts of the system. Included are a *detector array* encoding the current environmental and internal states, *resource reservoirs* keeping track of the needs and goals of the system, a set of *classifiers* constituting the procedural content of memory, a *message list* keeping track of some of the system's most recent internal state, and an *effector array* specifying the action to be taken.

For CS-1 the detector array consists of a set of individual sensors, each of which is either turned on (1) or off (0) at each time-step by the

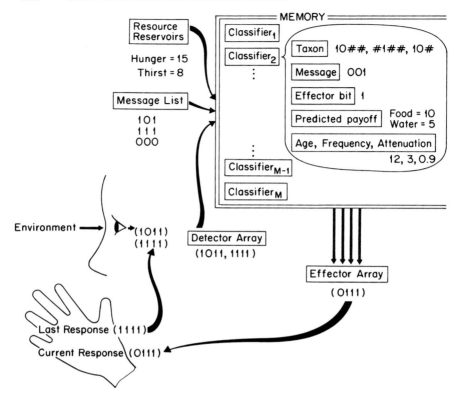

Fig. 1. Schematic diagram of structure of CS-1.

overall situation obtaining at that time. There are two sets of sensors, one set triggered by the external environment (such as retinal detectors or higher-order feature detectors), and one set by the state of memory and the effectors in the last response. Each classifier used in producing an actual response broadcasts a signal or message, also an array of 1s and 0s, stored on the message list. In the next time-step responses are chosen on the basis of both the message list and detector array, allowing the system to make an action conditional on past "thoughts" and actions. The resource reservoirs reflect simple biological needs, such as thirst and hunger, assumed in CS-1 to deplete regularly in time. Cognitive goals could be incorporated easily as needs that can be filled without introduction of externally presented rewards and that do not necessarily deplete continuously in time.

The memory of the system consists of a fixed large number of classifiers. Each classifier has a part that is sensitive to system input and messages, a signal that is emitted when the classifier is activated, and a series of parameters reflecting the value of the classifier to the system. The input side of the classifier, a taxon, consists of an array of 1s, 0s, and #s, where #s denote "I don't care." Each taxon will consequently match a number of detector and message list configurations, patterns of only 1s and 0s. For example, the taxon consisting of 1##1 will match four arrays, 1011, 1101, 1111, and 1001.

The output side of the classifier specifies a message and the condition of an effector, either on (1) or off (0), in the effector array. One set of classifiers exists for each separate effector. Actions can be coordinated because all sets of classifiers have access to the common message list and can read the last effector array setting.

Each classifier has associated with it parameters (single numbers of arrays) that determine its fate in the system. The most important is the predicted payoff, an array of the amounts and kinds of needs that were satisfied in the past when that particular classifier helped determine the responses. Predicted payoffs reflect the value of the classifier to the system and are the major determinants of the future influence of the classifier in the learning process. The three lesser parameters are called *age, frequency,* and *attenuation.* Age is a value that increases in time from the classifier's creation, but is reduced each time the classifier is used. Since it is a combination of the frequency and recency of use of a particular classifier, age appropriately determines when a particular classifier is to be deleted from memory. The second parameter, frequency, is a simple count of the number of times the classifier has been used. It allows adjustment of the predicted payoffs when a reward is issued to the system. The adjustment is less if the classifier has had heavier use and its predicted payoff can consequently be assumed to be more reliable. The third parameter, attenuation, figures in the adjustment of the predicted payoff when a reward is issued to the system, allowing appropriate allocation of this single reward value of the various classifiers that led to the reward. Between rewards, attenuation is incremented at every time t wherein an activated classifier has a successor (at time $t+1$) with a lower predicted payoff. This increment in attenuation is assigned to all classifiers activated between the last reward and time $t+1$. This gives early overpredicting classifiers less credit (an attenuated reward) than an accurately predicting one. This parameter is highly correlated with the delay between a response and the reward. On average, the classifier that is one step away from the reward will be less attenuated than one ten steps away; during the nine intervening steps, the early classifier is more likely to experience *attenuation.*

*The performance process.* The system performs in two cycles, one embedded in the other. In the smaller cycle, called a *stimulus-response cycle,* the input changes and a response (external or internal) is constructed. Many stimulus-response cycles can occur within each *epoch,* a larger cycle that is bounded by the issuance of a reward.

In the stimulus-response cycle, the set of classifiers is searched for those matching the particular current detector array and message list. Because many classifiers match each array (e.g., *taxa* 1 # # #, 10 # #, 101 #, and 1011 match array 1011), a competition is held for the one classifier whose taxon fits the specific details of the overall array (input and messages) *and* whose predicted payoff fits the current needs and goals of the system. Within each effector set, only classifiers having no direct mismatches with the detector array are considered for competition (e.g., taxa # 11 # #, 01 # # #, and # # # # 1 will all fit *detector array* 01101, but *taxon* 11110 # will not). A score is calculated for each matching classifier: the sum of the number of features specified in the taxon (giving weight to the more specific taxon) multiplied by the amount of the current needs fulfilled by this classifier's predicted payoff. Only the ten highest-scoring classifiers are assigned a probability of being activated; the probability is directly proportional to the classifier's relative advantage over the others in the high-scoring subset. The winner is then activated (turned on), its output condition is specified in the effector array, its message is left on the message list, the classifier's age is reduced by half, its frequency count is increased, and the attenuation parameters of other recently activated classifiers are adjusted. Within each stimulus-response cycle, many sets of classifiers hold simultaneous competitions, each set's winner producing an independent instruction for the effector array and a message for the common message list.

Briefly then, the system's performance is dependent in an interactive way on the input information (the detector array), an interpretation of that information dependent on context (the classifiers), recent actions and thoughts (the message list), the needs or goals (resource reservoir levels), and past long-term experience (the predicted payoffs).

*The simple learning process.* When a reward enters the system to replenish the depleting reservoirs, the epoch ends. All the predicted payoffs of the currently activated classifiers are then modified to reflect their accuracy in anticipating this reward. Those predicted payoffs that were consistent with (not greater than) this reward are maintained or increased; those that overpredicted are significantly reduced, all according to their attenuations. When the predicted payoffs of all the activated classifiers have been adjusted, the classifiers are inactivated and their attenuation parameters are returned to zero.

*The adaptation of the contents of memory.* The heart of the system's learning arises in continuous, autonomous changes occurring in the classifiers. The specific algorithm is a tailored genetic algorithm.

Genetic algorithms are defined and investigated in a general context in Holland [Holland75] and in a behavioral context in Holland [Holland76]. The algorithm combines variants of genetic operators (such as cross-over) with a "survival of the fittest" principle, to discover and exploit above-average feature combinations. At regular intervals, the contents of memory (the classifiers) are changed. The "survival of the fittest" aspect of the genetic algorithm is reflected in the fact that those classifiers that have performed better than average (have above-average predicted payoffs) are more likely to produce variants for trial in the next generation of memory. The variants in the next generation are produced by genetic operations such as a "crossing-over" applied to the taxa associated with good classifiers.

Specifically, the genetic algorithm proceeds as follows. From each set of classifiers controlling a single effector, two parent classifiers are chosen. Each candidate has a probability of being chosen proportional to its predicted payoff. The taxa and the signals (messages) of the two parent classifiers are crossed, respectively, at a random point, creating new taxa and signals. For example, if one "parent" taxon is #1111, the other is 00###, and the cross-over point is after the second position, the "children" *taxa* are #1### and 00111. One of the offspring is selected at random, and an entirely new classifier built around it. Its predicted payoff and effector setting are those of one of its parents, its age is an average of its parents' ages, and its frequency and attenuation parameters are set to zero.

Creation of a new classifier in a memory of fixed size requires that one be deleted; ideally, this should be a poor one. Recall that a classifier with a poor predicted payoff rarely wins competitions; without a win, its age increases steadily. Age therefore, reflects the classifier's quality as well as its frequency of use. To make room for the new classifier therefore, one with an old age is deleted. In particular, from the set of oldest classifiers, the one chosen for deletion is the one that most resembles the new classifier, resemblance being a simple count of the number of feature matches, a 1 for a 1, a # for a #.

This process, the selection of parent classifiers on the basis of good predicted payoffs, the creation of a new classifier, and the deletion of an old but similar classifier, continually revises memory. Useful productions that work well with others in memory persist; useless ones are replaced by new "trial" productions.

# 3.0 CS-1 IN OPERATION

CS-1 has been programmed in FORTRAN-IV on an IBM-1800 with 32K memory by Ted Wright (now at Bell Labs, Murray Hill, New Jersey) and Leslie Forman (a graduate student in Computer Science at The University of Michigan). All components of the proposed system are included in this version. Its simplicity comes from the following restrictions:

(1)  Each taxon has 25 features, 8 bits in the part that attends to the environment, 1 bit for the last effector setting, and 16 bits that attend to the internal signals encoded as messages on the message list.

(2)  One effector is included with two possible settings, 0 and 1.

(3)  Two needs are included and each grows one unit per time-step.

(4)  The environment consists of a set of positions or nodes in a graph, each node defined by a simple 8-bit array.

(5)  The memory consists of 100 classifiers: 50 directing the effector to be set to 1, 50 to 0.

The initial set of classifiers are built at random such that the probability that a specific taxon bit is on or off is 0.10. (This amounts to initializing with a fair amount of generality.) The initial predicted payoffs are all equally low (no biases built in).

Figure 2a illustrates the environment of the initial test, a one-dimensional array of nodes with a reward for one of the needs at one end and a reward for the other need at the other. Each position is labeled by an eight-tuple of 1s and 0s; the system can move left or right, depending on the effector setting chosen. At the beginning of each trial, the system is assumed to be in the middle, position 7. By attending to different features of the positions as well as keeping track of messages and the last effector settings, the system should learn to move to the two rewards, alternating in proportion to the amount of reward received and the depletion rate of its two reservoirs.

In this environment, the expected time to reach a reward on the first trial can be calculated from a simple random-walk model. For this environment, with choices of moves made randomly, the system should reach the goal in nine time-steps. Figure 3 shows the number of time-steps required by the system (an average of four runs of the system, each with a different random number seed). The rate of traversal to the reward quickly becomes far better than random, and improves regularly until CS-1 moves to the rewards in the correct two-to-one proportion, each trip requiring the minimum three steps.

To illustrate the power of the genetic algorithm, the dashed line in Fig. 3 shows the performance of the system *without* the genetic algorithm operating. This performance is dependent on updating the predicted payoffs after each reward is received, but is lacking experience with newly created and tested classifiers. Without the genetic algorithm, performance is better than random (as might be expected from the success of algorithms that change weights of features) but clearly not as good as that with the genetic algorithm operating. With-

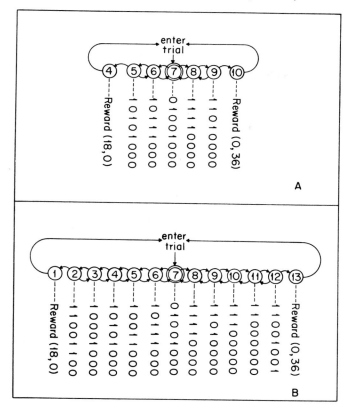

Fig. 2. Initial test (a) and transfer (b) environments for CS-1.

out the genetic algorithm, the system only reaches criterion (10 successive, three-step trials in the two-to-one proportion of alternating goal attainment) in 2161 time steps; with the learning algorithm, it reaches the criterion in 212 steps.

To demonstrate CS-1's ability to benefit from past experience, we tested it next in a simple transfer situation. First, the system experienced the environment in Fig. 2a to the criterion above. Then with memory intact, the system experienced the transfer environment illustrated in Fig. 2b, a larger one-dimensional array of nodes in which the first environment is embedded as the center seven nodes. The reward values remained the same but were positioned at the ends of this longer array. Random choices of moves in this environment result in an average of 36 time steps to reach a reward. Since the amount of the largest reward is 36 units and the reservoirs are assumed to deplete one unit per time-step, the system must do better than chance or perish!

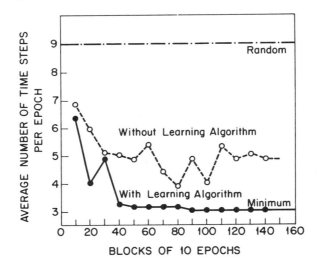

Fig. 3. Performance of CS-1 in the initial test environment with and without learning algorithm operating.

Figure 4 shows the performance of the experienced system compared to a naive system (traversing the same larger environment without prior experience). Having had even this limited experience with the seven center positions gave the system a 1865 time-step advantage over the naive system. To underscore the power of the genetic algorithm, we also tested the experienced system in the 13 position environment without the genetic algorithm. Even with the "tuned" classifiers provided by the prior learning, it failed to reach criterion in 10,000 time-steps.

## 4.0 EXTENSIONS

*Cognitive maps.* Our experiments to this point are of the "proof of principle" type. Consequently the environments used have only required the simplest cognitive maps (i.e., internal models of the environment). Nevertheless, extensive, learned cognitive maps are a major objective of these studies. Cognitive maps allow the system to use lookahead to explore, without overt acts, the consequences of various courses of action. Thus, procedures that use experience to generate good cognitive maps are of critical importance.

To see how the genetic algorithm generates coherent cognitive maps, attention must be focused on the "successful" (general and predictive) classifiers. The taxa of such classifiers generally achieve

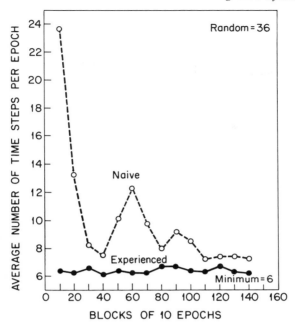

Fig. 4. Performances of naive CS-1 and experienced CS-1 in the transfer environment.

above-average match scores by attending to messages in the message list as well as environmental signals. (Recall that the messages are signals broadcast by the classifiers activated on the previous time-step.) To see this, consider two classifiers, one attending only to attributes of the environmental signals and another attending to these same attributes as well as to some correlated attributes of the message list. Clearly the latter classifier will have a higher match score than the former and will thereby tend to win out in competitions for activation. Thus the classifiers activated at time t-1 will, by the messages they place on the message list, increasingly influence which classifiers are activated at time t. Now consider a mode of operation where, at some point in time, the classifiers cease attending to environmental signals. At that point the internal signals, via the message list, would directly determine the set of classifiers activated next. These classifiers in turn would broadcast new signals activating a new set of classifiers, etc. This linking of classifiers via the message list (with environmental signals ignored) constitutes the system's cognitive map, as shown below. It is important that the cognitive map is produced automatically with no changes in the genetic algorithm.

Each classifier can be considered to name an environmental condition or pattern that has been significant in the system's experience. Each signal emitted is correlated with, and in fact represents, the system's response to that pattern. Overall, then, classifier-signal sequences constitute a kind of model of the environment; by defining the environment more carefully, this idea can be made more precise.

Assume that each response of the cognitive system alters the state of the environment according to a well-defined set of rules or laws. Technically, then, the environment can be defined (or approximated) by an automaton. The states and transition rules of the environment are initially unknown to the cognitive system; its task is to use experience to construct a model of them. Each state s of the environment gives rise to a set of environmental signals that elicit (via detectors, classifiers, etc.) a reponse from the cognitive system. The response produces a new environmental state s'. The system has constructed a good cognitive map of this part of the environment when the classifier that recognizes (is activated by) s' also has a good match with the signal emitted by the classifier recognizing s. Then the activation of the classifier for s is sufficient to activate the classifier for s' even if the environmental signals are ignored. In effect the cognitive system has enough internal information to predict the pattern (elicited by s') that will occur after the system makes its response to s. (Recall that the classifier activated by s determines the response to s.) Clearly this kind of linkage extends with no change to a whole chain s', s'', s''',...

The genetic algorithm, by favoring high match scores, enforces attention to internal signals. Thus each classifier will be sensitive to ⊄the signals originating from its immediate predecessors. At the same time it must be sensitive to the *current* environmental signals. This enforced combination automatically generates the cognitive map. Technically, the transition graph of the environment has been represented by the linked classifiers. Nodes of the graph, i.e., environmental states, are represented by taxa; edges, i.e., actions taken by the cognitive system, are represented by signals.

Once the system has enough experience with a part of the environment to have generated the relevant classifiers, lookahead is easily achieved. Given a classifier (or set of them) $\gamma$ activated by the current environmental state s, the system simply traces out a sequence of classifiers $\gamma'$, $\gamma''$, ..., $\gamma^{(n)}$ by using the message list alone. $\gamma^{(n)}$ amounts to the system's prediction of the condition or environmental pattern that will result from the sequence of reponses elicited by $\gamma'$, $\gamma''$, ..., $\gamma^{(n-1)}$.

*Using expert knowledge.* There is no reason to require the cognitive system to start with a "clean slate," if the designer has substantial knowledge of the task environment(s). It is easy to supply the system with an initial cognitive map, incorporating the designer's knowledge and conjectures. This requires writing an initial program for the system in the (computationally complete) "classifier language." The system itself corrects errors, misconceptions, etc., as experience accumulates. In addition, minor changes in the system's rules allow it to accept advice from experts unfamiliar with the cognitive system. The procedure is much like Samuel's [Samuel63] book-move technique.

One of us (Holland) has already produced the relevant theory (it was actually possible to prove some theorems!) and algorithms for these extensions (lookahead and advice-taking). The next year should see a substantial body of experiments along these lines.

*Further extensions.* There are also extensive sketches of algorithms (with supporting theorems) that allow the system to

(1) produce hierarchies of classifiers wherein a "higher-level" classifier attends to activation of "lower-level" classifiers, yielding hierarchical generalizations and searches employing analogy;

(2) develop and use key classifiers, "landmarks," in its cognitive map, so that lookahead can skip from landmark to landmark, thus permitting lookahead depth to depend on the detail required;

(3) fill in lacunae in its cognitive map by searching out unfamiliar parts of its environment when its "resource" needs are not pressing, thus providing a kind of "curiosity";

(4) develop a simple symbolic "language" (in the manner of the man-made chimpanzee languages), permitting one to induce associations, or pieces of the cognitive map, by presenting appropriate concatenations of abstract patterns ("symbols").

Each of these additions can be achieved parsimonously. They use the same basic mechanism to activate different sequences of classifiers via different sets of attributes. Exploring the effects of these additions, and discovering their limitations, should occupy a good deal of our time, and our students', over the next several years.

# Cognitive Modeling

# IMPLICATIONS OF HUMAN PATTERN PROCESSING FOR THE DESIGN OF ARTIFICIAL KNOWLEDGE SYSTEMS

Barbara Hayes-Roth

*Rand Corporation*

*Artificial knowledge systems typically embody several design principles that are also widely accepted as characteristic of human knowledge processing. These properties include canonical meaning representations for stored patterns; prototypes as representations of classes of stored patterns; pattern-matching processes that must evaluate fully all stored patterns that partially match a target pattern; and pattern-matching processes that are influenced by pattern complexity and limited processing capacity. This characterization of human pattern processing is critically evaluated in light of recent psychological studies. The implications of these results for the design of artificial knowledge systems are discussed.*

## 1.0 INTRODUCTION

Parallel theoretical developments in cognitive psychology and artificial intelligence are readily apparent in research in pattern processing, that is, in theories of pattern representation and matching and pattern-directed inference. Several common theoretical properties are considered in the present paper. These include canonical meaning representations of stored patterns; prototypes as representations of classes of stored patterns; pattern-matching processes that must evaluate fully all stored patterns that partially match a target pattern; and pattern-matching processes that are influenced by pattern complexity and limited processing capacity. The first two properties are theoretically motivated by presumed efficiencies of representation, matching, and inference. The second two properties are assumed to be inevitable

*333*

properties of all pattern-processing systems, even though they impair performance by increasing pattern-matching times and errors. Despite the wide acceptance of the theoretical assumptions introduced above, recent studies suggest that they are inconsistent with human pattern-processing capabilities. The assumptions are critically evaluated in light of the results below. The implications of these results for the design of artificial knowledge systems are also discussed.

## 2.0 CANONICAL MEANING REPRESENTATIONS OF STORED PATTERNS

In canonical meaning representations [Horowitz68, Schank73b, 74, Wilks72], the semantic constituents of patterns are abstracted and stored in standardized structures. Thus the meanings but not the surface features of patterns are stored in memory. It has been argued that canonical meaning representations provide several efficiencies. They minimize storage requirements because semantic redundancies among patterns can be factored out to avoid redundancies among representations. For example, the proposition "Mary handed John the book and he accepted it" includes two references to the transfer of the book, "handed" and "accepted." Both of these might be replaced by a single semantic verb primitive such as "physical transfer." Canonical meaning representations also facilitate pattern matching by eliminating the need to search among semantically equivalent representations of propositions. As Schank [Schank72] has argued:

> How should a proposition appear in memory? It simply cannot be stored in a form that bears a strong relationship to the original form of the input in natural language. Since it is possible to say the same thing in any number of different ways, it is unreasonable to suppose that people (or machines) are constantly checking to see if a proposition that they have stored one way in memory is the same as another they have stored somewhere else in a different form . . . . . . there must be a canonical form for meaning representations . . .

Canonical meaning representations facilitate inferential reasoning in two ways. First, the representation of a proposition makes explicit those meaning elements that support inference. For example, the proposition "John ran," implying movement of an agent x from location y to location z, would include a subrepresentation of the abstract inference, TRANSITION (x, y, z). Because the inference is represented explicitly in the meaning representation, inferential reasoning reduces from a deduction problem to a simple retrieval problem. Second, the use of canonical representations provides generality to inference rules that enable their application to a wider variety of situations. For example, because the propositions "Mary walked" and "Alice went" also imply movement of an agent x from location y to location z, their canonical representations would necessarily include subrepresentations of the same abstract inference, TRANSITION (x, y, z). As a result, the same general inferences would be entailed by all three propositions.

The assumption of canonical meaning representations is also consistent with prominent psychological theories, as illustrated in the following excerpt from Miller [G.A. Miller72]:

> It is usually not the precise words we happen to use in characterizing an experience that are stored and later recalled. Rather, it is some prelinguistic, conceptual representation that we seem to remember—something nonverbal, but with an affinity for verbal expression, couched in the dimensions of verbal thought.

Several kinds of empirical evidence have been adduced to support the assumption that people have canonical meaning representations. For example, people can recall studied information, given a recall cue that is a paraphrase of the verbatim cue present during study [R.C. Anderson71]. This suggests that the meanings of studied cues are stored in canonical representations. Any cue that preserves the meaning of a studied cue, regardless of its form of expression, will produce a successful match to the representation of the cue. People also frequently recall paraphrases of the material they have studied, rather than the literal wordings of the material [Brewer75]. This suggests that only meaning is retained from studied material. A meaning representation would predict recall of the gist, but not necessarily the exact wording of studied material. Finally, people frequently report that they recognize (have seen previously) paraphrases of material that they have seen previously [Anisfeld68, 69, Fillenbaum66, 69, Sachs74]. This also suggests that the meanings, but not the surface features, of studied materials are stored in memory. Thus any target that expresses the meaning of studied material will produce a successful match to its memory representation.

While these data are consistent with the assumption that people have canonical meaning representations, they do not exclude the possibility that people retain explicit information about the literal form of the material they acquire. In fact, it is possible to account for all of the data with a theory that assumes surface information, such as the specific words in a sentence, as the basic unit of representation [B. Hayes-Roth77c]. For example, consider the finding that people can recall material they have studied given a cue that paraphrases the originally presented cue. The theory assumes that people store literal representations of studied cues and associated material in an integrated semantic-propositional network. The theory also assumes that storage causes a spread of network "activation" to semantically related (including synonymous) information in the network and that activation creates a memory trace. In other words, this theory assumes that, during study, memory traces representing paraphrases of studied cues would be created along with memory traces representing the verbatim cues. These paraphrase cue traces would presumably enable subsequent recall of studied material, given a paraphrase cue. The other data described above can be accounted for in a similar manner.

Further, a reevaluation of the psychological data [B. Hayes-Roth77c] supports the assumption of literal representations over the assumption of canonical representations. For example, although people do sometimes recall studied material given a paraphrase cue, they recall it more often when given a verbatim cue [R. C. Anderson71]. If people had canonical representations of the cues, then either one should activate the appropriate representation equally well. Therefore, recall should be equally good given either cue. The literal representation theory, on the other hand, assumes that direct activation of the verbatim cue representation during study gives it a stronger memory trace than spreading activation gives the paraphrase cue representation. Therefore, it predicts that, as observed, the verbatim cue should be more effective. Similarly, although people do sometimes recall the literal form of the material at least as often as, and frequently more often than, any paraphrase [Brewer75]. If people had canonical representations of studied material, they should produce paraphrased expressions equally often during recall. The literal representation theory, on the other hand, again assumes that the literal form of the material has the stronger memory trace and so should be recalled better. Finally, although people frequently "recognize" material that paraphrases studied material, they recognize explicitly studied material more often and with greater confidence [Sachs74]. If people had canonical representations of studied material, any expression of the material should activate the appropriate representation. Therefore, studied and paraphrase forms should be recognized equally well. The literal representation theory again assumes that the literal form of the studied material has the stronger representation and so should be recognized better.

A recent study [B. Hayes-Roth77c]provided additional support for the literal representation theory. In the first experiment, people read 32 simple sentences, such as "The spy tore up the documents." They were told to try to remember the meanings of the sentences. Later, they were given a surprise recognition test. The test included the originally read sentences and some semantically equivalent sentences, in which the original verbs were replaced by synonyms (e.g., "The spy ripped up the documents"). The task was to identify the originally read sentences. Performance on the test indicated that the exact wordings of the sentences were present in memory. Originally read sentences were recognized with an average confidence rating of 2.14 (the maximum possible rating was 3), while synonymous wordings of the sentences were recognized with an average confidence rating of only 0.92. If the sentences had been stored in canonical meaning representations in memory, originally read and synonymous sentences should have been recognized with equal confidence. More confident recognition of originally read sentences suggests that the surface features of sentences, such as particular wordings, were retained as functional components of their memory representations.

In the second experiment, people again studied 32 sentences for meaning. Later, they were given a verification test. The test included two kinds of "true" sentences: the originally studied sentences and those same sentences with the verbs replaced by synonyms. It also included an equal number of "false" sentences, constructed by replacing the verbs in studied sentences with unrelated verbs. The task was to respond "TRUE" to the true sentences and "FALSE" to the false sentences. Performance indicated that the exact wordings of the sentences were present in memory. Reaction time to verify the originally studied sentences was 1.14 sec, while reaction time to verify the synonymous sentences was 1.41 sec. If the sentences had been stored in canonical meaning representations in memory, originally read and synonymous sentences should have been verified equally fast. Faster verification of the originally studied sentences suggests that the words in the sentences were retained as functional components of their memory representations.

In the third experiment, people studied 24 sentences for meaning. Eight of the sentences were unrelated to other studied sentences, eight shared a common verb with other sentences, eight contained verbs whose synonyms appeared in other sentences. Later, a verification task was given, in which people had to respond "TRUE" to the studied sentences and "FALSE" to an equal number of sentences whose verbs had been replaced by unrelated verbs. There was no difference between reaction times to verify sentences in the unrelated and synonymous verbs conditions (0.994 versus 1.006 sec). Reaction time to verify sentences in the common verbs condition, however, was significantly longer (1.092 sec). These results indicate that interference in memory for related sentences occurs when sentences share explicit surface information, not when they share only semantic information. It is generally assumed (cf.[J.R. Anderson74, Thorndyke74]) that interference in sentence memory arises from shared representational structures. When sentences share a common word, interference presumably derives from a shared representation of that word. If words and sentences have canonical meaning representations in memory, synonymous words in learned sentences should also produce shared representational structures and equivalent interference effects. The absence of interference effects among sentences sharing synonymous words suggests that distinctive surface information, rather than equivalent semantic information, is the basis for sentence representation in memory.

The results reviewed above rule out any typical theory of canonical meaning representation. Instead, they favor a more literal representational scheme, such as an integrated semantic-propositional network. Of course, the results do not rule out the coexistence of canonical meaning representations and corresponding representations of surface information. However, such a combined theory would be a less parsimonious description of human pattern matching, and such double representations would be considerably less efficient than either one alone for artificial knowledge systems.

Literal representations are, in some ways, more efficient than canonical representations. Because canonical representations minimize the number of representational component types, they maximize the number of component tokens and relations among tokens necessary to represent a given proposition. Thus, by employing a more informative code, literal representations require less storage than canonical meaning representations. Pattern matching should also be more efficient with literal representations than with canonical representations because they are less complex and, therefore, require fewer basic matching operations. Interference in pattern matching should be minimized with literal representations because, by increasing the number of distinctive symbols used to construct meaning representations, they minimize the number of partial matches for a given target pattern. Finally, literal representations support inference mechanisms that are as efficient as those based on canonical representations. For example, it is possible to express general inferences as productions. For the case described above, such a rule might be [x is the agent of verb w and w is an element of { "run," "walk," "go,". . .} → (there exist x, y, z) : x went from y to z]. Thus, in addition to being a better description of human pattern processing, literal meaning representations may, in fact, provide a more efficient data base for artificial knowledge systems.

## 3.0 PROTOTYPES AS REPRESENTATIONS OF CLASSES OF STORED PATTERNS

Many distinctive patterns represent variations on prototypic patterns. For example, there are numerous discriminable instances of the pattern "tree" or the pattern "dinner at a restaurant." Many designers of artificial knowledge systems (cf. [D.G. Bobrow76]) propose that pattern classes should be represented by single prototypes (frames, schemas, or scripts), rather than by representations of all individual instances of the pattern. The prototype emphasizes the similarities and obscures the peculiarities among instances. Prototypes apparently provide efficiencies in storage, matching, and inference. Because the information in a class of patterns can be concentrated in a single prototype, the amount of storage required is minimized. Similarly, the set of patterns that must be searched to match a class member is reduced from the set of all previously encountered class members to the single abstracted prototype. In addition, pattern-directed inference is facilitated, because the system can use the "typical" information present in the prototype to fill in any gaps in the information present in a target pattern.

Several kinds of empirical support have been adduced in support of the assumption that people represent classes of patterns as prototypes. For example, several studies have shown that when people experience many variations on prototypic patterns, their subsequent recognition and classification of both familiar and unfamiliar instances of the patterns are strongly influenced by the degree of similarity between the test pattern and the prototype [Franks71, Oldfield65, Posner69]. The more similar an instance is to the prototype, the better it is recognized and classified. The prototype is recognized and classified best of all, even if it has never been experienced previously. Other studies [Mandler77, Thorndyke77a] have shown that people's memory for texts that they have read can be predicted on the basis of prototypic text structures; higher-order propositions in the prototypic structure are remembered better than lower-order propositions.

Despite the consistency of these psychological results with prototype theory, a recent study [B. Hayes-Roth77b] has shown that people do not represent and process all classes of patterns in terms of their relationships to prototypes. In this study, people studied descriptions of individuals (name, age, education, marital status, hobby) who belonged to one of three classes. Each individual description was a variation on a prototypic description for the appropriate class. The goal for people in the experiment was to learn to classify individuals correctly. After studying 132 individual descriptions, they made recognition judgments (have I ever seen this particular description before?) and classification judgments (in what class does this description belong?) about familiar and unfamiliar descriptions.

The prototype theory assumes that during study people abstracted the most typical features of the individual descriptions in each class and stored them as prototypic class members. Subsequent recognition and classification judgments would be based presumably on the similarity of a test description to each of the stored prototypes. An alternative theory (property-set theory) assumes that during study, people stored and strengthened all features and combinations of features that they encountered in individual descriptions, along with appropriate class designations. Subsequent recognition and classification judgments would be based presumably on the stored strengths of the features and combinations of features in the test description. The two theories make a variety of differential predictions regarding recognition and classification judgments. For example, the prototype theory predicts that descriptions of prototypes should be recognized with greater confidence and classified with greater accuracy and confidence than any other descriptions. The property-set theory, on the other hand, predicts that descriptions should be recognized better and classified better and with higher confidence than the prototype whenever their constituent features and combinations of features occur more often than those in the prototype.

The prototype and property-set theories were comparatively evaluated in terms of their ability to predict relative recognition judgments for 24 critical pairs of descriptions (i.e., pairs for which the two theories made different predictions). These included six comparisons of prototypes to nonprototypic descriptions. For these, the prototype theory predicted more confident recognition for the prototype, while the property-set theory predicted better recognition confidence for the nonprototypic description. They also included 12 comparisons of nonprototypic descriptions that were equidistant from the prototype. For these, the prototype theory predicted equally confident recognition for paired descriptions, while the property-set theory predicted that one of the two should be recognized more confidently. The remaining six comparisons were between pairs of descriptions that were different distances from the prototype. For these, the prototype theory predicted better recognition of the descriptions that were nearer the prototype, while the property-set theory made the opposite prediction. The property-set theory fit the data considerably better than the prototype theory (23 of the 24 critical predictions confirmed). The two theories were also comparatively evaluated in terms of their ability to predict relative recognition and classification judgments for all pairwise combinations of 28 test descriptions. These included pairs of items varying in both distance from prototypes and frequencies of constituent feature combinations. The property-set theory provided a significantly better fit to both the recognition and classification data than the prototype theory.

These results indicate that people do not restrict the information stored in memory to those features that occur most often among a class of patterns, as assumed by the prototype theory. Rather, people appear to store all of the information present in the patterns they experience and they use all of it during pattern matching tasks such as recognition and classification.

In addition to modeling human pattern processing more accurately, representations that preserve all of the information in a class of patterns permit certain intelligent behavior that would not be possible if the data base were constrained to preserve only prototypic information. For example, there may be information among the instances that is not frequent enough to appear in a prototype (especially information that represents an alternative to information present in the prototype), but that is, nonetheless, diagnostic. This information will be available for appropriate use if all information in the class of patterns is stored, but not if only prototypes are stored. Also, it may not be possible to anticipate the importance of alternative values on prototypic dimensions in dealing with future situations. If only prototypes are stored, the system must make do with arbitrarily selected values. If all the information in the class of patterns is stored, the system has complete information available to be used as needed.

## 4.0 PROCESSING PARTIALLY MATCHED PATTERNS

In any reasonably sophisticated knowledge system, many stored patterns share common subpatterns. For example, a system that knows about U.S. history is likely to have many stored propositions about World War II. Each of these propositional representations will include a subrepresentation of the concept "World War II." When the system attempts to match a particular target proposition to its memory representation, the presence of other propositional representations with common subrepresentations will produce many partial matches. The pattern-matching process will be slowed by evaluation of all representations in memory that partially match the target proposition. This kind of interference occurs in several artificial pattern matching systems [J.R. Anderson76, D.G. Bobrow76, F. Hayes-Roth77g].

Interference is also one of the best known phenomena in human learning and memory. For example, several studies [J.R. Anderson74, B. Hayes-Roth75, 77c, Lewis76, Thorndyke74] have shown that reaction time to verify a stored proposition is an increasing function of the number of learned propositions that share concepts with the test proposition. Presumably, all learned propositions that include concepts present in the test proposition produce partial matches and therefore must be evaluated during the verification process.

While interference from partial matches is common, it is not inevitable. In a recent study [B. Hayes-Roth77a], it has been shown that interference occurs only when the target pattern is not well known. This seems intuitively reasonable when one considers, for example, that although most people know many more propositions about themselves than they do about anyone else, it is precisely those propositions that are the most accessible. In this study, people learned propositions that shared common concepts with zero, one, two, or five other learned propositions. They then had to verify (classify as true or false) the propositions they had studied, along with some false propositions. When one of the propositions was presented for verification, any other learned propositions with common concepts presumably produced partial matches to the target. These partial matches should have interferred with (slowed) the verification process. In fact, when people had learned the propositions well enough to verify them accurately (<5% errors), reaction time was an increasing function of the number of partially matched propositions in memory. However, as the amount of experience people had at verifying the propositions increased, interference decreased, ultimately to zero. That is, after a reasonable amount of practice (about 100 trials), reaction time was constant, regardless of the number of partially matching patterns in memory. Figure 1 illustrates these results. These data suggest that while it may be necessary to search all partial matches for complete desired matches to some learned patterns, it is not necessary for well learned patterns.

The ability to bypass partial matches in the search for a desired complete match should make pattern matching faster and more accurate. This ability is essential in a system that must acquire more than a few propositions regarding any one topic. It is generally true that the more important a certain topic is to a person or machine, the more propositions regarding that topic must be stored in memory. It is undesirable to have a knowledge system in which pattern matching gets slower as the number of related propositions increases. This would be tantamount to a system in which matching gets slower as the importance of the knowledge increases. People apparently respond to such conditions by making qualitative changes in the pattern-matching process, such that the process is no longer slowed down by the existence of partially matching patterns in memory. A comparable capacity in machine systems is an obvious goal of future research.

## 5.0 EFFECT OF PATTERN COMPLEXITY AND CAPACITY LIMITATIONS

All artificial pattern-matching systems operate under capacity limitations. A system has only finite resources. If pattern-matching

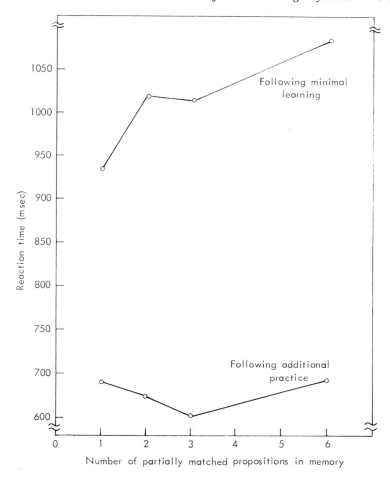

Fig. 1. Effect of partially matching propositions in memory on verification of target propositions.

operations are performed serially, the time required to complete a match must be directly related to the number of operations performed. The same must also be true of parallel matching processes once the number of requested simultaneous operations performed exceeds the system capacity. The number of operations performed is in turn determined by the complexity of the pattern to be matched, i.e., the number of elements and relations necessary to specify the pattern. For example, a human face is a more complex pattern than an equilateral triangle and therefore should take longer to match. In fact, it is widely believed [Aho74, F. Hayes-Roth76b, Karp72] that most interesting problems involving recognition, matching, and searching of general graph structures are intractable; the amount of computing needed for solution is an exponential function of the number of elements in the graph structures compared.

Similarly, it is a common assumption that because people have limited processing capacity, increasing the complexity of a pattern must decrease people's facility at processing it. This relationship is illustrated, for example, in the finding that the more elements in a proposition to be verified, the longer the verification time [Dosher76]. Other studies [Collins69, B. Hayes-Roth75] have shown that the time required to verify a semantic or relational proposition is an increasing function of the number of elements of the memory structure that must be activated (see also [Crowder69, Savin65]).

On the other hand, some researchers have shown that complex patterns are sometimes processed as well as or better than simpler patterns. For example, several studies [Chase73, DeGroot66, J.S. Reitman76] have shown that chess and Go masters operate on complex board configurations at least as well as nonmasters operate on simple configurations. These results suggest that, with experience, chess and Go players acquire the ability to process increasingly complex patterns without any decrement in performance. Other studies have shown that people can process some words and phrases as well as or better than they can process their constituent letters or words [Bower69, Horowitz68, LaBerge74].

A recent paper [B. Hayes-Roth77a] has argued that increasing experience can enable people to process complex patterns more easily than they process simpler patterns. In an earlier study [Dosher76], people studied subject-verb-object-location-time propositions. After they had learned the sentences minimally well (after seven trials), they verified two-part or three-part subsets of the propositions (e.g., subject-verb, subject-verb-object) along with the complete propositions. It was found that people verified two part subsets 5 msec faster than three-part subsets and verified three-part subsets 26 msec faster than complete (five-part) propositions. The latter study [B. Hayes-Roth77a] involved a similar procedure using subject-verb-object propositions. Here, when people had learned the complete propositions moderately well (after 18 trials), they verified one-part and two-part subsets equally fast. However, after they had gained considerably more experience with the complete propositions (after 100 trials), they verified two-part subsets 143 msec faster than one-part subsets. Thus, with minimal learning, simple patterns were matched faster than complex patterns, while with considerably better learning, complex patterns were matched faster than simpler patterns.

These results suggest that when propositions are moderately well learned, they are represented and processed as patterns of elements and relations. Matching a sub-proposition requires matching each of its substituent elements and relations. Because matching time is determined by the number of elements and relations that must be matched, simple propositions are matched faster than complex propositions. When propositions are very well learned, however, they are represented and processed as "unitary" events. Matching a subproposition requires matching and then "decomposing" the corresponding complete proposition. In addition, matching time for the complete proposition is assumed to be determined by the completeness of the target proposition. Thus, complex (more complete) patterns are matched faster than simpler patterns.

The acquired ability to match complex patterns as quickly and as accurately as simple patterns is a desirable goal for artificial knowledge systems too. A truly adaptive knowledge system should be sensitive to increases in the importance of certain stored patterns, as evidenced, for example, by frequency of access. People apparently respond to such conditions with qualitative changes in pattern representation and processing that compensate for apparent capacity limitations. Similarly, if artificial knowledge systems are to become as effective in their task domains as people are in theirs, effective means must be developed to increase their capacity to process important, but complex, structures.

## 6.0 CONCLUSIONS

Human cognition can provide an inspiring model for the design of artificial knowledge systems. This paper has presented evidence that four design principles commonly embodied in artificial knowledge systems are inconsistent with human cognitive capabilities. To summarize: Human memory representations appear to be knowledge extensive, preserving the surface features of each stored pattern, including those that are members of specifiable classes of patterns. Human pattern matching processes appear to be both powerful and flexible, overcoming apparent capacity limitations and bypassing the evaluation of partial matches in order to expedite the processing of important patterns. While such capabilities would be advantageous in intelligent systems, they are unfortunately beyond the state of the art in artificial intelligence. Memory and capacity limitations appear inevitable, and no search algorithm is yet known that can avoid extensive evaluation of all partial matches. While it is always possible to design functionally equivalent systems using alternative mechanisms, it has proven extremely difficult to discover *any* mechanism capable of producing anything approaching the intelligent and adaptive behavior typical of an average human being. Although several successful special-purpose artificial knowledge systems have been developed, their limitations are as salient as their capabilities. In the long run, the most promising avenue of approach toward the development of artificial knowledge systems may be to investigate and model human cognition as closely as possible. The four properties of human pattern processing described in this paper delimit a great gap between the technologies of natural and artificial intelligence. They illustrate both the difficulty and the potential rewards of modeling artificial intelligence systems after the human knowledge system.

# PATTERN-DIRECTED PROCESSING OF KNOWLEDGE FROM TEXTS

Perry W. Thorndyke
*The Rand Corporation*

*A framework for viewing human text comprehension, memory, and recall is presented that assumes patterns of abstract conceptual relations are used to guide processing. These patterns consist of clusters of knowledge that encode prototypical co-occurrences of situations and events in narrative texts. The patterns are assumed to be a part of a person's world knowledge and can be activated during comprehension to build associations among multiple linguistic propositions in memory according to their higher-order conceptual relations. During text reproduction from memory, these patterns provide retrieval plans for recall and a mechanism for sophisticated "guessing" when retrieval fails. Some data from human text learning tasks are presented as evidence for these higher-order conceptual patterns. Several structural and processing properties of the model are evaluated in light of these data. It is argued that the proposed pattern-directed processing model could be successfully implemented in artificial intelligence systems to provide adaptive error-handling mechanisms such as those observed in human behavior.*

## 1.0 INTRODUCTION

The comprehension of connected texts has recently emerged as a major area of research in cognitive psychology. Researchers have begun to explore characteristics of people's memory representations of learned prose [Crothers72, Frederiksen75, Kintsch74, 75, Mandler77, Meyer75, Rumelhart75, Thorndyke77a, 78]. Two problems in particular have been addressed in these and other studies of prose memory. The first problem is how to represent the meaning of a text in a way that is more than simply a concatenation of sentences. Clearly, texts have a structure that transcends the individual syntactic structures of the component sentences. People can easily discriminate

*347*

a well-organized, comprehensible text from a disorganized, confusing one, even when the two texts contain the same knowledge [Thorndyke77a]. The second problem is how to account for the fact that people are able to make inferences from texts that require the integration of knowledge across several sentences. At any point during the comprehension of a text, a reader can generate a vast number of plausible inferences. However, people typically generate only those inferences that promote integration of previous and current information, and inferences that establish expectations for subsequent information [Thorndyke76]. Thus, a model of human text memory should explain how and why certain inferences are produced and other equally plausible ones are not.

The purpose of this chapter is to argue for certain design considerations in the construction of computer systems that simulate human behavior. Text comprehension provides a particularly appropriate domain in which to formulate these arguments, since currently humans exhibit considerable success in this task while computers exhibit only limited success. The subsequent discussion is organized as follows. First, a process model is outlined for how people comprehend, store, and retrieve simple narrative texts in memory. The class of texts to be considered is sufficiently constrained to make the task of modeling human memory and performance a reasonable goal, yet it is sufficiently rich to provide a natural processing environment for people. Second, some of the more interesting observations of human performance on memory tasks using these texts are considered and evaluated against predictions of the processing model. These observations will serve to illustrate several desirable properties of successful information processing systems. In particular, it will be argued that these properties can be explicated in terms of pattern-directed recognition and generation mechanisms assumed by the psychological model. Finally, the implications of these observations for the design of artificial intelligence systems to simulate human performance are discussed.

## 2.0 OUTLINE OF A MODEL OF HUMAN TEXT COMPREHENSION

### 2.1 Prototypical Patterns for Story Organization

The model described here was designed to provide a representational scheme for the plot organization of a narrative, that is, the common configurations of situations and events in a well-formed passage. The class of texts considered by the model includes single-protagonist, single-goal, narrative stories. For example, a simple plot sequence might involve a problem facing the main character, a sequence of episodes in which the main character attempts to solve the problem, and some eventual resolution of the problem. The representational scheme formalizes these relationships as a grammar describing these narrative elements and the dependencies governing their occurrence in combination. The grammar thus provides a framework for encoding, or parsing, the organization of text information according to its narrative structure.

The grammar consists of a set of productions providing rules of narrative syntax and is independent of the linguistic content of any particular story. Each production in the grammar is a pattern of situation and event occurrences that characterizes some critical element in a story, such as the motivation and intention of characters. These patterns are abstract in that they are independent of particular semantic content. Furthermore, the patterns are hierarchically organized: combinations of patterns can organize into higher-order, more inclusive patterns. The successive application of the productions that formalize the structure of the patterns results in a hierarchical representation of a story that includes the semantic content of individual propositions and the organization of these propositions into abstract narrative patterns. Intermediate nodes in the structure represent patterns encoding narrative relationships among propositions. Terminal nodes represent actual propositions from the story. For example, consider the following simple story:

(1) Judy wanted a new dress for her birthday.
(2) So she went into town shopping for one.
(3) Finally, she found the one she wanted in a small boutique.
(4) She bought the dress and wore it home.

This story may be viewed as a single episode, and the narrative relations among the four events may be represented by the following rule:

(5) Episode → Goal + Attempt* + Outcome.

The goal, or desired state, can be matched to (1), Judy's desire for a dress. (2) and (3) represent attempts, that is, events initiated by Judy to attain the goal. (The "*" in (5) indicates that the element may be repeated). The outcome is an event or state that indicates either the success or failure in attaining the goal. Of course, the conceptual inferences required to satisfy the conditions for matching (1)-(4) to the narrative elements are not presented here. For example, the understander must identify (1) as a goal of Judy's, determine that in (2) and (3) "she" refers to Judy and "one" refers to a dress, and that buying the dress in (4) constitutes successful attainment of the goal. The problem of how these inferences are generated is treated elsewhere [Charniak72, Schank74, 77, Schmidt73, 76b, Thorndyke76]. The intent here, however, is to show how sequential events can be organized into higher-order patterns to produce a coherent text.

In more complex stories, simple episodes are embedded in a narrative that has a setting, a plot, and some resolution of the plot. The plot is some number of individual episodes comprising attempts to achieve the goal or some subgoal created by the main character. These episodes may be recursively embedded as attempts to resolve subgoals produced during efforts to satisfy higher-order goals. To illustrate the narrative patterns encoding story content, consider the following story:

(1) Circle Island is located in the middle of the Atlantic Ocean, (2) north of Ronald Island. (3) The main occupations on the island are farming and ranching. (4) Circle Island has good soil, (5) but few rivers and (6) hence a shortage of water. (7) The island is run democratically. (8) All issues are decided by a majority vote of the islanders. (9) The governing body is a senate, (10) whose job is to carry out the will of the majority. (11) Recently, an island scientist discovered a cheap method (12) of converting salt water into fresh water. (13) As a result, the island farmers wanted (14) to build a canal across the island, (15) so that they could use water from the canal (16) to cultivate the island's central region. (17) Therefore, the farmers formed a procanal association (18) and persuaded a few senators (19) to join. (20) The procanal association brought the construction idea to a vote. (21) All the islanders voted. (22) The majority voted in favor of construction. (23) The senate, however, decided that (24) the farmers' proposed canal was ecologically unsound. (25) The senators agreed (26) to build a smaller canal (27) that was 2 feet wide and 1 foot deep. (28) After starting construction on the smaller canal, (29) the islanders discovered that (30) no water would flow into it. (31) Thus the project was abandoned. (32) The farmers were angry (33) because of the failure of the canal project. (34) Civil war appeared inevitable.

By encoding this story according to the narrative grammar, the representation given in Fig. 1 is produced. The numbers at the terminal nodes of Fig. 1 correspond to the numbered propositions given above. The intermediate nodes encode the abstract narrative relations that organize the events of the story into a meaningful narrative according to the constraints specified by the grammar.

This approach to the analysis of text structure presumes a stereotypy in the organization of knowledge in this class of narratives. It further presumes that the conceptual patterns form an integral part of the story representation. While the narrative patterns provide some

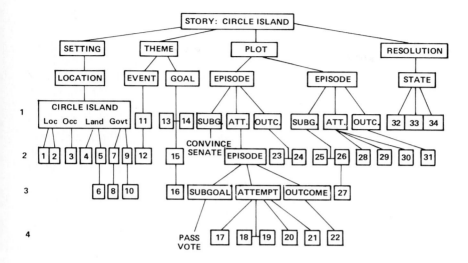

Fig. 1. Narrative structure for the Circle Island story.

constraints on the combination of events in a story, the framework can
be modified to fit the unique properties of a particular story. Thus
stories have invariant properties at some level of abstraction while
still varying in the details of particular events and states. This is
similar to Bartlett's [Bartlett32] notion that a story is represented in
memory as a general schema and a few specific details. More recently,
this general approach to knowledge representation has been embodied in the theories of frames [Minsky75], scripts [Schank77,
Schank75d], and schemata [Norman75a]. However, this theoretical
formulation has recurred in experimental psychology for 50 years (cf.
[Head20, Woodworth38]).

## 2.2 The Comprehension Process

Comprehension of stories is guided by the patterns of narrative
relations. The hierarchical organization of patterns specifies levels of
abstraction for matching input to the conceptual structure. The top
levels represent the integrating structural elements of a story, and the
lower levels represent specific event- and state-recognizing patterns.

Comprehension is viewed as the process of building a representation for the text using the prototypical structural patterns stored in
memory. Active processes attempt to match incoming propositions
from the story to narrative patterns using the constraints specified by
the grammar. For example, to build an episode representation of sentences (1)-(4), matches must be found for a goal, attempts, and an
outcome. Obtaining a desired object is frequently a goal, so (1) can be

tentatively matched to the goal portion of the episode pattern. Similarly, an effort would be made to match (2)-(4) to the attempt and outcome patterns. The success of these match attempts determines the ease of comprehension. When matches succeed, comprehension is facilitated because relationships among successive events can be inferred from the grammar, and the matched information along with its associated inferences can be represented in familiar well-learned structures in long-term memory (see [Thorndyke76]).

Processing proceeds both top-down (goal-directed) and bottom-up (data-driven). At any point during comprehension goal-directed processes actively attempt to match combinations of incoming propositions and instantiated patterns to more general structural patterns by fitting them to expectations provided by the grammar. Simultaneously, data-driven processes attempt to use raw data to fit low-level patterns for states or events to the input. Structural integration is produced by evaluating these input descriptions in a number of potential contexts and selecting the most reasonable overall interpretation.

## 2.3 Reconstruction from Memory

When a story has been comprehended, it is represented in memory in a hierarchical structure such as the one shown in Fig. 1. When asked to recall the story verbatim from memory, a person uses the encoded representation as a retrieval mechanism. His task is to gain access to and retrieve all the terminal nodes from the tree in Fig. 1 in correct serial order. Beginning at the highest or most general node in the representation, the subject retrieves information with a depth-first search through the hierarchy. The abstract narrative elements provide intermediate information about the type of knowledge being sought next. In particular, the narrative patterns encode the role of the to-be-recalled knowledge in the story. If the search process encounters a terminal node, that information is output as part of the recalled text.

In most cases, original learning of the passage is less than perfect. This is modeled in the representation as probabilistic strength parameters associated with each link in the hierarchy. Thus, the probability of successful retrieval of information in the hierarchy is a function of the probabilities associated with the path to that information. The deeper in the representational hierarchy a proposition is then, the lower the probability it can be recalled successfully. Another way to view this prediction is that over time, text-specific knowledge, especially low-level details of setting and plot, will decay faster than higher-order relational information.

The depth-first retrieval strategy provides a mechanism for recall of the stored information, directed by the narrative patterns encoding the plot structure of the story. When retrieval fails and details cannot be recalled, the subject is able to reconstruct information consistent with the functional role of the unretrieved information, based on the contextual knowledge supplied by the narrative patterns. This allows for a sophisticated guessing strategy, leading to recall errors that are functionally correct in the text as a whole even though the details of the recalled information are incorrect.

## 3.0 SOME OBSERVATIONS OF HUMAN PERFORMANCE

This model of story representation and the associated processes of comprehension and recall makes some interesting predictions for how knowledge is organized in memory, how it is retrieved, and what happens when retrieval attempts fail. In this section a few observations are presented that are consistent with predictions of the model. These observations are given to demonstrate some of the desirable properties of an information-processing system that must deal with imperfect information.

### 3.1 Transition Recall Probabilities

The model assumes that knowledge is organized according to meaningful narrative patterns. These patterns may be viewed as chunks of information that are conceptually related. If the chunks assumed by the theory are in fact used by people, propositions within one narrative pattern should be more strongly associated than propositions occurring in different patterns.

The data reported here (and later in this section) were obtained from 16 subjects who read and later attempted to recall the story represented in Fig. 1. Subjects were presented the story and instructed to recall it in exactly the same order in which it was presented. Thus recall was serial; that is, the input and output sequences were required to be the same. Note that this is the most natural recall order for connected discourse.

Associative strength between propositions in memory was determined by considering the conditional recall probabilities for adjacent propositions in the input sequence. That is, the probability of recall of proposition i is computed given correct recall of proposition i-1. This probability is termed the transition probability between propositions. If subjects are merely storing and recalling propositions independently of each other, the transition probabilities should be the same for all propositions. However, if the proposed model is correct, the transition probability should be low when propositions i-1 and i are in different narrative patterns, and high when they are in the same pattern.

Transition probabilities were first computed between and within the most general narrative constitutents (i.e., setting, theme, plot, or resolution). When the transition between two propositions was within one of these constituents (e.g., propositions 30 and 31), the mean conditional recall probability was 0.44. However, when the transition was between two constituents (e.g., propositions 31 and 32), the probability was .21. When constituents are defined at this most abstract level, the search distance between two adjacent propositions in different constituents is the maximum of all distances between adjacent propositions in the representation.

Now consider the episode as the basic conceptual constituent. The transition probability for two propositions within an episode was 0.45. However, the transition probability between adjacent items in two different episodes was 0.28. Here again a larger network distance between propositions, represented as a between-pattern transition, produced lower transition probabilities than the shorter network distance traversed in within-pattern transitions. These differences are consistent with data from studies of serial recall of hierarchical structures in other verbal learning paradigms (e.g., [Johnson72]).

This result suggests that one potential method for associating concepts effectively might be to unify or chunk them; that is, to integrate them into a single higher-order pattern or concept. At the same time, it should be possible to reduce associative strength between concepts by making them constituents of conceptually distinct patterns. This might be an effective storage technique for distinguishing and keeping separate potentially interfering sets of knowledge.

## 3.2 Intrusion Errors in Recall

When a subject unsuccessfully attempts to recall a portion of the studied story, the failure is often manifested not as a complete omission of information but as recall of information that was not in the original text. These intrusions of information in the recall protocol frequently indicate that the subject has forgotten the details of the story he read but has retained knowledge of the narrative structure of the passage. The evidence for this comes from the fact that the structural role of the intruded information in the narrative is identical to that of the correct information it replaced. That is, the intrusion errors, while incorrect in detail, serve the same function in the overall narrative sequence as the propositions that were actually presented. Consider the following examples:

(6) The senate, however, decided that the farmers' proposed canal was ecologically unsound. The senators agreed to build a smaller canal...

(6′) The senate had a vote and rejected the large canal idea and instead proposed a smaller canal...

(7) The islanders discovered that no water would flow into the canal.

(7') It was found that the rivers were dry.

(8) The farmers formed a procanal association and persuaded a few senators to join. The procanal association brought the construction idea to a vote. All the islanders voted. The majority voted in favor of construction.

(8') The farmers asked the senate to support the proposed canal.

The outcome of the first episode of the story is given in (6). (6') gives the recall of the corresponding information from one subject's protocol. Note that while the content of (6) and (6') are entirely different, the *effective* outcome of the two examples is the same. That is, in both examples the failure of the farmers to achieve their subgoal (convincing the senate to build the canal) is expressed. This knowledge, rather than the details themselves, is critical to the narrative since it provides the justification for the successive episodes.

Similarly, (7) represents part of the attempt to construct the smaller canal taken from the passage. (7') is taken from a subject's protocol. Again the details of the two are quite distinct, yet the failure of the smaller canal is expressed in both cases. In (8') a subject substituted in her recall a single sentence for an entire episode from the text (given in (8)). In this case the episode was embedded in another episode as an attempt to convince the senate to build the canal.

Examples such as these are commonly obtained in recall protocols for stories. In all of these cases subjects appeared to be guided in recall by knowledge of the narrative structure of the story. When memory for detail failed, the subject used the context information provided by the structure in which the information was embedded to generate plausible filler information consistent with the rest of the story. Thus the pattern-directed nature of the recall procedure provided a sort of error-recovery feature that allowed the subject to fill in missing information and continue his recall of the story.

## 3.3 Hierarchical Knowledge Organization

The story representation in Fig. 1 locates the passage content at the terminal nodes in the tree. These propositions appear at different levels in the hierarchy according to the number of productions required to produce the propositions from the top-level node. It may be noted that the higher in the hierarchy a proposition appears, the more global the structural element of the passage it represents. For example, propositions 13 and 14 of Fig. 1 refer to the text "The farmers wanted to build a canal across the island." This corresponds to the overall goal of the story, a critical structural element on which subsequent story events depend. Propositions 17-19, on the other hand, refer to the text "The farmers formed a procanal association and persuaded a few senators to join." These propositions represent an attempt to achieve an embedded subgoal and appear lower in the hierarchy. They are, then, less structurally central than propositions 13-14, because their function in the narrative is localized to a low-level pattern. The point here is that the hierarchical organization of knowledge provides an implicit ordering of the importance of information in the narrative structure. Information near the top of the hierarchy represents thematic knowledge of the narrative that is elaborated by details of setting and plot at lower levels in the hierarchy.

This feature of the representation has several implications for human performance. Since recall proceeds top-down and is a probabilistic function of search distance, recall probability of a proposition should be directly related to its location in the hierarchy. In fact, propositional recall was found to be a monotone decreasing function of hierarchical level. That is, the lower a proposition appeared in the hierarchy, the lower the probability of its recall. Thus the most structurally central information is most reliably recalled, while low-level details are less reliably recalled.

Another implication of the hierarchical organization of knowledge is that any proposition in the structure conceptually subsumes all information directly below it. Lower-order knowledge is a further specification or elaboration of knowledge represented in its higher-order parent. This means, for example, that an entire embedded episode may be omitted in recall, since its role in the narrative can be expressed at a higher level without explicit recall of the episode content. For example, in (8') above, a subject's recall protocol omitted entirely the embedded episode containing propositions 17-22. Instead, the subject inserted a reference to the subgoal of the higher-level episode (winning senate approval), then recalled the outcome of that episode. Although this deletion eliminated an entire episode from the protocol, the resulting transformed story remained a reasonable narrative account.

This knowledge stratification is also a useful framework for understanding subjects' behavior when they are required to produce concise summaries of the original story. A typical summarization protocol from a subject is given below:

| | |
|---|---|
| This passage basically describes the democratic attempt of a small island in the Atlantic Ocean | [SETTING] |
| to build a canal. | [GOAL] |
| Poor planning | [EPISODE 2] |
| and internal strife | [EPISODE 1] |
| finally lead to the project's abandonment. | [OUTCOME] |
| The people as well as the government are enraged | [RESOLUTION] |

and civil war seems inevitable between the two [RESOLUTION] bodies.

The propositions selected for inclusion in the summary correspond to the central elements of the narrative structure occurring near the top of the representational hierarchy. That is, the subject included minimal top-level setting information, the goal statement, two word summaries of each of the top-level episodes, the outcome of the second episode, and the story resolution. Details and specific actions from lower levels in the hierarchy have been systematically excluded from the summary. In general, summary content of this story is directly predictable from the representation: only knowledge designated as important (at the top of the hierarchy) will be included in summaries with high probability. In fact, an individual proposition from the top level in the hierarchy containing terminal nodes occurred in a summary with probability 0.45; from the second level, 0.20; and from the third level, 0.10. Thus the relative importance of story knowledge, reflected in hierarchical location of the knowledge, can be used to select best information to be used in constructing a good summary.

## 4.0 IMPLICATIONS FOR ARTIFICIAL INTELLIGENCE SYSTEMS

In Sections 2 and 3, a number of features of the representation of textual information in memory were presented. It was seen how this model of knowledge representation could be used to predict characteristic behaviors of people operating with that knowledge. It is evident that these behaviors, such as successful comprehension, summarization, error-recovery, and recall exhibit desirable performance properties of an information processing system. Since the model outlined here provides a mechanism for characterizing these behaviors, it seems reasonable that the model's features should be incorporated into the design of computer-based knowledge utilization systems. Some of the features of the human processor that seem particularly well-adapted for use in computer systems are discussed below.

### 4.1 Prototypes as Patterns

The present view of world knowledge is to consider it as a structural framework that guides the acquisition of new knowledge. Thus internal patterns may be considered to be clusters of knowledge that typically co-occur in the world and are often perceived and recognized together. One implication of this view is that the process of partial-matching input to stored patterns can be used as a basis for inference. For example, if an input sequence has been partially matched to a stored pattern, that pattern will contain residual information that needs to be instantiated to produce a completed match. So an inferential process may be initiated to attempt to match some information in the pattern to some unaccounted for information in the input.

Another type of inference directed by the stored pattern is determined by its association with other patterns. Since patterns combine into higher-order patterns, the recognition of one pattern via a successful match can lead to expectation for matching other patterns in the input sequence. Thus patterns can be used for prediction based on expectancies provided by earlier recognitions. This can effectively order the search for possible interpretations for successive information.

When some of the information that instantiates an instance of a pattern is missing due to its absence from the input or degradation in memory, knowledge of the correct pattern can supply the missing information. This knowledge might be in the form of "default" assignments [Kuipers75, Minsky75] or in the form of a "guess" that is functionally equivalent to the missing knowledge. This latter case was demonstrated in the recalls of subjects whose protocols contained information that was functionally correct but details that were incorrect. In this case, the fact that the pattern encoding the particular knowledge was well-learned resulted in better memory for the pattern than for the details instantiating it. This produced a graceful degradation of performance that is characteristic of humans but still an unattained goal for most computer systems. That is, rather than halting completely when information could not be retrieved, an incorrect response was produced that contained the correct functional properties of the missing information.

## 4.2 Hierarchical Knowledge Organization

The concept of organizing knowledge into hierarchies is certainly not a new idea to either computer scientists or psychologists. The use of generalization hierarchies for encoding information leads to convenient storage efficiencies and straightforward deductive mechanisms. In cognitive psychology, numerous models of semantic memory are based on the assumption of hierarchical knowledge representations. The novel concept proposed here is that information about hierarchical location can be used as a metric of information "importance." The knowledge at high levels of the hierarchy encodes the important structural information of the passage as well as the content that corresponds to this structural knowledge. In addition, this high- level knowledge conceptually subsumes and integrates other less important clusters of knowledge below it. Since access to the memory representation is assumed to occur at the top of the hierarchy, the most important content is the easiest to retrieve from memory. Less important details, on the other hand, are less readily retrieved but may be produced by searches through the structure.

This concept of importance ordering might be valuable in situations in which knowledge capacity is limited. A hierarchical representation scheme would permit memory to contain important information in quick-access storage while less salient knowledge could be stored remotely and addressed indirectly from conceptual parents. The memory organization scheme could thus be determined by the structural semantics of the knowledge domain.

## 4.3 Patterns as Knowledge Clusters

A fundamental feature of the model presented here is that knowledge units are actually collections of information that combine to produce a single conceptual pattern. For example, an episode is viewed as a pattern of situations, events, and relations among them. This higher-order pattern may be treated as a single unit (as in the deletion of an entire episode from a recall protocol), or it may be decomposed into its components if required.

This view of knowledge representation posits a mechanism for recognizing frequently associated concepts as unitized entities (patterns). The capacity of general patterns to integrate their components provides a basis for strengthening the association among the constituents that instantiate it. Thus, if one desires to associate strongly certain concepts with one another, a technique for accomplishing this might be to unify them under higher-order patterns that require conjunctions of recognized elements for their instantiation and produce representations reflecting the mutual dependencies.

On the other hand, if one desires to differentiate and maintain similar but distinct concepts, potential interference effects in memory should be minimized. Embedding the concepts in distinct patterns would effectively separate the concepts by distinguishing the contexts in which they were invoked or retrieved. The transition recall probabilities given above for subjects' story recall demonstrated this effect. Associations among items were found to be strong when they were embedded in the same higher-order pattern and weak when embedded in different patterns.

## 5.0 SUMMARY

The preceding discussion has sketched a psychological model for text learning. The model is based on the assumption that learned patterns in memory encode naturally occurring combinations of conceptual elements in narrative sequences. These patterns are used to guide the comprehension, representation, and reproduction of new information encountered through experience. Data have been presented here and elsewhere that are consistent with the predictions of the theory [Bartlett32, vanDijk77, Kintsch75, Mandler77, Thorndyke77a]. In addition to the large corpus of confirmatory evidence, substantial theoretical interest has emerged in the concept of prototypical patterns as models of memory [R.C. Anderson77, Minsky75, Norman75a, Rumelhart77, Schank77, Schmidt76a, Winograd75]. However, the viability of such schematic approaches as models of human memory has not yet been established. On the other hand, while confirmatory evidence in itself is never sufficient to accept a theory, it is the responsibility of researchers with alternative theories to formulate their predictions, demonstrate that their theories fit existing data equally well, and in addition make testable predictions that distinguish their theories from existing ones. To date, no other theories of human story comprehension have emerged satisfying these criteria.

This chapter has postulated a schematic representation of knowledge to account for available human data. However, no assumptions have been made that imply a particular representation of the knowledge units. The model described here could be implemented in software utilizing semantic networks, productions, frames, scripts, actors, etc. From a psychological point of view, the details of any computer implementation of knowledge utilization are unimportant. The important point is that an implemented system should behave in certain ways that are consistent with desirable human behaviors. Ultimately, the only decision criterion for choosing a representation should be how well it works. However, it should be noted that the most successful systems to date have utilized some form of prototypes for pattern recognition, memory encoding, and text generation [D.G. Bobrow76, Schank77, Schmidt76b].

# KNOWLEDGE-DIRECTED INFERENCE IN BELIEVER[1]

N.S. Sridharan and C.F. Schmidt

*Rutgers University*

*The BELIEVER theory is an attempt to specify an information processing system that constructs intentional interpretations of an observed sequence of human actions. A frame-based system, AIMDS, is used to define three domains: the physical world; the plan domain, where interpretations are con structed using plan structures composed from plan units; and the person domain, which consists of the psychological description of the actor. The system achieves a shift of representation from propositions about physical events to statements about beliefs and intentions of the actor by hypothesizing and attributing a plan structure to the actor.*

*A paradigm for approaching a part of the interpretation problem is described in this chapter. Understanding is viewed as a process of assimilating incoming patterns with existing knowledge and expectations. The essential process of "expectation matching" is attended to in detail and a simple example is presented to illustrate the paradigm and its possible extensions.*

## 1.0 INTRODUCTION

The task of the BELIEVER research group is to develop an information processing theory of how persons construct hypotheses and expectations to interpret the actions of others. This report outlines an approach to a part of the problem of interpretation. There are both psychological and AI aspects to this task. The construction of a psychological theory involves explicating psychological concepts within the framework of an information processing paradigm [Schmidt76a] and

[1] This research was sponsored by the NIH Special Research Resource on Computers in Bio-Medicine at Rutgers, The State University of New Jersey.

then developing experimental procedures that will test aspects of the information processing theory that has been defined. An AI representational framework is used to define the theoretical concepts and to exercise them in sample problems. The challenge of building an AI system to assist in theory construction lies (a) in developing rich descriptive formalisms and mechanisms for describing an information processing theory at a high level and (b) in maintaining its flexibility as it adapts to and evolves with the psychological theory.

The problem of organizing an input sequence of actions into a logical plan structure that satisfies psychological postulates about intentions, beliefs, and dispositions is new ground for AI. Earlier attempts that used a predictive top-down grammatical parsing technique [Schmidt73] and a postdictive bottom-up rule-based system using a semantic net [G. Brown74] have had major drawbacks, which the present approach [Sridharan75] attempts to remedy. The present system efforts are guided by the need (a) to use a context-sensitive notion of acts and plans; (b) to allow multiple hypotheses to be maintained; (c) to permit working with partial knowledge, especially in the domain of beliefs and intentions; (d) to separate the requirements imposed by the interpretation (possible worlds) from the actual situation (real world); and (e) to have a flexible control structure that allows expectations developed from the input to guide the system (the top-down process) yet stay tightly constrained by the incoming observations (the bottom-up process). The requirements on theory construction are to account for how human processing of input sequences (a) maintains a single-mindedness during interpretation; (b) works forward in time making predictions and using expectations to constrain further development; (c) moves up in levels of interpretation quickly; (d) uses well-defined specific ways of moving from hypothesis to hypothesis during revision of interpretation; and (e) is able to recognize interruptions to plans, side-effects of plans, failed plans and so on.

In this chapter we outline a general paradigm for act interpretation. We discuss the structure and the representation of knowledge in different domains and present an example showing how these ideas are utilized in the matching of input to the interpretive structure.

## 2.0  A PARADIGM FOR ACT INTERPRETATION

An interpretation I of observed actions is a *plan structure* composed of plan units. This plan structure organizes the actions that have already been observed and may also include expectations about future actions. The segment of the plan structure that is grounded in observations is referred to as the *hypothesis* H. The remaining segment of I that is not yet supported by observations forms the *expectations* E.

This partition of the plan structure into H and E changes as newly observed actions are accounted for under I. The term *expectation structure*, ES, is used to denote a *plan structure schema* containing schema variables to refer to objects, persons, and locations in the modeled world. When ES is initially set up as an interpretation, its H is empty and all its elements belong to E. As observations begin to support the expectations of I, the elements of ES shift and become supported elements of H. Additionally, details of the observations determine bindings for schema variables and serve to fill in the specifics of the hypothesis structure.

The current state of the observed world known to the system consists of a collection of statements known to be true or false and the pattern of dependency among these statements. Let us call this structure the *world model* WM. WM is a source of information for generating expectations, for making the plans in the hypothesis specific, and for resolving references to objects and places mentioned in the expectation structure. Changes to WM are initiated by giving to the system descriptions of actions. The system has the ability to derive an updated model structure WM' using the current model WM and the act description A (see Fig. 1).

Since we are interested in accounting for common sense reasoning about human action, the formation of an interpretation I involves the attribution of intent, beliefs, and expectations to the actor. This collection is referred to as PM, the *psychological model* of the person. PM serves as another important source of constraints guiding the construction and revision of the interpretation.

The definition of the plan structure and its rules of consistency are used to generate from a given structure E, two sets of *requirements*, MR and PR, that the world model and the person model should satisfy. These requirements take the form of propositions with designated truth values that should hold in the current model WM and the current person model PM.

The process of developing an interpretation consists of three main steps: (1) setting up an expectation structure based on initial information; (2) accepting input acts, updating the world model, and matching these acts against units in the expectation structure; and (3) verifying that WM and PM satisfy the requirements of the updated interpretation. This requirement matching provides bindings for variables and details to fill out schematic aspects of the plan structures.

## 3.0 THE SYSTEM ARCHITECTURE AND THE THEORETICAL FRAMEWORK

The MDS description formalism [Srinivasan76a, b] and compo-

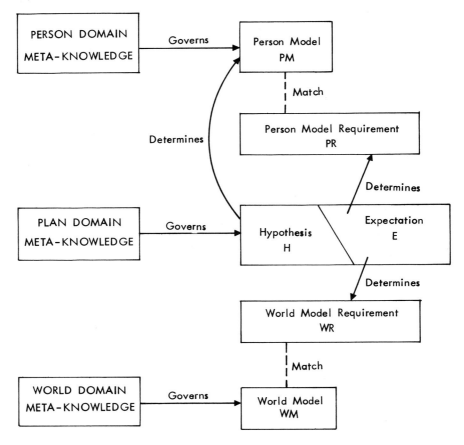

Fig. 1. Interpretation I ( = H + E) and its relation to knowledge sources.

nents of the MDS system architecture have been used to create a smaller system, AIMDS [Sridharan76a], customized and extended for act interpretation. AIMDS is a frame-based system that uses semantic knowledge of general classes of objects to perform modal as well as model-based reasoning. A system of *concepts, relations,* and *logical conditions* on these concepts and relations defined to AIMDS is called a *domain.* Each concept is described as a frame having three components. The first component, *template* specification, assigns a name for the class of objects denoted by the frame and defines a collection of names for relations that may exist between the frame and other frames in the domain. Associated with relation names are properties of the relations (e.g., irreflexive, symmetric, function) and metarelations (e.g., likes/dislikes are complementary, agent/agentof are inverses). The second component consists of the *rules of consistency,* which are written in a form of first-order logical language and anchored on specific relation names of the frame. These consistency conditions enable the system to preprocess the domain to generate a network of logical dependencies among frames and to use this network in verifying consistency during frame instantiation. The system offers a collection of uniform procedures for instantiation and inference-making. The user may compose procedures using this uniform collection and attach them individually to selected frames. The *procedural attachments* constitute the final component of a frame and are invoked when the frame is instantiated or when a relation in the frame is instantiated.

The collection of frame instances and their relations is always taken to be only partial knowledge and the checking of consistency proceeds using a three-valued logic of true/false/unknown. The concept of *residues* formulated by Srinivasan [Srinivasan76a, b, Hawrusik76] helps the system to remember dependencies between assertions, and thus aids in updating the state of the domain in a logical manner. Residues are logical expressions that the system associates with the acceptance or rejection of proposed instantiations. Residues are anchored on a relation within a frame instance and consist of subexpressions of a consistency condition and the associated collection of variable bindings that determine the truth value of the relation. If a proposed instantiation of a frame relation is unacceptable, the residue forms a method of *reporting* on the nature of the inconsistency so that corrective actions or alternative instantiations may be tried.

A *consistent* collection of frame instances and their relations (and associated residues) is a *state. Transition frames* (e.g., act schema) are used to accomplish state transition and constitute the model-based reasoning component of the system. Modal and hypothetical reasoning are accomplished by instantiating transition frames in logical relation to one another without performing state transitions. The inference rules of the system can answer questions about facts in a given state, dependency among facts in a given state, or changes caused by a transition. Furthermore, these rules can perform hypothetical reasoning and execute tests of consistency.

We have used the description facility of AIMDS to create three domains for BELIEVER: the physical world, the plan structures, and the psychological description of the planner. There is a strong separation among these domains both conceptually and within the system.

The physical domain consists of templates such as **Location, Person** and **Object** with relations such as "being at a location," "being near an object," and "holding an object." Act schema such as **Walk, Take, Carry** are given as transition frames.

The structure of the plan schema and the rules of plan composition [Schmidt76b] are part of the plan domain. The interpretation of actions is accomplished using these rules of composition to compose a **plan** structure with plan relations such as **InOrderTo**, **ByMeansOf**, **MotivatedBy**, and **EnabledBy**. This distinction between a representation in terms of **Acts** and that of **Plans** is an important aspect of the interpretation process. An **Act** describes changes in the physical world and is structured using a temporal linear order. The **Plan** representation is used to introduce the logical and psychological constraints entailed by our representation of the common sense assumptions about intentionality. An example may help to clarify this distinction. A person may move from one location to another. From an intentional point of view, the person may be seen as "getting away from" or as "going toward" a particular location since both of these are **Outcomes** of changing location. This distinction is captured by introducing the **Goal** proposition on the plan. This **Goal** proposition specifies the assumed intention of the actor in performing the action and is one of the **Outcome** propositions. One plan is in the **InOrderTo** relation to another plan only if the **Goal** proposition, not just any **Outcome** proposition, provides an **Opportunity** for a subsequent plan unit. Since only one proposition among the **Outcomes** may be chosen as the **Goal**, this restriction serves to focus the interpretation and also introduces the logical goal-subgoal structuring of plan units. Since the goal-subgoal structure defines only a partial order, it may be consistent with several temporal orderings of actions. Aside from providing a logical organization to observed act sequences, these plan structures also provide a basis for maintaining a structured set of expectations about what future actions should be observed if the plan is yet to be completed.

The plan domain forms a *bridge* between the model of the changing physical world and the psychological domain of the planner. The act description associated with a plan unit gives access to the system's knowledge about the physical domain, and the consistency conditions on the plan frame introduces the necessary psychological assumptions about the actor's beliefs and wants. Thus, the plan domain has, aside from the *rules of form* for plan structures, the bridge rules for *observational support* and rules for *motivational coherence*.

The concept of **Person** is principal in the psychological domain and includes relations such as **Believes**, **Knows**, **Wants**, and **Likes**. The truth of a statement in this domain does not logically depend upon the other domains, thus allowing "John believes the cup is empty" to be asserted and to remain uninfluenced by a physical world statement "The cup is not empty." However, a hypothesis may bridge the two and require a rule of inference or explanation to account for the divergence of belief from the state of the physical world.

## 4.0 INTERPRETATION PROCESS

The full process of interpretation involves developing a plan structure that is supported by and consistent with WM and PM. A basic step in this interpretive process is to match the "terminal" elements, the observables, with the "nonterminal" terms introduced by the interpretation structure. We will refer to this as the *basic matching* process and show by example how this process is carried out within the BELIEVER framework.

The process of interpretation for basic matching follows

*Basic Match Algorithm:*

(1) [Setting up an ES] Determine a suitable ES to set up. This can be done in *at least* three ways. (i) *Summoning:* Using the background knowledge of the actor, the physical and social setting, and the role of the actor, retrieve an appropriate ES. (ii) *Generation:* Using the motives and goal of the planner, generate a plan (Cf. [Sacerdoti 74, 75a]) (iii) *Postdictive reconstruction:* Assemble the observed actions, unit by unit, into a logical plan structure.

(2) [Requirement Matching]

(a) Calculate the requirements PR and MR from the set of expectations E.

(b) Use the subalgorithm RM (to be described later) to verify that the requirements are met by the current models PM and WM.

(3) [Accepting Input Act]

(a) Acquire the input act description A.

(b) Derive the updated model WM' from knowing A and WM.

(c) Select a plan unit from the expectations E to assign to the input A. The selected plan unit should be descriptively similar/compatible with the act description.

(d) Change the status of the selected plan unit so that it now belongs to H. Use the description of act A to get bindings and case descriptions for the plan unit. The updated H is H'.

(e) Derive the updated person model PM' using the updated H'.

(f) If conflict was generated in any of the steps 3(c), 3(d), and 3(e), proceed to perform extended constructive matching. See [Schmidt 77] for details.

(4) [Terminating]

(a) If the final plan unit of ES is grounded in observation, terminate this basic match algorithm with an evaluation of the interpretation I (=H+E).

(b) If the final plan unit of ES is not grounded, recycle from step 2 of this algorithm.

The *nonconstructive* basic matching process is designed to simply report the violations without remedial actions. The *extended constructive* matching process [Schmidt77] will recognize and revise the interpretation if the requirements do not match the models. The constructive operations of extended matching would include (a) postdictively constructing a new plan unit for an observed actions and inserting it into H, when no plan unit from the expectation can be found to match it; (b) predictively expanding the set of expectations on the basis of the observed act A, the current hypothesis H, and the current models WM and PM; and (c) revising the interpretation entirely after recognizing that the current one is no longer tenable.

## 5.0  BENEFITS OF THE SYSTEM ARCHITECTURE

The system framework of MDS, particularly the consistency checking of proposed assertions against a state of a domain and using residues as a method of conflict reporting, is helpful in programming the above algorithm. The assignment of a plan unit to an input description A causes the system to evaluate its consistency within the plan domain using metaknowledge about the construction of Plans (i.e., the description of the plan domain) and also to evaluate the propositions that are affected by that assignment, using the network of dependencies for that domain. The residue resulting from this gives the requirement sets MR and PR. The matching of these requirements against the respective models is accomplished by, once again, evaluating the consistency of the requirements with respect to the corresponding states. The requirements matching generates the candidate bindings for variables that are acceptable and reports through the residue any conflicts that may arise.

## 6.0  RELATION TO THE FRAME PROBLEM

The technique for recognizing, analyzing, and resolving inconsistency was demonstrated earlier [Sridharan76b] in the context of modeling actions. The standard treatment of the frame problem in the AI literature [Fikes71, Wilber76] concerns the logical and combinatorial aspects of transferring those propositions not explicitly modified using the act schema from the state before the action to the state resulting from the action. The extended form of the frame problem that we consider concerns checking and restoring consistency of the resulting state after the propositions are transferred. Our "context sensitive" formulation of the concept of "act" makes such a treatment necessary, because a specified action may induce additional state-dependent changes that are not (cannot be) given unconditionally in the act schema. The basic ideas described in [Sridharan76b] for recognition and resolution are usable in this general context for matching requirements against the model.

## 7.0  EXAMPLE PLAN STRUCTURE SCHEMA

The expectation structure provided for the system is a *plan structure schema* [Schmidt76b] in which the references to **Objects**, **Persons**, **Locations**, and other world objects are by means of variables. ES consists of a set of plan units that are organized into a structure using the **InOrderTo** relation. ES has thus a partial (weak temporal) ordering. Each plan unit has an associated description of an act, giving case information such as agent, object, instrument, and destination location. Presented below is the external syntax for describing the ES followed by a description of its internal structure when given to the system.

(a EXPECTATION STRUCTURE Assemble/Eat with

   [Parameters (LIST A L1 L2 L3 O1 O2 O3 O4)])

The actions embedded within the ES are listed below.

DESCRIPTION of Assemble/Eat Expectation Structure:
   (a **Walk**
      with
[**Agent** (a PERSON [ref: A] with [**PlannerOf** Assemble/Eat])]
      [**ToLoc** (a LOCATION [ref: L1])])
   (a **Take**
      with
      [**Agent** A]
      [**Object** (a **Object** [ref: O1] with [**Loc** L1]
         which **IsEdible**)]
      [**InOrderToOf** (the last **Walk**)])
   (a **Carry**
      with
      [**Agent** A]
      [**Object** O1]
      [**ToLoc** (a LOCATION [ref: L3])]
      [**InOrderToOf** (the last **Take**)])

(a **Walk**
  with
  [**Agent** A]
  [**ToLoc** (a LOCATION [ref: L2])])
(a **Take**
  with
  [**Agent** A]
  [**Object** (a **Object**
    [ref: O2]
    with
    [**Loc** L2]
    which
    IsEdible
    [ASSEMBLYPARTS O1 O2])]
  [**InOrderToOf** (the last **Walk**)])
(a **Carry**
  with
  [**Agent** A]
  [**Object** O2]
  [**ToLoc** L3]
  [**InOrderToOf** (the last **Take**)])
(a **Make**
  with
  [**Agent** A]
  [**Components** O1]
  [**Components** O2]
  [**Instrument** (a **Object** [ref: O3] with (**Loc** L3))]
  [**Assembly** (a **Object** [ref: O4]
    which
    (ASSEMBLYOF O1 and O2 using O3))]
  [**InOrderToOf** (the last **Carry**)]
  [**InOrderToOf** (the prev **Carry**)])
(a **Eat**
  with
  [**Agent** A]
  [**Object** O4]
  [**InOrderToOf** (the last **Make**)]))

The above style of description is adapted from KRL [D. G. Bobrow77]. The notation [ref: V] introduces a variable name and denotes the object in which the description is introduced. All subsequent uses of the variable designate the same entity. The "**InOrderToOf**" is a relation among the plan units, and the rest of the description of each unit is an act description. The "with" component of each description follows a relation name and related object format and the "which" component is a list of predicates using LISP conventions.

Internal description of the same expectation structure:

**(Walk1 Instanceof Walk) (Walk1 Agent** A**) (Walk1 ToLoc**
   L1**)**
**(Walk1 InOrderTo Take1)**
**(Take1 Instanceof Take) (Take1 Agent** A**) (Take1 Object**
   O1**)**
**(Take1 InOrderTo Carry1) (Take1 InOrderToOf Walk1)**
**(Carry1 Instanceof Carry) (Carry1 Agent** A**) (Carry1 Object**
   O1**)**
**(Carry1 ToLoc** L3**) (Carry1 InOrderTo Make1) (Carry1**
   **InOrderToOf**
   **Take1)**

. . .

(O1 **Instanceof Object**) (O1 IsEdible) (O1 **Loc** L1)
(O2 **Instanceof Object**) (O2 IsEdible) (O2 **Loc** L2)
(Assemblyof O1 O2) . . .

The above ES presents a frame for making and eating something, and Fig. 2 shows the graph of the plan units formed by the **InOrderTo** relation.

The **Make** assembles two **Objects** O1 and O2 to produce another **Object** O4, which is then eaten. The **Object** O3 is an **Instrument** used in the making of O4 from O1 and O2. The **Object** O1 and O2 need to be brought to the place of **Make** and the two **Walk-Take-Carry** sequences satisfy that requirement.

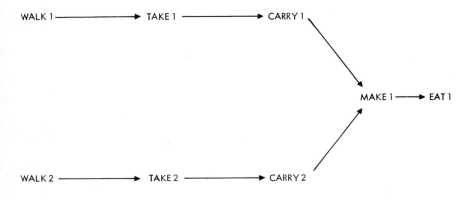

Fig. 2.

The example ES presented above is quite specialized to the task of assembling exactly two objects with an **Instrument,** and even the task of fetching the **Instrument** is left out. Using the **ByMeansOf** relation and its semantics one could develop hierarchical and more general plan structures for construct/consume schema and transportation schema, etc. However, even the specific structure shown above demonstrates some of the benefits of the representation adopted for BELIEVER. The ES is itself quite schematic and the linguistic description is terse. The knowledge of the meaning of **InOrderTo** and **Goal** relations and the rules of proper composition of **Plans** are *factored out* of this description, as are the psychological requirements on the plan structure. Similarly, many of the rules of the physical world concerning properties of locations, constraints on occupancy, and the consequences of action on the model world also need not be included in the ES. These *multiple sources of knowledge and metaknowledge* are represented in the independent domain descriptions. The architecture of the system allows this knowledge to be integrated at the time of action modeling and interpretation development. This not only affords simplicity of descriptions, as exemplified by the ES above, but also yields modularity and the attendant advantages of extensibility. This modularity gives us the opportunity to investigate the consequences of removing various consistency conditions and other components of domain knowledge.

In performing the basic match, each action in the input sequence is mapped onto a plan unit in the expectation structure. Consider the following input sequence in which Tom makes an ice cream cone for himself at the counter by scooping ice cream into the cone. In the starting model WM, Tom is in the kitchen in his house, there is ice cream in the freezer, cones on the cabinet, and a scoop on the counter. In the initial model PM, Tom is known to like ice cream cones, among other things.

(1) Tom walks to the cabinet.
(2) Tom takes a cone.
(3) Tom carries the cone to the counter.
(4) Tom walks to the freezer.
(5) Tom takes out ice cream.
(6) Tom carries the ice cream to the counter.
(7) Tom makes an ice cream cone using the scoop that is on the counter.
(8) Tom eats the ice cream cone.

Several points concerning the matching of the input to the expectation structure should be noted. First, the partially ordered ES can be matched in more than one way to the input sequence. Second, there is more than one input sequence that can be matched against an expectation structure with a fixed set of bindings to the schema variables of the ES. Further, not all linearizations of the partial order of the ES correspond to legitimate action sequences. An action sequence is legitimate if for any action in it, the action can be effectively carried out in the state resulting from the execution of the actions preceding it.

## 8.0 AN EXAMPLE OF BASIC MATCHING

### Step 2(a): Generating Requirements PR and MR

We assume that an ES has been set up and discuss here the use of this expectation structure in performing the basic match. Thus the example picks up from step 2(a) of the Basic Match Algorithm. The first substep is concerned with simply analyzing the given ES and extracting from it information whose ready availability will help the subsequent steps. The extracted information can be displayed using the following schematic form, a template definition:

```
(TDN: [ES
        (Name NAME)
        (Agent PERSON)
        (Goal PROPOSITION)
        ((Acts L) ACT)
        ((Plans L) PLAN)
        ((StartingUnits L) PLAN)
        ((FinalUnit FN) PLAN)
        ((EnablingProps L) [Tuple ACT PROPOSITION ACT])
        ((InOrderToProps L) [Tuple PLAN PROPOSITION
            PLAN])
        ((ModelRequirements L) [Tuple PROPOSITION
            PLAN])])
```

exactly one unit that is in the **InOrderTo** relation to no other plan unit. This unit is the **FinalUnit** of the ES and the **Goal** of the **FinalUnit** is the **Goal** of the ES. **StartingUnits** of ES are plan units of ES such that no other plan unit is in the **InOrderTo** relation to them. The following logical conditions capture the sense of the last three relations on ES. Here the variable X ranges over expectation structures; P, P1, P2 range over PLANS; A1, A2 range over ACTS; and S ranges over PROPOSITIONS.

(X **ModelRequirements** [S P])
  iff (X **Plans** P) and (P **Opportunity** S) and
  Not[(Thereis **Plan** Q) (Q **InOrderTo** P) and (Q **Result** S)]

(X **InOrderToProps** [P1 S P2])
  iff (X **Plans** P1) and (X **Plans** P2) and (P1 **InOrderTo** P2)
  and (P1 **Goal** S) and (P2 **Opportunity** S)

(X **EnablingProps** [A1 S A2])
  iff (X **Acts** A1) and (X **Acts** A2) and Not(A2 **InOrderTo*** A1)
  and (A1 **Outcomes** S) and (A2 **Precondition** S)

PROPOSITIONS that are **Opportunities** for a plan P in the ES and are not the **Result** of a plan in the **InOrderTo** relation to P, belong to the **ModelRequirements** of ES. The **InOrderToProps** of the ES is a collection of propositions that are involved in the **InOrderTo** relation between some two plans P1 and P2. Each such proposition is the **Goal** proposition of P1 and the **Opportunity** proposition of P2. The possible linearizations of the ES are not examined in detail during this analysis, but the **EnablingProps** forms the basis for performing this analysis at a later stage. The act descriptions are examined to determine if there are enabling connections between **Acts** (mediated by propositions in the **Outcome** set of one act and the **Precondition** set of the other) without regard to the **Goal** proposition of the corresponding plan unit. Enabling connections cannot be considered between the pair A1-A2 when A2 logically precedes A1. This is ensured in the above conditions through the use of the **InOrderTo*** relation, the transitive closure of **InOrderTo**.

The ES presented above has the following description associated with it as a result of this first step of analysis.

Name: Assemble/Eat
Agent: A
**Goal**: (A **Ate** O4)
**Acts**: **Walk1, Walk2, Take1, Take2, Carry1, Carry2, Make, Eat.**
**Plans**: **Walk1, Walk2, Take1, Take2, Carry1, Carry2, Make, Eat.**
**StartingUnits**: **Walk1, Walk2.**
**FinalUnit**: **Eat.**

**InOrderToProps**:
    [**Walk1** (A **Loc** L1) **Take1**]
    [**Take1** (A **Inhand** O1) **Carry1**]
    [**Carry1** (O1 **Loc** L3) **Make**]

[**Walk2** (A **Loc** L2) **Take2**]
[**Take2** (A **Inhand** O2) **Carry2**]
[**Carry2** (O2 **Loc** L3) **Make**]
[**Make** (A **Has** O4) **Eat**]

**EnablingProps**:
All of the **InOrderToProps** plus the following.
[**Walk1** (A **Loc** L1) **Carry1**]
[**Walk1** (A **Loc** L1) **Walk2** providing (**Walk2 Fromloc**
L1)]

[**Walk2** (A **Loc** L2) **Carry2**]
[**Walk2** (A **Loc** L2) **Walk1** providing (**Walk1 Fromloc**
L2)]

[**Carry1** (A **Loc** L3) **Walk2** providing (**Walk2 Fromloc**
L3)]
[**Carry1** (A **Loc** L3) **Eat**]

[**Carry2** (A **Loc** L3) **Walk1** providing (**Walk1 Fromloc**
L3)]
[**Carry2** (A **Loc** L3) **Eat**]

**ModelRequirements**:
[(O1 **Loc** L1) **Take1**]
[(O2 **Loc** L2) **Take2**]
[(O3 **Loc** L3) **Make**]

The above analysis for enabling connections and model requirements was carried out with the assumption that the three locations L1,
L2, and L3 are distinct and that the objects O1-O4 are distinct. This
assumption has eliminated some possible enablement connections.

From the **ModelRequirements** and the **Goal** of the ES, the system generates the set of requirements, PR, on the person model PM.
In this example, these requirements consist of a **Goal**-related proposition (A **Wants** (A **Ate** O4)) and a set of three belief propositions
derived from the **ModelRequirements**: (A **Believes** (O1 **Loc** L1)), (A
**Believes** (O2 **Loc** L2)), and (A **Believes** (O3 **Loc** L3)). In verifying
these wants and belief propositions, a weak form of plausibility is the
best that can be expected; thus no strict confirmation or validation
rules have been formulated. The consistency conditions on the structure of hypotheses assure internal consistency of hypotheses, but the
person requirements serve to keep the hypotheses coherent with a
psychological model of the person. The proposition (A **Believes** (O1
**IsEdible**)) does not appear in PR because, in a normal situation, a
planner A can be assumed to share with the system the knowledge of
such physical properties. If the system can determine for itself that a

knife is not edible, then (A **Believes** (Knife **IsEdible**)) can be taken to be false; and when the system can determine (Bread **IsEdible**), it can assume (A **Believes** (Bread **IsEdible**)). This would be true for all knowledge about "dispositional properties" of the physical world that is "normal" and unchanging in the current context.

## Step 2(b): Requirements Matching with the Models WM and PM

The system is presented with the initial model WM and the initial person model PM, which it assimilates into the ES. The assimilation should result in either acceptance of the ES and the making of predictions about the next act when possible, or the rejection of the ES. The rejection of the ES can be followed up (in the extended situation of matching) with various analysis and remedial measures, but those considerations do not arise for the basic matching. The initial model presented will be used to derive and refine candidate bindings for the variables of the ES, using the algorithm given below.

Initial Model WM:
(Tom **Loc** Kitchen) (Cabinet **In** Kitchen) (Cone **Loc** Cabinet)
(PeanutButter **Loc** Cabinet) (Refrigerator **In** Kitchen)
(Bread **Loc** Refrigerator) (Freezer **In** Kitchen)
(IceCream **Loc** Refrigerator) (Counter **In** Kitchen)
(Scoop **Loc** Counter)
accompanied with the general world knowledge:
(**Assemblyparts** IceCream Cone)
(**Assemblyparts** Bread PeanutButter)
(**Assemblyof** IceCream Cone Scoop ICC)
(**Assemblyof** Bread PeanutButter Knife PBS)
(IceCream **IsEdible**) (Cone **IsEdible**) Not(Knife **IsEdible**) etc.

In the above model, the occurrence of PeanutButter and other items should be taken to stand in for a collection of items of similar nature in those locations. We shall see in the example that the particular list of things used is unimportant.

Initial Person Model PM:
(Tom **Believes** (Scoop **Loc** Counter))
(Tom **Believes** (IceCream **Loc** Refrigerator))
(Tom **Believes** (Cone **Loc** Cabinet))
and so on, conforming to the model WM.
(Tom **Likes** (Tom **Ate** ICC))
(Tom **Likes** (Tom **Ate** PBS))

The subalgorithm RM is:

(0)  The given ES is acceptable only if the planner is known.

(1)  Use the person model PM to check that the **Goal**-related propositions of ES are not falsified in the model. Determine the **Objects** involved in the **Goal**.

(2)  Use general world knowledge about physical objects and locations to generate candidate binding lists for ES variables.

(3)  Use the model WM given and the model requirements of ES to refine candidate bindings.

(4)  Use the person model PM and the model requirements of ES to refine candidate bindings further.

(5)  If no candidate bindings are left for any of the variables, declare ES an unsuitable expectation structure.

The result of this analysis is given in the list of possible bindings:

A →(Tom),
L1→(Refrigerator, Freezer, Cabinet),
L2→(Refrigerator, Freezer, Cabinet),
L3→(Counter),
O1→(Cone, Bread, IceCream, PeanutButter),
O2→(Cone, Bread, IceCream, PeanutButter),
O3→(Scoop, Knife),
O4→(ICC, PBS).

In step 1 of the analysis, O4 is bound using what is known in model PM. In step 2, the possibilities O1→Knife and O2→Knife are eliminated for the knife is not edible. In Step 3, the absence of edible objects at the counter is used to eliminate the bindings L1→Counter and L2→Counter. For this example the step 4 has no effect. But one could consider cases where the planner has beliefs about the state of the world at deviance from the facts about that world. For example, if Tom does not know that there is PeanutButter in the cabinet, then the possibility that he would take it out (as part of his plan, not as part of his real actions) would have to be left out. If he does take out the PeanutButter as part of his actions, the person model would have to be revised using some explanatory note such as "He did not already know it was there, but he saw it."

## Step 3: Accepting Input Acts

The preceding processing makes the assignment of acts to plan units a straightforward process. The main interest in observing the input of act descriptions is in following how at each stage the variable binding possibilities are pared down and how the expectations about the next act are developed.

The input for the first act is "Tom walks to the cabinet." The assignment of this act to the expectation unit **Walk1** is similar to that of assigning it to **Walk2**. We shall gloss over whether and how the system might make that decision. Let us pursue the assignment to **Walk1**. The bindings are refined to L1→(Cabinet) from the act; L2→(Refrigerator, Freezer) from the requirement that variables denote distinct entities of the world; L3→(Counter); O1→(Cone, PeanutButter); O2→(Bread, IceCream); with O3 and O4 same as before. In the state resulting from the act, the **Preconditions** for **Take1** are fully satisfied (and according to ES **Walk1** is in enabling relation to **Take1**) giving **Take1** in the location Cabinet as the description of the next expected act. The **Object** of the **Take1** is uncertain with Cone and PeanutButter as possibilities.

The assignment of this act to **Walk1** requires that the status of **Walk1** is changed from being a unit in the expectation E to the hypothesis H. Accompanying this change, the starting set of units in the remaining expectation and its **ModelRequirements** are revised. Thus **Take1** and **Walk2** are now starting units. At this point lookahead analysis could reveal that the occurrence of **Walk2** would be indicative of failure. The system in its present conception would not perform this lookahead, but if the next act were indeed to be a **Walk** or if that were hypothetically submitted for analysis, the system should recognize the failure.

The second input act description is "Tom takes out the cone from the cabinet." Its assignment to the expectation **Take1** refines the bindings to: O1→(Cone), O2→(IceCream), O3→(Scoop), O4→(ICC), L3→(Counter) and L2→(Freezer). The binding of Cone to O1 allows the elimination of the possibility that O4 is PBS, O3 is Knife, O2 is Bread.

The third act description is "Tom carries the cone to the counter." Here the destination location could have been omitted and the matching of the expectation unit could be used to fill the description. The extended matching situation could conceivably use information from the expectation to override either the model information or the input description, thus developing deviations between the interpreter's model and the facts in the modeled world.

The current interpretation strongly guides the matching of the rest of the input acts. Consequently, they are matched with very little processing.

## 9.0  CONCLUSION

We have started with the assumption that our common sense knowledge of both the physical and the psychological domain is highly structured and interdependent. Consequently, a descriptive framework has been adopted to facilitate the expression of these dependencies. Once expressed, this rich set of domain specific knowledge can be used to define the notion of a consistent model of a domain. We have attempted to explain how this notion of consistency might be used for guiding and constraining a constructive process of interpretation that is underdetermined by the input. We apply these ideas to the problem of interpreting human action, where the knowledge of the physical and psychological worlds are separated. The plan domain captures the metaknowledge needed to bridge the gap between these two worlds. This plan domain provides the basis for focusing and collecting the implications that must hold between the physical and psychological domains under a given interpretation. Using such a plan structure, the triggering of inference and carrying out of conflict resolution can be highly knowledge-directed. We described a paradigm for the interpretation process employing both nonconstructive (basic) and constructive matching processes. In describing the knowledge structures and processes used for interpretation, a detailed example of the basic nonconstructive match illustrated how different knowledge domains are used to generate the constraints and candidate bindings that validate or invalidate a particular interpretation under consideration.

## ACKNOWLEDGMENTS

Frank Hawrusik and John Goodson have participated actively in our research, in system construction, and in experimental studies. Our most sincere thanks go to them. We thank Professor Saul Amarel, who has consistently given us expert guidance and support. We also thank Professor C. V. Srinivasan, whose system concepts have significantly influenced our research.

# Natural Language Understanding

# CONVERSATIONAL ACTION PATTERNS IN DIALOGS

William S. Faught[1]
*University of California at Los Angeles*

*Systems that interact in dialogs need to understand linguistic actions being used by one another and know which linguistic actions are appropriate for their own uses. We introduce a model based on conversational action patterns to describe and predict speech acts in natural language dialogs and to specify appropriate actions to satisfy the system's goals. A modified production system was used to implement the formalism. The salient characteristics of the production system are (1) affects (emotions) can modify the interpretation of external events and alter the flow of control of the system; (2) the system uses overlapping and parallel rules to predict and generate overlapping linguistic events in dialog situations. The same mechanism is used as a basis of cognitive functioning to model internal planning and inference functions.*

## 1.0 INTRODUCTION

Psychological simulation models of human behavior must perform three major tasks: (1) recognizing and analyzing the situation that the model is in, (2) performing actions that will accomplish the model's intentions, and (3) motivating its own behavior. For systems in natural language dialog situations, this includes the recognition of specific linguistic actions and their interpretation based on the linguistic context. Intentions are fulfilled by performing linguistic actions using the appropriate speech act. Motivation of the model stems from a third

[1] This research was supported by the National Institute of Mental Health under Grant PHS MH 27132-03. Computer facilities were provided by the Stanford University Medical Experimental Computing Resource (SUMEX) funded by the Biotechnology Resources Branch of the National Institutes of Health under Grant number RR-785.

*383*

function, called affect (emotion). Affect embodies the significant experiences of the entity (the self's needs, desires, and interests) and continually modulates the recognition of situations and the performance of actions.

We describe here a simulation model of the recognition and performance functions. The model is based on internal structures representing action patterns (APs). Specific instances of these APs dealing with conversation structure are called conversational action patterns (CAPs). The CAPs are implemented as rules in a production system in which several rules may be activated at once.

The production system execution is based on a five-step process:

(1) Update: The appraisal and affect conditions are updated to reflect the current state of the model.

(2) Activate: All of the APs (PS rules) whose initial conditions (left-hand sides) are true are activated.

(3) Match: All of the action elements of the activated APs are matched to select one action to perform.

(4) Execute: The selected action is executed.

(5) Book-keep: the working pool of active APs is cleared, except for APs specifying further actions for the next cycle.

The development and implementation of these processes are part of an attempt to construct a general simulation model for testing information processing theories of psychopathology. The model's only interface with the world is natural language. The task of the model is to exhibit its behavior, linguistically, as a participant in psychiatric interviews. The emphasis here will be on linguistic behavior of humans in dialog situations.

## 2.0 BACKGROUND

There are three major aspects of human thinking that psychological theories must attempt to explain: affect, conation, and cognition. Affect, or emotion, is the motivating force behind mental actions. Affect represents an evaluation of the significance that the entity places on an experience. Conation is the process of deciding on actions and then executing them. Cognition is the process of manipulating information or representations of the environment.

Difficulties usually arise in attempting to explain how actions originate. If one's explanation is "Process A starts the actions," then there is a danger of an infinite regress when process A is explained in terms of actions. Also, it is difficult to explain how emotions influence and are influenced by cognitive and conative processes. The requirement that our model participate in natural language dialogs with humans in order to exhibit its behavior motivated our study of the characteristics of dialog situations. We shall now examine some of those characteristics.

In order to fulfill desires and needs, human beings perform actions, and those actions tend to occur in patterns. Performing actions that are effectively correlated with their desires and needs is what enables them to ensure and enhance the quality of their survival. Further, these actions tend to occur in patterns so that humans may cope efficiently and effectively with the wealth of information and possible actions that surrounds them. One common example of action performance is the ringing of a telephone, and the action sequence of walking to the telephone, reaching for the receiver, picking it up, and saying "hello" into the mouthpiece. This is an example of a patterned action - a sequence of individual actions that tend to be performed in the same order, and that once started tend to run to completion of the sequence (unless interrupted by some higher priority process). An example from conversational interaction is the sequence

(Question → Clarification question → Clarification → Answer)

as in

"How do you like your work?" (Question)
"Why do you want to know?" (Clarification Question)
"I thought your job might upset you." (Clarification)
"Well, it's not too interesting; I look forward to leaving at night." (Answer)

Patterned action sequences manifest themselves in an individual's behavior because they are useful in predicting or specifying future events and states. A few observations can be made:

The fact that an action sequence is usually carried to completion seems to inhibit partially other possible actions from occurring [Dennett69]. For instance, once one's hand is on the telephone receiver, almost no thoughts or actions will interrupt putting the receiver to the head and saying "Hello." Thus actions are partially determined by the previous actions performed. Carrying this one step further we note that recognition and interpretation of situational inputs will also be partially determined by previous actions performed. In our example from a conversation, the final statement "Well, it's not too interesting..." is interpreted as an answer to the original question "How do you like your work?" and not to "I thought your job might upset you."

Because these action patterns or sequences seem to run to completion once begun, an economy of information processing can result [Dennett69]. For example, when first learning to drive a car with a stick shift, one must perform each step of the gear-shifting patterned action individually, and the state of the world must be verified after each one. After years of practice, one needs only to initiate the action pattern; since it is automatic, one is free to think about other things while shifting gears. In the same way, information storage about dialog participation is optimized by linguistic actions being formed into patterns.

Further, action patterns tend to be multi-attributed and overlap one another. The following is a sample of a portion of a psychiatric interview, with some example action patterns diagrammed on the right:

| Tell me about your job. | Question | |
|---|---|---|
| | ↓ | |
| I work at Sears. | Answer | |
| | | |
| How do you like it there? | Fear | Question |
| | ↓ | ↓ |
| Why do you want to know? | Protect | Clarification question |
| | | ↓ |
| Maybe it upsets you. | Topic add | Clarification |
| | ↓ | ↓ |
| It's ok. But I am upset. | New topic | Answer |
| | ↓ | |
| About what? | Accept new topic | |

The patterns correspond to several levels of actions: actions to control the conversation, actions to respond to affect needs (Fear→Protect), actions determining the syntactic form of the output expressions, actions guiding the topic of the conversation. Note that one linguistic expression can perform actions at several levels. For instance, the sentence "Maybe you are upset about it" serves to clarify a previous question, retain control of the conversation, and introduce a new topic. The fact that action patterns overlap and represent various levels of information extends the economies of information processing they make possible.

Our definition of an action has thus far been purposely vague so that we could allow recognition of situations (or interpretation of situations) to be considered an action. In our dialog example, the question from the interviewer "How do you like it there?" is not an action that the model can perform. Instead, the question is a condition or event in the world that should occur in order for the action pattern to fit. As it is, the interviewer's question must be performed by the interviewer; thus the action of the model is to wait, or even anticipate, the interviewer's next input expression. To generalize: actions are either events or states of the world that a person seeks to recognize in the world, or are instructions to perform.

Psychopathological models currently deal mostly with defensive cognition, i.e., strategies for manipulating beliefs and performing actions in accordance with those beliefs to minimize the overall occurrence of negative affects. These strategies are strongly dependent upon the notion of affect influencing other thought processing. One characteristic of these strategies is the biased interpretation of situations according to affect levels. For example, in the paranoid mode (according to the theory we are attempting to model), when the shame-humiliation affect rises to an extreme level, there is a strong bias toward interpreting another person's actions as persecutory. Another aspect is the use of unconscious strategies. In paranoia, a person may attempt to find evidence that another person is persecuting him, but the use of this strategy for avoiding or reducing humiliation may be unconscious. Finally, there can be thematic responses to particular affects. For example, the fear affect generally triggers an attempt to protect the self; the anger affect tends to trigger an action of locating the cause of the anger in someone else's actions and contending with them. In general, the recognition or interpretation of events and the selection of actions to be performed are determined by two sets of factors [Simon69]: the inner environment (the needs and desires of affect), and representations of the outer environment (beliefs and facts about the external world). If we consider these two factors both to be appropriate conditions for determining the use of patterned actions, then the strategies for defensive cognition become quite similar to patterned actions.

## 3.0 ACTION PATTERNS

Our theory of patterned actions will attempt to explain how actions are grouped into patterns and how these patterns are used in the recognition of situations and the performance of actions. The theory is based partially on differential emotion theory [Izard71] and on an extension of it into affect as motivation for other thought processing [Faught75]. According to differential emotion theory, there is a small number (approximately eight) of primary affects or emotions [Tomkins62] that identify the significant experiences for the entity, which in turn provide motivation for ensuring and enhancing the quality of survival of the entity. The important fact to note for the use of patterned actions is that the affects provide the criteria for determining the importance of events and information to the entity. Our theory will attempt to account for actions that might be considered automatic, unconscious, or not requiring deliberative planning to any great extent; i.e., those actions which are rich in situational factors and affect, but sparse in abstract thought.

The basic elements of the theory are (1) data structures called patterns, (2) an activation mechanism that activates patterns when they match a real-world situation, and (3) an interpreter that performs the actions specified by activated patterns.

Note that we will use the terms pattern and action pattern (AP) interchangeably. Action pattern helps convey the temporal aspect of a pattern existing over time; however, some patterns have no visible actions in them, and are better thought of as recognition or interpretation patterns that have system conditions as their antecedents and a recognition or interpretation of a situation as their consequent. The consequent still has the potential to alter the state of the system, e.g., to raise the fear affect. At the same time, patterns with actions may also have elements that interpret the situation.

In its simplest form, a pattern is a list, a data structure consisting of a one-dimensional set of elements that are linked. Each element of a pattern represents an event or state of the world. Elements are placed in a left-to-right sequence in a pattern according to the actual temporal order of the events' occurrence in the real world, making the elements time-dependent. For example, in a gear-shifting pattern (Disengage clutch → Shift gear lever → Reengage clutch) the elements correspond to the actual time ordering of the sequence in the real world, with earliest events leftmost.

A more complex pattern may be more than one-dimensional by having a number of elements in the same position. The events corresponding to these elements are all supposed to occur simultaneously. For example, we may expand the previous pattern to include the events surrounding the throttle:

Disengage clutch, close throttle
↓
Shift gear lever
↓
Re-engage clutch, open throttle

In this case, the two starting events (disengage clutch and close throttle) occur simultaneously, as if AND-ed together.

Conceptually, elements of patterns are representations of events or states of the world (facts about the external environment), or conditions (affects) of the internal environment. This allows one homogeneous representation of both factors influencing the behavior of the entity. Additionally, elements can be interpreted as events that have already occurred or as actions or states that should be brought about, depending on how far along in the pattern the real world situation matches. Thus, events in the patterns may be interpreted as situations to match or as actions to perform; affects may be interpreted as conditions on the inner environment to match, or as the affect response to the events in the pattern. Also, the elements of any one pattern are at a conceptually homogeneous level; i.e., the events that they represent are all of a similar nature. For example, the gear-shifting pattern would not contain elements from a pattern of conversational events, nor would it contain elements corresponding to specific muscular movements in the hands for shifting the gear lever. Such simultaneous pattern information on a different conceptual level would be included in a different pattern.

## 4.0 PATTERN ACTIVATION

Patterns may be active or inactive at any particular moment. A pattern is active when (part of) it matches the internal and/or external environment. Patterns are activated by an activation mechanism that matches their parts against conditions in the environment. Patterns match from left to right (to correspond to temporal order). Each element of the pattern must match; the last element matched must correspond to the most recent situation. When a pattern is activated, the remaining unmatched elements become available for further information processing. Inactive patterns are latent and unavailable for processing. An analogy may be made to short-term memory and long-term memory of psychological theories, in which the active concepts currently being processed are held in short-term memory, while the bulk of information is stored in long-term memory waiting to be called into short-term memory.

There are two forms of recognition of situations possible: recognition of new situations, and validation of on-going situations. The activation of a pattern represents a new situation being recognized, and all the appropriate information being activated for it. In our conversation example, the (question-clarification question) pattern provided a recognition of the local interaction as soon as the second element matched, and then provided the appropriate information to recognize the next input as a clarification of the original question. Validation of on-going situations occurs when a next event is correctly anticipated, as in recognizing the clarification input, or the next event is brought about through one's own actions, as in answering the question after clarification.

Patterns have initial conditions that determine whether they will be active or not. In general, initial conditions are the same inner and outer environmental factors that make up pattern elements. The necessity for making them special elements in patterns arises from having to keep a distinction between descriptive elements and prescriptive elements. In the (question-clarification question) pattern, we do not wish the fact that the other person asked a question to prescribe automatically a clarification question as the appropriate response. Instead, we need to add an initial condition that if the input was a question and if the question was not well understood, then a clarification is one of the possible appropriate actions to be taken. At that point, the two initial conditions plus the additional elements aready matched in the pattern become the initial conditions to the next element of the pattern.

The activation of patterns proceeds continuously and in parallel. An appropriate analogy to use is a network of AND and OR logical gates, with a set of level inputs, the propagation of signals, and the final output of level signals. The level inputs in our theory are the inner and outer environment variables, almost at the level of sensory inputs to the system. The logical gates are the patterns, with an input connection between the environment variable and the element of a pattern that it matches. The final output signals are the set of next states in the patterns that are to occur. The propagation of signals and the activations of patterns can occur quickly because no matching, graph searching, or back-tracking need occur.

It is this combination of instant assimilation of new information and at the same time tendency to stick with the same pattern or interpretation of a situation that gives this scheme its useful qualities for psychological models. For example, the input expression "How are you?" can have (at least) two different interpretations. At the beginning of a conversation:

"Hello."
"How are you?"

the appropriate response is "Fine." After saying "My girl friend has an exotic disease," the input "How are you" is undoubtedly more than a greeting. These can be distinguished by patterns of the following sort:

( "How are you?", Greetings → Standard greeting → Response = "Fine" )
( "How are you?", Nongreetings → Health question → Response = "No infection" )

Another example shows an interpretation of an input expression based on affect. The input expression "I find you interesting" can be interpreted in one of two ways: as a compliment, or as an insult.

( Enjoyment affect high, "I find you interesting" → Compliment )
( Humiliation affect high, "I find you interesting" → Insult )

Finally, while processing one piece of information, another may be discovered that changes the interpretation of the situation entirely.

For example, in a paranoid mode, the question "Are you sick?" can be interpreted to imply "You are crazy" if the person is sensitive to humiliation at that point. The implication of being abnormal is then interpreted as an attack and dealt with as such. The following patterns show how this phenomenon might be modeled:

( Humiliation high, Input="Are you sick?" → Interpretation= "Are you crazy?")

(Input="Are you crazy?" → Raise humiliation, Insult )

The input is dealt with as a question until the offending implication is found, at which point humiliation is raised. This immediately activates new patterns for dealing with humiliation and insults, which reinterpret the situation. In addition, some patterns may have been previously activated, based on initial conditions of high positive affect or low negative affect, to promote cooperation with the other person; those patterns are now deactivated and no longer figure in the interpretation of the situation, since their initial conditions are no longer true.

Another analogy for the structure and activation of patterns is one similar to semantic nets. Consider the system consisting of a set of concepts or conditions on the inner and outer environments. For instance, "Humiliation high," "Input is a question," and "Conversation in greetings mode" would be concepts or nodes. Consider the patterns as logical AND gates between concepts, so that the one concept "Humiliation high" would be linked to all of the patterns in which it was an element. (The time factor has been left out of this analogy.) Whenever an initial condition becomes true, if all the other initial conditions of a pattern were already true, the pattern would automatically be activated. Conversely, if a condition suddenly were invalidated, all the patterns in which it was an element would immediately be deactivated. Again, time-consuming matching processes are reduced by having each condition already tied to all the patterns of which it is a member. (Compilation of condition templates by network is more fully discussed in [F. Hayes-Roth75].)

## 5.0 PATTERN INTERPRETATION

Once activated, patterns are processed by an interpreter. Each pattern has a pointer that specifies the element corresponding to the present. For example, the pattern (Question → Clarification question → Clarification → Answer) would have a pointer to the third element after the clarification question had been asked. The elements preceding the pointer represent facts; the elements succeeding the pointer represent expectations; the element pointed to represents an action to perform or situation to recognize. The interpreter proceeds by (1) examining all of the elements currently pointed to, (2) determining an appropriate action (which may be to wait and interpret), and (3) performing the action. One might think of the interpreter stepping one element at a time across the patterns; actually, the stepping is accomplished by the pattern pointers moving across the patterns through the activation mechanism, rather than by the interpreter.

Note that the pointers are not moved across all of the patterns; only the patterns whose information was used in determining the action are likely to be changed. In particular, a pattern whose action is performed by a subpattern would not be completed until the subpattern concluded its processing. For instance, a conversational pattern

(Question → Answer → Comment on answer)

may have a subpattern performing part of its actions:

(Recognize input → Find answer → Say answer)

The pointer on the global pattern would point to question during recognize input, then would remain pointing to Answer during the last two elements of the subpattern.

The interpreter must determine a single action to be performed from all of the activated patterns, although this action may be a multilevel combination of several actions. For example, the linguistic output "Maybe you are upset about it" in the above clarification example was a result of two component actions (clarification) and (introduce new topic). The interpreter determines an action to perform by examining the current elements in the activated patterns and matching them with a small set of rules to compose multilevel actions. These are the only visible actions the system makes: the top-level loop of the system (assuming that the pattern activation is done continuously by an independent process) examines pattern elements, determines an action, and executes it (analogous to the fetch-decode-execute cycle of digital computers). Conflicts between patterns are kept to a minimum by (a) keeping the various levels of affects distinct in their interpretations of situations, (b) making the pattern elements as specific as possible in the conditions they represent, and (c) making certain categories of conditions mutually exclusive. If any conflicts arise concerning the correct action to take, one may either assume that all the remaining actions are appropriate, or that a state of confusion exists as to the best course of action. In any case, affect levels will change if no appropriate action is found, (e.g., shame is raised if the system detects confusion) until they are strong enough to dominate the system and insure some action.

Note that the interpreter can perform only one (multilevel) action or make one inference (if a pattern represents an inference) at a time, while the activation mechanism can recognize entire situations.

## 6.0 MODEL

The purposes of a computational model are (1) to help explicate the corresponding theory by requiring the theory-builder to specify its details, (2) to help formalize the theory by forcing it into a single notation, thus forcing the statements of the theory into a consistent form, and (3) to provide a testing ground that reveals consequences that may not be obvious in a complex theory. The first and second purposes have been realized by our model construction. We hope that the third will be possible as the model is improved.

There are two difficult aspects to modeling our theory: (a) the continuous and parallel activation of patterns, and (b) the appearance and disappearance of the right information at the right time. To preview our comments below, the patterns are activated after the interpreter has performed each action. The working memory is cleared of active patterns, except for those reactivated specifically by previous patterns and actions, and the entire set of patterns tested for activation. The right information is supplied at the right time by a wealth of initial conditions and pattern elements which narrow the scope of most patterns. Unfortunately, this also limits their generality.

The model comprises appraisal and affect conditions, patterns, and a five-step program for activating and interpreting patterns. The appraisal conditions and affects are the facts that the model must interpret. Examples of the appraisal conditions are the other person's linguistic input, "the model is tired," "30 seconds have elapsed since the last input." The appraisal conditions include all of the model's access to the external world. The affects are the eight primary affects referred to previously. These two sets of conditions are exogenous in the sense that any belief formed about them by the model will not change their values directly. They may, however, be indirectly modified by patterns or situations that occur.

The patterns in the model are conceptually equivalent to those in the theory, but have been broken up for ease of implementation. Each pattern is broken into a series of single-step patterns, such as could be done by the interpreter in one action. For example, the three-step pattern (Recognize input → Find answer → Say answer) is broken into three single-step patterns: (Input → Recognize input), (Recognized input, Question → Find answer), and (Answer found → Say answer). Each pattern has the form (Past, Present, Action, Future), where past is a set of initial or continuation conditions, present is a set of conditions that should be activated immediately, action is a recommended action for the interpreter to perform, and future is a set of conditions to activate for the next cycle. This decomposition into single-step patterns is done algorithmically by the program as the initial data are read in; tags are inserted to link single-step patterns that originated from a single multistep pattern.

The five stages of the program to perform the activation and interpretation are update, activate, match, execute, and book-keep. We shall give a brief description of each routine.

*Update:* updates the appraisal and affect conditions. The physical state of the model is assessed and the appraisal conditions updated (e.g., tiredness, cognitive overload). The affects are decremented slightly from the previous cycle and updated. The external inputs are tested, and any new information is noted in the corresponding appraisal variables. All of the conditions (internal and external environmental variables) that were set or are still true from the previous cycle are set true.

*Activate:* activates all patterns that are true based on the conditions set by update. This is accomplished by (a) testing all the conditions (stored on a list) for being true, (b) accessing the patterns for which the true conditions are pattern elements, and (c) testing to see if the other elements are true. If so, the pattern is activated, and any present conditions are set true and tested, recursively.

*Match:* collects all the action elements of the activated patterns and uses its set of rules (patterns) to combine the component actions into a few multilevel actions, then chooses the multilevel action with the highest affect to perform.

*Execute:* performs the (multilevel) action found by match, and determines which future conditions to update for the next cycle.

*Book-keep:* determines which conditions will be true at the start of the next cycle, and resets all other conditions.

For example, the following patterns are part of the processing for the input "I find you interesting." The general form is

Pn ( Past : Present → Action : Future )

where the several conditions within each part (e.g., past) are conjunctive.

P1 (INPUT, STMT, "I find you interesting" : Conclude INT → - : - )
P2 (INT, STMT, Shame high : INSULT, Raise anger → - : - )
P3 (INT, STMT, Joy high : COMPLIMENT, Raise joy → - : - )
P4 (INPUT, INSULT : - → DEFEND : Lower anger )

The first pattern P1, in the context of an INPUT from the interviewer and the input is a statement (STMT), asserts the belief INT, or that the interviewer believes that the model is interesting in some way. This is a global belief, adding to a model of the interviewer, and is accessible by all other patterns. P2 interprets the belief INT to be an insult if the shame affect is high, while P3 interprets INT as a compliment if the joy affect is high. P4 specifies the action DEFEND to respond to insults. If the DEFEND action is performed, anger is lowered, removing the motivation for further defense at this time.

If the interviewer's input were "I find you interesting" in a condition of high shame affect, the five-step process would perform as follows:

*Update:* detects the input statement, sets the input type to STMT, and activates the concept "interviewer interested in patient."

*Activate:* takes each condition and marks all patterns it is true in; for example, the STMT slot in P1, P2, and P3 is set true because STMT is true. Because INPUT, STMT, and the concept "I find you interesting" are true, P1 is activated. Immediately, the present condition of P1 is set true, and the belief INT is set true. Next, since INT, STMT, and (Shame high) are true, INSULT is set and the anger affect is raised. Finally, P4 is activated since INPUT and INSULT are now true. Note that some affect conditions have already been changed on the basis of the interpretation of the situation.

*Match:* collects all the actions (other actions could combine with DEFEND) and selects the multilevel action with the highest affect to perform.

*Execute:* executes the DEFEND action. DEFEND itself can be a multistep action pattern performed by the same five-step process.

*Book-keep:* deactivates P1 thru P4, with the exception of P4 if DEFEND is a multi-step pattern.

These five steps constitute a loop that continues indefinitely, the patterns determining what the program does at each step (i.e., the program does not have to await input to operate). Interesting conditions arise when no actions can be found, or when there is no external input to provide new information. Then the model must act on its own, striving to fulfill its own needs and desires by entertaining itself.

From a practical standpoint, APs allow a conversational action pattern such as (Question → Clarification question → Clarification → Answer) to be activated over a number of input-output pairs. At the same time, in the interval between producing output and recognizing the next input, the model can still activate other APs to perform inferences or evaluate its performance. Further, if an attack comes in the midst of a clarification AP, the attack response can interrupt the previous AP by choosing an action with a high affect content. Furthermore, the attack can change the conditions in the system so that the clarification AP is not reactivated, and the AP no longer interprets the situation.

## 7.0 IMPLEMENTATION

The model has been implemented in MLISP, a dialect of UCI-LISP at the SUMEX project at Stanford University. The language recognizer [Parkison77] is also written in MLISP and provides the natural language interface. About 500 action patterns have been necessary for an adequate conversational interaction. The performance demands upon our model are that it take no longer that 5 seconds of computer time, 15 seconds of real time to respond, and that it respond to an unrestricted set of English input. Our previous model [Faught77] was able to achieve these demands rather well. The current model required some optimization in its activation of patterns for faster response. Extension of the model will force further elaboration of the theory as we expand it to include more phenomena [Faught77a].

## 8.0 SUMMARY

There are three characteristics of patterned actions and their motivation by affect that are worth noting. These three are especially useful in psychological modeling and seem to fit our theory well.

(1) Patterned actions are multiattributed and overlapping. Conversational rules in particular consist of patterns of events and of linguistic forms interleaved at several levels of complexity. In addition, modifications made by affect to actions can be interwoven with the normal interaction rules, e.g., when a person answers a question, but angrily. This form of information is directly represented in the model and used in performing actions.

(2) The right control information is accessible at the right time. The traditional procedural approach to programming made it difficult to achieve the desired flow of control and interrupt capability based on changing situations. On the other extreme, traditional production systems sometimes made too much information available, with no discrimination. The solution here is to select information on the basis of previous interpretations of the situation, retain it until used, and then discard it. This allows a complex interaction between the stability of sticking with one pattern's interpretation and the flexibility of altering an interpretation due to changing conditions.

(3) Both internal variables (affects) and external representation variables (beliefs) are used in patterns. These relate to two of the presumed factors underlying human behavior: desire and habit. Desire is a function of the affect conditions of the person. Habit describes the tendency for a familiar external situation automatically to trigger appropriate patterns of behavior. One interesting feature in the use of these concepts in patterns is their role in modeling classical condi-

tioning. Conditioning is a matter of creating a new pattern with the operands placed as elements in the pattern. Reinforcement of the conditioning is modeled by raising the affect values of the pattern's elements. This same process is used for changing strategies for dealing with negative affects, as in defensive cognition. The free mixing of internal affect conditions and external conditions should make future psychological modeling more lucid.

# AN EXPECTATION-DRIVEN PRODUCTION SYSTEM FOR NATURAL LANGUAGE UNDERSTANDING[1]

Christopher K. Riesbeck
*Yale University*

*ELI, the English language interpreter for the SAM story understanding system at Yale, is a model of language understanding using productions. Productions are useful because they are flexible, but this flexibility means more work has to be spent controlling and manipulating them. ELI limits the number of productions that have to be manipulated with expectations. Expectations are constraints generated by frame structures that have been built by previously executed productions. Only productions that satisfy existing expectations are used.*

## 1.0 THE PROBLEM

A production system is a computer implementation in some domain where a significant portion of the content of the system is encoded as a set of condition-action pairs [Newell73]. Each condition-action pair is one production. In the simplest such system, these pairs are used in conjunction with the following two rules:

(1)  whenever new input enters the system, the conditions of all the productions are evaluated;
(2)  whenever the condition of a production is true, the action of the production is executed.

[1] This work was supported in part by the Advanced Research Projects Agency of the Department of Defense and monitored under the Office of Naval Research under contract N00014-75-C-1111.

Often the second rule is modified to cover situations where more than one condition is true. A conflict resolver is provided to choose the productions to be executed.

More important however is the modification that must be made to the first rule. While there are some tasks where the number of productions is reasonably small (e.g., puzzle solving), there are many where the number of productions is very large (e.g., natural language understanding). When there are only a few productions, it is reasonable to check all the conditions when there is new input, but as the number increases:

(1)    more time must be spent in evaluating conditions, most of which turn out to be false;
(2)    more time must be spent in conflict resolution, since increasing the number of productions increases the chance of unintended ones being executed.

In other words, in a simple-minded production system: "the more it knows, the dumber it gets."

One way to handle this problem is to make conflict resolution as painless as possible. For example hash tables can be used to index relevant productions quickly. Unfortunately it is nontrivial to develop a good hashing scheme for complex semantic structures, and hash tables will still take longer to access as they fill up and the number of conflicts increases.

Another way to handle large bodies of productions is to include mechanisms that delimit the set of productions active at any time. This chapter is about the mechanisms used in the ELI natural language understanding system [Riesbeck75b] to activate and deactivate productions.

## 2.0  THE ELI PROGRAM—OVERVIEW

ELI stands for English Language Interpreter. It is a program that is currently being used as part of the SAM and PAM story understanding systems at the Yale AI project [Schank75c]. It is the successor to the conceptual analyzer used in the MARGIE system [Schank75b]. ELI has the following important characteristics:

(1)    it produces Conceptual Dependency (CD) meaning representations for use in language-independent inference programs;
(2)    its dictionary entries are sets of productions, which perform most of the analysis;
(3)    it uses the constraints attached to the CD frames being built to control the activation of the dictionary productions.

A production-like formalism was used from the start because control of processing was a central topic of concern in the MARGIE analyzer. Processes written as sets of small condition-action pairs can be manipulated more easily than those written as monolithic programs. For example, it is easier to add or remove a production than it is to insert or delete an "if-then" clause. However, in real natural language processing, the number of lexical entries is in the thousands, and a significant effort has to be made to avoid an explosion of productions.

An obvious thing to do is to avoid using productions where other techniques are more reasonable. For example, lexical lookup could be done by using productions whose conditions ask "is the input a form of word x?" However this is not practical for implementation in a serial machine. Instead ELI makes use of the symbol table routines available in LISP to find dictionary entries in roughly constant time.

But each dictionary entry contains a lot of information, which means it contains a lot of productions. Further, the ELI system is built to use productions sent by other memory processes to guide its analysis, making the system as a whole sensitive to context. Therefore the ELI system contains several other mechanisms for delimiting the set of active productions.

One mechanism is to link to each variable of the system the set of productions that have conditions testing that variable. When a variable changes value, only the productions that are linked to it need to be checked. Another mechanism is to link to a production a set of other productions. When the first production is executed, then the set of productions linked to it is activated. In this way, some productions are ignored until other productions have been executed.

These two mechanisms are implemented in ELI by using a special kind of production called a *request*. Requests contain conditions, actions, and several additional fields. One of them is the *test focus*. This field specifies which variables the condition of the request depends upon. Another field is the *suggestions* field. This specifies new requests to activate if this request is executed.

The test focus and suggestions fields provide static information about a request. ELI does further pruning using dynamic frame constraints [Minsky75]. This is the *expectation* mechanism of ELI, whereby ELI keeps active only those requests that are consistent with the structures it has built so far.

To determine if a request is consistent with some existing structure, ELI needs to know what structure the action of the request produces, and what the existing structure needs for completion. The first task, recognizing what a request does, is an open-ended one. Currently ELI determines what a request does by executing it and saving the structure produced. One of the advantages of requests is that the work they do is split up over several fields. The action field is responsible only for structure building (not for setting global flags, or adding new requests, or anything else). Thus the action field is easily executed and undone, but it still contains the information necessary for deciding whether the request is consistent with the already built structures in the system.

The second task, recognizing what an existing structure needs for completion, is handled by keeping track of *gaps* and *constraints*. Gaps are the holes in the structures that ELI is building, i.e., the unfilled slots. For example, when analyzing the sentence "John told Mary Bill was coming," the dictionary entry program under "tell" sets up a structure for "someone transferred some information from self to someone else." "Someone," "some information," and "someone else" are the gaps in that structure and part of the analysis task is to fill in these gaps.

There are constraints on how these gaps can be filled. A "someone" gap must be filled with a person, while a "some information" gap must be filled with a full conceptualization (like "Bill was coming"). A request that built a descripion of a physical object would not be applicable to either of these gaps and would not have to be activated. Thus ELI can limit the number of productions it has to handle by removing productions whose actions do not fit the constraints of any gaps.

## 3.0  DATA STRUCTURES

ELI processes texts by reading words from the input text, looking up their definitions, handing them to the routine INCORPORATE, and putting the result, which is a set of requests, into the active memory (AM). The AM is where all the processing structures, i.e., the gaps, constraints, and active requests, are kept. Another routine, called CONSIDER, continually checks the active requests, executing those that have true conditions, and removing those that are no longer consistent with the other structures in the AM. A flow diagram of ELI is given in Fig. 1.

In the AM are three different kinds of data elements: *gap nodes* (GNs), *prediction nodes* (PNs), and *request nodes* (RNs). The gap nodes are the variables of the system. The request nodes are the productions, and they test and act upon the values of the gap nodes. The set of gap nodes changes dynamically. When a request node is executed, it fills a gap node, removing it from the system, but the structure built by the request node may contain several new gap nodes that must be added. The prediction nodes are the constraints placed upon the gap nodes.

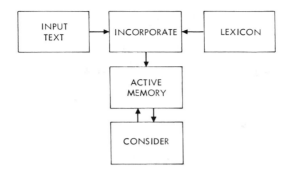

Fig. 1.

## 3.1  Gap Nodes

When ELI builds (by executing some request node) a conceptual or syntactic structure, it is frequently incomplete. It has holes that must be filled in using information taken from the rest of the text. These holes are represented using gap nodes.

For example, in undestanding the sentence "John gave Mary the book," ELI builds a CD form that says that John transferred a book from himself to Mary. Transfer of possession is represented in CD with the primitive ATRANS. ELI decides that ATRANS is the appropriate act after it reads "the book" (it waits because "give" can have other meanings, as in "John gave Mary a kiss"). This primitive has several associated conceptual cases: the donor (ACTOR case), the object (OBJECT case), and the recipient (TO case). When "the book" is read, ELI builds the following list structure:

(ACTOR GN1 < = > ATRANS OBJECT GN2 TO GN3 FROM GN1)

GN1, GN2, and GN3 are gap nodes. Each one is an unfilled slot in the ATRANS structure. Each one needs to be (and presumably will be) filled eventually, either by analyzing the text or by some inference procedure.

## 3.2  Prediction Nodes

Attached to gap nodes are constraints. These constraints specify what kind of conceptual objects can fill the gap nodes to which they are attached. A constraint is represented with a prediction node. The gap to which the prediction applies is called the *focus* of the prediction node. The predicate describing the constraint is called the *body* of the prediction node.

When ELI built the ATRANS form above, it also set up a prediction that the gap node GN1 would be filled with a human. That is, there is a piece of conceptual knowledge about the act ATRANS that says that only humans do it. The prediction node for this constraint looks like this:

FOCUS: GN1
BODY: (FEATURE HUMAN)

Each gap node in ELI has the property PREDLIST, which points to the prediction/constraint made for that gap.

For example, when ELI built the ATRANS structure for "John gave Mary the book," it had predictions for each of the gaps produced. The ACTOR gap was predicted to be a human, the OBJECT gap to be a physical object, and the TO gap to be an animate being. The gap node GN1 with its prediction node attached looks like this:

GN1:
    PREDLIST: (PN1)

PN1:
    FOCUS: GN1
    BODY: (FEATURE HUMAN)

### 3.3   Request Nodes

A production in the AM that may fill in a gap node according to the constraint specified by its prediction node is represented with a request node. The dictionary entries contain request templates. The routine INCORPORATE takes such templates, finds prediction nodes in the AM that would be satisfied by the structures the templates builds, and constructs request nodes from the templates, attaching them to the prediction nodes. No request node is ever put in the AM processing structures unless it can be attached to some prediction node.

A request node is basically a condition-action pair that has been attached to some prediction node. The request node may also specify special actions to be taken modifying other nodes in the AM, and it may contain pointers to other request templates to be given to INCORPORATE. Like the action, these parts of the request node are executed only if the condition of the request node becomes true.

Thus, a request node has the following parts:

(1)   a pointer to the prediction node that it satisfies;
(2)   a list of conditions specifying when the request node should be executed;

(3)  an action-function to build some structure;
(4)  a list (perhaps empty) of other actions to be performed;
(5)  a list (perhaps empty) of request templates.

For example, in the "John gave Mary a book" example that we have been following, when the word "John" is read, INCORPORATE looks it up and finds the following definition:

TEST: TRUE
ACTION: (#PERSON FIRSTNAME JOHN)

The structure built by the ACTION satisfies the prediction node PN1, whose BODY is (FEATURE HUMAN). Therefore the request template above is used to build a new request node RN1, which is attached to the prediction node PN1. Since PN1 is a constraint attached to the gap node GN1 (the ACTOR of the ATRANS), the request node built will fill GN1 when it is executed.

The new node RN1 has the following properties:

(1)  it is attached to the prediction PN1;
(2)  it has no conditions that are not already true;
(3)  it builds the structure for "a person named John."

RN1 looks like this:

RN1:
    SOURCE: PN1
    ACTION: (#PERSON FIRSTNAME JOHN)
    CONDITION: NONE

A prediction node can have zero or more request nodes under it, any one of which might eventually be the one to satisfy prediction. For example, in understanding the sentence "The book was ..." the verb "was" provides a number of equally likely requests for filling in the main conceptualization of the sentence. These requests include:

(1)  one that tests for adjectives; this handles "the book was red";
(2)  one that tests for past participles; this handles "the book was read";
(3)  one that tests for noun phrases; this handles "the book was a best seller";
(4)  one that tests for progressives; this handles "the book was falling."

Each of these requests becomes attached to the prediction that ELI sets up looking for the main conceptualization. Each prediction node has a property SUGGLIST, pointing to the list of request nodes focused on that prediction node.

In doing "John gave Mary a book," ELI builds the following chain of nodes to fill in the ACTOR of the ATRANS:

(ACTOR GN1 < = > ATRANS OBJECT GN2 TO GN3 FROM GN1)

GN1:

> PREDLIST: (PN1)

PN1:

> FOCUS: GN1
> BODY: (FEATURE HUMAN)
> SUGGLIST: (RN1)

RN1:

> SOURCE: PN1
> ACTION: (#PERSON FIRSTNAME JOHN)
> CONDITION: NONE

When a request node added to the AM has a condition, it is represented as a prediction node. That is, the condition of a request node is a gap node/prediction node pair. The condition is true if the gap node is ever filled with something satisfying the body of the prediction node.

For example, each word that is read is placed into the gap node GNWORD. Suppose INCORPORATE had just added to the AM a request node RN2 that builds the CD form for "the inside of a place," and this satisfies the prediction node PN2. Suppose further that RN2 is triggered if the word "to" is read. Then RN2 would look like this:

RN2:

> SOURCE: PN2
> ACTION: (INSIDE PART GN5)
> CONDITION: PN3

PN3:

> SOURCE: RN2
> FOCUS: GNWORD
> BODY: (EQUAL "TO")

The SOURCE property of the prediction node PN3 specifies the request node that generated this prediction node.

The complete set of links from gap node to prediction node to request node to prediction node (with its implicit gap node) forms a *processing tree*. With this structure ELI ties what it needs (the gaps and their predictions) to what it thinks will satisfy those needs (the requests), and at the same time it ties each request kept active to a reason (the gap and prediction) for keeping that request around. Graphically, a processing tree is shown in Fig. 2.

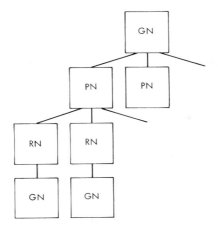

Fig. 2.

Remember that the gap node under a request node is the focus of the condition of that request. It is not one of the gap nodes that may have been generated by the structure built by the action of that request node.

When ELI interprets texts, it manipulates a number of these trees. Most of the gap nodes that ELI builds become the roots of processing trees that function to fill that gap. The trees terminate at special gap nodes (like GNWORD) where other processes (like a read routine) take care of filling the gap node.

At the start of a sentence, ELI initializes four gap nodes. These become the roots of the processing trees driving the rest of the analysis. These initial nodes are as follows:

(1) GNCONCEPT, which is to be filled with the main conceptualization of a clause; GNCONCEPT has a prediction node looking for a CD form representing an event;

(2) GNCLAUSE, which is to be filled with the main syntactic clause; GNCLAUSE has a prediction node looking for a syntactic form headed by a verb;

(3) GNSYNTOP, which is to be filled with the first noun phrase; GNSYNTOP has a prediction node looking for a syntactic form headed by a noun;

(4) GNCONTOP, which is to be filled with the conceptual meaning of the first noun phrase; GNCONTOP has a prediction node looking for a simple concept.

Each of these prediction nodes has a request node under it. The four request nodes have the same basic structure. Each looks at the input stream for anything that will satisfy the prediction node it is attached to.

The "input stream" in ELI means three special gap nodes that are always kept around:

(1)   GNWORD, where new words are put when read;
(2)   GNSYN, where new syntactic structures are placed when built;
(3)   GNCON, where new conceptual structures are placed when built.

Thus when a word is read, GNWORD contains the word itself, GNSYN contains its syntactic assignment, and GNCON contains its conceptual interpretation. These three gap nodes all have the following special properties:

(1)   They are the terminal nodes in processing trees, never roots.
(2)   They are not filled by requests, but by special routines in the main program of ELI itself; GNWORD is filled by the read routine, and GNSYN and GNCON are filled by the dictionary lookup routine.
(3)   Their values are not fixed; that is, once most gaps are filled, they stay unchanged from that point on; but these special gaps go through a cycle of being filled, emptied, and refilled.
(4)   All the prediction nodes on these gaps are inherited from the request nodes in the processing trees that terminate in these gaps.
(5)   A prediction node applied to them is always potentially true, because their values change; that is, when a normal gap is filled, any unsatisfied predictions on that gap are removed; this is not done for these special gaps with changing values.

Thus the monitor program in ELI fills GNWORD, GNCON, and GNSYN with values derived from the input text. Then the processing trees take these values and use them to fill the gaps in conceptual and syntactic frames.

ELI deals with multiple processing trees. In this way syntactic knowledge is merged with conceptual processing, without the use of a separate syntactic analysis phase. A processing tree that builds and fleshes out a syntactic description of a text can operate parallel to the more important trees that provide a conceptual interpretation for that text. At the same time, conceptual trees can be made with syntactic subtrees, when syntactic information is necessary to make conceptual decisions.

## 4.0   ANALYSIS EXAMPLE

As an example of ELI's processing trees in action, we trace how the syntactic description of "John thanked Mary" is arrived at. A linguistically trivial example has been chosen to avoid obscuring the interactions of the data structures. Keep in mind that when ELI interprets this sentence, the trees shown are only part of the total processing involved. Most of ELI's effort is spent on processing trees concerned with building a conceptual interpretation for the sentence.

The analysis starts with ELI setting up the two syntactic gap nodes, GNSYNTOP and GNCLAUSE, with a processing tree under each. The one under GNSYNTOP looks at the input stream gap node GNSYN for a noun phrase. The one under GNCLAUSE looks at the input stream gap node GNSYN for a verb clause. These two trees look like this:

GNSYNTOP:
    PREDLIST: (PN1)

PN1:
    FOCUS: GNSYNTOP
    BODY: (FEATURE NP)
    SUGGLIST: (RN1)

RN1:
    SOURCE: PN1
    ACTION: GNSYN
    CONDITION: PN2

PN2:
    SOURCE: RN1
    FOCUS: GNSYN
    BODY: (FEATURE NP)

GNCLAUSE:
    PREDLIST: (PN3)

PN3:
    FOCUS: GNCLAUSE
    BODY: (FEATURE CLAUSE)
    SUGGLIST: (RN2)

RN2:
    SOURCE: PN3
    ACTION: GNSYN
    CONDITION: PN4

PN4:
    SOURCE: RN4
    FOCUS: GNSYN
    BODY: (FEATURE CLAUSE)

Note that the request nodes RN1 and RN2 simply return the contents of GNSYN if it matches the condition predicate.

Graphically they are shown in Fig. 3.

With these two trees set up, ELI is ready to do the syntactic side of "John thanked Mary." Several other processing trees have also been set up to do the conceptual side of the sentence in parallel.

ELI reads the first word "John." The dictionary entry for "John" is matched against the prediction nodes attached to GNSYN, and the following request node is placed under PN2:

RN3:
        SOURCE: PN2
        ACTION: (JOHN)
        CONDITION: NONE

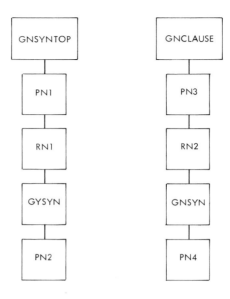

Fig. 3.

Because there is no condition, RN3 is executed immediately, filling the gap GNSYN with the proper noun phrase "John." This triggers RN1, which is looking at GNSYN for a noun phrase, and RN1 puts "John" in GNSYNTOP.

Now ELI reads the word "thank." The dictionary entry for "thank" is matched against the prediction nodes attached to GNSYN, and the following request node is placed under PN4:

RN4:

SOURCE: PN4
ACTION: (VERB THANK SUBJ GN1 OBJ GN2)
CONDITION: NONE

Because there is no condition, RN4 is executed immediately, filling the gap GNSYN with the verb clause for "thank." This triggers RN2, which is looking at GNSYN for a clause, and RN2 puts the clause in GNCLAUSE.

Adding this clause frame to the AM also adds the two gaps, GN1 and GN2, that are holes in the frame, with a processing tree hanging off each:

GN1:
    PREDLIST: PN5

GN2:
    PREDLIST: PN6

PN5:
    FOCUS: GN1
    BODY: (FEATURE NP)
    SUGGLIST: (RN5)

PN6:
    FOCUS: GN2
    BODY: (FEATURE NP)
    SUGGLIST: (RN6)

RN5:
    SOURCE: PN5
    BODY: GNSYNTOP
    CONDITION: PN7

RN6:
    SOURCE: PN6
    BODY: GNSYN
    CONDITION: PN8

PN7:
    SOURCE: RN5
    FOCUS: GNSYNTOP
    BODY: (FEATURE NP)

PN8:
    SOURCE: RN6
    FOCUS: GNSYN
    BODY: (FEATURE NP)

Graphically, the above processing trees are shown in Fig. 4.

GNSYNTOP already has a value, "John." This satisfies PN7, triggering RN5, which fills GN1 with "John." Thus the first noun phrase, previously saved in GNSYNTOP, is now placed in the subject slot of the clause frame for "thank."

Now ELI reads "Mary." The dictionary entry for "Mary" is matched against the predictions on GNSYN placing the following request under PN8:

RN7:
    SOURCE: PN8
    ACTION: (MARY)
    CONDITION: NONE

Because RN7 has no conditions on execution, it is executed as soon as it is added to the tree. This puts the proper noun phrase "Mary" in GNSYN, triggering RN6, which fills GN2, the object slot of the "thank" frame. This yields the final syntactic form:

(VERB THANK SUBJ (JOHN) OBJ (MARY))

This covers only the syntactic processing that happened during the interpretation of "John thanked Mary." There was one syntactic prediction that was set up and never used. This prediction said that the word "for" might appear, introducing the reason for John thanking Mary. In ELI this means that a prediction node was attached to the gap GNWORD waiting for GNWORD to be set to the word "for." This prediction node is the condition of a request whose action extends

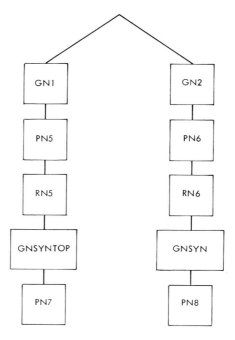

Fig. 4.

the conceptual representation of "John thanked Mary." Initially this representation says that John MTRANSed (i.e., mentally transferred) to Mary that she did something that pleased him. If "for" is seen, the request node triggered adds more requests to fill in what Mary did. One request would handle a succeeding verb phrase, as in "John thanked Mary for driving him home," while another would handle a succeeding noun phrase, as in "John thanked Mary for the book." In the second case, an ATRANS of the book from Mary to John is constructed.

## 5.0 CONCLUSIONS

The preceding sections have given the following four mechanisms used in the ELI system to reduce the problems of large numbers of productions:

(1) Using other methods where appropriate: e.g., the lexicon is indexed by standard LISP hash routines.

(2) Associating each production with the variables upon which it depends.

(3)   Having some productions kept off-stage until another production is executed and loads them.

(4)   Isolating the structures built by productions from their other effects, and eliminating any that build structures rejected by frame-generated constraints.

Among these mechanisms, this chapter has focused on the second and fourth. The second mechanism gives information about the conditions of productions and the fourth mechanism gives information about the actions of productions. A processing tree merges these two kinds of information, showing how the condition of one production becomes dynamically dependent on the action of another production.

However these two mechanisms are primarily concerned with controlling the testing and execution of productions after they have been retrieved from long-term storage. If we are to avoid the production explosion as the amount of information in long-term storage increases, the focus of work will have to be on the third mechanism, chaining productions so that many productions are only loaded by the execution of others. A production system with a large knowledge base will have many productions used primarily to index other productions; that is, it will have a lot of knowledge about how to use its knowledge.

# A GOAL-DIRECTED PRODUCTION SYSTEM FOR STORY UNDERSTANDING[1]

Roger C. Schank and Robert Wilensky
*Yale University*

*Using knowledge to make inferences is a crucial aspect of natural language processing. While the notion of a script has been useful in this regard, other forms of knowledge are also needed. In particular, knowledge about goals and knowledge about stories is crucial for story understanding. The understander must know what types of goals characters in a story can have so as to be able to interpret their behavior. Knowledge about the point of a story is needed to direct the understanding process. These forms of knowledge can best be applied by means of a hierarchical production system.*

## 1.0 INTRODUCTION

Work in natural understanding has, in general, been concentrated on issues related to parsing. In recent years, as research has moved away from dealing with individual sentences in isolation toward the understanding of coherent texts, there has been a spurt of interest in inference processes as well (e.g., [Charniak72], [Joshi76], [Schank74], [Wilks75a]. One of the major problems in this domain has been to build an inference mechanism that correctly determines which of the many plausible inferences it should make at any given point in the understanding process.

In trying to deal with the problem of the proliferation of inferences that occurred in MARGIE [Schank73b], the notion of a script was

[1] This work was supported in part by the Advanced Research Projects Agency of the Department of Defense and monitored under the Office of Naval Research under contract N00014-75-C-1111.

*415*

developed [Schank75d], and a computer program called SAM [Schank75c] was built that could use knowledge in the form of scripts to make the inferences necessary to understand stories about very well-structured knowledge domains. For example, SAM is now capable of processing car accident stories taken directly from a newspaper.

While we do not intend to demean this achievement, it is clear that SAM is not an entirely adequate solution to the problem of natural language understanding by computer. Much of what we can understand is extremely novel and thus we cannot have a script available to aid us in our processing. When such a situation occurs, there is need for a different kind of understanding apparatus. The following simple stories illustrate this difference:

(1a)   John wanted to go to Hawaii. He called his travel agent.
(1b)   John wanted to go to Hawaii. He called his mother.
(2a)   John was walking in the park with his wife Mary. Suddenly, some men jumped out from behind the bushes and held a knife to Mary's throat. They asked John for all his money. He gave it to them and they ran away.
(2b)   John was walking in the park with his wife Mary. Suddenly some men jumped out from behind the bushes and held a knife to Mary's throat. John could barely conceal his glee. The men killed Mary and ran away. John went back to his apartment to celebrate.

In examples 1 and 2, the "a" stories are more comprehensible than "b" stories. In the "a" stories, the information and processing strategy needed to connect together the pieces of the story is readily available from the appropriate scripts and necessary script interference rules (see [Schank77]). For example, in order to understand 1a, it is necessary to know the trip and the travel agency scripts and to understand that 1a refers to them. In the first sentence of 1a, there is a reference to the trip script (going to Hawaii), and in the second, there is a reference to one of the predictions made by accessing the trip script (calling a travel agent). Thus, the process of connecting these sentences is easy. The story is readily understandable because of the availability of knowledge in a standard form (a script) to connect it up.

In the "b" stories, the same predictions that made the "a" stories so comprehensible appear to be violated or ignored. In story 1b, for example, it is not likely that we have access to specific information about people and their mothers with respect to trips: in any reasonable model of the world, "mother" is not part of the trip script. In 2b, John's reactions to his wife's murder are not only not accounted for by any previous script-based predictions, but appear to be in direct contradiction to such expectations.

The "b" stories are not entirely nonsensical, however. We can connect up the sentences of these stories, but not with anywhere near as much certainty as before. For example, to make the connection in 1b, people often guess that either John's mother will supply the money for the trip, accompany him on the trip, or give permission for John to go on the trip. In 2b, people usually entertain the notion that John is crazy, or extremely callous, or that he was in on the murder in the first place. If we had continued the "b" stories with

(1c)   He asked her if she would give him the money for the trip.
(2c)   Later John met the men at a bar and paid them off.

the stories become perfectly comprehensible, in spite of the fact that our original expectations had been violated.

The fact that we can continue processing when our expectations have been violated is indicative of a language understanding capability beyond that of script processing. In particular, in order to understand the above examples, a person must be able to determine when a prediction has gone awry, ascertain actors' goals, and predict the plans that actors will use to attain those goals.

In order to perform these processes, knowledge in a form other than a script is necessary. The question we wish to pursue here is: What kind of knowledge do we need, and what sort of mechanism is best suited to apply it?

## 2.0 GOALS

As the beginning of the answer to the above question, we claim that an understander needs knowledge of the goals that people can normally be expected to have. A natural language processor needs to identify people's goals in a story, and thus be able to interpret their actions. Consider the following stories:

(3)   A suspicious looking man entered Bill's store. Bill slammed the buzzer.
(4)   John wanted to meet a politician. One day John spotted Ted Kennedy on a Boston street.

Once an understander determines a goal of a character, a set of predictions can be made that do a number of things for us. One important function these predictions have is to eliminate ambiguity and point out the correct sense or intent of an action. For example, one intention of a slamming action is to break something; another is to express one's frustration. However, neither comes to mind in (3). The reason is clear. We have already inferred Bill's goal to be "protect possessions" by virtue of what we know about people in general and store owners in particular. Thus we easily infer the sense of slammed here to be "hit excitedly," and the buzzer to be some sort of alarm system. Of course the buzzer could be a way of letting the man into the back part of the store but that seems unlikely because of our prior predictions. Similarly, in (4) we predict John's next action to be "go toward Kennedy with the intent of shaking his hand." That is, since we have a stated goal for John in the story, we can predict that John will take some action to fulfill his goal when the opportunity arises.

These simple examples demonstrate one role that goals play in the understanding process: They are organizers of a great deal of information about actions. It is through goals that scripts, and their more general counterparts, plans, are typically accessed (see [Schank75d]). Once we have accessed these sources of knowledge, we can generate predictions about actions. This aspect of using goals and plans for predictive understanding has been incorporated in a program called PAM, described in Wilensky [Wilensky76].

In addition to this information concerning actions, goals organize several other kinds of useful knowledge. For example, in understanding a story, we are prone to wonder if some goal underlies a goal stated in the story. In (4), the reader may assume John wanted to meet a politician so he could brag to his friends about it, or perhaps ask for a favor. Such considerations may become important in interpreting John's subsequent actions. Consider the following story:

(5)    John wanted to go to the train station. He couldn't get a cab, but he persuaded a friend to drive him. When the train got to New York, he rushed to the theatre only to find out that all the tickets were sold. He decided to go to a concert in Brooklyn. As luck would have it, he shared a taxi with a lovely redhead who invited him to her apartment. John enjoyed his trip to New York very much.

In order to understand this story, we claim that a person must have the following kinds of knowledge about goals:

1.  *The Origin of Goals:* What goals does each actor in a story have? Why does an actor have each of the goals attributed to him in the story? Where did these goals come from? If the story had ended with John going to the train station, would we assume that he had achieved his goal, since this was the goal explicitly stated in the story?

2.  *Goal Specification and Substitution:* What is an actor doing to satisfy a known goal? What is a reasonable substitute for a given goal? If John had decided to panhandle instead (when he found out the tickets were unavailable) would we have been able to make sense of it? If not, why not? If we can, what do we have to construct to do this and how to do we construct it?

Considering these issues let us look at story (5) in detail:

The first sentence of (5) explicitly states that John had the goal of going to the train station. However, most understanders are aware that neither the process of going to a train station nor the resulting state of being at a rairoad station is typically a goal in its own right. Instead, they make the inference that the stated goal is a subgoal arising from a plan to realize an unknown, "higher level" goal.

From what we know about trains and train stations, the reader can conjecture that being at the train station is a subgoal of the goal of being somewhere which the train will help John get to. Likewise, this latter, higher level goal is itself likely to be a subgoal of some other goal. However, we are still in suspense about what this goal really is until we hear that John "rushed to the theater."

The point here is that the understanding process is concerned with elucidating the "true" goals that the characters in a story possess, and that this process requires a great deal of knowledge. In order to make this determination, we must check each plausible goal against our knowledge of universal motivations, even if the goal is explicit. If the goal is not found among this set, we then have to apply a set of procedures that suggest what a higher level goal may be. These procedures may rely on our knowledge of the usual functions of objects and places, like trains and theaters. Often, it can be determined that a higher level goal must exist, although it cannot yet be specified. In this case an expectation must be set up looking for such a high-level goal, that would relate it to the lower level goals when it were found.

Two distinct high-level goals are inferred in story (5): "seek entertainment," and "satisfy sex." The entertainment goal is specified by "attend theater." When this fails, there is a rewrite into "attend concert." It is unclear whether this activity is ever pursued, since the sex goal interrupts, takes precedence, and apparently succeeds. The scenario never returns to the scene of the original goal pursuit; the reader never finds out whether John went to the concert, and furthermore, the reader doesn't find it essential to determine this. John has replaced one high-level goal with another one to which he gives higher priority.

The substitution or superseding of one goal by another is not an arbitrary affair. For example, while it is reasonable for John to substitute "attend concert" for "attend theater," the reader would be surprised if he decided to substitute the goal of "possess wealth" instead. The "satisfy sex" goal can reasonably supersede "attend concert," but it is unlikely that it could supersede "preserve health" if one's life were threatened. A natural language processor that was not capable of making these discriminations could not have really understood what was happening in a story such as (5).

In order to capture these distinctions in form that could be of use to a natural language unerstander, we have developed a taxonomy of goals. This taxonomy may be thought of as an organization of the knowledge about goals that resides in the understander's long-term memory. Whenever a stated goal appears in a text, or when the understander infers or predicts a goal, the knowledge specific to that goal's type will be accessed to determine the behavior of the goal, and hence to generate the appropriate predictions about and correct interpretations of subsequent events.

## 2.1 Types of Goals

The types of goals we identify are as follows:

2.1.1 *Satisfaction Goals (S-Goals).* These goals are for satisfying biological needs. They are useful in understanding because we must predict their satisfaction at the appropriate intervals as well as the consequences of their lack of satisfaction.

Some examples of S-goals are

S-HUNGER:  If unsatisfied for more than 3-5 waking hours predict plan to get food. If unsatisfied for a much longer time, predict weakness, ill health, etc.

S-SLEEP:  If unsatisfied in 18 hours predict plan to find a place to sleep. If unsatisfied for a much longer time, predict irritability, accident proneness, lack of logic, etc.

2.1.2 *Enjoyment Goals (E-Goals).* These goals are for enjoying certain activities. We can expect people to have some idiosyncratic set of E-goals that they pursue periodically. We can predict the kinds of substitutions he will accept for a given E-goal from the nature of the original choice. For example, suppose someone sets out to eat a lobster at a restaurant. We understand that he is trying to satisfy S-HUNGER as well as E-EATWELL. If no lobster is available he will substitute something he finds almost as enjoyable. So, "he ordered King Crab" is sensible. "He decided to go to McDonalds" is less sensible because of the abondonment of E-EATWELL. "He went bowling, instead" is far worse because of the abaondonment of both goals.

2.1.3 *Achievement Goals (A-Goals).* These goals refer to the achievement of someone's aims in life. A goal tends to be satisfied in a scriptlike manner. There are certain standard ways to accomplish

A-POWER or A-GOOD JOB.

2.1.4 *Preservation Goals (P-Goals).* These goals refer to preserving desirable states if those states are perceived to be in jeopardy. For example, we expect store owners to have the goal P-PROPERTY and husbands to have P-HEALTH(WIFE) should threats to these states arise. Understanders have strong expectations about the importance of satisfying P-goals. Thus in story 2, it is the prediction that John should act in accordance with the goal P-HEALTH(WIFE) that causes the confusion.

2.1.5 *Instrumental Goals (I-Goals).* These goals refer to the realization of a precondition in pursuit of another goal. If an I-goal is encountered, it usually indicates that some other, more fundamental goal is present. For example, being someplace is usually an I-goal of performing some function that being at that place enables. Thus in (5), we know that since John's stated goal is an I-goal, we should look for a high level goal to which it may be instrumental.

## 2.2 Using Knowledge About Goal Types

Knowledge about goals can best be applied to the understanding process by a hierarchical system of production rules. The rules are hierarchical in that only some of the rules in the memory of the understander are "active" at any given time, and a rule may be activated or deactivated as the result of firing off another production. Only active productions are examined in the subsequent processing. For example, one set of rules is activated whenever a new goal is encountered by the system. These rules use the goal classification just described to activate other production rules. For each goal type, there is the following production awaiting new goals:

If the goal is of type X, activate the following productions:

1. The "goal frustration" production for goal type X.
2. The "goal satisfaction" production for goal type X.
3. The "source" production for goal type X.

For example, if the goal is an E-goal, then the goal frustration reaction production activated will predict that another E-goal wil be substituted for this goal if the goal is frustrated. If the goal is an S-goal, no substitution is predicted. Likewise, the source production for an S-goal predicts that the source of the goal is a theme (see below). The source production for an I-goal, on the other hand, predicts that the source is some other goal. We will discuss the nature of this production system in more detail later on.

## 3.0 THEMES

The preceding goal classification is useful for determining the behavior of a goal once we know that the goal exists. Deciding that a goal is present requires knowledge about the origin of goals; as was demonstrated above, this knowledge is necessary even if the existence of a goal is explicitly stated in the text.

Where do goals come from? Goals often come in packages associated with certain *themes*. A theme is a standard relationship between a person and his world. A person may be involved in many themes at once. That is, a man might be a PROFESSOR, a FATHER, a HUSBAND, a HOME-OWNER, a DEMOCRAT as well as have as long-term themes LUXURY-LIVING, HONESTY, and KINDNESS.

The knowledge contained in a theme can be applied to the understanding process by a set of production rules that state what a person can be expected to do in a given circumstance. In general, each such rule predicts a goal that a person may have in a given situation. When a theme is encountered or inferred during understanding, the productions associated with that theme are made active. Then if a situation occurs that matches the test of one of these productions, the understander will be able to predict the appropriate goal. For example, the following are some of the productions that would be associated in memory with the theme for "A loves B" (where A and B are approximately the same age, of the opposite sex, etc.):

1.  If A is away from B for a period of time, predict A will have the goal of being with B.
2.  If A thinks B doesn't love A, predict A will have the goal of making B love A.
3.  If A is not married to B, predict A will have the goal of marrying B.
4.  If A thinks B has the goal X, predict B will have the goal X.
5.  If A thinks B is unhappy, predict A will have the goal of making B happier.
6.  If A thinks B is not well, predict A will have the goal of making B better.
7.  If A thinks some event X can make B happy, predict A will have the goal of bringing about X.
8.  If A thinks some future event X will make B unhappy, predict A will have the goal of preventing X from happening.
9.  If A thinks some future event X will adversely affect B's health, predict A will have the goal of preventing X from happening.
10.  If A thinks some future event X will harm B's physical condition, predict A will have the goal of preventing X from happening.

There are two points to be made about theme-associated productions. First, many themes are actually special cases of more general themes. The productions associated with the more general themes are inherited by the more specific ones, which also have their own unique set of productions. For example, the love theme described above is a special case of a more general love theme that would also characterize parent-child and friend-friend relationships. Most of the above productions are associated with this more general theme; production 3 is clearly associated only with the more specific relationship.

Second, these productions are meant to be true productions in the sense that they are not concerned about what other productions may do. For example, if B wants to marry C, then according to the above productions, A has the goals "B married C" and "A married B," a contradiction. However, it is not the job of these productions to note this problem. Instead, these productions blindly fire off, hoping that some other mechanism in the system will be on the lookout for just this sort of conflict.

The mechanism that identifies goal conflicts illustrates how productions may be used to organize knowledge application: the result of any production may be considered by a 'higher level' production that then decides how to interpret the result; productions that apply one kind of knowledge need not be concerned about other knowledge available to the understander.

Theme-driven productions organize knowledge that can be used predictively to explain the actions and intentions of actors about whom we have thematic information. While this knowledge is necessary for comprehension, other higher level forms of knowledge are also required. It is the nature of these other forms of knowledge that we will now consider.

## 4.0 STORIES

In order to bring our understanding apparatus to bear upon a story text, we need to understand what the nature of a story is. Most previous work on the nature of stories has been concerned with trying to elucidate the formal structure of a story (for example, see [Prince75], [Propp70], [Rumelhart75]. It is our conjecture that knowledge of the content of a story would be more useful to a story understander than knowledge of story structure, and furthermore, that the form of a story can only be understood in terms of the content that was to be expressed. Thus we will disregard such structural approaches for now, and concentrate on a more semantically based theory of stories.

We consider a story to be made up of one or more *points* that are expressive of some human dramatic event. A dramatic event is essentially a problem that is posed for a character, followed by some resolution or near resolution of that problem. Since these dramatic events are the points of stories, we will call them problem-solution points. We will also refer to the problem aspect and the solution aspect as problem points and solution points.

The "point structure" of a story is the highest level of organization of that story in memory. That is, the representation of a story in memory is a network of problem-solution points. Therefore the primary process the story understander is engaged in is to build such a structure, i.e., to identify and connect the points of the story. This has several implications:

1.   We are looking for points as we understand. To demonstrate that this is in fact going on, consider the following:

(6)   John loved Mary very much. One day, he asked her to marry him. She agreed, and they got married soon afterwards. Things went well for John at his job, so they were able to live comfortably.

If (6) were to end here, most readers would be left asking "What's the point?" (6) has goals, and actions that achieve those goals, but somehow does not seem to make it as a story. Our claim is that the understander is still waiting to hear a problem. For example, we can follow (6) by

(7)   Then, one night on his way home from work, John's car skidded off the wet pavement and struck a tree, killing John instantly. Mary went into a state of shock when the police told her what had happened. She had just gotten back from the doctor that afternoon, and had planned to tell John the good news that very evening: He was going to become a father.

This episode begins to legitimize the text by making a problem point: Mary is in a bad emotional state, has lost her husband, and must take care of herself and her child-to-be by herself. According to our theory, having made the problem point, we must get around to making a solution point. Thus the story cannot end here, as most readers will agree, but must be continued with a solution point, such as

(8)   Mary's friend Bill tried to comfort her as best he could. Eventually their friendship became something more than that. Bill told Mary that he loved her and wanted to take care of her and her newborn child. Mary agreed to marry Bill, and they lived happily ever after.

The importance of having a process that looks for problem-solution points is that it provides the understander with great predictive power. These predictions make it easier for the understander to connect together the conceptualizations in a story and make sense out of it, which is the understander's primary function. For example, consider the following story beginning:

(9) John and Mary had been happily married for a year. Then one day, John met Sue, a new employee at John's office. Soon afterwards, John told Mary he would have to work late many nights in the upcoming weeks.

By the time we read the second sentence of (9), we have a pretty good idea that John and Sue will have an affair. It is easy to make this prediction because we expect to find a problem point at this stage of the processing, and know that having an affair is a problem associated with marriage, and fits the data. This makes it very easy to interpret the next sentence, given our knowledge of how affairs are carried out. Furthermore, the point supplies ready-made inferences needed to connect together the conceptualizations in the text. For example, by finding the problem point in (9) we have inferred the motivation for John's actions.

2.  Because the point structure of a story is its highest level of organization, it should also be at the highest level of the "forgetting hierarchy." That is, the points of a story should be the last thing the understander forgets. For example, after reading the story composed of (6), (7), and (8), an understander should remember it as a "misfortune-screwing-thing-up" point followed by a "good-fortune-fixing-things-up" point. Thus we would predict that a person would forget the manner of John's death, or the details of the accident, before he would forget that Mary was left by herself, pregnant, or that she eventually became happily married to her friend Bill. Furthermore, a reasonable summary of the story could be made by following the point structure: "John died leaving his wife Mary pregnant. Mary's friend Bill tried to help her along. Eventually they fell in love and got married."

The following are brief summaries of the major types of problem-solution points.

## 4.1 Problem Points

A problem point is essentially something bad that happens that has to be rectified. The important types of problem points are

1. Failure to achieve a goal: An S-goal, E-goal, or A-goal arises, and the actor is unsuccessful in achieving it.
2. Subsumption state failure: A state that "subsumes" a goal fails. A state subsumes a goal if the existence of that state makes the goal easier to achieve. For example, the marriage relationship is a subsumption state that should make it easier for the members of the relationship to achieve the goal S-sex.
3. Troublesome physical or mental states: A physical or mental state that impairs normal functioning is inflicted upon a character.

4. Threats: Some valued state is perceived to be in jeopardy. This is essentially the same as a P-goal.

## 4.2  Solution Points

After detecting a problem point, we can expect to see a solution point. This is some sequence of events that affect the problem that has been introduced. Some solution points depend on the particular kind of problem point, while some are fairly general.

1. Fortuitous circumstances: Some event not motivated by the problem goal occurs and aids in the solution of the problem.
2. More desperate measures: Some plan that was previously considered to be too risky is now used.
3. Replanning a subsumption state: A problematic subsumption state can be mended, terminated, or replaced by a new subsumption state.

## 5.0  PROCESSING

How do we identify a point in story? How does the process of point detection interact with the goal-related processes described above? In general, how can we implement a system that applies all these kinds of knowledge in a coherent fashion?

We are presently implementing a version of PAM (Plan Applier Mechanism) as a point-oriented production system. This system has an "active memory," which holds the uncompleted meaning representation that the understander is trying to build (see [Riesbeck75b]). The purpose of the productions in the active memory is to fill the gaps in this meaning representation. Thus when a production's condition is met, and its action fills a gap in the representation, PAM removes all the active productions, including the one just fired, whose actions were intended to fill that gap. The fired production may also specify new productions to add to the active memory. Thus the productions in the active memory are dynamically added and deleted as other productions are fired off.

For example, if the meaning representation for a "plan-episode" (i.e., a sequence of events related to a goal by a plan) is being built, it will contain a gap for the outcome of the plan. The actions of the productions "aimed" at this gap will fill the gap with a meaning structure representing either success or failure. If one of these productions goes off and fills the gap, all the productions will be removed, since their purpose, to fill the outcome gap, no longer exists. The firing of one of these productions would cause new productions to be added; for example, if the failure production went off, then new productions would be added looking for replanning or goal-abondonment.

In addition, the condition of each production is focused either on a particular gap in the meaning representation, or on one of a few special gaps known to PAM. The condition of a production will be checked only if the gap upon which it is focused is filled. Thus, only a small number of the productions present in the active memory need to be tested each time something in the active memory changes. For example, a prediction about a subsequent event in a story will take the form of a production focused on the special gap in which the language analysis program places new conceptualizations as they are extracted from the story text. When a new conceptualization is placed in this gap, the productions that predict new conceptualizations are tested, while those productions that are waiting for internal events to transpire need not be considered.

## 5.1 Identifying Points

Let us now give some examples of the kinds of productions that would be needed to identify points, and activate other productions that do goal-oriented processing.

The overall model of point detection is that certain concepts "nominate" candidates as potential points. This means that the conceptualization has associated with it in long-term memory a set of points, and a set of productions that describe how subsequent conceptualizations might fill the gaps of that point. These productions are loaded into active memory when the conceptualization is encountered by the understander.

For example, if we are told that

(10) John and Mary had been happily married for about a year.

the conceptualization underlying this sentence nominates a set of problem points dealing with goal subsumption failure. That is, a set of productions are loaded that will build subsumption failure episodes if subsequent conceptualizations meets their conditions. Thus following (10) with

(11) Then John began working late at the office.

will cause one of these productions to be fired and build the skeleton of a "subsumption state inadequacy" problem point. This production also causes another production to be loaded stating that if we next see an actual problem state, then complete the problem point episode representation and move it into a gap in the representation for the entire story. For example, (11) may be followed with

(12) Mary found herself lonely and bored.

Then the problem state gap in the "subsumption state inadequacy" problem point episode will be filled out and the episode moved into a gap in the representation of the entire story.

At the start of the understanding process, the active memory contains a set of productions that expect a problem point. These productions would include the following:

(A)   1. If we encounter a subsumption state, activate the productions that look for the failure of that subsumption state.

2. If we encounter a goal, activate the productions that look for the various ways the goal can fail.

3. If we encounter a theme, activate its goal-producing productions.

These high-level productions serve to activate those productons that may be needed to detect a problem point. For example, the subsumption state failure productions would include the following rules:

(B)   1. If the object of a subsumption state is lost, then activate the productions predicting the problems associated with subsumption state termination.

2. If something interferes with how the state should subsume an intended goal, then activate the productions predicting the problems associated with subsumption state inadequacy.

These productions activate productions that will finally infer the problem point. For example, production B2 would activate productions that included

(C)   1. If the state that would result from the interference occurs, then incorporate the subsumption state inadequacy point into the story representation, and activate productions predicting the solution points for replanning a subsumption state.

Consider how the story composed of (10), (11), (12) would be handled by these production rules:

In the initial configuration of the system, productions A1, A2, and A3 are active.

| Sentence | Fired Off | Action Taken | Productions Added |
|----------|-----------|--------------|-------------------|
| 10 | A1 | — | B1 B2 |

Since marriage is a state that subsumes several goals, activate the subsumption state failure productions.

| 11 | B2 | build skeleton of "subsumption state failure" | C1 |

John being away from Mary will be found to interfere with the "social stimulation" goal subsumed by marriage.

| 12 | C1 | fill "problem state" gap, add episode to story rep. | solution point productions |

Being bored and lonely are problem states that would result if the subsumption state failed to satisfy the goal that was interfered with. Thus the subsumption state inadequacy point is instantiated, and the productions that predict the solution points typical of this problem point are activated.

What has all this work bought us? By instantiating the knowledge structure corresponding to a problem point, many inferences crucial for understanding are implicitly incorporated into the story representation. For example, the causal relations among the conceptualizations in the above story are contained in the problem point. If we were to later query the system to determine why Mary became lonely, it could use the causal information contained in the point to answer that her husband wasn't paying enough attention to her.

## 6.0 SUMMARY

We have described some of the kinds of knowledge needed for understanding stories and formulated a mechanism with which this knowledge can be applied. This mechanism is a form of production system in which productions are associated with conceptualizations in long-term memory and loaded into the active memory at the appropriate moments. The mechanism is designed to achieve these important effects:

1. Only a relatively small number of productions are active at any one time, even if the total knowledge and number of productions in memory is large.

2. This small set of productions are considered before performing other processes. Thus these productions constitute a predictive mechanism favoring a particular interpretation of events.

3. High-level expectations can motivate lower level tasks. Thus a high-level production (e.g., one concerned with story points) may acti-

vate lower level productions (e.g., those concerned with goal-plan processing) that perform the nitty-gritty of story understanding.

The use of productions in the manner described here is essentially an extension of the processing strategies we have used in our previous programs. For example, in our natural language analysis program [Riesbeck75a], we make extensive use of productions as predictive mechanisms that build structures when the predicted occurs. The production system described here may be thought of as an extrapolation of this notion to the domain of story understanding.

# INFERENTIAL SEARCHES OF KNOWLEDGE NETWORKS AS AN APPROACH TO EXTENSIBLE LANGUAGE-UNDERSTANDING SYSTEMS[1]

David McDonald
*Carnegie-Mellon University*

Frederick Hayes-Roth
*The Rand Corporation*

*A program has been constructed that implements some inference schemes for inferring the meaning of noun-noun, adjective-noun, and agent-verb-object phrases from the constituent words. Dictionary definitions of words are input directly into a semantic network using a context free grammar implemented in a production system. To interpret a novel phrase (e.g., lawn mower, car tire, car wheel) semantically, an intersection search originating from the nodes representing the constituent words is performed in the semantic network. If an intersection is found, a meaning for the phrase is produced; otherwise the phrase is not interpreted. During this interpretation, only knowledge provided by dictionary definitions and parts of speech of words is used.*

## 1.0 INTRODUCTION

Conventional language-understanding schemes attempt to interpret phrases by identifying arguments of predefined case frames [Fillmore68, Rumelhart72], by filling conceptual slots of externally pro-

[1] This research was supported in part by the Defense Advanced Research Projects Agency under contract no. F44620-73-C-0074 which is monitored by the Air Force Office of Scientific Research. The first author is partially supported by the National Research Council of Canada.

*431*

vided frames, schemata, or scripts [Schank77, Winograd75], or by processing semantic markers or primitive predicates [Schank73a, Wilks75a, b, Winograd72]. An alternative approach is to develop semantic interpretations at the surface level of linguistic tokens. The central hypotheses underlying our work are (1) that syntactic structures embody semantic knowledge that is sufficient for many understanding tasks and (2) that the actual words occurring, in text are a more desirable basis for representing meaning than predefined abstract semantic primitives. In particular, we propose that semantic analysis of novel phrases may be possible simply by rearranging certain components of the syntactic representations of the relevant word meanings as embodied in a semantic network representation of dictionary definitions. To achieve this "superficial" semantic analysis it is necessary to relate the words in a phrase to structures in the semantic network. As is well known, some relationships between concepts can be identified just by finding the paths that interconnect them [Quillian68]. It now appears that a large variety of interesting and difficult semantic problems can be solved by generalizing this idea. Thus, the chief questions that arise in this approach are (1) which paths are semantically interesting and (2) how can they be found efficiently?

Some of the initial impetus for the current work resulted from Quillian's [Quillian69] Teachable Language Comprehender. New text is comprehended in his system by relating each new assertion to existing factual assertions in a semantic network. As new assertions are understood, semantic network structures are created to represent their meanings. This is very similar to some of the inference strategies developed in the current work.

A second motivation for this work is a recent theory of Hayes-Roth and Hayes-Roth [B. Hayes-Roth76, 77c] proposing that specific words in text provide a better basis for representing meaning than abstract semantic entities proposed by conventional theories of meaning representation. The advantages of word-based meaning representations include simplified representation, faster input processing, faster retrieval of stored facts, reduced interference among conceptually similar memory structures, and easier inference. However, [B. Hayes-Roth77c] does not specify in detail how word-based semantic processing can be accomplished. This is the basic objective of our research.

The first goal is to develop methods to infer the meaning of novel phrases using only dictionary definitions of individual words. The meanings of words are provided by dictionary definitions stored in a semantic network [Quillian68, Schubert76, Woods75] in a format that closely approximates surface level English. Definitions in the semantic network are created by a simple production system used to parse definitions taken directly from the New College Edition of the American Heritage Dictionary. The semantic network structure is very similar to, but less complete than, that proposed by Schubert [Schubert76].

Since all the semantic inferential schemes employ semantic network searches, an efficient search algorithm is very desirable. The current algorithm has been adapted from the work on parallel automata for searching semantic networks by Fiksel and Bower [Fiksel76]. In their work, each node in a semantic network is a simple, finite-state automaton with connectors that link it to other automata.

Semantic network searches of various types can be performed by the distributed set of automata. Originally, the automaton at each node is idle. To find a connection between $node_1$ and $node_2$, start signals $s_1$ and $s_2$ are sent to $node_1$ and $node_2$, respectively. When an automaton receives a signal $s_i$ from a neighbor, it relays the signal to all of its neighbors and revises its state to reflect the type of signal encountered (i.e., $s_1$ or $s_2$). If any automaton has received both signals $s_1$ and $s_2$, it notifies a control program that an intersection has been found. The control program may then continue to search or to generate a response. This basic search mechanism is employed in the program for semantic interpretation of word sequences.

To determine the meaning of a phrase, an efficient intersection search is performed in the semantic net starting at the nodes corresponding to the words in the phrase. The order of the words in the phrase determines the syntactic form of the search. For example, novel noun-noun phrases (e.g., lawn mower, car tire, car wheel) are understood in terms of semantic relationships in which the first noun "modifies" the second. Work has begun on developing similar methods for adjective-noun and agent-verb-object phrases. Some encouraging results have been obtained for these types of interpretation problems.

The next sections briefly describe the semantic network structure as it is currently defined, the conversion of lexicographic knowledge into a semantic network, and the method used for searching the semantic network. Several examples are then given of the inference methods developed for understanding noun-noun, adjective-noun, and agent-verb-object phrases. Finally, conclusions from this work are considered, and some directions for future research in this area are indicated.

## 2.0 THE STRUCTURE OF THE SEMANTIC NETWORK

The semantic network is a directed graph allowing cycles. Each node in the network represents a concept that is either a word or a phrase. Each arc in the graph is labeled and is called a *link*. Links can be thought of as modifiers. If a link exists from $node_1$ to $node_2$, the concept represented by $node_2$ qualifies in some way the concept repre-

sented by node₁. The "meaning" of a node is defined by the collection
of all structures pointed to by links emanating from the node. Thus,
a node representing a word is meaningful, as far as the program is
concerned, only if it is linked to others.

Figure 1 displays the semantic network structures created to
represent the following definitions of "lawn" and "mower":

A lawn is a mown area or plot planted with grass or similar plants.
A mower is a machine that cuts grass, grain, or hay.

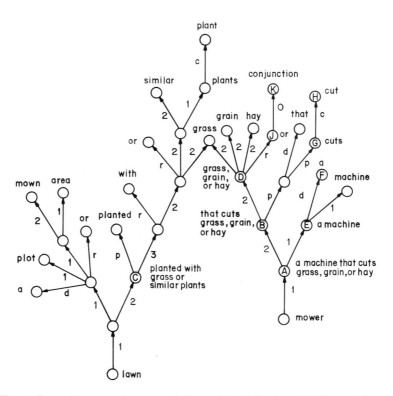

Fig. 1. Semantic network representations of the following definitions: A lawn is a
mown area or plot planted with grass or similar plants. A mower is a machine that cuts
grass, grain, or hay. For clarity, some nodes representing multiply occurring words (e.g.,
"a," "or") are shown more than once, although each such node occurs only once in the
semantic network. Nodes marked A, B, C, . . . are discussed in the text.

This figure shows several different types of links used to represent
the definitions. The 1 link represents the IS-A relationship. The 1 link
from "mower" to node A specifies that a "mower" is "a machine that
cuts grass, grain, or hay." The 2 link from node A to node B signifies

that "that cuts grass, grain, or hay" modifies "a machine." The 2 link is used whenever a noun is modified by an adjective, another noun, or other phrases.

The p link emanating from node C signifies that it is a predicate node with predicate "planted." A predicate is always a form of a verb. The 3 link specifies that "with grass or similar plants" is an argument to the predicate "planted."

The r link from node D to node J specifies that node D is a relation node with relation "or." The 2 links give the arguments ("grass," "grain," and "hay") to the relation "or." Since the relation "or" is symmetric, different link types are unnecessary. This symmetry is a property of most conjunctions. A different type of relation is the preposition, whose arguments have distinct roles. Different link types (2, 3, . . .) are used to point to functionally distinct arguments.

The d link from node E to node F specifies that node F represents a determiner that modifies the noun phrase ("machine") pointed to by the 1 link. In the current program, the d link is also used to point to relative pronouns (i.e., that, who, or which) from a node that points to a predicate.

The c link from node G to node H specifies that node H is the canonical form of node G. In the figure, "cut" is the infinitive of "cuts." This structure is similar for the different forms of nouns, adjectives, adverbs, and verbs.

The 0 link from node J to node K specifies that the part of speech of node J is a "conjunction."

## 3.0 KNOWLEDGE IN THE SEMANTIC NETWORK

The only information contained in the semantic network for performing semantic inferences consists of dictionary definitions of words. Definitions are used as an initial base of knowledge in the semantic network for two reasons. First, no bias is introduced by specially "tuning" definitions of words to facilitate inference, i.e., the data are clearly specified and objective. Second, dictionary definitions are prototypic real-world knowledge structures; if definitions can be freely added to the system without necessitating new inference methods, the goal of extensibility is achieved. It should then be possible to add other forms of knowledge in a similar way using English.

The current program allows only one definition for a word. Many words in English, however, have multiple meanings and parts of speech. Since all interpretations are represented as configurations of connections in the semantic network, multiple meanings simply permit alternative paths. Hence the problem of word ambiguity should not introduce any representational difficulties, although it can be expected to degrade efficiency by increasing the number of paths that must be followed.

A restricted subset of English is used to input the knowledge directly into the semantic network. Since the semantic network structure facilitates the representation of sentences and phrases at a surface structure level rather than a deep conceptual level, this approach entails a nearly direct mapping between definitions and corresponding semantic network structures.

Dictionary definitions usually exhibit one of a few fixed formats. In many cases, a simple context free grammar is sufficient to parse the definition. In the current program, a simple production system is used to perform a context free parse to transform definitions into semantic network structures. Each production has the form

$$C => A$$

where C is the condition part and is matched against structures in the semantic network, and A is the action part and may delete structures from or add structures to the semantic network, read the next word from the input stream, or create a new node in the semantic network. A variable in a rule specification may match any node in the semantic network. Variables are signified by a "?" as the first letter of their name.

Table 1 shows a fragment of a context-free grammar and the corresponding production system code to implement it. The production system uses the semantic network as its data base and thus needs to reference structures in the semantic network. The pattern $n:\{l_1:n_1, l_2:n_2, \ldots, l_m:n_m\}$ represents the semantic network structure in which node n has links $l_i$ pointing to nodes $n_i$. The link * is a special link employed to keep temporary information about the computation for the production system. The pattern phase:$\{\ldots\}$ specifies the state of the parse so as to restrict the set of productions allowed to fire at any given time.

Figure 2 shows the structures that match the condition and the new structures created by the action part of each production in Table 1 as the phrase "a similar plant" is parsed. Production (1) fires when the production system is looking for a phrase that matches an NP1 in the grammar and the current word is a determiner (which will have been input earlier). The action part of production (1) reads in the next word, deletes the current word and the information that an NP1 is wanted, creates a new node in the network to represent the noun phrase, and finally inserts the next word, the information that an NP2 is now wanted, and adds the determiner to the structure being built to represent the noun phrase. Figure 2a shows the structures neces-

| Context-Free Rules | Production Rules |
|---|---|
| (1) NP1 ::= DETERMINER NP2 | phase:{*:np1\|∧?x:{*:word, 0:determiner} => read(?w), delete(?x:{*:word}, phase:{*:np1}), create(?n), insert(?w:{*:word}, phase:{*:np2}, ?n:{*:np,d:?x}); |
| (2) NP2 ::= ADJECTIVE NP2 | phase:{*:np2\|∧?x:{*:word, 0:adjective} ?n:{*:np} => read(?w), delete(?x:{*:word}), insert(?w:{*:word}, ?n:{2:?x}); |
| (3) NP2 ::= NOUN | phase:{*:np2\|∧?x:{*:word, 0:noun} ?n:{*:np} => delete(?x:{*:word}, phase:{*:np2}), insert(?n:{1:?x}); |

Table 1. Product System Implementation of a Partial Noun Phrase Grammar.

sary for production (1) to fire and the resulting structures after its action part is executed. Figure 2b shows production (2) now adding the adjective "similar" to the structure. Figure 2c shows production (3) producing the final result. The * link and the node np are needed so that the phrase being built can be referenced easily by the productions. They are only temporary and are deleted once the phrase is stored permanently in the semantic network.

A BNF grammar can be mapped directly into the above production system formalism. Currently, only context free rules are used, but the production system could be augmented to handle context-sensitive rules. Context sensitive rules will probably be necessary when the production system is extended to process general text.

## 4.0 SEARCHING THE NETWORK FOR SEMANTIC INTERPRETATIONS

The key idea underlying the determination of meaning is a syntactically guided search of the semantic network. Semantic network searches for interpretation of a phrase are performed by independent, parallel processes emanating from the nodes corresponding to each word. Distinct starting signals are sent to each of these nodes, and the automata at each node perform the search by relaying the signals and

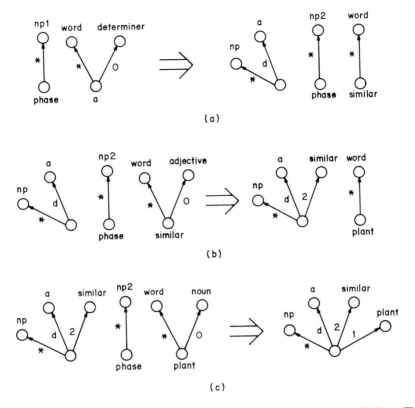

Fig. 2. (a), (b), and (c) correspond to productions (1), (2), and (3) in Table 1. The semantic network structures to the left of the large arrow are used to match the condition of the production; structures to the right are added to the semantic network by the action part of the production.

by changing states. Each signal in the system contains the following information:

(1) A mark-flag used to mark the nodes activated by this signal. Different signals leave different mark-flags. The mark-flag makes it possible to retrieve paths found by searches.

(2) Information about the *branching factor* encountered by the signal. This estimates the total number of paths in the search space from which this particular signal has been selected.

(3) The node and link causing the signal to be sent to the current node. This can be used to do simple inference during the search.

(4) A description of the type of inferential path sought. Currently this consists of a set of link types along which the search can explore for a solution path.

When a node receives a signal, it copies the signal using the same mark-flag and updating the values of the other types of information. It then forwards copies to whichever neighbors could be on the solution path, given the type of inferential path desired.

Since it is necessary to search the semantic network as efficiently as possible (i.e., to find an intersection as fast as possible), a metric has been designed to measure the goodness of a developing path. This metric is defined by the following formula:

$$S = ((1 - N / T) * B)^{-1},$$

where S is the *strength* assigned to all signals emanating from the current node. A signal is stronger and more preferred for larger values of S. N is the number of distinct signals that have intersected at the current node. T is the total number of distinct signals originally used to activate the initial nodes in the search. B represents the branching factor of the signal. Every time the signal is split n ways, each copy of the signal has a branching factor of n * B, where B is the branching factor of the parent signal. For lower branching factors, fewer copies of signals are processed.

Strength is used to decide which signal to process next. All active signals are kept in a list sorted by strength. When the search program has finished with one signal and wants to process the next, it picks the strongest one. The search is successfully terminated only when one node has been reached by all the distinct signals, and is unsuccessfully terminated if no more signals exist to process.

The search procedure outlined above will find any path between two nodes. Because the types of permissible links may be restricted, prior knowledge about properties of solution paths can significantly reduce search times. The search strategy works fastest when a solution exists and is "near" to the original nodes; it is slowest when no solution exists. Further improvements in processing time may be possible by ignoring signals with very small strengths relative to the best alternatives. Although such a heuristic may result in some search failures, it will surely reduce the search time in many situations. For the semantic net currently being used (about 2000 nodes), no such pruning is apparently necessary. However, this problem of combinatorics will probably be manifested in searches of networks having a significantly larger average number of links emanating from each node.

## 5.0 INFERENTIAL SEMANTIC INTERPRETATIONS

In this section, we give examples of the strategies that have been developed for handling noun-noun, adjective-noun, and agent-verb-object phrases. In these examples, the only information used is the part of speech and the dictionary definition of the words in the phrase (plus the definitions of the words used in defining these words, and so on).

To interpret a phrase, a search is initiated in the semantic network originating from all nodes representing words in the phrase. If the search terminates without finding an intersection node, no semantic interpretation of the phrase is attempted. When an intersection occurs, the system uses the paths discovered in the search to construct an interpretation. This interpretation depends on the structure of the relevant definitions and on the location of the intersection.

In generating the examples below, a data base consisting of about 180 definitions (about 2000 nodes in the semantic network) was used. Each inference takes between 0.2 and 2 sec of CPU time on a DEC PDP-10 (model KA10) computer. When an interpretation cannot be found, processing continues until no active signals exist. This usually takes between 1 and 2 sec.

## 5.1 Noun-Noun Phrases

In a noun-noun phrase (e.g., lawn mower, car tire, car wheel) the first noun modifies the second and is used basically as an adjective. A meaning for such a phrase is constructed by replacing a phrase (or word) in the definition of the second noun by either the first noun or a phrase used in the definition of the first noun. A new node is created in the semantic network to canonically represent this new concept. Subsequent references to that compound concept directly access the new node, thereby obviating repetitive inference.

First, the detailed inference strategy for one example will be given, then several more will be presented in less detail. In the examples below, italicized words in the generated phrase are the words used to replace a phrase in the definition of the second noun. The definitions used are identified as relevant by the search process and represent the information used to produce the "inferred meaning." The figures for these examples contain only the paths relevant to the inferences generated; other parts of the semantic network explored during the search are not shown. Nodes labeled by phrases actually point to structures representing these phrases. The nodes in the figures marked by * are the nodes created to represent the new concepts. The 1 and 2 links pointing from these nodes are the same as described previously. The 2' link specifies the node to be replaced in the definition of the second noun, and the 2" link specifies the node that replaces it.

(1) Interpret: lawn mower
Definitions used:
A lawn is a mown area or plot planted with grass or similar
  plants.
A mower is a machine that cuts grass, grain, or hay.
Inferred meaning: A lawn mower is a machine that cuts *grass
  or similar plants.*

Figure 3 displays the section of the semantic network used to construct the meaning of "lawn mower." A search is initiated at "lawn" and "mower" and fans out along all the possible paths from these two nodes. Eventually, the search intersects at "grass." The paths found during the search are used to create a meaning for the concept "lawn mower." First, the node to replace in the definition of "mower" is found. The program looks at the nodes on the intersection path between "grass" and "mower" starting at the node closest to "grass" and working backwards. Since the node Y ("grass, grain, or hay") points to a conjunction (by an "r" link), it is noted as the node to replace. This process always continues backward along the intersection path until a nonconjunction node is encountered. The node to

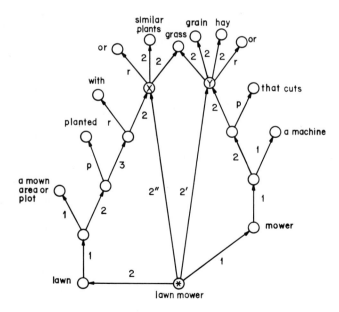

Fig. 3. Section of the semantic network used to construct an interpretation of "lawn mower," represented by newly created node *. Interpretation is constructed by replacing node X (pointed to by 2″ link) with node Y (pointed to by 2′ link) in the definition of mower (pointed to by 1 link).

replace this one must also be determined. If all the links on the inter-section path from "lawn" to "grass" were 1 links, "lawn" would be the replacement node, since it would be a more specific instance of the concept used in the definition. However, the path between "lawn" and "grass" does not contain only 1 links. Instead "grass" would be the replacement node, except that the node pointing to it is a conjunction node. Thus node X is selected as the replacement node using the same process as used to select node Y above. Hence, the program replaces node Y ("grass, grain, or hay") in the definition of mower by node X ("grass or similar plants") to form the meaning for "lawn mower." Such an inference gives an apparently more meaningful definition of "lawn mower."

(2) Interpret: computer program
Definitions used:
A computer is a device that computes.
A program is a procedure coded for a computer that solves a
    problem.
Inferred meaning: A computer program is a procedure coded
    for *a computer* that solves a problem.

Figure 4 gives the section of the semantic network involved in determining the meaning for "computer program." This example is

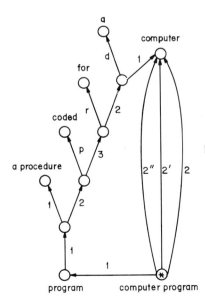

Fig. 4. Section of the semantic network used to construct an interpretation of "computer program."

particularly simple, since "computer" occurs directly in the definition of program. Hence a connection between computer and program can be established immediately, and the interpretation is produced without further processing. The important aspect here is that "computer" is used in a phrase modifying the word "procedure" in the definition of "program."

(3) Interpret: vegetable garden

> Definitions used:
> A vegetable is a plant cultivated for an edible part or parts.
> A garden is a plot of land used for the cultivation of flowers,
> vegetables, or fruit.
> Inferred meaning: A vegetable garden is a plot of land used for
> the cultivation of *a vegetable.*

Figure 5 shows the portion of the semantic network relevant to this example. Note that in this example also, the phrase "flowers, vegetables, or fruit" is replaced by "a vegetable." It would have been better to use "vegetables" as the replacement, but the program does not currently check for plurals of words and thus misses this obvious improvement.

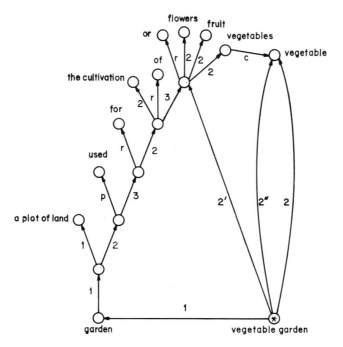

Fig. 5. Section of the semantic network used to construct an interpretation of "vegetable garden."

(4) Interpret: city planner

Definitions used:
A city is a town of significant size.
A planner is a person who forms a plan of something.
Inferred meaning: A city planner is a person who forms a plan
of *a city.*

Figure 6 presents the semantic network structures used to infer
the meaning of "city planner." Notice that the word "something" in
the definition of a planner is replaced by "a city." This is made possible
by finding a connection between "city" and "something" in the semantic network. In this case a chain of 1 links specify that a city is something.

(5) Interpret: car tire

Definitions used:
A car is an automobile.
A tire is a solid or air-filled covering for a wheel.
A wheel is a solid disk or rigid circular ring connected by
spokes to a hub that turns around the axle of a vehicle.

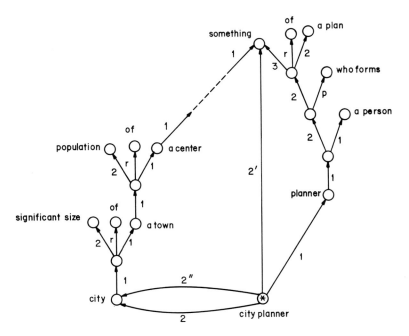

Fig. 6. Section of the semantic network used to construct an interpretation of "city planner."

Intermediate inference: A car wheel is a solid disk or rigid
   circular ring connected by spokes to a hub that turns around
   the axle of *a car.*
Inferred meaning: A car tire is a solid or air-filled covering for
   *a car wheel.*

Figure 7 shows the semantic network structures used to infer the
meaning of "car tire" and, in the process, the meaning of "car wheel."
The necessary inferences here are somewhat more complex than in
the previous cases. The word "wheel" in the definition of "tire" would
normally be replaced with "car." However, a more complete meaning
of "car tire" can be obtained by replacing "wheel" in the definition of
"tire" by "car wheel." This illustrates that multiple inferences may be
necessary to obtain an appropriate interpretation of a phrase. Here
the inference strategy has been applied a second time to "car" and
"wheel," producing an interpretation of the novel phrase "car wheel."
The phrase "car wheel" replaces "wheel" in the definition of "tire" to
produce an interpretation of "car tire." The inference strategy is always applied a second time to the first noun and the word it would
replace in the definition of the second noun. This second application
fails in most instances.

   In preceding examples, the program used only information contained in the dictionary definitions of the nouns. However, interpretation of some phrases requires more knowledge than these definitions
provide. In particular, consider the following examples.

(7) Interpret: computer music

Definitions used:
A computer is a device that computes.
Music is vocal or instrumental sound that has some degree of
   rhythm, melody, and harmony.
Inferred meaning: No relationship between computer and
   music was found.

   One possible answer is: "Computer music is music made or given
forth by a computer." This inference would require making a connection between the noun "sound" and the verb to "sound." In particular
the program would have to recognize that a computer can be an agent
of the verb to "sound." The the definition of "to sound" (to make or
give forth a sound) could be used to define the meaning of "computer
music." This would be done by replacing "sound" with "music" and
using "computer" as the agent of the sentence. This would produce

A computer makes or gives forth music.

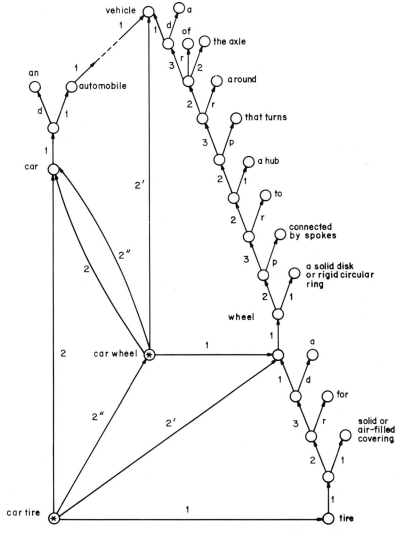

Fig. 7. Section of the semantic network used to construct an interpretation of "car tire."

or, using the passive form and inserting "computer music" at the beginning

Computer music is music made or given forth by a computer.

The mechanisms for performing this type of inference have not yet been built into the program.

(8) Interpret: lawn party

Definitions used:
A lawn is a mown area or plot planted with grass or similar plants.
A party is a social gathering for pleasure or amusement.
Inferred meaning: No relationship between lawn and party was found.

In this situation, no inference is made because there is not sufficient information in the definitions of the words involved. In particular, the knowledge that a party is held somewhere and that a lawn has the property of location is needed to produce: "A lawn party is a party held on a lawn."

(9) Interpret: fire department

(10) Interpret: fire hose

Definitions used:
A fire is a rapid persistent chemical reaction that releases heat and light from the exothermic combination of a combustible substance with oxygen.
A department is a distinct division of a large organization such as a government, company, or store that has a specialized function and personnel.
A hose is a flexible tube that conveys liquid or gas under pressure.
Inferred meaning: No relationship between fire and department was found.
Inferred meaning: No relationship between fire and hose was found.

In the two examples above, more knowledge about fires is necessary. In particular, it is sometimes necessary to fight fires and water is often used in doing so. Using this information, it should be possible to establish that a fire department has as a purpose fighting fires and that a fire hose conveys water for fighting fires.

(11) Interpret: bed room

> Definitions used:
> A bed is a piece of furniture for reclining and sleeping that
>   consists of a flat rectangular frame, mattress and bedclothes.
> A room is an area separated by walls or partitions from other
>   similar parts of a structure or building.
> Inferred meaning: No relationship between bed and room was
>   found.

This is another case in which the definition of a word provides insufficient information for inference. In particular, people know that a room normally contains furniture. Since a bed is a piece of furniture, it should be clear that a bed room is a room that normally contains a bed.

Examples 7 through 11 show that considerable knowledge exists about a concept or word beyond what is expressed by its dictionary definition. Much of this knowledge is apparently necessary in language-understanding tasks involving novel sentences. To gain the full advantage of inferential interpretation schemes, it will be necessary both to incorporate more knowledge and to permit more flexible types of associations in the semantic network.

## 5.2 Adjective-Noun Phrases

To interpret adjective-noun phrases, we use techniques similar to those for noun-noun phrases. These inferences seem to be less complex than those required for noun-noun interpretations. As for noun-noun phrases, a search in the semantic network determines if a connection between the adjective and the noun exists. If there is, a new concept is created in the semantic network to represent the meaning of the adjective-noun phrase. The definition of the adjective determines the meaning of the new adjective-noun phrase in the following way:

(a) If the adjective is defined in terms of a verb phrase, the new concept is defined by using the noun as the agent for the verb phrase.

(b) If the adjective is defined in terms of another adjective or adjectival phrase, the new concept is defined using only this definition.

(c) If the adjective is defined in terms of a noun phrase, the new concept is defined by replacing the head noun in the definition by the noun in the phrase.

Following are some examples illustrating the technique for adjective-noun phrases. The letter following the inferred meaning specifies which one of the above rules was used to obtain the meaning.

(12) Interpret: theoretical explanation

Definitions used:
Theoretical means based on theory.
An explanation is the act or process of making plain or
    comprehensible.
Inferred meaning: A theoretical explanation is an explanation
    based on theory. (a)

(13) Interpret: natural phenomenon

Definitions used:
Natural means present in nature.
A phenomenon is an occurrence or fact.
Inferred meaning: A natural phenomenon is a phenomenon
    present in nature. (b)

(14) Interpret: carnivorous animal

Definitions used:
Carnivorous means predatory.
An animal is an organism of the kingdom of Animalia.
Inferred meaning: A carnivorous animal is predatory. (b)

(15) Interpret: predatory animal

Definitions used:
Predatory means preying on other animals.
An animal is an organism of the kingdom of Animalia.
Inferred meaning: A predatory animal is an animal preying on
    other animals. (a)

(16) Interpret: essential constituent

Definitions used:
Essential means part of the essence of something.
A constituent is a component.
Inferred meaning: An essential constituent is a constituent of
    the essence of something. (c)

In the examples above, no test is made on the paths found in the
search. Currently, an insufficient number of test cases have been performed to see if any more complex strategy will be needed. The results
obtained using this simple strategy are encouraging and seem to indicate that nothing much more complex will be needed.

## 5.3  Agent-Verb-Object Phrases

The techniques developed for noun-noun and adjective-noun

phrases can be extended to handle agent-verb-object sentences. The inference strategy used here has not yet been fully developed and consequently does not work in all cases. Following are some examples.

(17) Interpret: A computer computes numbers.

> Definitions used:
> A computer is a device that computes.
> To compute is to determine by mathematics.
> Inferred meaning: A computer determines numbers by
>     mathematics.

(18) Interpret: A gardener plants a vegetable.

> Definitions used:
> A gardener is a person that works in a garden for pleasure or
>     profit.
> To plant is to place seeds, roots, cuttings, or young plants in
>     the ground.
> A vegetable is a plant cultivated for an edible part or parts.
> Inferred meaning: A gardener places a vegetable in the ground.

(19) Interpret: A computer operator operates a computer.

> Definitions used:
> A computer operator is a person that operates a computer.
> To operate is to control the function of something.
> A computer is a device that computes.
> Inferred meaning: A computer operator controls the function of
>     a computer.

(20) Interpret: People use computers.

> Definitions used:
> People is the mass of ordinary persons.
> To use is to employ for some purpose.
> Inferred meaning: People employ computers for some purpose.

Note that in the above example, more information than just "some purpose" could be provided. It would be much better to infer "People employ computers for computing numbers." This type of inference would require the program to take account of more information than is explicit in a definition. The current program does not continue its inference process to such "deeper levels."

(21) Interpret: A lawn mower cuts grass.

> Definitions used:
> A lawn mower is a machine that cuts grass.

To cut is to sever the edges or outer extensions of something.
Inferred meaning: A lawn mower severs the edges or outer
  extensions of grass.

(22) Interpret: An inference rule governs inference.

> Definitions used:
> An inference rule is a guide or principle that governs an
>   inference.
> To govern is to control the action of something.
> An inference is the act or process of inferring.
> Inferred meaning: An inference rule controls the action of
>   inference.

The preceding examples produce more complex sentences giving
fuller meanings to the initial phrases. This is accomplished as follows.
First a search is performed in the semantic network to see if the verb
and two noun phrases are connected. If no connection exists, the inference fails. When a connection exists, the program replaces or fills in
parts of the definition of the verb. Note that in the examples the object
in the initial phrase is not always the object in the new phrase. Where
to place the object is decided in the following way:

(a) If the definition of the verb contains only an object, the object
in the original phrase replaces this object.

(b) If the definition of the verb contains only an indirect object
without any specification for an object, the object in the original
phrase is used as the object in the new phrase (examples 17, 20).

(c) If the definition of the verb contains both an indirect and direct
object, the paths found in the original search are used to make the
decision. If the connection between the verb and the original object
was through the object in the definition of the verb, the original object
becomes the new object (examples 18, 21, 22). Otherwise, the noun
phrase in the indirect object is replaced by the original object to form
the new phrase (example 19).

These simple assumptions do not always work. For example consider
the following phrase:

(23) Interpret: People play tennis.

> Definitions used:
> People is the mass of ordinary persons.
> To play is to participate in a game or sport.
> Tennis is a game played with a racket and a light ball by two
>   players.
> Inferred meaning: People participate tennis in a game or sport.

This is not the desired effect. A better response would have been "People participate in tennis." But even this is lacking. A much better response would be "People participate in a tennis game." The program does not produce either of these responses, because it has no syntactic understanding of transitive and intransitive verbs. In particular, "participate" is an intransitive verb and thus may not have a direct object. This knowledge would enable the program to produce the first alternative response above. Note that for the second alternative, multiple-inference strategies must be combined. The current program does not have this capability.

## 6.0 SUMMARY AND CONCLUSIONS

A general strategy for inferring meanings of simple syntactic phrases was presented. A semantic network containing declarative (lexicographic) knowledge about concepts is searched efficiently to discover patterns of connections among concepts. These patterns are used to construct meanings at a verbal level of analysis. If no connection is found, no interpretation of a phrase is possible.

The assumption underlying this work is that the meaning of a phrase can be inferred by syntactically configuring the meanings of its constituent words. While the meanings of words derive both from their use in a phrase and from the context of previous sentences, the program currently utilizes only local (intraphrase) information to develop interpretations. An extension of these methods to permit more global sources of knowledge would obviously be required for fuller language understanding.

Currently, all knowledge is acquired by a primitive production system implementing a context-free grammar that transforms dictionary definitions into semantic network structures. This simple mechanism does not allow for defining a word whose definition contains words with multiple meanings (or parts of speech). The proposed inference methods can help by semantically interpreting the definitions themselves. The meaning for each word in a definition would be selected to be the one most semantically consistent with the meanings of the other words in the definition. Discovering how to exploit these inferences effectively during parsing is one of the areas in which future research is planned.

Dictionary definitions obviously cannot be the only source of knowledge in a language-understanding system. Which types of knowledge should be included and how they should be represented are thus two important questions. Clearly it would be best if additional knowledge could be supplied in declarative form (i.e., text) and successfully applied by a few simple and uniform inference strategies.

Finally, the proposed inferential techniques suggest a potential for realizing an extensible natural language-understanding system. Such a system would comprise a knowledge base and associated general inference mechanisms to develop word-level semantic interpretations of new phrases consistent with existing knowledge and expectations. The meanings of smaller phrases (and words) could be used to build up meanings for larger phrases until a semantic interpretation of a sentence or even a paragraph were constructed. The knowledge for such a system would be specified in a natural declarative form (i.e., English) and thus would be fundamentally extensible.

# RULE-BASED COMPUTATIONS ON ENGLISH

Robert F. Simmons
*University of Texas at Austin*

*A linear notation for expressing semantic networks as sets of semantic predicates is outlined. Rule forms are presented for translating from English discourse to semantic predicates. Rules for generating English sentences and for computing causal chains from semantic predicates are described. Each of these rule forms has been tested in an existing question answering system. A brief analysis of rule-based systems is given and a method for designing them is suggested.*

## 1.0 INTRODUCTION

A natural language such as English is an open set of symbols and reasonably well-formed symbol sequences. The set of sequences is potentially infinite. Any large English computational system, such as a mechanical translator or a text-based question answerer, can be expected to encounter new vocabulary items and new sequences that are meaningful to some people but beyond its definitions. Thus additional information must be added in the form of procedures or rules as the languages the system deals with evolve new symbols and expressions.

Even if we knew how to program a system to accomplish question-answering and translation over a vocabulary of 150,000 words and thousands of sequences, we could not complete the system; the very next new text might introduce new vocabulary and constructions. There exist a few truly large language processors, descendants of the mechanical translation (MT) effort of the fifties and sixties. Some of these have vocabularies including as many as 150,000 entries and thousands of sequence rules. (See Hays and Mathis [Hays76].) Al-

*455*

though the earliest experiments in MT were largely *ad hoc* programs that somehow computed the translation of a paragraph or two, an early version of the procedural-declarative controversy was resolved in favor of rule-based translators.

The consequence was that computer programmers (at least theoretically) could complete a program to manipulate rules to perform translations, even though the rule systems could never be completed. The benefit — actually realized in those few installations that found the quality of MT systems sufficient for their purposes — is that the users trained in rule writing add to the vocabulary and grammar to increase the capabilities of the system long after the system programmers have departed.

In recent work in natural language understanding Winograd [Winograd72], Riesbeck [Riesbeck75a], and Novak [Novak76], among others have favored a procedural approach to programming. Others such as Sager [Sager73], Heidorn [Heidorn72], and Wilks [Charniak76] prefer rule-based programming. The procedural approach is clearly justifiable by the argument that until we know the full extent of phenomena that can occur in a natural language, we need the flexibility provided by a high-level language such as LISP in order to account for the new and strange. Yet, powerful systems of rules such as Woods' augmented transition network [Woods73] or those recently published by Martin Kay [Kay73] offer either exactly the capabilities of the embedding programming language or something very close to it. Perhaps the argument reduces to one of stylistic preference, with those favoring free verse tending toward the procedural side and those preferring to write in meter liking rule forms.

I prefer systems that can easily be augmented with additional procedures in the form of vocabulary entries and rules, and find the rule forms a comfortable high-level language for describing meaning structures. This paper presents rule systems for analyzing English into semantic structures, augmenting these structures with rule-based inferences and generating English from them. The concluding discussion suggests a methodology for designing rule-based systems.

## 2.0 ANALYZING ENGLISH STRINGS

For some time we have used semantic networks to represent the meaning of an English discourse as a connected set of semantic case predicates. We have shown that this notation represents English meanings as a set of objects, relations among objects, and rules for inferring new relations from old [Hendrix76a, Simmons76]. The case notation for relations substitutes labeled argument positions (e.g., AGenT, THeme, LOCation, SUPerset, MODifier, FROM, TO, FOR) for the usual n-tuple conventions as exemplified below:

n-tuple: (BUY RUFOLO SHIP MERCHANT PRICE)

case predicate: (BUY AGT RUFOLO, TH SHIP, FROM MER-
CHANT, FOR PRICE)

The cases are signaled by morphological or syntactic cues in the English strings; they serve in question-answering and other inference
tasks to classify the semantic predicates by their argument patterns,
and are most useful in guiding the generation of English strings from
the predicates.

The case predicate notation also includes some similarity to English embedding conventions. Thus for a sentence such as

RUFOLO WAS A WEALTHY MAN WHO LIVED IN ITALY,

the case predicate notation,

(LIVE1 (AGT(RUFOLO1 SUP(MAN1 MOD WEALTH1)) LOC
ITALY1)

combines the following simple predicates:

(LIVE1 AGT RUFOLO1 LOC ITALY1)
(RUFOLO1 SUP MAN1)
(MAN1 MOD WEALTHY1)

There appears to be a small set of case names — we typically use
about 20-30. Case names have properties; SUPerset, and LOCus, for
example, are marked TRANSitive as are temporal and causal cases.
Agent has the property that (X AGT Y) implies the state (X WANT Y).
Generally these properties increase the implicative power and the
computational efficiency of a system. The subscripted words reveal a
convention for representing each new usage of an English word as a
new subscripted token of the lexical entry. This token is in the relation
SUP to the lexical entry and the entry has a list of INSTances that
includes every usage in the discourse.

A first step in the development of a grammar for a subset of
English is to define the desired semantic output. For this discussion,
a brief story about Margie's balloon has been selected. This is essentially the same discourse that Rumelhart [Rumelhart75] analyzed in
some detail. Figure 1 shows the discourse and a corresponding set of
semantic predicates to represent one level of its meaning. Each subscripted term in the semantic predicates is connected through its lexical entry to all the syntactic and semantic information associated with
that entry. Thus MARGIE1 is an INSTance of MARGIE W/C PRO-
PERNOUN, SUP GIRL, etc. Figure 1a shows the semantic graph or
network for the same predicates.

The semantic predicates of Fig. 1 are computed by a version of the

*Discourse:*[3]

Margie was holding her beautiful new balloon. Suddenly, a gust of wind caught it. The wind carried it into a tree. The balloon hit a branch and burst. Margie cried and cried.

*Semantic Case Predicates:*

(HOLD1 AGT MARGIE1 TH (BALLOON1 MOD
(BEAUTIFUL1 NEW1) R2* (OWN1 R1 MARGIE1)) TENSE PAST,
    PROGRESSIVE T)
(CATCH1 INSTR (WIND1 HASPRT GUST1) TH BALLOON1
    MANNER SUDDENLY1, TENSE PASE)
(CARRY1 INSTR WIND1 TH BALLOON1 TO TREE1 TENSE
    PAST)
HIT1 TH BALLOON1 LOC BRANCH1 TENSE PAST BEFORE
    BURST1)
(BURST1 TH BALLOON1 TENSE PAST)
(CRY1 TH MARGIE1 TENSE PAST BEFORE CRY2)
(CRY2 TH MARGIE1 TENSE PAST)

[3] Rumelhart's first sentence read, "Margie was holding tightly to the string of her beautiful new balloon." I have deleted "tightly to the string of" since it introduces some syntactic and semantic difficulties that are beyond the focus of this chapter. Note that "it" in the second and third sentences must refer to the "balloon" not the "string."

Fig. 1. Margie's balloon.

Cocke-Kasami-Younger algorithm programmed mainly by Dan Chester following Pratt's [Pratt75] description. We use this program as a semantic-grammar tester to calculate all paths that the grammar allows, then revise the grammar to minimize the number of interpretations. Each grammar rule is a 4-tuple as follows:

(PHRASENAME (LIST OF SYNTACTIC CONSTITUENTS)
    (CORRESPONDING LIST OF SEMANTIC CONSTRAINTS)
    (TRANSFORMATION))

For example:

(S(NP VP)(ANIMATE (ACT VPAS NIL)) (2 AGT 1))

The Phrasename is S. The syntactic constituents are the list (NP VP). The corresponding list of semantic constraints is (ANIMATE (ACT VPAS NIL)), which requires that the head of the NP have the feature ANIMATE, that the head of the VP constituent have the feature ACT,

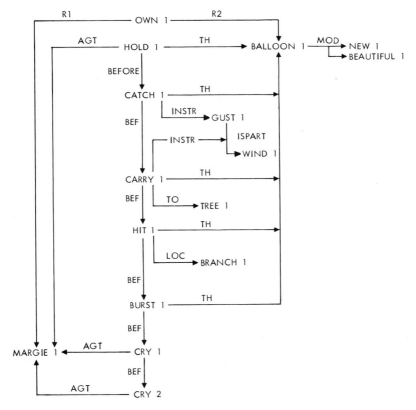

Fig. 1a. Semantic network representation of predicates from Fig. 1.

and that it not be a passive construction. If the syntactic and semantic patterns match, the fourth element (2 AGT 1) is applied as a transformation to construct a portion of a semantic predicate. If this rule is applied to the two constituents

(NP(MARGIE))
(VP(CRY TENSE PAST))

it constructs the following constituent:

(S(CRY TENSE PAST, AGT MARGIE))

A grammar of these rules sufficient to translate the Margie text into the semantic predicates of Fig. 1 is shown in Fig. 2.

At this writing our largest grammar is a set of 80 rules to analyze two paragraphs of text about coconut palms. Since the rules contain the same type of information that we have used in writing ATN gram-

Margie was holding her beautiful new balloon
(HOLD1 AGT MARGIE1 TH (BALLOON1 MOD (NEW1
   BEAUTIFUL1)
   R2* (OWN1 R1 MARGIE1))
   TENSE PAST, PROGR T)
(NP(PPRON NP1 OK (2 R2* (OWN R1 (ANTEC 1))))
(NP1 (ADJ NP1) OK (2 MOD 1))
(NP1 (N) OK (1))
(NP (NPR) OK (1))
(VP (VSTRNG NP) (ACT POBJ) (1 TH 2))
(VSTRNG (AUX VSTRNG) ((BE PAST) (ACT ING)) (2 TENSE
   PAST PROGR T))
(VSTRNG (V) ((OK PAST T)) (1 TENSE PAST))
(S (NP VP) (ANIMATE ACT) (2 AGT 1))

Suddenly a gust of wind caught it.
(CATCH1 ... ) See Figure 1.
(NP(ART NP1) (INDEF OK) (2 DET INDEF))
(NP1(NP1 PP) (CHANGE (FLUID PREP OF)) (2 HASPRT1))
(NP1(PRON) OK (ANTEC 1))
(PP (PREP NP) OK (2 PREP 1))
(S (NP VP ((OK ANIMATE NIL) ACT) (2 INSTR 1))
(S (ADVB S) (MANNER OK) (2 MANNER 1))

The wind carried it into a tree
(CARRY1 INSTR WIND1 ... )
(NP(ART NP1) (DEF OK) (2 DET DEF))
(VP(VP PP) (MOVE(POBJ PREP INTO)) (1 TO 2))

The balloon hit a branch and burst.
(HIT1 ... )
(BURST1 ... )
(S(S CONJVP) OK (1 BEFORE (ADDSUBJ 1 2)))
(CONJV(AND VP) OK (2))

Margie cried and cried.
(CRY1 ... )
(CRY2 ... )
No new rules needed!

   Note: ADDSUBJ seeks an AGT or an INSTR or a TH in the first
predicate and inserts it in the second

*Fig. 2. A grammar for Margie.*

mars for the same purpose, we naturally noticed that we could compile a form of ATN in which phrasenames such as S, NP, and VP corresponded to PUSH, arcs and wordclass names such as N, V, and ADJ corresponded to CATegory arcs. The semantic constraints and transformations correspond respectively to TST arcs and to the OPERATIONS that are allowed in ATNs. The following is an example of the S rule shown above expressed as an ATN path:

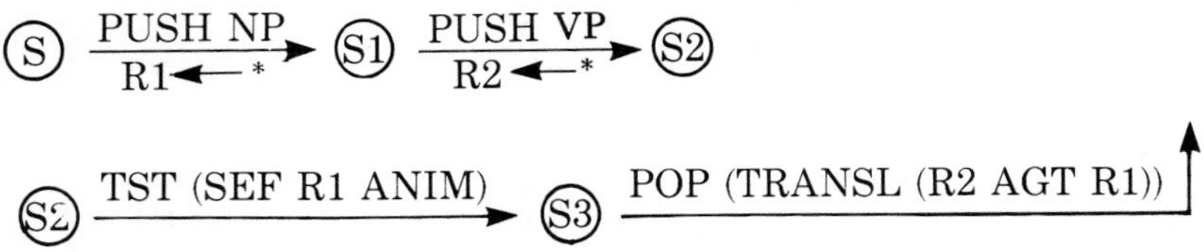

$$\text{(S)} \xrightarrow[\text{R1} \longleftarrow *]{\text{PUSH NP}} \text{(S1)} \xrightarrow[\text{R2} \longleftarrow *]{\text{PUSH VP}} \text{(S2)}$$

$$\text{(S2)} \xrightarrow{\text{TST (SEF R1 ANIM)}} \text{(S3)} \xrightarrow{\text{POP (TRANSL (R2 AGT R1))}}$$

SEF and TRANSL are functions that accomplish the semantic tests and transformations as described in the preceding paragraph. This is a strangely linear style for writing an ATN grammar, but the rule forms we present can be compiled by a fairly simple program into a form where an ATN system can interpret them.[1]

In our grammar tester, we compile the rules into a set of decision trees as illustrated in Fig. 3. This arrangement reduces storage cost and offers excellent accessing capabilities to the algorithm that applies the rules.

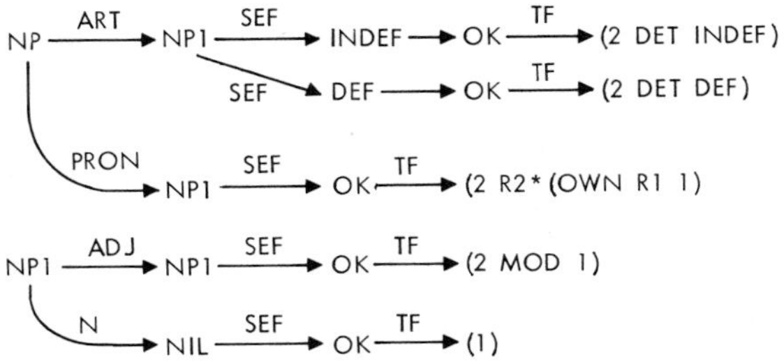

Fig. 3. Decision network for grammar rules.

When terminal elements such as V, N, and ADJ are encountered, it is necessary to construct tokens of the words. Each lexical entry contains an attribute NXT whose value is the number last used in a subscripted token of that word. The token is constructed by exploding the word and concatenating its letters with NXT + 1, then NXT is incremented in readiness for the next token. In the event that a token

---

[1] M. Kavenaugh Smith constructed such a compiling function early in 1976.

of the word already exists in the discourse, for example BALLOON1, then if the word is a noun not modified by such terms as OTHER, that token is used. (No complete solution is available for decision as to when to make a new token and when to use an old.)

When pronouns are encountered in the text, the function ANTEC is used to find some previous token agreeing in case, number, and gender with the pronoun. This function can be written easily for any simple text such as MARGIE, but generally the question of finding antecedents for pronouns and for discovering previous references is one of the areas that is beyond the present state of the art.

## 3.0 GENERATING ENGLISH FROM CASE PREDICATES

An analysis of the parsing rules described in the previous section showed us that they contain exactly the information required to generate the English constituents that they describe. This information is the correspondence of case names with syntactic forms.[2] Let us select from Fig. 1 the S rules

$$(S(NP\ VP)(\ldots)(2\ AGT\ 1))$$
$$(S(NP\ VP)(\ldots)(2\ INSTR\ 1))$$

and the semantic predicate

(CATCH1 INSTR WIND1 TH BALLOON1 TENSE PAST)

A two-argument function, GENerator, is called:

(GEN S CATCH1)

This function takes the transformation portion of the first S rule (2 AGT 1), binds "2" to the predicate CATCH1, attempts to match AGT to the predicate, and fails. It then repeats the process with the second S rule and succeeds in matching INSTR to the predicate, and so it recursively calls

(GEN NP WIND1) and (GEN VP CATCH1).

The generation of an NP by the following rule from Fig. 2

(NP(ART NP1) (...) (2 DET 1))

leads to

---

[2] For this kind of sentence generation where semantic predicates contain tokens of words the semantic constraints are not needed. For generation from deep conceptual structures, they would help select appropriate words.

(GEN ART THE) and (GEN NP1 WIND1)

which result in the string (THE WIND), and processing continues with the (GEN VP CATCH1) to eventuate in the sentence THE WIND CAUGHT THE BALLOON.

At first glance this symmetry of the rules appears to be an excitingly serendipitous side effect of the design of the parsing system. It may in fact be of importance but difficulties can arise if the transformations are allowed to contain arbitrary functions and constants other than case-names. The following two rules that are acceptable to the parser, impose difficulties for the generator:

(NP(ART NP1) (. . .) (2 DET DEF))
(NP(POSSPRON NP1) (. . .) (2 R2*(OWN R1 (ANTEC 1))))

In the (2 DET DEF) transform, we have to infer that the first element of the syntactic list is the one that is to generate the word corresponding to DEF. This is easy for binary rules and increasingly difficult for the n-ary form. In the second NP rule above, the transform is designed to map such strings as HER THING into (THING R2* (OWN R1 MARGIE)).[4] Discovering the "1" in the transformation in order to call (GEN POSSPRON THNG) is quite difficult in binary rules and increasingly so in n-ary forms. These difficulties can be surmounted by limiting the form of the transformation portion of the rule and by moving functions into the semantic constraint portion.

A second consideration is the fact that in using a generator, for example to generate reponses to questions, it may be awkward to access the large grammar required for parsing, when only 20 or so rules will in fact suffice to express the answers in a straight-forward subset of English. So although the grammar may be constrained to symmetry, it may still be desirable to select only a small subset for some tasks.

In our experience with generating English reponses from our question-answering system, rules in the form of 2-tuples were used:

(PHRASENAME (LIST OF FORMS))

Some examples will clarify the nature of the forms:

(S((AGT NP)VP) ((INSTR NP)VP) ((TH NP)VPAS))
(NP (DET NP) (MOD NP) (* PP) *)
(VP (VSTRNG COMPL))
(VSTRNG (AUX VSTRNG) *)
(COMPL ((TH NP) COMPL) ((TO PP)COMPL). . .#)

---

[4] Equiv to (OWN R1 MARGIE R2 THING). In general CASENAME* is the reverse pointing arc, for the casename.

In each form, the first element is either a list containing a casename and a syntactic phrasename, e.g., (AGT NP), or it is a phrasename, e.g., (VSTRNG ... ). The second element of a form is a phrasename. Two distinguished forms are "*" and "#"; the first of these signifies that the head of the semantic predicate is to be realized as a word, the second signifies that a null representation is acceptable. The set of forms associated with a phrasename are alternate ways of generating the phrase. It should be noted that the rules are recursive.

The generator for producing English applies a rule to a predicate in the fashion described earlier, resulting in recursive calls to generate new phrases until it reaches a terminal element, i.e., a wordclass instead of a phrasename. It then calls a function MORPH, which develops the appropriately inflected English word.

It must be remarked that both the generation grammar and the network of semantic predicates have many cycles. The generator must guard itself against infinite recursion of both rules and predicates, and so debugging the GEN function was not easy.

## 4.0 COMPUTING CAUSAL ORGANIZATION

Rumelhart's Margie story was selected to illustrate the use of rule forms because it represents a reasonably simple set of causally connected actions that have been analyzed in the form of a story grammar by Rumelhart. The story can also be analyzed as a temporal and causal succession of states such as those used in robotics work. Figure 4 displays a graph showing abbreviated semantic predicates and the states that enable them and that they enable. ENABLE is an arc that can connect any two predicates — actions or states — providing the first predicate precedes the second in time, and is a necessary or sufficient condition for the second. Thus, (MARGIE LOC BALLOON) is a necessary preconditon for (HOLD AGT MARGIE TH BALLOON), which itself is a sufficient precondition for (MARGIE CONTACT BALLOON). ENABLE is transitive and it implies BEFORE; so (X ENABLE (Y ENABLE Z)) allows us to infer (X ENABLE Z) and (X BEFORE Z).

The importance of finding causal chains has been discussed by Schank [Schank75a], who shows how a summary can be computed by extracting a main line of causality from a story. Van Dijk [vanDijk75] and Rumelhart offer deletion rules to construct summaries from comparable structures. Most of the hard inferences in question answering tasks require analysis of causal relations.

The causal organization of Fig. 4 can be computed with the aid of the set of inference rules shown in Fig. 5. The principle of these rules is that every action is characterized by a set of PREconditions and a set of POSTconditions. The rules are defined over variables X, Y, Z.

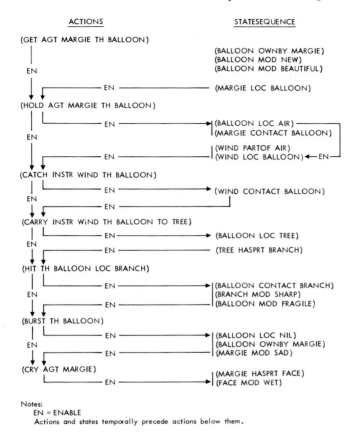

ACTIONS

(GET AGT MARGIE TH BALLOON)

EN

STATESEQUENCE

(BALLOON OWNBY MARGIE)
(BALLOON MOD NEW)
(BALLOON MOD BEAUTIFUL)

EN — (MARGIE LOC BALLOON)

(HOLD AGT MARGIE TH BALLOON)

EN — (BALLOON LOC AIR)
(MARGIE CONTACT BALLOON)

EN

EN — (WIND PARTOF AIR)
(WIND LOC BALLOON) ← EN

(CATCH INSTR WIND TH BALLOON)

EN — (WIND CONTACT BALLOON)

EN

EN

(CARRY INSTR WIND TH BALLOON TO TREE)

EN — (BALLOON LOC TREE)

EN

EN — (TREE HASPRT BRANCH)

(HIT TH BALLOON LOC BRANCH)

EN — (BALLOON CONTACT BRANCH)
(BRANCH MOD SHARP)

EN

EN — (BALLOON MOD FRAGILE)

(BURST TH BALLOON)

EN — (BALLOON LOC NIL)
(BALLOON OWNBY MARGIE)

EN

EN — (MARGIE MOD SAD)

(CRY AGT MARGIE)

EN — (MARGIE HASPRT FACE)
(FACE MOD WET)

Notes:
   EN = ENABLE
   Actions and states temporally precede actions below them.

Fig. 4. Some causal structure for Margie's balloon.

For each possible argument pattern of an action predicate, a different rule may be defined. In Fig. 5 the pattern (CATCH INSTR X TH Y) is defined; another pattern could be (CATCH AGT X TH Y). PREconditins for this pattern would include (X WANT Y) as well as (X LOC Y). Similarly (HOLD AGT X TH Y) includes the precondition, (X WANT Y) as would an entry for (GET AGT X TH Y). The rules of Fig. 5 are applied to the list of predicates shown in Fig. 1 (after the application of rules to convert from TENSE sequences to the BEFORE and AFTER relations that connect the predicates) to produce a discourse structure equivalent to that shown in Fig. 4. The first semantic predicate is matched against the set of rules; if a rule fits, the values of the predicate's arguments are substituted throughout the rule for the variables.

(HOLD AGT X TH Y)
 PRE ((X WANT Y)(GET AGT X TH Y)(X CONTACT Y))
 POST ((X CONTACT Y))

(CATCH INSTR X TH Y)
 PRE ((X LOC Y))
 POST ((X CONTACT Y))

(CARRY INSTR X TH Y TO Z)
 PRE ((X CONTACT Y))
 POST ((Y LOC Z))

(HIT INSTR X TH Y)
 PRE ((X LOC Y))
 POST ((X CONTACT Y))

(X CONTACT Y)
 PRE ((X LOC Y))
 POST ((X CONTACT Y))

(BURST TH X)
 PRE ((X CONTACT Y)(X MOD FRAGILE)(Y MOD SHARP))
 POST ((X LOC NIL))

(CRY AGT X)
 PRE ((X HASPRT FACE)(X MOD SAD))
 POST ((FACT MOD WET))

(X MOD SAD)
 PRE ((X OWN Y)(Y LOC NIL))

Fig. 5. Rules for computing pre- and postconditions.

Thus,

(HOLD1 AGT MARGIE1 TH BALLOON1)

matches

(HOLD AGT X TH Y).

The pre- and postconditions of the rule are bound as follows:

PRE (MARGIE1 WANT BALLOON1) (GET AGT MARGIE1 TH BALLOON1)
 (MARGIE CONTACT BALLOON1)
POST (MARGIE CONTACT BALLOON1)

At this point each precondition is matched against the discourse context (DCX); if the DCX is empty the precondition is asserted in the DCX; if the precondition directly matches a predicate in the DCX an ENABLE arc is created between the matching predicate and the action predicate that was bound to the rule. If there is no direct match, (as would be the case in comparing (A LOC B) and (A CONTACT B)) inference rules are attempted. Thus from Fig. 5, we find (X CONTACT Y) PRE (X LOC Y), and so (A CONTACT B) implies (A LOC B). Finally if no match can be inferred, the preconditions are asserted with ENABLE arcs to their action predicate. In every case the postconditions are then asserted in the DCX. In the event of no match, even though the predicate's preconditions are asserted as enabling the predicate, there is no further connection to preceding predicates and the causal chain is in fact broken, although some later predicate may reconnect it.

Alfred Correira has written a concise procedure to accomplish this computation from these rules and at this writing it works satisfactorily for the MARGIE story. The problem, however, is much deeper than the treatment presented here. The entire literature of frames, scripts, and story grammars is relevant, [D.G. Bobrow75b, Charniak76, Schank75b] and we must carry this form of rule much farther in order to account for such large units of inferential meaning as "birthday party," "trading voyage," "storm-at-sea," "supermarket," or "going-to-a-restaurant."


## 5.0 DISCUSSION AND CONCLUSIONS

The parsing, generation, and causal organizing systems that have been described are each examples of the class of translating systems. Each translator is given an input graph and a set of rules with which it computes an output graph; the parser and its rules map from English strings to semantic predicates, the generator maps from semantic predicates to strings, and the causal organizer maps from predicates to predicates.

Generally, given an input graph and a set of rules a translator computes a corresponding output graph. Thus a translator is a function of two arguments,

(TRANSLATOR INPUT-GRAPH, RULES) = OUTPUT-GRAPH

If we think of a language in extension as a set of 3-tuples:

L = ((INPUT-GRAPH-1 RULE-SET-1 OUTPUT-GRAPH-1)
    (INPUT-GRAPH-2 RULE-SET-2 OUTPUT-GRAPH-2)

    . . .

    (INPUT-GRAPH-n RULE-SET-n OUTPUT-GRAPH-n))

then a general translating function can be defined that given any two elements from a 3-tuple of L, will compute the third. Particular translation functions for parsing, generation, question-answering, etc., are very common in the natural language literature, but only a few examples currently exist for computing the rule system or grammar when given the input and output graphs. (See for examples Klein and Kuppin [Klein72], Harris [Harris72], and Hayes-Roth [F. Hayes-Roth76c].)

The importance of this conception is that it illuminates a method that humans use to define the rule-sets for translating output graphs. Refer again to Fig. 2 for an example of accumulating a grammar in this way. In making such a system of parsing rules, the first step is to select the input set of English sentences, then define the desired output structure, then write the rules that accomplish the transformation. In defining a system of rules for computing various types of causal organization, the method is similar. For a particular set of semantic predicates, the desired causal organization is defined and the rules that map the predicates into the causal organization can be written. A common flaw in preparation of such rule-sets or grammars is that the desired output graph is only dimly apprehended, with the consequence that the grammar is undefinable, or its output is unsatisfactory.

The search for useful representations of meaning that has characterized natural language research throughout its 20-year history reveals that there are many constraints on the form and content of output graphs that determine whether they will be useful for a given purpose. In Section 4, a particular causal organization was defined for the Margie story. Although it is useful for question-answering and for computing summaries, no claim was made that it is "the right one." In fact it defines only a causal chain, while what is needed is a hierarchical causal organization. For example, the verb PROPEL has the substates CATCH, MOVE, and HIT and the hierarchical causal organization of the story should include the fact that Margie's holding of the balloon ENABLEs the wind to PROPEL the balloon into a tree ENABLEs the balloon to burst. Such a hierarchical causal structure would require less computation to produce summaries than the causal chain structure.

I believe, in the final analysis, the definition of appropriate meaning representations, i.e., output graphs, is determined by the suitability of the output structure for its purpose. Semantic case predicates (semantic networks) have evolved as an excellent structure in which to encode aspects of the meaning of English statements for the purposes of question-answering, deeper causal analysis, and generation of natural language output. If we know suitable instances of the pairing of some input graphs, say English sentences, with output graph forms such as semantic predicates, then the necessary content of the rule forms is implied and the content for a given syntax of rule forms can be computed by a person or, eventually, by a computer.

# Multilevel Systems and Complexity

# A PRODUCTION SYSTEM FOR SPEECH UNDERSTANDING

David Jack Mostow
*Carnegie-Mellon University*[1]

Frederick Hayes-Roth
*The Rand Corporation*

*A production system was developed for syntactic and semantic processing within the Hearsay-II speech understanding system. The major properties of the system are discussed, including (1) conversion of static language descriptions into productions, (2) compilation and data-directed execution of productions, (3) dynamically modifiable thresholds on goodness of pattern matches, (4) partial matching, and (5) representation and integration of bottom-up, top-down, and horizontal searches. Several weaknesses of the production system paradigm in this application appeared during the course of this research. These arose from (1) the arbitrariness of canonical decompositions of patterns into subpatterns, (2) insufficient use of contextually confirming evidence for individual hypotheses due to the narrowness (literality) of monitored conditions, and (3) difficulty in evaluating the varying import of the same generic action in different contexts. Thus, while the uniformity and lack of explicit organization of production systems are touted as their most desirable features, attendant difficulties of dynamically organizing and controlling coherent problem solutions must be seriously considered in problem domains requiring careful allocation of computational resources.*

## 1.0 INTRODUCTION

In a speech understanding system, syntactic and semantic knowl-

[1] This work was supported in part by the Defense Advanced Research Projects Agency under contract no. F44620-73-C-0074 and monitored by the Air Force Office of Scientific Research. In addition, the first author was partially supported by a National Science Foundation Graduate Fellowship.

*471*

edge is used to choose among alternative lexical transcriptions of a spoken interval and to fill in unrecognized words. The data to which such knowledge is applied can be represented graphically as in Fig. 1. The chart in Fig. 1 shows the output of the Hearsay-II word recognizer [A.R. Smith76] in response to the utterance TELL ME ABOUT BEEF. In the chart, time proceeds from left to right and is measured in centiseconds elapsed since the beginning of the utterance. Words are distributed vertically according to the confidence with which they are recognized. For a typical utterance, the word recognizer hypothesizes 20 incorrect words in the same time interval as each correct word, 4 of them with higher confidence ratings. Of the correct words 20% are not hypothesized at all.

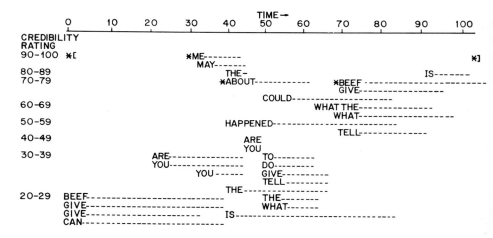

Fig. 1. Words hypothesized bottom-up in response to utterance TELL ME ABOUT BEEF. "*" marks correct hypothesis; "[" and "]" denote hypothesized beginning and end of utterance.

These data represent the task environment of Hearsay-II's syntax and semantics knowledge source module (SASS). Figure 2 shows the words hypothesized by SASS on the basis of the information shown in Fig. 1. Note that SASS predicts many incorrect words in addition to the correct word TELL. This happens because (1) SASS's predictions are based on errorful data, and (2) when several words are grammatically plausible in a recognized context, SASS hypothesizes all of them.

The words hypothesized by SASS are rated by Hearsay-II's word verifier [McKeown77]. Words that are verified (i.e., given high confidence ratings) are included in the data used for making further predictions and transcribing the utterance. Since the number of alternative

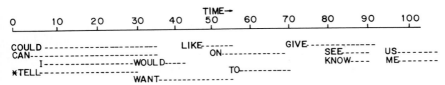

Fig. 2. Words predicted by SASS on the basis of the hypotheses shown in Fig. 1.

transcriptions is a combinatorial function of the number of recognized words, SASS must find the highest-rated grammatical (syntactically and semantically plausible) transcription.

Our experience with a production system implementation of SASS should be of interest to researchers who contemplate using production systems to solve other problems involving incomplete, uncertain information, or who are interested in the problems of controlling large production systems (i.e., containing several thousand productions).

## 2.0 A PRODUCTION SYSTEM APPROACH

### 2.1 Knowledge

Grammatical knowledge in HEARSAY-II is supplied by a case frame grammar describing expected types of utterances. For example, the case frame, or *semantic template* $GIVE $ME $RE $TOPICS describes a typical query in the subset of English understood by Hearsay-II, as shown in Table 1. Each sequential constituent of a template is either a word or another template representing a set of words and phrases. The sequence template $GIVE $ME $RE $TOPICS is itself an element of the class $QUERY. One utterance that matches this template is the earlier example TELL ME ABOUT BEEF. The present grammar contains about 200 templates and has a 1000-word vocabulary.

Table 1

Fragment of Hearsay-II Grammar

Knowledge

$QUERY ::= $GIVE $ME $RE $TOPICS
$GIVE ::= TELL | GIVE | SHOW
$ME ::= ME | US
$RE ::= ABOUT | CONCERNING | ON
$TOPICS ::= $TOPICS $CONJUNCTION $TOPICS | $FOOD | $POLITICS
$CONJUNCTION ::= AND | OR
$FOOD ::= BEEF

## 2.2 Production Types

Given grammatical knowledge of this sort, SASS must somehow use it to identify the spoken utterance among a large number of incorrect word hypotheses. Several types of knowledge-based behavior are used in this process.

The first, called *recognition*, identifies occurrences of grammatical templates in the data. For example, the word ME is recognized as an instance of the template $ME, the word ABOUT is recognized as an instance of $RE, and the word BEEF is recognized as an instance of $FOOD and hence of $TOPICS. The temporally adjacent instances of $RE and $TOPICS are then recognized as an instance of the sequence $RE $TOPICS.

A second behavior, called *prediction*, attempts to extend recognized grammatical patterns by hypothesizing contextually plausible constituents. For example, $GIVE is predicted in the temporal interval preceding a recognized instance of $ME.

A third behavior, called *respelling*, performs a type of goal reduction by enumerating the constituents of predicted templates. For example, the predicted $GIVE is respelled into the words GIVE, SHOW, and TELL, which can then be matched against the phonetic data by the word verifier. If the correct word TELL is rated credible by the word verifier, it can be recognized by SASS as an instance of $GIVE.

The fourth behavior, *postdiction*, boosts the credibility ratings of contextually consistent pattern constituents. Postdiction can be thought of as "prediction after the fact." For example, after the word TELL is recognized with a weak credibility rating, it can be postdicted by a preexisting expectation for $GIVE, which increases its credibility rating. The improved rating of TELL may enable SASS to recognize it as an instance of $GIVE. Thus postdiction provides a way to filter the recognition of weakly credible words so that only those which are contextually plausible are recognized.

In SASS, these four behaviors correspond to different types of condition-action productions. The condition of each production describes the circumstances in which the action is applicable. The action typically involves hypothesizing an instance of a template. In addition, each production has a *strength* between 0 and 100 measuring its reliability, i.e., the conditional likelihood that the result generated is correct given that the production condition is satisfied by correct data. The productions are generated automatically from the grammar by a program called CVSNET (Convert Semantic Net). The generated production system is nonadaptive in that all productions are generated a priori, rather than dynamically as needed during the analysis of each utterance. Some of the productions used to understand the example utterance TELL ME ABOUT BEEF are listed below. The condition precedes the arrow; the type of hypothesis to be created or supported follows the arrow and is followed by the appropriate action and its specific strength.

```
ME → $ME <RECOGNIZE (100)>
ABOUT → $RE <RECOGNIZE (100)>
BEEF → $FOOD <RECOGNIZE (100)>
$FOOD → $TOPICS <RECOGNIZE (100)>
$RE & $TOPICS → $RE+$TOPICS <IF ADJACENT
        THEN RECOGNIZE 100)>
$ME → $GIVE <PREDICT!LEFT (50)>
$GIVE → TELL <RESPELL (33)>
```

TELL ← $GIVE <POSTDICT (33)>

(This rule is shown with a reversed arrow because its effect is to modify (boost the rating of) an hypothesis for TELL on the basis of an existing expectation for $GIVE.)

TELL → $GIVE <RECOGNIZE (100)>

(This rule differs from the preceding one in that it creates an hypothesis for $GIVE based on the recognition of TELL.)

```
$GIVE & $ME → $GIVE+ME <IF ADJACENT THEN
        RECOGNIZE (100)>
```

## 2.3 Production System Characteristics

It is enlightening to consider the capabilities of this problem-solving system as a function of the (nonadaptive) production system architecture. This architecture is based on the premise that the situations appropriate for the various problem-solving actions defined above can be adequately described by a finite set of predetermined condition patterns. In the present domain this premise is invalid, as explained later.

The production system generated from the grammar is capable of the following behavior:

(1) It can recognize (parse) any sequence of recognized words instantiating a template (nonterminal) in the grammar. In particular, it can parse any grammatical utterance (sentential form).

(2) It can hypothesize the grammatical word neighbors of any instantiated template, by means of prediction and respelling.

(3) It can adduce additional (postdictive) support for contextually consistent templates instantiated in adjacent time intervals, as well as certain words and phrases that are semantically predictable. Semantic

predictions based on previous discourse [F. Hayes-Roth77c] or on recognized templates apply to the entire utterance rather than to a specific time interval. For example, the recognition of the utterance I AM INTERESTED IN FOOD justifies the prediction that $FOOD will be instantiated in the subsequent utterance. This prediction contributes postdictive support to the rating of the recognized word BEEF.

## 3.0 EXECUTION AND CONTROL

The preceding production system description leaves two aspects undefined: retrieval of applicable productions and conflict resolution between competing productions.

### 3.1 Retrieval

The feasibility of a production system implementation of SASS depends on the efficiency of the method used for dynamically identifying which productions are applicable to which data. The straightforward production system method matches each production against all the data during the recognize phase of each recognize-act cycle. This method is infeasible for SASS because of the number of productions (several thousand) and the amount of data (most of it incorrect).

Efficient retrieval of applicable productions is accomplished by embedding all production conditions in an *automatically compilable recognition network* (ACORN) that factors out common subexpressions [F. Hayes-Roth75]. An ACORN is a change-driven recognition network that generalizes the Pandemonium concept to enable general structured pattern recognition [F. Hayes-Roth76b]. Each node in the network corresponds to a template (or subtemplate) in the grammar and maintains a list of all existing instantiations of that template. Whenever a new instantiation of the template is created, this node is activated, and each production citing the template in its condition is retrieved. (The node contains a list of these productions.) The remainder of each condition is then evaluated by examining the existing instantiations of the other templates mentioned in the condition to find any combinations of instantiations satisfying the condition.

To simplify this task, all productions have at most two templates in their condition. This useful property is achieved by transforming the grammar in CVSNET before generating productions. CVSNET adds new templates corresponding to subsequences of existing sequence templates, and redefines the latter in terms of the former so that all sequence templates have length two. The resulting grammar is said to be in *template normal form* [F. Hayes-Roth75]. For instance, the template $GIVE $ME $RE $TOPICS is redefined as the sequence of new templates \$GIVE+\$ME \$RE+\$TOPICS, and is recognized by the productions

\$GIVE & \$ME → \$GIVE+\$ME <IF ADJACENT THEN
    RECOGNIZE (100)>
\$RE & \$TOPICS → \$RE+\$TOPICS <IF ADJACENT THEN
    RECOGNIZE (100)>
\$GIVE+\$ME & \$RE+\$TOPICS → \$GIVE+\$ME+\$RE+\$TOPICS
    <IF ADJACENT THEN RECOGNIZE (100)>

## 3.2 Search Space

Once the relevant productions have been retrieved, SASS must choose which ones to execute. The importance of this choice can be appreciated by considering the task of SASS as a search problem. The search space is the combinatorially large set of sequences of hypothesized words. A (partial) solution consists of a grammatical sequence spanning (part of) the utterance. The search strategy is to identify possible partial solutions and combine them hierarchically into a complete solution (i.e., a parse). Since the search space is generally incomplete, it must be extended by predicting words that may be present but were not hypothesized bottom-up. Such prediction expands the search space by a combinatorial degree corresponding to the number of words predicted. The number of plausible predictions in a given recognized context is called the *branching factor*. Clearly, the implicative strength (reliability) of a prediction is inversely related to its branching factor. This relationship is used by CVSNET to estimate production strength.

## 3.3 Thresholds

To keep the search space manageable, it is necessary to control its initial size and to restrict its growth. Accordingly, the search space is defined to contain only those words rated higher than a minimum validity threshold. This threshold value is dynamically modifiable and location-specific to reflect the variations in data quality between different utterances and between different temporal regions of the same utterance. Predictive expansion of the search space is controlled by thresholds on validity of predictors, conditional strength of predictions, and likelihood of prediction correctness. Thus the decision whether to execute a production depends both on pattern-match confidence (the overall validity of the data satisfying the production condition) and on the importance of the result. Pattern-match goodness also depends on the degree of satisfaction of flexible constraints, such as fuzzy temporal adjacency.

A focus-of-attention mechanism described elsewhere [F. Hayes-Roth76g] manipulates these thresholds so as to control the size, shape, and growth of the search space. Since lowering a threshold may necessitate reconsideration of previously rejected productions, the production retrieval mechanism must respond to threshold changes as well as to data changes. This is accomplished roughly as follows. Whenever a production is rejected for failing a threshold test, the data instantiating the production condition are marked with the type of threshold failed. If this threshold is subsequently relaxed in the temporal region containing the data, the ACORN nodes instantiated by the data are reactivated, and the appropriate production is retrieved.

### 3.4 Scheduling

Further control of processing is achieved by executing instantiated productions in order of priority. The numerical priority of an instantiated production should estimate the expected usefulness of the result produced by executing it. A result is useful [F. Hayes-Roth76g] to the extent that it is: (1) *reliable*, likely to be correct; (2) *necessary*, unlikely to duplicate an existing result; (3) *relevant*, likely to contribute toward the overall understanding of the utterance.

Thus the usefulness of executing a production depends not only on the data instantiating it but also on global, dynamically changing properties of the data. Hence the simple conflict resolution schemes typical of many production systems, e.g., production ordering and data recency [J. McDermott77b], are inadequate to implement the complex priority scheduling required. Therefore priorities, instead of being defined a priori, are assigned by a central scheduling mechanism [F. Hayes-Roth76g] based on a global model of the state of the search. Priorities are recomputed periodically to reflect changes in that state.

The separation of production system control from the production system itself is a significant methodological advantage. Such a separation makes it possible to explore, evaluate, and compare different search strategies, search models, and priority schemes without modifying the production system.

### 4.0 COMBINATORIAL EXPLOSION

The production system architecture proved inadequate to perform SASS's task. Since the set of production conditions was finite and precomputed, and the conditions were matched on an all-or-none basis, the production system could only recognize certain types of grammatical patterns for use as predictors. Specifically, these patterns (word sequences) corresponded to completely matched templates in the grammar. Although the data often contained grammatical sequences several words long (e.g., ME ABOUT BEEF, Fig. 1), which would have made highly reliable predictors, these sequences seldom corresponded to complete templates and hence could not be detected by the precomputed production conditions. Instead, subsequences (e.g., ME) corresponding to lower-level templates ($ME) were used most frequently as predictors. These subsequences were usually only one or two words in length, and from SASS's viewpoint appeared no more reliable as predictors than the large number of incorrect one- and two-word sequences. To fill in the unrecognized words, it was necessary to make many incorrect predictions along with the correct ones. The execution of an excessive number of unreliable productions tended to explode the search space combinatorially.

In short, SASS was able to recognize only those patterns corresponding to the templates of the grammar and their canonically but arbitrarily decomposed subtemplates. SASS's consequent inability to recognize the most reliable data patterns in a set of incomplete, errorful data caused a combinatorial explosion of unreliable inference activity.

## 5.0 NEW SOLUTION

The cause of the combinatorial explosion was SASS's inability to recognize the most credible data patterns, i.e., those subsets of data that could be integrated into consistent interpretations and that satisfied a maximum number of constraints unlikely to be satisfied by random data. In order to remedy this inability, it is necessary to recognize partial instantiations of templates. Since it is infeasible to precompute recognition productions for every possible partial instantiation of every template, partial-matching of templates must be performed. The most credible partial matches can then be extended by predicting and verifying grammatically consistent adjacent words.

Thus efficient partial-matching is a fundamental problem in the current task domain. Because of the large number of templates and the amount of incorrect data, it is not practical to match every template "top-down" against all the data. An alternative method is to allow the execution of recognition productions whose conditions are only partly satisfied. This method (which was tried and rejected) leads to a combinatorial explosion of partial-matching activity, since each word partial-matches many templates and many incorrect words are partial-matched. Moreover, many inferior matches (short sequences) are identified along with the desired best matches, which is a waste of computation.

The new, non-production-system syntax and semantics module

solves the partial matching problem by using a cheap filter to detect potential good partial matches, i.e., word sequences that are likely to be good matches. The word sequence filter (WOSEQ) finds highly rated sequences of pairwise language-adjacent (grammatically consistent) words [Lesser77]. A pair of words is language-adjacent if it occurs in some grammatical utterance. Language adjacency information is pre-computed from the grammar and stored in a boolean matrix for fast retrieval. Since the sequences found by WOSEQ are only pairwise grammatical, they must be parsed to determine whether they are in fact grammatical. WOSEQ makes partial-matching efficient by greatly reducing the number of word sequences that must be parsed. Parsing is done by searching a graph representation of the grammar.

Grammatical sequences are extended by predicting and verifying their grammatical word neighbors, found by another graph search. A sequence is extended word-by-word until it spans the utterance or becomes blocked, i.e., has no verifiable grammatically consistent word neighbors. The global scheduling mechanism described earlier decides at each point in the analysis which sequence to extend next.

## 6.0 IMPLICATIONS FOR PRODUCTION SYSTEM THEORY AND APPLICATIONS

Our experience with the production system version of SASS has clarified some issues affecting the applicability of production systems in general. This section discusses the properties of a task that make it amenable to production system solution and then shows how the SASS task, among others, lacks some of these properties.

### 6.1 Production System Applicability

To be appropriate for execution by a nonadaptive production system, a computational task must have certain characteristics. (1) The computation must consist of a sequence of actions drawn from some fixed set. (2) The applicability conditions of each action must be economically expressible by a predetermined boolean combination of properties of the computational state. (3) The sequence of actions should be unpredictable a priori due to the richness of possible behaviors appropriate to different data; if this is not the case, cheaper control structures (e.g., sequential execution and iteration) are more appropriate. Finally, (4) the usefulness of applying a condition-action production should depend only on the credibility of the data matching the condition, the closeness of this match if the match is inexact, and the relative import of the action. All of these must be computable locally, i.e., independent of outside context.

## 6.2 Violators of the Presumed Problem Characteristics

Several tasks, including SASS's, have characteristics violating some of these properties. (1) The interesting conditions for the SASS task cannot be expressed economically as finite boolean expressions. (2) The significance of an action depends on context external to the data satisfying the condition justifying the action. Finally, (3) since the SASS task involves only two basic kinds of actions (partial matching and prediction), the right-hand sides of the productions lose their practical interest. One highly touted property of production systems is their modular specification of which actions to perform under different conditions; when there are only two basic actions, this property loses much of its appeal.

## 7.0 CONCLUSION

The unsuitability of the pure production system architecture for SASS-like parsing and tasks with similar characteristics derives from its limitations in detecting and evaluating interesting conditions. Specifically, the static encoding of interesting conditions in the production conditions is inadequate to capture the dynamically most interesting conditions. It appears that this inadequacy can be remedied only by introducing a pattern-matching mechanism that can integrate and evaluate configurations of data dynamically. Whether the introduction of such a mechanism signifies the abandonment of the production system framework or simply its enrichment is merely a matter of terminology.

## ACKNOWLEDGMENTS

WOSEQ was designed and implemented by Rick Hayes-Roth, Victor Lesser, and Mark Birnbaum. The partial-parser was designed and implemented by Rick Hayes-Roth, Lee Erman, and Mark Fox. Several useful clarifications were suggested by the referee.

# RULE-BASED UNDERSTANDING OF SIGNALS[1]

H. Penny Nii and Edward A. Feigenbaum
*Stanford University*

*SU/X and SU/P are knowledge-based programs that employ pattern-invoked inference methods. Both tasks are concerned with the interpretation of large quantities of digitized signal data. The task of SU/X is to understand "continuous signals," that is, signals that persist over time. The task of SU/P is to interpret protein X-ray crystallographic data. Some features of the design are (1) incremental interpretation of data employing many different pattern-invoked sources of knowledge, (2) production rule representation of knowledge, including high-level strategy knowledge, (3) "opportunistic" hypothesis formation using both data-driven and model-driven techniques within a general hypothesize-and-test paradigm, and (4) multilevel representation of the solution hypothesis.*

## 1.0 INTRODUCTION AND SUMMARY

This chapter describes a design of knowledge-based programs that employ pattern-invoked inference methods. Domain and strategy knowledge are represented as production rules to be invoked when appropriate situations arise in the problem-solving process. The same basic design philosophy is utilized in two task domains, both of which are concerned with the interpretation of large volumes of digitized physical signals. The tasks are (1) the understanding of continuous signals produced by objects and (2) the interpretation of protein X-ray crystallographic data in terms of a three-dimensional model of the molecule. The programs associated with these tasks are called SU/X and SU/P, respectively.

[1] This work was supported by the Department of Defense, Advanced Research Project Agency, ARPA Contract DAHC15-73-6-0435.

*483*

Some of the design concepts in SU/X and SU/P are rooted in the HEARSAY-II program [Erman75, F. Hayes-Roth76g, Lesser75]. Concepts that have been borrowed are (a) a global data base, called the blackboard, for the integration of knowledge sources and (b) a multilevel representation of the solution hypotheses. These basic concepts are integrated into a system design that emphasizes (a) the representation of knowledge in production rules, (b) the representation of the control structure as sources of knowledge related to problem-solving methods and strategies, (c) the capability of the program to explain its reasoning steps, and (d) a level of generality of the basic design concepts leading to application in different tasks or domains.

### 1.1 Major Themes

The "understanding" of physical signals often requires using information not present in the signal data themselves. Examples of such information are (a) in the continuous-signal problem, the characteristics of the signal-producing objects, (b) in the protein-modeling problem, the amino acid sequence and the stereochemical and protein chemistry constraints. Each such source of knowledge may at any time provide an inference that serves as a basis for another knowledge source to make yet another inference, and so on, until all relevant information has been used and appropriate inferences have been drawn.

Essential to the operation of the program is its *model* of the developing hypothesis. The model is a symbol-structure that is built and maintained by the program, contains what is known about the unfolding situation, and thus provides a context for the ongoing analysis. The model is used as a reference for the interpretation of new information, assimilation of new events, and generation of expectations concerning future events. It is the program's "cognitive flywheel."

SU/X and SU/P are "knowledge-based" programs.[2] Their powers are largely derived from the knowledge given to them by "expert" human analysts and/or "expert" algorithms. Major problems in the design of such systems show up vividly in these two programs:

(a) *Knowledge acquisition.* This is a task of systematically ferreting out the informal and semiformal knowledge held by the expert. The breadth and sheer volume of an expert's knowledge is what makes his analysis general and powerful; yet, obtaining that knowl-

---

[2] SU/X was implemented in the context of a military signal-understanding application. It is a large INTERLISP program that performed well on a variety of complex signal-interpretation tasks within the domain. SU/P, also written in INTERLISP, is under development.

edge, which he often does not realize he is using, is a painstaking and inexact process.

(b) *Knowledge representation*. Having acquired the knowledge in its "human" form, we must represent it in a form that is convenient and efficient for machine processing and at the same time reasonably "natural" (bear in mind that the knowledge rarely boils down merely to a set of numbers), a difficult and time-consuming task.

(c) *Integration of multiple, diverse sources of knowledge*. Program and information structures must be created by which the various kinds of knowledge can "work together" to form a coherent and accurate hypothesis. When the knowledge exists at many different levels of abstraction and aggregation (say, from alpha-helix substructure all the way down to electron density values in an electron density map), one has a major design problem.

## 1.2 Major Terms and Concepts

The task of "understanding" the data is accomplished at various *levels of analysis*. These levels are exhibited in Fig. 1a for the continuous-signal interpretation problem and in Fig. 1b for the protein-modeling problem. The most integrated—the highest—levels for the two problems involve the description of the signal-producing objects, and the three-dimensional model of the protein. The lowest levels, that is, the levels closest to the data, consist of the line features derived from the signal data, and the atoms and their coordinates in three-space.

At each level, the units of analysis are the *hypothesis elements*. These are symbol-structures that summarize what the available evidence indicates in terms that are meaningful at that particular level.

Bridging between the levels of analysis are *sources of knowledge* [Erman75, Lesser75]. A knowledge source (KS) is capable of putting forth the *inference* that some hypothesis elements present at its "input" level imply some particular hypothesis elements(s) at its "output" level. A source of knowledge contains not only the knowledge necessary for making its own specialized inferences, but also the knowledge necessary for checking the inferences made by other sources of knowledge. The inferences that draw together hypothesis elements at one level into a hypothesis element at a higher level (or that operate in the other direction) are represented symbolically as links between levels (See Figs. 1a and 1b). The resulting network, rooted in the input data and integrated at the highest level into a description of the hypothesized problem solution, is called the *current best hypothesis*, or *the hypothesis* for short. Each source of knowledge holds a considerable body of specialized information that a human expert would generally consider "ordinary." Sometimes this is rela-

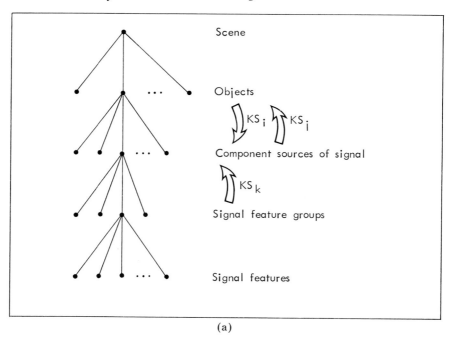

(a)

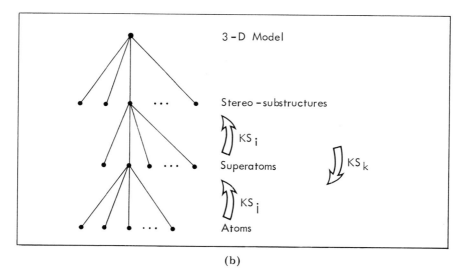

(b)

Fig. 1. (a) Hypothesis structure (SU/X)* (b) Hypothesis structure (SU/P)*
*The nodes represent hypothesis elements. The arrows represent KSs which infer
hypothesis element(s) on one level from hypothesis elements on another level.

tively "hard" knowledge or "textbook" knowledge. Also represented are the *heuristics,* that is, "rules of good guessing" a human expert develops in his area of expertise. These "judgmental" rules are generally accompanied by estimates from human experts concerning the *weight* that each rule should carry in the analysis.

Each KS is composed of "pieces" of knowledge. By a piece of knowledge we mean a *production rule* , that is, an IF-THEN type of implication formula. The IF side, also called the *situation* side, specifies a set of conditions or patterns for the applicability of the particular rule. The THEN side, also called the *action* side, symbolizes the implications to be drawn (more precisely, various processing events to be caused) if the IF conditions are met. (Refer to [Davis76b] for an excellent overview of production rules.)

The *knowledge of how to perform,* that is, how to use the available knowledge sources, is another kind of knowledge that experts possess. This type of knowledge is also represented in the system in the form of *control/strategy* production rules, which promote flexibility in specifying and modifying strategies of analysis.

Hypothesis formation is an "opportunistic" process. Both *data-driven* and *model-driven* hypothesis formation techniques are used within the general *hypothesize-and-test* paradigm. One of the tasks of the control/strategy knowledge source is to determine the applicability of these methods to different situations. The unit of processing activity is *the event.* Events symbolize such things as "what inferences to make," "what symbol-structures to modify," and "what to look for in the data." The basic control loop for these *event-driven programs,* is one in which lists of events (events sometimes include new data) and the set of control/strategy rules is periodically scanned to determine the "next thing to do".[3]

In the following sections we discuss issues related to the representation of the hypothesis, the knowledge sources, and the control structure. Before continuing, however, we will briefly describe the two tasks that have been implemented and list some guidelines for choosing applications in which this type of system organization may be useful.

---

[3] The events are stored in three lists, each of which requires its own special treatment; *knowledge-based events,* i.e., events specifically related to changes in the hypothesis; *time-based events,* i.e., those events specifically related to expectations of "what will happen when"; and *problems,* i.e., expectations from the programs' "model of the situation" for which the clinching confirmatory or disconfirmatory evidence has not yet been found.

## 2.0  THE TASKS

### 2.1  Interpretation of Continuous Signals

The signal-understanding program performs analysis of data derived from a digitized plot of continuous signals, the interpretation of which is to a considerable degree a function of time. Examples of data having this characteristic are electromagnetic and acoustic signals, and signals from hospital patients monitored in an intensive care unit. The "front-end" signal- processing hardware and software detect energy "packets" appearing at various spectral frequencies, and follow these packets in time. The current system is designed to analyze a digitized description of these data. At the end of each time period, say, a few minutes, the user is given an integrated analysis of the interpreted objects within its data purview [Feigenbaum75].

### 2.2  Interpretation of Three-Dimensional Signal Data: Protein Crystallography

The task of this program is to infer three-dimensional models of protein molecules. The model is derived from an interpretation of the electron density map of the crystallized protein. The density map is, in turn, derived from X-ray diffraction data. These data typically yield a poorly resolved distribution of the electron density within the protein molecule, and the location of individual atoms are generally not identifiable. Traditionally, the protein crystallographer embodies his interpretation of the electron density map in a "ball and stick" molecular model fashioned from metal parts. These parts are strung together to build a model that conforms to the electron density map and is also consistent with protein chemistry and stereochemical constraints.

The current system tries to simulate humans who build models incrementally from the most "obvious" regions of the electron density map. The incremental, opportunistic strategies used by our program to form hypotheses closely resemble the problem-solving methods used by human model builders. Refer to [Engelmore77] for a more complete description of the problem.

## 3.0  SUITABLE APPLICATION AREAS

Building a signal interpretation system within the program organization summarized above can best be described as "opportunistic" analysis. Bits and pieces of information must be used as the opportunity arises to build slowly a coherent picture of the world—much like putting a jigsaw puzzle together. Some thoughts on the characteristics of problems suited to this approach are listed below:

(1)  *Large amounts of signal data need to be analyzed.* Examples include the interpretation of speech and other acoustic signals, X-ray and other spectral data, radar signals, and photographic data. (A variation involves understanding a large volume of symbolic data; for example, the maintenance of a global plotboard of air traffic based on messages from various air traffic control centers.)

(2)  *Formal or informal interpretive theories exist.* By informal interpretive theory we mean *lore* or heuristics that human experts bring to bear in order to "understand" the data. These inexact and informal rules are incorporated as KSs in conjunction with more formal knowledge about the domain.

(3)  *Task domain can be decomposed hierarchically in a "natural way" [Erman 75].* In many cases the domain can be decomposed into a series of data reduction levels, where various interpretive theories (in the sense described above) exist for transforming data from one level to another.

(4)  *"Opportunistic" strategies must be used.* That is, there is no computationally feasible "legal move generator" that defines the space of solutions in which pruning and steering take place. Rather, by reasoning about bits and pieces of available evidence, one can incrementally generate partial hypotheses that will eventually lead to a more global solution hypothesis.

## 3.1 Data-Driven vs. Model-Driven Hypothesis Formation Methods

We have combined data- and model-driven methods of hypothesis formation in the design of SU/X and SU/P. By "data-driven" we mean "inferred from the input data." By "model-driven" we mean "based on expectation," where the expectation is inferred from knowledge about the domain. For example, a hypothesis generated by a KS that infers an amino acid side chain from the electron density data is a data-driven hypothesis. On the other hand, a hypothesis about the existence of an amino-acid side chain that is deduced from topological knowledge of the protein is a model-based hypothesis. In the former case, the data are used as the basis for signal analysis; in the latter case, the primary data are used solely to verify the expectation.

There are no hard-and-fast criteria for determining which of the two hypothesis formation methods is more appropriate for a particular signal-processing task. The choice depends, to a large extent, on the nature of the KSs that are available and on the power of the analysis model available. Our experience points strongly toward the use of a combination of these techniques; some KSs are strongly data dependent while others are strongly model dependent. In the continuous-signal interpretation program, for example, the majority of the inferences are data-driven, with occasional model-driven inferences. The converse is true in the protein model-building, which places more emphasis on model-driven hypothesis generation. The following are guidelines we have used in determining which of the two methods is more appropriate:

(1) *Signal to Noise Ratio.* Problems with inherently low S/N ratios are better suited to solutions by model-driven programs; the converse is true for problems with high S/N ratios.

(2) *Availability of a model.* A model, sometimes referred to as "the semantics of the task domain," can be available in various forms: (1) input to an abstract level of the hypothesis structure, (2) general knowledge about the task domain, or (3) specific knowledge about the particular task. In the protein crystallography problem, for instance, the amino acid sequence (the topology of the protein) serves as a model for guiding the interpretation of the primary data. However, in the continuous-signal interpretation problem, the model is drawn from general knowledge about the signal sources and from other relevant external sources of information that serve to define the context. If a reliable model is available, the data-interpretation KSs can be used as verifiers rather than generators of inferences; this reduces the computational burden on the signal-processing programs at the "front end."

## 4.0  THE NATURE OF THE HYPOTHESIS

In order to integrate a diversity of knowledge about the task domain, the domain is decomposed hierarchically into levels of analysis. We will describe briefly some of the basic ideas on the nature of the hypothesis.[4]

A signal interpretation problem can be viewed as a problem of "transforming" signals representing an object into a symbolic description of the object on a more abstract level. We use the word "transformation" to mean a shift from one representation of an object (digitized signals) to another (symbolic description) using any formal or informal rules.

The data structure hierarchy reflects a plan for the utilization of the various data transformation KSs that contribute to the total data

---

[4] As mentioned earlier, the design of the hypothesis structure in SU/X and SU/P is based on the concepts found in HEARSAY-II. Refer to [Erman75, Lesser75] for a more detailed description.

interpretation process. Generally these transformational steps involve data reductions of the primary data in a stepwise fashion from the detailed to the more abstract description of the object. However, we have found that some of the most useful KSs generate inferences spanning several levels. For example, in the protein-modeling problem, a human can "see" helical substructures in the electron density data, without knowing or observing the details of each atom placement. This kind of knowledge is usually very specific to situations; human experts know, and use, many of these specialized, informal bodies of knowledge.

The data structure of the solution hypothesis is a linked network of nodes, where each node (hypothesis element) represents a meaningful aggregation of lower level hypothesis elements. A link between any two hypothesis elements represents a result of some action by a KS and indirectly points to the KS itself. A link has associated with it directional properties. In general, the direction indicates one of the following:

(1) A link that goes from a more abstract to a less abstract level of the hypothesis is referred to as an "expectation-link." The node at the end of an expectation-link is a model-based hypothesis element, and the link represents "support from above" (i.e., the reason for proposing the hypothesis element is to be found at the higher level).

(2) A link that goes in the opposite direction, from lower levels of abstraction to higher, is referred to as a "reduction-link." The node at the end of a reduction-link is a data-based hypothesis element, and the link represents "support from below" (i.e., the reason for proposing the hypothesis element is to be found at a lower level). (These directions correspond loosely to "top-down" and "bottom-up" path generation.) Examples of KSs and hypothesis elements generated by the KSs are shown in Fig. 2.

The protein-modeling problem posed some difficulties in the design of its hypothesis structure. These can be attributed to several factors. First, the decomposition of the solution space (the three-dimensional model) and the abstractions of the primary data (electron density) do not result in one consistent data hierarchy but result in two hierarchies. Second, the two hierarchies overlap semantically at some levels but are not representationally compatible. Third, very little is known about mapping the object between the two spaces. As indicated in Fig. 3, however, the two hierarchies, with a network of links, can be merged into a single representation of the problem space. This representation indicates that the hypothesis need not be represented as a strict hierarchy; it can be represented as a more general network of related elements. (Refer to [Engelmore77] for more detailed description.)

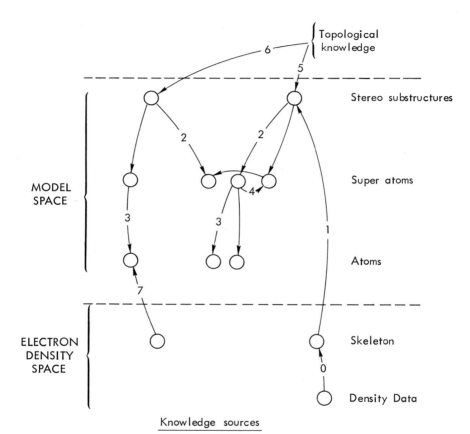

Knowledge sources

0. Skeletonization
1. Helix identification (Skeletal)
2. Sidechain identification
3. Bond rotation
4. Sequence identification
5. Helix identification (topological)
6. Cofactor identification
7. "Heavy Atoms" identification

Fig. 2. Knowledge source utilization in hypothesis formation.

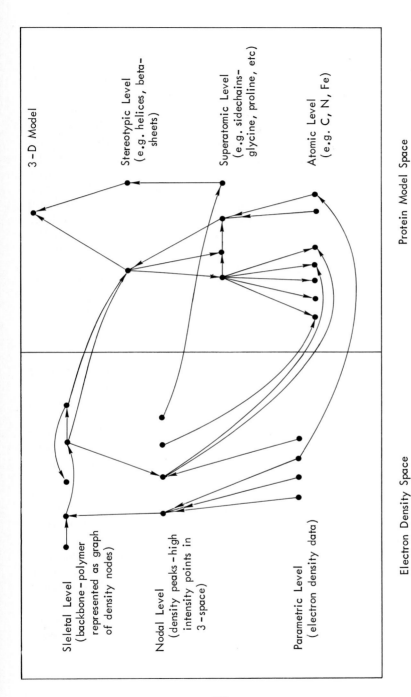

Fig. 3. Hypothesis construction in the protein modeling problem.

## 5.0  THE NATURE OF THE "CONTROL"

A system's performance depends both on the competence of each KS and on the utilization of these KSs within the context of the goals of the task domain.

There are two separate but equally important issues involved in a design of a knowledge-based performance program: (1) the availability and the quality of the specialist KSs that cooperate in the building of a hypothesis. (These KSs define the hierarchy of abstractions of the hypothesis.) (2) the optimal utilization of these KSs. If we view the KSs as resources that are available for solving a problem, then the optimal resource allocation strategy is determined by the quality, the size, and the cost of the KSs, and the state of the current hypothesized solution. The control structure must be sensitive to, and be able to adjust to, the numerous possible solution states that arise in the course of solving a problem. Within this viewpoint, then, what is commonly called the "control structure" becomes another totally domain-dependent knowledge source. The notion of a "hierarchic control" is an attempt to come to grips with the issues of resource allocation and "control" strategies.

### 5.1  Hierarchically Organized Control Structures

In a "hierarchically organized control structure," problem-solving activities themselves form a hierarchy of knowledge necessary for solving the problem. On the lowest level is a set of knowledge sources the tasks of which are to make the primary inferences in the hypothesis network previously described. We refer to this level of knowledge as the "hypothesis-formation" level. At the next level are "meta" KSs that have knowledge about the capabilities of the KSs in the hypothesis-formation level. We refer to this level as the "KS-activation" level; a KS on this level represents a policy on knowledge utilization. At the highest level is the strategy-KS, which analyzes the quality of the current solution to determine what region of the data to analyze next; it also determines what kind of strategy to use.

Another way to describe this organization is as follows: The KSs are organized hierarchically—much like the management structure in a corporate environment—in terms of the scope of their knowledge and the specificity of their functions.

*Example:* A KS capable of deciding whether to look for helices or to continue looking for a large amino acid side chain would possess a higher level of knowledge than a KS whose function is to infer the placement of atoms of some amino acid side chain. It is at a higher level because its area of expertise (choosing the best problem-solving strategy for a given situation) is broader in scope and narrower in the knowledge of the processing specifics. It does not have, and it need not have, any knowledge of the details of the execution of the problem-solving strategy it chooses.

This control hierarchy should be clearly distinguished from the hierarchy of hypothesis levels. The hypothesis hierarchy represents an *a priori* plan for the solution presented by a "natural" decomposition of the analysis problem. The control hierarchy, on the other hand, represents the organization of the problem-solving activities necessary for the formation of the hypothesis. Figure 4 shows a general relationship between the organization of the hypothesis structure and the organization of the control structure. Table 1 summarizes the scope of KSs on each level of control hierarchy.

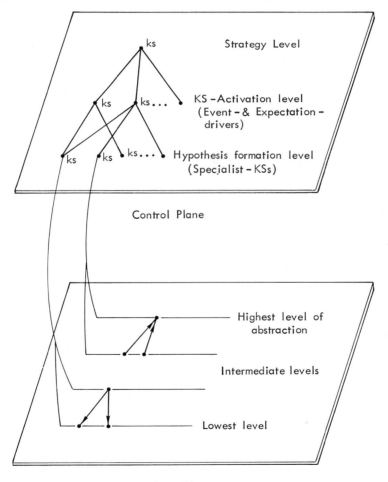

Fig. 4. Relationship between hypothesis hierarchy and control hierarchy.

Table 1. Summary of KS Activities on Different Levels of Control

Specialist-KS (on Hypothesis-Formation Level)

*Has access to*
1. primary data
2. hypothesis elements
3. facts, and
4. events in the event history list

*May act to*
1. change the values of attributes of hypothesis elements, or
2. change the links (relationships) in the hypothesis structure, and
3. inform the system of its actions by
   a. putting on the eventlist the type of changes that were made, or
   b. putting unresolved problems on the problems-list, or
   c. ask to be recalled at a later time (generate time-based event)

Event- and Expectation-Driver (on Knowledge-Source-Activation Level)

*Has access to:*
1. events on the eventlist
2. items on the problems-list, and
3. time-based events

*May act to*

invoke appropriate specialist-KSs in an appropriate sequence

Strategy-KS  (on Strategy Level)

*Has access to*
1. eventlist
2. problems-list
3. time-based events
4. current-best-hypothesis (or a summary of CBH if available), and
5. event- and expectation-drivers

*May act to*
1. choose the appropriate KSs on the KS-activation level, and/or
2. change the focus of attention (i.e., choose an event, a problem, dormant region of the hypothesis, or a different region of the data to process next)

## 5.2 Control Structure Implementation

All information needed by the different KSs is contained in a global data structure called the "blackboard." The blackboard concept has its origin in HEARSAY [Erman75] and is extended in SU/X and SU/P. The contents of the blackboard in SU/X and SU/P consist of

(1)  The current best hypothesis (CBH).

(2)  The event-list: A list of changes in the hypothesis that have not yet been processed by any KS. An event also contains the name of the KS and the identifier of the rule that caused the change.

(3)  The event: A global variable containing the currently "active event," that is, an event currently being processed by some KS. The event also represents the current focus of attention.

(4)  The problems-list: A list of unresolved problems encountered by various KSs. Such problems range from expected data not yet available, to detectable "errors" in the program (e.g., insufficient knowledge).

(5)  The event history list: The event, together with its predecessor and successor events form a causal chain of reasoning. In the continuous-signal understanding problem, the event history list is sometimes used by a KS to analyze a series of events that occurred over a period of time. More generally, it serves as a data base from which reasoning traces are generated and "how" and "why" questions answered. (See reference [Davis77d, Shortliffe75b] for some examples of this type of trace.)

### 5.2.1 Hypothesis Formation Level

At the lowest level of control—the most data-specific level—are the inference-generating KSs, or the specialist-KSs. Each specialist-KS has the task of creating or modifying hypothesis elements, evaluating inferences generated by other specialist-KSs, and cataloging missing evidence, which is essential for a KS to generate meaningful inferences.

Each specialist-KS has access to the blackboard. Its focus of attention is that portion of the blackboard containing the latest change(s) made to the current hypothesis. Although a KS has access to the entire hypothesis, it normally "understands" only the descriptors contained in two levels, its input level and its output level.

*INFERENCE-GENERATION*. Inference-generation is the creation or modification of hypothesis elements; it is the "hypothesize" part of the hypothesize-and-test paradigm. An inference-generator may use a data- or model-driven hypothesis formation method. As mentioned earlier, a KS is represented as a set of production rules consisting of "situation-action" pairs . The "situation" for the infer-ence-generator is a particular state of those hypothesis elements con-taining data relevant to the KS. A match between a description in the hypothesis element and the situation side of a rule indicates that a KS can make some conjectures regarding that hypothesis element. When the appropriate KS is invoked, the "action" part will transform the current hypothesis to a new current hypothesis by adding new links to the structure, creating new hypothesis elements, or changing the attribute values of a hypothesis element (see Table 1 for a summary).

*INFERENCE-EVALUATION.* Inference evaluation involves the appraisal of inferences generated by other KSs; it is the "test" part of the hypothesize-and-test paradigm. For each inference level there is usually more than one specialist-KS capable of generating inferences on that level. When a KS is invoked because of a particular event, another KS may already have processed the salient event. In such a circumstance, the currently active KS evaluates the inference gener-ated by the other KS. The evaluation can result in the KS agreeing with, disagreeing with, or being indifferent about the particular infer-ence being evaluated. If there is agreement, the confidence in that inference is increased; if there is disagreement, either the confidence value is decreased or an alternative hypothesis is generated. There is no action taken for "I don't know" situations.

*PROBLEM-CATALOGING.* Problem cataloging involves attempt-ing to identify missing evidence essential for a KS to generate mean-ingful inferences. If a KS is unable to make new inferences when called upon to do so, it may be due to lack of knowledge about the particular situation or due to lack of necessary information, that is, the current situation does not meet the conditions on the situation sides of the rules. If the specialist-KS is "ignorant" then its knowledge-base must be augmented in some way. If the cause is due to lack of particular evidence, a KS can request it by placing notice on the problems-list. This calls the system's attention to a particular situation in which a solution is possible ". . . if x were true." Since a specialist-KS is not aware of the importance (or the unimportance) of its own im-mediate needs within the general framework of the solution, the deci-sion to pursue or not to pursue the needs of the specialist-KSs is made by a higher level KS.

### 5.2.2 KS-Activation Level

At the level immediately above the hypothesis-formation level are the KS-activators whose tasks are to invoke the specialist-KSs as appropriate. The KSs on this level represent various policies and prob-lem-solving strategies related to the utilization of the specialist-KSs. If, for example, events are processed on an earliest-occurrences-first policy, we would have a breadth-first strategy; if events are processed on a latest-occurrences-first policy, we would have a depth-first strategy.

If there is more than one specialist-KS available to process an event, some policy is needed to guide the order in which these KSs are to be utilized. Different KS-activators can be made to reflect different policies, ranging from fastest-first to most-accurate-first.[5] There are currently two kinds of KS on the KS-activation level, the event-driver and the expectation-driver. For each event the event-driver activates specialist-KSs based on the degree of specialization (and assumed accuracy) of the KSs. The expectation-driver processes items on the problems-list on the basis of how critical the needed evidence is to the emerging hypothesis. This evaluation of how-critical for the continuous-signal problem is sharply defined as part of the knowledge of the domain. In the protein-modeling problem, however, the evaluation criteria are much more heuristic, and in fact are just another element of the overall analysis strategy.

*The event-driver.* An event type represents an *a priori* grouping of similar changes to the hypothesis, that is, it represents the abstractions of possible changes to the hypothesis. The changes, together with the identity of the rules that produced the changes, are put on a globally accessible list called the "event-list." The event-driver invokes the appropriate specialist-KSs based on the information contained in the event or group of events.

*The Expectation-driver.* The task of the expectation-driver is to monitor the items on the problems-list to see if any events that might satisfy the conditions on the problems-list have occurred. If the conditions have occurred, it will activate the specialist-KS that had arranged the request.[6]

### 5.2.3 Strategy Level

The set of rules at the strategy level captures a human expert's knowledge of how to solve a problem. The task of the strategy-KS—the highest control level—is to choose the best problem-solving strategy for the current state of the solution. Its expertise lies, first, in determining how close the current hypothesis is to the actual solution.

---

[5] The issues of focus of attention and resource allocation policies, as described by Hayes-Roth and Lesser [F. Hayes-Roth76g], are important ones. A subsequent paper will describe the implementation of these policies within the SU/X and SU/P framework.

[6] The problems that are "need-for-evidence" can be viewed as "subgoals-to-be-achieved." The systems are currently biased toward an opportunistic mode of hypothesis formation, and the implicit strategy for such subgoals is "wait and see."

In neither SU/X nor SU/P are there formal mechanisms to measure the differences between the current best hypothesis and the "right answer." The program detects when the solution hypothesis is "on the right track" by use of heuristic criteria. For example, in the protein-modeling problem a large number of connected nodes on the stereo-substructure level may imply that the hypothesis is approaching a solution.

A consistent inability to verify expectation-based hypothesis elements may signal an error in the hypothesis. A more general indication of ineffective hypothesis formation appears as a consistent generation of conjectures whose confidence values are below a threshhold value, and which therefore indicates that the analysis is "bogged down."

A strategy-KS must also decide on a course of action once a difference between the hypothesis and the "right answer" is found. Note that these two functions of the strategy-KS—noticing weak parts of the hypothesized solution and choosing the appropriate corrective actions—correspond to the situation and the action parts of production rules. Currently, the strategy-KS can take one of three possible actions:

(1) invoke the expectation-driver to see if the local needs/goals are satisfiable by recent event(s);

(2) invoke the event-driver to process the latest changes in the hypothesis;

(3) decide what region of the data space to work on next, i.e., determine the region of minimal ambiguity in the data.

## 6.0 GOAL-DIRECTED ACTIVITY: SOME SPECULATIONS

Our experience indicates that although the data- and model-driven hypothesis formation methods in combination are powerful, some situations are best handled with a goal-driven method, i.e., utilizing a goal structure and goal-seeking search processes. In the programs described, the occasional lack of certain evidence can halt the whole problem-solving process. However, the need for missing evidence may already be known and catalogued on the problems-list. Under such a circumstance the obvious solution is to set a goal for "seeking" that evidence. Within the context of the current implementation, a goal-directed search through the solution space can be accomplished by (1) adding a goal-driver on the KS-activation control level, (2) implementing a backward-chaining mechanism for the rules as in the MYCIN system [Davis77d], and (3) adding rules to the strategy-KS to choose between data-driven, model-driven, and goal-driven methods of hypothesis formation as appropriate.

## 7.0 SUMMARY AND CONCLUDING REMARKS

SU/X and SU/P are two application programs that have been written to reason toward an understanding of digitized physical signals. The essential features of the programs' design are (1) data- and model-driven, opportunistic modes of hypothesis formation in which the "control" is organized hierarchically, and (2) a globally accessible hypothesis structure augmented by focus-of-attention and historical information, which serve to integrate diverse sources of knowledge. The basic design is similar in many ways to the HEARSAY-II speech-understanding system design. It is applicable to many different types of problems, especially to those problems that do not have computationally feasible "legal move generators" and must therefore resort to opportunistic generation of alternate hypotheses.

The use of production rules to represent control/strategy knowledge offers the advantages of uniformity of representation and accessibility of knowledge for purposes of augmentation and modification of the knowledge base. Because the line of reasoning is often a complex compounding of the elemental steps indicated by the rules, a dynamic explanation capability is needed. We did not discuss this important feature of the programs. Nor did we discuss the facility that allows assignment of an expert's degree of uncertainty for each rule entered. The use of this facility is not well developed currently in the programs discussed. (See [Shortliffe75a, b] for similar but better developed capabilities in the MYCIN program.) We believe that facilities for explanation and for inexact inference must be integrated into the program design at the initial stages.

# PATTERN RECOGNITION AND PATTERN-DIRECTED INFERENCE IN A PROGRAM FOR PLAYING GO[1]

Walter Reitman and Bruce Wilcox
*University of Michigan*

*Skilled human Go play presumes the ability to recognize and make inferences from many different kinds of complex patterns. The Go playing program described here deals with these various pattern recognition activities in terms of a small set of basic scanning and recognition mechanisms. All of the program's inference processes are defined with respect to these mechanisms. The treatment of pattern similarity is conservative. Novel configurations are broken down into subpatterns, and subsequent inferences regarding such configurations are based upon the properties of the subpatterns and the relations among them. The basic functions carried out by the recognition and inference system include establishing appropriate multilevel pattern organizations; maintaining and updating pattern interrelations as the board situation changes; recognizing configurational identities and similarities; monitoring and filtering situational changes with respect to their implications for higher-level planning and problem solving functions; and providing predictively useful pattern information for planning. Although still very weak by human standards, the program is demonstrably stronger than previous Go programs. In particular, tests of its performance resulted in the first reported win by a program against a nonnovice human player.*

## 1.0 INTRODUCTION

Go often is thought of as a protracted game heavily dependent on strategic planning and on skill in reading out the tactical and strategic

[1] Support for this work received under NSF grant MCS77-00880 is gratefully acknowledged. We also thank David McArthur, Robert Nado, David Reitman, Judith Reitman, and Henry Rueter for helpful comments on an earlier draft.

consequences of long hypothetical move sequences. Boorman [Boorman69], for example, focuses mainly upon strategic concepts in contending that Maoist revolutionary strategy was influenced by Mao's familiarity with Go; and the Nobel prize winner Yasunari Kawabata has constructed an entire novel [Kawabata72] around a single famous game, played in 1938, that took 14 sessions and 54 hours to complete. In such a game, it is not unusual for a single critical move to be preceded by an hour or more of analysis and lookahead, with hypothetical move sequences running 30 or more moves deep. As these statistics suggest, the scope in Go for tactical and strategic analysis, planning, and problem solving is substantial. Bozulich, in his introduction to Nagahara's *Strategic Concepts of Go* [Nagahara72], goes as far as to argue that "the essence of Go strategy and in fact the essence of Go itself" lies in the strategy concepts presented in Nagahara's book.

By themselves, however, such characterizations give a one-sided impression of the information processing capabilities skilled Go performance requires. In particular, they convey nothing of the need to recognize, represent, and utilize many different kinds of patterns over the course of a game. Our studies of skilled human Go play [Kerwin73, W.R. Reitman76] suggest, for example, that the extended lookahead sequences just referred to depend very heavily upon pattern-directed inference processes. In many cases, our data show that the one or two correct responses to an oppponent's move are identified almost immediately; the time that elapses before actually responding is spent not in finding a candidate response but in investigating the consequences that follow from playing it. The fundamental role of pattern-directed inference in Go becomes still clearer when we consider such phenomena as the NHK lightening Go tournaments [Rilley72]. These matches, which are telecast on Japanese TV, permit each player only 15 minutes for initial analysis. Each move thereafter must be made in 30 seconds or less. In view of these time limits and the impressive levels of performance attained in such tournaments, it seems reasonable to suggest that pattern-directed inference processes are both a fundamental component of skilled human Go play and a basic desideratum in any attempt to explicate human Go play by means of a Go playing program.

The interim program described below is the first result of an effort to construct an intelligent Go playing program modeled upon the pattern recognition and problem-solving capabilities of highly skilled human Go players. Almost all of the components programmed so far are designed to realize the pattern recognition, representation, and utilization capabilities involved. In this chapter, after a brief introduction to Go, we consider the general functions served by the primary pattern components, and then briefly describe how these components work. We conclude with test results for the interim program, and a brief summary of our views on the role of pattern-directed inference in this domain.

## 2.0 THE BASIC ELEMENTS OF THE TASK ENVIRONMENT

Go is a board game contest for territory between two players, black and white. Ignoring captures for the moment, whoever controls more territory when the game ends wins. The game board is a 19 × 19 grid, with territory consisting of the 361 points defined by the intersections of the grid. The two players move by turns. A legal move is made by placing a stone (token) upon any vacant intersection. A player kills (captures) an enemy stone and removes it from the board whenever he succeeds in surrounding the stone. This involves placing four of his own stones, using four turns, on the vacant grid points (referred to as *liberties* or dame) horizontally and vertically adjacent to the enemy stone (see Fig. 1). Every enemy stone killed adds one point to the player's final score. Direct capture of a single stone as in the above example is not a very profitable idea in itself, however, since it takes four moves and gains just two points (the captured stone and the one enclosed board point). The possibility of capture is significant mainly because it gives rise to moves that threaten important higher-order units, such as groups.

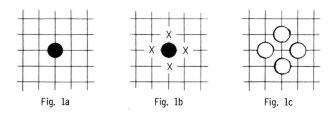

Fig. 1. (a) Placement of a single stone on a portion of the board. (b) The four liberties for the stone also are indicated. (c) The results of capturing the single black stone in Fig. 1a by playing on all of its liberties. From Iwamoto [Iwamoto72].

*Strings.* In addition to the individual stones, the Go program recognizes a variety of higher-order units. A string consists of a single isolated stone or two or more stones of the same color located on immediately adjacent grid points. In Fig. 2, for example, the two white stones at Q7 and Q8 form a string. Multistone strings are captured just as one-stone strings are, by depriving them of liberties. A string is extended by placing a token of the same color on a grid point vertically or horizontally adjacent to any token already in the string. Extension

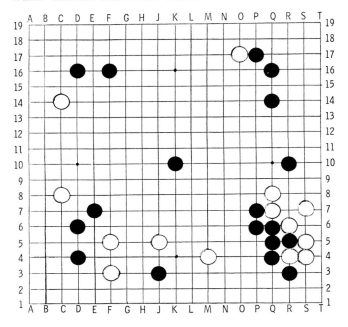

Fig. 2. Early stage in a five-stone handicap game, i.e., a game beginning with black stones at D4, D16, Q16, Q4, and K10. From Kerwin and Reitman [Kerwin73].

of a string may occur, for example, when a player resists a threatened capture of the string by placing another stone on a vacant grid point anywhere immediately adjacent to the string to increase its liberty count.

*Linkages and chains.* Two strings of the same color, in close proximity, with no intervening enemy stones, are considered by the program to be linked together to form a chain. In Fig. 2, for example, the white stones at J5 and M4 are considered to be joined by a "large knight's move" linkage. Strings in close proximity to the edge of the board, with no intervening enemy stones, are considered to be linked to the edge.

*Enclosure and territory.* The single black stone at J3 is enclosed by an uninterrupted set of links running from the edge point F1 through the white stones F3, F5, J5, M4, and back to the edge at M1. The territory presently enclosed by the four white stones and their linkages is worth about 20 points. Linkages and enclosures under some conditions may be broken by the interposition of enemy stones, but this can lead to fighting disadvantageous to the player attempting to break through.

*Groups.* A group consists of a single isolated string or two or more strings of the same color in close proximity, with no intervening enemy stones or links. Groups usually are attacked and defended as units, not string by string. Under certain well-defined conditions, groups may become relatively or absolutely alive (i.e., stable, secure, not subject to capture). The seven white stones on the lower right side in the figure form a group. So do the four white stones at the bottom center of the figure since there are uninterrupted links connecting each stone in the group to at least one other and, therefore, by transitivity, to all of the others. In addition, a collection of chains interrupted by a dead enemy group, i.e., a group that currently cannot achieve life, also forms a group. The extent and degree of prospective territorial control exercised by each side at any time during the game is a function of the relative stability of each side's groups and the interacting dispositions of the two sets of groups over the board. In Fig. 2, for example, black has some measure of control over the upper right side, and white is strong around the middle of the bottom.

*Options and multifunction moves.* Each group may be thought of as having associated with it a set of options. These are general ways in which that particular group may be developed, protected, and used. The white group at C8 in Fig. 2 may develop in subsequent moves along the left side or out towards the center. Similarly, the white group at 017 may develop along the upper side or escape out into the center or serve as a sacrifice stone to minimize black's territorial profits along the upper side or in the upper-right corner. As a single move may serve multiple functions, a play at one point, in addition to affecting the options in its immediate area, also may augment, modify, or reduce the options of groups elsewhere on the board. Just as a car emerging from a side street may affect the choices open to other cars at some distance from it on the main road, so the play of a white stone may alter the developmental options of a remote black group, for example by obstructing a potential escape route of that group. Thus groups interact at a distance through the interrelations among their options. Notice also that a group that earlier had several options for development and protection may, as a result of several unanswered remote attacking plays by the opponent, be left with only one. Consequently, protection of that group becomes urgent, since otherwise, with a single additional move, the opponent may be able to disrupt the group entirely. In this sense, changes in option sets significantly affect the focus of the game.

## 3.0 THE PATTERN RECOGNITION SYSTEM AND ITS FUNCTIONS

A program capable of effective pattern-directed inference in Go needs components analogous to the pattern recognition and representation capabilities that a human employs over the course of a game. This section introduces these components and the general functions they serve. Their design is based upon analyses of detailed records of skilled human Go play [Kerwin73]. Note that the individual mechanisms are not meant to correspond to individual components of the human pattern recognition system. Instead, each is designed to carry out one class of the functions the human system as a whole performs in this domain. Thus each is defined with respect to the distinct kind of pattern information it provides.

Some of these components deal with the lower-level task elements described above. Thus there are components that segregate the stones on the board into elements at various levels, recognizing and representing strings, linkages, chains, territories, and so on. Other pattern components also correspond to task elements, e.g., groups, but the functions carried out by the systems at this level are more broadly defined. The edge perception system, for example, provides information analogous to that obtained when a human player scans the periphery of the board, and the web perception system is designed to scan along and out from the irregular boundaries of groups. The information the edge and web perception systems return for a group about the arrangement and locations of the other groups and empty regions that constitute its environment are used both tactically and strategically, both for attack and for defense. Thus these systems correspond to more generalized classes of perceptual scanning activities rather than being tied to particular patterns or functions. The information provided by these more general components is used in making inferences in many different ways in the course of the program's analysis and planning.

## 3.1 The Basic Functions of the Pattern Recognition System

The basic functions of the system as a whole include establishing an appropriate multilevel pattern organization ; maintaining and updating pattern interrelations as the board situation changes; recognizing configurational identities and similarities; monitoring and filtering situational changes with respect to their implications in higher-level planning and problem solving functions; and providing predictively useful pattern information for planning.

*Multilevel pattern organization.* A game in progress, for example the one shown in Fig. 2, may be represented at the most elementary level as a collection of black, white, and unoccupied points. The skilled Go player is only partly concerned with individual points, however. He also will be thinking about higher-order units, such as groups and territories, and about the interrelations among them. If a system is to solve problems in a domain containing patterns at several levels, it must organize lower-order patterns into whatever higher-order units are to be used in planning and problem solving. In Go the problem of organization is made more difficult by the fact that unlike the pieces of a jigsaw puzzle, the elements returned by the pattern segregation and organization mechanisms are not required to be fixed, bounded, or restricted in any way. There are no *a priori* limits on the shape or extent of individual patterns at any level, nor any requirement that they be confined to particular subregions of the board.

A great benefit for a system that can organize an appropriate multilevel pattern framework is that it may substantially amplify the effective power of those mechanisms, e.g., selective lookahead, that carry on detailed point by point computations. Although remote interactions among higher-level units become very important for long-range strategic planning, they often may be ignored for local tactical purposes. To a first approximation, then, establishing an appropriate multilevel pattern framework breaks down the whole board situation into a set of parts, each one of which may be considered separately. Given this set of local situations, we may now define the concept of focus, which in turn makes it possible to restrict detailed point by point examination to whichever situation is most important at the moment.

The pattern components not only organize the board into patterns at each level; they also provide basic information about their interactions. Stability and proximity, for example, are two of the main determinants of the importance of interactions among groups. Two opposing unstable groups in close proximity are likely to interact strongly. The interactions between neighboring stable groups, or between two unstable ones with a stable group intervening, are likely to be much weaker and much less important. The pattern components yield information both about group stability and about spatial interrelations around the board.

*Maintaining and updating the multilevel pattern correspndence as the board situation changes.* To someone not familiar with the game, the Go board does not seem a very dynamic perceptual situation. Except for captures, which are relatively infrequent, stones once played remain where they are until the game ends. Thus, the changes that occur seem to come slowly, in discrete increments, as black and white take turns placing one stone at a time upon the board. To the skilled Go player, however, the unfolding of a game looks very different. "Although the stones themselves do not move during the game there is always a feeling of powerful movement over the board; of advance and retreat, of growth and withering, of stability and change" [Iwamoto72]. In part, the two descriptions differ because they focus on different levels within the pattern framework. The skilled Go player looks at a move that links to an existing group and sees that group swell out in a new direction. A move that links several existing groups can merge them quite suddenly into a new, much larger whole. And a move that breaks a critical linkage in an enemy group may shatter the group into two fragments, neither of which is to be identified with any previously existing pattern in the representation. Since planning and problem solving require accurate current information about the patterns at various levels on the board, the system must take account of all of the changes that follow as a consequence of each new move.

Generally speaking then, the updating objectives for the pattern components are to describe and monitor the changing spatial relations among a collection of patterns, and to do so in ways that make efficient use of all the information available. Most of these patterns persist from one move to the next, and their overall spatial locations do not change. As we have seen, however, their sizes and shapes may change, and these alterations will affect the description of the spatial interrelations among them. There also may be occasional abrupt transformations, such as the creation of a new larger pattern from a subcollection of old ones, or the creation of a new collection of smaller patterns from the destruction of an old one. Finally, a move may initiate a new element at any unoccupied point in the space. This also will affect the description of the spatial relations among all of the patterns in that general area. At every level in the representation affected by any such event, old patterns and relationships will have to be deleted, and new patterns, properties, and relationships established.

Though such drastic changes will occur, they are relatively infrequent and their effects are to some extent localized. Thus, by making use of the current description, and of the system's knowledge of the effects different kind of changes can produce, intelligent updating procedures for such a domain can maintain an accurate current description of patterns and spatial relations without having to search, scan, and completely reanalyze the whole board after each new move. In this way, whenever any component of the system needs to make further inferences about any aspect of the current task environment, it knows where to look and what pattern analysis components to call.

*Recognizing configurational identities and similarities.* Each new stone placed on the board may alter some existing local configurations and set up new ones. Both immediate tactical play and the long-run strategic options associated with a situation will vary with the properties of these configurations. Thus the system must be able to identify patterns and significant subpatterns if it is to utilize its knowledge of configuration properties to infer locally useful plays. Notice that when new stones are played, the resulting transformations from one pattern to another are generally purposeful and therefore to some extent predictable. Thus an intelligent system should be able to use its knowledge of transformation possibilities, and of the patterns presently on the board, to avoid having to recognize new patterns from scratch. Entirely novel transitions and patterns do sometimes occur, however, and so the system must be able to deal with these situations as well. Notice also that in all cases, appropriate play will depend not only upon inferences about options based upon the local pattern context, but also upon the goals to be achieved in this situation. The program's mechanisms for recognizing local patterns must therefore be closely integrated with its knowledge of the uses to which such patterns may be put. In Section 4 we describe the lens perception system, the means the program uses to achieve these results.

*Filtering.* In many artificial intelligence systems, a major objective is to reduce the information flow from one function to another. This is true of the present system as well. For example, a lens (a data structure monitoring a particular occurrence of a pattern) will not pass on information about just any move played within its field of view, only about those moves that threaten the intended purpose of the configuration. Similarly, a move played within web scope of several groups will result in a considerable amount of web modification activity. But only after all web modifications have been completed will any information be passed on to other components, and then only if, in the light of the information resulting from the web reorganization, a local expert infers that the move threatens the stability or the options of a group. Thus, the pattern components serve not only as recognizers, reorganizers, and monitors, but also as highly selective filters.

*Generating predictively useful perceptual information.* In real world problem domains, functional relations often depend upon spatial ones. This also applies in Go. If the multilevel pattern representation is accurate and up to date, and if it corresponds to the way skilled Go players perceive and think about board situations, it should be useful in predicting likely outcomes for many different lines of play.

During most of a Go game, there are about 100 to 300 legal move possibilities at each turn, and the game may go on for 200 moves or more. Thus the generation and evaluation of whole board lookahead trees quickly becomes an impossibility. The information returned by the pattern components often provides valuable surrogates for detailed move-by-move lookahead, however, and the functions that analyze the representation make use of these surrogates wherever they can. Even in the interim program, which has no planning or strategic capability at all, pattern-based tests are used to infer whether a group encloses sufficient territory for stability, for example, or whether it is likely to be enclosed. As we proceed from local tactical considerations to components meant to plan out strategy over large areas of the board and long segments of a game, pattern-based surrogates for detailed move-by-move lookahead become still more important.

## 4.0 THE PRIMARY PATTERN COMPONENTS AND HOW THEY ARE USED

The preceding section discussed the general functions of the pattern recognition system. Here we briefly describe both the main pattern components and the interim program's control structure for using them.

### 4.1 The Lens Component

Local stone configurations and the sequences of moves that transform one configuration into another are fundamental in Go. The lens system is the component that recognizes and monitors such configurations. The interim Go program uses lenses to monitor three types of configurations: linkages, corners, and patterns near the edge of the board (yose). The description that follows uses linkage lens examples, but it applies to the other configuration types as well.

*The purpose of lenses.* The move patterns involved in defending and attacking linkages recur constantly. Thus a skilled Go player comes to recognize them directly. He also builds up information about the strengths and weaknesses of particular linkages, and about the standard attack and defense sequences for each linkage type. The first purpose of the lens system is to associate the program's permanent information about patterns of a particular type (two-point jump linkages, for example) with occurrences of that pattern in particular orientations and positions on the board.

If standard local configurations always were generated in some single fixed order, associating knowledge with a particular occurrence would involve nothing more than converting the information to the appropriate board coordinates. In general, however, this is not the case. Patterns may be affected, for example, by plays arising out of nearby situations. Or a player may deliberately make a move out of sequence, either to force his opponent away from the standard patterns, or because the particular point enters into several possible sequences, and his move thus gives him several options for further development. Even in relatively small local areas, the number of possible patterns quickly becomes quite large. Ignoring symmetry and equivalences under rotation and translation, a $5 \times 5$ area of the board may contain any of $3^{25}$ different patterns, and neither human player nor computer program can store specific information about more than a very small fraction of them. Thus the lens system must be able not only to recognize known patterns but also to characterize new ones in terms of part properties and subpatterns, i.e., in terms of their significant similarities to standard patterns whose properties already are known.

The detection of patterns and the analysis of similarity is organized under each lens by field types. Each field type is stored in canonical form as part of the program's permanent information about the lens. As instantiated with respect to some particular configuration on the board, a field is a collection of points, including both the points of the configuration itself and a subset of the points immediately around the configuration. There are no restrictions on field size or shape, but fields in the interim Go program typically include no more than 25 board points. When a new stone is played anywhere near the configuration monitored by the lens, any field containing that point becomes a source of expert information about the implications of the play. If the point is represented in several fields, each may be called upon for suggestions about how to respond. Notice that larger fields may overlap one another substantially, and the points in a smaller field may be entirely contained in some larger one. The reasons for this will become clear when we consider how the fields function.

*Setting up a new lens data structure.* When a move creates a new linkage, MOVE, the top level updating routine, calls *LINKLENS, which creates a lens data structure to monitor the new linkage. (Routines that create and updata data structures are prefixed with (*) and ($) respectively.) *LINKLENS retrieves the canonical representation of the set of all points to be monitored by this lens, and the list of all field types associated with it. These data are then transformed to fit the location and orientation of the linkage on the board. When *LINKLENS has finished, the result is a data structure containing the following elements:

(1)  The center of the lens. For a linkage lens, this is one of the linkage endpoints.

(2)  The lens type (here, LNK), and a pointer to the particular linkage data structure this lens monitors.

(3)  The primary orientation of the lens, determined by the orientation of the two endpoints of the linkage.

(4)  A list, initially NIL, of moves serving the purpose associated with the configuration being monitored (here, connecting or forming a barrier). These are provided by PHOTOANALYSIS, as described immediately below.

(5)  A pointer, initially NIL, to the lens field PHOTOANALYSIS is currently still **examining**.

(6)  A compound list containing all actual board points monitored by the lens, and pointers for PHOTOANALYSIS to the lens fields currently still relevant.

Once the lens data structure has been created, pointers to the lens in the LENSBOARD array from each of the points monitored by the lens are set up. Then PHOTOANALYSIS is called.

*Using an existing lens to recognize a modified configuration.* Referring again to Fig. 2, suppose for purposes of illustration that black's next play is at H6. That play, which threatens to break through the two-point jump linkage between F5 and J5, will be seen by the lens monitoring that linkage. More precisely, since H6 is included in one or more of the fields for that lens, it points to that lens in the LENS-BOARD array. Thus, after the program has recorded the play at H6, when MOVE begins to update the lens data structures, it will access this lens. (If there is more than one linkage through a point and, consequently, more than one lens monitoring the point, all of them will be accessed.) MOVE now calls PHOTOANALYSIS. PHOTOANAL-YSIS takes each field that includes this point, beginning with the largest fields first, and passes it to PIC. PIC takes the field and the occupancy status of each point in it and returns a characterization of the pattern. The characterization includes the linkage type, the name of the field, and the canonical bit-pattern representing the occupancy status of all the points in the field. In this form, the information now may be compared with the program's permanent canonical pattern representations. If the pattern cannot be identified, this field subsequently is ignored. Thus, early in the game many fields will be relevant to any given configuration. Later, as the configurations become more complex, most of them will be eliminated either because they do not match or because they have no useful suggestions to make. If the pattern is identified, the relevant permanent data are checked to see whether moves further attacking or defending the linkage may be inferred for either side. Larger fields may provide exact matches for larger configurations or matches for smaller configurations in a particular context. Smaller fields may match smaller configurations or significant subpatterns in larger ones. If there is no match at all from any of the fields, PHOTOANALYSIS fails, and since the lens has no good move to suggest, it is ignored thereafter.

As this example suggests, the theory of similarity and pattern recognition upon which the lens system and the program as a whole are based is a conservative one. A doctor selects a particular test on the basis of an hypothesis deriving from a pattern of observed symptoms. If the test is inconclusive, he may turn to other tests suggested by symptom subpatterns. If all of his tests are inconclusive, he simply does not know what the problem is, and he may be at a loss to know what to do. The one thing he probably should not do is to regard each of the many tests he has run as defining a dimension in a multidimensional space and then take the nearest known disease entity in the space, as defined by some arbitrary global distance measure, as a basis for prescribing treatment. This global distance approach to similarity and pattern classification may work for some areas, but since it ignores conditional relations and interactions, it probably is inappropriate for problem domains such as Go, in which conditional relations and interactions are a dominant feature.

## 4.2 The Edge Component

Most Go games begin with plays in the corner and along the sides, typically on the third or fourth lines out from the edge of the board. Looking again at Fig. 2, if we imagine a band running all around the board and containing all the points from the edge out to and including the fourth line from each side, we see that all but six of the 32 stones on the board so far fall within that band. Corner and side plays have high priority in the opening stage of the game because with the loose linkages they form with the edge, they enclose territory more quickly than plays in the center would. As a result, the perceptual activity of the skilled Go player includes many scans around the edge of the board during the opening stage of the game. Such scanning continues to be important later on as well. The edge component makes possible inferences analogous to those resulting from such perceptual scans around this band of points. The edge data structure may be thought of as a closed loop around the edge. Individual points in the edge data structure index sets of four points running out, perpendicular to the edge, to the fourth line in the edge band. The structure is organized as a circular list of blocks, each corresponding to one of the black or white positions around the board. Each block is implemented as a list containing the following information:

(1) The number of open points between this position and its next left neighbor. If the two positions are in contact, this number is zero. Otherwise, the number increases for each unit distance between the two as measured along the edge.

(2) The leftmost boundary point of this position.

(3) The maximum extent of the position, measured parallel to the edge. For example, the extent of a third line position consisting of two stones with a two-point jump between them is four.

(4) The rightmost boundary point of this position.

(5) The number of open points between the rightmost boundary point and the nearest neighbor to the right.

Once the edge data structure has been updated, it is scanned to locate and record those empty regions within the edge band that may be of interest to the analysis and inference routines, e.g., EXTEND, that propose extension moves from groups, moves that invade areas between groups, plays that secure a group by expanding it along the side, and plays at the end of the game that push out the boundaries of a group to increase the territory it encloses as much as possible. In addition, the information about the extent of any empty areas to the left or right of a group also is used in making inferences about its stability.

## 4.3 The Web Component

Imagine each group on the Go board as having its own two-dimensional radar, which operates in the plane of the board. Radar waves from the group pass through vacant points, but are reflected back by stones, links, and the edges of the board. Now imagine that each group on the board also has its own spider. Each group's spider spins a web in all directions, over exactly those points of the board passed through or reached by that group's radar. The web terminates wherever it runs into a stone, a link, an edge of the board or a radar shadow cast by some other stone. The range of the radar and the scope of the resulting web are controlled by a program parameter. In the interim program, the scope of a web is set to a limit of five intersections out in any direction from the boundary of the group it surrounds. This web scope provides all of the proximate, tactically significant data about the group's environment the interim program can handle.

*Web generation.* The procedure responsible for producing a web is $WEB. The first circumferential strand of the web is spun immediately around the group's boundary, forming a complete ring. To generate the second level circumferential strand from the first, or more generally, the $(n+1)$th level strand from the nth, $WEB calls REWEB. REWEB determines each node in the $(n+1)$th strand from three contiguous nth strand nodes. Generation of nodes on the $(n+1)$th strand halts when REWEB either reaches its starting node in the previous strand, or else comes across a nonvacant board point. If all of the nodes of a strand are vacant, all of the nodes of the next level strand are generated in one uninterrupted sequence by the process just described. In this case, the nodes just generated form a complete $(n+1)$th level ring. If REWEB encounters in the previous strand a node corresponding to a blocked point, however, it treats that node as a boundary node. In this case, the nodes just generated form not a complete ring but a ring arc. In either case the ring or arc just created now is taken as the new basis, and generation of nodes on the next strand out begins.

When the outermost strand of the present web segment has been finished, that is, when no further strands can be generated because the current strand consists entirely of boundary nodes or has reached the scope limit, REWEB moves back in one strand, to the right-hand boundary node of the immediately preceding strand. If that right-hand boundary node has an unprocessed vacant node anywhere after it in the strand, the spinning of another segment begins there. Otherwise, REWEB again moves inward one level and proceeds in the manner just described. At some point, REWEB either finds some portion of an inner circumferential strand that can be spun out further, in which case the process continues as before, or it reaches its starting point on the innermost level strand, and the web for the group is finished.

*Updating the webs.* The web for a group will be updated whenever a friendly or enemy stone is played within its scope. Consider first what happens when a stone is added that extends an existing string outward across the group boundary. Note that the new stone must always be played at a point corresponding to a node in the level 1 strand of the old web. This node already is tied to a level 1 node immediately to its left.

Now, beginning from that node, REWALKR (i.e., REWALK to the right) adds to the strand appropriate new level 1 nodes. When it reaches a still valid level 1 node in the existing strand, it reconnects the two ends of the level 1 strand at that point. Each successive $(n+1)$th strand of the web is then augmented in its turn.

A similar web modification process is initiated when a friendly stone is played within linking distance of an existing group. The details of this process are more complex because a number of possibilities are involved. Consider, for example, a white play at D11 in Fig. 2. That stone forms links to both white C8 and White C14. Thus two webs have to be modified and merged in order to come up with an appropriate web structure for the new three string group. The now incorrect portions of the old webs also must be deleted. The scope of the new web structure always includes all those board points in direct line of sight from any string or linkage in the group, out to the scope limit. Consequently, once the web modification process is complete for all affected webs, each group can "see" the arrangement of all friendly and hostile patterns within its web scope and thus can infer exactly what the immediate effects upon its options are.

## 4.4 Updating GAMEMAP after a Move

The interim program's representation of the current state of the game is implemented as a multilevel collection of interrelated GAME-BOARDS. Each board is an array that indexes a particular type of data structure. Together, the set of boards and data structures comprise GAMEMAP. Some boards, e.g., STRINGBOARD and LINK-BOARD, index the basic game elements (strings, linkages, etc.). Others, such as the WEBBOARD, index higher levels, e.g., webs, that may be thought of as analogs of the higher level perceptual and cognitive elements constituting a skilled Go player's representation of the current task environment. In most of these boards, the individual array positions correspond to the individual points of the $19 \times 19$ grid. Should the program require information, for example, about the white stone at Q8 in Fig. 2, it can access the appropriate position in STRING-BOARD to determine the string that white stone belongs to, or the corresponding position in WEBBOARD to identify all webs that impinge on this stone.

MOVE is the top-level routine responsible for updating GAME-MAP after each new play. MOVE begins by calling PHOTOANALYSIS to update any existing lenses affected by the play. MOVE takes each lens from the list at the LENSBOARD array position corresponding to the board point just played upon and provides it as an argument to PHOTOANALYSIS. When all existing lenses have been updated, MOVE calls $STRINGS to update strings. If the latest move has created a new string, $STRINGS calls *STRING to initialize a new string data structure. The elements of a string data structure are lists of the stone(s) in the string, the vacant points (liberties) immediately adjacent to the string, and any immediately adjacent enemy stones.

MOVE next calls $LINKS, which updates the set of linkages on the board to take account of any new linkages created by the latest move. $LINKS uses FINDLINK, which iteratively takes information about each possible displacement for each of the possible linkage types and passes this information together with the locus of the latest move to TESTLINK. TESTLINK checks to see whether the point reached is occupied, and if so, whether all of the other conditions for that linkage type are satisfied. If so, it creates an appropriate new linkage data structure. TESTLINK now calls *LINKLENS to create a new lens data structure to monitor the new linkage. Finally, $LINKS call UN-LINK to alter or remove linkage data structures representing linkages weakened or broken by the move.

Next, MOVE calls $FRIENDCHAINS and $ENEMYCHAINS to update friendly and enemy chains, respectively. Assuming that the latest move was made by the program, $FRIENDCHAINS examines each of the new linkages created, and combines chains involving its endpoints into new, updated ones. If the program's latest move has destroyed any enemy linkages, $ENEMYCHAINS will regroup the strings involved into new chain data structures.

Now MOVE calls $WEB to update webs, and then $TERRITORY, which updates territory data structures to reflect any changes produced by the most recent move. Finally, $EDGE and $GROUPS are called to update the edge and group data structures, respectively. Among other things, $GROUPS updates the stability information for each group, making the following checks. Has the latest move enclosed the group? If not, is the group threatened with enclosure? Is the territory the group encloses adequate for making life? Are there any unsafe linkages? Are any significant group linkages threatened? Are any significant strings in the group short of liberties or threatened with capture? Is the group involved in any locally urgent contact fight situations? All of this information is combined into a single stability rating for the group, along with an estimate of the value of the group. With GAMEMAP now fully updated to reflect the effects of the latest play, MOVE terminates.

## 4.5 How the Interim Program Selects a Move

Move selection is determined rather directly by the pattern information accessed through GAMEMAP. The process is under the control of REFLEX, which is called after MOVE terminates. REFLEX begins with a call to DEFENSE-ALERTS. DEFENSE-ALERTS calls WORST-GROUPS, which orders all of the program's groups for stability, using the stability data generated by $GROUPS. Now DEFENSE-ALERTS takes each group in turn, beginning with the least stable, and calls DEVELOPGROUP. DEVELOPGROUP considers each group to determine whether it has any currently available development options. In doing so, it makes use of such analysis and inference routines as KILLANY, DEFENDSTRINGS, EXTEND, RUNGROUP, BREAK-OUT, and FORMEYES. Each of these, in turn, makes use of pattern information from one or more of the data structures maintained under MOVE. If DEVELOPGROUP finds a group having such an option, it calls REFLEX1, whch makes the move. At this point, DEVELOP-GROUP, DEFENSE-ALERTS, and REFLEX all terminate.

If no development moves are available for any group, or no group needs development, DEFENSE-ALERTS exits back into REFLEX. REFLEX now calls TAKESENTE (i.e., take the initiative). If the game is still in its early stage, and if there are any important opening moves that can be found using the edge data structure information, the best of those moves will be made. Otherwise, TAKESENTE considers in turn various classes of moves that would improve the position of one of the program's groups. If no improvement move is returned, TAKE-SENTE calls WORSTGROUPS for the opponent's groups, and then, beginning with the least stable, calls KILLGROUP to find a good attack against the group. In doing this, KILLGROUP uses most of the same analysis experts used by DEVELOPGROUP as well as several new ones, e.g., ENCLOSEGROUP. By means of these routines, KILL-GROUP makes use of information from the edge data structure to infer moves that would block possible extensions; it uses information from the group's web data structure to infer possible enclosing moves; it uses information about weak linkages included in the group's stability data to look for moves that might fragment the group; and using information about the territory enclosed by the group, it will try to find moves that would deprive the group of the use of that enclosed space for making life.

If KILLGROUP fails to return a move, then having gotten this far in REFLEX, the program now considers the game to be in the end-game stage, and TAKESENTE calls YOSE. YOSE is a routine that looks for good end-game moves, working mainly from edge and territory pattern information. If YOSE fails to find a next move, the program passs. If the opponent also passes, the game is over. Otherwise, after the opponent's latest move, it is once more the program's turn and MOVE and REFLEX are called again.

## 5.0 SYSTEM PERFORMANCE

This section reports the results of three test games played against human opponents by the interim Go program. The program consists basically of the pattern and representation components just described; the inference routines that work from the multilevel representation the pattern components produce; MOVE, which coordinates updating; and REFLEX, which controls the choice of a next move.

The interim program is written in LISP/MTS. It cycles through four steps: (1) the opponent's latest move is read in and placed on the board; (2) MOVE updates GAMEMAP; (3) REFLEX chooses the program's next move; and (4) MOVE again updates the representation to reflect the effects of the program's move. The program runs on The University of Michigan's AMDAHL/470 computer and its main files at run-time occupy about 80,000 words of core. The program has played a total of about 15 full board games over the course of its development. The games reported below, run under test conditions, were the last three of these.

To provide a basis for assessing the work done to date, the results from the interim program's games are compared in what follows with seven games presented by Ryder [Ryder71] and Zobrist [Zobrist70]. So far as we have been able to determine, these are the only complete games by a Go program that have been reported. The one game Ryder describes was played against a novice. The program's play was quite interesting at many points, but it eventually lost by a substantial margin. Scores for all six of the completed games Zobrist reports, together with scores for the three games by the interim program, are presented in Table 1.

Before discussing the results, it will be helpful to have a brief explanation of the basis for estimating rankings. Rankings for beginning and intermediate amateur Go players begin at 35 kyu, the rank assigned to novice players, and proceed downward to 1 kyu. After this come the advanced amateur ranks, measured in dan units. At least two years of serious play and study are required to reach 1 kyu. In games between players of unequal rank, one handicap stone is allowed to compensate for each unit difference in rank. There is a standard

Table 1

Comparative Results for Zobrist's Program
and the Interim Program

| Program | Opponent | Opponent's rank (kyu) | Handicap taken by the program | Score difference* | Estimated program rank (kyu) |
|---|---|---|---|---|---|
| Zobrist, 1969 version | GC | 35 | — | 7 | 34 |
| | SS | 35 | — | 35 | 31 |
| | EM | 25 | — | -116 | 37 |
| | LL | 12 | 13 | -255 | 50 |

Average estimated program rank: 38

| Program | Opponent | Opponent's rank (kyu) | Handicap taken by the program | Score difference* | Estimated program rank (kyu) |
|---|---|---|---|---|---|
| Zobrist, 1970 version | EM | 16 | — | - 94 | 25 |
| | WB | 7 | 13 | -181 | 38 |

Average estimated program rank: 31.5

| Program | Opponent | Opponent's rank (kyu) | Handicap taken by the program | Score difference* | Estimated program rank (kyu) |
|---|---|---|---|---|---|
| Interim program | BS | 22 | 9 | 42 | 27 |
| | JH | 4 | 9 | -112 | 24 |
| | GH | 34 | — | 40 | 30 |

Average estimated program rank: 27

*A positive score indicates a game won by the program.

way to get a rough estimate of a player's strength, using results from his games against a player of known strength. The procedure starts with the rank of the rated player, subtracts one rank for each handicap stone he gives the other, and then adds or subtracts one rank for every 10 points of difference in final score. This is the procedure used to get the estimated program rank listed in the last column of Table 1. To illustrate, the first of the three games played by the interim program was against BS, a regular participant at the local Go club whose ranking at the time was 22 kyu. BS gave the program a nine-stone handicap, and lost by 42 points. The estimate of the program's rank based upon this game is 27 kyu $(22 + 9 - 4 = 27)$.

Turning now to Table 1, we see that the stronger of Zobrist's two programs ranked about 31 or 32 kyu. This would correspond to a player who had played perhaps 15 or 20 previous games. The interim program also does no better than a beginner, but its estimated rank of 27 kyu is what might be expected of someone who had played perhaps 40 to 50 previous games. If we order the results from the ten games that have now been reported (one by Ryder, six by Zobrist, and three here), all but one of the best four scores are from the games played by the interim program. We may note further that so far as can be determined from published and unpublished sources, the games reported here are the first in which a Go program has won against anyone other than a complete novice, i.e., a 35 kyu player.

The restricted range of the estimated ranks for the preliminary program (24 to 30 kyu) also is of interest. Examination of the detailed game records indicates that this can be attributed almost entirely to the ability of the pattern and representation components to define and keep track of the program's groups over the course of a game. The interim program cannot yet analyze and take advantage of interactions among situations, it cannot construct moves with multiple purposes, and it has no ability to plan. Moreoever, the interim control structure is unnecessarily conservative in defending itself and it takes the offensive only when it has no other alternative. As a result, the game records contain many instances of easy attacks and kills that the program never even considered. But ignoring bugs, the only cases in which the program loses a group are those in which several groups are inferred to be unstable and in need of defense at the same time. However complex the patterns on the board may become, the program's representation of the structure of its groups remains intact; and when it recognizes moves that threaten its groups, it reacts accordingly.

## 6.0 CONCLUDING COMMENTS

In Go, the ability to recognize and utilize pattern information is presumed at all levels. Some patterns are straightforward local configurations of stones. Others are higher level structures whose elements are themselves complex patterns. It remains to be seen how well the interim program's pattern recognition and inference components will work in conjunction with the analysis, planning, and problem solving components still to be developed. The game results and move-by-move records suggest, however, that these components do return information quite comparable to that provided by the recognition and inference capabilities of a skilled Go player.

Insofar as the interim program plays primarily on the basis of direct inferences from patterns, it may be regarded as modeling a highly intuitive human player, one who uses "perceptualized" surrogates in place of the complex planning processes a more analytic player would employ. In designing the interim program we have tried to aggregate the many different kinds of pattern recognition activities into a small set of basic scanning and recognition mechanisms (the lens, edge, and web components) and to define all of the interim program's inference processes with respect to these mechanisms. Given our limited present understanding of the ways in which the human perceptual system operates, we would suggest that the strategy adopted here, identifying and developing analogs for a limited set of basic recognition and scanning mechanisms appropriate to a given domain, should prove useful in investigating skilled performance in other complex, perceptually rich domains as well.

Finally, as indicated in discussing the lens system, the treatment of pattern-directed inference throughout the program is quite conservative. The Go board is not a continuous space. Differences of a single line can have large effects. Furthermore, interactions among patterns must always be considered. In domains with these characteristics, the generation of inferences on the basis of some uniform notion of "similarity" probably is inappropriate. Instead, the present system deals with novel configurations by breaking them down into identifiable and characterizable subpatterns, and then trying to infer, e.g., by lookahead analyses of the interactions among the subpatterns, what an appropriate response might be. We will not be able to assess the real effectiveness of this treatment until the full set of analysis, planning, and problem solving components has been completed. Once these components are operational, however, we anticipate that recognition and inference problems that seem unmanageable in isolation often will turn out to be quite tractable, because pattern recognition is treated not as a complete process in and of itself, but as one essential component of a more general information processing system. If this expectation is confirmed, the approach to pattern-directed inference taken here should prove useful as a general scheme for dealing with other domains as well.

# THE PRODUCTION SYSTEM: ARCHITECTURE AND ABSTRACTION

Stanley J. Rosenschein
*Technion-Israel Institute of Technology*

*The use of production systems as the primary method for encoding knowledge in large knowledge-based systems is discussed at two levels; their suitability as an architecture that can be efficiently supported and their appropriateness as a language of expression. Questions of efficiency are posed in the framework of a broad class of pattern-directed rewrite systems. Factors governing efficiency are discussed informally, and the usefulness of production systems as an information processing abstraction is examined critically. In this regard, several problems suggested by work on lexically motivated inference are described. It is argued that the use of a particular class of production systems demands a more detailed justification in domain-specific terms than is often given.*

## 1.0 INTRODUCTION

A large knowledge-based system is ordinarily judged by its performance, extensibility, psychological validity, comprehensibility, and other similar criteria. It follows then that a general formalism for encoding knowledge in such a system must be judged by how well it promotes these qualities. Two central issues are involved in the evaluation:

(a) *(Architecture)* Is the formalism a powerful and efficient way to embody the knowledge of the domain in a computer program, regardless of its expressiveness for human users of the program? What are the hidden costs of the formalism? Can they be reduced in principle and in practice by using clever implementation techniques?

(b) *(Abstraction)* Is the formalism a natural way to express a human's understanding of the domain, regardless of its relative efficiency? What are the properties of the formalism viewed as a vehicle for conceptualization and communication?

These questions are raised in an attempt to explore the feasibility of using pattern-directed rewrite systems (production systems) in large-scale programs. For an overview of production systems in the context of knowledge-based systems, see [Davis76b].

On the question of architecture, production systems raise many of the same issues as ordinary programming languages. Both programming languages and production systems shield the programmer from implementation costs, which generally rise in proportion to the "level" of the formalism being implemented. Techniques for improving efficiency include optimizing compilers for high-level languages and clever preprocessors for production system rules. However, the use of certain types of production rules entails severe run-time inefficiency even if preprocessing is allowed.

The potential loss of efficiency makes it essential that a high-level formalism at least serve as a good *abstraction*, one that aids the process of composing solutions for the class of problems for which it was intended. Production systems have two shortcomings in this regard. First, they lack convenient facilities for the hierarchical description of processes. Second, because the operations are not abstract but rather are oriented toward particular syntactic transformations, production systems encourage the premature choice of representations for the computation structures. This point is illustrated in Section 4.2 by considering the problem of syntactic reorganization of propositions during matching.

The present exposition is not concerned with defining a single production system but rather delineating a class of such systems. A particular production system can then be viewed as an instance of a production system type. It is hoped that this framework (or a similar one) might sharpen comparisons of production systems and clarify design decisions. Although the current treatment is informal, it is felt that such a framework will ultimately be needed as the basis for a careful formal study of the computational complexity of production systems.

In Section 2 the class of production systems under consideration is defined more precisely. Implementation problems for the case of unrestricted rules are discussed in Section 3, along with suggested restrictions allowing more efficient run-time behavior. Section 4 is devoted to a brief critique of production systems as an abstraction and an examination of related difficulties in trying to express lexical inference in a pattern-based rewrite system. Section 5 summarizes by suggesting the need for more careful justification of production systems.

## 2.0 CLASSES OF PRODUCTION SYSTEMS

A *production system* will be taken to be a set of *rules* (possibly with additional structure) together with a *control strategy* for selecting the rule(s) to be applied. By a rule we mean an antecedent-consequent pair drawn from a certain set of symbolic objects. An antecedent can be *matched* against a *data object*, which in different versions of the production system formalism may be referred to as the data base, short term memory, symbol string, etc. The results of the match are used together with the consequent to derive a new data object in one step (conceptually). As stated above, the present goal is the description of a broad class of production systems. The first stage of this description involves the definitions of classes of objects from which the *data object* and *rule* structures can be chosen, while in the second stage the class of permissible *control* structures is defined.

### 2.1 A Universe of Symbolic Objects

Of central interest here are production systems that do what has been called "syntactic pattern matching," [D.G. Bobrow75a] i.e., that test only equality of symbols and conformability of syntactic structure. As such, the domains of interest comprise sets of symbolic structures similar to the data types of QLISP [Sacerdoti76, Wilber76]. The basic symbols are drawn from three disjoint, potentially infinite sets of *atomic types*:

CONST = {A, FOO, BAR, ...}       (constants)
IVAR = {?x33, ?foo, ?a-variable, ...}   (unit variables)
SVAR = {$x41, $bar, $seg, ...}    (segment variables)

The uses for the two variable types are explained in Section 2.2 (formal definitions are contained in the Appendix):

I.  *Sequences over B: seq(B)*

Examples:  1.  (FOO BAR GLITCH) $\epsilon$ *seq*(CONST)
2.  ((AA BB CC) (X Y Z)(FOO BAR))
$\epsilon$ *seq*(*seq*(CONST))
3.  ((AA BB CC)?x (FOO))$\epsilon$ *seq*(IVAR$\cup$ *seq*(CONST))

II.  *Sets over B: set(b)*

Examples:  1.  ({FOO, BAR} {AA, BB, CC}) $\epsilon$ *seq*(*set*(CONST))
2.  {(FOO BAR), (AA BB CC)} $\epsilon$ *set*(*seq*(CONST))

III.  *Sequences recursively embedded to any level: seq\*(B)*

Examples:  1.  (AA BB CC (((D E) F)) G) $\epsilon$ *seq\**(CONST)
2.  (AA BB (C ?x)((C) ?y)) $\epsilon$ *seq\**(CONST$\cup$IVAR)

IV.  *Sets recursively embedded to any level: set*\*(B)*

Example:  {(AA  BB), {{(FOO BAR), {}} , (J K)}} ∈ *set*\*(*seq*(CONST))

V.  *Sets and sequences mutually embedded to any level: set/q*\*(B)*

Example:  ({AA, BB} (C D){{Q}, ((AA BB)(FOO BAR))})
    ∈ *set/q*\*(CONST)

The *universe* is defined as UNIV = *set/q*\*(CONST ∪ IVAR ∪ SVAR). Clearly all sets constructible from CONST, IVAR, and SVAR using set union and the operations given above (*set, seq,* etc.) are contained in this set.

One distinguished structure-building operation is provided: *pair*(B) = {(b₁ → b₂) | bᵢ ∈ B, i = 1,2}. (A pair can be thought of a special kind of sequence.) b₁ is called the *antecedent* and b₂ the *consequent*. Rule structures are taken from some set

$$struct_1(pair(struct_2))$$

where *struct₁* is a composition of *set, seq,* etc., while *struct₂* is obtained from atomic types through zero or more operations of set union, *set, seq, ..., set/q*\*. For every different *struct₁* and *struct₂* we get a different class of rule structures. Having specified the rule structure, we require that the data object be drawn from *struct*₂₂ (in many cases from the subset over CONST).

An example of a valid rule structure is

$$set(seq(pair(set(seq(CONST ∪ IVAR))))).$$

To give this structure an intuitive basis, the following interpretation might be imagined:

*seq*(CONST ∪ IVAR) will represent individual assertions (possibly with variables), e.g., (GIVE JOHN ?x MARY)

*pair*(*set*(*seq*(CONST ∪ IVAR))) would be the rewrites whose antecedents and consequents are *sets* of such assertions, representing the conjunction of the assertions in the set

*seq*(*pair*(*set*(*seq*(CONST ∪ IVAR)))) represents sequences of rewrite rules, perhaps to be tried in the order given

*set*(*seq*(*pair*(*set*(*seq*(CONST ∪ IVAR))))) could be viewed as sets of alternative rewrite sequences (perhaps to describe backup, alternate data interpretation rules, etc.)

## 2.2 The Control Component

The specification of rule and data object structure drawn from some set of possibilities is only part of the task of defining a production system; a control structure must also be specified. Of course not all the possibilities can be enumerated, especially since there are so many diverse types of rule structure. Instead some weak conditions are given that a program must satisfy in order to be considered a control structure for the purposes of this discussion.

First we will define some predicates and functions to be used by control structures.

Assume the following predicates are given:

(1) nullset(x): true if x = { }.

(2) nullseq(x): true if x = ( ).

(3) of-type(x,t): true if at the top level x is of type t, where t is one of the type indicators SET,SEQ,CONST,IVAR, or SVAR.

(4) equal(x,y): defined recursively: Elements of atomic type are equal only if they are identical; two sets are equal if every member of each is equal to some member of the other; and two sequences are equal if they are componentwise equal.

Assume further that three functions are given for manipulating an associative memory (denoted AM) allowing any pair of elements of UNIV to be linked. (Such a memory will be used during matching, but may be used elsewhere as well.)

(5) nullmem( ): returns an initialized associative memory.

(6) store(a,b,mem): returns a new AM that is like mem except that a is linked to b.

(7) get(a,mem): returns the element of UNIV that is linked to a in mem. If there is no such element, *error* is returned as a value.

Nothing is assumed about how the AM is implemented, but it is often convenient to denote by $(b_1/a_1 \ldots b_k/a_k)$ that mem such that get($a_1$,mem) = $b_1$, etc.

We have a substitution function:

(8) subst(e,mem): where e $\epsilon$ UNIV and mem is an AM.

This function instantiates expressions from UNIV. It works in the ordinary way, and we shall just illustrate its use rather than define it:

$$\text{subst}(\{\$x, C, B, (G H \$y ?q), ?q\},$$
$$(\{C, D\}/\$x (H E F)/\$y \{M\}/?q))$$
$$= \{C, D, B, (G H H E F \{M\}), \{M\}\}$$

Constants map into themselves, and item variables can map into any element of UNIV. However, segment variables must map into structures the same as that of the level in which they appear so that these values might be "union-ed" or "spliced in"(according to whether that structure is a set of a sequence).

A *control structure* will be considered to be any program (defined in a conventional way) that uses this instruction set, augmented by instructions for iterating over sets and sequences (e.g., *head* and *tail*), subject to the following constraints: The program must process the rule structure and must contain a distinguished variable D (data object) taking values from UNIV. In addition, the program must have at least one "update" statement of the form

$$D \leftarrow \text{subst}(consqt, \ bindings)$$

whose use can be described as follows: if *val* is the value of D just before executing the statement, there must be some $(antcdt \rightarrow consqt)$ rule occurring in the rule structure such that subst($antcdt, \ bindings$) = $val$. No other statements may modify D, except possibly input statements.

## 2.3 Sample Production System

Let us illustrate the preceding definitions with an example of a particular production system, P = (RULES, CONTROL). Let RULES be a member of $seq(pair(seq(\text{CONST} \cup \text{SVAR})))$

$$
\begin{aligned}
\text{RULES} = \ &(((\$x \ A \ B \ \$y) \rightarrow (\$x \ B \ A \ \$y)) \\
&((\$x \ A \ \$y) \rightarrow (\$x \ G \ G \ \$y)) \\
&((\$x \ B \ \$y) \rightarrow (\$x \ H \ H \ \$y))).
\end{aligned}
$$

CONTROL will be a program written in an Algol-like language that meets the requirements stated above. In this program the function leftmost__match (form$_1$, form$_2$) is assumed to return an associative memory mem such that

$$\text{subst}(\text{form}_1, \text{mem}) = \text{form}_2$$

and such that the segment variables in order from left to right match the shortest sequences possible. (Note that the null sequence is the shortest sequence of all and will match a segment variable.)

```
CONTROL =
  while (true)
    do remaining_rules ← RULES;
      success ← false;
      while (not(nullseq(remaining_rules)) and not(success))
        do curr_rule ← head(remaining_rules);
        remaining_rules ← tail(remaining_rules);
        bindings ← leftmost_match(antecedent(curr_rule),D);
        if bindings ≠ error then
        /* UPDATE STATEMENT */
```

*do* D ← subst(consequent(curr_rule), bindings);
    success ← *true*
  *end*;
  *end*;
  *If not(success)then* HALT;
 *end*;

The program CONTROL allows for no input from the external environment and thus, together with RULES, defines a transformation that will cause D to receive the following values if its initial value is (A B B A B A):

(B A B A B A) → (B B A A B A) → ... → (H H H H H H G G G G G G)

## 3.0 SOME EFFICIENCY CONSIDERATIONS

Most models of computation assume some universe of structures divided into a finite number of equivalence classes by some primitive tests and mapped onto other structures by a function determined by the equivalence class. Unit cost may be assumed for each primitive transformation at the abstract level only. If the model is to be implemented on some device, each unit of computation ordinarily entails overhead.

### 3.1 How to Sort in "Linear" Time

A simple illustration of the above principle in the context of production systems involves sorting positive integers . Let us symbolize the number n by the sequence (NUM n n-1 n-2 ...1). Thus, for example, our somewhat extravagant representation of "5" is (NUM 5 4 3 2 1). With such a representation we can express a sorting algorithm as a rewrite system that successively transforms a pair of lists of "numbers," one containing numbers to be sorted and the other containing numbers already sorted. For example, if the list (4 7 1 5) were to be sorted, the production system would be given the following input:

D = ((UNSORTED (NUM 4 3 2 1) (NUM 7 6 5 4 3 2 1) (NUM 1)
      (NUM 5 4 3 2 1))

  (SORTED))

Assuming the sample control structure (CONTROL) described in Section 2.3, consider the following rule structure (the rules are numbered for convenience):

```
(
1. (((UNSORTED   (NUM ?largest-digit $rest)
                 $other-unsorted-nums)
       (SORTED   $smaller-sorted-nums
                 (NUM $big-digits ?largest-digit $rest)
                 $also-sorted))
          → ((UNSORTED $other-unsorted-nums)
             (SORTED    $smaller-sorted-nums
                 (NUM ?largest-digit $rest)
                 (NUM $big-digits ?largest-digit $rest)
                 $also-sorted)))
2. (((UNSORTED   ?some-num
                 $other-nums)
       (SORTED   $any-sorted-list))
          → ((UNSORTED $other-nums)
             (SORTED    $any-sorted-list
                 ?some-num))))
```

The idea behind rule 1 is to find the spot in the sorted list where the first yet-unsorted number is to be inserted. Rule 2 is used to take care of the case where the first unsorted number is larger than all the sorted ones, as will be the case initially.

The sequence of values taken by D during the computation is as follows:

```
((UNSORTED (NUM 4 3 2 1)
           (NUM 7 6 5 4 3 2 1)
           (NUM 1)
           (NUM 5 4 3 2 1))
      (SORTED))
rule 2
=> ((UNSORTED (NUM 7 6 5 4 3 2 1)
              (NUM 1)
              (NUM 5 4 3 2 1))
         (SORTED (NUM 4 3 2 1)))
rule 2
=> ((UNSORTED (NUM 1)
              (NUM 5 4 3 2 1))
         (SORTED (NUM 4 3 2 1)
                 (NUM 7 6 5 4 3 2 1)))
rule 1
    ((UNSORTED (NUM 5 4 3 2 1))
    => (SORTED (NUM 1)
               (NUM 4 3 2 1)
               (NUM 7 6 5 4 3 2 1)))
```

```
rule 1
=> ((UNSORTED)
      (SORTED  (NUM 1)
               (NUM 4 3 2 1)
               (NUM 5 4 3 2 1)
               (NUM 7 6 5 4 3 2 1))))
```

Because each step involves exactly one rewrite, if each rewrite were of unit cost we would have a linear sort. Of course the "linear" sort depends on the judicious use of hidden tests in the control structure that are not counted. In fact, a direct implementation of this production system would yield an $O(n^2)$ sort.

### 3.2 Production Systems and Optimization

It is not difficult to construct production systems that solve NP-complete problems in a "single" step, and it seems that a pattern-matching operation can be used to do almost an arbitrary amount of work. Such examples are plentiful but of course do not in themselves discredit production systems or make any *particular* production system infeasible. The question naturally arises whether a "compiler" or "preprocessor" could be presented with a rule structure in advance and come up with a more efficient program equivalent to a given control program P in the sense of determining the same sequence of D values (or in some other suitable sense). (See also [Davis76b, F. Hayes-Roth76b]).

Since it is easy to show that the detection problem is very hard in the general case—no matter what equivalence preserving transformation we allow—several alternative approaches suggest themselves:

(1) The programmer may be encouraged to refrain "voluntarily" from employing certain legal but inefficient constructs.
(2) The formalism may be constrained to allow only as much flexibility as the domain seems to demand.
(3) Optimizations may be employed to improve performance.

Each approach has its drawbacks:

(1) Having the programmer consider implementation costs run counter to the goals of a high-level formalism.
(2) It may be difficult to estimate in advance how much flexibility will be required for a certain domain.
(3) Optimizations may not be known or may themselves be impractical to implement.

For these reasons, no solution will be completely satisfactory in the general case. Nonetheless, the convenience of a high-level formalism is seen as justifying a certain degree of inefficiency, which hopefully can be minimized in various ways. Here is a partial list of properties characterizing production systems with efficient run-time behavior (possibly after optimization). This list is based on practical experience with an experimental system for pattern-based inference [Joshi76, Rosenschein75a, b], although additional formal study would be quite useful.

(1) *seq* is used instead of *set* wherever possible, whenever the whole structure is to be matched.

(2) Segment variables are avoided, especially contiguous segment variables for *seq* and any multiple segment variables for *set*.

(3) The rule structure contains a distribution of constants that differentiate the rules well, so that indexing can be used to choose candidates for matching.

(4) Control structures that allow unrestricted, syntactically based partial matches are avoided.

(5) In a single pattern, formulas are avoided which are identical except for a different distribution of variables, e.g.,

$$\{(R \ ?x \ ?y \ ?x), (R \ ?x \ ?x \ ?y) \ \ldots\}.$$

(6) A rule structure of the form

$$((\ldots ?x \ldots) \to (FOO \ ?x)$$
$$((FOO \ ?x) \ldots) \to \ldots$$
$$((FOO \ ?x) \ldots) \to \ldots \quad )$$

is preferable to one of the form

$$( \ (\ldots ?x \ldots) \to \ldots$$
$$(\ldots ?x \ldots) \to \ldots$$
$$\ldots \qquad )$$

where $(\ldots ?x \ldots)$ is a complicated expression that would have to be repeatedly matched otherwise; this may be thought of as the pattern-match equivalent of the assignment statement often introduced in programs to avoid repeated evaluation of identical subexpressions.

(7) The data object is kept small and "hierarchical" so that where an exhaustive match must be performed, failure can occur quickly. That is, deep, heterogeneous structures are preferred to broad, homogeneous structures. For example, {( )}( )( )}} is better than {{}{}}{}{}{}}.

The extent to which such guidelines will appear natural will depend on the problem domain and the designer's conception of it.

# 4.0 THE PRODUCTION SYSTEM AS AN ABSTRACTION

## 4.1 Process Abstraction and Data Abstraction

The primary method by which abstraction is achieved in a programming language is by allowing the programmer to treat sequences of steps as a single step. That is, complex operations (i.e., compositions of primitive operations) can be named and treated as though they were primitive, and the language promotes this by providing appropriate dictions. The definition of ever more complex operations in this way results in the hierarchical structure obtainable in all but the most primitive of programming languages.

In production systems, abstraction is achieved in another way. The built-in tests and transformations are very sophisticated and are designed to implement constructs found useful in various applications. However, there is generally no way to symbolize composition of operations in a transparent way. Complicated tests and actions have to be simulated by groups of rules whose coordination is not symbolized in the program or graced with a mnemonic name. The more complicated the tests and actions, the more severe the coordination problems. This is typical of programs written at one level of abstraction, no matter how sophisticated the primitive operators.

Inflexibility in composing operations has immediate effects on choice of representations. One would like data objects to be abstract, i.e., structural attributes of a data object should be logically determined by the operations performed on it [Liskov75]. If new manipulating operations are definable, then new data abstractions can be created *ipso facto*. If, on the other hand, new operators are *not* definable, the tendency is to make the conceptualization of the problem fit the available data structures. The class of data structures UNIV constructed in Section 2.1 is a very rich class, but even though all problem domains could be represented as appropriate structures in UNIV, these structures may still be the most natural choice.

## 4.2 An Experimental Inference System:  Partial Match and Syntactic Reorganization

Let us examine this problem in the context of a production system for inference that, on the surface, appears to be a domain quite well suited for this approach. The most straightforward way to implement an inference system is to conceive of the database as a set of "facts" (symbolic representations of propositions). The syntactic structure chosen for propositions might be arbitrary nested sequences of constants, yielding databases in *set(seq*\*(CONST))*. Rules transform one set of facts into another. For example:

(1)  {(LIKE ?x ?y), (PERSON ?x), (PERSON ?y) $z}
     → {(WANT ?x (LIKE ?y ?x)),(LIKE ?x ?y),
        (PERSON ?x) (PERSON ?y), $z}
(2)  {(WANT ?x (LIKE ?y ?x)), (KNOW ?x (WANT ?y ?a)), $z}
     → {(TRY ?x (CAUSE ?x ?a)), (WANT ?x (LIKE ?y ?x)),
        (KNOW ?x (WANT ?y ?a)), $z}

Given such rules, an initial data base

{(LIKE JOHN MARY), (PERSON JOHN),
    (PERSON MARY),
(KNOW JOHN (WANT MARY
    (HAVE MARY BOOK)))}

would be transformed in two steps to

{(LIKE JOHN MARY), (PERSON JOHN), (PERSON MARY),
(WANT JOHN (LIKE MARY JOHN)),
(KNOW JOHN (WANT MARY (HAVE MARY BOOK))),
(TRY JOHN (CAUSE JOHN (HAVE MARY BOOK)))}.

Part of the effort reported in [Joshi76, Rosenschein75a, b] was to develop a theoretically sound pattern-matching system for lexically grounded inferences. Two types of inferences in particular were of interest: (1) automatic instantiation of definitions (or in general, replacing a group of propositions by a single summarizing proposition), and conversely (2) automatic expansion of such definitions or summaries. Many aspects of this problem were considered, and on the whole, models based on rewrite systems were well suited to the domain. There were several areas, however, that highlight deficiencies of the approach. These areas have to do with the flexibility of matching and the lack of facilities for hierarchical process description.

Consider the problem of partial match. The goal here was to find criteria to allow a rewrite rule to be invoked even when some of the antecedent propositions have no instance in the database. (Imagine the example above with (PERSON JOHN) deleted from the initial database.) The reason for permitting such a match is to develop a more "robust" system. However, implementation difficulties arise because partial match essentially treats each rule as a class of rules whose antecedents are the various approximating patterns. This generally has a pronounced negative effect on the efficiency of the matcher because the partial matcher must persist in its search even *after* discovering a mismatch on a symbol, making blind alleys that much more time consuming.

Some treatment was also given to the problem of matches that necessitate syntactic reorganization of the proposition . For example, "John does something . . ." might be represented by

(?p JOHN).

When this pattern is matched against

(SEE JOHN MARY)

the following substitution would be obtained:

(LAMBDA(X)(SEE X MARY))/?p.

This then necessitates the introduction of a new equivalence relation into the pattern matcher to take into account the equivalence of the two expressions

((LAMBDA(X)(SEE X MARY)) JOHN)

and

(SEE JOHN MARY).

This is not complicated, but it reduces efficiency considerably.

In an inference system, tests and transformations that one would like to perform on a proposition are often more complex than simple pattern matching and instantiation support: equivalence of logical expressions, occurrence of subexpressions at an arbitrary level of recursion, lambda abstraction , etc. Several approaches are possible in dealing with these problems, each with its own shortcomings. The first alternative is to write a more sophisticated pattern matcher, providing even fancier primitives. The drawback here is the introduction of general inefficiency to solve a local problem.

Alternatively, a complex operation, e.g., testing equivalence of two propositions by reduction to canonical form, can be simulated using a set of coordinated rewrites to carry out the reduction. Here the drawback is comprehensibility; the details of the reduction algorithm are not interesting at the level at which we want to use the equivalence test, yet this approach would require that they be specified as rewrites.

A third possibility, one often employed in practice, is to allow for the evaluation of arbitrary expressions in the antecedent and/or consequent. By embedding the production system in a programming language, the language's resources can be drawn upon to compensate for the production system's clumsiness in certain instances. While this solution takes us outside the class of systems we are considering, it may be noted in passing that it also impedes efforts to develop syntactically based match optimizations.

## 5.0 CONCLUSIONS

If a production system is to be something more than a very high level assembly language with an exorbitantly expensive interpreter, its use should be carefully scrutinized. Problems of efficiency, together with conceptual problems, indicate that a detailed justification of the use of production systems be formulated for every domain to which they are applied. This justification should first attempt to analyze the domain without representational bias; it should then be shown how the data structures and operations needed for the domain are just those provided by a particular production system type (rule class and control structure). Because the procedure is often reversed, the resulting efficiency and comprehensibility are significanty reduced.

## APPENDIX

*Definitions of Structure-Building Operations*

I.    $seq(B) = \{(b_1 \ldots b_n) \mid b_i \in B, 1 \leqslant i \leqslant n, n \geqslant 0\}$.

II.   $set(B) = \{\{b_1, \ldots, b_n\} \mid b_i \in B, 1 \leqslant i \leqslant n, n \geqslant 0\}$.

III.  $seq^*(B)$ is the least set S such that
    a) $B \subseteq S$
    and b) $x_1, \ldots, x_n \in S \Rightarrow (x_1 \ldots x_n) \in S, n \geqslant 0$.

IV.   $set^*(B)$ is the least set S such that
    a) $B \subseteq S$
    and b) $x_1, \ldots, x_n \in S \Rightarrow \{x_1, \ldots, x_n\} \in S, n \geqslant 0$.

V.    $set/q^*(B)$ is the least set S such that
    a) $B \subseteq S$
    b) $x_1, \ldots, x_n \in S \Rightarrow (x_1 \ldots x_n) \in S, n \geqslant 0$
    and c) $x_1, \ldots, x_n \in S \Rightarrow \{x_1, \ldots, x_n\} \in S, n \geqslant 0$.

# PRODUCTION SYSTEMS WITH FEEDBACK

Steven W. Zucker[1]
*McGill University*

*Production systems provide a methodology for using knowledge embedded in (condition → action) pairs. An action is performed when its conditions match the state of a current data base. When multiple conditions match the data base simultaneously, however, the problem arises of which productions should be executed. Such multiple matches can derive from ambiguity and uncertainty in the data base and condition patterns. One solution to this multiple matching problem is to extend the production system with a form of feedback. This chapter describes the implementation of feedback directed toward global data base consistency. Specific examples are chosen from a low-level vision system.*

## 1.0 INTRODUCTION

Production systems provide a framework for implementing pattern-directed computations. As an introductory example of a production system (PS), Newell and Simon ([Newell72b], p. 44) suggested modeling a thermostat:

*Thermostat:*

PD1: temperature > 70° and temperature < 72° → stop.
PD2: temperature < 32° → call-repair-man; turn-on *electric heat.*
PD3: temperature < 70° and furnace-state = off → turn-on *furnace.*
PD4: temperature > 72° and furnace-state = on → turn-off *furnace.*

[1] The preparation of this chapter was supported by a grant from the Graduate Faculty of McGill University.

This production system consists of four rules. The left-hand side or condition of each rule indicates a pattern of predefined variables that must be matched to the data base. When one of these patterns matches successfully, the action sequence indicated by the right-hand side is executed.

Production systems (PSs) have been used in a number of recent attempts at modeling psychological processes [Moran73, Newell73, Waterman75] and at implementing expert systems [Shortliffe76]. Their popularity derives from the advantages they offer for expressing knowledge in a fine-grained and modular form. However, some of these attempts have uncovered a fundamental problem with the PS methodology: How should the system function when there are a number of activation-condition partial matches and no perfect matches?

To illustrate how such a problem situation could arise, consider the thermostat example once again. As long as the value for the temperature variable is known precisely, the interpreter can select the proper rule for execution. However, actual temperature sensors are never perfect; there is always some uncertainty (or noise) in their response. If the temperature is only approximately 72° (i.e., 72 ± 1°) should the interpreter select PD1 or PD4? Or, should both fire, with the system somehow maintaining a record of the different possibilities? In the first case, the performance of the PS becomes nondeterministic. A "best" production is selected on some basis, such as noise statistics. However, the consequences of this selection are not known until many subsequent productions have fired. In the second case the combinatorial explosion of possibilities would rapidly cripple any system even moderately more complex than this simplified example (e.g., [Mostow77]).

The central theme of this chapter is that a form of feedback can be used as a control structure to deal with these multiple partial match situations. The feedback embodies a mechanism for eliminating the incorrect or noise matches by evaluating each of their effects in terms of data base consistency. Multiple partial matches arise both when uncertainty is introduced into the data base, as in the sensor noise of the thermostat example, and when there is ambiguity in the specification of the data base (or activation-condition) patterns. These two cases are discussed in more detail in Section 2, after which the essential properties of a feedback mechanism and certain of its implementations are described.

## 2.0 PATTERN AMBIGUITY AND UNCERTAINTY

In this section, a low-level vision problem is considered that lends itself to a discussion of ambiguity and uncertainty in data base and production rule patterns. One purpose of low-level vision systems is to build a description of the intensity changes in an image in terms of a vocabulary of low-level symbols. This is analogous to the lower levels of speech understanding systems that attempt to interpret the acoustic waveform into a sequence of phonemes. The specific vision problem considered is the interpretation of local binary patterns into a space of linelike objects. Locally this will require attaching assertions about the presence (or absence) of oriented unit line segments to the various pictorial positions.[2] The process of attaching appropriate assertions can be formulated as a PS with productions of the form shown in Fig. 1. Each condition is a $3 \times 3$ binary pattern, and the associated action is to assign the right-hand side assertion to the pictorial position corresponding to the center of the pattern. Figure 1a shows productions for describing perfect line segments in any of four quantized orientations. Figure 1b shows some of the additional productions necessary to describe line segments whose end points lie in the $3 \times 3$ pattern. Even more productions would be necessary if the line segments were to have varying thicknesses, intermediate orientations, etc.

As long as the data base (i.e., the picture) only contains clearly distinct examples of these patterns, the selection of appropriate productions is a feasible task for the interpreter. When combinations of the condition patterns are allowed, however, the individual pattern states become less distinct, and the task facing the interpreter becomes much more complex. Many of the productions match the data base at least partially, making them all possible candidates for execution. For example, productions PL1, PL5, PL7, and PL9 all match the pattern shown in Fig. 2, and some even match in more than one way.

The problem of selecting one production over another in ambiguous situations such as this has been dealt with in a number of different ways. Some systems, e.g., PSG [Newell73], scan the rules in a predetermined order until one match evaluates successfully. The interpreter then executes this rule and begins another scan through the productions. Other systems find the rules whose activation-conditions evaluate successfully. This set of rules is called the conflict set. A single rule is chosen from this set by a scheme based on the following (from [Davis76b], p. 30):

(1) Rule order: there is a complete ordering of all rules in the system, and the rule in the conflict set with the highest priority is chosen.

(2) Data order: elements of the data base are ordered, and that

---

[2] A more complete vocabulary for gray-level images would be much larger, probably including additional assertions about the presence or absence of edge segments and certain blob or regionlike constructs [Marr75]. However, a larger vocabulary would only complicate this example further.

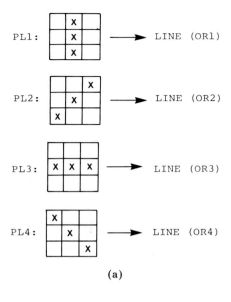

(a)

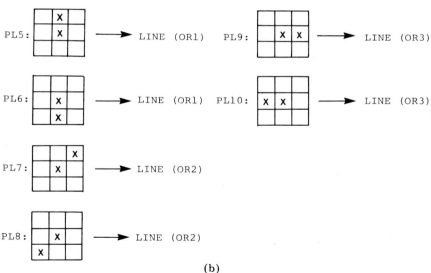

(b)

Fig. 1. (a) Sample productions for four ideal line patterns. (b) Some of the additional productions necessary for lines that end.

rule which matches element(s) in the data base with highest priority is chosen.

(3)  Generality order:  the most specific rule is chosen.

(4)  Rule precedence:  a precedence network (perhaps containing cycles) determines the order of execution.

Fig. 2. An ambiguous pattern to which many productions match.

(5) Recency order: choosing either the most recently executed rule, or the rule containing the most recently updated element of the data base.

All of these schemes can lead to reasonable resolutions of the multiple matching problem as long as the individual knowledge states (i.e., the data base patterns) are clearly distinct from one another. This is not the case for the low-level vision problem, however, and therefore none of these schemes is particularly applicable. Furthermore there are no theoretical guidelines for suggesting which one should be attempted.

The problems of multiple and partial matching become even more complicated when the PS data base contains inexact information. This occurs in systems dealing with realistic or judgmental data, such as Hearsay-II or MYCIN. Inexact information was the cause of the problem in the thermostat example, and it enters the low-level vision example in many forms. One form is as quantization errors in line orientation. That is, the actual orientation of the line segment is the indicated quantized orientation plus a small error. Another form is as noise points in the binary image. These noise points could block correct productions from matching by falling within a line, or they could enable incorrect productions by falling between or adjacent to actual lines. As a specific illustration, consider the different sets of productions that would match Fig. 2 if an additional dark square were added or if a current dark square were deleted. For both of these cases, the degradation in performance would be in proportion to the amount of corrupting noise.

The previous schemes for dealing with multiple matches provide little guidance for inexact or noise matches. For example, the first production in the system will almost always partially match, and any precedence scheme would require knowing the noise sample properties *a priori*. Furthermore, the definition of additional productions capable of detecting every possible noise situation with the accompanying line pattern is an impossible task, since even for this simplified example there are $2^9$ possible activation-conditions for each $3 \times 3$ pattern in the image.

An analogous situation from the Hearsay-II speech understanding system is shown in Fig. 3 (from [Mostow77]). Multiple matches are shown as various hypothesized words attached to positions in the utterance. They derive both from the lack of a one-to-one correspondence between the acoustic waveform and the actual spoken words and from noise in the transduced waveform.

The conflict set of multiple matches can be thought of as containing true matches and noise matches. Normally the noise matches, when selected, lead the PS to apply many incorrect productions. This in turn entails nondeterminism (i.e., necessitates backtracking) and in many situations leads to thrashing [D.G. Bobrow74]. As will be shown in Section 3, structuring a system in a closed-loop configuration provides the feedback necessary for it to function in the presence of such noise sources. This feedback also provides the capability for coarser encodings of knowledge than that suggested in these opening examples.

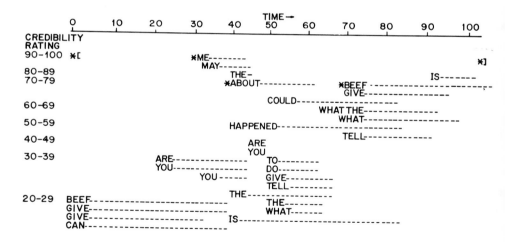

Fig. 3. Words hypothesized by Hearsay II in response to utterance "Tell me about beef" (from Hayes-Roth and Mostow, 1976).

## 3.0 FEEDBACK AND CONTROL THEORY

The theory and use of feedback have been developed within the context of control systems engineering. For this reason some background information about control systems will be helpful in understanding how feedback works.

Control engineering is concerned with the problem of regulating mechanisms so that they perform properly and stably, even in the presence of noise disturbances. A block diagram of a canonical regulator system is shown in Fig. 4a. For this system, the reference input defines the desired state of the system, while the controlled output indicates its present state.[3] The instantaneous behavior of the system is determined by an error signal that is proportional to the difference between the desired state (i.e., the reference input) and the current state as it is indicated by the feedback transducer.

In terms of our original thermostat example, the state variable to be controlled is temperature. The component under control (i.e., the furnace) is activated by the difference between the current temperature (a portion of the current state) and the desired temperature. If this difference is negative (i.e., the desired temperature is warmer than the current temperature), the furnace turns on. If the difference is positive, the furnace turns off.

There are two basic types of regulator system configurations: open-loop systems, in which there is no feedback between the current state and the desired state (Fig. 4b), and closed-loop systems, in which there is feedback (Fig. 4a). For deterministic systems, i.e., systems containing no random components, open-loop and closed-loop behavior are, in an important sense, equivalent.[4] In both cases the control input is derived from an exact knowledge of the state of the system. When an accurate model for the system exists, knowledge of the initial state can be used to compute the state at any later time. Thus an open-loop controller can compute the state from its model for the system, and it can then compute the control input on the basis of both this computed current state and the desired final state. In the closed-loop configuration, the state can be measured directly, or it can be computed from measurements of the system.

As soon as uncertainty appears in the state description of the system, however, the fundamental difference between open-loop and closed-loop configurations becomes paramount. Knowledge of the current state, the system's dynamics, or perhaps both may be degraded by a disturbing random noise source. This makes closed-loop models manditory. The description of a random system can no longer be represented by a deterministic model, but now requires a stochastic, nondeterministic model. (For an introduction to stochastic control theory,

[3] In control theoretic terms, the system is assumed to be controllable and observable; a standard reference for these and other terms in control theory is Zadeh and Desoer [Zadeh61].

[4] There are, however, important practical differences in the behavior evidenced by systems in each of these configurations. These differences appear in dynamic criteria such as stability, bandwidth, and response time.

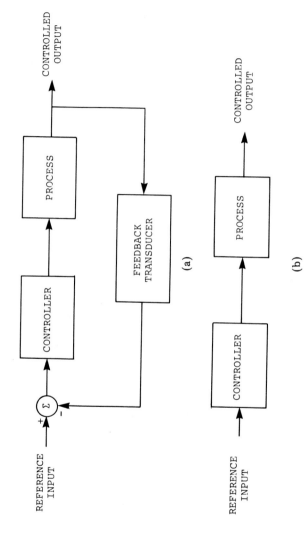

Fig. 4. (a) A closed-loop regulator configuration. (b) An open-loop regulator configuration.

see [Astrom70].) Random open-loop systems perform poorly because they must operate (compute the control input) with no specific knowledge of the disturbing noise processes and hence no exact knowledge of the current state. The controller can only assume that the system is operating according to a prespecified plan, e.g., a deterministic differential equation, and it must prescribe inputs on this basis. However, the noise source will eventually (with probability 1) cause the system to deviate from this planned track, in which case the open-loop control input may be completely wrong. Such would be the case for a vehicle traveling along a given trajectory. At each instant the velocity of the vehicle, or similarly its control, can be determined from its position on the trajectory. If, however, it deviated from this trajectory in a random direction, then applying the thrust determined by the trajectory would no longer propel the vehicle toward its goal. In terms of the thermostat example, the open-loop controller could not know whether or not the termperature had deviated from its prescribed, deterministic path. If it believed the temperature to be 71°, it would turn the furnace on. If the actual temperature was $71° + \xi$, where $\xi$ is a random variable distributed in the range [0,2], then the furnace could remain on above its cutoff temperature, even to the point of becoming critically explosive.

Closed-loop configurations allow the controller to accumulate information about the noise disturbances. This almost immediate feedback permits a constant updating of the estimate for the current state of the system that is used to compute the next control input. Thus if the actual temperature were 73° (i.e., $\xi = 2°$), this would be fed back to the comparator, which would yield a negative value, and the furnace would turn off. Or, in the case of the vehicle, the immediate past value for the deviation could be used to compute the next increment of thrust to orient it more directly toward its goal. Of course, the noise process could then perturb the vehicle in another random direction in the next increment of time, but this would be corrected by the next control input. This cycle of disturbance and compensation is repeated until the system reaches its final state.

In order to minimize the total time taken to reach the designated final state, or some other overall criterion, an optimal control strategy can be selected. For the case of linear systems with quadratic optimality criteria, the optimal strategy is given by the separation theorem [Astrom70], Chapter 8). This theorem is illustrated in block diagram form in Fig. 5. It states that the optimal strategy is to first compute an optimal estimate $\hat{X}$ of the state X. Then, assuming that this estimate is correct, use it to solve the deterministic control problem that results when all noise sources are set to zero.

In summary of this brief discussion of control theory, one of the primary advantages of systems with feedback is that they can con-

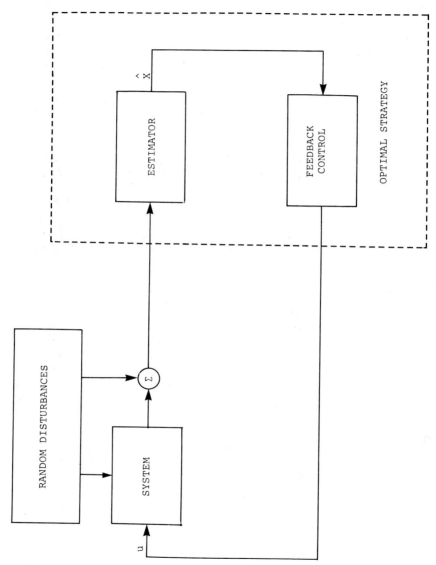

Fig. 5. Block diagram illustration of the separation theorem (after Astrom, 1970).

548

tinue to function under uncertain and noisy conditions. In other words, feedback reduces the system's dependency upon an accurate knowledge of the current state. Exactly this sort of uncertainty in the data base of a PS underlies the multiple partial pattern-matching problems discussed in Sections 1 and 2. Section 4 shows that a form of feedback can be used to reduce this data base uncertainty, leading to improved closed-loop behavior analogous to that of regulator systems.

## 4.0 REDUCING DATA BASE UNCERTAINTY WITH RELAXATION LABELING PROCESSES

Multiple partial pattern matches derive from either uncertainty in the data base or from production rules with partially overlapping activation-condition patterns. As shown in Section 3, the operation of the PS under uncertainty with proper conflict resolution requires a selection mechanism incorporating feedback. The essential property of feedback is its iterative comparison of the current state with the desired state in a way such that the results of the comparison can be used to correct the system toward this desired state.

A crude form of feedback does take place in PSs operating in depth-first search modes. However, the wrong choices remain undetected until many productions have fired and a contradiction is noticed. Only then does the system begin to backtrack, thrashing until the correct choice is stumbled upon.

Feedback can be implemented by allowing various forms of interaction between the data base and the production rules before a single rule is selected. Such feedback is provided by relaxation labeling processes (RLP) through their iterative rule for accumulating evidence [Rosenfeld76, Zucker76]. Metaphorically, RLPs can be viewed as a scheme for allowing all of the productions in the conflict set to fire simultaneously with a resultant consistency or compatability check on the new data base. The likelihood of each production being the correct one is then adjusted in an appropriate direction. This process continues, iteratively, with the various possibilities cooperating and competing with one another until only a minimally ambiguous set remains. Thus while the desired final state of the data base (i.e., the true pattern) is initially only implicit, the minimal ambiguity or maximal global compatability criterion is sufficient for obtaining it.

The symbolic aspect of a relaxation labeling process consists of a set of labels attached to each node in a graph. The labels indicate possible assertions about or interpretations of the objects denoted by the nodes. For the low-level vision example considered in this chapter, the objects are the $3 \times 3$ pictorial regions and the labels are the assertions shown in Fig. 1. An additional assertion indicating that no line segment is present at each location is also necessary. Thus the label set at each position corresponds to the conflict set of possible productions that could fire there. Each overlapping $3 \times 3$ area of the picture has such a label set attached to it.

The edges of the graph underlying the RLP indicate which nodes can interact with one another. For this example it is sufficient for each node to examine only its surrounding neighbors. The mutual compatibility between different labels on neighboring nodes is given by a list of compatibility functions. This is the way that *a priori* knowledge is built into the RLP. Note that such a representation is modular and uniform in the same sense that production rules are. More specifically, let $\lambda$ be a label attached to node i and let $\lambda'$ be a label attached to its neighbor j. Then $r_{ij}(\lambda,\lambda')$ indicates the compatibility between them. If $\lambda$ on i is strongly compatible with $\lambda'$ on j, then $r_{ij}(\lambda,\lambda') \simeq 1$; this corresponds, for example, to the situation in which two neighboring line segments are perfectly aligned or to a no-line label being completely surrounded by other no-line labels. If $\lambda$ on i is highly incompatible with $\lambda'$ on j, then $r_{ij}(\lambda,\lambda') \simeq -1$; this corresponds to neighboring line segments that are aligned perpendicularly, or to line segments that are oriented directly into no-line labels. In general, most compabitility pairs are intermediate between these two extremes, such as the many pairs of intermediately aligned line segments [Zucker77a]. The compatibilities for these intermediate situations take values in the interval [-1, 1].

The different labels associated with each node are ordered according to a measure of confidence or probability attached to each one. The initial values for these probabilities can be obtained from a local inspection of the data base. For the line example, this amounts to evaluating a local line detector over the picture in each quantized orientation. The results can then be scaled into the range [0,1] and associated with the proper label. These results are ambiguous, however, because line detectors respond not only to the presence of line segments, but also to various noise configurations. They are, furthermore, sensitive to differences in contrast. Thus in many highly ambiguous situations the label with the highest initial probability will not be the correct one. Or, in terms of productions, the initial "best" match is not the correct match.

The RLP updates the initial probability estimates by using the knowledge represented in the compatibilities to exploit global data base (i.e., pictorial) consistency. Letting $p_i(\lambda)$ denote the probability that label $\lambda$ is correct for node i, it is updated according to the following formula:

$$p_i^{K+1}(\lambda) = \frac{p_i^K(\lambda)\,[1+q_i^K(\lambda)]}{\sum_\lambda p_i^K(\lambda)[1+q_i^K(\lambda)]}$$

where K is the iteration number and $q_i^k(\lambda)$, the neighborhood contribution to $p_i(\lambda)$, is given by

$$q_i^K(\lambda) = \sum_j c_{ij} \sum_{\lambda'} r_{ij}\,(\lambda,\lambda')\,p_j^K(\lambda').$$

In other words, each neighboring label $\lambda'$ contributes an amount proportional to its current strength $p_j^K(\lambda')$, multiplied by its compatibility with the label being updated. The contribution is summed over all the labels on each node, and then a weighted ($c_{ij}$) sum over all the neighbors is computed. The updating is computed in parallel in order to update every label on every node simultaneously. The process terminates when stable equilibrium values are obtained. These equilibrium values are often of the form $p_i(\lambda_k) = 1$, for one label $\lambda_k$, with the probability for all other labels at that node equal to zero [Zucker 78]. Such unique labelings leave no doubt about which production should be executed at that location. Even when the RLP terminates with nonunique labelings at some nodes, the probabilities still provide an ordering over the labels reflective of the global state of the data base. This is because, as the rule iterates, information propagates through longer and longer distances.

The basic point of this section was that the mechanism for selecting productions should be capable of evaluating the effect that a given production could have through some means of immediate feedback. The specific means explored was to partition the global data base into many local patterns and to attempt to find the proper production to match each local pattern. The feedback was accomplished by the iterative rule in a RLP, with the comparison component based on consistency between neighbors. Each iteration adjusted the probability distributions toward a more globally consistent state. More general updating rules are of course possible. These would permit many other knowledge sources to exert cooperative and competitive influences during this disambiguation process with many different processes acting concurrently [Zucker76].

At this stage, disambiguation has been taking place at a single level of symbolic abstraction within the system. Each production replaced an intensity pattern with a line (or no-line) assertion. Data bases have been partitioned into local chunks of either spatial positions, as in the image understanding example, or temporal positions, as in the speech understanding example. Consistency-based feedback has been provided by mechanisms such as the iterative updating rule in the RLP.[5] Another dimension for characterizing data bases is the degree of abstraction indicated by the symbols attached to the positional nodes. Such multiple-level systems are considered next.

## 5.0 MULTIPLE-LEVEL SYSTEMS

Most complex problem solving and understanding systems can be organized into many internal levels, where each level consists of symbols that are increasingly more abstract than the original data. Such organizations apparently reduce the overall complexity of associating correct high-level constructs with low-level data. In vision systems, the lower levels attempt to translate intensity data into a description of the edge, line, and region content. Slightly higher levels might consist of vertex labels, which are groupings of these low-level symbols out of which occlusion, orientation, and depth relationships might be computed. Finally, at the highest levels, the labels correspond to final semantic interpretations for the objects in the scene being processed.

In Section 4 an RLP for disambiguating a portion of the low-level processing was demonstrated. In a similar manner, an RLP could have been designed to operate with symbols at another level. Barrow and Tenenbaum [Barrow76], for example, have developed a type of RLP for disambiguating high-level symbolic assignments such as DOOR and BASEBOARD, in the domain of office scenes, and Waltz [Waltz75] has developed a discrete relaxation algorithm for disambiguating the vertex interpretations in "blocks-world" scenes. Without such disambiguation, the combinatorial explosion of potential interpretations arising in any realistic domain can cripple almost any system. For example, Yakimovsky and Feldman [Feldman74], although they formulated their problem in an optimal fashion, had to settle for a final solution that was suboptimal and heuristic. One reason for this was that their program attempted to assign high-level interpretive labels directly to low-level region data without considering the intermediate levels.

Levels of abstraction arise naturally in speech understanding systems as well as in image understanding systems. In Hearsay-II the levels that are considered explicitly are parametric, segmental, pho-

---

[5] Since PSs are universal programming languages, the feedback could, in principle, be written in terms of addtional productions. However, this would appear to be in violation of the "spirit" of PSs [Davis76b].

netic, syllabic, lexical, phrasal, and conceptual. The blackboard data base, which lies at the heart of this system, is thus organized along two dimensions: position in time and level of abstraction. Similarly the structure of plans and behavior can be organized into levels, separating major steps from specific or practical details [Sacerdoti75a].

The information processing within these systems takes place through the levels in a top-down, bottom-up, or more heterarchical fashion. Although there may be various expert modules operating on these different symbolic levels in parallel, in effect the final result can be characterized as a search through a state space as broad as the possibilities at each level and as deep as the number of levels (see Fig. 6). The feedback discussed in Section 4 served to reduce the number of possibilities at one level, i.e., to prune the breadth of this search space.

When single level feedback does not lead to unique labelings, feedback between levels can be used. This opens the entire range of multilevel possibilities, perhaps the simplest of which is feedback between adjacent levels. Such feedback can once again be based on a criterion of data base consistency. In speech understanding, for example, the word sequence hypothesizer (WOSEQ) has been found to be one of the

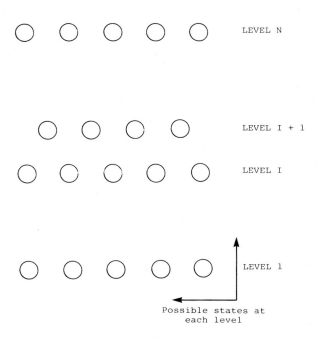

Fig. 6. A state characterization of multiple-level systems.

most important knowledge sources in Hearsay-II. It implements feedback, although of a very simple form, between the word level and the phrase level [Lesser77]. Its consistency criteria derive from the redundancies in English. Briefly, WOSEQ begins with hypothesized words that are highly likely. Temporally adjacent words are joined together into a phrase if they are also language-adjacent, i.e., if they form a grammatical two-word sequence. This process is repeated recursively, with phrases as the unit to be extended. Termination is controlled by the ratio of the number of words in a phrase with the expected increase in search space provided by each word.

When levels of processing are not indexed according to abstraction, but are indexed according to detail, hierarchical organizations provide a rigid architecture for implementing a restricted kind of feedback. Such architectures can be seen in image processsng as pyramidal data structures (e.g., [Tanimoto75, Kelly71]) and in planning systems [Sacerdoti75a]. In both of these structures processing is accomplished at the higher, more coarse levels so that the fine, noiselike details do not cause too many incorrect searches. Or, in terms of PSs, so that fewer incorrect productions fire. This is precisely the rationale for using metarules in MYCIN [Shortliffe76]. The fundamental reason why these schemes work is that the symbols at the coarser levels function like constraints over symbols at the finer levels. Each coarse symbol defines a set of possible fine symbols. By operating with the coarse symbols, the system is effectively functioning with the implicit uncertainty in the fine symbols. While such specific architectures do permit more efficient operation through restricted feedback, they do not provide the general feedback and noise reduction capabilities of systems such as RLP.

Finally, during the operation of feedback mechanisms at both single and multiple levels, data bases may still not be disambiguated completely. More than one production may remain in certain conflict sets. There will, however, be an improved ordering over the possibilities at each level imposed by the attached probabilities. This provides an additional source of current information to be propagated around the data base network. Some recent attempts to accomplish this have been described by Shortliffe [Shortliffe76] and Duda, *et al.* [Duda76].

## 6.0 CONCLUSIONS

Hypothesize-and-test is one of the most basic paradigms of artificial intelligence programming. It is sufficiently general so that its realization within any particular programming system can take many forms. Production systems are currently a popular methodology for AI programming. They admit many ways for implementing hypothesize-

and-test, one of which was considered in this chapter. This was the specific use of feedback, both at a single level of abstraction and across multiple levels, to cope with the problem of multiple productions partially matching the data base at any given time.

Multiple partial pattern matches can derive from both pattern ambiguity (i.e., lack of detailed specificity) and from pattern uncertainty due to random disturbances. Both of these sources can be modeled as noise processes, and both can be controlled by systems structured in a closed-loop, feedback configuration. Most PSs have, in effect, been open-loop configurations, and have therefore been inadequate in dealing with noise-corrupted data. Relaxation labeling processes, on the other hand, can be described as single-level PSs with feedback. To extend this sort of disambiguation to multiple levels, RLPs can be developed to disambiguate symbolic structures (i.e., graphs and label sets) at various levels of abstraction. They could use traditional production rules to rewrite the symbols both across and between levels (when their confidence levels were within an appropriate range). In short, such a system would function like a hierarchy of RLPs with multiple interconnections.

The kinds of feedback discussed in this chapter were based on a consistency or compatability criterion between local chunks of the data base. This required that the global pattern at each descriptive level be partitioned into local pieces affected by noise processes. The quantities of noise that such local schemes are capable of handling, as well as more powerful schemes for implementing feedback when they fail, still remain to be worked out.

# THE ROLE OF PARTIAL AND BEST MATCHES IN KNOWLEDGE SYSTEMS

Frederick Hayes-Roth[1]
*The Rand Corporation*

*Partial matching is a comparison of two or more descriptions that iden-*
*tifies their similarities. Determining which of several descriptions is most*
*similar to one description of interest is called the best-match problem. Partial*
*and best matches underlie several knowledge system functions, including ana-*
*logical reasoning, inductive inference, predicate discovery, pattern-directed*
*inference, semantic interpretation, and speech and image understanding. Be-*
*cause partial-matching is both combinatorial and ill-structured, admissible*
*algorithms are elusive. Economical solutions require very effective use of con-*
*straints that apparently can be provided only by globally organized knowledge*
*bases. Examples of such organizations are provided, and promising avenues*
*of research are proposed.*

## 1.0 INTRODUCTION: WHAT IS THE PARTIAL-MATCHING PROBLEM?

A partial-match is a comparison of two or more descriptions that identifies their similarities. Because typical descriptions are formulated as symbolic property-lists or propositional formulas, a partial-match of two descriptions includes three components: an *abstraction*, consisting of all properties or propositions common to both compared descriptions; and two *residual* terms, representing the properties that are true of only one or the other of the descriptions. If the two compared descriptions are A and B, the partial-match of A and B, denoted PM(A,B), is (A*B, A-A*B, B-A*B), where A*B denotes the abstraction

[1] This research was supported in part by Grant MCS77-03273 from the National Science Foundation to the Rand Corporation.

*557*

of A and B, and A-A$^*$B and B-A$^*$B denote the properties of A and B, respectively, that are not contained in A$^*$B. In other papers, partial-matching has been variously referred to as *interference matching, generalization,* or *correspondence mapping* [F. Hayes-Roth76a, c, h, 77f, Vere75, Winston75].

The premise of this chapter is that the partial-matching problem is of fundamental importance for pattern-directed inference and other knowledge-based activities. While some well-structured problems may be solvable by conventional algorithmic methods, it appears that the majority of complex problems cannot be solved with a small set of predefined, pattern-matching rules that are applied in an all-or-none fashion, exactly as coded. In this regard, knowledge systems can be likened to social systems. Just as the complexities of ordinary social interactions force judicial decisions to integrate many diverse and flexibly interpreted laws, so the complexities of real problems usually require that solutions be *influenced* by many elements of knowledge without being *dominated* by any. In systems applying large amounts of knowledge to complex problems, many diverse sources of influence must be pooled to identify the *best* or *most strongly indicated* course of action at each moment in time. Partial matching and best matching are the mechanisms for accomplishing this control.

In addition to its role in pattern-directed inference, partial-matching can be used in two other ways. The second role of partial-matching is to ascertain how well an observed event satisfies the prescribed constraints of an *ideal* or *prototypic* situational description. Identifying the best match between the description of an observed event and alternative prototypes enables the current situation to be *recognized* as an *instance* or special case of one of the prototypes. Those relationships shared by both descriptions are the *constraints* of the prototype that the observed event satisifies. Any residual properties of the prototype are unsatisfied constraints. Classifying an event according to its best match among alternative prototypes is tantamount to pattern recognition by constraint satisfaction (cf. [Barrow76]).

The third role of partial-matching is similar to constraint satisfaction. In this case, too, a description of data is compared with descriptions called *templates, case frames, schemata,* or *frames* (cf. [D.G. Bobrow77, F. Hayes-Roth76h, 77g, Minsky75]). These frames are usually hierarchically organized, empirical or conceptual descriptions of observable phenomena. In short, frames constitute a system's knowledge of its world. Once the best matching frames have been ascertained, the data are *interpreted* by imposing the frame structure upon them. For example, in a speech understanding task the data might consist of an array of hypothesized words, and the templates would be empirical phrase structures of the language. The best-matched templates determine how the words should be parsed and semantically interpreted. As a general rule, it appears that semantic interpretation is best conceived as the mapping between current data and previously inferred schemata. Because the superficial aspects of most observed situations differ substantially from all previously encountered ones, semantic interpretation is fundamentally a problem of partial-matching.

In the next section, several applications of partial and best matches are presented to convey the generality and difficulty of the partial-matching problem. Subsequently, a criterion for the admissibility of partial-matching algorithms is discussed that, though simple and reasonable, is difficult to realize. In the last sections, the principal features of the partial-matching problem are discussed, and some promising approaches toward its solution are proposed.

## 2.0 SOME APPLICATIONS OF PARTIAL-MATCHING

In this section, several applications are briefly discussed to illustrate the generality, importance, and difficulty of the partial- and best-matching problems. The applications considered include analogical reasoning, inductive inference, predicate discovery, semantic interpretation, and speech and image understanding. In each case, the central problem is finding a best match between two data descriptions or between a data description and existing knowledge. This nearly always entails searches of exponential problem spaces.

*Analogical Reasoning.* While this category properly embraces numerous problems of widely varying specificity, the most well studied is "A is to B as C is to which, D1, D2, ..., Dn?" As several researchers have shown (cf. [Evans68]), an effective program for solving these problems is as follows:

(1) Compute the partial matches PM(A, B), PM(C, D1), . . , PM(C, Dn).

(2) Determine the best match between PM(A, B) and one of PM(C, D1), . . ., PM(C, Dn). If the best match is PM(C, Dk), Dk is the best solution to the problem.

Recall that PM(X, Y) comprises three terms, the abstraction X*Y and the residuals of X and Y. Thus, the partial match between A and B defines a viewpoint for interpreting what changes were necessary to transform A into B; i.e., the pair A-B induces a *transformation* [A → B]. This transformation is implicit in the structure PM(A, B) = (A*B, A-A*B, B-A*B): A*B specifies which properties of A were retained, A-A*B specifies which properties of A were deleted, and B-A*B specifies which new properties were introduced by the transformation of A into B.

The partial match between PM(A, B) and PM(C, Di) (for some i) can be viewed as a comparison of two ordered lists and is defined as PM(PM(A, B), PM(C, Di)) = (((A*B)*(C*Di), (A-A*B)*(C-C*Di), (B-A*B)*(Di-C*Di)), R1, R2), where R1 and R2 are the appropriate residual terms. The abstraction of this partial match consists of three terms: (A*B)*(C*Di) comprises all properties common to all of the descriptions, A, B, C, and Di (the partial-matching operator * is associative); (A-A*B)*(C-C*Di) comprises all properties removed from *both* A and C in transforming them to B and Di, respectively; and, similarly, (B-A*B)*(Di-C*Di) comprises all properties added to *both* A and C in transforming them to B and Di, respectively. Thus, the original analogy problem is reducible, through partial-matching, to a question of choosing the one combination of common, deleted, and added properties that is most persuasive or plausible. Because any answer to this question must rest on empirical or subjective criteria, nothing of general validity can be added to this analysis.

Another use of partial-matching for analogical reasoning occurs in Merlin [Moore74]. In this system, any object can be interpreted as a special case of another whenever their differences do not outweigh their similarities. As an example, suppose we wished to play baseball with only a bat and a tennis ball. In Merlin's framework, the feasibility of playing should be directly related to the reasonability of viewing a tennis ball in the role of a baseball. Such a viewpoint can be achieved by partial-matching their descriptions. Suppose tennis ball were defined as a "bouncy, hollow, fuzzy, light, three-inch spheroid that is forcefully hit in the game of tennis" and a baseball were defined as a "hard, solid, leather-covered, moderately heavy, three-inch spheroid that is forcefully hit in the game of baseball." In this case, the abstraction of the two descriptions specifies that both objects are three-inch spheroids hit forcefully in games. The residuals, however, specify that whereas the baseball is hard, solid, leather-covered, moderately heavy, and used in the game of baseball, the tennis ball is bouncy, hollow, fuzzy, light, and used in the game of tennis.

To decide if the tennis ball will suffice as a makeshift baseball, these residuals must be reconciled. One simplifying approach to reconciliation employs semantic categories. If correspondences between pairs of residual properties can be established so that each difference is interpretable as a specific dimensional variation, the significance of the overall difference can be decomposed and thus easily apprehended and evaluated. A hierarchical organization of the system's knowledge greatly facilitates such a decomposition. For example, the difference hollow-solid can be reconciled by interpreting it as a variation on the dimension of "structure" or "construction type." As a result, a tennis ball can be viewed as a type of baseball that is hollow (rather than solid), light (rather than moderately heavy), fuzzy (rather than leather-covered), used in the game of tennis (rather than baseball), and bouncy (rather than some unspecified related property of a baseball). If these differences do not outweigh the similarities of the two, the tennis ball will serve admirably.

Before leaving this example, consider the role of partial-matching and residuals in establishing the correspondence (bindings) between objects. First, the two objects' descriptions were obtained from a dictionary or semantic network. Second, the properties common to both were abstracted by intersecting their property-lists. Third, the residuals were forced into possible corresponding value pairs by finding dimensions that embraced both values. Note that, in general, reconciling the difference between two arbitrary values requires a recursive application of the partial-matching scheme. Finally, the best match maximizes the similarities and minimizes the differences (according to exogenous criteria) between the compared descriptions.

Other sorts of analogical reasoning tasks can be formulated easily. For example:

(1) If I know a detailed procedure (ordered operations on operands) to accomplish a specific function (establish particular relationships on the operands), how do I modify the procedure to accomplish similar objectives on qualitatively different operands? Answer: try to find related operations applicable to the new operands that perform similar functions.

(2) If I want to persuade someone that X causes Y but don't have specific examples, what can I do? Answer: find an example where $X'$ caused $Y'$ and X is to $X'$ as Y is to $Y'$.

Despite the fact that such arguments are not strictly logical, many people find them persuasive when the underlying analogies are plausible.

*Inductive Inference.* Several researchers have shown that patterns, concepts, and production rules can be inferred by partial-matching examples to discover the consistently repeated, hence presumably criterial, properties [J.S. Brown73, Bruner56, F. Hayes-Roth74, 76a, c, h, 77f, Hunt62, Hunt75, Stoffel74, Vere75, Winston75]. To illustrate, consider the following examples of several classes:

Example 1: Tom and Jack are brothers. Jack is the father of a boy named Bill who is under 10. Both Tom and Jack are in their fifties. Jack's brother is Bill's Uncle Tom.

Example 2: Mary is the mother of twin sons, Bill and Jim. Mary is in her forties, while the boys are both 14. Mary has two brothers who are the boys' Uncles Tom and Steve.

Example 3: Sue has no brothers or sisters. Her mother is Jane, and Jane has has a brother named Fred. Fred is Sue's uncle.

Example 4: Fred was a brilliant Negro who lived all of his life in a predominantly white, racist country. Because he was powerless and intimidated, Fred was humiliatingly subservient to the whites in his community. Fred was an Uncle Tom.

Example 5: Because John, an aging, impoverished Negro, was humiliatingly subservient to Southern whites, the young blacks in his town called him Uncle Tom.

These examples will support a number of both correct and incorrect inferences that are equally plausible. If Examples 1 and 2 are partial-matched, one inference is that parents are at least 40 years old and children are 14 or younger. However, the type of inference that I want to draw attention to here has to do with notions of "Uncle." By partial-matching Examples 1 and 2, it is reasonable to infer that an uncle of x is the brother of the parent of x. However, the best partial match of these two examples would entail the stronger inference that x's Uncle Tom is the brother of x's parent, who is at least forty, while x is no older than 14.

A valid inference of the concept of "uncle" requires partial-matching all of Examples 1, 2 and 3, whereas a valid inference of the concept of "Uncle Tom" requires comparing Examples 4 and 5. This illustrates one of the perplexing problems regarding the role of partial-matching in inductive inference. While it is possible to infer valid rules by partial-matching enough examples to eliminate all irrelevant properties, partial-matching is also necessary to determine which examples illustrate the same concept. Knowing that Examples 4 and 5 should be compared to infer the meaning of "Uncle Tom," rather than comparing Examples 1, 2, 4, and 5, requires additional knowledge.

Suppose a learning system were asked to decide, based only on its knowledge of the five examples, if a certain 55-year-old Negro named Sam could be considered an uncle. To answer, it would necessarily seek similarities between the properties of Sam and previous examples of uncles. If, instead of actually retaining all examples, the system had only stored some "sufficient" set of rules induced by partial-matching arbitrarily selected subsets of examples, its current classification would have a good chance of being incorrect. Because most systems do, in fact, attempt to store only a minimal set of rules that can "cover" the data [Michalski73, Stoffel74], they are prone to errors caused by decisions, about what combinations of properties are important, made before the properties of a test item are known. A system that stores its examples and postpones inference until the item to be classified is fully specified has a significantly reduced probability of error. In the current example, such a system would be guaranteed to have sufficient evidence to infer both that: if Sam is the brother of a parent, he may be labeled an uncle; and if he is subservient to whites, he may be an Uncle Tom.

The important point to observe is that the properties of the item to be classified, *not the properties of the training data*, determine which inferences should be made. Obviously, then, many inferences cannot be anticipated or generated until the problem is fully specified. In short, optimal performance in inductive inference requires a "wait-and-see" approach. In actual applications of the partial-matching mechanism to pattern classification, the improved performance of wait-and-see classifiers has repeatedly been observed [Burge76, F. Hayes-Roth76e].

The general learning framework that revolves about partial-matching has been applied to the induction of several kinds of knowledge, including speech and image patterns [Burge76, F. Hayes-Roth-76a, 76e, Stoffel74], structured or relational concepts [J.S. Brown73, F. Hayes-Roth76a, c, h, 77f, Vere75, Vere77b, Winston75], transformational grammar rules [F. Hayes-Roth76a, c, Vere77b], and other [condition → action] productions [Vere77b].

*Predicate Discovery.* While the type of induction discussed in the previous section assumes the prior discovery and encoding of those properties needed to express a rule, partial-matching provides a basis for discovering new predicates too. For example, the following sentences provide a good basis for several interesting inductions:

Example 1: Because John is so tall, it is difficult to find clothes that fit him.

Example 2: Because Mary is so short, it is hard to get clothes that can fit her.

Example 3: Because Joanne is so fat, it is impossible to get apparel that is the right size.

Example 4: Because Tom is so skinny, it is not possible to find clothes that are suitable.

Using only superficial characteristics of the string representations of these examples, the following common abstraction would be produced by partial-matching:

(Because $u$ is so $v$, it is $w$ to $x$).

The corresponding residual values from the four examples associated with each variable $u$, $v$, $w$ and $x$ are as follows:

$u$: (John, Mary, Joanne, Tom)
$v$: (tall, short, fat, skinny)
$w$: (difficult, hard, impossible, not possible)

*x:* (find clothes that fit him, get clothes that can fit her, get apparel that is the right size, find clothes that are suitable).

Thus, provided that enough knowledge exists to motivate their comparison, these four examples generate reasonable inferences regarding four apparent categories of natural language. The four distinct values associated with each of the variables are apparently subsets of the possible domains of associated (unknown) predicates. For example, John, Mary, Joanne, and Tom are four of the possible values of the attribute "name." If this attribute had already been known to the system, partial-matching of the examples would have preserved the common "name" attribute, and a slightly more informative abstraction would have been produced, such as

(Because the thing named $u$ is so $v$, it is $w$ to $x$

Thus, $u$, $v$, and $w$ contribute to the discovery of the categories of *name*, *body shape attributes*, and *expressions for "difficult to achieve"*. For the purposes of machine learning, knowledge of these interpretations *per se* is unnecessary. All that apparently *is necessary* is to infer the existence and composition of such categories (unary predicates), and this may be done whenever different constants are correspondents in correctly partial-matched descriptions.

Continuing with the previous example, it is also interesting to compare the residuals associated with variable $x$ by a recursive application of partial-matching like that employed in Merlin. As a result of recursive partial matches of the four residual $x$ strings, the following sequence of inferences will be produced:

(1) Infer the category FIND = {find, get}.
(2) Infer the category CLOTHES = {clothes, apparel}.
(3) Infer the category FIT = {fit him, can fit her, is the right size, are suitable}.

Then the abstraction of the residuals of $x$ is

(FIND(a) CLOTHES(b) that FIT(c)).

Notice that this abstraction is itself a candidate for a new type of ternary relation that, by definition, is true of any triple (a, b, c) constituted from the categories FIND, CLOTHES, and FIT, respectively. Any such triple is an *instance* of this general template and has the obvious interpretation. Such a template is a plausible model of the natural language expression for *finding clothes that fit*. In any case, a capacity exists to identify plausible syntactic categories and semantic templates by partial-matching even a small number of similar verbal strings. This approach to predicate discovery has been successfully applied to a number of restricted languages [F. Hayes-Roth76a, Hirschman75, Tretiakoff74].

*Semantic Interpretation.* One of the concepts that has captured the imagination of many computer scientists and psychologists is that of frames, prototypes, templates, scripts or schemata [D.G. Bobrow77, Minsky75]. Frames are supposedly knowledge units that delineate the elements of physical or conceptual events and express the constraints by which they are related. Distinct frames have been proposed for every ordinary physical object, typical configurations of objects, and most observable phenomena (e.g., dining at a restaurant or shopping for food). While there is *prima facie* evidence supporting the theory that people have such knowledge, there is little concrete understanding of how this knowledge can be exploited to simplify reasoning processes. What can be universally agreed upon is trivial: whenever a situation is encountered where existing knowledge is applicable, that knowledge should be applied to constrain the possible interpretations attributed to observed phenomena.

In this framework, the key issues are how relevant knowledge can be identified efficiently and applied effectively. Thus, for the moment, it will be assumed that a frame exists for describing every interesting pattern of relationships. Suppose, for example, that the number of frames relevant to image processing is about 100,000, including ones for familiar faces, buildings, automobiles, buses, bodies, trees, mountains, furniture, and implements of various sorts. Now, suppose that someone presents a photograph selected randomly from a magazine and asks how knowledge should be employed to assist in interpreting it. Simply asserting that we should apply whatever knowledge is needed to resolve the a priori uncertainty about the identity of various objects and their interrelationships is not an answer, for this is presumed by the question. The question asks *how* the relevant knowledge can be identified. Once again, the answer appears to be that the best-matching frames should be chosen to interpret the data. In most cases, even best-matched frames will only be partially satisfied, because observed objects are occluded or otherwise fail to conform perfectly to the preconceived frame constraints. Once the best-matched frames have been identified, their knowledge can be exploited to hypothesize and test the apparently missing or erroneous data constituents.

Because no frame, by itself, can be expected to give a thorough account of the significant features of any normal, reasonably complex scene, satisfactory interpretations will normally require the integration of several partially matched frames. Two ways of determining the appropriate combination of frames can be proposed: (1) frames should be tried one-at-a-time, and additional frames should be incorporated as needed to resolve residual or anomalous properties; (2) some identifying characteristics of appropriate frames should be discerned through an analysis of global properties of the problem, and then frames satisfying these dynamically determined criteria should be invoked. In the next subsection some recent results of speech and image understanding research are presented favoring the second alternative.

There is a second way in which partial-matching supports semantic interpretation. In this case, two or more concepts sharing certain syntactic relationships stimulate restricted sorts of "spreading activation" searches of a semantic network. When the searches emanating from the original concepts intersect, the connecting path defines the semantic interpretation of the syntactic structure [McDonald77, Quillian68]. For example, a novel noun-noun phrase encountered in a text, such as "lawn mower," can be semantically interpreted simply by finding the best match among the relationships that radiate from the two concepts "lawn" and "mower" in a network embodying dictionary definitions. When "lawn" is defined as a "mown area or plot planted with grass or similar plants" and "mower" is defined as "a machine that cuts grass, grain, or hay," the best such match entails the following paraphrased interpretation: a "lawn mower" is a machine that cuts grass or similar plants [McDonald77]. Spreading activation, intersection searches are now widely applied in computer science and psychology (cf. [J.R.Anderson76,Collins75]). Their similarity to the search techniques employed by Merlin is apparent. Regardless of the particular knowledge representation adopted, the essential function of these systems is to find good partial matches under the constraints imposed by the current knowledge.

*Speech Understanding.* Speech understanding systems face the task of finding the best-fitting interpretation for a noisy, parametric time series. The parameters are acoustic measurements and the interpretation is a hierarchical tree whose root is a semantic template from the language and whose intermediate levels represent phrases, words, syllables, phones, and acoustic segments [F. Hayes-Roth77g, Lesser75]. An interpretation is constructed by applying knowledge of possible mappings between intermediate levels. In the Hearsay-II system in particular, the interpretation process occurs basically in two phases. First, knowledge about the acoustic realization of words is used to hypothesize, bottom-up, plausible words at various temporal locations within an utterance. For example, if the sentence contains 10 words chosen from a 1000-word vocabulary, about 7 or 8 on the average are correctly hypothesized. In addition, approximately 200 incorrect words are hypothesized, and about 40 of these are actually rated higher than valid word hypotheses.

In the second phase, missing words are hypothesized and rated and the entire sequence of words in the sentence is parsed and assigned an overall semantic interpretation. The key problem in this phase is to generate and rate the most plausible, missing words. Even when the vocabulary and grammar are highly constrained, the size of the search space for possible grammatical word sequences is extraordinarily large. In the Hearsay-II system several approaches to this problem were tried, and only one approach apparently derived sufficient constraint, by applying enough knowledge simultaneously, to succeed. The method used was to partial-match the entire collection of bottom-up word hypotheses against all templates of the grammar, in parallel, in the hope of finding one sequence of highly-rated words that was grammatical and most probably valid. If such a sequence could be identified, the system predicted and rated its plausible word extensions, iteratively, until a complete interpretation of the sentence was constructed.

Two knowledge sources were involved in computing the partial match between the matrix of hypothesized words and the grammatical case frames. These were WOSEQ [Lesser77], a word sequence hypothesizer, and PPARSE [F. Hayes-Roth77a], a partial parser. In overview, WOSEQ uses knowledge about the adjacency of words in the language to form hypothetical word sequences by stringing together bottom-up word hypotheses that are both language-adjacent and time-adjacent. It prunes the search space further by terminating the concatenation process for any sequence when the expected benefit is less than the cost, i.e., when the increase in credibility obtainable by concatenating additional word hypotheses is insufficient to warrant the attendant multiplicative increase in the total number of word sequences generated. Each of the most credible word sequences identified by WOSEQ is then evaluated by PPARSE to determine whether it is actually grammatical, i.e., whether it is a subsequence of some sentence in the language. Each of these partial-matching procedures is now explained in more detail.

WOSEQ uses a precomputed bit matrix that specifies for each possible word pair (u, v) whether the sequence u v can occur in a sentence of the language. For the 1000-word vocabulary, this requires approximately 30K 36-bit words of memory. Given a collection of bottom-up word hypotheses, WOSEQ selects a few of the most credible ones as *seeds* for its sequence-growing process. Each seed is a one-word sequence, and the following procedure is applied repeatedly to all sequences until quiescence occurs:

(1) For each word sequence W, construct the sets P(W) and S(W) of word hypotheses that can precede and succeed W. P(W) contains all hypotheses that are both language-adjacent and time-adjacent to the first word in W. The set S(W) contains all hypotheses that are time- and language-adjacent to the last word of W.

(2) For each w in P(W), evaluate the credibility of the sequence (w,W). This is an increasing function of the credibility of w and W, an

increasing function of the total number of syllables spanned by (w, **W**), and a decreasing function of the number of words in P(**W**). If the credibility of the sequence (w, **W**) is greater than that of **W**, add (w, **W**) to the set of hypothesized sequences. For each word w in S(**W**), similarly process the potential sequence (**W**, w).

When WOSEQ quiesces, it will have identified sequences of pair-wise-grammatical words that appear to be most credible over the entire set, both because they incorporate at least one of the individually most credible bottom-up hypotheses and because they satisfy a maximum number of low-probability constraints. WOSEQ is usually successful at its task, because it continually increases the credibility of the objects it processes. It does this by adducing contextual support in the form of numerous, consistent, unlikely observations. The algorithm is efficient because the time- and language-adjacency constraints are easily computed. In a later section we suggest that easily computable, global attributes of the problem space may provide a promising, general approach to the partial-matching problem.

The next step in the linguistic partial-matching problem is to test each word sequence for grammaticality. This requires a parser capable of recognizing the grammaticality of any word sequence, even if it is only a subsequence of the string derivable from a nonterminal. In Hearsay-II, this is accomplished by a program PPARSE. PPARSE is a bottom-up, left-to-right Kay-type parser with the following modifications: Any rewrite rule such as X → A B can be applied, and the parse node X constructed, whenever the leftmost derivative of B in the parse tree is the first word of the sequence being partial-parsed. Similarly, any rewrite like Y → C D can be applied whenever the rightmost derivative of C is the last word of the sequence being partial-parsed. These are the only cases in which incomplete tree structures are built.

WOSEQ and PPARSE succeeded at controlling the combinatorics of the search problem, while a number of production systems failed [F. Hayes-Roth77g, Mostow77], because hypotheses that satisfy many of WOSEQ's constraints are likely to be valid. Furthermore, the truly expensive operation in this partial-matching, instantiating and hypothesizing incomplete grammatical case frames, is allowed only for nonterminals that can derive the first or last word of a sequence selected by WOSEQ. Compared to any simplistic conception of how a frame system can operate to hypothesize and then fill in partially instantiated frames, WOSEQ and PPARSE constitute a significantly superior solution to the best match problem.

*Image Understanding.* In numerous ways (e.g., noisiness of data, frame-based interpretation), the speech and image understanding problems are quite similar. However, the last example of partial-matching considered is a problem unique to vision, that is, determining stereo disparity between two images that are left- and right-eye views of one scene. To resolve the disparity between two images of this sort, it is necessary to partial-match them to identify the corresponding (same) objects in each image. Once this is done, the lateral displacement or disparity between the two is a cue for the distance of the object from the viewer. The human visual system is capable of resolving such disparity, even when there are no distinguishable objects in either view (as in random-dot stereograms). Recently Marr and Poggio [Marr76] have shown how the necessary partial-matching computations can be performed locally by spatially distributed, cooperative processes. Their approach rests on the observation that, while the disparity between any two corresponding points is initially unknown, any hypothesis regarding some particular disparity value between two points in the two images implies approximately the same disparity value between neighboring points. By constructing a problem representation in which every possible pair of corresponding points, with disparity d, influences the neighboring points with matching properties toward correspondences under the same disparity, a difference equation is constructed that can be applied iteratively and locally to choose correspondences that maximize constraint satisfaction. A solution in this algorithm is just a steady-state reached by the difference equation.

This application of partial-matching is particularly interesting, because it shows how global features of the problem space, such as disparity and spatial position, can constrain the search for the best match. The global communication of constraint is accomplished by directly connecting neighboring points whose hypothetical disparity values influence one another. To develop a mechanism capable of this sort of information sharing, a representation had to be discovered that clarified the relationship between global data attributes (location and disparity) and local computations involved in partial-matching (determining the gray-scale similarity of two potentially corresponding points). The role of this integrated global-local problem representation is comparable to that played by the precomputed language-adjacency matrix used by WOSEQ to hypothesize word sequences in Hearsay-II. This suggests some interesting properties of the partial-matching problem that are pursued in the subsequent sections.

## 3.0 PRINCIPAL PROPERTIES OF THE PARTIAL-MATCHING PROBLEM

From the preceding illustrations, it is possible to identify four principal characteristics of the partial-matching problem. In this section, these are briefly discussed.

*The desirability of analyzing any particular configuration of data can only be determined dynamically.* In the large class of problems where partial-matching is necessary and computationally expensive, the number of distinct partial matches that can arise is virtually limitless. As a result, it is not possible to predetermine all combinations of observable properties that may, at some time, most warrant some response. A fortiori, it is not possible to rank order the potential situations in terms of import or interest value. Rather, the choice of which configurations of data deserve further processing resources is determinable only as a result of dynamic partial-matching between the data in hand and the frames or templates specifying known constraints.

*Partial-matching, as a general computational problem, is intractable.* Because partial-matching subsumes the graph monomorphism, the k-clique, and other NP-complete problems, the amount of time apparently needed to solve worst-case problems is at least exponential in the complexity of the structures being matched. It follows that if partial-matching is to be applied successfully, problem complexity must be reduced. The principal way in which such complexity reduction can be accomplished is by choosing rich, high-order predicates as a basis for description. As the grain of description is reduced toward uniform, low-level predicates (e.g., simple graphs, retinal arrays of on-off detectors, semantic primitives), the partial-matching problem is made inherently more complex and less feasible.

*Partial-matching is fundamentally nondeterministic.* Any partial-matching problem can produce a large number of alternative solutions of varying plausibility. Thus far in this chapter the nondeterminism of partial-matching algorithms has been neglected, primarily because one partial-match solution is usually best. Thus, while any program designed for partial-matching must incorporate logic that permits it to pursue multiple solutions simultaneously, effective mechanisms will quickly prune poor alternatives from consideration.

*Good partial matches traverse a priori boundaries and multiple levels of hierarchically organized knowledge structures.* This point is of the utmost importance for understanding why simple approaches to pattern-directed inference or frame-theoretic analysis of real data are likely to fail. Simple approaches will attempt to hypothesize all partial-matched frames and then predict and verify their missing constituents. In any reasonably complex domain, the best interpretation of data will traverse a priori boundaries of several low-order frames and will only be apparent when multiple levels of partial-matched frames are integrated. The simple approach entails extensive unwarranted searching of many levels of frames, because hundreds of frames can be consistent with at least some properties of the observed data. The search for a best overall interpretation can be effective only if many properties of the data, providing multiple sources of constraints, are considered simultaneously.

# 4.0 THE PARTIAL-MATCH ADMISSIBILITY CRITERION

Any proposed algorithm for partial-matching two structures A and B ought to satisfy the following criterion:

The more similar A and B are (everything else held constant), the faster the partial match should be.

This criterion is called the *partial-match admissibility criterion.* Its reasonableness and desirability are intuitively apparent. Yet, even in the simplest applications of partial-matching, it is rarely achievable [Rivest76]. The cause is that typical partial-matching algorithms evaluate properties one-at-a-time. For example, if we wish to find a document that has keys (attributes) g, h, and k, most procedures accomplish this by intersecting the inverted lists of documents associated with each of the three keys. Thus, it takes longer to find a document that matches 10 keys than to find one that matches 3, and so forth.

Avenues of approach toward realizing admissible algorithms are suggested by considering partial-matching as a search problem in which each partial match corresponds to a state. The initial state is represented as a three-tuple, (( ), A, F), where A is the observed data representation (or query) and F is a set of frames against which A can be compared. As before, the first component represents the abstraction or partial match thus far constructed, the second component represents the residual of A with respect to this abstraction, and the third component represents the residuals of the frames vis-a-vis the current abstraction.

By applying typical admissibility criteria of general searches [Nilsson71], it is apparent how one should move through this search space. At each decision point in the algorithm, the most promising partial solution should be extended. The most promising extension is the one providing the most complete partial match for the least expense. Here, expense is defined as the total computation required to arrive at any given state, including both the computation time spent developing the particular partial match as well as the time spent constructing collateral matches from expanded partial solutions on the same path. Thus, the best step at each point is the one that adduces the most constraint for the least cost. Constraint in this case is exactly definable as the reduction in the remaining uncertainty regarding which frames of F are involved in the best match of A.

From this viewpoint, it appears that there is only one interpretation of constraint. A transformation from one partial-matching state to another is constraining to the extent that it eliminates possible elements of F from further consideration.

Two useful concepts in this context are the *diagnosticity* of a test and its *performance.* Diagnosticity is a measure of the ability of a test to rule out possibilities. Performance is a composite measure of the expected utility of a test, combining its diagnosticity with its expected frequency of satisfiability [F. Hayes-Roth74]. An optimal algorithm would apply, at each decision point, the most diagnostic test that is satisfiable. Expected cost can be minimized by applying the tests with highest performance values at each decision point. Such an approximation is important, because we know of no reasonable way to determine dynamically the most diagnostic tests. Some avenues of approach to these problems are suggested in the next section.

## 5.0 IMPLICATIONS FOR THE DESIGN OF KNOWLEDGE SYSTEMS

From this study of partial-matching, four general implications for the design of knowledge systems are drawn. Each of these is considered in turn.

*Analyses should be synthetic and dynamic.* This criterion, although sounding superficially like a suggestion for analysis-by-synthesis, is diametrically opposed to that approach. In analysis-by-synthesis [Hunt75], patterns are interpreted by top-down methods: one most likely, highest-level frame is selected arbitrarily to apply and, at each point, unfilled frames are expanded downward until they can fit (interpret) the data. Because such search strategies are insensitive to properties of the data at hand, they will perform badly unless more constraint is available from the top-down structure of the frame system than from tests based on diagnostic combinations of data and frames. To be *synthetic* means choosing tests to perform which, in view of the properties exhibited by the data, apply maximal constraint. Knowledge systems designed along these lines would employ a basic three-step cycle: (1) a small number of highest-performance tests are applied to the best partial solutions (initially, to the most credible data); (2) the most promising matches are extended; and (3) the new best matches are identified for evaluation by another set of highest-performance tests. Note how this paradigm embraces the WOSEQ-PPARSE methodology described earlier.

*Descriptions should be rich and simple.* To reduce the complexity of the search problem, descriptions should be as rich and simple as possible. This criterion implies that high-level descriptors are more desirable than low-level ones. For example, language processing systems representing knowledge in terms of lexemes are more efficient than those representing such knowledge in the form of equivalent graphs of semantic primitives [B. Hayes-Roth77c]. One particularly interesting aspect of Merlin is its use of hierarchical descriptions permitting partial-matching to be performed at the highest-level of description possible. Merlin's partial matcher descends into the depths of low-order descriptions only if matches of rich, high-level terms fail.

This criterion is actually a heuristic for achieving maximally constraining tests for the least cost. Its actual effectivness depends on the
exact performance of tests at high and low levels; in reasonable problem domains, however, the heuristic should be generally valid.

*Scheduling of computational resources, based on diagnosticity or
performance, should be considered a primitive function in partial-
matching systems.* Complex partial-matching systems must include
mechanisms to ensure that the most desirable actions are executed
first. Two properties of schedulers are proposed. First, desirability
should primarily reflect the diagnosticity of a pending action. Second,
since scheduling is a primitive operation, the costs of calculating
desirabilities and sorting the pending actions should be minimized. In
this context, it is interesting to note that previous studies of knowledge system scheduling [F. Hayes-Roth76g] and conflict resolution in
production systems [J. McDermott77b, Newell72a] have completely
neglected the concept of diagnosticity.

*Problem representations should integrate characteristics of the
knowledge base with properties of the data to maximize the constraint
provided in search.* This criterion suggests that one approach to improved performance in partial-matching is to develop globally organized representations whose attributes can be exploited to reduce
uncertainty during partial-matching. The work of Marr and Poggio
[Marr76] on stereo disparity is a good example of the use of such a
globally organized problem space. Each locus of computation is influenced by all relevant cooperative loci, and these are efficiently identifiable because they are in the same neighborhood of the problem
space. The essence of such spatial organizations is an ability to reduce
the number of computations involved in similarity judgments. Similar
benefits were provided to the partial matcher in Merlin as a result of
its hierarchical organization of knowledge.

In the future, representations should be sought that support the
use of proximity measures or directionality to identify good partial
matches. These could provide cheap and constraining tests for a variety of tasks. For example, semantic networks might be superimposed
upon the type of metric semantic spaces that humans apparently possess [Rips73, Shephard75, Voss76]. The value of such organizations
would derive from an improved capacity to detect that two objects are
likely correspondents (are highly similar) just because they are close
in the metric representational space. Moreover, such integrated spatial and symbolic representations could significantly improve intersection searches by favoring spread of activation in the "area" between
two concepts of interest. Given the coordinates of two nodes to be
connected by a best path, preference should be given to out-going links
that are oriented in appropriate directions.

Other types of organization should also be sought that can facilitate computation of approximate similarity. For example, in early experiments in rule induction, Hayes-Roth and McDermott [F. Hayes-Roth77f] showed how transformational grammar rules could be inferred by partial-matching before-and-after examples. Their program employed no knowledge about either the structure of productions or sentences. By incorporating properties of these structures as attributes of the representations, Vere was able to reduce the computation time by two orders of magnitude [Vere77b]. The organizing properties he exploited included a three-part decomposition of each production, corresponding to the three components of the partial match of the before and after parts of each example, and a hierarchical representation of sentences. The additional constraints provided by these global attributes of problem organization greatly simplify this particular partial-matching problem.

## 6.0 CONCLUSIONS

I have tried to show that partial-matching is central to many interesting functions of knowledge systems. A few years ago, the foremost problem of knowlege system design was how knowledge should be represented. While knowledge representations are continually improving, many good frameworks have already been developed. Since pattern-directed function invocation is obviously desirable for many applications of these knowledge systems, attention has recently focused upon good methods to invoke appropriate knowledge units. Within the framework of all-or-none knowledge application, the major topics of interest concern matters of efficiency, such as developing methods for common subexpression elimination, efficient techniques for all-or-none pattern matching, and strategies for conflict resolution. While these are surely important considerations in implementing systems for simple or well-structured tasks, the most difficult problem arising in very large and flexible knowledge systems is to determine, as quickly as possible, the *most useful* knowledge for the task at hand. Because many diverse elements of knowledge may be weakly contributory to an overall solution, new ways of organizing computation must be developed to prevent intractable, combinatorial searches. In the future, a major shift in attention can be anticipated toward the the deceptively easily stated but fundamental question: How should partial and best matches be computed?

# Conclusion

# PRINCIPLES OF PATTERN-DIRECTED INFERENCE SYSTEMS

Frederick Hayes-Roth and D. A. Waterman
*The Rand Corporation*

Douglas B. Lenat
*Carnegie-Mellon University*

*The general class of pattern-directed inference systems (PDISs) is defined and its general properties are investigated. Within a taxonomy of PDISs, the special properties of rule-based systems and two subclasses, production systems and transformation systems, are considered in detail. A comparison between these PDIS properties and contemporary information processing conceptions of human cognition suggests that PDISs provide an excellent basis for cognitive modeling. Principles for knowledge representation and system architecture are developed that suggest guidelines for controlling the combinatorial explosion that will accompany efforts to implement intelligent systems with extensive amounts of knowledge.*

## 1.0 INTRODUCTION

The programs described in this volume are members of a class of systems that are called pattern-directed. In this chapter we examine this specific class of computer systems to identify important principles regarding their design and use. In the process of formulating these principles for pattern-directed inference systems (PDISs), a number of central questions are addressed.

First, what distinguishes PDISs from other computer programs? The answer should provide an explicit definition of what we mean by *pattern-directed inference*. Second, how can PDISs be classified? This can be adddressed through a discussion of both functional and struc-

*577*

tural characteristics of PDISs. Third, what insight does the PDIS formalism provide for builders of information-processing models of human cognition? In answering this, a parallel will be drawn between human memory structures and the structure of PDISs. Finally, what features of PDISs have been identified that make them worth distinguishing? The main focus here is on the architecture of PDISs and the related design principles that underlie their generality and usefulness.

This chapter is organized as follows. Sections 2 and 3 contain a definition and classification of PDISs and describe in some detail an important category of PDISs called *rule-based systems*. Section 4 discusses the relationship between computational models of intelligence based on the PDIS model and modern psychological models of intelligence based on more general information processing conceptions. The contrast between these two approaches sets the stage for the consideration of knowledge representation and system architecture that follows in Sections 5 and 6. Section 7 investigates the difficulties that may be expected to arise as PDISs are extended to incorporate large amounts of knowledge, and the last section presents our conclusions regarding the current state and future of the PDIS concepts.

## 2.0 THE SCOPE OF PATTERN-DIRECTED INFERENCE

Almost all programs of consequence are dependent upon *data*: initial conditions, parameters, dynamic interactive responses from a human being, digitized representations of signals received by instruments, outcomes of earlier computations, etc. Typically, the flow of control and the utilization of data are rigidly fixed by the program's code. The default kind of program step is *sequential*; branching is performed only at points—and in ways—explicitly provided for in the program code. While this is an appropriate structure for certain kinds of computations (e.g., routinely solving a set of simultaneous linear equations), it is ill-adapted for some others (e.g., simulating a human's responses to a complex, rapidly changing and unfamiliar environment). In these latter situations, branching may be the norm, not the exception. That is, the program will examine the state of the world at each step and react appropriately. When no new important stimulus is perceived, the current "context" (history or last state) may be the controlling factor that causes the program to advance sequentially one step further. However, if an important new stimulus is detected, the program's next step will depend upon the properties of that stimulus as well as upon context. In situations where new stimuli are continually arising (either from an external environment or from conditions internally generated by the program itself), "straight-line" sequential code may be inappropriate. In these situations the program is better viewed as a loosely organized collection of *pattern-directed modules* (PDMs) that are responsible both for detecting various situations and for responding appropriately to them.

Each PDM is a bundle of mechanisms for examining and modifying one or more data structures that model critical aspects of the external environment. In one sense a PDM is a miniature program for accomplishing some specialized task: PDMs can range in complexity from arbitrarily complex pattern-evoked functions to simple stylized production rules. Examination of a data structure by a PDM will be called *reading*, and modification will be called *writing*. Acquisition of data from "the outside," (another program or a user) involves writing information into one of the existing data structures. One very important kind of macro-operation that PDMs employ involves reading information in a data structure and then checking to see if it matches a particular template associated with the PDM. This activity is called *pattern-matching* and is what gives PDMs their name. Another less ubiquitous operation involves finding all items in a particular data structure that match a particular template pattern. Ordinarily, PDMs search for data items of special interest using pattern-matching reads, use these items to help compute some intermediate result, and then write the newly computed values into one of the data structures. Thus, what is written is often logically or functionally related to what was just previously read.

The flow of control in a PDIS is governed by a part of the system called the *executive*.[1] This program is tasked with the jobs of controlling pattern matching, monitoring data base changes, deciding which PDM should be executed next, and then actually carrying out the execution. The executive may select PDMs by simply cycling from one PDM to the next, executing those deemed appropriate, or it may employ some more complicated scheduling strategy.

Any system composed of several PDMs that performs pattern-matching reads and modifications to the data structures, coupled with an executive to schedule and run the PDMs, is called a *pattern-directed inference system*. No stronger general assumptions can be made about the structure of a PDM; for example, in some systems PDM write accesses may be interleaved with read accesses, or the data structures being examined and modified may include PDMs themselves.

Two important features of a PDIS are its separation of permanent and temporary information and its modular organization, i.e., the interacting community of stimulus-driven "knowledge units" or "ex-

---

[1] In contemporary production system architectures this part of the system is called an *interpreter*.

perts" called PDMs. These and other characteristics of PDISs are described below (and throughout this chapter) together with the advantages associated with each.

C1.    PDISs separate permanent knowledge (the knowledge base containing the PDMs themselves) from temporary knowledge (the working memories).
C2.    PDIS modules are structurally independent.
C3.    PDIS modules faciltate functional independence.
C4.    PDIS modules may be processed by a variety of control schemes.

The separation of permanent and temporary knowledge provides for many of the mechanisms embodied in human memory models currently employed in psychology. Presumably, human short-term memory (STM) and external memories (EM) corresponds to the dynamic working memories (data structures) of the PDISs, and human long-term memory (LTM) corresponds to the memory in which the PDMs themselves are stored.

The structural independence of PDIS modules facilitates incremental expansion of the system. Hence the PDIS may approach competence, or expertise, by gradually incorporating a large body of knowledge over a long period of time. This also facilitates combining code written by several individuals, or understanding code that is too massive for any one person to comprehend and master easily.

It is not difficult to incorporate into an individual PDM a cohesive body of knowledge that can be treated as a unit. It is generally useful for individual modules to convey some intrinsic meaning to an expert in the domain of application, i.e., represent chunks of knowledge that can reasonably be interpreted as units. This provides a simple way for the program to "trace" or explain its behavior: it need only keep a human observer informed of which PDM has control at any moment. In a related way, the modularization of the program's function along dimensions of "knowledge" and "meaning" facilitates the evaluation of which units are playing critical roles in the decision making that occurs during the operation of the PDIS. The capacity within PDISs for assessing individual PDMs and for removing or modifying PDMs selectively provides an inviting framework for studying and modeling learning.

A variety of systems can be realized as PDISs with widely varying control structures. For example, the PDMs can be treated as competing actors [Hewitt77], as cooperating beings [Lenat75] or knowledge sources [Erman75], as frames [Minsky75], or even as Petri-net nodes [Zisman77a].

## 3.0 RULE-BASED SYSTEMS

Most of the PDISs discussed in this book satisfy one very important constraint: all the reads (examination of data) in a PDM are bundled together and precede all the writes (modification of data). These two parts of a PDM are called the *antecedent* or left-hand side (LHS) and *consequent* or right-hand side (RHS). The antecedent is responsible for examining items in the data structures, for testing them for matches against the PDM pattern templates. Such functionally partitioned PDMs will be called *rules*, and PDISs composed of rule sets will be called *rule-based systems* (RBSs). The location of RBSs in the hierarchy of PDISs is shown in Fig. 1. Of the two main subclasses of PDISs, the rule-based system is the one examined in detail in this chapter.

### 3.1 Characteristics of Rule-Based Systems

The characteristics and associated advantages of RBSs include C1 through C4 (from Section 2), plus the following:

C5. RBSs separate examination of data from modification of data.

C6. RBSs use PDMs (called rules) that have a high degree of structure imposed on them.

Because each rule has bundled all its tests (bundles of reads and pattern matches) together in the rule's antecedent, the executive can now be specified in more functional detail: it examines the left-hand sides of rules for satisfaction (which may be logical, numeric, or symbolic), and uses the results of such tests to decide which rules to execute next. No general principles have yet been formulated regarding algorithms for deciding which rules to examine or to fire. However, different specifications of the executive may permit qualitatively different sorts of behavior to occur as the system runs (see, for example, [F. Hayes-Roth77e]).

Separation of data examination from data modification within a PDM facilitates debugging. When a bug occurs, the programmer can track down the rule that is in error (or that is missing). If it is an existing rule, he decides whether the bug arises from a rule firing at an inappropriate time (in which case he modifies the antecedent of the rule appropriately) or from performing some activity incorrectly (in which case the consequent is patched). In case a new rule is called for, the RBS builder can isolate two separate subproblems, instead of merely facing a monolithic task of constructing a new PDM. This separation of reading from writing also suggests a ready analogy to

PROGRAM

An arbitrary collection of instructions that can be executed by a computer. Behavior is dependent upon both external and internal (intermediate) data.

PATTERN-DIRECTED INFERENCE SYSTEM (PDIS)

A program organized as a collection of individual Pattern-Directed Modules, operating on data structures to match patterns and modify data via an executive that controls execution of the PDMs.

RULE-BASED SYSTEM (RBS)

A PDIS composed of PDMs called rules, each with a separate left-hand side containing most of the read accesses and a separate right-hand side containing most of the write accesses.

NETWORK-BASED SYSTEM

A PDIS composed of PDMs that are located at nodes in a network and are activated by signals received on incoming arcs.

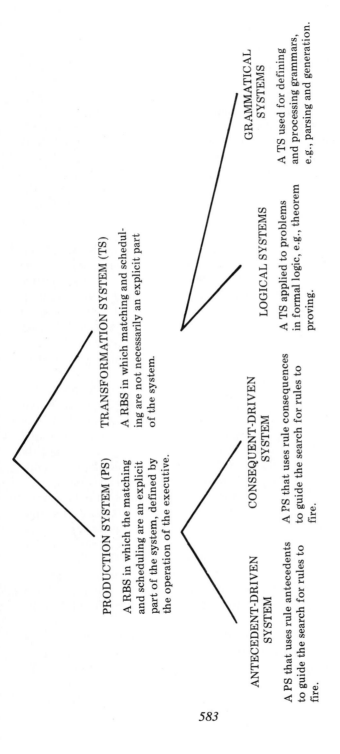

PRODUCTION SYSTEM (PS)

A RBS in which the matching
and scheduling are an explicit
part of the system, defined by
the operation of the executive.

ANTECEDENT-DRIVEN
SYSTEM

A PS that uses rule antecedents
to guide the search for rules to
fire.

CONSEQUENT-DRIVEN
SYSTEM

A PS that uses rule consequences
to guide the search for rules to
fire.

TRANSFORMATION SYSTEM (TS)

A RBS in which matching and scheduling are not necessarily an explicit part
of the system.

LOGICAL SYSTEMS

A TS applied to problems
in formal logic, e.g., theorem
proving.

GRAMMATICAL
SYSTEMS

A TS used for defining
and processing grammars,
e.g., parsing and generation.

Fig. 1. A partial hierarchy of types of pattern-directed inference systems.

psychological stimulus-response pairings, to codes of law, to causal relationships, to IF-THEN programming constructs, and to logical implication.

The high degree of structure imposed on the rules tends to give RBSs a simple organization. The original concept of a massive, complex, interwoven PDM provided a basis for an individual PDM to carry out fairly complex activities. By contrast, an individual rule in a RBS is often a simple, intelligible, and inferrable piece of code. After a flurry of testing of left-hand sides, essentially no more contingency (no more testing and branching) occurs while the right-hand side (the list of actions to perform) is carried out. Rules may—for many tasks—be more easily conceptualized as primitive entities, than can arbitrary PDMs.

Notice that some of the advantages of general PDISs have been sacrificed in RBSs. It is no longer possible to realize naturally all the varied control methodologies mentioned earlier (e.g., actors, beings, and knowledge sources), since a rule cannot be arbitrarily complex (cannot be conceived as a full-fledged "expert" module). For the sake of efficiency and power the executive must be of a special kind. It must distinguish between left-hand sides (LHSs or antecedents) and right-hand sides (RHSs or consequents) of rules, and treat them quite differently.

The other branch under PDISs in Fig. 1 leads to a category of systems called *network-based* systems. These systems typically have PDMs represented as nodes in a network containing specifications about what actions to take if a message is received from one or more input arcs to the node. Semantic network-based PDISs fall into this category as do other systems that activate selected modules by sending them messages or signals that match their invocation patterns.

Within the semantic network system, nodes represent concepts or propositions, and links (arcs) between nodes represent relationships. Nodes can send or receive messages to and from neighboring nodes along their common arcs. A variety of problems can be formulated as searches within these networks, and frequently such search procedures can be implemented simply by associating pattern-directed modules with each node to examine, modify, and relay incoming messages. See, for examples, [J.R. Anderson76, Collins75, Duda77, Fiksel76, McDonald77, Shapiro77,].

Other types of network-based systems have been developed by modifying some of the characteristics of semantic nets. For example, if nodes are distributed spatially so that the concept of *neighborhoods* based on explicit links can be replaced by that of neighborhoods defined by proximity, the network-based PDIS effectively performs scene analysis functions [Zucker77b].

A variety of other applications has been investigated within this general framework. Aside from differences reflecting domain-specific information, the networks used in these diverse applications differ chiefly in their values on three primary dimensions: *structural permanence* — are the networks static or dynamically changeable; *neighborhood definition* — are neighborhoods represented explicitly by the net structure or induced implicitly by some function such as proximity, similarity, or dependency; and *relational heterogeneity* — are there multiple (e.g., spatial proximity, set inclusion, attribute-value relations) types of relationships between adjacent nodes and, if so, how are they differentially processed? See, for examples, [Hewitt77, W.R. Reitman77, Woods75, Zisman77a].

## 3.2 Classification of Rule-Based Systems

Additional constraints may be imposed on RBSs. Figure 1 illustrates the "tree" of increasingly specialized kinds of PDISs that seem worth naming and discussing separately. The major division below RBS distinguishes between production systems (PSs) and transformation systems (TSs). Production systems are composed of antecedent-consequent rules operating against a data base with the matching and scheduling an implicit part of the system [Newell72b, Davis76b, Waterman76b, 77e]. Transformation systems, by contrast, comprise rules and data but do not necessarily specify an executive to control the application of the rules. Examples of TSs are logical systems for theorem proving and grammatical systems for language definition. Logical systems are amenable to formal manipulation techniques such as resolution theorem proving [Minker77] and have been proposed as alternatives to more complex inference system architectures [Hayes77]. Grammatical systems are often useful when problems can be solved by parsing (see, for example, [Fu74, Wilks75a]).

Production systems can be divided into two categories based on rule syntax and control structure (see Fig. 1). The *antecedent-driven* system (ADS) is the one more commonly known as a production system. The antecedent is a logical combination of propositions about the data base or working memories. When the antecendent is "true" the consequent, a collection of actions that may modify the working memories, is processed and the associated actions are executed. These systems (or sometimes, just their *executives*) are called antecedent-driven since the scheduling and execution of rules is controlled by pattern-matching rule antecedents against working memory. The *consequent-driven* system (CDS) has both antecedents and consequents that are assertions about the data. Here scheduling and execution of rules is guided by *backward chaining* [Waterman77e], involving matching rule consequents against the assertions to be proven. In this way a CDS may attempt to deduce a theorem or achieve a goal by recursively establishing the antecedents of matched rules as lower-order subgoals. When the lowest-order subgoals match valid assertions in the data base, the entire process halts and the goal is achieved.

Two types of PSs have gained prominence in recent years. The first is the *pure* production system, an ADS with many formal constraints concerning the structure of the antecedents, consequents, and working memory. These constraints generally lead to relatively simple, parsimonious systems and make this type of system attractive for modeling human cognition and memory. Thus a primary advantage of the pure production system is the strong analogy to cognitive models (LTM corresponding to production memory, and STM to working memory) [Newell72a, b, 73, J.R. Anderson76, 77a, b]. Several recent studies have addressed principles of representation and control of pure production systems, and the reader is directed to them [J. McDermott77a, 77b, Rychener77, Vere77a, Zisman77]. The second type of PS that has been in wide use of late is the so-called *performance* system, a system designed to perform at an expert level on some particular (usually narrow) problem. For example, Meta-DENDRAL is an ADS that induces new rules of mass spectroscopy theory [B.G. Buchanan77], while MYCIN is a CDS that performs medical diagnosis of infectious blood diseases [Shortliffe76]. There are many fewer "simplicity and purity" constraints for expert performance systems, hence they often formally are esthetically unattractive. However, their builders have achieved higher levels of expertise than has been possible to date within the pure PS design. The expert systems also claim that their rules are more natural, since each one can be a huge chunk of domain-dependent expertise. (See for example [Lenat77d].)

Many of the performance systems use causal reasoning, making long chains of deductions or integrating multiple, diverse sources of information to reach composite decisions. Examples of this type of system include common-sense reasoning world models [Rieger77c] and speech understanding systems that relate observable characteristics of speech at one level of abstraction (e.g., lexical) to their realizations at adjacent levels (syllabic or phrasal, [Mostow77]).

Some additional characteristics and associated advantages of productions systems are as follows:

C7.   PSs have many constraints on the form and processing of rules.

C8.   ADSs have consequents that are actions.

C9.   CDSs have consequents that are assertions.

The many constraints placed on PS rules, especially in pure PSs lead to a much stronger analogy to psychological stimulus-response behaviors than do arbitrary RBSs. They also facilitate the use of a simpler executive for controlling system operation. Furthermore, the ADSs provide natural models of dynamic physical activity since the rules' RHSs actually do things that simulate changes in the real world. An interesting advantage of the CDS results from both left- and right-hand sides being similar constructs. This permits the system to be run both forward (where A → B means "if you see A asserted, then assert B") and backward (where A → B means "to establish B it will suffice to establish A").

# 4.0 HUMAN COGNITION AND PATTERN-DIRECTED INFERENCE SYSTEMS

Within the theoretical framework of information processing systems, major topics in both psychology and artificial intelligence have been converging. Although both fields are interested in problem solving, language understanding, and learning they have proceeded somewhat independently in a search for the mechanisms and functions underlying intelligent behavior. Psychologists have focused primarily on problems of acquisition, storage, and retrieval of knowledge, while researchers in computer science have focused on the representation and application of knowledge. In this section we shall investigate this schism from the viewpoint of the pattern-directed inference system formalism.

Figure 2 represents a very simplified view of a contemporary information-processing model of human cognition. Its major components include mental behavior mechanisms for perceiving, thinking, and learning, and memories for storing and accessing information.

Two different types of memories are identified here. The *long-term memory* contains two subsets of knowledge, differing in both type and accessibility. *Quiescent knowledge* consists of background information that is not currently accessible to reasoning processes. It is the remotely accessible warehouse for the bulk of human experiences. Knowledge that is currently relevant and can be accessed quickly is called *active knowledge*. The essential difference between active and quiescent knowledge is the availability and readiness of the active knowledge. Presumably, knowledge is activated by a variety of both passive and purposive search processes in response to conditions of the current situation. At any one time, the subset of knowledge actually included in the active knowledge is presumably but a small fraction of the total knowledge in long-term memory. Within this model, selec-

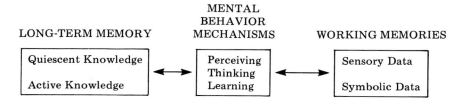

Fig. 2. A contemporary information processing model of human cognition.

tion and activation of appropriate knowledge are necessary precursors of the inference processes that apply that knowledge.

Figure 2 shows the other key component of the information-processing model of human cognition, the set of *working memories*. These memories hold information of a temporary nature and include memories for *sensory data* and *symbolic data*. The sensory data memories hold the results of sensory stimulation (e.g., visual, auditory, and proprioceptive stimuli), while the symbolic data memories hold temporary or intermediate results of cognitive processing.

Although psychological investigations of human cognition have contributed enormously to our understanding of where, when, and why knowledge is acquired, stored, and retrieved, they have glossed over the questions of what the knowledge actually is and how it is applied.

A contemporary pattern-directed inference system combining the principal features of systems discussed in earlier chapters is shown in Fig. 3. This model consists of an *executive* and two types of memory. The executive, or pattern-directed inference mechanism, has five components that communicate with various memories to detect conditions of interest and initiate appropriate actions. It employs a *change monitor* to detect perturbations in the memories that may require attention and a *pattern matcher* to compare the observed situations with those defined as warranting responses by the inference rules. Every action that is suggested by the pattern matcher is stored in an *agenda* that is used as a basis for ordering the computations. The *scheduler* selects the most important potential action and the *processor* calculates and implements the action thus selected. The *knowledge modifier* effects the changes to the knowledge base representing temporary modifications (knowledge activation) and assists in making permanent modifications such as rule or data reformulations.

In addition to the agenda, the PDIS model contains two other

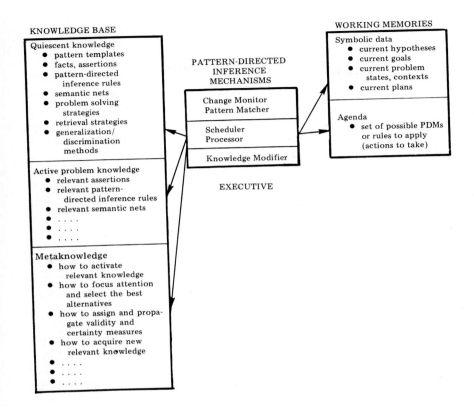

Fig. 3. A model of a contemporary pattern-directed inference system (PDIS).

memory units that are similar to those in the human cognition model: the knowledge base and the working memories. The knowledge base is similar to long-term memory, and contains three subcomponents: *quiescent knowledge*, all information not currently involved in inferential activity; *active knowledge*, all permanent information relevant to the problem at hand; and *metaknowledge*, information describing how knowledge should be activated or how alternative actions should be selected and executed.

The three major types of knowledge employed by contemporary PDISs are pattern-directed inference rules, assertions, and semantic nets. The rules are the antecedent-consequent pairs described in Section 3.2. The assertions are statements about data in the knowledge base, and the semantic nets are networks of additional facts and relationships that can be oganized, stored, and searched efficiently because of their hierarchical (general-to-specific) structure.

The other memory unit similar to that in the cognitive model is also called *working memory*. It can be viewed as having two main components: the *agenda*, containing the set of possible rules (or PDMs) to apply in the current situation, and the *symbolic data* store, the repository of problem representations, goals, and intermediate results.

Most PDISs incorporate global goals that affect the outcomes of inference. For example, a PDIS used for real-time speech understanding applications may be forced to choose between speed and certainty of response [F. Hayes-Roth77e, Mostow77]. Other goals that may affect the way the system operates include various requirements concerning interpretability, explicability, modifiability, and extensibility of the PDIS behavior. These goals usually are reflected in design decisions regarding the structure of the working memory stores and the modularity and granularity of the knowledge and data representations employed.

The PDIS model of Fig. 3 can be thought of as one realization or specification of the cognitive model of Fig. 2. Where the goal of psychological research has been to understand *when, where,* and *why* knowledge is stored, the goal of AI research has been to understand *what* knowledge is needed to perform some task (knowledge representation) and *how* that knowledge should be matched to appropriate data conditions and applied to alter them (architecture for inference systems). Thus, the two fields offer nearly complementary theories of information processing. In the remainder of this chapter the topics of knowledge representation, system architecture and the imminent knowledge explosion are reconsidered in light of recent research. We shall suggest that inference systems designed for general, "intelligent" applications will require a synthesis of both the knowledge engineering techniques garnered from the study of PDISs as well as the principles of memory architecture garnered from the study of human intelligence.

## 5.0 THE REPRESENTATION OF KNOWLEDGE

The antecedent-consequent (A-C) rule form that is the basis of many current PDISs provides a natural and concise representation of behavioral knowledge of the sort, "If a situation occurs with characteristics A, the appropriate thing to do is C." This knowledge representation has a number of useful features. The same form of rule can be used either to build a machine for a specific task (given A it performs C), to model a system (if the system is observed to do C whenever A occurs, the A-C rule models it), or to represent judgmental knowledge and apply it (if A implies C and A is true then assume C is true). In addition, an antecedent-consequent rule is easily interpreted, both by people who wish to understand what effects it will have and by machines that actually apply it to data.

As noted in Section 1.3, PDISs are more complex than pure production systems, which incorporate only symbol manipulating rules, a working memory, and an executive. PDISs permit additional types of knowledge representations, including semantic networks, procedural methods invoked implicitly in pattern matching or directly by action components of rules, heuristically estimated strength measures (credibility and validity) of working memory elements, metaknowledge rules and procedures that regulate the scheduler or propagate analog measures through working memory, and specialized working memory representations for multiple levels of abstraction and analog dimensions of time and space.

For some problems, the pure production system formalism is not as useful as the more complex and comprehensive PDIS formulation. One important characteristic of pure production systems is

C10.   Pure PSs are highly constrained with regard to the structure and processing of rules and working memory.

The constraints on the structure of rules and working memory can lead to rules so fine-grained that they lack both clarity and generality [Mostow77, Davis76b, 77d]. Reasoning power and scope could be extended, however, by increasing the level of abstraction and richness of the rule components [Lenat77a, b, d]. Also, certain behaviors are difficult to represent in terms of rigid symbol manipulation rules, despite the grain size. These include temporal sequences, procedural invocation, and recursion. Thus, complex behavior can be represented more naturally if the strict syntax of the rules is adequately generalized [Lenat77c]. The constraints on working memory promote generality but tend to restrict power. Many problem solving methods could benefit from specialized working memory structures that transcend the simple symbolic format used with most pure production systems.

The constraints on rule processing in pure PSs make it difficult to create metarules for governing selection of actions for execution and activation of relevant knowledge. Many complex tasks require careful selection of the most appropriate action for immediate execution when numerous actions are warranted and combinatorial explosions are often possible [F. Hayes-Roth77b, e, Joshi77, Mostow77, Rosenschein77a]. This type of focusing is best accomplished through the use of a special agenda memory and metaknowledge to affect the scheduler directly. Many tasks also require the selection and inclusion of assertions and procedural knowledge from a quiescent knowledge base. These interactions seem to be beyond the scope of most pure production system representations.

## 6.0 THE ARCHITECTURE OF PATTERN-DIRECTED INFERENCE SYSTEMS

Contemporary PDISs have developed specialized architectures far beyond the early production systems that motivated them [Post43, Newell72a, 72b]). As Fig. 3 illustrates, architectural elaborations include more developed working memories, more sophisticated knowledge bases, and more complex pattern matching and scheduling. The architectural techniques and principles currently employed in PDISs will be discussed and evaluated in this section.

### 6.1 Working Memory

Working memory was originally conceived as an analog of human short-term memory. Thus, it would contain approximately seven chunks of symbolic list structures [Newell73, G. A. Miller56]. Some of the simplest production system applications have operated under such constraints. Other production system architectures eliminate this constraint simply because the restriction to a small number of chunks (or lists) seems arbitrary and provides no apparent benefits [Rychener77]. Of course, very little is yet understood about the methods that humans use to reduce computation to the apparently limited amount of human short-term memory, and the relaxation of the working memory constraint in computer systems may be a possible reflection of a lack of understanding and appreciation of its value.

Various PDISs differ in the types of elaborate working memories allowed. Nearly all allow an unlimited number of symbols to be created, maintained, and monitored in working memory for pattern matches (up to the storage limits of the systems). A consequence of this relaxation on total capacity has been a perceived need to make the pattern matching process faster. The expected time to compare the contents of working memory to the rule antecedents is approximately a linear function of the number of elements in working memory. This unfortunate fact has given rise to two lines of research to alleviate the problem. One line (see Section 6.3) has led to improved matching algorithms that simply do not have a linear time relationship with working memory size [J. McDermott 77a]. The other is based on architectural innovations such as specialized working memories, as discussed below.

Specialized working memories have been developed primarily to reduce the cost of pattern matches. For example, several systems have introduced multilevel representations of data, so that rules could be compared for applicability with data at appropriate levels [Nii77, Mostow77, W.R. Reitman77, Soloway77, Sridharan77]. In addition, a number of systems have incorporated into working memories other dimensions of the problem space (such as time or location) to provide coordinates for pattern matches and retrievals [F. Hayes-Roth76j, 77e, g, Lesser75, Zucker77b].

Analog weights to represent the validity or certainty factors associated with statistical or judgmental data have also been widely applied [Shortliffe75a, F. Hayes-Roth77i, Lenat76, 77a, Zucker77a, b, 78, Duda76, 77]. These values are usually integrated into the working memory representations by attaching them to symbolic data representing hypotheses or inferences. Their magnitude is either determined by metaknowledge rules, by executive procedures, or by fundamental memory processes (as in relaxation labeling [Zucker76, 77c]). The utility and significance of weights depends on the problem domain. In a complex domain such as speech or image understanding, weights are needed to prune the least significant data from memory and to schedule preferentially those actions associated with the most significant data [F. Hayes-Roth77e]. In a problem domain such as medical diagnosis or geological classification, weights may be essential only for the ultimate choice of the most strongly supported judgment [Shortliffe76, Duda77].

It is clear from these developments that specialization of memory representations has proven useful. As knowledge and understanding of various problem domains grow, additional ways to constrain the working memory design for efficiency should be discovered.

## 6.2 The Knowledge Base

The architecture of knowledge bases has become increasingly complex and sophisticated. As the bulk of knowledge and its complexity have increased, the concept of a uniform knowledge base has been extended to incorporate distinctions between quiescent and active knowledge and between problem-level and metalevel knowledge. These distinctions have led to several principles concerning the way in which knowledge is activated and the way in which knowledge itself is acquired and evaluated.

What does it mean for knowledge to be *activated* and how should knowledge be transferred from the quiescent to the active state? The primary distinction between quiescent and active knowledge is that only the latter participates in pattern-directed inference. Thus, knowledge is active if it is considered by the pattern matcher and quiescent otherwise. In simple systems possessing little knowledge, this distinction is unnecessary. However, for systems possessing knowledge about multiple problem domains or numerous alternative strategies for approaching a single problem, selectivity is needed. A number of systems have now been built that activate knowledge selectively, including [D. McDermott77a, Joshi77, D.G. Bobrow77, 77a, McDonald77, Lenat76].

The most typical method for selectively activating assertions that may be relevant for current inference problems is *spreading excitation* in semantic networks ([W.R. Reitman65, Quillian68, Collins75]). In this scheme, the knowledge base is partially organized in terms of concept nodes and relational links. When an input datum or intermediate result is identified as an instance of a particular concept node, that node is "excited," and this excitation is propagated to neighboring nodes via their connecting links. Neighboring concepts are thus excited and considered relevant to the current problem. Assertions about their properties and relationships are then added to the active knowledge base. The first system to employ this technique was Reitman's ARGUS [W.R. Reitman65], and several chapters in this book present contemporary approaches to this selective activation notion [McDonald77, Duda77, Reiger77c] Other recent papers on this problem include [Minker77, J.R. Anderson76, 77a, Hobbs77].

A more general methodology for selectively transferring quiescent knowledge to the active state depends on a *partial match* between working memory data characteristics and properties of knowledge elements. This approach attempts to apply to the inference process just the knowledge that is most likely to be relevant or useful. Two chapters in this book that discuss the role of partial matches for the selection of appropriate knowledge are [Joshi77] and [F. Hayes-Roth77b]. As these chapters point out, the use of partial matches to select knowledge is a very general associative retrieval mechanism that is computationally complex and still poorly understood. (See also [Rieger77c].)

Another type of architectural innovation in the realm of knowledge bases concerns the use of metaknowledge. What methods have been developed for incorporating and exploiting metaknowledge? Three principles for dealing with metaknowledge have emerged and are concerned with the activation of knowledge, the execution of potential actions, and the acquisition of new knowledge. These are discussed in turn.

The first principle concerns the selective activation of quiescent knowledge: *Metaknowledge is required to determine what quiescent knowledge is relevant and when it should be included in inference processes.* While several systems have been developed that embody this principle, none to our knowledge has achieved a rule-based representation of that knowledge. Instead, as previously discussed, the primary methods for selection are spreading excitation and partial matching.

The second principle underlying the use of metaknowledge concerns the selective execution of potential actions: *The most desirable rules to execute first are those whose consequents maximize the probability of producing correct or important results while minimizing the computational cost of processing.* The implementation of this principle can take many forms. Alternative actions within a rule or set of rules whose antecedents are satisfied can be ordered heuristically and consecutively explored. This requires either backtracking or generator mechanisms. However, the most widely adopted method of scheduling employs the concept of an agenda of possible actions that are sorted according to desirability values computed by applying metaknowledge evaluators. This general scheme covers both explicit desirability calculations based on notions of validity, importance, interest, etc. [F. Hayes-Roth77e, Lenat76] as well as implicit desirability calculations based on syntactic approaches to conflict resolution [J. McDemott77b].

The third principle dealing with metaknowledge concerns knowledge acquisition: *New rules can be generated from examples of their behavior.* This underlies a number of successful efforts to augment an original knowledge base by discovering new rules. For example, several chapters in this book (Chapters 13-15 [Vere77b, B. G. Buchanan77, Holland77]) discuss techniques for discovering and adding new rules to the data base. Vere's method of generalizing specific behavior sequences into sets of general production rules is similar to that proposed by Hayes-Roth [F. Hayes-Roth76c, 77f] and Becker [Becker73]. Buchanan and Mitchell discuss a less general but computationally more economical approach to rule discovery that employs model-based hypothesis generation. Holland and Reitman explore constrained (less general) rule representations that permit the use of exponentially faster algorithms for evaluating hypothetical rules. The chapter by Waterman [Waterman77d] significantly extends this notion of learning from examples by applying it to the generation of complete production systems that act as agents (see also [R.H. Anderson77a]). While his programs require some interaction with an expert instructor, Waterman's approach shows how organized sets of behavior rules can be generalized from specific exemplary behavior sequences.

## 6.3 Pattern Matching and Scheduling

The success of a PDIS depends on many things, including the quality of incorporated knowledge, the efficiency with which working memory data is compared with rule conditions, and the methods used to schedule alternatives. Both the pattern-matching efficiency problem and the problem of scheduling (conflict resolution) are discussed in detail in this section.

Three principles have emerged from the study of pattern matching. These concern filtering data prior to pattern matching, more efficient methods of common subexpression evaluation, and adoption of high-level representations to reduce complexity and processing time. These three principles are explained and illustrated below.

The filtering principle can be stated as: *Inexpensive heuristic tests can reduce the amount of data that need to be compared to condition patterns.* Two different sorts of filters have been developed. A *syntactic filter* winnows data based on superficial characteristics relevant to some characteristics of the condition patterns, such as specific predicates or arguments (see [J. McDermott77a]). A more sophisticated type, the *global selection* filter, employs high-level approximations of detailed knowledge representations to search for data that satisfy important constraints or reflect global coherence. Data thus identified are considered to be prime candidates for more detailed pattern matching operations (see [Mostow77, Zucker77b, F. Hayes-Roth77b], as well as [Mark77]). Both types of filters serve the important function of reducing the average number of computations required to identify the set of possible consequents to be executed.

The second principle concerns a technique for avoiding redundant calculations in pattern matching: *Subexpression evaluation can and should be minimized.* One way to accomplish this is by saving the evaluations of subexpressions common to several condition elements (the software analog of "caching"). The chapter by McDermott, Newell, and Moore explores the use of such a technique for improving the efficiency of execution. Related work is described in [Forgy77, F. Hayes-Roth75].

The third principle for improving pattern matching efficiency is: *High-level representations should be preferred to low-level ones.* This follows from the fact that high-level representations can be compared more easily than low-level ones. For example, once a box is defined and recognizable, representing it in terms of the high-level predicate "box" is preferable to representing it in terms of a configuration of low-level predicates, such as "line," "orientation," and "vertex." Matching a datum labeled "box" to a rule condition containing the same label is trivial. On the other hand, matching two box descriptions encoded in low-level primitives can be very complex (see [Rosenschein77a, F.

Hayes-Roth77b]). In general, the use of high-level descriptors reduces the probability of chance agreement between data and rule antecedents and thus reduces the expected time to compute actual matches (see also [B. Hayes-Roth77c]).

The problem of conflict resolution or scheduling in PDISs is a difficult one, and a number of scheduling techniques have been devised ([J.McDermott 77b, F. Hayes-Roth77e, Lenat77d, Zisman77]). The need for choosing among alternative consequents can arise from having multiple PDMs match the data at the same time. This may occur for several reasons, including ambiguity or error in the data, incomplete or erroneous rule antecedents, or the use of redundant methods for achieving comparable goals.

To facilitate selection, contemporary PDIS executives employ a four-step process. In the first step, data are filtered relative to the antecedents of rules. In the second step, detailed pattern matching is performed to instantiate PDM conditions or rule antecedents. All satisfied rules or PDMs (the conflict set) are added to an agenda of invoked but not yet executed actions. In step three, pending agenda items are assigned priorities by applying metaknowledge rules that determine the scheduling priority of each alternative. In step four, the highest priority item is executed. Modifications made to working memory are noted by a *change monitor* ([Lesser75]) and are used to reinitiate the cycle at step one.

## 6.4 Guidelines for Constructing PDISs

Various principles have emerged concerning methods for creating and applying PDIS architectures to specific problems. These principles (see Sections 4.2 and 4.3) suggest a number of guidelines to follow when constructing PDISs. Some of the most general are discussed in this section.

The PDIS formalism derives much power from its factorization of complex problems into manageable, largely independent subproblems. Thus each PDM should[2] be written as a single and separate unit that is independently meaningful within the task domain of the PDIS. This facilitates incremental growth, explanatory power, and many types of experiments that aid in determining the location of the effective "intelligence" (e.g., experiments in which various PDMs are modified, deleted, or traced). It also simplifies debugging since individual PDMs can be held accountable for specific tasks. For the same reasons, strong coupling between PDMs (one PDM explicitly calling another) should be minimized. In situations where two PDMs couple inseparably, they

---

[2] This is the "should" of homilies and maxims. They rest primarily upon empirical experience and intuition rather than upon formal justification.

should be merged into one unit, if this can be done without violating the other guidelines for PDIS construction.

Each PDM in a PDIS should be supplied with certain key information to facilitate system operation. This should include information about the *origin* of the PDM, an English *paraphrase* of what it does, details on how to estimate its expected *running time* in different situations, and some measure of the PDM's *utility* or overall worth to the PDIS. This information may be useful to the human monitor (programmer or user) in communicating with the PDIS (e.g., for keeping the user abreast of what the system is doing), may be used by the PDIS itself in inducing new PDMs (e.g., by analogy to the most successful existing ones), or may be used by the executive in selecting the PDM to be executed next.

Finally, PDIS knowledge representations should incorporate more programming language constructs to represent a wider variety of behaviors. For example, rules that can handle procedure calls, recursion, and mechanisms for local and global contexts and variable bindings will be useful in combatting the combinatorial explosion inherent in processing huge amounts of information. Of course, these programming language constructs all tend to reduce the modularity and independence of PDMs. Thus, there is a trade-off between reducing the knowledge explosion on the one hand and facilitating incremental and adaptive behavior on the other.

## 7.0 THE KNOWLEDGE EXPLOSION AND INTELLIGENCE

A critical problem facing designers of intelligent systems is the acquisition, integration, and application of vast amounts of knowledge. Increasing the amount and complexity of knowledge can cause major difficulties and lead to new theoretical developments, as evidenced in the historical progression from simple production systems to complex PDISs. The main problem with incorporating massive amounts of knowledge in an inference system is that it can precipitate a combinatorial explosion of possible behaviors. Thus the problem of paramount interest becomes controlling the attendant *knowledge explosion*. Some suggestions for handling this problem will now be presented.

The efficiency of pattern matchers underlying pattern-directed inference must be improved to help combat the knowledge explosion. The development of improved filters and state-saving memories is certainly a step in the right direction. Another feasible approach might be to explore specialized hardware for data description and pattern matching.

A clever choice of data representations can help reduce computational complexity. Improved methods for discovering and employing high-level descriptors are needed, since the use of low-level predicates seems to contribute significantly to the combinatorial explosion. In a related way, embedding complex matching processes within a pattern matcher to allow simple descriptions of rule antecedents is very misleading (see [Rosenschein77a]). What is needed is more elaborate description processes with correspondingly simpler matching requirements.

Special problem representations and memory structures may exploit the possibilities of global organization and hierarchical decomposition. Increasing the amount of knowledge without simultaneously increasing the ability to identify the relevant relationships involved would be deleterious. Directions for research in this area include improved metaknowledge representations, multilevel problem representations, and hierarchically organized knowledge representations.

Partial matching techniques need to be refined and extended. This is especially important for domains where the match between data and rule antecedents is inherently imperfect. As the amount of knowledge is increased, the importance of effective use of partial matching is paramount, particularly in domains such as vision and speech that are characterized by noise, error, ambiguity, and incompleteness.

Alternative methods for monitoring events and triggering activity should be explored in the attempt to find methods for controlling the knowledge explosion. The basic pattern matching and scheduling cycle discussed previously seems robust, but could be developed and refined further. For example, more explicit control structures can be developed for relaying data changes to condition monitors of interest. Thus, the concept of filtering is just one way of improving communication between actions that cause events and conditions that monitor and respond to them. As an example, Reitman's system (Chapter 26 [W. R. Reitman77]) generates spiderlike webs around situations where changes should be sensed. These webs monitor the area and relay events to the condition monitors specifically associated with that area. This is one example of the type of structural specialization possible within the PDIS framework. For other examples see [Lenat77d, Zisman77a, Rieger77c].

## 8.0 CONCLUSIONS

In the realm of intelligent systems, two general types of inferential relationships prevail. The *causal* connection, A causes B, is the essence of scientific understanding of physical systems. Such a relationship is easily captured and exploited within a PDIS by the inference rule, "If A occurs, perform an action that causes B." The second type of relationship is logical implication, the key to deductive inference. This relationship is captured by the rule, "If A is true then B is true." The ease with which such rules can be used to represent both causal and logical implications makes them very powerful and general bases for knowledge representation.

However, contemporary PDISs offer as many challenges as opportunities. As our understanding of problem solving in specific task domains improves, the syntactic and semantic complexity of our rules and the logic of the executive that schedules and interprets actions increase accordingly. We therefore expect PDISs to become more frequent topics of study within the areas of programming languages and operating systems. While even the simplest PDISs satisfy the minimal requirement of computational universality, it must be conceded that the diversity of PDIS formalisms and associated executives reflects both a lack of understanding of their semantics and a lack of accepted programming conventions. Just as algorithmic languages have evolved in elegant ways about the concepts of procedures, contexts, and recursion, so will PDISs probably evolve about the concepts of quiescence and activation, assertions, inference rules, working memory, pattern matchers, schedulers, and executives. In this process, essential notions of modularity and granularity of knowledge must surely be addressed.

As the chapters in this book illustrate, PDISs are already being used for a variety of applications, including program synthesis, knowledge engineering, natural language understanding, vision and speech, and cognitive modeling (see [Waterman77e] for a survey of this work). Additional domains that would appear well suited to such approaches include computer-generated instructions for troubleshooting or operating devices, experimental design, situation assessment and presentation, tactical or operational planning and control, and circuit design and analysis. Each of these domains is associated with a number of applications that are typically approached by first modeling causal or contingent relations and then manipulating representations of these relations to work backward from a goal to a set of initial conditions or to work forward from initial conditions to a desirable result.

PDISs provide an excellent and experimentally tested framework for the representation of knowledge and its application to inference problems. Individual rules seem to satisfy the desirable requirements of independent verifiability, interpretability, explicability, and learnability. As a result, PDISs based on antecedent-consequent rules make a strong claim to being the best available scheme for knowledge representation, and the pattern-directed inference systems that have evolved to select and apply these rules present an equivalently strong claim to being appropriate architectures for behavioral complexity and intelligence.

# BIBLIOGRAPHY

[Aho74]
Aho, A. V., Hopcroft, J. E., and Ullman, J. D. *The design and analysis of computer algorithms.* Addison-Wesley, Reading, Massachusetts, 1974.

[J. R. Anderson73]
Anderson, J. R., and Bower, G. *Human associative memory.* Winston-Wiley, Washington, D.C., 1973.

[J. R. Anderson74]
Anderson, J. R. Retrieval of propositional information from long-term memory. *Cognitive Psych.* 6, 1974, 451-474.

[J. R. Anderson76]
Anderson, J. R. *Language, memory, and thought.* Lawrence Erlbaum Associates, Hillsdale, New Jersey, 1976.

[J. R. Anderson77a]
Anderson, J. R., and Kline, P. J. Design of a production system for cognitive modeling. *Proc. Workshop Pattern-Directed Inference Systems, SIGART Newsletter* 63, 1977, 60-65.

[J. R. Anderson77b]
Anderson, J. R., Kline, P. J., and Lewis, C. A production system model for language processing. *In Cognitive processes in comprehension* (Carpenter, P., and Just, M., eds.). Lawrence Erlbaum Associates, Hillsdale, New Jersey, 1977.

[R. C. Anderson71]
Anderson, R. C. Encoding processes in the storage and retrieval of sentences. *J. Exp. Psych.* 2, 1971, 338-340.

[R. C. Anderson77]
Anderson, R. C. The notion of schemata and the educational enter-
prise. *In Schooling and the acquisition of knowledge* (Anderson,
R. C., Spiro, R. J., and Montague, W. E., eds.). Lawrence Erlbaum
Associates, Hillsdale, New Jersey, 1977.

[R. H. Anderson76a]
Anderson, R. H., and Gillogly, J. J. The Rand intelligent terminal
agent (RITA) as a network access aid. *AFIPS Proc. 45,* 1976,
501-509.

[R. H. Anderson76b]
Anderson, R. H., and Gillogly, J. J. Rand intelligent terminal agent
(RITA): design philosophy. R-1809-ARPA, The Rand Corpora-
tion, Santa Monica, California, 1976.

[R. H. Anderson77a]
Anderson, R. H. The use of production systems in RITA to construct
personal computer "agents." *Proc. Workshop Pattern-Directed
Inference Systems, SIGART Newsletter 63,* 1977, 23-28.

[R. H. Anderson77b]
Anderson, R. H., Gallegos, M., Gillogly, J. J., Greenberg, R. B., and
Villanueva, R. RITA Reference Manual, R-1808-ARPA. The
Rand Corporation, Santa Monica, California, 1977.

[Anisfeld68]
Anisfeld, M., and Knapp, M. Association, synonymity, and directionality in false recognition. *J. Exp. Psych. 77,* 1968, 171-179.

[Anisfeld69]
Anisfeld, M. False recognition produced by semantic and phonetic
relations under two presentation rates. *Psychonomic Sci. 17,*
1969, 366-367.

[Astrom70]
Astrom, K. *An introduction to stochastic control theory.* Academic
Press, New York, 1970.

[Bachman75]
Bachman C. W. Trends in database management—1975. *Proc. 1975
Nat. Comput. Conf.,* 569-576.

[Bajcsy78]
Bajcsy, R., and Joshi, A. K. Partially ordered world model and natural
outdoor scenes. *Proc. Workshop Machine Vision,* Amherst, 1977
(Riseman, E., ed.). Academic Press, New York, 1978.

[Balzer67]
Balzer, R. M. Dataless programming. *Proc. 1967 Fall Joint Comput. Conf.*, 535-544.

[Balzer72]
Balzer, R. M. Automatic programming. Tech. Memo, USC/Information Sciences Institute, Marina del Rey, California, 1972.

[Balzer73]
Balzer, R. M. A global view of automatic programming. *Proc. 3rd Int. Joint Conf. Artificial Intelligence*, Stanford, California, 1973, 494-499.

[Barrow76]
Barrow, H. G., and Tenebaum, J. M. MSYS: a system for reasoning about scenes. Tech. Note 121, Artificial Intelligence Center, Stanford Research Institute, Menlo Park, California, 1976.

[Barstow76]
Barstow, D., and Kant, E. Observations on the interaction between coding and efficienty knowledge in the PSI program syntehsis system. *Proc. 2nd Int. Conf. Software Engineering*, San Francisco, 1976.

[Barstow77a]
Barstow, D. A knowledge base organization for rules about programming. *Proc. Workshop Pattern-Directed Inference Systems, SIGART Newsletter 63*, 1977, 18-22.

[Barstow77b]
Barstow, D. A knowledge-based system for automatic program construction. *Proc. 5th Int. Joint Conf. Artificial Intelligence*, Cambridge, Massachusetts, 1977, 382-388.

[Bartlett32]
Bartlett, F. *Remembering*. Cambridge Univ. Press, Cambridge, 1932.

[Becker73]
Becker, J. D. A model for the encoding of experiential information. *In Computer models of thought and language* (Schank, R. C., and Colby, K. M., eds.). Freeman, San Francisco, 1973.

[Biermann74]
Biermann, A. W., and Krishnaswamy, R. Constructing programs from example computations. Report CISRC-TR-74-5, Computer and Information Science Research Center, Ohio State Univ., Columbus, Ohio, 1974.

[Biermann76]
Biermann, A. W. Regular LISP programs and their automatic synthesis from examples. Report CS-1976-12, Dep. Comput. Sci., Duke Univ., Durham, North Carolina, 1976.

[Biermann77]
Biermann, A. W., and Smith, D. R. A production rule mechanism for generating LISP code. Dep. Comput. Sci., Duke Univ., Durham, North Carolina, 1977.

[Bledsoe72]
Bledsoe, W. W., Boyer, R. S., and Henneman, W. H. Computer proofs of limit theorems. *Artificial Int. 3*, 1972, 27-60.

[Bledsoe74]
Bledsoe, W. W., and Bruell, P. A man-machine theorem-proving system. *Artificial Int. 5*, 1974, 51-72.

[Bledsoe75]
Bledsoe, W. W., and Tyson, M. The UT interactive prover, Automatic Theorem Proving Project Report No. 17, Depts. of Math. and Comput. Sci., Univ. of Texas at Austin, 1975.

[D. G. Bobrow68]
Bobrow, D. G. Natural language input for a computer problem solving system. *In Semantic information processing* (Minsky, M., ed.). MIT Press, Cambridge, Massachusetts, 1968.

[D. G. Bobrow74]
Bobrow, D. G., and Raphael, B. R. New programming languages for artificial intelligence research. *ACM Comput. Surv. 6*, 1974, 153-174.

[D. G. Bobrow75a]
Bobrow, D. G. Dimensions of representation. In *Representation and understanding* (Bobrow, D. G., and Collins, A., eds.). Academic Press, New York, 1975.

[D. G. Bobrow75b]
Bobrow, D. G., and Collins, A. (eds.). *Representation and understanding: Studies in cognitive science.* Academic Press, New York, 1975.

[D. G. Bobrow77]
Bobrow, D. G., and Winograd, T. An overview of KRL, A knowledge representation language. *J. Cognitive Sci. 1*, 1977, 3-46.

[D. G. Bobrow77a]
Bobrow, D. G., Winograd, T., and the KRL Research Group. Experi-

ence with KRL-0: One cycle of a knowledge representation language. *Proc. 5th Int. Joint Conf. Artificial Intelligence*, Cambridge, Massachusetts, 1977, 213-222.

[R. Bobrow75]
Bobrow, R., and Brown, J. S. Systematic understanding. *In Representation and understanding: Studies in cognitive science* (Bobrow, D. G., and Collins, A., eds.). Academic Press, New York, 1975.

[Boorman69]
Boorman, S. A. *The protracted game.* Oxford Univ. Press, New York, 1969.

[Bower69]
Bower, G. H. Chunks as interference units in free recall. *J. Verbal Learning Verbal Behav.* 8, 1969, 610-613.

[Brewer75]
Brewer, W. F. Memory for ideas: Synonym substitution. *Memory and Cognition* 3, 1975, 458-464.

[Brooks75]
Brooks, R. A model of human cognitive processes in writing code for computer programs. Ph.D. Dissertation, Dep. Psych., Carnegie-Mellon Univ., Pittsburgh, Pennsylvania, 1975.

[Brooks77]
Brooks, R. Production systems as control structures for programming languages. *Proc. Workshop Pattern-Directed Inference Systems, SIGART Newsletter* 63, 1977, 33-37.

[D. Brown75]
Brown, D. J. H. Concept formation and exposition. Ph.D. Dissertation, Univ. of the Witwatersrand, Johannesburg, South Africa, 1975.

[D. Brown77]
Brown, D. J. H. Concept learning by feature value interval abstraction. *Proc. Workshop Pattern-Directed Inference Systems, SIGART Newsletter* 63, 1977, 55-60.

[G. Brown74]
Brown, G. The BELIEVER System. Report RUCBM-TR-33, Dep. Comput. Sci., Rutgers Univ., Camden, New Jersey, 1974.

[J. S. Brown73]
Brown, J. S. Steps toward automatic theory formation. *Proc. 3rd Int. Joint Conf. Artificial Intelligence*, Stanford, California, 1973, 121-129.

[Bruner56]
Bruner, J. S., Goodnow, J. J., and Austin, G. A. *A study of thinking.* Wiley, New York, 1956.

[B. G. Buchanan69]
Buchanan, B. G., Sutherland, G., and Feigenbaum, E. A. Heuristic Dendral: A program for generating explanatory hypotheses in organic chemistry. *In Machine intelligence,* Vol. 4 (Meltzer, B., and Michie, D., eds.). American Elsevier, New York, 1969, 209-254.

[B. G. Buchanan72]
Buchanan, B. G., Feigenbaum, E. A., and Sridharan, N. S. Heuristic theory formation: Data interpretation and rule formation. *In Machine Intelligence,* Vol. 7 (Meltzer, B., and Michie, D., eds.). Edinburgh Univ. Press, Edinburgh, 1972.

[B. G. Buchanan73]
Buchanan, B. G., and Sridharan, N. S. Analysis of behavior of chemical molecules: Rule formation on non-homogeneous classes of objects. *Proc. 3rd Int. Joint Conf. Artificial Intelligence,* Stanford, California, 1973, 67-76.

[B. G. Buchanan75]
Buchanan, B. G. Applications of artificial intelligence to scientific reasoning. *Proc. 2nd USA-Japan Comput. Conf..* AFIPS and IPSJ, Tokyo, 1975, 189-194.

[B. G. Buchanan76a]
Buchanan, B. G. Scientific theory formation by computer. *Proc. NATO Advanced Study Inst. Computer Oriented Learning Processes.* Noordhoff, Leydon, 1976.

[B. G. Buchanan76b]
Buchanan, B. G., Smith, D. H., White, W. C., Gritter, R. J., Feigenbaum, E. A., Lederberg, J., and Djerassi, C. Automatic rule formation in mass spectrometry by means of the Meta-DENDRAL program. *J. Am. Chem. Soc. 98,* 1976.

[B. G. Buchanan77]
Buchanan, B. G., and Mitchell, T. Model directed learning by production rules. In this volume.

[J. R. Buchanan74]
Buchanan, J. R. A study in automatic programming. Dep. Comput. Sci., Carnegie-Mellon Univ., Pittsburgh, Pennsylvania, 1974.

[J. R. Buchanan77]
Buchanan, J. R., and Fennell, R. D. An intelligent information system

for criminal case management in the federal courts. *Proc. 5th Int. Joint Conf. Artificial Intelligence,* Cambridge, Massachusetts, 1977, 901-902.

[Burge76]
Burge, J., and Hayes-Roth, F. A novel pattern learning and classification procedure applied to the learning of vowels. *Proc. 1976 IEEE Int. Conf. Acoustics, Speech, and Signal Processing.* Philadelphia, Pennsylvania, 1976, 154-157.

[Chang73]
Chang, C. L., and Lee, R. C. T. *Symbolic logic and mechanical theorem proving.* Academic Press, New York, 1973.

[Charniak72]
Charniak, E. Towards a model of children's story comprehension. AI TR-266, MIT, Cambridge, Massachusetts, 1972.

[Charniak76]
Charniak, E., and Wilks, Y. *Computational semantics.* North-Holland, New York, 1976.

[Chase72]
Chase, W. G., and Clark, H. Mental operations in the comparison of sentences and pictures. *In Cognition in learning and memory* (Gregg,L., ed.). Wiley, New York, 1972, 205-232.

[Chase73]
Chase, W. G., and Simon, H. A. Perception in chess. *Cognitive Psych.* 4, 1973, 55-81.

[Chomsky57]
Chomsky, A. N. *Syntactic structures.* Mouton, The Hague, 1957.

[Collins69]
Collins, A. M., and Quillian, M. R. Retrieval time from semantic memory. *J. Verbal Learning Verbal Behav.* 8, 1969, 240-247.

[Collins75]
Collins, A. M., and Loftus, E. F. A spreading-activation theory of semantic processing. *Psych. Rev.* 82, 1975, 407-428.

[Crothers72]
Crothers, E. Memory structure and the recall of discourse. *In Language comprehension and the acquisition of knowledge* (Carroll, J., and Freedle, R., eds.). Winston, Washington, D. C., 1972.

[Crowder69]

Crowder, R. G. Behavioral strategies in immediate memory. *J. Verbal Learning Verbal Behav.* 8, 1969, 524-528.

[Dahl72]

Dahl O., Dijkstra E., and Hoare A. *Structured programming.* North-Holland, New York, 1972.

[Davies73]

Davies, D. J. M. Poplar 1.5 Reference Manual, TPU Report No. 1, Univ. of Edinburgh, Edinburgh, 1973.

[Davis76a]

Davis, R. Application of meta level knowledge to the construction, maintenance and use of large knowledge bases. Memo AIM-283, Artificial Intelligence Laboratory, Stanford Univ., Stanford, California, 1976.

[Davis76b]

Davis, R., and King, J. An overview of production systems. *In Machine intelligence,* Vol. 8 (Elcock, E. W., and Michie, D., eds.). Wiley, New York, 1976, 300-332.

[Davis77a]

Davis, R. Generalized procedure calling and content directed invocation. *Proc. Symp. Artificial Intelligence Programming Languages, SIGPLAN Notices 12, SIGART Newsletter 64,* 1977, 45-54.

[Davis77b]

Davis R. Interactive transfer of expertise: Acquisition of new inference rules. *Proc. 5th Int. Joint Conf. Artificial Intelligence,* Cambridge, Massachusetts, 1977, 321-328.

[Davis77c]

Davis R., and Buchanan B. G. Meta level knowledge: Overview and implications. *Proc. 5th Int. Joint Conf. Artificial Intelligence,* Cambridge, Massachusetts, 1977, 920-927.

[Davis77d]

Davis, R., Buchanan, B. G., and Shortliffe, E. Production rules as a representation for a knowledge-based consultation program. *J. Artificial Intelligence 8,* 1977, 15-45.

[Davis77e]

Davis, R. Knowledge acquisition in rule-based systems: Knowledge about representation as a basis for system construction and maintenance. In this volume.

[DeGroot66]
DeGroot, A. D. Perception and memory versus thought: Some ideas and recent findings. *In Problem solving* (Kleinmuntz, B., ed.). Wiley, New York, 1966.

[DeJong75]
De Jong, K. A. An analysis of the behavior of a class of genetic adaptive systems. Ph.D. Dissertation, Univ. of Michigan, Ann Arbor, 1975.

[deKleer77]
deKleer, J., Doyle, J., Steele, G. L., and Sussman, G. J. AMORD: Explicit control of reasoning. *Proc. Symp. Artificial Intelligence Programming Languages, SIGPLAN Notices 12, SIGART Newsletter 64*, 1977, 116-125.

[Dennett69]
Dennett, D. C. *Content and consciousness.* Humanities Press, New York, 1969, 114-131.

[vanDijk75]
vanDijk, T. A. Recalling and summarizing complex discourse, Department of Gen. Lit. Studies, Univ. of Amsterdam, 1975.

[vanDijk77]
van Dijk, T. A., and Kintsch, W. Cognitive psychology and discourse: Recalling and summarizing stories. *In Trends in textlinguistics* (Dressler, W. U., ed.). de Gruyter, New York, 1977.

[Dijkstra72]
Dijkstra, E. W. Notes on structured programming. *In Structured programming* (Dahl, Dijkstra, and Hoare, eds.). Academic Press, London, 1972, 1-82.

[Dosher76]
Dosher, B. A. The retrieval of sentences from memory: A speed-accuracy study. *Cognitive Psych. 8*, 1976, 291-311.

[Duda76]
Duda, R. O., Hart, P. E., and Nilsson, N. J. Subjective Bayesian methods for rule-based inference systems. *Proc. 1976 Nat. Comput. Conf. (AFIPS Conf. Proc.) 45*, 1976, 1075-1082.

[Duda77]
Duda, R. O., Hart, P. E., Nilsson, N. J., and Sutherland, G. Semantic network representations in rule-based inference systems. In this volume.

[Egan74]
Egan, D. E., and Greeno, J. G. Theory of rule induction. *In Knowledge and cognition* (Gregg, L.W., ed.). Wiley, New York, 1974, 43-103.

[Engelmore77]
Engelmore, R. S., and Nii, H. P. A knowledge-based system for the interpretation of protein x-ray crystallographic data. Heuristic Programming Project Report HPP-77-2 (also STAN-CS-77-589), Stanford Univ., Stanford, California, 1977.

[Erman75]
Erman, L. D., and Lesser, V. R. A multi-level organization for problem solving using many, diverse, cooperating sources of knowledge. *Proc. 4th Int. Joint Conf. Artificial Intelligence*, Tbilisi, USSR, 1975, 483-490.

[Evans68]
Evans, T. G. A program for the solution of geometric-analogy intelligence test questions. *In Semantic information processing* (Minsky, M., ed.). MIT Press, Cambridge, 1968, 271-353.

[Farber64]
Farber, D. J., Griswold, R. E. and Polonsky, I. P. SNOBOL, a string manipulation language. *JACM 11*, 1964, 21-30.

[Faught75]
Faught, W. S. Affect as motivation for cognitive and conative processes. *Proc. 4th Int. Joint Conf. Artificial Intelligence*, Tbilisi, USSR, 1975, 893-899.

[Faught77]
Faught, W. S., Colby, K. M., and Parkison, R. C. Inferences, affects, and intentions in a model of paranoia. *Cognitive Psych. 9*, 1977, 153-187.

[Faught77a]
Faught, W. S. Motivation and intensionality in a computer simulation model. AIM Memo 305, Stanford Artificial Intelligence Laboratory, Stanford, California, 1977.

[Faught77b]
Faught, W. S. Conversational action patterns in dialogs. In this volume.

[Feigenbaum71]
Feigenbaum, E. A., Buchanan, B. G., and Lederberg, J. On generality and problem solving: A case study using the DENDRAL pro-

gram. *Machine intelligence,* Vol. 6 (Meltzer, B. and Michie, D., eds.). American Elsevier, New York, 1971, 165-190.

[Feigenbaum75]
Feigenbaum, E. A., Nii, H. P., Brooks, S., Miller, J. L., Miller, N. L., and Model, M. *HASP Final Report,* Vols. 1-4, Technical Report under ARPA Contract M66314-74-C-1235, Systems Control, Inc., Palo Alto, California, 1975 (classified document).

[Feigenbaum77]
Feigenbaum, E. A. The art of artificial intelligence: I. Themes and case studies of knowledge engineering. *Proc. 5th Int. Joint Conf. Artificial Intelligence,* Cambridge, Massachusetts, 1977, 1014-1029.

[Feldman74]
Feldman, J., and Yakimovsky, Y. Decision theory and artificial intelligence: I. A semantics-based region analyzer. *Artificial Int. 5,* 1974, 349-371.

[Fikes71]
Fikes, R. E., and Nilsson, N. J. STRIPS: A new approach to the application of theorem proving to problem solving. *Artificial Int. 2,* 1971, 189-208.

[Fikes72]
Fikes, R. E., Hart, P. E., and Nilsson, N. J. Learning and executing generalized robot plans. *Artificial Int. 3,* 1972, 251-288.

[Fiksel76]
Fiksel, J. R., and Bower, G. H. Question answering by a semantic network of parallel automata. *J. Math. Psych. 13,* 1976, 1-45.

[Fillenbaum66]
Fillenbaum, S. Memory for gist: Some relevant variables. *Language and Speech 9,* 1966, 217-227.

[Fillenbaum69]
Fillenbaum, S. Words and feature complexes: False recognition of antonyms and synonyms. *J. Exp. Psych. 22,* 1969, 400-402.

[Fillmore68]
Fillmore, C. J. The case for case. *In Universals in linguistic theory* (Bach and Harms, eds.). Holt, Chicago, 1968.

[Fine73]
Fine, T. L. *Theories of probability.* Academic Press, New York, 1973.

[Floyd61]
Floyd, R. W. An algorithm for coding efficient arithmetic operations. *Communications of the ACM 4*, 1961, 42-51.

[Forgy76]
Forgy, C., and McDermott, J. The OPS reference manual. Carnegie-Mellon Univ., Dep. Comput. Sci., Pittsburgh, Pennsylvania, 1976.

[Forgy77]
Forgy, C. A production system monitor for parallel computers. Tech. Report, Dep. Comput. Sci., Carnegie-Mellon Univ., Pittsburgh, Pennsylvania, 1977.

[Forgy77a]
Forgy, C., and McDermott, J. OPS, a domain-independent production system language. *Proc. 5th Int. Joint Conf. Artificial Intelligence*, Cambridge, Massachusetts, 1977, 933-939.

[Franks71]
Franks, J. J., and Bransford, J. D. Abstraction of visual patterns. *J. Exp. Psych. 90*, 1971, 65-74.

[Frederiksen75]
Frederiksen, C. Representing logical and semantic structure of knowledge acquired from discourse. *Cognitive Psych. 7*, 1975, 371-458.

[Friend73]
Friend, K. An information processing approach to small group interaction in a coalition formation game. Dep. Psych., Carnegie-Mellon Univ., Pittsburgh, Pennsylvania, 1973.

[Fu74]
Fu, K. S. *Syntactic methods in pattern recognition*. Academic Press, New York, 1974.

[Galler70]
Galler, B., and Perlis, A. *A view of programming languages*. Addison-Wesley, Reading, Massachusetts, 1970.

[Goldberg72]
Goldberg, A., and Kay, A. SMALLTALK-72 User's Manual. Xerox Palo Alto Research Center, Palo Alto, California, 1972.

[Goldberg75]
Goldberg, P. C. Automatic programming. *In Programming Methodology* (Goos, G. and Hartmanis, J., eds.). *Lecture Notes Comput. Sci. 23*. Springer-Verlag, New York, 1975.

[Goldstein77]
Goldstein, I. P., and Grimson, E. Annotated production systems: A model for skill acquisition. *Proc. 5th Int. Joint Conf. Artificial Intelligence*, Cambridge, Massachusetts, 1977, 311-317.

[Green69]
Green, C. C. Theorem proving by resolution as a basis for question-answering systems. *In Machine intelligence*, Vol. 4 (Meltzer, B., and Michie, D., eds.). Edinburgh Univ. Press, Edinburgh, 1969, 183-205.

[Green75]
Green, C. C., and Barstow, D. Some rules for the automatic synthesis of programs. *Proc. 4th Int. Joint Conf. Artificial Intelligence*, Tbilisi, USSR, 1975, 232-239.

[Green76]
Green, C.C. The Design of the PSI Program Synthesis System. *Proc. 2nd Int. Conf. Software Engineering*, San Francisco, 1976, 4-18.

[Harris72]
Harris, L. R. A model for adaptive problem solving applied to natural language acquisition. TR 72-133, Dep. Comput. Sci., Cornell Univ., Ithaca, New York, 1972.

[Hawrusik76]
Hawrusik, F. CONCHECK: A mechanism for maintaining model state consistency in a frame-based system. Report RUCBM-TM-57, Dep. Comput. Sci., Rutgers Univ., Camden, New Jersey, 1976.

[Hayes77]
Hayes, P. J. In defense of logic. *Proc. 5th Int. Joint Conf. Artificial Intelligence*, Cambridge, Massachusetts, 559-565.

[B. Hayes-Roth75]
Hayes-Roth, B., and Hayes-Roth, F. Plasticity in memorial networks. *J. Verbal Learning Verbal Behav. 14*, 1975, 506-522.

[B. Hayes-Roth76]
Hayes-Roth, B. Lexical information in memory for text. P-5832, The Rand Corporation, Santa Monica, California, 1976.

[B. Hayes-Roth77a]
Hayes-Roth, B. The evolution of cognitive structures and processes. *Psych. Rev. 84*, 1977, 260-278.

[B. Hayes-Roth77b]
Hayes-Roth, B., and Hayes-Roth, F. Concept learning and the recogni-

tion and classification of exemplars. *J. Verbal Learning Verbal Behav. 16,* 1977, 321-338.

[B. Hayes-Roth77c]
Hayes-Roth, B., and Hayes-Roth, F. The prominence of lexical information in memory representations of meaning. *J. Verbal Learning Verbal Behav. 16,* 1977, 119-136.

[B. Hayes-Roth77d]
Hayes-Roth, B. Implications of human pattern processing for the design of artificial knowledge systems. In this volume.

[F. Hayes-Roth74]
Hayes-Roth, F. Schematic classification problems and their solution. *Pattern Recognition 6,* 1974, 105-114.

[F. Hayes-Roth75]
Hayes-Roth, F., and Mostow, D. J. An automatically compilable recognition network for structured patterns. *Proc. 4th Int. Joint Conf. Artificial Intelligence,* Tbilisi, USSR, 1975, 246-251.

[F. Hayes-Roth76a]
Hayes-Roth, F. Patterns of induction and associated knowledge acquisition algorithms. *In Pattern recognition and artificial intelligence* (Chen, C.H., ed.). Academic Press, New York, 1976.

[F. Hayes-Roth76b]
Hayes-Roth, F. Representation of structured events and efficient procedures for their recognition. *Pattern Recognition 8,* 1976, 141-150.

[F. Hayes-Roth76c]
Hayes-Roth, F. Uniform representations of structured patterns and an algorithm for the induction of contingency-response rules. *Informat. Control 33,* 1976, 87-116.

[F. Hayes-Roth76e]
Hayes-Roth, F., and Burge, J. Characterizing syllables as sequences of machine-generated labelled segments of connected speech: A study in symbolic pattern learning using a conjunctive feature learning and classification system. *Proc. 3rd Int. Joint Conf. Pattern Recognition.* Coronado, California, 1976, 431-435.

[F. Hayes-Roth76g]
Hayes-Roth, F., and Lesser, V. R. Focus of attention in a distributed logic speech understanding system. *Proc. 1976 IEEE Int. Conf. Acoustics, Speech and Signal Processing.* Philadelphia, Pennsylvania, 1976, 416-420.

[F. Hayes-Roth76h]
Hayes-Roth, F., and McDermott, J. Learning structured patterns from examples. *Proc. 3rd Int. Joint Conf. Pattern Recognition.* Coronado, California, 1976, 419-423.

[F. Hayes-Roth76i]
Hayes-Roth, F., and Mostow, D. J. Organization and control of syntactic, semantic, inferential and world knowledge for language understanding. *Proc. 1976 Int. Conf. Computational Linguistics,* Ottawa, Canada, 1976.

[F. Hayes-Roth76j]
Hayes-Roth, F., and Mostow, D. J. Syntax and semantics in a distributed logic speech understanding system. *Proc. 1976 IEEE Int. Conf. Acoustics, Speech, and Signal Processing,* Philadelphia, Pennsylvania, 421-424.

[F. Hayes-Roth77a]
Hayes-Roth, F., Erman, L. D., Fox, M., and Mostow, D. J. Syntactic processing in Hearsay-II. *In Speech understanding systems: summary of results of the five-year research effort.* Dep. Comput. Sci., Carnegie-Mellon Univ., Pittsburgh, Pennsylvania, 1977.

[F. Hayes-Roth77b]
Hayes-Roth, F. The role of partial and best matches in knowledge systems. In this volume.

[F. Hayes-Roth77c]
Hayes-Roth, F., Fox, M., Gill, G., and Mostow, D. J. Semantics and pragmatics in the Hearsay-II speech understanding system. *In Speech understanding systems: summary of results of the five-year research effort.* Dep. Comput. Sci., Carnegie-Mellon Univ., Pittsburgh, Pennsylvania, 1977.

[F. Hayes-Roth77d]
Hayes-Roth, F., Gill, G., and Mostow, D. J. Discourse analysis and task performance in the Hearsay-II speech understanding system. *In Speech understanding systems: summary of results of the five-year research effort.* Dep. Comput. Sci., Carnegie-Mellon Univ., Pittsburgh, Pennsylvania, 1977.

[F. Hayes-Roth77e]
Hayes-Roth, F., and Lesser, V. Focus of attention in the Hearsay-II speech understanding system. *Proc. 5th Int. Joint Conf. Artificial Intelligence,* Cambridge, Massachusetts, 1977, 27-35.

[F. Hayes-Roth77f]
Hayes-Roth, F., and McDermott, J. Knowledge acquisition from struc-

tural descriptions. *Proc. 5th Int. Joint Conf. Artificial Intelligence*, Cambridge, Massachusetts, 1977, 356-362.

[F. Hayes-Roth77g]
Hayes-Roth, F., Mostow, D. J., and Fox, M. S. Understanding speech in the Hearsay-II system. *In Natural language communication with computers* (Bolc, L., ed.). Springer-Verlag, Berlin, 1977.

[F. Hayes-Roth77h]
Hayes-Roth, F., Waterman, D. A., and Lenat, D. Principles of pattern-directed inference systems. In this volume.

[F. Hayes-Roth77i]
Hayes-Roth, F., Lesser, V. R., Mostow, D. J., and Erman, L. D. Policies for rating hypotheses, halting,and selecting a solution in Hearsay-II. *In Speech understanding systems: summary of results of the five-year research effort.* Dep. Comput. Sci., Carnegie-Mellon Univ., Pittsburgh, Pennsylvania, 1977.

[F. Hayes-Roth78]
Hayes-Roth, F. Learning by Example. *In Cognitive psychology and instruction* (Lesgold, A. M., Pellegrino, J. W., Fokkema, S., and Glaser, R., eds.). Plenum, New York, 1978.

[Hays76]
Hays, D. G., and Mathis, J. (eds.). FBIS Seminar on Machine Translation. *AJCL*, 1976, MF 46.

[Head20]
Head, H. *Studies in neurology.* Oxford Univ. Press, New York, 1920.

[Hedrick74]
Hedrick, C. L. A computer program to learn production systems using a semantic net. Ph.D. Dissertation, Graduate School of Industrial Adm., Carnegie-Mellon Univ., Pittsburgh, Pennsylvania, 1974.

[Hedrick76]
Hedrick, C. L. Learning production systems from examples. *Artificial Int.* 7, 1976, 21-49.

[Heidorn72]
Heidorn, G. E., Natural language inputs to a simulation programming system. Naval Postgraduate School, Monterey, California, 1972.

[Hendrix75]
Hendrix, G. G. Expanding the utility of semantic networks through partitioning. *Proc. 4th Int. Joint Conf. Artificial Intelligence*, Tbilisi, USSR, 1975, 115-121.

[Hendrix76a]
Hendrix, G. G. Partitioned networks for modeling natural language semantics, Dissertation, Dep. Comput. Sci., Univ. of Texas, Austin, 1976.

[Hendrix76b]
Hendrix, G. G. The representation of semantic knowledge. *In Speech understanding research* (Walker, D., ed.). Final Report, SRI Project 4762, Stanford Research Institute, Menlo Park, California, 1976.

[Hendrix77]
Hendrix, G. G. LIFER: A natural language interface facility. *Sigart Newsletter 61*, 1977, 25-26.

[Hewitt71]
Hewitt, C. Procedural embedding of knowledge in PLANNER. *Proc. 2nd Int. Joint Conf. Artificial Intelligence.* Brit. Comput. Soc., London, 1971, 167-184.

[Hewitt72]
Hewitt, C. Description and theoretical analysis (using schemata) of Planner: A language for proving theorems and manipulating models in robots. TR-258, MIT AI Lab., Cambridge, Massachusetts, 1972.

[Hewitt75]
Hewitt, C., and Smith, B. Toward a programmer's apprentice. *IEEE Trans. Software Eng. 1*, 1975, 26-45.

[Hewitt77]
Hewitt, C. Viewing control structures as patterns of passing messages. *Artificial Int. 8*, 1977, 323-364.

[Hirschman75]
Hirschman, L., Grishman, R., and Sager, N. Gramatically-based automatic word class formation. *Informat. Process. Management 11*, 1975, 39-57.

[Hobbs77]
Hobbs, J. R. Coherence and interpretation in English texts. *Proc. 5th Int. Joint Conf. Artificial Intelligence*, Cambridge, Massachusetts, 1977, 110-116.

[Holland75]
Holland, J. H. *Adaptation in natural and artificial systems.* Univ. of Michigan Press, Ann Arbor, 1975.

[Holland76]
Holland, J. H. Adaptation. *In Progress in theoretical biology* , Vol. 4 (Rosen, R., and Snell, F. M., eds.). Academic Press, New York, 1976, 263-293.

[Holland77]
Holland, J. H., and Reitman, J. S. Cognitive systems based on adaptive algorithms. In this volume.

[Holt70]
Holt, A. W., and Commoner, F. Events and conditions, *Rec. Project MAC Conf. Concurrent Systems and Parallel Computation.* ACM, New York, 1970.

[Holt71]
Holt, A. W. Introduction to occurrence systems. *In Associative information techniques* (Jacks, E. L., ed.). American Elsevier, New York, 1971.

[Horowitz68]
Horowitz, L. M., Day, R. S., Light, L. L., and White, M. A. Availability growth and latent verbal learning. *J. Gen. Psych.* 78, 1968, 65-83.

[Hunt62]
Hunt, E. B. *Concept formation: An information processing problem.* Wiley, New York, 1962.

[Hunt74]
Hunt, E. B., and Poltrock, S. E. The mechanics of thought. *In Human information processing: tutorials in performance and cognition.* (Kantowitz, B. H., ed.). Lawrence Erlbaum Associates, Hillsdale, New Jersey, 1974, 277-350.

[Hunt75]
Hunt, E. B. *Artificial intelligence.* Academic Press, New York, 1975.

[Iwamoto72]
Iwamoto, K. *Go for beginners.* Ishi Press, Tokyo, 1972.

[Izard71]
Izard, C. E. *The face of emotion.* Appleton-Century-Crofts, New York, 1971.

[Jackendoff75]
Jackendoff, R. A system of semantic primitives. *In Theoretical issues in natural language processing, Proc. Interdisciplinary Workshop Computational Linguistics Artificial Intelligence,* Cambridge, Massachusetts, 1975, 24-29.

[Johnson72]
Johnson, N. Organization and the concept of a memory code. *In Coding processes in human memory* (Melton, A., and Martin, E., eds.). V. H. Winston, Washington, 1972.

[Joshi75]
Joshi, A. K., and Rosenschein, S. J. A formalism for relating lexical and pragmatic information. *Proc. Workshop Theoretical Issues in Natural Language Processing*, Cambridge, Massachusetts, 1975.

[Joshi76]
Joshi, A. K., and Rosenschein, S. J. Some problems of inferencing: Relation of inferencing to decomposition of predicates. Special issue of *Statistical Methods in Linguistics*, Skriptor, Stockholm, 1976.

[Joshi77]
Joshi, A. K. Some extensions of a system for inferencing on partial information. In this volume.

[Jurs74]
Jurs, P. C. *In Computer representation and manipulation of chemical information* (Wipke, W. T., *et al.*, eds.). Wiley-Interscience, New York, 1974.

[Karp72]
Karp, R. M. Reducibility among combinatorial problems. *In Complexity of computer computations* (Miller, A. E., and Thatcher, J. W., eds.). Plenum, New York, 1972.

[Kawabata72]
Kawabata, Y. *The master of Go*. Knopf, New York, 1972.

[Kay73]
Kay, M. The mind system. *In Natural language processing* (Rustin, R., ed.). Algorithmics Press, New York, 1973.

[Kellogg71]
Kellogg, C. H., Burger, J., Diller, T., and Fogt, K. The CONVERSE natural language data management system: Current status and plans. *Proc. Symp. Informat. Storage Retrieval*, ACM, New York, 1971, 33-46.

[Kellogg76]
Kellogg, C. H., Klahr, P., and Travis, L. A deductive capability for data management. *In Systems for large data bases* (Lockemann, P. C., and Neuhold, E. J., eds.). North-Holland, Amsterdam, 1976, 181-196.

[Kellogg77]
Kellogg, C. H., Klahr, P., and Travis, L. Deductive methods for large data bases. *Proc. 5th Int. Joint Conf. Artificial Intelligence*, Cambridge, Massachusetts, 1977, 203-209.

[Kelly71]
Kelly, M. D. Edge detection by computer using planning. *Machine intelligence* (Meltzer, B., and Michie, D., eds.), Vol. 6, Edinburgh Univ. Press, Edinburgh, 1971, 397-4

[Kerwin73]
Kerwin, J., and Reitman, W. Video game #3: A Go protocol with comments. Unpublished paper, Mental Health Research Institute, Univ. of Michigan, Ann Arbor, 1973.

[Kibler77]
Kibler, D. F., Neighbors, J. M., and Standish, T. A. Program manipulation via an efficient production system. *Proc. Symp. Artificial Intelligence Programming Languages, SIGPLAN Notices 12, SIGART Newsletter 64*, 1977, 163-173.

[Kintsch74]
Kintsch, W. Memory representations of text. *Proc. 3rd Loyola Symp.* (Solso, R., ed.). Lawrence Erlbaum Associates, Potomac, Maryland, 1974.

[Kintsch75]
Kintsch, W. Memory for prose. *In The structure of human memory* (Cofer, C., ed.). Freeman, San Francisco, 1975.

[D. Klahr73]
Klahr, D. A production system for counting, subitizing and adding. *In Visual information processing* (Chase, W.G., ed.). Academic Press, New York, 1973.

[D. Klahr76]
Klahr, D., and Wallace, J. G. *Cognitive development: An information processing view*. Lawrence Erlbaum Associates, Hillsdale, New Jersey, 1976.

[P. Klahr75]
Klahr, P. The deductive pathfinder: Creating derivation plans for inferential question-answering. Ph.D. Dissertation, Comput. Sci. Dept., Univ. of Wisconsin, Madison, 1975.

[P. Klahr77]
Klahr, P. Planning techniques for rule selection in deductive question answering. In this volume.

[Klein72]
Klein, S., and Kuppin, M. A. An interactive heuristic program for learning transformational grammars. *Comput. Stud. Humanities Verbal Behav. 3*, 1972, 144-162.

[Kowalski75]
Kowalski, R. A proof procedure using connecting graphs. *JACM 22*, 1975, 572-595.

[Kuipers75]
Kuipers, B. A frame for frames. In *Representation and understanding* (Bobrow, D. G., and Collins, A.M., eds.). Academic Press, New York, 1975.

[Kulikowski72]
Kulikowski, C. A., and Weiss, S. M. Strategies of data base utilization in sequential pattern recognition. *Proc. IEEE Conf. Decision Control, 11th Symp. Adaptive Processes*, New York, 1972, 103-105.

[LaBerge74]
LaBerge, D., and Samuels, S. J. Toward a theory of automatic information processing in reading. *Cognitive Psych. 6*, 1974, 293-323.

[Lakatos76]
Lakatos, I. *Proofs and refutations*. Cambridge Univ. Press, Cambridge, 1976.

[Larson77]
Larson, J., and Michalski, R. S. Inductive inference of VL decision rules. *Proc. Workshop Pattern-Directed Inference Systems, SIGART Newsletter 63*, 1977, 38-44.

[Lenat75]
Lenat, D. BEINGs: Knowledge as interacting experts. *Proc. 4th Int. Joint Conf. Artificial Intelligence*, Tbilisi, USSR, 1975, 126-133.

[Lenat76]
Lenat, D. AM: An artificial intelligence approach to discovery in mathematics as heuristic search. SAIL AIM-286, Stanford Artificial Intelligence Laboratory, Stanford, California, 1976. Jointly issued as Computer Science Dept. Report No. STAN-CS-76-570.

[Lenat77a]
Lenat, D. Automated theory formation in mathematics. *Proc. 5th Int. Joint Conf. Artificial Intelligence*, Cambridge, Massachusetts, 1977, 833-842.

[Lenat77b]

Lenat, D. The ubiquity of discovery: 1977 computers and thought lecture. *Proc. 5th Int. Joint Conf. Artificial Intelligence,* Cambridge, Massachusetts, 1977, 1093-1105.

[Lenat77c]

Lenat, D., and McDermott, J. Less than general production system architectures. *Proc. 5th Int. Joint Conf. Artificial Intelligence,* Cambridge, Massachusetts, 1977, 928-932.

[Lenat77d]

Lenat, D. and Harris, G. Designing a rule system that searches for scientific discoveries. In this volume.

[Lesser75]

Lesser, V. R., Fennell, R. D., Erman, L. D., and Reddy, D. R. Organization of the Hearsay-II speech understanding system. *IEEE Trans. Acoustics, Speech, Signal Processing ASSP-23,* 1975, 11-33.

[Lesser77]

Lesser, V. R., Hayes-Roth, F., Birnbaum, M., and Cronk, R. The word sequence hypothesizer in Hearsay-II. *Proc. IEEE Int. Conf. Acoustics, Speech, Signal Processing,* Hartford, Connecticut, 1977.

[Lesser77a]

Lesser, V. R., and Erman, L. D. A retrospective view of the Hearsay-II architecture. *Proc. 5th Int. Joint Conf. Artificial Intelligence,* Cambridge, Massachusetts, 1977, 790-800.

[Lewis76]

Lewis, C. H., and Anderson, J. R. Interference with real world knowledge. *Cognitive Psych. 8,* 1976, 311-335.

[Liskov74]

Liskov, B., and Zilles, S. Programming with abstract data types. *SIGPLAN Notices,* 1974, 50-59.

[Liskov75]

Liskov, B., and Zilles, S. Specification techniques for data abstractions. *IEEE Trans. Software Eng. 1,* 1975, 7-19.

[Lucking75]

Lucking, J. R. Essential features of a data descriptive methodology. *In Data base description* (Dongue and Nijssen, eds.). North-Holland, Amsterdam, 1975, 111-119.

[McCracken77]
McCracken, D. A parallel production system architecture for speech understanding, Ph.D. Dissertation, Dep. Comput. Sci., Carnegie-Mellon Univ., Pittsburgh, Pennsylvania, 1977.

[McCune77]
McCune, B. P. The PSI program model builder, synthesis of very high-level programs. *Proc. Symp. Artificial Intelligence Programming Languages. SIGPLAN Notices 12, SIGART Newsletter 64,* 1977, 130-139.

[D. McDermott74]
McDermott, D., and Sussman, G. The CONNIVER Reference Manual, Memo 259a, MIT AI Lab, Cambridge, Massachusetts, 1974.

[D. McDermott77a]
McDermott, D. A deductive model of control of a problem solver. *Proc. Workshop Pattern-Directed Inference Systems, SIGART Newsletter 63,* 1977, 2-7.

[D. McDermott77b]
McDermott, D. Vocabularies for problem solver state descriptions. *Proc. 5th Int. Joint Conf. Artificial Intelligence,* Cambridge, Massachusetts, 1977, 229-234.

[J. McDermott77a]
McDermott, J., Newell, A., and Moore, J. The efficiency of certain production system implementations. In this volume.

[J. McDermott77b]
McDermott, J., and Forgy, C. Production system conflict resolution strategies. In this volume.

[McDonald77]
McDonald, D., and Hayes-Roth, F. Inferential searches of knowledge networks as an approach to extensible language understanding systems. In this volume.

[McKeown77]
McKeown, D. M. Word verification in the Hearsay-II speech understanding system. *Proc. IEEE Int. Conf. Acoustics, Speech, Signal Processing,* Hartford, Connecticut, 1977.

[Mandler77]
Mandler, J. M., and Johnson, N. S. Remembrance of things parsed: Story structure and recall. *Cognitive Psych. 9,* 1977, 111-151.

[Manna75]
Manna, Z., and Waldinger, R. J. Knowledge and reasoning in program synthesis. *Artificial Int.* 6, 1975, 175-208.

[Manna77]
Manna, Z., and Waldinger, R. The automatic synthesis of systems of recursive programs. *Proc. 5th Int. Joint Conf. Artificial Intelligence*, Cambridge, Massachusetts, 1977, 405-411.

[Marcus74]
Marcus, M. Wait-and-see strategies for parsing natural language. Working Paper 75, MIT AI Lab, Cambridge, Massachusetts, 1974.

[Mark77]
Mark, W. S. The reformulation approach to building expert systems. *Proc. 5th Int. Joint Conf. Artificial Intelligence*, Cambridge, Massachusetts, 1977, 329-335.

[Markov54]
Markov, A. A. *Theory of algorithms.* National Academy of Sciences, USSR, 1954.

[Marr75]
Marr, D. Early processing of visual information. AI Memo 340, MIT AI Lab, Cambridge, Massachusetts, 1975.

[Marr76]
Marr, D., and Poggio, T. Cooperative computation of stereo disparity. Memo 364, MIT AI Lab, Cambridge, Massachusetts, 1976.

[Martin77]
Martin, N., Friedland, P., King, J., and Stefik, M. Knowledge base management for experiment planning in molecular genetics. *Proc. 5th Int. Joint Conf. Artificial Intelligence*, Cambridge, Massachusetts, 1977, 882-887.

[Mathlab74]
Mathlab Group. The MACSYMA reference manual. MIT, Cambridge, Massachusetts, 1974.

[Meyer75]
Meyer, B. J. F. *The organization of prose and its effects on memory.* North-Holland, Amsterdam, 1975.

[Michalski73]
Michalski, R. S. AQVAL/1—Computer implementation of a variable valued logic system VL1 and examples of its application to pat-

tern recognition. *Proc. 1st Int. Joint Conf. Pattern Recognition,* Wash., D.C., 1973, 3-17.

[G. A. Miller56]
Miller, G. A. The magical number seven, plus or minus two. *Psych. Rev. 63,* 1956, 81-97.

[G. A. Miller72]
Miller, G. A. English verbs of motion: A case study in semantics and lexical memory. *In Coding processes in human memory* (Melton, A. W., and Martin, E., eds.). Wiley, New York, 1972.

[R. A. Miller76]
Miller, R. A., and Thorson, S. J. Control concepts in theories of governmental decision making: A structural approach. *In Mathematical systems in international relations research* (Gillespie, J. V., and Zinnes, D. V., eds.). Praeger, New York, 1976.

[R. E. Miller73]
Miller, R. E. A comparison of some theoretical models of parallel computation. *IEEE Trans. Comput. C-22,* 1973, 710-717.

[Minker73]
Minker, J., Fishman, D. H., and McSkimin, J. R. The Q* Algorithm—a search strategy for a deductive question-answering system. *Artificial Int. 4,* 1973, 225-243.

[Minker77]
Minker, J. Control structure of a pattern-directed search system. *Proc. Workshop Pattern-Directed Inference Systems, SIGART Newsletter 63,* 1977, 7-14.

[Minsky63]
Minsky, M. Steps toward artificial intelligence. *In Computers and thought* (Feigenbaum, E. A., and Feldman, J., eds.). McGraw-Hill, New York, 1963, 406-450.

[Minsky67]
Minsky, M. *Computation:finite and infinite machines.* Prentice-Hall, Englewood Cliffs, New Jersey, 1967.

[Minsky75]
Minsky, M. A framework for representing knowledge. *In The psychology of computer vision* (Winston, P. H., ed.). McGraw-Hill, New York, 1975.

[Mitchell77]
Mitchell, T. M. Version spaces: A candidate elimination approach to

rule learning. *Proc. 5th Int. Joint Conf. Artificial Intelligence,* Cambridge, Massachusetts, 1977, 305-310.

[Mitchell78]
Mitchell, T. M., and Schwenzer, G. M. A computer program for automated empirical 13C NMR rule formation. *Organic Magnetic Resonance,* 1978, in press.

[Moore74]
Moore, J., and Newell, A. How can Merlin understand? *In Knowledge and cognition* (Gregg, L. W., ed.). Lawrence Erlbaum Associates, New York, 1974, 201-252.

[Moran73]
Moran, T. P. The symbolic nature of visual imagery. *Proc. 3rd Int. Joint Conf. Artificial Intelligence,* Stanford, California, 1973, 472-477.

[Moran74]
Moran, T. P. The symbolic imagery hypothesis: An empirical investigation via a production system simulation of human behavior in a visualization task. Ph.D. Dissertation, Dep. Comput. Sci., Carnegie-Mellon Univ., Pittsburgh, Pennsylvania, 1974.

[Mostow77]
Mostow, D. J., and Hayes-Roth, F. A production system for speech understanding. In this volume.

[Nagahara72]
Nagahara, Y. *Strategic concepts of Go.* Ishi Press, Tokyo, 1972.

[Nevins74]
Nevins, A. J. A human oriented logic for automatic theorem proving. *JACM 21,* 1974, 606-621.

[Newell57]
Newell, A., Shaw, J., and Simon, H. Empirical explorations of the logic theory machine: A case study in heuristics. P-951, The Rand Corporation, Santa Monica, California, 1957.

[Newell60]
Newell, A., Shaw, J. C., and Simon, H. A. Report on a general problem-solving program for a computer. *Proc. Int. Conf. Informat. Processing,* UNESCO, Paris, 1960, 256-264.

[Newell65]
Newell, A., and Simon, H. A. An example of human chess play in the light of chess playing programs. *In Progress in biocybernetics* (Wiener, N., and Schade, J. P., eds.). Elsevier, Amsterdam, 1965.

[Newell67]
Newell, A. Studies in problem solving: Subject 3 on the cryptarithmet-
ic task: DONALD GERALD = ROBERT. Carnegie-Mellon
Univ., Pittsburgh, Pennsylvania, 1967.

[Newell68]
Newell, A. On the analysis of human problem solving protocols. *In
Calcul et formalisation dans les sciences de l'homme (Gardin, J.
C., and Jaulin, B., eds.). CNRS, Paris, 1968, 146-185.*

[Newell72a]
Newell, A. A theoretical exploration of mechanisms for coding the
stimulus. *In Coding processes in human memory* (Melton, A. W.,
and Martin, E., eds.). Winston, Washington, D.C., 1972, 373-434.

[Newell72b]
Newell, A., and Simon, H. A. *Human problem solving.* Prentice-Hall,
Englewood Cliffs, New Jersey, 1972.

[Newell73]
Newell, A. Production systems: models of control structures. *In Visual
information processing* (Chase, W. G., ed.). Academic Press, New
York, 1973, 463-526.

[Newell75]
Newell, A., and McDermott, J. PSG manual. Dep. Comput. Sci., Carnegie-Mellon Univ., Pittsburgh, Pennsylvania, 1975.

[Newell77]
Newell, A., McCracken, D., and Robertson, G. L*: an interactive, sym-
bolic implementation system. Tech. Report, Dep. Comput. Sci.,
Carnegie-Mellon Univ., Pittsburgh, Pennsylvania, 1977.

[Nii77]
Nii, H. P., and Feigenbaum, E. A. Rule-based understanding of signals.
In this volume.

[Nilsson71]
Nilsson, N. J. *Problem solving methods in artificial intelligence.*
McGraw-Hill, New York, 1971.

[Norman75a]
Norman, D., and Bobrow, D. On the role of active memory processes
in perception and cognition. *In The structure of human memory*
(Cofer C., ed.). Freeman, San Francisco, 1975.

[Norman75b]
Norman, D., and Bobrow, D. On data-limited and resource-limited
processes, *J. Cognitive Psych.* 7, 1975, 44-64.

[Novak76]
Novak, G. S. Computer understanding of physics problems stated in natural language, *AJCL*, 1976, MF53.

[Oldfield65]
Oldfield, R. C. Memory mechanisms and the theory of schemata. *Brit. J. Psych. 56*, 1965, 349-358.

[Parkison77]
Parkison, R. C., Colby, K. M., and Faught, W. S. Conversational language comprehension using integrated pattern-matching and parsing. *Artificial Int. 9*, 1977, 111-134.

[Petri66]
Petri, C. A. Communication with automata. Supplement 1 to Tech. Report RAD C-TR-65-337, Vol. 1, Griffiss Air Force Base, New York, 1966 (translated from *Kommunikation mit Automaton*, Univ. Bonn, Germany, 1962).

[Pohl71]
Pohl, I. Bi-directional search. *In Machine intelligence*, Vol. 6 (Meltzer, B., and Michie, D., eds.). Edinburgh Univ. Press, Edinburgh, 1971, 127-140.

[Polya54]
Polya, G. *Mathematics and plausible reasoning*, Vols. 1, 2. Princeton Univ. Press, Princeton, New Jersey, 1954.

[Pople75]
Pople, H. E., Jr., Myers, J. D., and Miller, R. A. DIALOG: A model of diagnostic logic for internal medicine. *Proc. 4th Int. Joint Conf. Artificial Intelligence*, Tbilisi, USSR, 1975, 848-855.

[Posner69]
Posner, M. I. Abstraction and the process of recognition. *In Psychology of learning and motivation* (Bower, G. H., and Spence, J. T., eds.), Vol. 3. Academic Press, New York, 1969.

[Post43]
Post, E. L. Formal reductions of the general combinatorial decision problem. *Am. J. Math. 65*, 1943, 197-268.

[Pratt75]
Pratt, V. R. Lingol — a progress report. *Proc. 4th Int. Joint Conf. Artificial Intelligence*, Vol. 1, A.I. Lab., Cambridge, Massachusetts, 1975, 422-428.

[Prince75]
Prince, G. *A grammar of stories*. Mouton, The Hague, 1973.

[Propp70]
Propp, V. *Morphology of the folktale.* Univ. of Texas Press, Austin, 1970.

[Quillian68]
Quillian, M. R. Semantic memory. *In Semantic information processing* (Minsky, M., ed.). MIT Press, Cambridge, Massachusetts, 1968.

[Quillian69]
Quillian, M. R. The teachable language comprehender: a simulation program and theory of language. *Comm. ACM 12,* 1969, 459-476.

[Raphael64]
Raphael, B. A computer program which "understands". *Proc. Fall Joint Comput. Conf. 26.* Spartan Press, Baltimore, Maryland, 1964, 577-589.

[Reboh73]
Reboh, R., and Sacerdoti, E. A Preliminary QLISP Manual. Tech. Note 81, Artificial Intelligence Center, Stanford Research Institute, Menlo Park, California, 1973.

[Reiter73]
Reiter, R. A semantically guided deductive system for automatic theorem-proving. *Proc. 3rd Int. Joint Conf. Artificial Intelligence.* Stanford Research Institute, Menlo Park, California, 1973, 41-46.

[J. S. Reitman76]
Reitman, J. S. Skilled perception in Go: Deducing memory structures from inter-response times. *Cognitive Psych. 8,* 1976, 336-356.

[W. R. Reitman65]
Reitman, W. R. *Cognition and thought.* Wiley, New York, 1965.

[W. R. Reitman76]
Reitman, W. R., and Wilcox, B. A program for playing Go: Interim report. Unpublished paper, Univ. of Michigan, Ann Arbor, 1976.

[W. R. Reitman77]
Reitman, W. R., and Wilcox, B. Pattern recognition and pattern-directed inference in a program for playing Go. In this volume.

[Rhyne77]
Rhyne, J. R. On finding conflict sets in production systems. Working Note, Dept. Comput. Sci., Univ. of Houston, Texas, 1977.

[Rieger75a]
Rieger, C. The commonsense algorithm as a basis for computer models of human memory, inference, belief and contextual language comprehension. *Proc. Theoretical Issues in Natural Language Processing Workshop*, MIT, Cambridge, Massachusetts, 1975.

[Rieger75b]
Rieger, C. Conceptual memory. *In Conceptual information processing* (Schank, R.C., ed.). North-Holland, Amsterdam, 1975.

[Rieger76a]
Rieger, C. An organization of knowledge for problem solving and language comprehension. *Artificial Int. 7*, 1976, 89-127.

[Rieger76b]
Rieger, C. The representation and selection of commonsense knowledge for natural language comprehension. *Proc. Georgetown Univ. Linguistics Roundtable*, 1976.

[Rieger76c]
Rieger, C., and Grinberg, M. The causal representation and simulation of physical mechanisms. TR-495, Univ. of Maryland, College Park, 1976.

[Rieger77a]
Rieger, C., and Grinberg, M. The declarative representation and procedural simulation of causality in physical mechanisms. TR-513, Univ. of Maryland, College Park, 1977.

[Rieger77b]
Rieger, C., and London, P. Subgoal protection and unravelling during plan synthesis. TR-512, Univ. of Maryland, College Park, 1977.

[Rieger77c]
Rieger, C. Spontaneous computation and its roles in AI modeling. In this volume.

[Rieger77d]
Rieger, C. Spontaneous computation in cognitive models. *Cognitive Sci. 1*, 1977, 315-354.

[Riesbeck75a]
Riesbeck, C. Conceptual analysis. *In Conceptual information processing* (Schank, R. C., ed.). North-Holland, Amsterdam, 1975.

[Riesbeck75b]
Riesbeck, C., and Schank, R. C. Comprehension by computer: expectation-based analysis of sentences in context. Research Report 78,

Dep. Comput. Sci., Yale University, New Haven, Connecticut, 1975.

[Riesbeck77]
Riesbeck, C. An expectation-driven production system for natural language. In this volume.

[Rilley72]
Rilley, J. S. (ed.). *GO: International handbook and dictionary.* Ishi Press, Tokyo, 1972.

[Rips73]
Rips, L. J., Shobin, E. J., and Smith, E. E. Semantic distance and the verification of semantic relations. *J. Verbal Learning Verbal Behav. 12,* 1973, 1-20.

[Rivest76]
Rivest, R. Partial-match retrieval algorithms. *SIAM J. Comput. 5,* 1976, 19-50.

[Robinson65]
Robinson, J. A. A machine-oriented logic based on the resolution principle. *JACM 12,* 1965, 23-41.

[Rosenfeld76]
Rosenfeld, A., Hummel, R., and Zucker, S. W. Scene labeling by relaxation operations, *IEEE Trans. Systems, Man Cybernet. SMC-6,* 1976, 420-433.

[Rosenschein75a]
Rosenschein, S. J. Structuring a pattern space, with applications to lexical information and event interpretation. Ph.D. dissertation, Univ. of Pennsylvania, Philadelphia, 1975.

[Rosenschein75b]
Rosenschein, S. J. How does a system know when to stop inferencing. *Am. J. Comput. Linguistics,* Microfiche 36, 1975.

[Rosenschein77a]
Rosenschein, S. J. The production system: Architecture and abstraction. In this volume.

[Rosenschein77b]
Rosenschein, S. J., and Joshi, A. K. A system for inferencing on partial information, forthcoming.

[Rulifson68]
Rulifson, J. F., *et al.* QA4, A language for writing problem-solving programs, *Proc. IFIP Congr.,* 1968.

[Rulifson72]
Rulifson, J. F., Derksen, J. A., and Waldinger, R. J. QA4: a procedural calculus for intuitive reasoning. Stanford Research Institute, Menlo Park, California, 1972.

[Rumelhart72]
Rumelhart, D. E., Lindsay, P. H., and Norman, D. A. A process model for long term memory. *In Organization of memory* (Tulving, E., and Donaldson, W., eds.). Academic Press, New York, 1972.

[Rumelhart75]
Rumelhart, D. E. Notes on a schema for stories. *In Representation and understanding: studies in cognitive science* (Bobrow, D., and Collins, A., eds.). Academic Press, New York, 1975.

[Rumelhart77]
Rumelhart, D. E., and Ortony, A. The representation of knowledge in memory. *In Schooling and the acquisition of knowledge* (Anderson, R. C., Spiro, R. J., and Montague, W. E., eds.). Lawrence Erlbaum Associates, Hillsdale, New Jersey, 1977.

[Rustin73]
Rustin, R. (ed.). *Natural language processing.* Algorithmics Press, New York, 1973.

[Rychener76]
Rychener, M. D. Production systems as a programming language for artificial intelligence applications. Tech. Report, Dep. Comput. Sci., Carnegie-Mellon Univ., Pittsburgh, Pennsylvania, 1976.

[Rychener77]
Rychener, M. D., and Newell, A. An instructable production system: Basic design issues. In this volume.

[Ryder71]
Ryder, J. L. Heuristic analysis of large trees as generated in the game of Go. Ph.D. Dissertation, Stanford Univ., Stanford, California, 1971. Microfilm No. 72-11,654.

[Sacerdoti74]
Sacerdoti, E. D. Planning in a hierarchy of abstraction spaces. *Artificial Int.* 5, 1974, 115-135.

[Sacerdoti75a]
Sacerdoti, E. D. A structure for plans and behavior. Tech Note 109, Artificial Intelligence Center, Stanford Research Institute, Menlo Park, California, 1975.

[Sacerdoti75b]
Sacerdoti, E. D. The nonlinear nature of plans. *Proc. 4th Int. Joint Conf. Artificial Intelligence*, Tbilisi, USSR, 1975, 206-214.

[Sacerdoti76]
Sacerdoti, E. D., Fikes, R. E., Reboh, R., Sagalowicz, D., Waldinger, R. J., and Wilber, B. M. QLISP — a language for interactive development of complex systems. *Proc. Nat. Comput. Conf.*, AFIPS Press, 1976, 349-356.

[Sachs74]
Sachs, J. S. Memory in reading and listening to discourse. *Memory and Cognition 2*, 1974, 95-100.

[Sager73]
Sager, N. The string parser for scientific literature. *In Natural language processing* (Rustin, R., ed.). Algorithmics Press, New York, 1973.

[Samuel63]
Samuel, A. L. Some studies of machine learning using the game of checkers. *In Computers and thought* (Feigenbaum, E. A., and Feldman, J., eds.). McGraw-Hill, New York, 1963, 71-105.

[Savin65]
Savin, H. B., and Perchonock, E. Grammatical structure and the immediate recall of English sentences. *J. Verbal Learning Verbal Behav. 4*, 1965, 348-353.

[Schank72]
Schank, R. C. Conceptual dependency: A theory of natural language understanding. *Cognitive Psych. 3*, 1972, 552-631.

[Schank73a]
Schank, R. C. Identification of conceptualizations underlying natural language. *In Computer models of thought and language* (Schank, R. C., and Colby, K. M., eds.). Freeman, San Fransisco, 1973.

[Schank73b]
Schank, R. C., Goldman, N., Rieger, C. J. III, and Riesbeck, C. MARGIE: Memory, analysis, response generation, and inference on English. *Proc. 3rd Int. Joint Conf. Artificial Intelligence*, Stanford, California, 1973, 255-261.

[Schank74]
Schank, R. C., and Rieger, C. J. III. Inference and the computer understanding of natural language. *Artificial Int. 5*, 1974, 373-412.

[Schank75a]
Schank, R. C. The structure of episodes in memory. *In Representation and understanding* (Bobrow, D. G., and Collins, A., eds.). Academic Press, New York, 1975.

[Schank75b]
Schank, R. C. *Conceptual information processing.* North-Holland, Amsterdam, 1975.

[Schank75c]
Schank, R. C. SAM — a story understander. Research Report 54, Dep. Comput. Sci., Yale University, New Haven, Connecticut, 1975.

[Schank75d]
Schank, R. C., and Abelson, R. P. Scripts, plans, and knowledge. *Proc. 4th Int. Joint Conf. Artificial Intelligence,* Tbilisi, USSR, 1975, 151-157.

[Schank77]
Schank, R. C., and Abelson, R. P. *Scripts, plans, goals, and understanding.* Lawrence Erlbaum Associates, Hillsdale, New Jersey, 1977.

[Schank77a]
Schank, R. C., and Selfridge, M. How to learn/What to learn. *Proc. 5th Int. Joint Conf. Artificial Intelligence,* Cambridge, Massachusetts, 1977, 8-14.

[Schank77b]
Schank, R. C., and Wilensky, R. A goal-directed production system for story understanding. In this volume.

[Schmidt73]
Schmidt, C. F., and D'Addamio, J. A model of the common-sense theory of intention and personal causation. *Proc. 3rd Int. Joint Conf. Artficial Intelligence,* Stanford, California, 1973, 465-471.

[Schmidt76a]
Schmidt, C. F. Understanding human action: Recognizing the plans and motives of other persons. *In Cognition and social behavior* (Carrol and Payne, eds.). Lawrence Erlbaum Associates, Hillsdale, New Jersey, 1976, 47-67.

[Schmidt76b]
Schmidt, C. F., Sridharan, N. S., and Goodson, J. Recognizing plans and summarizing actions, *Proc. AISB Conf.,* Edinburgh, 1976, 291-306.

[Schmidt77]
Schmidt, C. F., and Sridharan, N. S. Plan recognition: A hypothesize

and revise paradigm. Report RUCBM-TR-77, Dep. Comput. Sci., Rutgers Univ., Camden, New Jersey, 1977.

[Schubert76]
Schubert, L. K. Extending the expressive power of semantic networks. *Artificial Int.* 7, 1976, 163-198.

[Schneiderman74]
Schneiderman, B., and Scheuermann, P. Structured data structures. *Comm. ACM 17*, 1974, 566-574.

[Schwarcz70]
Schwarcz, R. M., Burger, J. F., and Simmons, R. F. A deductive question-answerer for natural language inference. *Comm. ACM 13*, 1970, 167-183.

[Shapiro77]
Shapiro, S. C. Representing and locating deduction rules in a semantic network. *Proc. Workshop Pattern-Directed Inference Systems, SIGART Newsletter 63*, 1977, 14-18.

[Shepard75]
Shepard, R. N., Kilpatrick, D. W., and Cunningham, J. P. The internal representation of numbers. *Cognitive Psych.* 7, 1975, 82-138.

[Shortliffe73]
Shortliffe, E. H., Axline, S., Buchanan, B., Merigan, T., and Cohen, S. An artificial intelligence program to advise physicians regarding antimicrobial therapy. *Comput. Biomed. Res. 6*, 1973, 544- 560.

[Shortliffe74]
Shortliffe, E. H. MYCIN: A rule-based computer program for advising physicians regarding antimicrobial therapy selection. Memo AIM-251, Artificial Intelligence Laboratory, Stanford Univ., Stanford, California, 1974.

[Shortliffe75a]
Shortliffe, E. H., and Buchanan, B. G. A model of inexact reasoning in medicine. *Math. Biosci. 23*, 1975, 351-379.

[Shortliffe75b]
Shortliffe, E. H., Davis, R., Axline, S., Buchanan, B., Green, C., and Cohen, S. Computer-based consultations in clinical therapeutics: explanation and rule acquisition capabilities of the MYCIN system. *Comput. Biomed. Res. 8*, 1975, 303-320.

[Shortliffe76]
Shortliffe, E. H. *Computer-based medical consultations: MYCIN.* American Elsevier, New York, 1976.

[Shostak76]
Shostak, R. F. Refutation graphs. *Artificial Int.* 7, 1976, 51-64.

[Sickel76]
Sickel, S. A search technique for clause interconnectivity graphs. *IEEE Trans. Comput. C-25,* 1976, 823-835.

[Siklossy75]
Siklossy, L., and Sykes, D. A. Automatic program synthesis from example. *Proc. 4th Int. Joint Conf. Artificial Intelligence,* Tbilisi, USSR, 1975, 268-273.

[Simmons72]
Simmons, R. F., and Slocum, J. Generating English discourse from semantic networks. *Comm. ACM 15,* 1972, 891-905.

[Simmons76]
Simmons, R. F. Inferential question answering in a textual data base, *ACM76 Proc.,* New York, 1976.

[Simmons77]
Simmons, R. F. Rule-based computations on English. In this volume.

[Simon63]
Simon, H. A., and Kotovsky, K. Human acquisition of concepts for sequential patterns. *Psych. Rev. 70,* 1963, 534-546.

[Simon69]
Simon, H. A. *The sciences of the artificial.* MIT Press, Cambridge, Massachusetts, 1969.

[Simon73]
Simon, H. A., and Lea, G. Problem solving and rule induction: a unified view. CMU Complex Information Processing Working Paper 227 (revised), Carnegie-Mellon Univ., Pittsburgh, Pennsylvania, 1973.

[Sloan77]
Sloan, K. R., and Bajcsy, R. World model driven recognition of natural scenes. *Proc. IEEE Workshop Picture Data Description,* Chicago, 1977.

[A. R. Smith76]
Smith, A. R. Word hypothesization in the Hearsay II Speech System. *Proc. IEEE Int. Conf. Acoustics, Speech, Signal Processing,* Philadelphia, Pennsylvania, 1976, 549-552.

[D. H. Smith74]
Smith, D. H., Masinter, L. M., and Sridharan, N. S. Heuristic DEN-

DRAL: Analysis of molecular structure. *Proc. NATO/CNNA Advanced Study Inst. Comput. Representation Manipulation of Chem. Inf.,* 1974.

[M. J. Smith77]
Smith, M. J., and Sleeman, D. H. APRIL: A flexible production rule interpreter. *Proc. Workshop Pattern-Directed Inference Systems, SIGART Newsletter 63,* 1977, 28-33.

[R. G. Smith77]
Smith, R. G., Mitchell, T. M., Chestek, R. A., and Buchanan, B. G. A model for learning systems. *Proc. 5th Int. Joint Conf. Artificial Intelligence,* Cambridge, Massachusetts, 1977, 338-343.

[Soloway76]
Soloway, E. M., and Riseman, E. M. Mechanizing the common-sense inference of rules which direct behavior. *Proc. AISB Summer Conf.,* Edinburgh, 1976, 307-321.

[Soloway77]
Soloway, E. M., and Riseman, E. M. A common sense approach to learning. *Proc. Workshop Pattern-Directed Inference Systems, SIGART Newsletter 63,* 1977, 49-55.'

[Spitzen75]
Spitzen, J., and Webgreit, B. The verification and synthesis of data structures. *Acta Informatica 4,* 1975, 127-144.

[Sridharan75]
Sridharan, N. S. The architecture of BELIEVER Part I. Report RUCBM-TR-46, Dep. Comput. Sci., Rutgers Univ., Camden, New Jersey, 1975.

[Sridharan76a]
Sridharan, N. S. A Frame-based system for reasoning and interpretation tasks. Report RUCBM-TM-56, Dep. Comput. Sci., Rutgers Univ., Camden, New Jersey, 1976.

[Sridharan76b]
Sridharan, N. S. The frame and focus problems: Discussion in relation to the BELIEVER system. *Proc. Conf. Artificial Intelligence Simulation of Behavior,* Edinburgh, 1976, 322-333.

[Sridharan77]
Sridharan, N. S., and Schmidt, C. F. Knowledge-directed inference in BELIEVER. In this volume.

[Srinivasan76a]
Srinivasan, C. V. The architecture of coherent information system: A

general problem solving system. *IEEE Trans. Computers*, 1976, 390-402.

[Srinivasan76b]
Srinivasan, C. V. The Meta-Description System (MDS). Report RUCBM-TR-50, Dep. Comput. Sci., Rutgers Univ., Camden, New Jersey, 1976.

[Stallman76]
Stallman, R., and Sussman, G. J. Forward reasoning and dependency-directed backtracking in a system for computer-aided circuit analysis. Memo 380, MIT AI Lab, Cambridge, Massachusetts, 1976.

[Stoffel74]
Stoffel, J. C. A classifier design technique for discrete variable pattern recognition problems. *IEEE Trans. Comput. C-23*, 1974, 428-441.

[Stonebreaker75]
Stonebreaker, M. Implementation of integrity constraints and views by query modification. *Proc. ACM SIGMOD Conf.*, 1975, 65-78.

[Sussman71]
Sussman, G. J., Winograd, T., and Charniak, E. MICRO-PLANNER Reference Manual, Memo 203a, MIT AI Lab, Cambridge, Massachusetts, 1971.

[Sussman72]
Sussman, G. J., and McDermott, D. V. Why conniving is better than planning. Memo 255A, MIT AI Lab., Cambridge, Massachusetts, 1972.

[Sussman75a]
Sussman, G. J. *A computational model of skill acquisition*. American Elsevier, New York, 1975.

[Sussman75b]
Sussman, G. J., and Stallman, R. Heuristic techniques in computer aided circuit analysis, Memo 328, MIT AI Lab., Cambridge, Massachusetts, 1975.

[Sussman77]
Sussman, G. J. Electrical design: A problem for artificial intelligence research. *Proc. 5th Int. Joint Conf. Artificial Intelligence*, Cambridge, Massachusetts, 1977, 894-900.

[Suzuki76]
Suzuki, N. Automatic verification of programs with complex data

structures. AI Memo 279, Comput. Sci. Dep., Stanford Univ., Stanford, California, 1976.

[Sylvan77]
Sylvan, D. A., Thorson, E., and Thorson, S. J. Processing styles and theories of foreign policy decision making. International Studies Association, St. Louis, 1977.

[Szolovits77]
Szolovits, P., Hawkinson, L. B., and Martin, W. A. An overview of OWL, a language for knowledge representation. MIT/LCS/TM-86, Lab. for Comput. Sci., MIT, Cambridge, Massachusetts, 1977.

[Tanimoto75]
Tanimoto, S., and Pavlidis, T. A hierarchical data structure for picture processing. *Comput. Graphics Image Processing 4*, 1975, 104-119.

[Teitelman74]
Teitelman, W. Interlisp reference manual. Xerox Palo Alto Research Center, Palo Alto, California, 1974.

[Tesler73]
Tesler, L. G., Enea, M. J., and Smith, D. C. The Lisp70 pattern matching system. *Proc. 3rd Int. Joint Conf. Artificial Intelligence*, Stanford, California, 1973, 671-676.

[Thorndyke74]
Thorndyke, P. W., and Bower, G. H. Storage and retrieval processes in sentence memory. *Cognitive Psych. 6*, 1974, 515-543.

[Thorndyke76]
Thorndyke, P. W. The role of inferences in discourse comprehension. *J. Verbal Learning Verbal Behav. 15*, 1976, 437-446.

[Thorndyke77a]
Thorndyke, P. W. Cognitive structures in comprehension and memory of narrative discourse. *Cognitive Psych. 9*, 1977, 77-110.

[Thorndyke77b]
Thorndyke, P. W. Pattern-directed processing of knowledge from texts. In this volume.

[Thorndyke78]
Thorndyke, P. W. Knowledge transfer in learning from texts. *In Cognitive psychology and instruction* (Lesgold, A. M., Pellegrino, J. W., Fokkema, S., and Glaser, R., eds.). Plenum, New York, 1978.

[Tidhar74]
Tidhar, A. Flexible recognition of 2-D patterns. Ph.D. Dissertation, Univ. of Pennsylvania, Scranton, 1974.

[Tomkins62]
Tomkins, S. S. *Affect, imagery, and consciousness.* Springer, New York, 1962.

[Travis77]
Travis, L., Honda, M., LeBlanc, R., and Zeigler, S. Design rationale for TELOS, a PASCAL-based AI language. *Proc. Symp. Artificial Intelligence Programming Languages, SIGPLAN Notices 12, SIGART Newsletter 64,* 1977, 67-76.

[Tretiakoff74]
Tretiakoff, A. Computer-generated word classes and sentence structures. *Inform. Processing 1974, Proc. IFIPS Cong. 74,* 1974.

[Trigoboff76]
Trigoboff, M. Propagation of information in a semantic net. *Proc. AISB Summer Conf.,* Edinburgh, 1976, 334-343.

[Trigoboff77]
Trigoboff, M., and Kulikowski, C. A. IRIS: A system for the propagation of inferences in a semantic net. *Proc. 5th Int. Joint Conf. Artificial Intelligence,* Cambridge, Massachusetts, 1977, 274-280.

[Vere75]
Vere, S. A. Induction of concepts in the predicate calculus. *Proc. 4th Int. Joint Conf. Artificial Intelligence,* Tbilisi, USSR, 1975, 281-287.

[Vere76]
Vere, S. A. Composition of relational productions for plans and programs. Dep. Inform. Eng., Univ. of Illinois at Chicago Circle, 1976.

[Vere77a]
Vere, S. A. Relational production systems. *Artificial Int. 8,* 1977, 47-68.

[Vere77b]
Vere, S. A. Inductive learning of relational productions. In this volume.

[Vere77c]
Vere, S. A. Induction of relational productions in the presence of background information. *Proc. 5th Int. Conf. Artificial Intelligence,* Cambridge, Massachusetts, 1977, 349-355.

[Voss76]
Voss, J. F., Bisanz, G., and LaPorte, R. Semantic memory and semantic context. Paper presented at the Annual Meeting of the Psychonomic Society, St. Louis, 1976.

[Waldinger75]
Waldinger, R. Achieving several goals simultaneously, SRI Tech Note 107, Stanford Research Institute, Menlo Park, California, 1975.

[Walser76]
Walser, R. L., and McCormick, B. H. Organization of clinical knowledge in MEDICO. *Proc. 3rd Illinois Conf. Med. Inform. Syst.*, 1976.

[Walser77]
Walser, R. L., and McCormick, B. H. A system for priming a clinical knowledge base. *Proc. Nat. Comput. Conf.*, 1977, 301-307.

[Waltz75]
Waltz, D. Understanding line drawings of scenes with shadows. *In The psychology of computer vision* (Winston, P.H., ed.). McGraw-Hill, New York, 1975.

[Waterman68]
Waterman, D. A. Machine learning of heuristics. Ph.D. Dissertation, Comput. Sci. Dep., Stanford Univ., Stanford, California, 1968.

[Waterman70]
Waterman, D. A. Generalization learning techniques for automating the learning of heuristics. *Artificial Int. 1*, 1970, 121-170.

[Waterman71]
Waterman, D. A., and Newell, A. Protocol analysis as a task for artificial intelligence. *Artificial Int. 2*, 1971, 285-318.

[Waterman75]
Waterman, D. A. Adaptive production systems. *Proc. 4th Int. Joint Conf. Artificial Intelligence*, Tbilisi, USSR, 1975, 296-303.

[Waterman76a]
Waterman, D. A. Serial pattern acquisition: A production system approach. *In Pattern recognition and artificial intelligence* (Chen, C. H., ed.). Academic Press, New York, 1976, 529-553.

[Waterman76b]
Waterman, D. A. An introduction to production systems. P-5751, The Rand Corporation, Santa Monica, California, 1976.

[Waterman76c]
Waterman, D. A., and Newell, A. PAS-II: An interactive task-free version of an automatic protocol analysis system. *IEEE Trans. Comput.* C-25, 1976, 402-413.

[Waterman77a]
Waterman, D. A. A rule-based approach to knowledge acquisition for man-machine interface programs. P-5895, The Rand Corporation, Santa Monica, California, 1977.

[Waterman77b]
Waterman, D. A. Rule-directed interactive transaction agents: An approach to knowledge acquisition. R-2171-ARPA, The Rand Corporation, Santa Monica, California, 1977.

[Waterman77c]
Waterman, D. A. and Jenkins, B. Heuristic modeling using rule-based computer systems. P-5811, The Rand Corporation, Santa Monica, California, 1977.

[Waterman77d]
Waterman, D. A. Exemplary programming in RITA. In this volume.

[Waterman77e]
Waterman, D. A., and Hayes-Roth, F. An overview of pattern-directed inference systems. In this volume.

[Wesson77]
Wesson, R. B. Planning in the world of the air traffic controller. *Proc. 5th Int. Joint Conf. Artificial Intelligence*, Cambridge, Massachusetts, 1977, 473-479.

[Wilber76]
Wilber, B. M. The QLISP reference manual. Tech. Note 118, Artficial Intelligence Center, Stanford Research Institute, Menlo Park, California, 1976.

[Wilensky76]
Wilensky, R. Using plans to understand natural language. *Proc. ACM, Houston, 1976*, ACM, New York, 1976.

[Wilks72]
Wilks, Y. *Grammar, meaning, and the machine analysis of language.* Routledge and Kegan Paul, London, 1972.

[Wilks75a]
Wilks, Y. A preferential pattern-seeking, semantics for natural language inference. *Artificial Int. 6*, 1975, 53-74.

[Wilks75b]
Wilks, Y. An intelligent analyzer and understander of English. *Comm. ACM 18*, 1975, 264-274.

[Winograd72]
Winograd, T. *Understanding natural language.* Academic Press, New York, 1972.

[Winograd75]
Winograd, T. Frame representations and the declarative/procedural controversy. *In Representation and understanding: Studies in cognitive science* (Bobrow, D. G., and Collins, A., eds.). Academic Press, New York, 1975.

[Winston75]
Winston, P. H. Learning structural descriptions from examples. *In The psychology of computer vision* (Winston, P. H., ed.). McGraw-Hill, New York, 1975.

[Woods70]
Woods, W. A. Transition Network Grammars for Natural Language Analysis, *Comm. ACM 13*, 1970, 591-606.

[Woods73]
Woods, W. A. An experimental parsing system for transition network grammars. *In Natural language processing* (Rustin, R., ed.). Algorithmics Press, New York, 1973.

[Woods75]
Woods, W. A. What's in a link: foundations for semantic networks. *In Representation and understanding: Studies in cognitive science* (Bobrow, D. G., and Collins, A., eds.). Academic Press, New York, 1975.

[Woodworth38]
Woodworth, R. *Experimental psychology.* Holt, New York, 1938.

[Yngve58]
Yngve, V. H. A programming language for mechanical translation. *Mech. Transl. 5*, 1958, 25-41.

[Young73]
Young, R. M. Children's seriation behavior: A production system analysis. Ph.D. Dissertation, Dep. Psych., Carnegie-Mellon Univ., Pittsburgh, Pennsylvania, 1973.

[Young77]
Young, R. M. Mixtures of strategies in structurally adaptive produc-

tion systems: Examples from seriation and subtraction. *Proc. Workshop Pattern-Directed Inference Systems, SIGART Newsletter 63*, 1977, 65-71.

[Zadeh61]
Zadeh, L., and Desoer, C. A. *Linear system theory: The state space approach.* McGraw-Hill, New York, 1961.

[Zadeh65]
Zadeh, L. A. Fuzzy sets. *Inform. Control 8*, 1965, 338-353.

[Zisman76]
Zisman, M. D. A representation for office processes. Working Paper 76-10-03, Dep. Decision Sci., The Wharton School, Univ. of Pennsylvania, Scranton, 1976.

[Zisman77]
Zisman, M. D. Representation, specification and automation of office procedures. Ph.D. Dissertation, Working Paper 77-09-04. Dep. Decision Sci., The Wharton School, Univ. of Pennsylvania, Scranton, 1977.

[Zisman77a]
Zisman, M. D. Use of production systems for modeling asynchronous, concurrent processes. In this volume.

[Zobrist70]
Zobrist, A. L. Feature extraction and representation for pattern recognition and the game of Go. Ph.D. dissertation, Univ. of Wisonsin, Madison, 1970. Microfilm No. 71-3,162.

[Zucker76]
Zucker, S. W. Relaxation labeling and the reduction of local ambiguities. *In Pattern recognition and artificial intelligence* (Chen, C.H., ed.). Academic Press, New York, 1976.

[Zucker77a]
Zucker, S. W., Hummel, R. A., and Rosenfeld, A. An application of relaxation labeling to line and curve enhancement. *IEEE Trans. Comput. C-26*, 1977, 394-403, 922-929.

[Zucker77b]
Zucker, S. W. Production systems with feedback. In this volume.

[Zucker78]
Zucker, S. W., Krishnanurthy, E. V., and Haar, R. Relaxation processes for scene labeling: Convergence, speed, and stability. *IEEE Trans. Syst., Man, Cybernet. SMC-8*, 1978, 41-48.

# AUTHOR INDEX

# SUBJECT INDEX

## A

Abstraction, 334–335, 339, 351, 485, 490–491, 499, 526, 557, 561
  lambda, 537
Acquisition, knowledge, 17, 101, 103, 106, 139–140, 265, 297, 310–311, 357, 484, 595
Act, 5, 362–369, 373–378, 385, 491
Action patterns, 28, 91, 384, 388, 401
Activation, 336, 344, 593
Actor, 29, 361, 363, 366–367, 580
Actual cost, 159–160, 163, 165–166
Adaptive capability, 311, 322, 474
Affect, 383, 390
Agent, 261, 334, 335, 338, 369
Aging, 319, 321, 323
AIMDS, 361, 364–365
Ambiguity of conditions, 300, 305, 540
Analogical reasoning, 36, 43, 282, 559
Analysis
  linguistic, 347, 349
  means–ends, 135, 151
  syntactic, 347
Antecedent–consequent rules, 4, 6, 209, 224, 242, 244, 263, 283, 338, 527, 581, 585
Applicability, 284, 484
Architecture, 16, 364, 372, 475, 525–526
  PS, 16, 26, 49, 136–137, 140, 151, 156, 158, 165, 262, 475, 478, 586, 588
Associative network, 75, 336, 338, 584
Asynchronous processes, concurrent, 17, 54, 64, 551
ATN, 65, 459
Attenuation, 321
Augmentation, 252, 302, 498

## B

Backward chaining, 10, 47, 90, 216, 224–225, 230, 263, 585
Before-and-after examples, 286, 292, 574
Behavior, sequence of, 286, 385
Belief, 362–363, 366, 375, 377, 394
  degree of, 213
Best match, 242–243, 335, 342, 540, 550

Bindings, 206, 246, 248, 284, 561
  candidate, 368, 376–377, 573
  variable, 43, 74, 206, 225–226, 365
Bridge, 366, 379

## C

CAI, 72
Calculus, predicate, 205, 238, 365
Candidate bindings, 368, 376, 377, 573
Canonical representations, 334–338, 513–514, 596
Capability, explanatory, 119, 204, 264, 484
Capacity
  limitations, 342, 345
  limited, 344, 592
Case frames, 431, 473, 558, 563
  semantic, 456
Causal inference, 89, 464, 484
Causal network, 89, 584
Causal relationship, 46, 464, 599
Chaining
  backward, 10, 47, 90, 216, 224–225, 230, 263, 585
  foreward, 216, 225, 230, 263, 316
Channels, 80
Characteristics, PS, 27, 151, 262
Classification, pattern, 333, 339–341, 345
Classifiers, 315–316, 318, 327
Closed-loop control, 545, 547
Cognition, 345–346, 383
Cognitive map, 314, 326
Cognitive model, 70, 83, 328, 345–346, 348, 353, 359–360, 393, 504
Cognitive modeling, 6, 20, 383, 587
Cognitive psychology, 333, 347, 358, 384, 580, 587
Common generalization, 43, 289, 309
Complexity in pattern matching, 28, 49, 334, 341–345, 509, 596, 599
Comprehension, story, 87, 347, 353, 400
Computation, 69, 315, 480
  order of, 480, 595–596
Computer, personal, 261
Conation, 383–384